# UK Agenda for Children

A systematic analysis of the extent to which law, policy and practice in the UK complies with the principles and standards contained in the UN Convention on the Rights of the Child

Produced by the staff of the Children's Rights Development Unit:

Gerison Lansdown,  Director
Issy Cole-Hamilton,  Assistant director
Saskia Jackson,  Administrator
Phil Treseder,  Youth development worker
Alison Cleland,  Scottish policy co-ordinator
Miriam Titterton,  N Ireland policy co-ordinator

Edited by:
Gerison Lansdown
Peter Newell, Chair, CRDU Council

**Published by the Children's Rights Development Unit:**
**April 1994**

# Preface

*From the chair of the United Nations Committee on the Rights of the Child.*

The adoption by the United Nations of the Convention on the Rights of the Child represented a considerable leap forward in respect of children's rights. However, the process of translating those rights into effective change in children's lives will take a little longer. A critical part of that process is the need for detailed monitoring and evaluation of how far the rights contained in the Convention are respected in individual countries. Only with such information is it possible to begin to identify the changes that are needed. Only through such a process is it possible to open up a debate about the rights and status of children in society. Non-governmental organisations have a vital part to play in this process, and this is expressly recognised in Article 45 which states that the Committee is entitled to seek their expertise on the implementation of the Convention.

I therefore welcome the process which has led to the preparation of this report, through collaboration of the widest possible number of non-governmental organisations, which seeks to undertake a systematic evaluation of children's rights in the UK. It represents a major innovatory contribution to the methodology of monitoring the state of children's rights within an individual country and as such may be of much interest internationally.

Mrs Hoda Badran
Chair of the UN Committee on the Rights of the Child
Palais des Nations
Geneva

# Contents

# International obligations to promote children's rights

# Introduction

Two years have passed since the UK Government ratified the United Nations Convention on the Rights of the Child. The Convention, article by article, sets out principles and detailed standards for our treatment of children, for laws, policies and practice which affect children, and for both formal and informal relationships with children.

Worldwide, the Convention has been ratified - fully accepted - by 154 countries, leaving only 20 countries in membership of the UN which have neither signed nor ratified it. It has been accepted more quickly and more comprehensively than any other international convention. UNICEF is seeking universal ratification by the turn of the millennium. In September 1990 71 heads of state and government came together for the World Summit on Children in New York, the largest gathering of world leaders in history. They included Margaret Thatcher and they pledged: 'The well-being of children requires political action at the highest level. We are determined to take that action. We ourselves make a solemn commitment to give high priority to the rights of children'.

If consistent action follows signatures and good intentions, then the lives of the world's children and thus the future of the world, no less, could be transformed. The stakes could hardly be higher.

### The UK's response

It would be good to be able to report that in the UK the obligations of ratification were being taken seriously, that there was an open commitment to giving a high priority to the best interests of children throughout the political agenda. Such a priority would require a careful audit of the state of UK children and the law, policy and practice which affects them, and energetic implementation of the duty in the Convention to make its contents widely known, 'by appropriate and active means', to adults and children alike. Discrimination in children's access to basic social, economic, health and education rights would be openly acknowledged and actively challenged. There would be a new recognition that children's views must be heard and properly considered when decisions that affect them are made.

Sadly, none of this has happened. While the decision to ratify is of course welcome, from the perspective of children the lack as yet of any serious attempt at implementation must be deplored. The Department of Health was named as the department with lead responsibility for implementation and for preparation of the initial report to the UN Committee on the Rights of the Child on progress towards implementation, due in January 1994, two years after ratification. Since then derisory resources in terms of a small proportion of a few officials' time have been devoted to the task. In relation to the duty to disseminate the Convention, it has been put on sale in government bookshops, circulated to local authorities, and a few hundred thousand leaflets distributed. Nothing has been directed at the UK's 13 million under 18 year-olds.

During Parliamentary sessions since ratification, the Government has on several occasions declined to consider the implications of the Convention for new legislation. In debates on what is now the Education Act 1993, for example, ministers dismissed the idea of legal duties to consult pupils to fulfil Article 12 of the Convention. Criminal justice legislation introduced in the current (1993/94) session and proposals to remove rights to permanent housing for homeless parents and their children both appear to breach the Convention.

There has been no attempt to place Government policy as it affects children (and most of it does) within the context of the Convention. In a growing number of countries, governments have moved logically to appoint ministers for children and independent ombudspeople or commissioners with statutory powers. In the UK, such proposals have been rejected by the Government as entirely unnecessary.

In England and Wales, it is often suggested by ministers that the Children Act 1989 does all that is needed to fulfil the Convention. The Act was certainly a major and welcome reform of aspects of the law affecting children, and much of it reflects (and in some cases even exceeds) principles and standards in the Convention. But it does so only in relation to relatively small numbers of defined children, to particular services - child care and child protection in particular - and to particular court hearings. It has no influence at all on many services and many aspects of most children's lives. It can be seen as a staging post, but no more, on the journey towards adequate legal recognition of children's rights. As yet current reviews of children's law in Scotland and N Ireland have not led to major advances beyond the Children Act reforms and in line with the full implications of the Convention.

The UK's initial report to the UN Committee illustrates not progress but complacency. It is dishonest by omission, highlighting particular laws and statistics that indicate compliance, without adequate recognition of gaps, inconsistencies and blatant breaches. It does not give a true picture of the state of our children. In itself, it breaches Article 44 which sets out detailed requirements for reports which must 'contain sufficient information to provide the Committee with a comprehensive understanding of the implementation of the Convention in the country concerned'. And the Committee expanded on this in its guidelines for reporting: the need for a 'comprehensive review', a process which 'encourages and facilitates popular participation and public scrutiny of government policies'. In the UK, there has been none of that.

## Aims of the UK Agenda

The aim of drafting the **UK Agenda for Children** was to attempt, with very limited resources, the exercise which should be carried out by Government: to review the full implications of the Convention for all areas of law, policy and practice affecting children in the UK, and propose action needed for compliance. The Children's Rights Development Unit, a small, independent and short-life project, has worked collaboratively with a very wide range of organisations and individuals, and consulted with children and young people, individually and in groups, throughout the UK. It is a start, and no more: a basis for policy development which pays proper respect to children's rights. Many organisations have endorsed the **Agenda** (see page xvi).

While so far the Unit appears to have had little impact on the Government's attitude to the Convention, it has certainly helped to focus interest and generate activity beyond central government. More than 250 local government bodies, health authorities and trusts, and voluntary and professional organisations have taken up the Unit's proposal that they should formally 'adopt' the Convention and commit themselves to using it actively to inform all aspects of their work. In its final year, the Unit will produce detailed briefings and guidelines on using the Convention. In particular, it is convening meetings of children and young people to provide guidelines on the implementation of Article 12, on consultation and participation in decision-making. The Unit also hopes to aid the development of local and UK-wide organisations of children and young people.

The **UK Agenda** will be submitted to the UN Committee, together with a detailed analysis of the shortcomings of the Government's initial report. When the Committee comes to examine the report, probably in 1995, it will need to consider carefully to what degree the UK is fulfilling its obligations. It has already formally considered about 20 initial reports from other countries, and shown that the exercise is by no means one of rubber-stamping. There has been rigorous interrogation, requests for detailed further information, and in one case a state has been asked to withdraw its report and submit a more detailed one.

There is a common perception that the Convention's standards are only challenging to those developing countries where children's basic survival is at stake, where lack of resources prevents fulfilment of basic rights to education and health. But the **Agenda** makes clear that there can be no justification for complacency over the state of UK children. Judged against other industrialised, resource-rich countries, we spend comparatively little on the basic services which affect the quality of children's lives - health and personal social services, education, housing and social security: in 1989 we ranked 17th out of 21 OECD countries. On health spending alone, we ranked 22nd out of 24 OECD countries in 1990.

While there has been a welcome halving of the UK's overall infant mortality rate in the last 14 years, at 7.5 per 1,000 live births it is still significantly higher than that of other European countries. More seriously, when these and other basic indicators of child welfare are analysed in more detail, gross discrimination - in particular on grounds of socio-economic class - appears. A baby born into a manual worker's family is twice as likely to die in his or her first year of life than a baby born into a professional or managerial family. And now there is evidence that such differences are widening, reflecting an overall increase in inequality. The massive rise in unemployment together with changes in the structure of employment, with more workers in part-time and temporary jobs, has led to a vast growth in poverty. Since 1979, there has been a three-fold increase in the numbers of children living in poverty, measured by a standard accepted across Europe; a threefold increase in numbers of children living in families dependent on basic benefit. The real income of the poorest 10 per cent has reduced, while the richest have got even richer. Poverty, together with Government policies on housing during the 1980s, have led to vast increases in the numbers of children in homeless families; the sight of young people begging and sleeping on our city streets has become commonplace.

In relation to the social and economic rights in the Convention, there is a very clear dissonance between a professed commitment to children's welfare, and the effective implementation of that commitment. There is evidence that in some very fundamental ways things are getting worse, not better, for many children. Article 2 of the Convention insists that the rights within it must be implemented for all children without discrimination on any ground. Yet it is clear that whether for reasons of poverty, ethnicity, disability, sexuality, immigration status or geography, many children are denied fundamental rights in the Convention. Black children are more likely to be living in families where the parents are unemployed or low paid, they are more likely to experience homelessness or to be living in poor quality housing. They are more likely to experience difficulties in gaining access to health and social services that they need. The services that they do receive will often fail to address their particular cultural and religious needs. Afro-Caribbean children are more likely to be excluded from school. There is serious cause for concern about the rising numbers of racist attacks being experienced by members of minority ethnic communities.

We have no legislation rendering it unlawful to discriminate on grounds of disability. Disabled children remain substantially marginalised from most mainstream activities which able-bodied children take for granted. Article 23 stresses the right of disabled children to opportunities for the fullest possible social integration. Yet, despite education legislation which provides a qualified duty to place children with special educational needs in ordinary schools wherever possible, there has been only a very small decrease in segregation on grounds of disability. Many disabled children remain excluded from mainstream schools, from mainstream play opportunities, from integrated day care, and from access to cultural opportunities available to other children.

The Convention is not just about social and economic rights. It also guarantees children civil and political rights but there is not yet the beginnings of any real understanding of the implications of these issues. Article 12 states that the Government *shall assure to the child who is capable of forming his or her own views the right to express those views freely in all matters affecting the child, the views of the child being given due weight in accordance with the age and maturity of the child*. Legislation, policy and practice in the UK is far from achieving recognition of this principle. Attitudes both within and outside the family continue to accept the legitimacy of excluding children from participation in decisions that affect their lives. The theme which emerged from every group of children and young people consulted by CRDU was that they felt that adults did not listen to them, respect them, take them seriously, or value what they had to say. They felt this in respect of their personal relationships with parents, in school, in foster- and residential care, and in the outside world in relation to the media, politicians and policy makers. There is a general feeling amongst many young people that childhood is characterised by low status, little power and almost no control over the outcomes of their lives. These views were echoed by many of the professionals working with young people.

All this and much, much more which is impoverishing and in some cases immediately threatening the lives of UK children is detailed in the reports which follow and together form the UK Agenda.

The Convention gives us a framework for judging commitment to children, and progress for children. How could there be a more worthy, a more compelling and obvious priority? Yet there is no sign of political action at the highest level for children in the UK. Children have a right to be taken seriously as citizens, to civil and political liberties, to adequate protection, to adequate resources for their development. There must be recognition at all levels of the changes that need to take place if these rights are to be respected. Making the rights within the Convention a reality for all the UK's children challenges all of us. Unless and until we accept that challenge children will not achieve justice in our society and the Convention will remain little more than a set of pious aspirations.

## How the UK Agenda was drafted

The Children's Rights Development Unit opened in March 1992 and has worked collaboratively with as wide a range of individuals, organisations and young people as possible to draw up the **UK Agenda for Children.** The Agenda aims to cover the implications for law, policy and practice of all articles of the Convention, setting out changes needed and identifying gaps in current knowledge which make it impossible to tell whether the Convention's standards are being met.

*Creating a network of interested organisations and individuals*

The Unit drafted a questionnaire which was circulated to all health authorities and trusts, local authorities, key national voluntary organisations, interested academics and professional associations. The questionnaire was intended to alert them to the Convention, the Unit's existence and the proposal to draw up an Agenda for Children; it asked if they were interested in participating in a consultative process and, if so, with which articles of the Convention they were concerned. More than 1,000 questionnaires were distributed in England and Wales, and a further circulation was sent out in both Scotland and N Ireland. Several hundred were completed and returned, forming the basis of an extensive network.

*Production of consultation papers*

The Convention contains more than 40 articles relating to different rights of children. It was decided that rather than produce papers in relation to each article, it would be more constructive to identify the key policy areas addressed by the Convention and then to examine all the articles of relevance within that policy framework. The areas identified were: personal freedoms; care of children; physical and personal integrity; an adequate standard of living; health and health care services; the environment; education; play; youth justice; child labour; immigration, nationality, and refugees; children and violent conflict: N Ireland; abduction; international obligations. These are the titles of the 14 reports which make up the UK Agenda. In each policy area, there are three underlying principles which have application - **Article 2,** the requirement that all the rights in the Convention apply to all children without discrimination, **Article 3,** the requirement that in all actions affecting them, the welfare of children must be a primary consideration, and **Article 12,** the rights of children to express views and have them taken seriously in all decisions that affect them. The implications of these articles were considered in drafting each report.

Having established the central themes, initial research was undertaken to explore relevant law, policy and practice in each area and evaluate it against the standards and principles embodied in the Convention. In some policy areas, an exploratory seminar was convened with interested experts to identify current concerns in relation to children's rights. Consultation papers were then produced which identified key areas where there was either an explicit breach of the Convention or where there would need to be changes to legislation, its implementation or levels of resourcing if the UK was to achieve full compliance. Action necessary to achieve compliance was identified. Most of the papers were produced by the Unit itself but in some areas other organisations were commissioned to produce a draft. The draft papers were then sent out for consultation to every organisation or individual who had expressed an interest in that policy area.

### Ensuring a UK-wide perspective

There are marked differences in legislation, administration of statutory services and cultural experiences within the four jurisdictions in the UK. It was obviously essential that these differences should be reflected in the UK Agenda. The Unit identified a number of areas where the experience in Scotland and N Ireland was of sufficient difference to require a separate paper being produced - for example, youth justice in Scotland and armed conflict in N Ireland. Where the differences were more marginal or were quantitative rather than qualitative, such as in issues around poverty, it was agreed to circulate the same paper and rely on the feedback from participants to identify critical regional concerns that needed to be addressed. Separate consultations and seminars were convened for a number of the policy areas in Scotland and N Ireland. A close dialogue was established with the Children in Wales organisation which ensured wide circulation of draft papers in Wales in order that any specific issues concerning Welsh children were adequately addressed.

### Involving children and young people

The Agenda needed to be informed as fully as possible by the views of children and young people. We approached this objective through two routes.

(a) With each policy paper that was drafted, we also produced a shorter document, setting out the key rights addressed in the paper and asking a number of questions about how far those rights were respected in practice. When we distributed the papers we asked every participant to use the document as a basis for discussion with any groups of young people with whom they were in touch and to send us details of the results.

(b) We set up over 40 consultation sessions with children and young people throughout the UK (see page xvii). These groups ranged in age from six to 18 and sought to reflect the wide disparities in life experience of children in different circumstances. For example, some discussions were based in schools or youth clubs, others with young people looked after by local authorities, or who were leaving care, others with young people who were caring for sick or disabled parents or who had been abused, or were homeless. The discussions were wide-ranging and produced a wealth of material which was able to inform and strengthen the analysis in the Agenda, and which is reflected by a selection of direct quotes in the text of the reports.

### Finalising the Agenda

Once comments had been received, each paper was redrafted into a final report listing action required for compliance with the Convention. The Scottish, Welsh and N Ireland perspectives were incorporated together with the views and experiences of young people. In some subject areas, a follow-up seminar was convened prior to redrafting to explore any contentious or unresolved issues.

## Support for the UK Agenda for Children

Each section of the UK Agenda for Children was circulated for consultation amongst key voluntary, statutory and professional organisations. Many responded and the final draft has been amended to incorporate the detailed and constructive comments that were submitted. In view of the very considerable numbers of individuals and organisations who have contributed to the report and provided their support in its production, it is not possible to make individual acknowledgments. The following 183 organisations which were amongst those contributing to the process of drawing up the UK Agenda have endorsed the following statement:

'We are committed to the fullest possible implementation of the UN Convention on the Rights of the Child in the UK. We also recognise the need to undertake a continuous audit of the promotion of children's rights in line with the Convention. We support the UK Agenda for Children drawn up by the Children's Rights Development Unit (while not necessarily endorsing every action proposed for compliance and every individual interpretation of articles in the Convention). It represents a detailed analysis of what needs to be done to bring law, policy and practice throughout the UK into conformity with the principles and standards of the Convention. Implementation of the action required in the UK Agenda would represent a considerable step forward in achieving compliance with the principles contained in the UN Convention on the Rights of the Child.'

A Voice for the Child in Care
Aberlour Child Care Trust
Action for Sick Children (NAWCH Scotland)
Action for Sick Children
Advice, Advocacy & Representation Services for Children
Advisory Centre for Education Ltd
Aids Helpline NI
All Wales Play Forum
Anti-Slavery International
Article 19
Association for all Speech-Impaired Children - Overcoming Speech Impairment
Association of British Orchestras
Association of Combined Youth Clubs
Association of County Councils
Association of London Authorities
Association of Metropolitan Authorities
Barnardos
Barnardos Northern Ireland
Barnardos Scottish Adoption Service
Boys Brigade
British Agencies for Adoption & Fostering
British Association for the Study & Prevention of Child Abuse & Neglect
British Association for Community Child Health
British Association of Social Workers
British Deaf Association
British Journal of Special Education
British Medical Association
British Youth Council
Brook Advisory Centre (in Scotland)
Bryson House (in N Ireland)
Campaign for State Education
Carers National Association
Catholic Family Care Society (in N Ireland)
Centre for Citizenship Studies in Education
Centre for Studies on Integration in Education
Centre for the Study of the Child & Society
Centre for the Study of Conflict
Child Accident Prevention Trust
Child Care (NI)
Child Poverty Action Group
ChildLine
Children in Wales
Children's Community Holidays (in N Ireland)
Children's Legal Centre
Children's Society
Childwatch
Committee on the Administration of Justice
Commonwork Land Trust
Community Development Foundation
Community Relations Council (in N Ireland)

Community Technical Aid (NI) Ltd
Community Transport Association
Confederation of Indian Organisations (UK)
Council for Disabled Children
Council for Environmental Education
Daycare Trust
Disability Action
Dyslexia Institute (Scotland)
Early Years Trainers Anti-Racist Network
Educational Institute of Scotland
Epilepsy Association of Scotland
EPOCH (Scotland) - End Physical Punishment of Children
EPOCH - End Physical Punishment of Children
Equal Opportunities Commission for Northern Ireland
Extern Organisation
Fair Play for Children
Family Care (in Scotland)
Family Mediation (Scotland)
Family Planning Association (in N Ireland)
Family Planning Association
Family Rights Group
Family Service Units
Gingerbread Northern Ireland
Health Promotion Agency for Northern Ireland
Housing Rights Service (in N Ireland)
Howard League for Penal Reform
Independent Panel of Special Education Advisers
Independent Representation for Children in Need
Institute for Social Inventions
Institute of Environmental Health Officers
International Play Association (UK)
International Year of the Family (NI)
Kids Clubs Network
Law Centre (NI)
Law Society
Liberty
London Homelessness Forum
Low Pay Unit
Maternity Alliance
National Aids Trust
National Association for Special Educational Needs
National Association for the Care & Resettlement of Offenders
National Association of Nursery Nurses
National Association of Social Workers in Education
National Association of Youth Orchestras
National Association of Head Teachers
National Childminding Association
National Children's Bureau
National Coalition Building Institute
National Council for Voluntary Child Care Organisations
National Council for Voluntary Youth Services

National Federation of City Farms
National Foster Care Association
National Foster Care Association (in Scotland)
National Society for Education in Art & Design
National Union of Students/Union of Students in Ireland
National Union of Teachers
National Voluntary Council for Children's Play
National Youth Agency
NCH Action for Children (Scotland)
NCH Action for Children
Nexus Institute
Northern Ireland Association of Community Based Training Organisations
Northern Ireland Association for the Care & Resettlement of Offenders
Northern Ireland Association of Citizens Advice Bureaux
Northern Ireland Committee - Irish Congress of Trade Unions
Northern Ireland Council for Travelling People
Northern Ireland Intermediate Treatment Association
Northern Ireland Preschool Playgroups Association
Northern Ireland Youth Forum
NSPCC (National Society for the Prevention of Cruelty to Children)
One World Centre for Northern Ireland
Parents Advice Centre
Parents for Safe Food
Pedestrians Association
Phab (Northern Ireland)
Playboard
Playlink
Playtech
Professional Association of Teachers (in Scotland)
Public Health Alliance
Quarriers Homes (in Scotland)
Re-Unite National Council for Abducted Children
Refugee Arrivals Project
Refugee Legal Centre
Relate - Northern Ireland
Royal Association for Disability & Rehabilitation
Royal College of Nursing
Royal College of Surgeons of England
Royal Institute of Public Health & Hygiene
RSSPCC (Royal Scottish Society for the Prevention of Cruelty to Children)
Save the Children Fund - Scottish Division
Save the Children Fund-UK
Scottish Association for Mental Health
Scottish Association of Youth Care & Justice
Scottish Childminding Association
Scottish Council for Single Homeless
Scottish Council for Spastics
Scottish Council for Single Parents
Scottish Council for Civil Liberties
Scottish Health Visitors' Association
Scottish Out of School Care Network
Scottish Pre-School Play Association
Scottish Secondary Teachers' Association
Scottish Traveller Education Project
Shelter (Scotland)
Simon Community Northern Ireland
Society of Teachers of Speech & Drama
Stepping Stones in Scotland
Town & Country Planning Association
Transport 2000

Turning Point
UK Sports Association for People with Learning Disability
Ulster Cancer Foundation
Underground Power
UNICEF-UK
Union of Muslim Organisations of UK & Eire
United Reformed Church
University of East London
Voluntary Organisations Liaison Council for Under Fives
Volunteer Tutors Association (in Scotland)
Welsh Joint Education Committee
Who Cares? Scotland
'Who Cares?' Trust
Women's Resource & Development Agency
Woodcraft Folk
YMCA Glasgow
Young People's Trust for the Environment & Nature Conservation
Youth Clubs UK
Youth Council for Northern Ireland
Youthaid

**Groups of children and young people who participated in the consultation exercise contributing to the UK Agenda**
(For reasons of confidentiality some of the groups consulted did not wish to be listed)
Albany Centre Children's festival, Lewisham
Artscape Centre, Shrewsbury
Blyton Youth Club, Lincolnshire
Clanmannock Youth Council, Alloa
Co-operation North, Belfast
Craiglands Residential Unit, Lincoln
Durham in Care
Eastfields High School, Merton
Extern Project, West Belfast
Fourth Friend, Alloa
Horizon Youth Centre, Gainsborough
Islington Play Training Unit, play day
Lifechance Project, Oxford
Markfield Project, North London
Mary Webb Secondary School, Shropshire
Menzies High School, Birmingham
National Members Group, Youth Clubs UK
North Dulwich & Nunhead Guides
North East Care Conference
Northern Ireland Youth Forum
Off The Record, Sterling
Pentwyn Youth Forum, Cardiff
Queens Park Family Service Unit, London
S.C.F. Project, Annadale
S.C.F. Project, Ardomonagh
Schools Environment Project, Manchester
Shrewsbury Sixth Form College
St Paul's Primary School
Underground Power
Voices from Care Cymru
Wilfred Owen Primary School, Shropshire
Woodcraft Folk, Cholten Manchester
Y.M.C.A., Belfast
Young Carers, Liverpool
Ysgol Bryn Clwyd, Llandyrnog Clwyd
11th Antrim Beaver Scouts, West Belfast
123 Project, North Belfast

**CHILDREN'S RIGHTS**
DEVELOPMENT UNIT

# UK Agenda for Children

**1**

**Personal freedoms**

# Contents

*The unreferenced quotations in this report are comments made during a consultation exercise undertaken by the Children's Rights Development Unit with groups of young people throughout the UK.*

# 1 Introduction

**1.1** The adoption by the UN General Assembly of the Convention on the Rights of the Child represents a step forward of considerable magnitude in its explicit recognition that children have civil and political rights, in addition to the more generally accepted rights to protection and provision. Many of these rights are already included in other conventions and covenants applying to people of all ages but the UN Convention draws all these rights together and adds others for the first time in one treaty. In so doing, it lends greater emphasis to the importance of recognising children as people with human rights and places substantial obligations on governments to promote and respect children's civil and political rights. Such a recognition is long overdue in the UK, where children's lack of effective voice in the political, judicial and administrative systems that impinge on their lives renders them peculiarly vulnerable to exploitation, abuse, and neglect.

**1.2** In the absence of a written constitution or Bill of Rights in the UK, we currently have few rights as such. Rather, there is a presumption that unless an action is expressly forbidden it is permitted. The UK is the only country in the European Union (EU) not to have explicit rights, such as the right to freedom of conscience, assembly, religion and speech, embodied within its laws and is also the only country in the EU or the Council of Europe without a written constitution or enforceable Bill of Rights. Without either, the opportunity for individuals to seek redress against the state for infringement of rights or to gain adequate protection against such infringements by other individuals is seriously restricted. In *The people's charter*, a draft Bill of Rights produced by Liberty, it is emphasised that: 'From the empowerment perspective, the greatest value of a Bill of Rights is ... the chance it offers to enhance the rights of those who are most vulnerable to abuse of power by the state[1]'. Power is unevenly distributed within our society but, without doubt, it is children who are the weakest members of that society. It is therefore of particular importance that the principles contained in the Convention which assert the right of children to fundamental civil and political liberties are incorporated within legislation.

**1.3** Article 4 stresses the obligation on governments to undertake '*all appropriate legislative, administrative and other measures for the implementation of the rights recognised in the present Convention*'. Whilst, in respect of economic, social and cultural rights, governments are required to introduce measures '*to the maximum extent of their resources*', no such qualification exists in respect of civil and political rights. It is therefore incumbent on the Government to pursue fully the implementation of these rights.

**This report does not cover civil and political liberties for children involved in armed conflict (see UK Agenda Report 12, page 259) or youth justice (see UK Agenda Report 9, page 199). The right of children to physical integrity is covered in UK Agenda Report 3, page 51.**

# 2 Relevant articles in the Convention

## 2.1 General principles

**Article 2:** all rights in the Convention must apply without discrimination of any kind irrespective of race, colour, language, religion, national, ethnic or social origin, disability or other status.

**Article 3:** the duty in all actions to consider the best interests of the child.

**Article 12:** the right to express an opinion and to have that opinion taken into account in any matter or procedure affecting the child.

## 2.2 Articles relevant to the right to personal freedoms

**Article 5:** the duty of the Government to respect the rights and responsibilities of parents to provide guidance and direction to children which is appropriate to their evolving capacity.

**Article 7:** the right to a name from birth and to be granted a nationality.

**Article 8:** the right to preserve an identity including name, nationality and family relations.

**Article 13:** the right to freedom of expression and to obtain and impart information.

**Article 14:** the right to freedom of conscience, thought and religion.

**Article 15:** the right to freedom of association and peaceful assembly.

**Article 16:** the right to protection from interference with privacy, family, home and correspondence.

**Article 30:** the right of children from minority communities to enjoy their own culture and practise their own religion and culture.

*For the full wording of the articles, see the UN Convention on the Rights of the Child, page 311.*

# 3 Freedom from discrimination
## Article 2

**3.1** Article 2.1 states that all the rights in the Convention must apply to all children '*without discrimination of any kind, irrespective of the child's or his or her parent's or legal guardian's race, colour, sex, language, religion, political or other opinion, national, ethnic or social origin, property, disability, birth or other status*'. Article 2.2 goes on to require that the Government takes '*all appropriate measures to ensure that the child is protected against all forms of discrimination or punishment on the basis of the status, activities, expressed opinions, or beliefs of the child's parents, legal guardians, or family members*'. Legislation exists in England, Wales and Scotland rendering it unlawful to discriminate on grounds of race. In N Ireland there is legislation which makes it unlawful to discriminate in matters of employment on grounds of religion or political opinion but, although there is currently a Government consultation paper on proposals regarding race relations, there is as yet no race relations legislation in N Ireland. The Committee on the Administration of Justice, a civil rights group based in Belfast, has argued that the absence of such legislation contravenes the UN Convention on the Elimination of Racial Discrimination. Certainly, the failure to provide the same rights to protection from discrimination throughout the UK represents a breach of Article 2 of the Convention on the Rights of the Child. The defence of its absence in N Ireland that there is not a problem of discrimination is totally unsatisfactory. Organisations working with minority ethnic communities in N Ireland have identified a substantial body of evidence of racial attacks and discrimination.

**3.2** No legislation exists in the UK to protect disabled people including children from discrimination on grounds of their disability. There have been repeated attempts by Members of Parliament, supported by disability organisations, to introduce legislation but they have been rejected by the Government on the grounds that elimination of discrimination is best promoted by encouragement of good practice. But without the protection of law it remains impossible for disabled children to challenge decisions or actions which are discriminatory.

**3.3** There is no protective legislation rendering it unlawful to discriminate against people, including children, on grounds of sexual orientation. Article 2 states that all rights must be respected '*irrespective of the child's ... race, colour, sex, language, religion, political or other opinion, national ethnic or social origin, property, disability, birth or other status*'. 'Other status' is being increasingly understood within the European Union, the USA and in international forums to include sexual orientation. The current age of consent for homosexuality in the UK is 21, as compared with 16 for heterosexuals. This is clearly discriminatory and also out of step with other European countries, almost all of whom have a common age of consent or plans to introduce one. This discrimination within the law, together with the lack of legal protection against discriminatory acts towards homosexual young people, allows a level of hostility and prejudice within society to go unchallenged. It causes many young people to deny their sexuality for fear of attack, isolation, abuse or rejection. Not only is the discriminatory consent legislation and lack of legal protection against discrimination in breach

of Article 2, but it also represents a failure to comply with Article 13, the right to freedom of expression without discrimination. An attempt to end this discrimination is being made during the passage of the Criminal Justice and Public Order Bill currently( Feb 1994) before parliament.

> '*The most relevant issue for gay and lesbian teenagers is the age of consent which is a major problem for many young people. I know that it is difficult to enforce anyway and there is a test case on at the moment but in principle I still believe it should be an equal age of consent for homosexual and hetrosexual activity. I think it also goes against freedom of self expression; we cannot advertise our gay and lesbian youth group because there are a few British National Party activists in the area.*'
> (17 year-old, Scotland)

**3.4** The discrimination experienced by many Travellers and Gypsies fundamentally affects their enjoyment of many of the rights contained in the Convention. The lack of adequate sites and the appalling standard of many of those that do exist and the proposals in the current (1994) Criminal Justice and Public Order Bill to remove local authority responsibility for provision of sites and to introduce criminal penalties for unauthorised stopping on land without permission have major implications for children living in Traveller and Gypsy families (see also **UK Agenda Report 4 on poverty,** page 79). Such children are effectively being denied respect for their cultural rights in breach of Article 30 as the Government seeks, through its proposals, to restrict the opportunities for a nomadic way of life. The combined impact of limiting the provision of authorised sites and the restriction of access to other land will make it very difficult for Travellers and Gypsies to continue their traditional way of life. This also represents an interference with the right to privacy and family life as described in Article 15. The European Commission of Human Rights has accepted the applicability of this principle to discrimination in relation to life style. Under Article 8 of the European Convention on Human Rights a minority group is, in principle, entitled to claim the right to respect for the particular life style it may lead as being 'private life', 'family life' or 'home'[2].

**3.5** Travellers and Gypsies, including their children, are frequently maligned and abused by the media in a manner which would be considered quite unacceptable and in many cases unlawful in respect of other racial minorities. Articles such as one published by a national newspaper headed 'Curse of the gypsies', which makes sweeping accusations to the effect that they are all cheats and scroungers, should be prosecutable under the race discrimination legislation[3]. Inflammatory articles such as these not only provoke and heighten prejudice and discrimination but are also clearly in conflict with the requirement contained in Article 17 which stresses the importance of developing '*appropriate guidelines for the protection of the child from information and material injurious to his or her well being*'.

**3.6** There is increasing concern particularly in many inner-city areas about growing levels of racism and racial violence. There were nearly 8,000 racial attacks recorded in 1992, up from just over 6,000 in 1990. The Commission for Racial Equality estimates that these attacks are under-reported by a factor of 10, which suggests that there could be as many as 80,000 attacks each year. Whilst not all these attacks are against children, they nevertheless create an environment of terror for many children who are unable to exercise many of the rights in the Convention as a consequence of fear of violence. Many black children are unable to exercise their right to protection of privacy (Article 16), to freedom of expression (Article 13), freedom of association (Article 15) or freedom of religion (Article 14) because of fear of reprisals. Legislation does exist rendering it unlawful to discriminate on grounds of race (see para 3.1), but there is no legislation creating a specific criminal offence of racial violence. Without this, many cases are not recorded as racially motivated even where the victim considers the attack to be such and it is therefore impossible to assess the extent of racial harassment.

**3.7** There are a number of other areas of law where differential and discriminatory treatment of children exists on the basis of gender, status of the child or his or her parents or geography. The other reports in the **UK Agenda** cover many examples of discrimination. These include:

● non-marital children are not able to acquire British citizenship through their father (see **UK Agenda Report 11 on immigration, nationality and refugee children,** page 243);

● children in care in N Ireland have no right to have their wishes and feelings ascertained when decisions concerning their welfare are being made. The current (Feb 1994) Draft Children (NI) Order proposes similar rights to those applying under the Children Act in England and Wales, but is unlikely to come into force until 1995 (see **UK Agenda Report 2 on care of children,** page 19);

● the age of criminal responsibility is 10 for children in England, Wales and N Ireland but eight in Scotland (see **UK Agenda Report 9 on youth justice,** page199);

● children in care have more restricted rights than other children in England and Wales to apply to the court for leave to apply for orders for example concerning contact with other family members (see **UK Agenda Report 2 on care of children,** page 19);

● admissions procedures in some schools serve to discriminate against children from black and minority ethnic communities (see **UK Agenda Report 7 on children's rights to education,** page 149).

racist abuse, and assault and would provide greater protection from racist attacks.

### ACTION REQUIRED FOR COMPLIANCE

**Compliance with Article 2, the right not to be discriminated against, requires that:**

● **race relations legislation is introduced in N Ireland;**

● **legislation is introduced rendering it unlawful to discriminate on grounds of disability;**

● **the age of consent is equalised for all young people irrespective of sexual orientation, and legislation is introduced to make it unlawful to discriminate on grounds of sexual orientation;**

● **the rights of Travellers and Gypsies including children to continue their traditional way of life must be respected in law. Any proposed legislation must take account of the right embodied in Article 2 that no child may be discriminated against in respect of any of the rights in the Convention;**

● **racial harassment legislation is introduced which would cover offences such as arson, damage to property and places of religious worship, verbal**

# 4 Right to an identity
## Article 7

**4.1** Article 7 states that the child has the right *'as far as possible ... to know and be cared for by his or her parents'*. There are a number of groups of children for whom this right is not protected in law. The Government has entered a declaration to the Convention stating that it interprets 'parents' to mean 'only those persons who, as a matter of national law, are treated as parents'. This declaration implies that the Government is not prepared to comply with Article 7 in so far as it gives children a right to knowledge of the identity of biological parents irrespective of their legal relationship with the child. The right to this information is of fundamental significance to the child as confirmed by the ruling of the European Court of Human Rights in the 'Gaskin' case which asserted that 'respect for private life' under the European Convention on Human Rights means that 'everyone should be able to establish details of their identity as an individual human being'[4].

**4.2** Children who are adopted do not have a right in law to know the identity of their biological parents until they are 18 (17 in Scotland) when they have a right of access to their full birth certificate. In other words the right to knowledge of identity only exists for adults. However, Article 7 states that children defined in the Convention as *'every human being below the age of 18 years'* have this right. Whilst adoptive parents are encouraged to inform a child that they have been adopted there is no requirement in law that they do so.

> *'I don't know who my real parents are but I know my file will tell me. But I am not allowed to read it. It's not as if I'm going to go around knocking on the door and say I'm your long-lost daughter and you're my mother. I don't want to see them. I just want to see what my identity is.'*
> (17 year-old, Oxfordshire)

**4.3** The current White Paper *Adoption: the future*, for England and Wales states that: 'There must be arrangements to ensure that adopted children are made aware of their adoptive status at a suitable stage in their lives and can if and when they wish obtain more information about their birth parents, provided that the birth parents agree'[5]. However, this recommendation falls short of proposing a legal duty on adoptive parents to provide the child with this information. Ensuring that the child has a right to know their parents *'as far as possible'* would be best achieved by a change in the law requiring adoptive parents to provide children with this information. This provision would give formal recognition of the significance of this right for the child.

**4.4** Similar issues are raised for children born by artificial birth methods such as surrogacy or donor insemination. These represent a small but increasingly significant number of births each year (approximately 4,000 in 1988). The Human Fertilisation and Embryology Act 1990 seeks to tackle some of the complex dilemmas raised by the new practices of assisted reproduction but its attempts to normalise and legitimise the family life of donor children, have disregarded their right to knowledge of their genetic inheritance[6]. The child has no significant rights to information about genetic parentage. The Act defines, for example, the legal mother as the woman who carries the child irrespective of her genetic relationship to that child. The Family Law Reform Act 1987 defines the husband of a married woman who receives embryo implantation or insemination as the father of the child. The identity of the biological father, then, is shrouded in secrecy. Once a child reaches the age of 18, (or 16 if they are marrying) they will be given the limited right to seek information about whether they might be genetically related to their proposed spouse but, as they may have received only limited information about their real identity, there is little reason for an individual to consider that they need this information.

**4.5** There appears to be a greater importance attached in the legislation to the protection of adults' needs than the child's rights under Article 7. Arguments in favour of donor anonymity have been given precedence over the child's right to know. Adopted children have the right of access at 18 to all the information recorded about their parentage but donor children will not have access to all the information contained in records maintained under the Human Fertilisation and Embryology Act. They are, therefore, discriminated against in relation to adopted and all other children, in breach not only of Article 7 but also Article 2 and the requirement that all the rights in the Convention should apply equally to all children.

**4.6** Non-marital children do not have a right to knowledge of their father. The mother can enter the father's name on the birth certificate by agreement but the father has no right to enter his name unless there is proof of paternity and a court order. The mother is under no obligation to reveal the identity of the father to the child. In addition there is an assumption in law that a man married to the child's mother is the father of her children even if this is known not to be the case. It is not possible to introduce a requirement on all mothers to provide this information to children - there will be situations for example where the mother does not know the father's identity. However, it would be consistent with the child's right to know *'as far as possible'* who their parents are, to introduce a requirement that, wherever known, the father's name should be entered on the birth certificate. The child should have the right to all available information.

### ACTION REQUIRED FOR COMPLIANCE

**Compliance with Article 7, the right to a name and knowledge of parents, requires:**

- **the introduction of a legislative duty on adoptive parents to inform a child that they are adopted as soon as the child is capable of understanding and on the adoption agency involved to provide details of the biological parents as soon as the child requests the information;**

- **a review of the current legislation on assisted birth techniques which addresses the issues of identity and parenthood from the perspective of the right of a child to knowledge of his or her identity, in line with article 7;**

- **that the child has access to available information on both biological parents. Such information should be recorded in the full birth certificate which should be accessible to the child.**

# 5 Preservation of child's identity
## Article 8

## 5.1 Access to personal files

**5.1.1** Article 8 requires that a child has the right to '*preserve his or her identity, including nationality, name and family relations*'. Children must have a right of access to personal files if their right to preserve identity is to be protected. Rights of access to records and reports written about them by professionals and others involved in education, care and treatment need to be examined in the light of this Article. Recent legislation has improved children's rights of access to their reports and records in social services and the health service. However, in education children under 16 have no rights of access to files. The general rights of access for individuals on data kept on computers contained in the Data Protection Act 1984 were specifically restricted to prevent children who were the subject of a statement of special educational needs under the Education Act 1981 having access to their statement if it was stored on a computer. As noted above in England and Wales adopted children have no rights of access to their birth records until they are 18 (17 in Scotland).

> '*I think it's really important that you can sit down and discuss files which are kept on you. They can write things in files which you can't challenge which may affect your whole future.*'
> (18 year-old, Yorkshire)

**5.1.2** In a recent judgement by the European Court of Human Rights on an application made by Graham Gaskin, a young man who had been in care and was denied access to his records, the Court stated that '[he had] a vital interest, protected by the [European Human Rights] Convention in receiving the information necessary to know and to understand his early development'.

**5.1.3** The Court found that the procedures followed 'failed to secure respect for Mr Gaskin's private and family life as required by Article 8 of the Convention'. In its report on the application the European Human Rights Commission stated that the right to respect for family life 'requires that everyone should be able to establish details of their identity as individual human beings and that in principle they should not be obstructed by authorities from obtaining such very basic information without specific justification'.

**5.1.4** In this particular case Graham Gaskin had been taken into care at a very early age and the Commission found that the Government had been in breach of the European Convention and that 'the file compiled and maintained by the local authority provides the only coherent record of the applicant's early childhood and formative years. Hence the Commission finds that the refusal to allow the applicant access to the file is an interference with his right to respect for family life'.

**5.1.5** This case highlights two issues of relevance. The right to identity implies that children have a right of retrospective access to files which is not included in current legislation. The decision also implies that there must be a right of appeal to an impartial authority against any refusal of access and current legislation also fails to provide this right.

> '*You can't see the file until you are 18 and then you have to wait months for an appointment and then they will only let you see the bits they want you to see or they tell you, "Sorry, we can't find it", and they just stash it in some store cupboard somewhere.*'
> (18 year-old, Oxfordshire)

### ACTION REQUIRED FOR COMPLIANCE
**Compliance with Article 8, the right of the child to preserve his or her identity, requires the recognition in law that the child has a right of access to all files held about him or her and that support is provided in accessing files and understanding their implications.**

## 5.2 The right to preserve identity

**5.2.1** The right of a child to preserve his or her identity under Article 8 clearly includes the right to retain a name. Parents in the UK have a duty to register a child within 42 days of the child's birth and to give the registrar a surname by which the child will be known. If a child is adopted, the adoptive parents can change the child's name whereupon the new names are entered in the adopted children's register held by the Registrar of Births and this replaces the original birth certificate. A shortened form of the birth certificate can be obtained which makes no reference to the child's biological parents or to the adoption. When an adoption order is being made by the courts, there is an obligation to consider the ascertainable wishes of the child but the child has no right to retain his or her name. The child therefore can lose his or her name and identity through adoption. Whilst for many children there is a wish to take on the name of the adoptive parents, this may not always be so and compliance with this Article requires that the child who understands the implications of the adoption order should be able to exercise a choice.

**5.2.2** Parents can change the name of a child following a separation or divorce and under the Children Act 1989 courts in England and Wales would be required to take account of the child's wishes, although they would not be under an obligation to follow them. In such proceedings, the child is not normally represented and may not be given any effective opportunity to make their views known to the court.

### ACTION REQUIRED FOR COMPLIANCE
**Compliance with Article 8 together with Article 12, the right of the child to express a view and have it taken seriously, requires that children should be given the opportunity to express their views about any proposal to change their name and to have that opinion taken into account in any judicial or administrative proceedings subject to their age and understanding.**

# 6 The right to express views
## Article 12

**6.1** Article 12 requires that a child who is capable of forming his or her own views has '*the right to express those views freely in all matters affecting the child, the views of the child being given due weight in accordance with the age and maturity of the child*'. This right is not adequately reflected within current legislation. The Children Act in England and Wales does require that courts and local authorities have regard to the wishes and feelings of the child when decisions in respect of them are being made but there is no comparable requirement in respect of decisions made within the family. Nor is there any such provision in legislation in Scotland and N Ireland.

**6.2** The right of children of sufficient understanding to make decisions for themselves were enhanced by the 'Gillick' decision in the House of Lords which gave children under 16 an independent right to consent to treatment if they are judged to have sufficient understanding. The judgement which made clear that it applied to decision-making on any important matter and not just medical treatment, stated: 'The parental right to determine whether or not their minor child below the age of 16 years will have medical treatment terminates if and when the child achieves a sufficient understanding and intelligence to enable him or her to fully understand what is proposed'[7]. However, a subsequent ruling from the Appeal Court in 1992, in the case of Re W, concerning a young woman suffering from anorexia nervosa, sought to distinguish between consent and refusal to consent to treatment[8]. As a result, a competent child under the age of 18 who refuses treatment which a doctor considers necessary could be required to have that treatment against his or her will if any person with parental responsibility consents to that treatment.

**6.3** The 'Gillick' judgement was significant in recognising children's rights to growing self-determination and is consistent both with Article 12 and Article 5 which stresses that parents and others with responsibility for children must provide appropriate direction and guidance to children '*in a manner consistent with the evolving capacities of the child*'. The Re W ruling, although from a lower court, has put in question this principle of individual competence by suggesting that those with parental responsibility can overrule the child's refusal to consent. There is therefore some confusion at present in respect of the law pertaining to children's right to self-determination which needs clarification.

**6.4** Whilst the most effective means of achieving recognition of this right will rest with changes in attitudes towards children, children also need to be able to challenge breaches of it through the courts. If parents were under a clear obligation in law to ascertain the wishes and feelings of children when decisions are being made relating to the child and to give due consideration to them, two objectives would be achieved. First, the principle of taking children's views seriously would be firmly established in legislation and secondly, there would be the opportunity in cases where there was a major breach of this principle, for a child to take the issue to court for independent consideration.

*'What really annoys me is when your parents decide to move. You have settled into a new school and met new friends and you don't get any choice in it and that's it. And your parents don't have to worry about having to go to a new school and making new friends because they can keep in contact that much easier.'*
(14 year-old, London)

**6.5** The Children Act 1989 for England and Wales introduces the concept of 'parental responsibility' to replace the common law concept of parental rights. However, it fails to provide any detailed definition of what is meant by the term 'parental responsibility' other than to describe it as 'all the rights and duties, power, responsibilities and authority which by law a parent of a child has in relation to a child and his property' (section 3.1). It places no obligation on parents to ascertain their children's wishes and feelings when making decisions that affect them.

*'Parents should not have the right to choose your direction in life, like sexual orientation, religion, education and all that. Parents should not impose their own beliefs, and disregard what we think. We have the right to our own opinion.'*
(16 year-old, N Ireland)

**6.6** The Scottish Law Commission's *Report on family law* proposed that there should be in law a requirement that: 'Before a person reaches a major decision which involves fulfilling parental responsibility or exercising a parental right, the person shall, so far as is practicable, ascertain the views of the child concerned regarding the decision, and shall give due consideration to those views, taking account of the child's age and maturity'[9]. They found that there was widespread support for such a provision, which already exists in a number of other countries including Germany, Sweden, Norway and Finland. If such a requirement were introduced into legislation it would provide a more explicit definition in law of the responsibilities associated with parenthood and would impose a clear duty on parents to consider their children's wishes and feelings in a manner consistent with the requirements embodied in Article 12 and Article 5.

**(See also the other UK Agenda Reports, each of which addresses the issue of Article 12 within the context of the relevant policy area).**

### ACTION REQUIRED FOR COMPLIANCE

**Compliance with Article 12 requires that the relevant family law in each jurisdiction in the UK is amended to introduce a duty on those with parental responsibility, in reaching any major decision relating to the child, to ascertain the child's wishes and give them due consideration subject to age and understanding.**

# 7 Freedom of expression
## Article 13

## 7.1 In the home

**7.1.2** Article 13 states that a child has the right to *'freedom of expression; this right shall include freedom to seek, receive and impart information and ideas of all kinds, regardless of frontiers, either orally, in writing or in print, in the form of art, or through any other media of the child's choice'*. This Article has major implications for the relationship between parents and their children and the degree of freedom children are allowed. The traditional approach to parenting in the UK has not been one which is consistent with a recognition that children have a right to express views independently of their parents. Rather, there is a presumption that parents have rights of control over their children's activities, access to the media, dress and so on. Where children do exercise control, it is often interpreted, by other parents, by the media, by professionals and politicians, as a failure on the part of the children's parents to exercise their responsibilities sufficiently effectively.

**7.1.2** Compliance with the right of the child to freedom of expression will require a change in attitudes to children which affords them greater respect. There is certainly a widespread perception amongst many children that their views and opinions are not adequately respected or acknowledged. The introduction of a legislative duty on those with parental responsibility to ascertain the wishes and feelings of children when reaching any major decision relating to the child (see para 6.6) would contribute to a process of beginning to afford greater significance to the views of children.

## 7.2 In school

**7.2.1** Schools have an important role to play in promoting children's freedom of expression and developing their skills and opportunities for freedom of expression. However, the school system throughout the UK tends to operate in a formal and authoritarian way which does not encourage children to explore and contribute their ideas for the provision and development of education. Concerns have been expressed that the introduction of the National Curriculum in the Education Reform Act 1988 ( Education reform (NI) Order 1989 in N Ireland) with its imposition of a detailed structure and content are inhibiting the capacity of schools to respond with sufficient flexibility to the right of children to freedom of expression. The pressures of meeting the demands of the National Curriculum allow for little room for child-directed initiatives or issues of concern to children which are not part of the prescribed work programme. The National Curriculum does not extend to Scotland and therefore Scottish children would appear to be offered a greater degree of flexibility.

**7.2.2** The Education Act 1993 diminishes the rights of school pupils in England and Wales to receive sex education, apart from basic details of human development and reproduction. In particular the changes remove any right to be taught about HIV/AIDS and other sexually transmitted diseases. Provisions due to come into effect in August 1994 enable parents to withdraw their children from all or part of sex education, except that provided as part of the National Curriculum. But the Act specifically states that National Curriculum science from which parents will not be able to withdraw pupils must not include any reference to HIV/AIDS, other sexually transmitted diseases or aspects of human sexual behaviour.

> *'I am very worried about parents being able to opt you out of sex education lessons because that is an infringement of freedom of information, children and young people have the right to this information and parents should not have the right to deny them this. It would be very irresponsible of them. The chances are that if parents will not allow a teacher to do it then they won't be prepared to do it either, and then the person will be seriously disadvantaged by not knowing about diseases or contraception or AIDS, and therefore will be at a disadvantage when it comes to making decisions about whether or not to have sexual relationships'.*
> (17 year-old, Scotland)

**7.2.3** Previously, under the Education (No 2) Act 1986, pupils' right to receive sex education has been at the discretion of school governors, who could decide whether it should be taught and, if it were taught, to determine the methods and content of courses. The new provisions leave governors with the discretion over whether to provide sex education for primary age pupils. Sex education must be provided for secondary age pupils: governors are required to devise a policy and disseminate to parents.

**7.2.4** Thus, primary age pupils' rights to sex education are dependent both on governors discretion and their parents' right to withdraw them from any teaching which goes beyond basic biological facts. Secondary age pupils' rights may be diminished by governors decisions about the content and method of sex education teaching and parents' rights to withdraw them from any teaching which goes beyond basic biological facts (see **UK Agenda Report 5 on health,** page 105 for a more detailed discussion of these issues).

**7.2.5** A recent survey by the Consumers' Association revealed that amongst 150 young people questioned a third stated that they had learned about sex too late and that they did not consider that there was any truth in the fear that learning about sex acted as an encouragement to experiment before they were ready to. Findings from the *National survey of sexual attitudes and lifestyles* indicate that about 30% of young people now have sex before the age of 16 and without adequate information they are placing themselves at unnecessary risk of unwanted pregnancy as well as HIV infection[10].

> *'They always teach it too late because they have this fear that if they teach it early everyone is going to rush out and start having sex. That's total rubbish! People start having sex because their bodies have got to that stage, not because of some outside influence. And when they do, it's here is a penis and here is a vagina and off you go - nothing about how you feel before or after - and some very basic contraception because you won't be needing it because you're not sixteen and not married.[11]'*

**7.2.6** The Education (No 2) Act 1986, section 44, also limits the right of younger pupils in maintained schools in England and Wales to freedom of expression by giving local education authorities, governing bodies and head teachers a duty to forbid 'the pursuit of partisan political activities by any of those registered pupils at the school who are junior pupils'. Many junior school pupils will have political views, and the denial of the right to express those views simply on grounds of age appears to be a clear breach of Article 13 as well as Article 2 and the right of **all** children to **all** the rights in the Convention. Indeed, far from being discouraged, children should be actively encouraged to explore political views as part of their eduation.

**7.2.7** The right to freedom of expression should also include the right to self-expression through dress. However, dress, hair styles and the wearing of jewellery are sources of frequent conflict between pupils and schools. Compulsory school uniform is a curtailment of freedom of expression but many schools have strict uniform rules and will exclude children who fail to comply with the requirements. To exclude a child from school is a very serious punishment, which often results in a child being denied a right to education in breach of Article 28. The courts have supported head-teachers who have imposed strict dress codes. The qualification in Article 13.2 on the exercise of freedom of expression does not appear to justify the limitations imposed by many schools on pupils' style of dress. In many cases the restrictions imposed are discriminatory; for example, where girls are banned from wearing trousers and as such are in breach of Article 2; these particular cases may be challengeable under the Sex Discrimination Act 1975. Other examples have arisen where a child is denied the right to wear clothing or a headdress which is a requirement within their religion and as such are in breach of the Race Relations Act 1976 as well as Article 2. In 1983 an orthodox Sikh boy sued a school for refusing him admission unless he removed his turban and cut his hair. The court found that this amounted to unlawful discrimination.

> '*School uniform can seem like a trivial issue, but in reality it is highly indicative of the head and governing body's attitude towards the pupil, that they wish to reduce them to identical components, without any sense of character or individuality, as the word uniform suggests. For many children and young people clothing is an important means of self-expression, a way in which they can define both to themselves and others who they are.*'
> (17 year-old, Humberside)

**7.2.8** The Local Government Act 1988, section 28, prohibits the intentional promotion of homosexuality through publishing material or teaching by local authorities in England, Wales and Scotland. In particular, authorities are banned from promoting the teaching in any maintained school of the acceptability of homosexuality as a 'pretended family relationship'. The restrictive nature of this legislation and its explicit denial of the validity of homosexual relationships may mean that children are denied the opportunity to understand and learn about different expressions of sexuality. They may also be effectively denied the right to express their own homosexuality and to discuss it with sympathetic adults who might be able to help them come to terms with the choices available to them and affirm the legitimacy of their sexuality.

> '*When I first felt I may be gay the support I needed at the time was some education to say yes, it is possible that I might be gay, because I never considered it as a serious possibility, because it's something that happens to other people or in books, but not real life. Maybe if I had some formal education or had seen a more positive potrayal of gay people*

*in the media then maybe I would have considered it as being realistic.*'
(17 year-old, Scotland)

**7.2.9** All these restrictions on the freedom of expression of children in schools are indicative of a system in which children are the recipients of an adult-designed education rather than participants in a process of education which progresses through a dialogue between children and adults. The Government view, expressed frequently during the passage of the Education Act 1993 and in the White Paper that preceded it, is that parents and not children are the consumers of education. Until this view is challenged, children will continue to be denied the right to freedom of expression within the educational system.

## 7.3 In the arts

**7.3.1** There is growing concern that opportunities for freedom of expression through the arts in schools are being seriously curtailed by cutbacks in provision and through the increasing practice of charging for lessons such as music. There is also widespread variation in availability: some children have far less opportunities for education in the arts than others. The current encouragement of schools to opt out of local authority control, thus diminishing the role of authorities, is raising fears of the demise of provision of inter-school music tuition and drama and, with it, a considerable loss of arts education for children (see **UK Agenda Report 8 on play, leisure and the arts,** page 181 for a more detailed discussion of these issues).

### ACTION REQUIRED FOR COMPLIANCE

**Compliance with Article 13, the right to freedom of expression, requires:**

● **a fundamental shift in prevailing attitudes towards children's status in the education system. It requires that rights to freedom of expression of children should be protected in the same way as for adults. So, unless restrictions are '*necessary for the respect of the rights or reputations of others or for the protection of national security or of public order, or of public health or morals*', there should be a presumption in law that the child has a right to freedom of expression. All education legislation should be reviewed in the light of this fundamental right. Further, policies which enhance freedom of expression in schools would be advanced by the introduction of school councils in all schools. They would provide children with the opportunity to contribute to the implementation of this right in the day to day running of the school;**

● **careful monitoring of the provision of music, drama and other arts in schools during changes in the control and administration of education to ensure that any reduction is identified. Compliance with the spirit of Article 13 rests on a Government commitment to introduce measures to restore any reductions or inequalities in provisions that are identified.**

(See also UK Agenda Report on health, page 106 for details of action required for compliance in respect of sex education)

# 8 Freedom of thought, conscience and religion

## Article 14

## 8.1 Choice of religion

**8.1.1** Article 14 stresses that the Government *'shall respect the right of the child to freedom of thought, conscience and religion'* and further that they must *'respect the rights and duties of the parents and, when applicable, legal guardians, to provide direction to the child in the exercise of his or her right in a manner consistent with the evolving capacities of the child'*.

**8.1.2** Children under 18 do not have a statutory right to choose their own religion in England and Wales or N Ireland. In Scotland, children have the right to choose their own religion at 16. It is discriminatory that children in different parts of the UK have uneven access to these rights. The only course of action which a child in England and Wales could take to vary aspects of his or her upbringing would be to seek to apply under section 8 of the Children Act 1989 for a specific issues order to override the imposition of religion against his or her wishes. However, it is not at all clear that the courts would be sympathetic to such applications. Similarly, in Scotland a child could apply for an order under section 3 of the Law Reform (Parent and Child) (Scotland) Act 1986 relating to the exercise of parental rights.

**8.1.3** The wording of Article 14 makes clear that, while parents have a responsibility to provide direction to the child, this must be in a *'manner consistent with the evolving capacities of the child'*. This balance is also reflected in Article 5 which states that a parent's responsibilities for the upbringing of a child must be undertaken in a manner consistent with the evolving capacity of the child. As a child becomes capable of articulating a view in relation to religious practice it should be respected by the parent. The implication of the 'Gillick' judgement (see para 6.2) is that if children have 'sufficient understanding and intelligence' they have the right to make their own decisions about important matters, including religion, independent of their parents. In practice this can be an area of considerable conflict between parents and children.

> *'Children and young people should not be forced into deciding on their parents religion. We have our own views but sometimes we go to church because my parents are Christian, but they never ask me if I am.'*
> (13 year-old, London)

**8.1.4** The issue of religion and beliefs within a family can be a matter of extreme sensitivity and a child's rights to freedom of conscience and religion cannot be promoted fully by providing legal redress. While legal reform is essential, full implementation of the child's rights in this, as in many other areas of civil rights, will only arise through a change in attitudes towards children and a shift in the prevailing widespread and powerful belief that parents 'own' their children and have the right to control their spiritual as well as their physical activities. There is concern that recognition of children's rights, in this context in particular, may lead to the undermining of the role of the parents. This can engender conflict where the exercise of the child's right conflicts with deeply-held beliefs within a family. But compliance with the Convention and its recognition of children as people with civil and political rights requires that these issues and their implications for the status of children are recognised by parents, professionals working with children, as well as by politicians and the media.

### ACTION REQUIRED FOR COMPLIANCE

**Compliance with Article 14, the right to freedom of thought, conscience and religion, requires that the law clarifies the right of the child to freedom of conscience and religion in line with the 'Gillick' principle with a presumption that children acquire sufficient understanding at the latest at 12. It will also be necessary for schools both to encourage children to articulate and develop their own views and to understand their rights in law where these rights are not respected.**

## 8.2 Children looked after by local authorities

**8.2.1** The Children Act 1989 in England and Wales requires that a child being looked after by the local authority cannot be brought up 'in any religious persuasion other than that in which he would have been brought up if the order had not been made' (section 33.(6)). Comparable provisions exist in Scotland and the Draft Children (NI) Order will introduce similar provisions in N Ireland. This provision was introduced in order to protect the right of parents to determine the religion of their child and clearly represents an area of very deep concern to many parents. It is also a recognition of the right embodied in Article 30 that a child from a minority ethnic community has a right to 'profess and practice' their religion. This section of the legislation imposes an absolute duty on the local authority and is not subject to the general principle that the welfare of the child is the paramount consideration.

**8.2.2** Whilst it is important that a child's personal history, culture and religion is respected when placements are being arranged, this provision must not impede the right of a child under Article 14 either to withdraw from the religion of her or his parents or to choose an alternative religion. Children looked after by the local authority do not have the right to apply for a section 8 order in the same way as children living at home and are therefore offered less opportunity to challenge the imposition of religion against their will. The requirement under the Children Act to 'ascertain the wishes and feelings of the child' when decisions are being made should therefore apply when decisions are made about the child's religion. The 'Gillick' principle should apply to any child judged to be competent to exercise a choice.

### ACTION REQUIRED FOR COMPLIANCE

**Compliance with Article 14, the right of children looked after by local authorities to freedom of religion, requires an amendment to the Children Act in England and Wales (and draft Children (N Ireland) Order): the right of parents whose child is looked after by the local authority to determine the religion in which their child will be brought up should be subject to the evolving capacity of the child to exercise a choice. Children should be consulted about their views on religion and, where they are competent to exercise a choice, their wishes should prevail.**

## 8.3 Religion in schools

**8.3.1** Parents have the right to withdraw their children from religious education and worship in school and can request lessons in a particular religion. But children have no such rights in school. Equally, a child has no right to participate in religious education where the parents wish the child to be excluded. Where a child has the competence to exercise a choice, Article 14 is quite clear that the child has a right to freedom of conscience and religion. The lack of respect for this right in education law, imposing as it does a requirement on children to participate in acts of worship which they may object strongly to and potentially denying them access to participation in a religion of their choice, breaches this Article.

**8.3.2** The Education Reform Act 1988 changed the provisions on religious education and worship in schools in England and Wales so that collective worship in maintained schools 'shall be wholly or mainly of a broadly Christian character [reflecting] the broad traditions of Christian belief without being distinctive of any particular Christian denomination'. The legislation does allow for relevant circumstances relating to the family backgrounds of pupils and their ages and aptitudes to be taken into account but nevertheless the prescriptive nature of this provision in England and Wales would appear to breach the right of all children to practice their religion. The Education Act 1993 requires that all local education authorities in England and Wales which have not introduced a new religious education syllabus since 1988 must undertake a review of their existing syllabus and may only continue to use it if it meets the requirements of section 8(3) of the 1988 Act. This states that syllabuses must 'reflect the fact that the religious traditions in Great Britain are in the main Christian whilst taking account of the teaching and practices of the other principle religions represented in Great Britain'.

> *'If you don't learn about other religions then you only get one view of how the world should be.'*
> (12 year-old, London)

**8.3.3** Many local authorities and Standing Advisory Councils for Religious Education (local bodies established to advise on religious education) have taken the view that these requirements giving a pre-eminent place to Christianity are discriminatory. The UK is a multi-cultural and multi-religious society and the syllabus for religious education should fully reflect this. The current legislation denies children from Muslim, Hindu and other non-Christian faiths equal opportunities to learn in school about their religion. This would appear to be a breach of both Article 14 and Article 2. Furthermore, Article 29.1(c) and (d) states that education must be directed to '*the development of respect for the child's parents, his or her own cultural identity, language and values, for the national values of the country in which the child is living, the country from which he or she may originate, and for civilizations different from his or her own; and the preparation of the child for responsible life in a free society, in the spirit of understanding, peace, tolerance, equality of sexes, and friendship among all peoples, ethnic, national and religious groups and persons of indigenous origin*'. Such respect will not be achieved if one religion, Christianity, is given an explicitly higher status than others.

### ACTION REQUIRED FOR COMPLIANCE

Compliance with Article 14 requires that children are given a right in law to exercise a choice over religion in schools subject to the child's evolving capacity.

Compliance with Articles 2, 14 and 29.1(c) and (d) requires that the provision in the Education Reform Act 1988, that Christianity is given pre-eminence both in collective acts of worship and in religious syllabuses, is repealed in favour of a recognition of the equal value and importance of all religions.

# 9 Freedom of association
## Article 15

## 9.1 Environmental restrictions

**9.1.1** Article 15 states that children have the right '*to freedom of association and to freedom of peaceful assembly*'. Children have comparatively few opportunities for freedom of assembly and association. The environment we have created has led to children being far less free today to move about cities and meet freely with friends independently of adults than was the case for previous generations of children. This has occurred not through deliberate intent but rather as a consequence of the design of cities, growing levels of traffic and heightened awareness and possibly incidence of attacks and assaults on children. Far fewer children, for example, go to school alone now than did only 20 years ago. A study by the Policy Studies Institute revealed that in 1971 80% of 7-8 year-olds were allowed to go to school alone but that by 1990 this figure had fallen to 9%[12]. The report comments: 'The freedom gained from the growth in the ownership and use of cars has resulted in freedom lost for another sector of the community'.

**9.1.2** This generation's children are being denied a whole range of opportunities for autonomy, for social development and for recreational activity that their parents and grandparents enjoyed when they were children. It is important to address the implications of this Article not only in relation to the adequacy of legislation to explicitly recognise and protect these rights but also in relation to the construction of an environment which creates and facilitates opportunities for young people to express their right to freedom of association and assembly. Adequate youth service provision, availability of transport, availability of places where young people can meet without harassment or interference are as necessary to the promotion of this civil right as the existence of protective legislation. (See also **UK Agenda Report 6 on environment,** page 134 for a more detailed discussion of these issues).

> '*We need more bridges over the road so we can get to the park.*'
> (8 year-old, Bristol)

### ACTION REQUIRED FOR COMPLIANCE

**An active commitment to the promotion of Article 15, the right to freedom of association, requires the development of a child-centred approach to environmental planning. Local authorities should be required to consider the implications of any proposed development on children living in the area in respect of public transport, social facilities, road safety and meeting places, all of which have considerable impact on their opportunities for association and assembly.**

## 9.2 School policies

**9.2.1** Children's rights to freedom of assembly are restricted in schools with no rights to form associations or to organise meetings. In the 1970s the National Union of School Students was proscribed by some head teachers, and young people therefore experienced great difficulty in organising and recruiting members. Some head teachers have refused to allow CND branches to be formed and meetings to be held in schools. Within social services the National Association of Young People in Care has had difficulty in organising in some areas. Without any written constitution which enshrines these principles it is particularly difficult for young people to enforce these rights and to challenge any failure to respect them.

**9.2.2** Children currently have no formal structures through which they can raise concerns about school policies on matters such as these. Nor do they have formal avenues of complaint.

> '*We want to be consulted about the running of the school and discuss issues, not just asked for ideas for stupid things like the school concert.*'
> (14 year-old, N Ireland)

### ACTION REQUIRED FOR COMPLIANCE

**Compliance with Article 15 would be promoted by the introduction of school councils and complaints procedures in all schools. They would provide opportunities for a dialogue between pupils and staff about the recognition of the right to freedom of assembly and how it could be protected.**

# 10 Protection of privacy
## Article 16

## 10.1 Privacy in residential institutions

**10.1.1** Article 16 states that: '*No child shall be subjected to arbitrary or unlawful interference with his or her privacy, family, home or correspondence, nor to unlawful attacks on his or her honour and reputation*'. The Children Act 1989 in England and Wales does provide important safeguards for children in some institutions. Regulations provide that there are facilities for children to meet parents and others privately and that pay phones are available in a setting where it is possible to make and receive telephone calls in privacy. These regulations also provide that sanctions cannot be imposed on children which refuse them visits or contact with family or friends unless this is judged to be in the child's best interests. There are regulations requiring provision in maintained schools for children aged 16 and over for storing pupil's belongings and space for private study and social purposes. Guidance issued by the Department of Health on the Children Act stresses the need for children accommodated in independent boarding schools to have lockable cupboards for personal belongings and to be able to enjoy a degree of privacy where they can opt to be alone from adults or their peers.

**10.1.2** However, there are still significant gaps in the protection available. The right to private correspondence is not guaranteed in all institutions for children and young people. If correspondence needs to be opened on grounds of safety or security, such as on suspicion of drugs or other forbidden articles, it should be possible for this to be done in front of the child without reading the contents of the letter. Children who live in schools or health institutions often for up to 52 weeks in the year do not, in many cases, have any formal right to protection of their privacy. Similarly, children and young people in wards in long-stay hospitals and shared cells in young offender institutions and prisons may have no privacy whatever. In some children's homes, including secure accommodation and some health units, closed-circuit video cameras and one-way mirror screens are used to observe children, often without their knowledge or consent. Some residential institutions run by social services, health and education departments and some day schools remove doors or door-locks from toilets and only have communal washing areas.

'*There is no such thing as privacy in a children's home.*[13]'

**10.1.3** The inquiries following a recent series of scandals concerning abuse of children in residential care have demonstrated the fundamental importance of respecting children's civil rights if they are to be able to challenge and prevent recurrences of such episodes. Unless children have access to basic civil rights, including the right to privacy, they will continue to lack the opportunities to take steps to protect themselves. The right to speak and write in confidence and the right to be alone are central to this process. However, for staff to feel able to respect young people, they themselves need to feel valued. Both the Scottish report on residential care, *Another kind of home*, and a report into children's homes in England and Wales, *Choosing with care* acknowledged that there is an urgent need for more training, management support and supervision of residential staff if the quality of care is to be enhanced[14][15]. Serious commitment to the implementation of Article 16 would necessitate regulations and guidance based on the child's right to privacy in all institutions in which children live subject, obviously, to such restrictions as are necessary in the interests of the safety both of the child and others.

### ACTION REQUIRED FOR COMPLIANCE
**Compliance with Article 16, the right to privacy, requires that the new rights to privacy introduced under the Children Act are monitored through consultation with children about the effectiveness of their implementation. Children's privacy should be safeguarded in regulations and guidance applying to all institutional settings, both day and boarding, which include children.**

## 10.2 Rights to confidentiality

**10.2.1** Article 16 needs to be considered in the context of a child's right to have confidences respected. This is of particular significance in the situation of a child wishing to discuss sexual or physical abuse with an adult. The growing recognition of the extent of sexual abuse within our society and the level of concern amongst practitioners and policy makers has led to a range of measures designed to protect children from continued abuse. Social workers and the police are required by law, and many others are required contractually, to notify the relevant authorities once a child has disclosed abuse. The need to protect the child is seen to take precedence over the child's right to respect for confidentiality or privacy. The danger is that the outcome of disclosure with all its profound consequences for children in relation to their own and their family's lives can be experienced as another form of abuse. In its way, the failure to respect the confidence of the child is a betrayal of trust just as the original abuse is.

**10.2.2** There has been considerable progress in recent years in both recognising and responding to child abuse. There is a danger that in the understandable efforts to protect the child experiencing abuse other rights are being forfeited. There is now a greater willingness to listen to the child disclosing abuse. It is equally important to listen to the child's concerns about how disclosure is handled. Child protection procedures need to reflect the principle of respect for children's privacy and confidentiality and the implications of overriding a child's wishes must be weighed against the cost to the child of a breach of confidentiality.

### ACTION REQUIRED FOR COMPLIANCE
**Compliance with Article 16 requires that there is a wide-ranging review of child protection procedures which draws on and is informed by the experiences of children and which takes as its framework all the principles of the Convention and does not focus exclusively on protection but also considers children's rights to confidentiality and privacy.**

# 11 Language, culture and religion
## Article 30

**11.1** Article 30 states that a child has the right to enjoy '*his or her own culture, to profess and practise his or her own religion, or to use his or her own language*'. This Article is of particular significance in the UK where there are many different minority ethnic communities each with their own language, religion and culture. In Wales, Welsh is the indigenous language of the country and continues to be spoken by a substantial minority of the population. Language is inextricably linked to the social system where all the elements of home, work, school and community interact and have consequences for children who are unable to live their everyday lives through the language of their choice.

**11.2** The importance of the Welsh language has been acknowledged in the Welsh Language Act 1993 which imposes a duty on public bodies to provide a bi-lingual service. The Welsh Language Board has responsibility for monitoring the provision of these services. However, whilst the legislation represents a welcome step forward, it is limited in its scope: it fails to impose a duty on all organisations providing services to do so bi-lingually, and it has not been backed up by a Government commitment to resource the changes that are necessary. Unless the requirements it contains are comprehensive and adequately funded, the impact of the legislation in ensuring the right of children to use their own language will be limited.

(see UK Agenda Report 7 on education, page 167 for a broader discussion of Article 30)

### ACTION REQUIRED FOR COMPLIANCE

**Compliance with Article 30, the right of a child to enjoy his or her own language, requires that the duty introduced in the Welsh Language Act 1993 on public bodies to provide a bi-lingual service are extended to all services in Wales and that the Government commits sufficient resources to facilitate this process.**

# Summary of action required for compliance

**1** Compliance with Article 2, the right not to be discriminated against, requires that:

- race relations legislation is introduced in N Ireland;

- legislation is introduced rendering it unlawful to discriminate on grounds of disability;

- the age of consent is equalised for all young people irrespective of sexual orientation, and legislation is introduced to make it unlawful to discriminate on grounds of sexual orientation;

- the rights of Travellers and Gypsies including children to continue their traditional way of life must be respected in law. Any proposed legislation must take account of the right embodied in Article 2 that no child may be discriminated against in respect of any of the rights in the Convention;

- racial harassment legislation is introduced which would cover offences such as arson, damage to property and places of religious worship, verbal racist abuse, and assault and would provide protection from racist attacks.

**2** Compliance with Article 7, the right to a name and knowledge of parents, requires:

- the introduction of a legislative duty on adoptive parents to inform a child that they are adopted as soon as the child is capable of understanding and to provide the child with access to his or her full birth certificate as soon as the child requests the information. They should also provide as much information to the child as is available about his or her origins;

- a review of the current legislation on assisted birth techniques which addresses the issues of identity and parenthood from the perspective of the right of children to knowledge of their identity, in line with article 7;

- that the child has access to available information on both biological parents. Such information should be recorded in the full birth certificate which should be accessible to the child.

**3** Compliance with Article 8, the right of the child to preserve his or her identity, requires the recognition in law that the child has a right of access to all files held about him or her and that support is provided in gaining access to files and understanding their implications.

**4** Compliance with Article 8 together with Article 12, the right of the child to express a view and have it taken seriously, requires that children should be given the opportunity to express their views about any proposal to change their name and to have that opinion taken into account in any judicial or administrative proceedings subject to their age and understanding.

**5** Compliance with Article 12 requires that the relevant family law in each jurisdiction in the UK is amended to introduce a duty on those with parental responsibility, in reaching any major decision relating to the child, to ascertain the child's wishes and give them due consideration subject to age and understanding.

**6** Compliance with Article 13, the right to freedom of expression, requires:

● a fundamental shift in prevailing attitudes towards children's status in the education system. It requires that rights to freedom of expression of children should be protected in the same way as for adults. So, unless restrictions are '*necessary for the respect of the rights or reputations of others or for the protection of national security or of public order, or of public health or morals*', there should be a presumption in law that the child has a right to freedom of expression. All education legislation should be reviewed in the light of this fundamental right;

● careful monitoring of the provision of music, drama and other arts in schools during changes in the control and administration of education to ensure that any reduction is identified, and in Government commitment to introduce measures to restore any reductions or inequalities in provisions that are identified.

**7** Compliance with Article 14, the right to freedom of thought, conscience and religion, requires:

● that the law clarifies the right of the child to freedom of conscience and religion in line with the 'Gillick' principle with a presumption that children acquire sufficient understanding at the latest at 12. It will also be necessary for schools both to encourage children to articulate and develop their own views and to understand their rights in law where these rights are not respected;

● an amendment to the Children Act in England and Wales (and draft Children (N Ireland) Order) rendering the right of parents whose child is looked after by the local authority to determine the religion in which their child will be brought up to be subject to the evolving capacity of the child to exercise a choice. Children should be consulted about their views on religion and, where they are competent to exercise a choice, their wishes should prevail;

● that children are given a right in law to exercise a choice over religion in schools subject to the child's evolving capacity.

**8** Compliance with Articles 2, 14 and 29.1(c) and (d) requires that the provision in the Education Reform Act 1988, that Christianity is given pre-eminence both in collective acts of worship and in religious syllabuses, is repealed in favour of a recognition of the equal value and importance of all religions.

**9** An active commitment to the promotion of Article 15, the right to freedom of association, requires:

● the development of a child-centred approach to environmental planning. Local authorities should be required to consider the implications of any proposed development on children living in the area in respect of public transport, social facilities, road safety and meeting places, all of which have considerable impact on their opportunities for association and assembly;

● the introduction of school councils and complaints procedures in all schools which would make a significant contribution towards protecting children's rights within the schools system. It would provide opportunities for a dialogue between pupils and staff about the recognition of the right to freedom of assembly and how it could be protected.

**10** Compliance with Article 16, the right to privacy, requires:

● that the new rights to privacy introduced under the Children Act are monitored through consultation with children about the effectiveness of their implementation. Children's privacy should be safeguarded in regulations and guidance applying to all institutional settings, both day and boarding, which include children;

● a wide-ranging review of child protection procedures which draws on and is informed by the experiences of children and which takes as its framework all the principles of the Convention and does not focus exclusively on protection but also considers children's rights to confidentiality and privacy.

**11** Compliance with Article 30, the right of a child to enjoy his or her own language, requires that the duty introduced in the Welsh Language Act 1993 on public bodies to provide a bi-lingual service are extended to all services in Wales and that the Government commits sufficient resources to facilitate this process.

# References

1. *A people's charter: Liberty's Bill of Rights: a consultation document*, NCCL (1991)
2. Application no 9278/81 and 9415/81 to the European Commission: G&E v Norway
3. *Curse of the gypsies*, Daily Star (23 October 1991)
4. European Court of Human Rights: Gaskin v UK, Strasbourg judgement (7 July 1989)
5. *Adoption: the future*, Department of Health, Welsh Office, Home Office and Lord Chancellor's Office, HMSO (1993)
6. *Birth secrets*, Blyth E, Childright (June 1991)
7. Gillick v West Norfolk and Wisbech AHA, 3 All ER 402 (1985)
8. Re W (A Minor: Consent to medical treatment), 1 FLR 1 (1993)
9. *Report on family law*, Scottish Law Commission, HMSO (1992)
10. *Sexual lifestyles and HIV risk*, Johnson A M et al, Nature (1992)
11. 'Let's talk about sex', Bell A, *Scottish Child* (February/March 1993)
12. *One false move: a study of children's independent mobility*, Hillman M, Adams J and Whitelegg J, Policy Studies Institute (1990)
13. *Not just a name: the views of young people in residential and foster care*, Fletcher B, National Consumer Council (1993)
14. *Another kind of home: a review of residential child care*, The Social Work Services Inspectorate for Scotland, The Scottish Office, Edinburgh HMSO (1992)
15. *Choosing with care: the report of the committee of inquiry into the selection, development and management of staff in children's homes*, chaired by Norman Warner, HMSO (1992)

UK Agenda for Children

**2** Care of children

# Contents

> *The unreferenced quotations in this report are comments made during a consultation exercise undertaken by the Children's Rights Development Unit with groups of young people throughout the UK.*

# 1 Introduction

**1.1** All children have basic needs for day to day care. The preamble to the Convention states that children '*for the full and harmonious development of [their] personality, should grow up in a family environment, in an atmosphere of happiness, love and understanding*'. A number of the articles proceed to establish the right of every child to have those needs met. The primary responsibility for the provision of care clearly rests with a child's parents but the Convention makes explicit that child care is not and should not be an isolated task. There is an important function for the State in both supporting parents in their parenting role and in providing care for children where, for whatever reason, parents are not able to fulfil that role.

**1.2** In England and Wales the Children Act 1989 is the main legislation addressing the need to promote and safeguard the welfare of children within the family and to provide alternative care when the family is unable to meet the needs of a child. This Act, which came into force in October 1991, is based on a number of principles consistent with those in the Convention:

- parents are generally the best people to care for children (Articles 5 and 18);
- the best interests of the child must be a primary consideration of local authorities and the paramount consideration of certain courts when decisions are made concerning the child (Article 3);
- local authorities have a duty to give support to children in need and their families (Article 18);
- the views of the child must be taken account of when decisions are made that affect the child (Article 12).

**1.3** However, although the Children Act provides a constructive legislative framework for working towards full implementation of the relevant articles in the Convention, progress is impeded by a number of factors. The Act includes both public child care law, when local authority social services become involved in the care of children, and private family law involving parental responsibilities. There are serious differences between the two:

- certain courts and local authorities are required to have regard to the wishes and feelings of children when making decisions on their behalf. But, within the family, no such requirement applies to parents;
- children in public law proceedings have automatic party status whereas in private law court proceedings they do not;
- children who are in the care of the local authority are denied the right available to other children to apply for leave to apply to the court for an order determining their upbringing, for example for contact with a relative. They can only apply for a residence order;
- parents, unlike courts and local authorities, are under no duty to ensure that the child's welfare is a primary consideration when making decisions that affect the child.

**1.4** There is as yet a considerable gulf between, on the one hand, the legal provisions in the Act concerning the requirement in the sphere of public care of children to listen to children and take them seriously, and on the other hand, our prevailing attitudes towards children which tend to exclude and marginalise them from decision-making in their lives. And there are serious concerns over whether the level of resourcing of the legislation is sufficient to permit the effective implementation of its principles. There is also a disjuncture between the policy thrust of the Children Act and other recent legislation such as the Child Support Act 1992 (see **UK Agenda Report 4 on an adequate standard of living,** page 67), the Education Act 1993 (see **UK Agenda Report 7 on education,** page 149) and criminal justice legislation relating to young people (see **UK Agenda Report 9 on youth justice,** page 199).

**1.5** In Scotland, there is no comprehensive piece of legislation covering public and private law as the Children Act does. The Scottish Law Commission *Report on Family Law* 1992 has suggested reforms of private law which go further towards defining parental responsibilities to children and towards reflecting principles in the Convention. Public law is contained within the Social Work (Scotland )Act 1968 and is currently the subject of a White Paper *Scotland's Children* published in August 1993. However, there is a need for a common set of principles underpinning both areas of law and to date there is no Government commitment for an integrated Act for children.

**1.6** In N Ireland, the primary child care legislation is the Children and Young Persons Act (NI) 1968 which closely resembles the Children and Young Persons Act 1963 in England and Wales. A major review of legislation and services took place in the late 1970s resulting in the Black Report (1979) and an expectation of new legislation. Minor consultative documents were issued during the 1980s but it was not until 1993 that draft legislation, in the form of the draft Children (NI) Order, was published. It is anticipated that the new legislation will be enacted in 1994 and be in operation by 1996.

**1.7** The draft Children (NI) Order proposes legislation closely resembling the Children Act 1989 and in so doing can be criticised for failing to give serious consideration to the particular features of N Ireland society - the extent of multiple deprivation, the large proportion of young people, the religious and cultural divide and the political instability and violence. It also fails to address the local characteristics of child care services such as the organisationally integrated health and personal social services and the presence of training schools with both justice and welfare populations.

**1.8** Legislation on adoption in England and Wales is contained in the Adoption Act 1976 but the Department of Health (DH) and Welsh Office have led a major inter-departmental review of adoption law and, following consultation, a White paper was published in November 1993. A similar review of adoption law is taking place in Scotland.

Issues relating to poverty, youth justice, protection of children from all forms of violence while in the care of parents and others, and international adoption are addressed in other Reports in the UK Agenda.

# 2 Relevant articles in the Convention

## 2.1 General principles

**Article 2:** all rights in the Convention must apply without discrimination of any kind irrespective of race, colour, language, religion, national, ethnic or social origin, disability or other status.

**Article 3:** the duty in all actions to consider the best interests of the child.

**Article 12:** the right to express an opinion and to have that opinion taken into account in any matter or procedure affecting the child.

## 2.2 Articles relevant to care of children

These principles relate directly to the day to day provision of care for children and provide the framework for assessing the extent to which the rights of children in the sphere of the home and alternatives to the home are currently respected:

**Article 3.2:** the duty of the Government to provide the necessary care and protection for the child's well-being and introduce appropriate legislative and administrative procedures to achieve this end.

**Article 3.3:** the duty of the Government to ensure that the standards of services provided for the care and protection of children are adequate, particularly in relation to safety, health, staffing and supervision.

**Article 5:** the duty of the Government to respect the rights and responsibilities of parents to provide guidance and direction for children which is appropriate to the evolving capacity of the child.

**Article 8:** the right to preserve identity including name, nationality and family relations.

**Article 9:** the right to live with one's family unless this is not in the child's best interests and, where separation does take place, the right to maintain contact with both parents on a regular basis.

**Article 18:** the duty of the Government to recognise that both parents have joint responsibility for bringing up their children and to support them in this task.

**Article 19:** the right to protection from all forms of violence while in the care of parents and others.

**Article 20:** the duty of the Government to provide special protection for children unable to live with their family, and the right to appropriate alternative care which takes account of children's need for continuity and their ethnic, religious, cultural and linguistic background.

**Article 21:** the duty of the Government to ensure that where adoption takes place, it is only carried out in the best interests of the child with all necessary safeguards.

**Article 23:** the right of disabled children to special care, education and training to ensure the fullest possible social integration.

**Article 24:** the right to the highest level of health possible and to access to health care services.

**Article 25:** the right for children placed in the care of the State to periodic reviews of treatment.

**Article 28:** the right to education, including vocational education, on the basis of equality of opportunity.

**Article 30:** the right of minority groups to enjoy their own culture, language and religion.

*For the full wording of the articles, see the UN Convention on the Rights of the Child, page311.*

# 3 The right to family life

## 3.1 Background

**3.1.1** The preamble to the Convention stresses that '*the family, as the fundamental group in society and the natural environment for the growth and well-being of all its members and particularly children, should be afforded the necessary protection and assistance so that it can fully assume its responsibilities within the community*'. The Convention therefore constructs a model of partnership between parents and the state in which there is acknowledgement of the importance to children of their family life and the need for broad social support to enhance the opportunities of all children to be brought up within their family wherever possible. This section examines how far existing law, policy and practice ensures that the family is able to protect and promote the rights of children and the extent to which state support, consistent with the principles of the Convention, is available to families throughout the UK.

## 3.2 Parental responsibilities (Article 18)

**3.2.1** Article 18 states that governments must '*ensure the recognition of the principle that both parents have common responsibilities for the upbringing and development of the child ... The best interests of the child will be their basic concern*'. Article 3 extends the responsibility for promoting children's welfare to '*private or public social welfare institutions, courts of law, administrative authorities or legislative bodies*'. Parents' relationship to their children is clearly defined in terms of responsibilities and not in terms of parental rights. Such rights as exist for parents only exist in so far as they are necessary in order to promote their children's welfare. This approach is confirmed in Article 5 which states that parents should exercise their responsibilities towards children in a manner '*consistent with the evolving capacities of the child*'.

**3.2.2** The Children Act 1989 for England and Wales introduces the concept of 'parental responsibility' to replace the traditional common law concept of parental rights. However, it fails to provide any detailed definition of what is meant by the term 'parental responsibility' other than to describe it as 'all the rights and duties, power, responsibilities and authority which by law a parent of a child has in relation to a child and his property' (section 3.1). In N Ireland pending the implementation of the new Children (NI) Order, the legal concept of parental responsibility does not exist. In Scotland, the relevant legislation is the Law Reform (Parent and Child) (Scotland) Act 1986 which does not contain a principle of parental responsibility. The Scottish Law Commission in its *Report on family law* explored the proposal that there should be, in legislation, a general statement setting out the statutory obligations of parenthood. They concluded it would be advantageous a) to clarify exactly what those responsibilities were, b) to counteract the view that parenthood conferred rights but no responsibilities, and c) to enable the law to make it clear that parental rights were conferred in order to enable parents to meet their responsibilities[1]. They therefore recommended that there should be such a statement in law and proposed the following wording:

● It should be provided that a parent has in relation to his or her child a responsibility so far as it is practicable or in the interests of the child:

(i) to safeguard and promote the child's health, development and welfare;

(ii) to provide, in a manner appropriate to the child's stage of development, direction and guidance to the child;

(iii) if not living with the child, to maintain personal relations and direct contact with the child on a regular basis;

(iv) to act as the child's legal representative and, in that capacity, to administer in the interests of the child any property belonging to the child.'

**3.2.3** If such a statement were introduced into legislation it would provide a more explicit definition in law of the responsibilities associated with parenthood and would impose a clear duty on parents to promote their children's welfare in a manner consistent with the requirements embodied in Article 18 and Article 5. It would also be consistent with the state's obligation under Article 3 to promote the welfare of children for legislation to incorporate this principle, rather than leaving the responsibility within the individual confines of the family.

### ACTION REQUIRED FOR COMPLIANCE

**Compliance with Articles 18, 5 and 3, the responsibility to promote children's welfare in a manner consistent with their evolving capacity, requires that family law in each jurisdiction in the UK should be amended to introduce a definition of parental responsibility which makes explicit those obligations and avoids discrimination between children in different jurisdictions, in line with Article 2.**

## 3.3 Views of the child within families (Article 12)

**3.3.1** Article 12 states that '*the child who is capable of forming his or her own views [has] the right to express those views freely in all matters affecting the child, the views of the child being given due weight in accordance with the age and maturity of the child*'. Whilst the Children Act, in line with this principle, does require local authorities and courts to have regard to the wishes and feelings of the child when decisions in respect of that child are being made, no comparable requirement exists with regard to decisions made within the family. Similarly, there is no provision in law in Scotland or N Ireland for children's views to be taken seriously.

**3.3.2** There is provision within the Children Act in England and Wales under section 8 for a child to apply for leave to apply to the court for an order relating to residence, contact or any other matter relating to parental responsibility. (Parents, by contrast, have an absolute right to apply for such orders). This provision has been used by children, for example, to challenge decisions made by adults about where they should live. In Scotland, whilst it is technically possible for a child to seek an order relating to parental rights, under the Law Reform (Parent and Child) (Scotland) Act 1986, section 3, in practice no child has ever succeeded in doing so. In N Ireland no such provisions exist.

**3.3.3** However, whilst having rights to apply to court for an order would represent an important step forward for children, it is clearly a right which should only be exercised when discussion and negotiation have failed. It is a measure of last resort. There is therefore a need to introduce an obligation to listen to children's views at an earlier stage if the principle embodied in Article 12 is to have any real significance in children's lives. This could be achieved by introducing into law a requirement that all parents should listen to the views of children and give them due consideration when taking significant decisions that affect the child. Such a requirement would give legal recognition to the principle that children have a right to participate in matters that affect them. It would seem sensible to ensure that, if children do have such a right, it is exercised at the earliest possible stage in order to avoid where possible the need for adversarial proceedings. It is an issue about which many young people feel very strongly:

> *'We should have rights, to some extent, to go where we want, rights to take part in family decisions, rights to make our own decisions about our future, rights to live our own life and not what our parents want us to do, the right to our own opinion.'*
> (15 year-old, N Ireland)

**3.3.4** The Scottish Law Commission *Report on family law* proposed that there should be in law a requirement that: 'Before a person reaches a major decision which involves fulfilling parental responsibility or exercising a parental right, the person shall, so far as is practicable, ascertain the views of the child concerned regarding the decision, and shall give due consideration to those views, taking account of the child's age and maturity'[2]. They found that there was widespread support for such a provision which already exists in a number of other countries including Germany, Sweden, Norway and Finland.

> *'I'm looking to be able to have a say in what happens to me. My parents are talking of moving at the moment and I'd quite like to be in on that decision.'*
> (14 year-old, Manchester)

**3.3.5** The Scottish Law Commission also proposes limits on parents' rights to physically punish their children, going some way to meet the requirement in Article 19 that children in the care of parents and others should be protected from '*all forms of physical or mental violence*'. (The right of the child to physical and personal integrity is covered in the **UK Agenda Report 3 on physical integrity,** page 51).

### ACTION REQUIRED FOR COMPLIANCE

**Compliance with Article 12 requires that the relevant family law in each jurisdiction in the UK is amended to introduce a requirement that, in reaching any major decision relating to the child, parents are required to ascertain to those views and give due consideration subject to age and understanding.**

## 3.4 Family support services (Article 18)

**3.4.1** Article 18.2 states that the Government must provide '*assistance to parents ... in the performance of their child rearing responsibilities and shall ensure the development of institutions, facilities and services for the care of children*'. Article 18.3 goes on to state that '*the children of working parents have the right to benefit from child care services and facilities for which they are eligible*'. These provisions spell out the practical obligations that ensue from the commitment in the preamble to the Convention which stresses that the family must be afforded the necessary assistance and protection to enable it to carry out its responsibilities. The Articles and the preamble describe a responsibility for the provision of services for the

care of **all** children.

*Children in need*

**3.4.2** It is difficult to reconcile this broad-ranging commitment to a shared approach to provision and services for children with the potentially restrictive implications of the gate-keeping concept of 'in need' which applies in the Children Act 1989 for England and Wales. Section 17 requires local authorities to provide appropriate services for children in need. A child in need is defined in the legislation as any child whose health or development is likely to be impaired without the provision of services, or is unlikely to achieve or maintain a reasonable standard of health and development without the provision of services, or who is disabled. While the Convention describes a responsibility on the part of the state in respect of all children, the Children Act restricts responsibility to those children who are perceived as vulnerable in some way. It was precisely this narrowing of potential entitlement to family support services that united voluntary organisations against the concept during the passage of the Act through Parliament. Furthermore, any public policy in respect of family support must also reflect the requirement in Article 3 that '*in all actions ... the best interests of the child shall be a primary consideration*'. It is necessary, therefore, to examine the existing provision of support for families against this welfare principle.

> *'We were living in really bad circumstances and my mum started drinking. I suppose it was her way of escape and I can remember literally starving with hunger.'*
> (18 year-old, Merseyside)

**3.4.3** The White Paper *Scotland's children* expressed concern that the existing legislation to provide support for families emphasised the use of powers to prevent reception into care under section 12 of the 1968 Social Work (Scotland) Act. It recommended a more positive promotion of the welfare of children, referring to a 'broad emphasis to allow support of children within their family and community'. This approach appears more consistent with the concept of state responsibility for the provision of services for all families, but the White Paper fails to provide any detail on how this provision should be introduced.

**3.4.4** In practice, the Children Act definition of 'in need' is open to widely different interpretations by local authorities. Both the Association of Metropolitan Authorities (AMA) and the Association of County Councils (ACC) have stressed the need for a wide application of 'in need'. The ACC point out that all children may come into the broader 'in need' net at some time[3]. However, it is already becoming clear that many local authorities are constructing a narrow definition of need which requires individual families to undergo assessment before being able to qualify for access to any services. The Social Services Inspectorate (SSI) in its initial research on the Act comments that one of its most worrying findings is the failure to give high priority to families on income support and family credit, one parent families or unemployed parents[4]. This low rating is of particular concern in view of the known high correlation between material deprivation and the use of accommodation or care. The SSI comment that: 'There would seem to be a conflict between some of [the priority ratings] and the intention of the Act to make family support services the cornerstone of local authority child care systems and to encourage a broad definition of need'. *The Children*

*Act Report 1992* confirms this pattern with only a quarter of authorities identifying children in low-income families as being in need[5]. It further reveals that there is a continuing tendency to give highest priority to those children for whom authorities already had an existing responsibility. Budgets for children in need are resource rather than needs led and with local authorities currently experiencing severe constraints on expenditure, there is little provision for any development of family support services.

**3.4.5** Concern has also been expressed at the stigmatising effect of services which can only be offered if a family is perceived as being or having a problem[6]. Many families may be unwilling to go through an assessment process, others may be unaware of the services available or the criteria for eligibility. Either way, the children will not be receiving services that they may well need and would benefit from. In the *1990 Report for the European Commission's Children's Network*, Bronwen Cohen comments that: 'The single greatest disappointment of the [Children] Act, however, is the continuing restriction of duties of local authorities in providing services to those children defined as being in need, perpetuating the use of rationing systems such as the stigmatising admissions system to local authority nurseries, so widely condemned by organisations consulted for the initial UK report and in contrast to the increasing abandonment of similar policies within the European Community'[7].

**3.4.6** Restrictions on services to those families where children are seen to be at risk of abuse may lead to both families and professionals lending an over-emphasis to child protection perspectives in order to gain the services. It may also lead to any request for help being perceived as an acknowledgement of abuse or neglect. Certainly, research into the implementation of section 17 of the Act amongst Welsh local authorities confirms that initial concerns that child protection would take the major share of resources with insufficient left over for family support services were well-founded. Children suffering from abuse or neglect were rightly receiving the highest priority but senior managers felt that putting more resources into family support would reduce the numbers of children at risk[8]. The NSPCC have commented that because resources are scarce, children have to be deemed to be in need of protection to get help[9].

**3.4.7** The findings of Department of Health commissioned research conducted by Jane Gibbons and as yet unpublished shows that only one in six of all child protection referrals result in a child being placed on the child protection register and further that of the remaining five in six, most need family support services and yet fail to receive them. These findings appear to confirm that social workers will intervene to protect children from their families but are more reluctant to intervene to promote parent's capacities to protect their children for themselves as required by Article 18.2.

**3.4.8** An approach to definitions of need which fails to recognise that the problems for many families are rooted in long-term acute structural poverty and not individual pathology, will inevitably create a narrow route of access which will deny many families the *'appropriate assistance to parents ... in the performance of their child-rearing responsibilities'*. (For a more detailed analysis, see **UK Agenda Report 4 on an adequate standard of living**, page 67) Comprehensive needs assessment of children in each local authority area should be undertaken, based on a broad interpretation of

need which looks at causes as well as symptoms of need. There should also be longitudinal research which examines the impact of family support services over a period of time to assess their efficacy.

> *'It's an ongoing cycle of deprivation; our parents are unemployed, we are unemployed and it will go onto a third generation and a really bad situation of debt and malnutrition.'*
> (17 year-old, Merseyside)

*Levels of family support*

**3.4.9** Day care provision for children represents a central plank in the range of support services that parents require in bringing up their children. Publicly-funded provision for under-fives in the UK is very low compared with most other European countries. The most recent figures on nursery education places Britain eleventh in a league table of European countries with only Portugal providing lower levels. Day care is available for 2% of under-threes as compared with 30% in France and 48% in Denmark. More than 95% of French and Belgian children are in nursery schools from the age of three, as are 85% of Italian and Danes[10]. In Britain the figure is about 25% with most attending only part-time.

**3.4.10** There is substantial evidence of the benefits to children of receiving nursery education in terms of academic achievement and yet even our current limited provision may be under threat from the Education Act 1993. As the budgets currently held at local authority level for nursery education are devolved down to each individual school, the amount received by a school is, at present levels of funding, unlikely to be sufficient to enable the development of nursery classes. Commitments made by the Government to continue providing funding for schools with nursery classes which opt out of local authority control only apply to full-time provision. There is therefore a serious threat that a service of primary importance for children, already woefully inadequate, may in the future deteriorate much further. These policies demonstrate a clear lack of commitment to the principles embodied in Article 18 of a partnership between parents and the State in the provision of services for children. The Association of Metropolitan Authorities in its 1991 report *Children first: services for young children*, argues the need for a broader-based level of under-fives provision to meet the developmental needs of children. It observes that investment in pre-school education can have a significant impact in countering the damaging effects of early deprivation[11].

**3.4.11** Substantial numbers of children under five attend some form of social care provision. Half a million children attend playgroups which are an important source of social experience for children. However, many of these groups operate on tiny and often precarious budgets and are run by volunteers. There is a need to sustain and develop playgroups as a resource for children which is affordable for parents. Playgroups, however, are of little help to working parents. They only operate for 2-3 hours a day. For many pre-school-age children whose parents are working, the two main forms of child care are childminders and day nurseries. Childminding, whilst in many ways a desirable option for very young children, is prohibitively expensive for many low income families, particularly lone-parents and those families with more than one school-age child. There is substantial evidence of unmet demand for day care, the lack of which currently inhibits opportunities, particularly for women, to obtain paid employment. Bradshaw and Millar found that among lone mothers who were not employed, 28% would have liked to obtain work straightaway if affordable child care was available[12]. The rate of full-time employment amongst single mothers is the lowest in the European Community (6% in 1988) primarily because of the lack of affordable publicly funded day care[13]. Day nurseries in England provide for less than 1% of under-fives, 0.5% in N Ireland and a mere 0.14% in Wales and the figures are falling. There was a smaller proportion of under-fives in day nurseries in 1989 than in 1985.

> *'All of us were keen to get a job but the lack of, or the expense of child care facilities was making it impossible. Society does not give us the opportunity to show that we are intelligent, worthwhile people.'*
> (18 year-old, Oxfordshire)

**3.4.12** The problem is not exclusive to under-fives. Provision of 'out-of-school care' for children of working parents is extremely limited. The Department of Employment in 1993 allocated £45 million through the Training Enterprise Councils (TECs) to promote out-of-school clubs in the UK. This development is very welcome and represents the first Government money available for this type of provision. The explicit recognition of the importance of training for play work evidenced by the decision to provide the money through the TECs is also welcome. However, the money is only for start-up costs and schemes are expected to become self-financing in the longer term. There is real concern therefore that fees will have to be charged by providers of out-of-school care and these will serve to exclude children from low-income families. Without subsidies, new provision is unlikely to be of any real value to such families.

**3.4.13** Although this recent initiative is a significant breakthrough, it needs to be remembered that there are serious inadequacies in the level of provision generally available. Prior to the TEC grants there were only 500-600 out-of-school clubs in the whole of the UK. Many are currently under threat because of the withdrawal in England of the Urban Aid Programme and the severe cuts in local authority expenditure. This form of care is a vital resource for working parents without which many parents are faced with the stark choice of giving up work or allowing their children to come home to empty houses, neither of which is likely to be in the child's best interests. Commitment to Article 18. 3 and support for working parents has been advanced by the injection of new money but this will need to be expanded and sustained if we are to achieve full compliance with the principle it embodies.

**3.4.14** Section 19 of the Children Act requires local authorities to undertake reviews of their day care provision for under-eights. This requirement extends to Scottish as well as English and Welsh authorities and should provide a detailed analysis of the level and availability of provision. Clearly such information is essential to compliance with Article 18.2 and the provision of '*appropriate assistance*' to parents. However, whilst local authorities in England and Wales have a statutory duty under section 18 of the Children Act to provide day care for children in need, Scottish authorities are currently under no such obligation. This distinction would appear to be in breach of the obligation in Article 2 that all the rights in the Convention must apply without discrimination to all children.

**3.4.15** The reviews of day care have to be conducted jointly with the relevant education authority in recognition of the importance of co-ordination in the provision of services for under-eights. However, the proposals in the Education Act 1993 to promote increased numbers of opted-out schools and establish a Funding Agency for Schools would appear to threaten moves towards a more collaborative approach. The role of the local education authority as the agency responsible for overall planning and development of services including nursery provision will be substantially diminished with an inevitable fragmentation of services as budgets are devolved to individual schools.

**3.4.16** There has traditionally been little commitment by local authorities to consulting with parents and children over the type of services needed and the most effective ways of providing these services. Local authorities in England and Wales are now required under the NHS and Community Care Act 1992 to consult with local communities, users and providers of services about plans for future services. However, in many authorities, community care plans only extend to adult services and there is no comparable requirement in respect of children's services. Effective compliance with Article 18 requires that services are developed in line with the wishes and views of both parents and children. Furthermore, in order for parents to take advantage of what services do exist they need information about what is available and how to gain access to it.

### ACTION REQUIRED FOR COMPLIANCE

**Compliance with Article 18, and the broad-based duty to provide support for all parents, requires:**

- **longitudinal research into the cost effectiveness of family support services and into the impact on children of differing interpretations of 'in need';**

- **all local authorities to undertake needs assessments of children in their area based on a broad definition of need, backed up by a central Government commitment to provide sufficient resources to fund the identified need;**

- **consultation with parents and children in the planning of services, and parents to be provided with information about the availability of and criteria for access to these services;**

- **flexible and appropriate educational (and care) provision for all three and four year-olds, publicly funded day care services available to the under-three population and out-of-school provision for all who require it, together with adequate central government grants to achieve it;**

- **close monitoring of the impact of these changes on the overall provision of services to under-eight year-olds to ensure that the obligations under Article 18 are not being undermined by administrative changes to the educational system.**

## 3.5 Standards of day care provision
(Article 3.3)

**3.5.1** The guidance to the Children Act sets out detailed advice on the standards that should be applied by local authorities when registering day care providers[14]. These standards are consistent with the requirement in Article 3.3 that '*institutions, services and facilities responsible for the care or* *protection of children shall conform with the standards established by competent authorities, particularly in the areas of safety, health in the number and suitability of thier staff as well as compenent supervision'.* However, since the publication of the guidance, the DH has issued a circular which substantially undermines these standards by arguing that too rigid an interpretation of the guidance is leading to a reduction in the availability of provision and encouraging local authorities to adopt a more flexible approach to registration.

**3.5.2** It is the view of many of the major organisations representing providers of day care both in the voluntary and statutory sector that this circular may be detrimental to children, potentially jeopardising standards of safety and protection that are essential to the provision of high quality care. It is not appropriate to rely on the reduction of standards as the means of achieving growth in provision. To do so is merely to sacrifice one set of principles – namely that of the right of the chld to high quality and safe provision – in favour of the principle of expanding the service. The promotion of day care is of immense importance but the growth in provison must remain a separate issue from the maintenance of standards.

**ACTION REQUIRED FOR COMPLIANCE**

**Compliance with Article 3.3, the duty to ensure appropriate standards of provision requires that the advice on standards contained in the original guidance on the Children Act issued by the Department of Health should be adhered to for purposes of registration of all day care provison, and that basic standards should be included in regulations, not merely guidance.**

## 3.6 Maternity rights and parental leave
(Article 18)

**3.6.1** Article 5 stresses the obligation on the part of the state to *'respect the responsibilities, rights and duties of parents'*, and *Article 18 goes on to emphasise the 'recognition of the principle that both parents have common responsibilties for the upbringing and development of the child'.* Statutory employment rights for working parents to enable them to fulfil responsibilities towards their children are very limited in the UK. The Trade Union Reform and Employment Rights Act 1993 incorporates measures to implement the proposals contained in the EC Directive on the protection of pregnant women at work, but offers only 14 weeks entitlement to paid maternity leave[15]. Given that this leave can commence 11 weeks before the baby is due this means that, for many mothers, they will be liable to return to work when the baby is only three weeks old. Where the baby is born after the due date, this thrce weeks will be even further reduced. Most employers have no child care or breast-feeding facilities and therefore the consequences of such an early rcturn to work is likely, in many instances, to be detrimental to the best interests of the child. It inhibits the possibility of the mother continuing to breast-feed in contravenion of Article 24.2(e) which states that the Government must ensure that *'parents . . . are informed, have access to and are supported in the use of basic knowledge of . . . the advantages of breast feeding'.* It is also virtually impossible to find child care for a baby aged three weeks or less. The mother is therefore faced with the choice of losing her job or, if she can get child care, separating from a newborn baby. If she has two years service with her

employer she has the right to maternity leave of up to 29 wecks after the baby is born but for many women this is not a practical option because they are dependent on their earnings. An increase in statuory maternity leave would go some way towards achieving a greater commitment to the principle embodied in Article 18.

**3.6.2** Despite the right contained in the Employment Act 1980 'not to be unreasonably refused time off to attend ante-natal appointments', a report by the National Association of Citizen's Advice Bureau, *Not in labour* found continuing evidence of employers flouting the legislation and, indeed, evidence that many employers and employees were unaware that the right existed[16]. Clearly, it is unacceptable and in breach of Article 24.2(d), which imposes a duty on the state *'to ensure appropriate pre-natal and post-natal health care for mothers',* that women should be denied access to necessary health care during pregnancy. There is a need for a publicity campaign to inform both employers and employees of their obligations and rights, including the right to ante-natal care.

**3.6.3**. Article 18 states that *'both parents have common responsibilities for the upbringing and development of the child'.* To date in the UK, there is no recognition in employment law of the responsibilities of fathers towards their children. There is no statutory provision of parental leave to enable parents to carry out their child cae responsibilities and indeed the UK Government is currently blocking the draft *EC Directive on parental leave and leave for family reasons.* Comparatively few employers offer contractual provision of this right. Even where they do such leave is restricted to a few days. There is no provision, as is the case for example in Sweden, for parents to choose who will take time off to care for a baby. This continued failure to introduce the necessary legislative change giving fathers these rights denies them the capacity to exercise their responsibilities in respect of their children in line with Article 18.1.

**3.6.4** Nor is there any statutory provision of dependence leave for sick children. This can present problems for all parents but in particular those with disabled children who often need time for hospital and other appointments.

**ACTION REQUIRED FOR COMPLIANCE**

**Complaince with Article 18, the duty on the Government to promote the principle of parents having common responsibility for their children requires that:**

● **statutory maternity leave is increased to at least 18 weeks;**

● **statutory paternity leave is introduced which provide opportunities for fathers to be more involved in the care of their children;**

● **statutory leave to care for children whilst they are ill is introduced for all employees;**

● **publicity campaigns are developed to ensure that both employees and employers are aware of the statutory rights of pregnant women to time off for ante-natal care.**

## 3.7 Services for disabled children
(Article 23)

**3.7.1** The Children Act does for the first time bring the responsibility for providing services to disabled children within the mainstream of child care legislation, requiring local authorities 'to minimise the effect on disabled children of their disabilities and to give such children the opportunities to lead lives which are as normal as possible'[17]. This change represents significant progress in recognising that disabled children are children first and foremost and is consistent with the obligation in Article 23 to '*recognise that a mentally or physically disabled child should enjoy a full and decent life, in conditions which ensure dignity, promote self reliance and facilitate the child's active participation in the community*' and to '*ensure that the disabled child has access to and receives education, training, health care services, rehabilitation services ... in a manner conducive to the child's receiving the fullest possible social integration*'. In Scotland and N Ireland there is no legislation which parallels these duties in the Children Act and there will need to be legislative change in order to achieve the necessary framework for compliance with Article 23.

**3.7.2** However, there are concerns throughout the UK about the very considerable shortfalls between the standards established for disabled children in Article 23 and actual practice and service provision on a day to day level. Disabled children experience both direct and indirect discrimination and continue to be marginalised from much mainstream activity not by virtue of their disability but by the failure to create the necessary opportunities for them to participate.

*The right to special care*
**3.7.3** Local authorities in England and Wales have a duty under section 17 of the Children Act to identify children in their area who are in need and this must include children with disabilities and provide or make available services which might benefit them.

**3.7.4** Appropriate levels of integrated services can mean that families are better able to care for their children with reduced likelihood of breakdown and that the quality of life for those children is improved with greater opportunities to participate in everyday activities. Thus the principle of non-discrimination (Article 2), of non-separation from families (Article 9) and of special care and help towards social integration (Article 23) can all be promoted by imaginative and well-resourced services. The Act introduces duties to develop arrangements for liaison between social services, education and health authorities in line with a recognition of the advantages of an integrated approach. In practice, however, the implementation of these principles is variable. Research undertaken by the London Region of the Social Services Inspectorate in 1992 indicated that of the 30 London authorities responding to the survey, only 18 had a named officer in each department, only seven had identified joint planning arrangements and only one had established specific arrangements with the education department[18]. There is recent research by Barnados and Keele University which indicates that for many disabled children assessments at birth were poorly handled by medical and social work staff, continuous assessment was poorly co-ordinated and service provision was determined by the level of resources, not needs[19]. The Council for Disabled Children has also stressed the need for much better co-ordination in the delivery of services to avoid the fragmented, inefficient and inconsistent arrangements which currently characterise much of the provision which is available.

**3.7.5** Local authorities in England and Wales are obliged under the Children Act to keep a register of children with disabilities, and guidance advises that this should be undertaken jointly between social services, education departments and health authorities. However, by June 1992, only five registers had been established jointly between the three authorities and only a further eight between a social services department and one other authority[20]. In Scotland, there is no such legislative duty but in the White Paper *Scotland's children* the Government stated its intention to legislate to require local authorities to assess the social care needs of children affected by disability and to publish information about services for disabled children. Such an approach would clearly enhance the opportunity for disabled children to receive '*special care ... and assistance ... appropriate to the child's condition and to the circumstances of the parent or others caring for the child*' as required by Article 23.2.

**3.7.6** Article 23.2 recognises '*the right of the disabled child to special care ... [and] assistance which is appropriate to the child's condition and to the circumstances of the parents or others caring for the child*'. Respite care is a vital resource for families caring for children with disabilities, providing as it does opportunities for rest and emotional and psychological renewal. But it should reflect the views of the child as well as those of the caring members of the family if it is to comply not only with Article 23 but also with Article 12 and the child's right to participate in decisions that affect them. Research undertaken in 1992 reveals that in the six local authority homes surveyed, children had little control over the length, frequency or nature of their stays, since both the service and the parents viewed the main purpose as offering respite for the carers[21].

**3.7.7** In addition, all placements must be consistent with the requirement under Article 3 that the child's welfare must be a primary consideration. Local authorities, if they are to meet these obligations, must have the resources and commitment to develop a range of facilities for respite care including provision within the child's own home, within families, and specialised residential homes. The type of accommodation provided, its location and the opportunity to return to the same placement and to construct continuing relationships with the carers involved are all relevant considerations in ensuring that the child's interests are adequately acknowledged. Compliance with Article 12 and Article 3 requires that children and young people are consulted both in relation to individual placements and in the planning and development of a respite care service.

**3.7.8** Article 23.2 emphasises that placements for disabled children must be '*appropriate to their condition*'. The Department of Health guidance on the welfare of children in hospital states that any use of National Health Service provision for respite care must be justified on specific medical needs and that long-stay mental handicap hospitals are inappropriate placements for children[22]. However, hospitals continue to be used. In practice in 1988/9 there were 11,000 individual respite care placements in mental handicap hospitals. Nearly all respite care schemes have waiting lists and the OPCS survey estimates that of the 165,000 children with severe disabilities only 3.7% currently have access to family-based respite care[23]. The continued problem of both inappropriate placements and lack of provision would appear to be a breach of the Government's obligations under Article 23.

**3.7.9** An important first step towards achieving

improvements would be the implementation of the requirement in the Children Act for comprehensive regularly reviewed child care plans. A study of respite care under the new regulatory framework for accommodated children introduced by the Children Act found that a number of local authorities were accommodating children for short periods of time without a child care plan. Shortages of staff and pressure of other work had led to an absence of specific planning thus rendering those children particularly vulnerable. Research into six local authorities in 1992 showed that only half ever used plans for short stay placements and even then they were not used for all children[24]. Without proper planning it is not possible to ensure compliance with Article 3 and the best interests of the child, nor can proper consideration be given to Article 20.3 and the suitability and continuity of care necessary for the child.

## ACTION REQUIRED FOR COMPLIANCE

**Compliance with Article 23, the right of disabled children to special care and assistance requires careful monitoring of the implementation of the Children Act with regard to:**

- **co-ordination between social services, education and health authorities;**

- **interpretation of 'in need';**

- **assessments based on need rather than on levels of resources available.**

**Compliance with Article 23 and the right of disabled children to appropriate services requires that:**

- **procedures are established in local authorities to consult with children as well as parents, both about individual placements and the planning and development of services;**

- **local authorities develop a range of provision of care in order that the wishes and feelings of children in relation to placements can be acted on;**

- **the requirements under the Children Act in England and Wales for child care plans for all children who are accommodated are fully applied to children in respite care.**

*Social integration*
**3.7.10** Article 23 states that disabled children have the right to special care and to *'enjoy a full and decent life, in conditions which ... facilitate the child's active participation in the community'* and that services which are provided must be *'conducive to the child's achieving the fullest possible social integration'*. However, serious concerns exist with regard to the provision of day care and out of school care for disabled children and those with special needs. There is inadequate availability of integrated publicly funded day care provision for disabled children. Childminders taking children with special needs face particular pressures and often lack the training and support necessary to provide a high standard of appropriate care. At present, the lack of adequate provision means that disabled children often have even less access to day care than other children. In consequence, not only does the lack of provision mean that we are not complying with Article 23, but also disabled children are being discriminated against in contravention of Article 2 in the opportunities available to them.

**3.7.11** Further difficulties are experienced by parents with disabled children. Many general services to children including leisure, play and recreational facilities do not cater for disabled children, thus both discriminating against those children in breach of Article 2 and placing considerably increased burdens on their parents. The lack of access for wheelchair users to many public buildings, public transport systems, shops and restaurants further isolates some children and parents. The OPCS survey of disability in 1989 suggested the need for further attention to family support to avoid discrimination against these children[25].

> *'It would be nice shopping or out to the pub or for meals more often but most of the time I take the easy way out and stay in so I don't have to bother anybody.'*
> (18 year-old, Shropshire)

**3.7.12** There is a need for local authorities to develop corporate strategies to address these issues if they are to begin to achieve compliance with the requirements of Article 23 to *'ensure that the disabled child has effective access to and receives education, training, health care services, rehabilitation services, preparation for employment and recreation opportunities in a manner conducive to the child's achieving the fullest possible social integration'*. At present, there is often a lack of co-ordination between different local authority departments which means that no coherent approach exists to ensure that the services needed by disabled children and their families are developed. This is of particular importance in view of the current Government strategy to encourage more service provision by the voluntary sector. There is a danger that unless services are properly co-ordinated disabled children will receive an increasingly fragmented service than is currently the case.

**3.7.13** Families with disabled children, as well as children themselves should be consulted on the types of services they require and on how best to ensure opportunities for participation in everyday life. Failure to do so renders it unlikely that the requirements of Article 23 can be attained. Without such a commitment to listening to them, disabled children are more likely than able-bodied children to encounter social isolation, discrimination and the risk of family break-down through stress.

**3.7.14** The Children Act 1989 and the NHS and Community Care Act 1990 in England and Wales both establish the principles of consultation and provision of support for families within the community. The legislative framework therefore exists for compliance with the relevant rights in the Convention. However, it will be necessary to monitor very closely the implementation of that legislation. Local authorities are experiencing serious financial crisis at the present time and without the necessary resources to maintain and to develop services such as respite care, home care, home helps, opportunity play groups, transport, integrated adventure playgrounds, specialist advice services, the principles in the legislation will remain little more than pious aspirations.

> *'The buses are no good for the disabled and it's embarrassing being carried around like a little baby, being shoved into a car and then shoved back out again.'*
> (17 year-old, Shropshire)

## ACTION REQUIRED FOR COMPLIANCE

**Compliance with Article 23, the right of disabled children to the fullest possible social integration,**

requires that:

- **local authorities ensure that their equal opportunities policies address the rights of disabled children and that procedures are established for evaluating all policies and practice to ensure that they do not discriminate against disabled children;**

- **local authorities develop strategic plans for the development of integrated services including day care, leisure, play and recreation;**

- **children and their parents are consulted on the development of services and facilities to ensure that they reflect their needs;**

- **there is a commitment to providing necessary resources to ensure that disabled children are not discriminated against in their access to services and facilities.**

## 3.8 Young carers (Articles 12, 28 and 31)

**3.8.1** The preamble to the Convention states that *'childhood is entitled to special care and assistance'*. Yet it is estimated that there are around 10,000 young people in the UK caring for adult relatives. Many of these young people are coping in isolation with minimal social support from the state and in consequence are being denied a number of basic rights. Recent research into the experiences of young carers, *Children who care*, reveals that although many young people who are caring for their sick or disabled parents are undertaking almost complete responsibility for their day to day care, they are not respected or acknowledged by professionals who are involved[26]. Of the 15 young people in the survey, none was consulted by social workers, doctors, or district nurses about their needs or the role they were fulfilling. This failure would appear to breach the requirement in Article 12 to ensure that young people are able to express their views on all matters of concern to them. Indeed, many young people state that they are frightened to involve professionals in case they are removed from their caring role without consultation.

*'When you go and see about getting some help, they just patronise you and tell you to tell your mum that they will sort it out and to go home and play with your dolly. So you're old enough and mature enough to look after your mum, to bathe, toilet her and everything, but you're not old enough to fight for her rights.'*
(18 year-old, Merseyside)

**3.8.2** *Children who care* also reveals that both informal and formal support networks for young carers are extremely limited. Many carers are having to bear the full burden of physical and emotional support of their parents almost completely alone. Young people describe the lack of recognition of the stresses they experience and the lack of sympathy with young people:

*'When an adult comes to breaking point, they scream out and people run to them, but when a young person is screaming for help, they are told to behave, to pull yourself together.'*

*'It's understandable if you are an adult breaking down, you cannot cope. But if you are a child, then you are attention-seeking.'*
(17 year-old, Merseyside)

**3.8.3** Many young people want to continue their caring function but also want support and recognition of their needs. The all too common experience is a fear that asking for help will be perceived as an expression of failure and result in the removal of the parent. Many young people therefore struggle on alone in isolation; undervalued and unsupported. The consequences of this lack of recognition combined with the level of responsibility that they are having to shoulder, results in many young carers being denied the right, described in Article 31, to *'rest, leisure, to engage in play and recreational activities appropriate to the age of the child'*. They are also often unable to benefit fully from their education as required by Article 28. Article 17 states that children must have access to information *'aimed at the promotion of his or her social, spiritual and moral well-being and physical and mental health'*. However, it is evident that many young people lack the information necessary for them to benefit fully from services and benefits that are available and which would enhance their capacity to care.

*'At the age of thirteen I was looking after the house, looking after my mum, shielding my mum from attacks from my dad which is a hell of a lot for a thirteen year-old to take on. I missed out on a lot, being trapped in the house with the person you are caring for, not being able to go out, not being able to have a social life and friends.'*
(17 year-old, Merseyside)

### ACTION REQUIRED FOR COMPLIANCE

**Compliance with the obligation to recognise the special needs of childhood and to ensure rights of young carers to play and leisure (Article 31), education (Article 28) and to participate in decisions that affect their lives (Article 12) requires that social services departments, in conjunction with health and education authorities:**

- **identify those young people within their area who carry caring responsibilities;**

- **develop in consultation with young people, comprehensive information about services and benefits available, and how to gain access to them;**

- **ensure that all support from professionals takes full account of the contribution being made by the young person and respects their views on service needs;**

- **develop support services which reflect the expressed needs of the young people.**

## 3.9 Discrimination and racism
(Article 2)

**3.9.1** The Children Act in England and Wales, for the first time in child care legislation, places specific duties on local authorities 'to give due consideration to the child's religious persuasion, racial origin and cultural and religious background' when making decisions in respect of a child. In their arrangements for day care, local authorities must 'have regard' to the different racial groups to which children in their area who are in need belong (schedule 2, para 11)[27]. These requirements, together with the provisions of the Race Relations Act 1976, which renders racial discrimination unlawful in England, Wales and Scotland, provide a legal framework for the implementation of Article 2, the need to ensure that all the rights in the Convention are respected 'without discrimination of any kind' and Article 30, the right of children from minority ethnic groups, to 'enjoy [their] own culture, to profess [their] own religion and to use [their] own language'. In N Ireland, there is no legal protection from discrimination on grounds of race or ethnicity for Traveller children and other minority ethnic groups. There is no equivalent to the Children Act duties in N Ireland or Scotland.

**3.9.2** However, throughout the UK, the day-to-day reality for many black and other minority ethnic children is far from that which the legislation seeks to achieve. There is widespread and continuing racism within the UK which perpetuates discrimination and unequal access to services for children from ethnic minority communities. There is evidence from numerous surveys and studies showing difficulties many black families experience in their contacts with both social services departments and voluntary organisations providing services. These difficulties arise from failure to address the implications of equal opportunities:

● failure to ensure that services are provided which reflect the needs of both children and their families from black and minority ethnic communities. To achieve this, it is imperative that providers consult with representatives from those communities and do not rely on their own assumptions about what is needed;

● failure to provide the necessary training for staff to promote understanding or knowledge of racism, different cultures and religions and the implications for service development;

● failure to recruit staff, including foster carers and prospective adopters, from local minority ethnic communities. Unless recruitment policies achieve equal opportunities for all applicants, the services provided will continue to promote a white image which will not encourage families from ethnic minority communities to use services. Nor will it provide the range of skills, expertise and knowledge necessary to provide an anti-discriminatory and anti-racist service.

**3.9.3** The Children Act guidance and regulations on day care provision require that local authorities have the necessary information about their local community to ensure that they can make appropriate provision reflecting the linguistic, cultural and religious needs of children[28]. These provisions are consistent with the principles in Articles 2 and 30 and provide a framework for day care services which are anti-discriminatory and provide equal opportunities for all children. However, a great deal of work is needed to translate these principles into practice. Many families from black and other minority ethnic communities find that services are not designed for the needs of their children. Many anticipate hostility and racism and are therefore reluctant to use the service that is available.

> *'I felt discriminated against while I was in care and now I am homeless and pregnant and I'm still not getting any help from social services.'*
> (17 year-old, London)

**3.9.4** Research into disabled children in Asian families published in 1992 paints a bleak picture of isolation, discrimination and racism[29]. Of the 35 families interviewed 88% said the social workers had no understanding of their beliefs and cultures, 80% of families had no knowledge that short-term or respite care was available, 62% did not know where the social services department was located. The families described poor communications, inappropriate reliance on children as interpreters and lack of confidence in the cultural appropriateness of services offered. The research further identified wide-ranging false assumptions on the part of professionals about attitudes, beliefs and support levels within the Asian community.

**3.9.5** The findings of this research are not unique. Another study, funded by the Department of Health over three years, into respite care facilities in three local authorities found the same problems - lack of information about services, difficulties with communication and failure to ensure the services provided appropriate food and access to religion[30]. A survey in the London Borough of Lewisham found that black families with disabled children felt excluded and isolated from a key support network run in the borough[31]. They saw the organisation as patronising, racist and off-hand. It failed to accommodate people whose first language was not English. They felt excluded from access to information and indeed from the information itself which was exclusively white in its imagery, language and content.

**3.9.6** These experiences are replicated throughout the UK and demonstrate vividly that there is a very long way to go before achieving the standards of anti-discrimination required by Article 2 and recognition and promotion of minority culture, language and religion required by Article 30. Research, funded by the Department of Health over three years, examined social services development, implementation and monitoring of equality for black and minority ethnic communities. The project surveyed all 133 social services departments in the UK. Its report *Equally fair* is based on a response rate of 69%. Findings from the survey indicate that most authorities have undertaken some initiatives in service delivery to black and minority ethnic groups but the picture is very uneven with large gaps in provision in many areas[32].

## ACTION REQUIRED FOR COMPLIANCE

**Compliance with Articles 2 and 30 requires that:**

● **Section 20 of the Social Work (Scotland ) Act 1968 is amended to include reference to racial origin and cultural background;**

● **research is undertaken into the operation of the requirement under the Children Act to take account of children's religious persuasion, racial origin and cultural and linguistic background;**

● **local authorities appoint officers to monitor the quality of child care to assess whether it meets the standards of care expected by black and minority ethnic communities. This should also be tested by research studies into other aspects of the Act;**

● **policies relating to recruitment, training, admissions, publicity and information are established which ensure that discrimination, either direct or indirect is not taking place;**

● **services are developed in consultation with representatives of all minority ethnic communities to ensure that they fully reflect the linguistic, cultural and religious needs of all children;**

● **equal opportunities policies in organisations providing services whether in the statutory or voluntary sector specifically address the rights of children;**

● **equal opportunities policies are monitored, eg collection of ethnic data in employment and service delivery, evaluation and review of practice to** ensure that policies are being implemented and procedures are in place for tackling inequalities or discrimination that are identified. In the context of increasing levels of provision by voluntary organisations, it is also vital that adequate levels of support and funding are allocated to organisations to ensure that they are able to develop effective equal opportunities policies and that they are also monitored and evaluated;

- the provisions of the Race Relations Act 1976 are extended to N Ireland.

## 3.10 The child's views in divorce
(Article 12)

**3.10.1** There are about 150,000 divorces in England and Wales each year. In England and Wales a court cannot make an order in respect of a child in divorce proceedings unless it is satisfied that the order will positively contribute to the child's welfare. It was intended to restrict the making of orders to situations where it was demonstrably necessary in the expectation that this would reduce conflict and promote parental agreement and co-operation. This principle does not extend to Scotland or N Ireland.

*Uncontested proceedings in England and Wales*
**3.10.2** In situations where the parents agree over where the child lives and the level of contact with the absent parent, they have to complete a form for the court setting out the details of the proposed arrangements for the children which, in the majority of cases, will be accepted and no further investigation undertaken. In practice, there has been some concern raised by a number of organisations advising children and young people that the lack of court intervention does mean that their views and wishes are not being heard by the courts. Article 12 states that children have '*the right to express [their] views freely in all matters affecting [them]*' and shall '*be provided with the opportunity to be heard in any judicial and administrative proceedings affecting [them]*'. However, in uncontested cases there is no opportunity for children to express a view on what they wish to happen as is required by Article 12 and no opportunity for children to challenge a decision with which they are unhappy.

**3.10.3** Section 8 of the Children Act does allow for the child to apply for leave to apply to the court to make an order but not all children are aware of this right and the court retains the discretion whether to hear their application. Furthermore, the President of the Family Division has issued a Practice Direction requiring that such applications for leave are heard by the High Court[33]. The impression amongst many practitioners is that this requirement has been imposed with a view to discouraging children from seeking leave.

**3.10.4** Where a child has been given leave to apply to the court for an order, and the court has made the child a party to the case the court will appoint a guardian ad litem to represent the interests of the child. The guardian, in contrast to those appointed in public law, is not bound by court rules and is not required to provide the court with evidence of the child's wishes and feelings, but the court must ascertain them.

**3.10.5** Obviously application for section 8 orders is a last resort when all other measures for resolving the conflict have failed. But while some parents will obviously consult their children and take their wishes into account when deciding on residence and contact, they are under no duty to do so and it is therefore probable that children will have decisions imposed on them in which they have taken no part and with which they are unhappy. The extent of the problem is, by its very nature, hidden. If we are to take seriously the requirement in Article 12 to ensure that children are able to express their views and to give them due consideration, it will be necessary to investigate the workings of the Children Act in this respect and to undertake research to ascertain whether the current procedures in divorce do adequately protect children's rights. It will also be necessary to explore ways of providing children and young people with access to free legal advice.

*'You should have the right to decide where you want to go and to take part in family decisions and decisions about your future. It's about having the right to live your own life and not just what parents want you to do.'*
(14 year-old, N Ireland)

*Contested proceedings in England and Wales*
**3.10 6** Only if the parents fail to agree or if the judge is dissatisfied with the proposals will there be any further scrutiny of the case and the possibility of the appointment of a court welfare officer to determine what would be in the best interests of the child. The child in these circumstances is not normally party to the proceedings and will not be legally represented. Research undertaken by James and Hay reveals that court welfare officers do not always consult children[34]. In fact, in nearly one fifth of all reports there was no mention that children were seen during the inquiries and in nearly one half there was no reference to their wishes and feelings. The Children's Legal Centre, which runs an advice service for young people, also has evidence that court welfare officers do not always consult children, particularly where they are younger[35]. Compliance with Article 12 and the right to be heard in all relevant proceedings would require that children were made automatic parties. Children in public law proceedings have this right so such a change would also be consistent with the requirement in Article 2 that all the rights in the Convention must apply equally to all children.

*Divorce proceedings in Scotland*
**3.10.7** Concern has been expressed by the Scottish Child Law Centre that children's wishes and feelings are not adequately catered for in Scottish private law as required by Article 12. The Scottish Law Commission has recognised this and in its draft Family Law (Scotland) Bill (1992) it provides that parental responsibilities will include a duty to maintain personal relations and direct contact with the child on a regular basis, thus moving away from viewing contact as an adult right to a focus on the right of the child to contact[36]. In theory, a child can apply to the court for an order in private proceedings under section 3 of the Law Reform (Parent and Child) (Scotland) Act 1986 but in practice no child has ever done this successfully. Without ultimate access to legal redress the child has no means of exercising the right to contact or participation in the decision making process. It seems therefore that there is a need for greater awareness on the part of solicitors of the possibilities of section 3 and clearer legal aid rules which make it explicit that children may instruct solicitors in order to raise actions on their own behalf. The Scottish Law Commission has proposed that children's rights to apply to court should be spelt out in legislation.

Compliance with Article 12, the right of children to
have their wishes and feelings considered and taken
seriously requires that:

- in cases being heard by the courts which affect
children, they should be entitled to automatic party
status;
- the child should be entitled to separate legal
representation in all proceedings;
- a review of Scottish court and mediation processes
should be undertaken leading to a revised strategy
and new court rules on children raising actions;
- research is undertaken into the operation of the 'no
order' principle under the Children Act in respect
of its impact on children in divorce proceedings.

# 4 Children unable to live with their families

## 4.1 Background

**4.1.1** Article 20 states that *'a child temporarily or permanently
deprived of his or her family environment, or in whose best interests
cannot be allowed to remain in that environment, shall be entitled
to special protection and assistance provided by the State'*. Whilst
the Children Act has substantially revised and improved the
legislation on public care of children in England and Wales,
there remain serious concerns relating to some aspects of its
provisions and its implementation. The concerns relate to
certain gaps within the legislation, the interpretation of the
legislation, the extent to which practice has adequately
changed to embody its principles and the level of resourcing
necessary to render the Act effective. In Scotland, children
and young people who may require compulsory measures of
care are referred to the children's hearings system. The
relevant legislation is the Social Work (Scotland) Act 1968 as
amended; more recently the White Paper, *Scotland's children,*
published in 1993, proposes further changes[37].

## 4.2 Placements (Article 2)

**4.2.1** Article 20.3 sets out very clear requirements on
placements; stipulating the need for care which is suitable for
the child's needs, that regard is paid to the importance of
continuity and that, in making placements, full account is
taken of the child's race, language, religion and culture.

*Suitability*

**4.2.2** The majority of the 60,000 children looked after by
local authorities in England and Wales are now cared for in
foster homes. Similar patterns apply in Scotland and N
Ireland. Whilst for many children, it is the most appropriate
form of care, this is certainly not the case for all children.
Article 3 and the requirement that *'in all actions, ... the best
interests of the child shall be a primary consideration'* will
necessitate that choice is available. It cannot be possible to
ensure the best interests of the child if there is only one
option available for placement. A recent study of foster care
in Warwickshire reported that 'in well over half of the cases
when a placement was needed there was only one placement
available and that was sometimes with carers who did not
appear wholly suitable'[38]. Whilst Warwickshire has gone
further than other authorities in closing residential homes, it
is certainly not unique in facing this problem. Many local
authorities have reduced their provision of residential care.

> *'They put me into a foster home where the foster mother was
> having an affair with the lodger and the foster father was
> talking about killing himself all the time and would get drunk
> and pretend to be affectionate by trying to snog me.'*
> (18 year-old, Merseyside)

**4.2.3** Article 12 insists that children are able to express a
view on all decisions affecting them. However, unless there
are options available, opportunities for participation are
meaningless. There is little research data available on the
extent to which children's preferred options for placements
are achieved, but there is anecdotal evidence which suggests
that young people experience difficulty in making any impact
on the decisions that are made. Packman commented in

1981 that 'what is clear is that a voice for the child is useless or even dangerous when it is not accompanied by high standards of substitute care and a range of options which enable choice to be made'[39]. Many young people do not wish to be placed in foster care. The emotional intensity of family life may well be inappropriate for their needs or they may find that the demands of the foster family conflict with their attachments to their birth family. Compliance with Articles 12 as well as Articles 3 and 20 must mean that local authorities should strive to achieve a broad range of provision which allows a flexible and individual response to the needs of each child.

> *'We eventually went to a foster home but by that time it had been so long that I just couldn't handle being inside a house. It was really foreign to me and they just didn't understand these little things and so my younger brother stayed and I just run away.'*
> (18 year-old, Merseyside)

4.2.4 Residential care has for some time been perceived as a service of 'last resort'. It has suffered from low status, poorly paid and inadequately trained staff and a failure to address its role within an integrated framework of provision of care for children. It has been seen consistently as 'second best' to foster care and as such the quality of much of the care provided and its suitability for the vulnerable children using it is seriously open to question. It is evident from the recent series of inquiries established to investigate aspects of residential care that there is widespread failure to comply with Articles 3 and 20; there are concerns about the suitability of many of the staff and the homes in which children are placed to provide an even minimally adequate standard of care. The lack of consistent safeguards applying to the various forms of residential care breaches the requirement in Article 3.3 to ensure *'that the institutions, services and facilities responsible for the care or protection of children shall conform with the standards established by competent authorities, particularly in the areas of safety, health, in the number and suitability of their staff as well as competent supervision'*. The Warner Report published in 1992 on management of children's homes comments that: 'Society as a whole has shown considerable indifference to the position of children in residential care' and goes on to observe that: 'National and local government has shown a lack of interest in defining the role and purpose of children's homes or in obtaining information about how the sector was changing ... Children's homes have too often been a backwater neglected by politicians, managers and professionals alike'[40].

4.2.5 Each of these inquiries has made detailed recommendations for improvements in recruitment and selection practice, supervision procedures, management of homes and staff training. There has been a remarkable degree of consistency among the findings and in the words of the Warner report: 'If employers and managers fail to tackle the problems we have identified within a reasonable timescale there will be more neglected and abused children, more frustrated and ill-prepared staff and more scandals'.

4.2.6 The focus in most of the inquiries has been the development of strategies for improving the protection of children and removing the opportunities through both omission and commission for the continued abuse and neglect of children. However, one of the reasons for children's vulnerability has traditionally been their lack of

civil rights. The Kirkwood inquiry into children's homes in Leicestershire makes clear that the reason the abuse it documents was able to continue unchecked for years was the failure to listen to children and take them seriously[39]. The requirements in the Children Act to take account of the wishes and feelings of children and to establish complaints procedures introduces the potential for the child to be heard and to have a means of redress in line with the principle contained in Article 12. It is imperative that these provisions are introduced by local authorities in such a way that children's civil rights are properly respected. Children are then empowered themselves to take action to challenge injustice, poor quality provision, failure to consult and bad decision-making. Genuine commitment to the principle of participation contained in the Convention will be the most powerful mechanism for ensuring the future protection of children.

> *'For complaints they have a white card you send in to social services and the staff just say, so what, we will send in a yellow card, who do you think they are going to believe?'.*
> (15 year-old, North East)

## ACTION REQUIRED FOR COMPLIANCE

**Compliance with Article 20, the requirement to ensure suitable placements for children and young people requires that:**

- **local authorities maintain and develop a broad range of foster and residential provision which allows for young people to exercise real choice over placements and enhances the possibility of achieving placements which promote the child's best interests;**
- **the broad range of recommendations proposed from the series of inquiries into residential care relating to staffing, management, training, policy and planning of the service are implemented as a matter of urgency.**

(See also action required under consultation and participation).

*Continuity*

4.2.7 Public care is frequently characterised by disruption, change and broken relationships for children and as such, often fails to meet the requirements in Article 20.3 for continuity in a child's upbringing. This lack of continuity is evidenced in many aspects of public care:

- many local authorities continue to operate structures which involve initial placement for assessment in one institution followed by a change to a longer-term placement once that assessment is complete. For children who have already experienced rejection and loss, this process can serve to compound their sense of alienation and loneliness. There is a need to consult children on their experiences of care and build the outcome of that consultation into the development of future structures of care provision;

> *'It's so cold when you walk into a children's home for the first time. It's frightening.'*
> (17 year-old, London)

- continued contact with a child's family, including parents, siblings, grandparents and others is a vital key to the welfare of children looked after by local authorities. There are obviously some children who cannot or would not want to sustain contact with their families but for many it is their own family to whom they return once they leave accommodation or care and with whom they maintain contact throughout their adult lives. Severance of this relationship in childhood denies children access to their family, not just in childhood, but for the whole of life. Young people in the consultation process commented on their concerns about lack of contact with family members. A typical comment was:

*'I've been in care for a long time now and I miss my brothers and sisters. I would love to see them regularly as I have only seen them once or twice. It would help if I could get a court order saying that I could see them regularly so no-one could stop our visits.*[42]*'*

*'I had my family near me so I would go home often and my brothers and sisters would come and visit me all the time and that made me feel a lot better.'*
(18 year-old, London)

There is a considerable body of research evidence demonstrating the value of continued contact with families for children in accommodation or care. Continued contact with families is shown to be associated with fewer fostering breakdowns. However, there has been a widely prevailing ethos within social services in recent years of the need to sever contact with a child's birth-parents in order to achieve security and permanence with foster carers. Research from the Dartington Social Research Unit demonstrates that 75% of children in care experience difficulty in maintaining contact with their parents[43]. The barriers that exist are sometimes as a result of specific restrictions imposed by social workers on contact with family members and sometimes due to non-specific restrictions such as hostility, distance and inaccessibility. The Children Act endorses the need for contact. It will be necessary now to ensure that practice developing with local authorities is consistent with their duty to promote contact;

● many children experience loss of continuity within the care system through the breakdown of placements. Research indicates that amongst short-term foster placements, as many as 20% did not last as long as was planned whereas amongst adolescent placements with professional foster carers, up to half resulted in breakdown[44]. There is now considerable research evidence on placement outcome which needs to be reflected in decision-making. Whilst placement breakdown is often associated with a complex range of inter-related factors, there are known indicators of risk which can be borne in mind when placing a child. There are plans to improve national and local child care statistics which can provide details on what happens to children looked after by local authorities and make it possible to begin to build up pictures of 'care careers' rather than just snap-shots of numbers, in particular forms of accommodation or care at any given time. It is important that there is consistency in monitoring in order to allow comparisons to be drawn;

● staff turnover in residential establishments can be significantly disruptive for children, often experienced as a personal rejection. Whilst it is obviously not possible to prevent staff leaving or changing jobs there are measures that can be introduced to minimise the rate of turnover and the consequences when staff do leave. The Warner report on residential care documents a depressing picture of poorly trained low-paid and inadequately supported residential staff through the care system[45]. The provision of good quality training and improved adequate staffing levels, supervision and management would achieve a great deal in raising morale and reducing turnover with substantial benefits to the quality of care being provided. When staff do leave, however, it is essential that the implications for children in their care are fully recognised and dealt with. Children need to be given as much information as possible about the change, the reasons for it and the implications for the future. When appropriate, arrangements for continued contact should be made and remaining staff need to be aware of the significance of the loss for the child and to understand any subsequent behaviour changes which might ensue.

## ACTION REQUIRED FOR COMPLIANCE

**Compliance with Article 20.3, the requirement that due regard is paid to the continuity of care requires that:**

● **local authorities examine their policy and practice with regard to continuity within the care system. This examination must include rigorous consultation with young people who have been and are currently looked after by the local authority. Guidelines to improve continuity need to be developed following this consultation;**

● **authorities make a commitment to finding placements for children as near to their home as possible; making use of their powers to help family members with costs associated with visiting, and encourage and support family members to recognise the value of their continued involvement with the child.**

*Race, culture, language and religion*
**4.2.8** Children from minority ethnic groups are substantially over represented amongst children looked after by local authorities. Research published in 1989 which examined 9,000 placement starts in six local authorities found: 'Black children were over-represented in admissions to care of all six authorities ... Asian groups were under-represented in all age groups. African and Afro-Caribbean children were over-represented particularly in the pre-school and 5-10 groups where their admission rates were more than twice that of white children'[46].

**4.2.9** Even more striking are the findings that children of mixed race parentage are two and a half times as likely to enter care as white children[47]. These figures raise profound questions. Why are children from some minority ethnic groups at such increased risk of coming into care? Of equal importance is to discover the reasons for the under-representation of Asian children in public care. It is easy to rely on preconceptions that Asian families are able to draw on support from the extended family and their own community groups, thus minimizing the need to rely on public care as a resource. However, this view may disguise the extent to which the Asian community lack confidence in the willingness and ability of local authorities to offer a service which is culturally appropriate and free from racism and discrimination. Research into these areas is necessary if we are to develop policies and practice which ensure adequate compliance with Article 2 and non-discrimination in relation to the rights of children to live with their families (Article 9).

**4.2.10** Children Act, section 22(5)(c) requires that placements are made with due consideration of the child's religion, culture, race and language. This requirement is consistent with the obligation in Article 20.3 to ensure that *'due regard shall be made to the ... child's ethnic, cultural and linguistic background'* as well as Article 8, the right to preservation of identity and Article 30, the right of a child *'to enjoy his or her own culture, to profess and practice his or her religion, or to use his or her own language'*. White people's awareness of race as central to a child's identity has grown in recent years and this has led to increasing recognition of the importance of respecting a child's right to preserve and retain their identity in placement practice. There have also been considerable developments through the introduction of equal opportunities policies in promoting awareness of the extent to which black children experience racism and discrimination and in beginning to introduce strategies to challenge those practices and attitudes.

**4.2.11** However, it is still the experience of many black children and their families that their culture is inadequately understood and that many social workers operate with stereotyped images and assumptions which are inaccurate and often racist. These attitudes impede good practice and appropriate decision-making; for example, the placement of Muslim children in Hindu families, false assumptions about attitudes towards discipline and education, inadequate expectations of educational achievement, particularly of Afro-Caribbean children. These problems can influence decisions about whether to place children in residential care, the type of placement made and the work that is undertaken with the child and the family once a placement is made. The British Agencies for Adoption and Fostering take the view that 'the placement of choice for a black child is always a black family'. Clearly this does not mean that in every situation a same race placement will be made but it does mean that local authorities need to invest heavily in the recruitment of foster carers from all minority ethnic communities within their locality if they are to comply with the requirement in Article 30 that a child's right to their culture, religion and language must be respected.

> *'You get some white staff won't give the time of day to black kids. They hate us and they will let you know that they think they are better than you, more superior. You still get that in children's homes.'*
> (18 year-old, London)

**4.2.12** There is evidence from black children which indicates the difficulties that can be experienced by growing up in a white family - a lack of any sense of belonging, a loss of identity, no sense of who they are or what being black means. These experiences do not reflect the failure of foster carers to provide the best possible care for the children they are looking after, but the inability of a white family to bring up a child as a black person.

> *'I didn't realise I was black when I was with my foster parents. The whole area was white. I didn't realise I was any different. It was never discussed'*[48].

**4.2.13** Any serious analysis of the extent to which this requirement is fulfilled is hampered by the lack of any comprehensive statistics on ethnicity and cultural and linguistic background of the children who are looked after by local authorities. There is no statutory requirement on local authorities to collect this information.

**ACTION REQUIRED FOR COMPLIANCE**

**Compliance with Article 9 coupled with Article 2, the equal rights of all children, requires research into the reasons for differential rates of admission to care from different minority ethnic groups and exploration of measures to tackle underlying causes.**

**Compliance with Article 30 and the duty to respect a child's identity requires:**

● **collection of relevant data at a national and local level;**

● **regular analysis of that data to assess its implications for policy and service planning;**

● **an active commitment to the recruitment of staff and foster carers from all ethnic and religious groups represented within the community;**

● **training for all staff on the implications of a child's cultural background for planning and provision of services.**

## 4.3 **Disabled children** (Article 23)

**4.3.1** Article 23 states that a disabled child has a right to *'enjoy a full and decent life in conditions which ensure dignity, promote self-reliance and facilitate the child's active participation in the community'*. This principle must form the framework against which all services for disabled children are evaluated and developed. The recognition in the Children Act that services for disabled children should be integrated and subject to the same principles as those for all other children represents a significant move forward. However, practice has not yet fully matched the principle.

**4.3.2** In recent years, there has been a shift in policy away from the traditional pattern of caring for disabled children in long-stay NHS hospitals. More disabled children are now cared for in residential educational establishments or with foster carers. The Scottish White Paper *Scotland's children* recommends ending the practice of placing disabled children in long-stay hospitals. The Office of Population and Census Studies (OPCS) studies of children with disabilities found that there were approximately 5,000 children in residential care[49]. Of these it was estimated that a third were there because their parents could not cope with either behaviour or health problems. These problems were not specified but it could be reasonably assumed that better levels of care and support might have enabled those children to live with their families in local communities. Certainly it is clear that there is a dearth of appropriate community support systems to avoid recourse to residential care. Thus, for a significant number of disabled children, the principle embodied in Article 9 that children should not be separated from their families is not being met.

**4.3.3** There are however some disabled children who will continue to require residential care. There has been a growth in the provision of integrated residential care which is to be welcomed but it remains limited. Where it does exist, appropriate staff training is essential. Without the necessary skills and expertise on the part of staff working with disabled children it will not be possible to comply with Article 20.3 and Article 3.3 which require suitable staff and institutions for the appropriate care of all children. Inspection arrangements also need to take account of special factors relating to disability such as controls and sanctions used and complaints procedures (see also para 4.8).

**4.3.4** A disabled child faces a greater likelihood of being placed some distance from home. Whilst this practice might in some cases be unavoidable, it is clearly important that these should be kept to a minimum. Long distance placements can lead to isolation of children from their family and communities which is contrary to their best interests (Article 3) and rights to family life (Article 9) and render them more isolated and therefore potentially more at risk of neglect and abuse. Where a child is placed at some distance from home, it is imperative that parents are encouraged, and where appropriate, supported financially to visit. It is also of particular importance that complaints procedures are accessible and promoted and backed up with independent advocacy (see para 4.8 on complaints procedures).

ACTION REQUIRED FOR COMPLIANCE

**Compliance with Article 23, the rights of disabled children to the greatest possible participation and integration requires that:**

- **all local authorities develop policies and procedures for the development of integrated residential care;**

- **training is provided for residential staff and foster carers which will promote their skills and expertise;**

- **all local authorities have policies for promoting parental and other family contact with children who are placed in residential care, including measures of practical support with travel and child care.**

**Compliance with Article 12, the rights to express their views and have them taken seriously requires:**

- **effective access to complaints procedures developed in consultation with children and young people themselves as well as family members;**

- **access to confidential advocacy services for all disabled children and young people in residential institutions.**

## 4.4 Reviews (Article 25)

*Reviewing duties*
**4.4.1** Article 25 stresses the importance of regular reviews of every child who has been placed for the purposes of care, protection or treatment. In England and Wales regulations issued under the Children Act impose reviewing duties on local authorities for all children whom they look after. These duties also apply to children in care in voluntary and private children's homes. Children in secure accommodation in community homes must also have their detention reviewed on a regular basis. However, no comparable duties exist with regard to children in secure accommodation provided in youth treatment centres or by health or education authorities. Nor are there obligations to review cases of children in private foster care.

> *'My gran was ill so they told me I would be with foster parents for a week. That was nine years ago.'*
> (16 year-old, North East)

**4.4.2** The Children Act does place duties on social services departments to ensure that the welfare of children placed by health and education authorities is adequately safeguarded and promoted and the provisions cover children placed in residential schools, residential care homes, nursing homes

and mental nursing homes. However, they do not specify any requirement to visit or review children regularly in the way described for children looked after by the local authority. Nor is there any requirement to review the placement and treatment of children admitted as informal patients to psychiatric hospitals. Article 2, the requirement for all children to be equally respected implies that this unevenness of provision is unacceptable and that comparable requirements should be introduced for all children.

**4.4.3** Compliance with Article 25 for all children requires that arrangements for formal reviews of placement and treatment, involving children themselves, should extend to all children being accommodated in institutions and quasi-institutional settings (for example, private foster care) throughout the UK.

*Participation in reviews*
**4.4.4** Section 22(4)(a) of the Children Act requires that the local authority must obtain and take account of the feelings of a child before making any decisions in respect of a child whom they look after. The Department of Health guidance on the legislation further states that a child's attendance at reviews should be the norm rather then the exception and that the child should only be excluded where it is clear that their attendance is not appropriate or practicable[50]. This requirement is consistent with Article 12. However, the reality for many young people is far from satisfactory in this respect and, in order for a child to be able to participate effectively in reviews, it is necessary to undertake a great deal more work than merely inviting them to be present.

> *'Staff always have meetings to discuss where you are going next but they never involve you. You should have the right to know what they are thinking of doing with you.'*
> (16 year-old, London)

> *'They held a meeting and pretended to involve me by calling me in at the end and saying, "We think it would be best for you to go to a secure unit. What do you think?" but I wasn't prepared, so I didn't really say much. But it was a farce anyway, because they had a social service minibus parked outside with a driver waiting for me to be taken there.'*
> (18 year-old, South Wales)

**4.4.5** A survey of 600 young people in care revealed that almost 40% felt that they were not listened to at reviews:

> *'Sometimes I feel that they do not want to listen because they do not value your opinion. But if it is you they are discussing they should listen to your point of view.'*

> *'They never ask me anything about how I'm doing in care - they just pretend I'm not there.'*

> *'All I ask for in my reviews is to see my brothers and sisters to see if they are OK, but nothing ever gets done about it.'[51]*

ACTION REQUIRED FOR COMPLIANCE

**Compliance with Article 12, the provision of genuine opportunities for children to express their views and Article 25, the right to periodic reviews requires:**

- **provision for participation in reviews to be incorporated into regulations throughout the UK and not simply left to guidance as is currently the case;**

- **consultation with young people about how to improve the review structure to make it more** accessible;

- participation in the whole review and not just in the part where the decision is made;

- proper preparation before the review about the structure of the meeting, who will be there, and why, how long it will last, what decisions need to be made and why and how the child will be able to take part;

- the review being followed up if necessary by a meeting to explain the decisions that were made, how they will take effect and when;

- if a decision is made which runs counter to the child's wishes, he or she is made aware of the reasons and informed about the complaints procedure and how to use it, and is offered independent advocacy to help them make their case.

## 4.5 Leaving accommodation or care
(Articles 20 and 2)

**4.5.1** Every year over 6,000 18 year-olds leave the care system in England and Wales and possibly as many as 10,000 16-17 year-olds. Considerable numbers of these young people end up homeless on the streets of our cities or trapped into a cycle of admissions to psychiatric hospitals and prison. The Convention sets out very clear responsibilities for the State towards young people: it seems clear these are not being met for many young people leaving accommodation or care.

> *When you leave care you are worse off because you don't know how to pay your bills; always in debt, you never have any food in the cupboard and you just sit back and leave it all to go on around you. And you wish that one day you will do this or that and it's just a big dream because you are left there and nobody calls to see if you are managing okay and before long the flat is taken away, you become homeless and social services just say it's your own fault.'*
> (18 year-old, London)

**4.5.2** The preamble to the Convention states that children have a right to '*special care and protection*'. Article 20 stresses the need for continuity of care. Articles 26 and 27 describe the rights of young people to an adequate standard of living including nutrition, clothing and housing. It states that those responsible for the child have the primary responsibility for securing the conditions necessary for the child's development. These Articles construct a framework of continuing responsibility for children throughout their childhood. They take account of children's vulnerability, deriving from inexperience, physical and emotional immaturity and lack of knowledge. The Children Act for England and Wales recognises the importance of the provision of continuity after accommodation or care. Section 24 sets out the powers of local authorities to advise, assist and befriend a young person after she or he ceases to be looked after. The legislation therefore does in principle broadly comply with the rights of children set out in the Convention. The guidance from the Department of Health elaborates in detail how that legislation should be interpreted by local authorities[52]. In Scotland, there are no comparable duties to those established in section 24 and the White Paper *Scotland's children* is also lacking in clear recommendations in this field. In N Ireland there are serious concerns about the lack of responsibility for after-care for young people leaving training schools.

**4.5.3** However, the application of the Children Act in England and Wales in both policy and practice at a local level falls far short of meeting the standards necessary to ensure that children leaving accommodation or care are provided with even minimally adequate support. Initial research one year on from the implementation of the Children Act conducted by the Campaign for the Homeless and Roofless (CHAR) among 20 social services departments found that:

- 80% did not produce adequate information on leaving care policies;

- 75% did not have an audit of local need;

- 67% did not have criteria for accepting homeless 16-17 year-olds as in need[53].

*'They should tell us more about when we leave. They should teach us more about how to budget and ow to get flats and benefits, basically prepare us for when we leave care.[54]'*

**4.5.4** First Key, an organisation that advises those leaving accommodation or care, carried out a survey supported by the Department of Health during the summer of 1992 into provision of after-care[55]. The responses from 75 authorities indicated a clear failure to fulfil their duties in the first year of implementation of the Children Act. 47% of the sample had no policies on after-care and in only 21% of cases had social services and housing departments developed co-ordinated policy and criteria for assessment of housing need, an essential pre-requisite to ensure that young people are able to get appropriate accommodation preparatory to and after leaving accommodation or care. Evidence from both Scotland and N Ireland confirm similar patterns.

**4.5.5** Meanwhile, there is a continuing problem of 'abandonment' of young people:

- those leaving accommodation or care are over-represented amongst the homeless and destitute young people found in London and other major cities. Centrepoint, a night shelter for young people, has found that over 30% of 16-17 year-olds who were homeless had been in care[56];

- even when not actually homeless, those leaving accommodation or care often experience insecurity with the only available housing options being squatting, staying with friends, frequent moves between poor standard bedsits;

*'I left care and had nowhere to go and ended up living with my boyfriend and his parents which I think is wrong, but I had nowhere else to go.'*
(18 year-old, London)

- where housing is obtainable loneliness and inability to cope caused by lack of adequate preparation often result in rising debts and the loss of the accommodation;

- there is growing evidence from local authorities that children are being discharged to independence earlier. Recent research indicates that 28% of young people leaving care left at 16 and 31% at 17[57]. Stein and Carey point out that in the general population only 0.5% of 16-17 year-olds live alone and yet 'a group of young people regarded as being in need of care and control up to the age of 16-18 are catapulted into a position of greater vulnerability than that of other people of their age'[58];

- one survey found over three quarters of young people leaving care had no educational qualifications[59];

- 40% of care leavers were unemployed after leaving care

according to another survey[60].

**4.5.6** Most families retain a strong sense of continuing responsibility and involvement with their children not just in childhood but throughout their lives. A decision to remove a child from their family must take on board the implications of severing that child's loss of contact with family, possibly for ever. The preamble to the Convention states that the '*child, for the full and harmonious development of his or her personality, should grow up in a family environment*' and Article 9 stresses that children '*shall not be separated from his or her family against their will except when ... such separation is necessary for the best interests of the child*'. Both the preamble and Article 9 are acknowledging the importance to children of the security and stability that family life can provide. Where this is not possible within the child's own family, the child is entitled to 'special care and protection provided by the State' (Article 20.1). The nature of that protection must take account of the principle in Article 2 that all children have rights without discrimination to all the rights in the Convention. So local authorities must ensure that the rights of young people leaving care to an adequate standard of living, to material assistance with housing (Article 27) and to protection from drug abuse (Article 33) and sexual exploitation (Article 34) are as well safeguarded as they would be for children living within their own family. The evidence to date indicates that for many young care leavers this standard of care is not being provided.

> '*I'm pregnant and they want me to go and live on an estate that the postman won't risk going to, and then they tell me that if I have not sorted myself out by the time the baby is born then they will put it on the at risk register which is not what I need to hear right now.*'
> (18 year-old, London)

**4.5.7** Unless policies are developed at local authority level, backed up with the necessary resources these obligations under the Convention are being breached. There are models of good after-care provision which have been developed and which, if disseminated, could be widely adopted.

### ACTION REQUIRED FOR COMPLIANCE

**Compliance with Articles 2 and 20 together with other rights to protection from abuse and exploitation of young people leaving care requires that:**

● **for England and Wales the Children Act is strengthened to place clear duties on local authorities to assist young people leaving accommodation or care; local authorities should be required to provide continuing help after a young person has left accommodation or care and they need to be adequately resourced to achieve this. Comparable provisions must be introduced in Scotland and N Ireland;**

● **the current policies of very early preparation for independence are reviewed in consultation with young people. Practice in this field needs to allow flexibility of approach which acknowledges the different needs of different children and also allows them to experiment with independence with the option of returning to accommodation or care or getting levels of support if they wish to do so;**

● **service development in the field of leaving accommodation or care is based on genuine consultation with young people. It is imperative**

**that any consultation that does take place is undertaken at a corporate level to ensure that all the services on which young people depend are provided in a co-ordinated and consistent manner. This will therefore need to include social services, housing, education, and welfare rights services.**

## 4.6 Children with parents in prison
(Article 9)

**4.6.1** Article 9 states that children should not be separated from their parents unless this is in their best interests and that, where separation must take place, the child has a right to maintain contact with the parent with whom she or he is not living.

**4.6.2** When a parent is imprisoned a separation is imposed on a child, not because it is necessary in the interests of the child, but as a result of a punishment imposed on the parent. Such separation, whilst nearly always causing distress for a child, may take on a more acute significance when it is the mother who is imprisoned. Recent estimates by the Howard League indicated that in 1990 as many as 6,000 children were affected by the imprisonment of their mother. Once a mother is imprisoned there are substantial difficulties for her children in maintaining regular or meaningful contact. Convicted prisoners are only allowed two visits per month of between half an hour and an hour, which is totally inadequate for renewing and sustaining contact with a child. There are very few women's prisons so that children often have to travel long distances to see their mother and visits are rarely allowed in the evenings, which would allow greater flexibility where the child is at school or the accompanying adult is working. The physical environment in which visits to parents takes place is often hostile, constraining and unfriendly, further adding to the stress and discomfort experienced by children in such situations. Lack of money for visits, distress experienced during visits, the infrequency and unsatisfactory nature of contact all add up to a picture of very clear failure to acknowledge the rights of children whose parents are imprisoned. The current arrangements fail to take account of children's best interests (Article 3), of children's rights to maintain contact with both parents (Article 9) and of their right not to be discriminated against because of the status of a parent (Article 2).

**4.6.3** Young children do experience profound emotional and psychological effects when separated from, in particular, their mother, often with long-term harmful consequences. In most cases, separation from either parent is traumatic. If the principles of the Convention are to be applied it is important to take the impact of imprisonment on children into account in determining public policy in this field. This would necessitate always considering children's best interests when sentencing parents, examining both the practice of imposing prison sentences on women and reviewing the quality, frequency and resourcing of prison visits when parents are imprisoned.

**4.6.4** Many women are imprisoned for offences which would not merit a custodial sentence if committed by a man. Indeed, very few women are in prison for offences which constitute a threat to others. This being so, and in the context of the grave consequences for children of their imprisonment, there needs to be a review of sentencing practice with a greater emphasis placed on the use of non-custodial sentences. Equally, there should be a review of sentencing of men who pose no threat to society. The Convention also requires that the best interests of children should also be considered when sentencing of a parent is taking place. In England and Wales arguably section 1 of the Children Act should apply, given the profound effect on children's upbringing of imprisoning a parent. But as yet criminal courts have shown no respect for the principle.

**4.6.5** The concerns for women are well illustrated by Judge Tumin, Her Majesty's Inspector of Prisons, in his Annual Report (1992) where he criticized Holloway prison's general visiting area which had 'a first floor visitor's room with no children's play area and refreshments available only from a vending machine. The room was divided by 3-foot high partitioning. Visitors sat on one side of this and inmates on the other on hard chairs bolted on the floor set sideways to their visitors. We found no good reason for this absurdly unwelcoming and uncomfortable arrangement'[61].

**4.6.6** But meaningful contact can be developed within prisons. The Safe the Children Fund have helped to develop at Holloway Prison a scheme of extended day visits for children which provide an environment akin to that in a community centre, allowing mother and children to share activities such as reading, painting and swimming, as well as simply being together.

**4.6.7** Particular concerns are raised by the growing number of African women undergoing long sentences for drug-related offences. They are arrested for bringing drugs into the country and it is invariably the case that they are deported on release from prison. Some are pregnant on arrival in this country and are separated from their babies once they are between 9-18 months-old. These children are later deported with their mother who is often almost a complete stranger to them as is the language and culture to which they return. It is imperative that the children's best interests are considered when sentencing and, if mothers are imprisoned, these children are helped to maintain as high a level of contact as is possible with their mothers during the period of imprisonment. The current failure to address the problems of these children is a clear breach of Articles 3 and 9. Furthermore, where such children are not cared for by a family of the same race and culture as that of their mother the rights contained in Article 30, to allow a child to enjoy their own culture, are not being respected.

## ACTION REQUIRED FOR COMPLIANCE

**Compliance with the best interests principle in Article 3 and with Article 9, the right of children to maintain contact with their parents requires that:**

● **there is a review of sentencing policy of parents with a greater emphasis on non-custodial sentences;**

● **visiting arrangements for children similar to those developed by the Save the Children Fund at Holloway Prison should be extended to all prisons including men's prisons.**

## 4.7 Consultation and the evolving capacity of the child (Article 12)

**4.7.1** Article 12 establishes the centrality of the principle that children have a right to express their views on all matters of concern to them and that their views must be given due consideration appropriate to their age and understanding. Article 5 is also significant in that it affirms that the rights of parents derive from their responsibility to promote the rights of their children and that the direction and guidance they provide must be consistent with the evolving capacity of the child.

**4.7.2** In the field of child care, the Children Act in England and Wales requires that children's wishes and feelings are considered where decisions about them are being made. Comparable provisions exist in Scotland and the draft Children (NI) Order will introduce the requirement in N Ireland. However, practice still lags a long way behind the principle.

**4.7.3** Organisations established to represent the rights of young people looked after by local authorities such as the National Association of Young People in Care (NAYPIC) have pointed to consistent failure to involve young people in decisions as broad-ranging as policies within children's homes, children's home closures, placements, contact with families, participation in case conferences, development of child care plans and moves towards independence. Many young people experience a lack of control over their lives - being moved without consultation and sometimes without warning, waiting months for meetings to determine their future, attending case conferences hoping to express their views only to find that decisions had already been made. Research published in 1993 reveals the extent to which young people in both residential and foster care continue to feel marginalised from decisions that affect their lives. Of over 600 young people responding to a questionnaire about their experience of care, nearly all felt that there were areas of their lives where they needed more involvement. Nearly half of those in foster care felt that they had no say in daily decisions. Two in five young people felt that they were not listened to in case conferences or reviews.

*'A lot of decisions I wish to make are not carried out or negotiated. I feel I don't have the power, therefore I feel I have very little say in decisions that are made.'*

*'You have a case conference and the staff used to talk about it for about one and a half hours and they would call you in for about 5 minutes.'*

*'I never have the courage to talk because I am alone in the room with about five types of social worker. When I do speak, everyone doesn't listen.'*

*'As soon as I talk, someone interrupts then they change the subject so when I do get to talk they tell me the subject has been discussed and we are on to something else.'[60]*

**4.7.4** There is also a need for the development of skills to enable the voice of disabled children to be heard. Children with physical and sensory disabilities and learning difficulties can be particularly excluded unless staff working with them have developed the commitment and expertise to ensure that they are helped and encouraged to have greater involvement in decisions that affect their lives.

**4.7.5** Serious application of the principle requires that local authorities and voluntary organisations looking after children:
ensure that children have adequate information appropriate to their age with which to form opinions;

● provide them with proper opportunities to express their views and explore options open to them;

● listen to those views and consider them with respect and seriousness;

● tell children how their views will be considered;

● let them know the outcome of any decision and, if that decision is contrary to the child's wishes, ensure that the reasons are fully explained;

● provide children with effective and accessible avenues of complaint, backed up by access to independent advocacy.

> 'You get moved from one place to another. I went through about six places in a year and you never have a choice. They just tell you to get packed.'
> (14 year-old, North East)

**4.7.6** It will be necessary for local authorities and voluntary organisations caring for children to ensure that policies are introduced which establish the basis for good practice and provide detailed guidelines for practitioners. We do not, as a society, have a tradition of taking children seriously and the requirements of Article 12 will necessitate some fundamental shifts in working practices if they are to create real change. The process of change should directly involve young people; they will necessarily have experience and views about how agencies fail to involve them and what might be done to put things right.

**4.7.7** Young people need to be involved not only in decisions that affect them as individuals but also in broader matters of policy and service planning. Without their input as service users into the provision of care, the service will not be complying with the spirit of Article 12 and young people will not be investing their valuable experiences to improve the quality of care both for themselves and for other young people in the system. The recent Department of Health circular on *Inspection of community homes* makes a welcome recommendation that local authorities should include young people who have experienced the residential care system on their inspection teams[63]. This involvement needs to be encouraged at all levels of service development.

> 'I would like a say about what happens in residential care, the decisions that the managers make about me and what would be best for me. I think the residential staff should listen to the young people and acknowledge their needs and hear us, as I don't think young people are taken seriously. I would like to have a say about who works with me.[64]'

**4.7.8** Local authorities could usefully address the following questions in examining how far their practice is consistent with a commitment to Article 12:

● Are young people consulted over matters of importance to them; for example, placements, policies in children's homes, after care, schooling, health care, information needs?

● Are there any written policies on consultation?

● Is there any training for staff on the implications of consulting young people and how to do that effectively?

● Is there any monitoring of the impact of consultation?

● Are young people informed about how their views will be

considered and, where they are not followed, helped through the consequences?

**4.7.9** Effective involvement of young people will not happen until there is a major shift in the training of social work practitioners and in the culture of social services departments towards recognition of the civil rights of young people being looked after, and the fundamental importance of respecting those rights.

## ACTION REQUIRED FOR COMPLIANCE

**Compliance with Article 12 in respect of children looked after by local authorities and voluntary organisations requires that:**

● **local authorities and voluntary organisations produce guidelines on procedures for consulting with young people both in relation to decisions that affect them as individuals and in relation to broader service planning and development;**

● **the guidelines should be drawn up in consultation with young people;**

● **guidelines should be backed up by staff training and monitoring and evaluation of the effectiveness of consultation procedures;**

● **the Government make clear through guidance or preferably legislation that where children's views conflict with other considerations, local authorities must take into account that the children's views should take precedence.**

## 4.8 Complaints procedures (Article 12)

**4.8.1** Complaints procedures are central to a commitment to respecting children's and young people's right to have their views heard. Rights are meaningless if there is no means of redress where they are not properly respected. Section 26(3) of the Children Act requires local authorities in England and Wales to establish complaints procedures in respect of children defined as being in need. Children, as well as adults with an interest in the child, must have access to the procedure. This requirement represents a considerable step forward; however, an effective right to challenge decisions requires an active and thoughtful response to the legal requirements. Certainly, the evidence from *Not just a name* indicates that current arrangements for making complaints are failing to provide an adequate service for many young people. Half those in foster care did not know how to make a complaint, nearly half thought they were not covered by the procedure. One child in six felt that there was no-one to whom they could talk when things went wrong. A key problem identified was the lack of access to a phone in privacy when they needed help; around a third of those in both foster and residential care said they did not have access to a phone in private.

**4.8.2** When establishing procedures, local authorities and voluntary organisations need to consider:

● Do many young people make complaints? If not, is this because the service is good or because they do not know about the complaints procedures, do not trust them, or think complaints will be followed up by punishment?

● Do children have the privacy to make complaints?

● Have they been consulted about setting up complaints

procedures, what information would be useful, and methods of dissemination?

● Are staff trained in the working and importance of the complaints procedures?

● Does the local authority generate a culture that sees complaints as a means of improving services?

● Does the local authority fund any independent child advocacy service to ensure that there is access to independent advice and support for children and for others acting on their behalf?

● How independent are the 'independent persons' required by the complaints procedure? Are past service users invited to act in this capacity?

*'I had an incident where I was restrained by three members of staff while three others sat and laughed. They cut my arm in the process, so I put in a complaint but before it went further they just intimidated me by telling me that they would rip me to shreds by bringing up everything from my past and I just wasn't prepared to put myself through that.'*
(14 year-old, North East)

**4.8.3** It is also of particular importance that the difficulties that disabled children may have in using complaints procedures are addressed. Disabled children may be significantly more vulnerable within the care system to abuse, neglect or inadequate consultation. If a child has complex needs or communication difficulties, every effort should be made to establish his or her views. Decisions may be made incorrectly about children with disabilities because of ignorance about the implications of the disability and the child's potential for growth and development. Children with disabilities have the same rights as other children to express choice. Even children with severe learning disabilities or very limited expressive language can communicate preference if they are asked in the right way by people who understand their needs and have the relevant skills to communicate with them. No assumptions should be made about 'categories' of children with disabilities who cannot share in decision-making or give consent to or refuse examination, assessment or treatment. These views are strongly expressed in the DH guidance on children with disabilities but need reiteration because they are often misunderstood[65]. Unless complaints procedures are established which ensure access to **all** children entitled to use them, local authorities caring for disabled children may be in breach of Article 2 as well as Article 12.

**4.8.4** There is a need to recognise that parents have continuing responsibility for children who are looked after by the local authority and will often play a key role in supporting a child wishing to make a complaint. The complaints procedure therefore must be accessible to parents and recognise the concern and commitment that most parents will sustain for their child while they are looked after.

## ACTION REQUIRED FOR COMPLIANCE

**Compliance with Article 12, the provision of effective means of redress necessary for its implementation requires that:**

● **complaints procedures are established, promoted and monitored in full consultation with young people. Particular attention needs to be given to the access of disabled children to the complaints procedures;**

● **children in care should have the same access as**

other children to the courts to seek redress (for example, Children Act section 8 orders and wardship) where complaints procedures do not provide satisfaction.

# 5 Adoption

## 5.1 Background

**5.1.1** Historically, adoption has tended to be viewed as a service for adults wanting a child rather than one promoting the rights of children. The strong emphasis within adoption legislation of the creation of a new family severing all links with the birth family is testimony to the priority given to the desire of adopters for their 'own' child. 'Ownership' of the child has been a central feature of the adoption process with a legislative framework which discourages and often makes impossible any continuing contact with the child's immediate or wider family. The very language used - 'available for adoption' - implies a commodity for parents rather than a service for children.

**5.1.2** In recent years, as the number of babies 'available for adoption' has diminished, the focus has moved to the permanent placement of older children from within the care system. Whereas in 1974, 22,500 children were adopted of whom more than 5,000 were under one year-old, by 1991 only 7,000 children were adopted, 88% of whom were older children. Of these, about 3,500 were step-parent adoptions. As research into placement outcomes became available during the 1980s there was growing concern about the numbers of children left within the care system without any real prospect of returning home and with no alternative family. Adoption was increasingly used as a solution for these children. One of the difficulties has been that this process involved using legislation that was drafted to provide homes for new-born babies who were placed almost at birth. The needs of older children cannot adequately be reflected within the constraints of that legislation. The Department of Health and Welsh office as well as the Scottish Office have recently published major reviews of adoption law[66]. A White Paper has also now been published for England and Wales *Adoption; the future* with a view to introducing new legislation which more accurately reflects current thinking in this field and which addresses itself to the needs of children who are likely to be experiencing the adoption procedures[67].

## 5.2 A principled framework for adoption

**5.2.1** Having ratified the Convention, the Government should have used the opportunity of the White Paper on adoption law to propose a new framework for the legislation based on principles in the Convention. Article 21 of the Convention sets out very clear standards that should operate with regard to adoption both within this country and in the context of inter-country adoption. However, there are a number of other rights contained in the Convention which need to be considered in developing procedures which are genuinely child-centred and do not serve to perpetuate a system of catering for the needs of the adopters at the expense of the child. Article 12, the involvement of the child in decision making, Article 8, the right of the child to preserve her or his identity, Article 9, the right to maintain contact with one's family, and Article 30, the right to enjoy one's own culture, religion and language, all need to be considered in evaluating both current and proposed adoption law.

## 5.3 Alternatives to adoption
### (Articles 8 and 9)

**5.3.1** Adoption is a permanent and irrevocable process which severs all legal ties between a child and her or his birth family. Compliance with the right to preserve identity (Article 8) and the right when separated from family to maintain contact (Article 9) would require that every possible effort is made to seek security for the child within their own family before any alternatives are considered and that when an alternative family is needed then the child is enabled to sustain contact and knowledge of her or his birth family as far as is possible.

**5.3.2** Adoption is too often regarded by practitioners as the only way of securing permanence for children, and the White Paper proposes that when considering an application for adoption, the courts should have a duty to consider alternative orders that are available and might better promote the interests of the child. However, given the prevailing view amongst many practitioners and prospective adopters that adoption is the most desirable route to security for children, there is reason to have concern that other orders, such as the proposed inter vivos guardianship order may well not be sufficiently used as an alternative to adoption. These orders would bestow parental responsibility on the guardian and would carry almost all the rights and duties of a guardian under the Children Act until the child was 18 years-old. Their strength is that they provide security and permanence for the child without severing entirely the legal links with the birth family. As such they have a number of advantages over adoption:

- because they do not sever all legal links with the birth family, they may well be easier for families to accept and could well have the effect of reducing the numbers of contested adoptions which would clearly be of benefit to children who are caught up in the conflict of those contests; they are also consistent with a commitment to promote the best interests of the child (Article 3). Reduced conflict over the process itself would also be likely to enhance the possibilities of continued contact with the family after the order is made;

- they focus on the **responsibility** of the person caring for the child rather than on the **ownership** of the child. In this way they remove the presumption which still prevails widely within adoption that it is possible to cut out a child's history and family background and provide a new beginning for a child. An inter vivos guardianship order describes the legal status of the carer in terms of parental responsibilities and would help direct practice in this field more appropriately towards a recognition that adoption is not about replacing birth parents but about providing long-term care and security for a child.

**5.3.3** The right to an identity and the preservation of family relationships embodied in Article 8 is the right that is perhaps most at risk in the process of adoption. Promoting the use of inter vivos orders is a means of overcoming these problems and would be best achieved by requiring that the courts should be under a duty not to make an adoption order unless it is satisfied that it would be significantly better for the child than making an inter vivos guardianship order. This would go some way towards challenging existing practice that assumes a hierarchy of orders with adoption traditionally at the apex of that hierarchy.

**Compliance with Articles 8 and 9, the right of the child to an identity and to preserve family relationships requires that courts considering applications for adoption orders should always first consider whether the child's best interests would not be more appropriately met under an order for inter vivos guardianship.**

## 5.4 Same-race placements (Article 30)

**5.4.1** Article 30 states that children from minority ethnic groups must not be denied the right to '*enjoy [their] own culture, to profess and practice [their] own religion and to use [their] own language*'. There has been considerable debate over the past few years relating to the placement of children for adoption in families of the same race. The Children Act acknowledges the importance to children of having the opportunity to be brought up by a family who can sustain the child's links with their language, culture and religion. Section 22(5)(c) requires local authorities, when making decisions in respect of children, to take account of their 'religious persuasion, racial origin and cultural and linguistic origin'. It is certainly the view of the key organisations working in the field of adoption that same-race policies are central to good practice. This approach is fully consistent with Article 30 and the child's right to enjoy their own culture, religion and language. However, the White Paper *Adoption; the future* appears to be backtracking from that commitment. It comments that these issues should be considered but given no greater weight than that attached to other concerns. Whilst it is undoubtedly true that all placements will need to take account of a range of factors of relevance to the child, and in particular the views of the child, the tone of the White Paper would seem to be overly dismissive of the centrality of race and culture to a child's identity. Clearly, issues of race and culture should not override all other considerations and, in particular, they should not override the views and feelings of the child. But it would be helpful if the principle of respect for the child's race, culture and language was embedded in the legislation as an issue to be given serious consideration whenever placing children from minority ethnic groups.

**5.4.2** There are still only around one third of adoption agencies that have a policy on placements of black children. Unless there is a policy in place, it is unlikely that the necessary work that is needed to recruit black adoptive parents is being done. It is often argued by agencies that the issue of primary importance for a child is that a permanent and secure home is found and that the racial dimension is of secondary concern. As a result inadequate work is undertaken to recruit black adoptive parents. The practice of trans-racial adoption is then defended on the grounds that no alternatives exist.

**5.4.3** Planning and developing appropriate resources for placing black children relies on accurate information being available about the ethnicity, language and religion of children placed and the adoptive parents with whom they are placed. However, there are no nationally collected statistics available on the ethnicity of children placed for adoption nor on the ethnicity of the adopters. The only information that is collected relates to the gender and age of the child placed and the marital status of the parents. This lack of access to information means that it is difficult for agencies to assess the levels of need that exist for adoptive families of different racial origins. In consequence, they are unable to comply adequately with Article 30 in ensuring that full account is taken of a child's race and culture in making placements.

**Compliance with Article 30, the right of all children to enjoy their own culture and language requires that:**

● **all adoption agencies develop policies for ensuring that children are able to be placed wherever possible in same race families and also introduce strategies for implementing the policy;**

● **research on the experience of children in trans-racial adoptions is undertaken in order that future law and policy can draw on an informed understanding of the implications for children of growing up in a family of another culture;**

● **statistics are collected on the ethnicity of both children who are adopted and their adoptive parents.**

**Compliance with Article 12 requires that the views of children should inform decisions that are made in respect of them and this should happen not only at the level of individual decision-making but also at the level of public policy.**

## 5.5 Information about adoption (Article 8)

**5.5.1** The White Paper on adoption recognises the fundamental importance of informing a child about the adoption and recommends that adoption agencies should have a responsibility to advise adoptive parents of the necessity of explaining this to the child. It further recommends that adoptive parents should be provided with a package of information about the child's background to be given to the child when he or she is of an age to understand it. These proposals are welcome and entirely consistent with the requirement in Article 8 that a child has a right to knowledge of his or her identity. However, if the requirement to inform the child was written into adoption law, this would further strengthen the significance attached to this issue. To do so would be a means of asserting the principle in primary legislation as a fundamental right of all children and would highlight the importance attached to ensuring that it is respected by adoptive parents.

**Compliance with Article 8, the right to knowledge of identity, requires that adoptive parents should have a legal duty to inform a child that he or she is adopted as soon as he or she is competent to understand.**

## 5.6 Welfare test (Articles 8 and 30)

**5.6.1** The White Paper recommends that the framework for making decisions in respect of an adoption should be based on the same principles as those in the Children Act. This means that courts will consider the welfare of the child, the need to avoid delays in decision making and a welfare checklist which includes the wishes of the child, the emotional, physical and educational needs of the child, the age, sex, background and other relevant factors, any harm the child has suffered or is at risk of suffering, and the capacity of relevant adults to meet the child's needs. In addition, it is proposed that the courts should also consider the effect on the child when an adult of an adoption order and the implications of an order on the child's relationships with the birth family. These proposals are consistent with the requirement in Article 3 to consider the best interests of the child in all actions that affect them. However, no reference is made in this checklist to the need to consider the child's race, culture, religion and language when decisions are being made, as is required by Article 30. Nor is there any requirement to consider the implications of adoption for the child's nationality and immigration status. These matters are of critical significance to the child and it is therefore essential that the court be required to take account of them.

**ACTION REQUIRED FOR COMPLIANCE**

**Compliance with Articles 8 and 30 as well as with Article 3 requires that when considering an application to adopt, the courts should be required to have regard to the child's race, culture, religion and language and to the implications of the adoption order for the child's nationality and immigration status.**

## 5.7 The child's consent (Article 12)

**5.7.1** Article 12 stresses the right of the child to express his or her views in all matters of concern to them. It is therefore welcome that the White Paper acknowledges this principle in recommending that the courts should not be able to grant an adoption order in respect of a child of 12 years or over unless the child has agreed to the adoption. This principle has existed in Scottish law for some time. However, concerns have been expressed by a number of organisations working in the adoption field. These concerns include:

- it has been argued that 12 years is an arbitrary age limit to introduce and that many children under that age are fully capable of understanding the issues involved and taking a view on the proposed adoption. There is also a concern that children under 12 years will not be adequately consulted if such a cut-off point is introduced;

- the introduction of an age limit at which consent is required does not necessarily mean that there will be an improvement in practice. It has been argued that this would be better achieved by requiring guardians ad litem to produce detailed evidence to the court of the measures taken to ascertain the wishes and feelings of the child;

- the introduction of a right of veto for the child to any proposed adoption would ensure that no adoption could go ahead if the child was unhappy with it but would avoid the necessity of the requirement for formal agreement in every case;

- the critical decisions with regard to a child's future are often made much earlier than the point at which consent to an adoption is required. By that stage the decision can be merely a formality. Involving a child effectively in decisions for the long-term future needs to happen at the very early stages of planning;

- the requirement to give consent could be experienced as a pressure imposing an undue responsibility on some children. It may be felt that they are being actively required to reject their parents in order to agree to the adoption and this may make some children reluctant to

agree to an adoption that they might otherwise want.

Some of these concerns could be met if the 'Gillick' principle were applied; that a child should have an independent right to exercise a choice if they are judged to have sufficient understanding. There should be a presumption of competency at 12 years.

**5.7.2** The White Paper proposes that only children over the age of 12 years should be party to adoption proceedings. Compliance with Article 12 would require that all children should be represented in court, as they are in all proceedings under the Children Act. It is difficult to understand why a different approach should be taken in the context of adoption where the decisions being made are of such profound and irrevocable significance to the child.

**ACTION REQUIRED FOR COMPLIANCE**

**Compliance with Article 12, the right of children to be involved in decision making in respect of adoption, requires that all children should have the right to give consent if they are judged to have sufficient understanding, and a presumption of competence should apply at 12. All children should be independently represented in adoption hearings irrespective of age**

# Summary of action required for compliance

1 Compliance with Article 12, the right of children to express a view on matters of concern to them, requires that:

- the relevant family law in each jurisdiction in the UK is amended to introduce a requirement that in reaching any major decision relating to the child, parents are required to ascertain the child's views and give due consideration to those views subject to age and understanding;

- in all cases being heard by the courts which affect children, they should be entitled to automatic party status and should be entitled to separate legal representation in all proceedings;

- children in care should have the same access as other children to the courts to seek redress (for example, Children Act section 8 orders and wardship) where complaints procedures do not provide satisfaction;

- a review of Scottish court and mediation processes should be undertaken leading to a revised strategy and new court rules on children raising actions;

- all children should have the right to give consent to adoption if they are judged to have sufficient understanding, and a presumption of competence should apply at 12. All children should be independently represented in adoption hearings irrespective of age;

- provision for participation in reviews is incorporated into regulations throughout the UK and not simply left to guidance as is currently the case. Consultation is undertaken with young people about how to improve the review structure to make it more accessible;

- local authorities and voluntary organisations produce guidelines on procedures for consulting with young people both in relation to decisions that affect them as individuals and in relation to broader service planning and development. The guidelines should be drawn up in consultation with young people and backed up by staff training and monitoring and evaluation of the effectiveness of consultation procedures;

- complaints procedures are established, promoted and monitored in full consultation with young people. Particular attention needs to be given to the access of disabled children to the complaints procedures;

- access is available to confidential advocacy services for all disabled children and young people in residential institutions.

2 Compliance with Articles 18, 5 and 3, the responsibility to promote children's welfare in a manner consistent with their evolving capacity, requires that family law in each jurisdiction in the UK should be amended to introduce a definition of parental responsibility which makes explicit those obligations and avoids discrimination between children in different jurisdictions, in line with Article 2.

3 Compliance with Article 18, the broad-based duty to provide support for all parents, requires:

- longitudinal research into the cost effectiveness of family support services and into the impact on children of differing interpretations of 'in need';

- all local authorities to undertake needs assessments of children in their area based on a broad definition of need, backed up by a central Government commitment to provide sufficient resources to fund the identified need;

- consultation with parents and children in the planning of services, and parents to be provided with information about the availability of and criteria for access to these services;

- flexible and appropriate educational (and care) provision for all three and four year-olds, publicly funded day care services available to the under-three population and out-of-school provision for all who require it, together with adequate central government grants to achieve it;

- close monitoring of the impact of these changes on the overall provision of services to under-eight year-olds to ensure that the obligations under Article 18 are not being undermined by the reduced role of local education authorities following the Education Act 1993;

- statutory maternity leave is increased to at least 18 weeks;

- statutory paternity leave is introduced which provide opportunities for fathers to be more involved in the care of their children;

- statutory leave to care for children whilst they are ill is introduced for all employees;

- publicity campaigns are developed to ensure that both employees and employers are aware of the statutory rights of pregnant women to time off for ante-natal care.

4 Compliance with Article 20, the requirement to ensure suitable placements for children and young people with due regard to the need of continuity, requires that:

- local authorities maintain and develop a broad range of foster and residential provision which allows for young people to exercise real choice over placements and enhances the possibility of achieving placements which promote the child's best interests;

- the broad range of recommendations proposed from the series of inquiries into residential care relating to staffing, management, training, policy and planning of the service are implemented as a matter of urgency;

- local authorities examine their policy and practice with regard to continuity within the care system. This examination must include rigorous consultation with young people who have been and are currently looked after by the local authority. Guidelines to improve continuity need to be developed following this consultation;

- authorities make a commitment to finding placements for children as near to their home as possible; making use of their powers to help family members with costs associated with visiting, and encourage and support family members to recognise the value of their continued involvement with the child.

5 Compliance with Articles 2 and 20 together with other rights to protection from abuse and exploitation of young people leaving care requires that:

- for England and Wales the Children Act is strengthened to place clear duties on local authorities to assist young people leaving accommodation or care; local authorities should be required to provide continuing help after a young person has left accommodation or care and they need to be adequately resourced to achieve this. Comparable provisions must be introduced in Scotland and N Ireland;

- the current policies of very early preparation for independence are reviewed in consultation with young people. Practice in this field needs to allow flexibility of approach which acknowledges the different needs of different children and also allows them to experiment with independence with the option of returning to accommodation or care or getting levels of support if they wish to do so;

- service development in the field of leaving accommodation or care is based on genuine consultation with young people. It is imperative that any consultation that does take place is undertaken at a corporate level to ensure that all the services on which young people depend are provided in a co-ordinated and consistent manner. This will therefore need to include social services, housing, education, and welfare rights services.

**6** Compliance with Article 23, the right of disabled children to special care and assistance, appropriate services and the fullest possible social integration, requires:

- careful monitoring of the implementation of the Children Act with regard to co-ordination between social services, education and health authorities, interpretation of 'in need', assessments based on need rather than on levels of resources available;

- that procedures are established in local authorities to consult with children as well as parents, both about individual placements and the planning and development of services;

- that local authorities develop a range of provision of care in order that the wishes and feelings of children in relation to placements can be acted on;

- that the requirements under the Children Act in England and Wales for child care plans for all children who are accommodated are fully applied to children in respite care;

- that local authorities ensure that their equal opportunities policies address the rights of disabled children and that procedures are established for evaluating all policies and practice to ensure that they do not discriminate against disabled children;

- that local authorities develop strategic plans for the development of integrated services including day care, leisure, play and recreation;

- that children and their parents are consulted on the development of services and facilities to ensure that they reflect their needs;

- that there is a commitment to providing necessary resources to ensure that disabled children are not discriminated against in their access to services and facilities;

- that all local authorities develop policies and procedures for the development of integrated residential care;

- that training is provided for residential staff and foster carers which will promote their skills and expertise;

- that all local authorities have policies for promoting parental and other family contact with children who are placed in residential care, including measures of practical support with travel and child care.

**7** Compliance with Articles 2, the equal rights of all children, and Article 30, the right for respect for cultural identity, requires that:

- Section 20 of the Social Work (Scotland ) Act 1968 is amended to include reference to racial origin and cultural background;

- research is undertaken into the operation of the requirement under the Children Act to take account of children's religious persuasion, racial origin and cultural and linguistic background;

- local authorities appoint officers to monitor the quality of child care to assess whether it meets the standards of care expected by black and minority ethnic communities. This should also be tested by research studies into other aspects of the Act;

- policies relating to recruitment, training, admissions, publicity and information are established which ensure that discrimination, either direct or indirect is not taking place;

- services are developed in consultation with representatives of all ethnic minority communities to ensure that they fully reflect the linguistic, cultural and religious needs of all children;

- equal opportunities policies in organisations providing services whether in the statutory or voluntary sector specifically address the rights of children;

- equal opportunities policies are monitored, eg collection of ethnic data in employment and service delivery, evaluation and review of practice to ensure that policies are being implemented and procedures are in place for tackling inequalities or discrimination that are identified. In the context of increasing levels of provision by voluntary organisations, it is also vital that adequate levels of support and funding are allocated to organisations to ensure that they are able to develop effective equal opportunities policies and that they are also monitored and evaluated;

- the provisions of the Race Relations Act 1976 are extended to N Ireland;

- when considering an application to adopt, the courts should be required to have regard to the child's race, culture, religion and language and to the implications of the adoption order for the child's nationality and immigration status;

- all adoption agencies develop policies for ensuring that children are able to be placed wherever possible in same race families and also introduce strategies for implementing the policy;

- research on the experience of children in trans-racial adoptions is undertaken in order that future law and policy can draw on an informed understanding of the implications for children of growing up in a family of another culture;

- statistics are collected on the ethnicity of both children who are adopted and their adoptive parents;

- collection of relevant data at a national and local level;

- regular analysis of that data to assess its implications for policy and service planning;

- an active commitment to the recruitment of staff and foster carers from all ethnic and religious groups represented within the community;

- training for all staff on the implications of a child's

cultural background for planning and provision of services.

**8** Compliance with Articles 8 and 9, the right of the child to an identity and to preserve family relationships, requires that:

● courts considering applications for adoption orders should always first consider whether the child's best interests would not be more appropriately met under an order for inter vivos guardianship;

● adoptive parents should have a legal duty to inform a child that he or she is adopted as soon as he or she is competent to understand.

**9** Compliance with Article 9 coupled with Article 2, the equal rights of children from different minority ethnic groups, requires research into the reasons for differential rates of admission to care and exploration of measures to tackle underlying causes.

**10** Compliance with the best interests principle in Article 3 and with Article 9, the right of children to maintain contact with their parents requires that:

● there is a review of sentencing policy of parents with a greater emphasis on non-custodial sentences;

● visiting arrangements for children similar to those developed by the Save the Children Fund at Holloway Prison should be extended to all prisons including mens prisons.

**11** Compliance with Article 3.3, the duty to ensure appropriate standards of provision, requires that the advice on standards contained in the original guidance on the Children Act issued by the Department of Health should be adhered to for purposes of registration of all day care provision, and that basic standards should be included in regulations, not merely guidance.

**12** Compliance with the obligation to recognise the special needs of childhood and to ensure rights of young carers to play and leisure (Article 31), education (Article 28) and to participate in decisions that affect their lives (Article 12) requires that social services departments, in conjunction with health and education authorities:

● identify those young people within their area who carry caring responsibilities;

● develop in consultation with young people, comprehensive information about services and benefits available, and how to gain access to them;

● ensure that all support from professionals takes full account of the contribution being made by the young person and respects their views on service needs;

● develop support services which reflect the expressed needs of the young people.

# References

1. *Report on family law*, Scottish Law Commission, HMSO (1992)
2. see reference 1
3. *A new deal for children: implementation of the Children Act 1989 in the counties*, Cohen P, Association of County Councils Publication (1992)
4. *Capitalising on the Act: a working party report on the implementation of the Children Act 1989 in London*, London Regional Social Services Inspectorate (1992)
5. *Children Act Report*, Department of Health and Welsh Office, HMSO (1992)
6. *Flaws in the partnership*, Holman B, Community Care, no 903 (2 March 1992)
7. *Caring for children: services and policies for child care and equal opportunities in the UK*, Cohen B, a report for the European Commission's Child Care Network (1990)
8. *Summary of report on stage 1 of research project on children in need under the Children Act 1989*, Colton M and Drury C, Department of Social Policy and Applied Social Studies, University of Wales (1993)
9. *No room for doubt*, Community Care, (21 October 1993)
10. *Childcare in the European Community 1985-1990*, Moos P, Commission of the European Communities (1990)
11. *Children first: report of the AMA working party on services for young children*, Association of Metropolitan Authorities (1991)
12. *Lone parent families in the UK*, Bradshaw J and Millar J, HMSO (19 *Child care in the European Community 1985-90*, Moss P, Commission of European Communities (1990)
14. *The Children Act 1989 guidance and regulations: volume 2, family support, daycare and educational provision for young children*, Department of Health, HMSO (1991)
15. *EC Directive on the protection of pregnant women at work*, Commission of the European Communities (1993)
16. *Not in labour: Citizen's Advice Bureaux evidence on pregnancy dismissal and employment*, NACAB (1992)
17. *Children Act 1989*, schedule 2 para 6, HMSO (1989)
18. see reference 4
19. *The implications of the Children Act 1989 on children and young people with severe learning difficulties*, Lyon C M, University of Keele and Barnardos (1991)
20. see reference 5
21. *Room for improvement*, Robinson C, Minkes J and Weston, Norah Fry Research Centre, University of Bristol, reported in Community Care (8 July 1993)
22. *The welfare of children and young people in hospital*, NHS Management Executive, HSG(91)1 Department of Health, London (1991)
23. *Disabled children's services, transport and education*, Survey of Disability in Great Britain No 6, OPCS, HMSO (1989)
24. see reference 21
25. The prevalence of disability among children, Bone M and Meltzer H, OPCS, HMSO (1989)
26. *Children who Care: Inside the World of Young Carers* Becker S and Aldridge J, Loughborough University (1993)
27. see reference 14
28. see reference 14

29. *The silent minority: children with disabilities in Asian families*, Shah R, National Children's Bureau (1992)

30. *National study of respite care service to disabled children*, Nora Fry Research Centre, University of Bristol (June 1991)

31. *Reaching black families: a study of Contact a Family in Lewisham and the relevance of services for black families who have children with disabilities and special needs*, Contact a Family (1989)

32. *Equally fair: a report of the Ethnic Monitoring Social Services Project*, Department of Health (1992)

33. Practice Direction (1993 1 FLR 668) Application by Children, Children Act 1989 S10(8) (22 February 1993)

34. *Court welfare work*, James A and Hay W (1992)

35. *Stifled voices*, Wyld N, Community Care (29 October 1992)

36. see reference 1

37. *Scotland's children: proposals for child care policy and law*, Scottish Office Social Work Services Group, HMSO (1993)

38. *An end to residential care*, Cliffe D, text of paper to National Children's Bureau/Warwickshire County Council Conference (11 October 1990)

39. *The child's generation*, Packman J, Blackwell (1981)

40. *Choosing with care: the report of the committee of inquiry into the selection, development and management of staff in children's homes*, chaired by Norman Warner, para 6.44, HMSO (1992)

41. *The Leicestershire Inquiry 1992: the report of an inquiry into aspects of the management of children's homes in Leicestershire between 1973-1986*, Kirkwood A, Leicestershire County Council (1993)

42. *Not just a name: the views of young people in residential and foster care*, Fletcher B, National Consumer Council (1993)

43. *Access disputes in child care*, Milham et al, Gower (1989)

44. *Patterns and outcomes: messages from current research and their implications*, Department of Health, HMSO (1991)

45. see reference 40

46. *Child care now*, Rowe J, Hundleby M and Garnett L, Research Series 6, British Agencies for Adoption and Fostering (1989)

47. 'The background of children who enter local authority care', Bebbington A and Miles J, *The British Journal of Social Work*, vol 19, no 5 (October 1989)

48. *Placed in a white family: views of young black people*, Childright No 6 (October 1989)

49. *The prevalence of disability amongst children*, OPCS, HMSO (1989)

50. *The Children Act 1989 guidance and regulations: volume 3, family placements* Department of Health, HMS0 (1991)

51. see reference 42

52. *The Children Act 1989 guidance and regulations: volume 4, residential care* Department of Health, HMSO (1991)

53. *Plans no action*, Goldman R, CHAR (1992)

54. see reference 42

55. *Prepared for living: a survey of young people leaving the care of three local authorities*, Biehal N, Clayden J, Stein M and Wade J, National Children's Bureau (1992)

56. *No way back: homelessness and 16-17 year-olds in the 90s*, Strathdee R, Centrepoint (1992)

57. see reference 55

58. *Leaving care*, Stein M and Carey K, Blackwell (1989)

59. *Housing our children*, Strathdee R, Centrepoint (1993)

60. Leaving care and after, Garnett L, National Children's Bureau (1992)

61. *Report of Her Majesty's Inspector of Prisons*, Home Office, HMSO (1992)

62. see reference 42

63. *Inspection of community homes*, LAC (92)14, Department of Health, HMSO (1992)

64. see reference 42

65. *The Children Act 1989 guidance and regulations: volume 6, children with disabilities*, Department of Health, HMSO (1989)

66. *Review of adoption law: report to Ministers of an inter-departmental working group: a consultation document*, Department of Health and Welsh Office, HMSO (October 1992)

67. *Adoption: the future*, Department of Health, Welsh Office, Home office and Lord Chancellor's Office, HMSO (1993)

# CHILDREN'S RIGHTS
## DEVELOPMENT UNIT

# UK Agenda for Children

A right to have your apinyon
and to argue with your mum
or dad with out getting
smacked or sent to bed

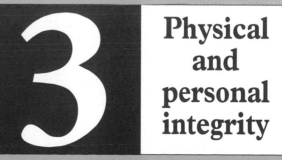

## 3 Physical and personal integrity

# Contents

*The unreferenced quotations in this report are comments made during a consultation exercise undertaken by the Children's Rights Development Unit with groups of young people throughout the UK.*

# 1 Introduction

## 1.1 Background

**1.1.1** The right to physical and personal integrity, to protection from all forms of inter-personal violence, is regarded as a fundamental human right. Articles in the Convention emphasise that this right extends to children, who are also entitled to *'special care and assistance'*. But in the UK, legislation, policy and practice and prevailing social attitudes still condone a high level of violence to children. Physical punishment of children is the only form of inter-personal violence now tolerated under the law. Outside the home, there has been some progress to limit physical punishment and other humiliating practices. But the reforms have not been consistent between different jurisdictions within the UK, nor between different institutional and quasi-institutional settings. In some instances only guidance, rather than legislation, protects children.

**1.1.2** The Convention insists that States protect children from *'all forms of physical or mental violence'*, from *'inhuman and degrading treatment and punishment'*, from harmful traditional practices, and from all forms of exploitation including sexual exploitation. It insists on adequate and consistent standards of care for children in institutions, on regular reviews of care and treatment, and on proper help and rehabilitation for victims.

**1.1.3** Public and professional concern over child abuse has escalated in the last few years, and there has been much publicity over a series of scandals involving serious physical, sexual and emotional abuse of children over long periods, both in their own homes and in many different institutions. A succession of judicial and other inquiries and a flow of major reports has followed.

**1.1.4** There has been significant law reform (notably the Children Act 1989 for England and Wales) but it has provided neither consistent nor comprehensive safeguards and has fallen short of implementing the Convention's principles and standards.

**1.1.5** Significantly in Scotland the first recommendation of the 1992 Orkney Inquiry report was: 'Reform in the field of child law and in particular in matters of child protection should proceed under reference to the European Convention on Human Rights and the UN Convention on the Rights of the Child'[1].

**1.1.6** The degree to which basic social and economic rights in the Convention are fulfilled for children is obviously relevant to aspects of child abuse and child protection: these, including rights to life and healthy development (Articles 6 and 24), an adequate standard of living, social security (Articles 26 and 27), and proper levels of support for parents (Article 18) are covered in **UK Agenda Report 2, on the care of children; 4 on standard of living; and 5 on health and health care services.**

## 1.2 Indicators of effective protection

**1.2.1** Because of the cultural conditioning that leads our society to accept a significant level of physical and mental violence to children, there are no established indicators of the full implementation of the child's right to physical and personal integrity.

The following are some suggested indicators:

- a legislative framework which provides children with effective protection from all forms of physical or mental violence, at least equal to that provided to adults, both in their homes and in other institutional and quasi-institutional settings where they may spend significant periods;

- wide knowledge of and respect for public policies, supported by government, which encourage positive, non-violent child-rearing, education and caring;

- evidence from children that they feel safe, in their homes, their neighbourhoods, their institutions;

- indications that children are satisfied with the form and effect of interventions intended to protect them from violence;

- acceptance, rather than denial, of the true level of intra-familial and institutional abuse of children;

- indications that those who suffer violence are offered appropriate treatment and rehabilitation.

# 2 Relevant articles in the Convention

## 2.1 Underlying principles

**Article 2:** all rights in the Convention must apply without discrimination of any kind irrespective of race, colour, language, religion, national, ethnic or social origin, disability or other status.

**Article 3:** the duty in all actions to consider the best interests of the child.

**Article 12:** the right to express an opinion and to have that opinion taken into account in any matter or procedure affecting the child.

The preamble to the Convention emphasises the *'equal and inalienable rights of all members of the human family'*, and also children's rights to *'special care and assistance'*.

## 2.2 Articles relevant to physical and personal integrity

**Article 3.2:** the duty to ensure the protection and care necessary for the well-being of the child.

**Article 3.3:** the duty to ensure that services and facilities are provided to an agreed standard.

**Article 19:** the right to protection from all forms of violence, injury, abuse, neglect or exploitation.

**Article 20:** the duty of the Government to provide special protection and assistance to children deprived of their family environment.

**Article 24.3:** the duty to move towards abolition of traditional practices prejudicial to the health of children.

**Article 25:** the right of children placed in the care of the State to periodic review of treatment.

**Article 28.2:** school discipline must respect the personal dignity of pupils and conform with other articles in the Convention.

**Article 30:** the right of children from minority communities to enjoy their own culture and practise their own language and religion.

**Article 34:** the right to protection from sexual exploitation.

**Article 36:** the right to protection from all other forms of exploitation.

**Article 39:** the duty of the Government to take measures to ensure that child-victims of armed conflict, torture, neglect or exploitation receive treatment for recovery and social integration.

*For the full wording of the articles, see the UN Convention on the Rights of the Child, page 311.*

# 3 Available information on protection of physical and personal integrity

**3.1** It is only recently that any statistical information on the prevalence of child abuse has been collected centrally and published. The Government now publishes yearly returns of numbers of children on child protection registers. These cannot of course be taken as a measure of the true extent of child abuse. Some children are placed on registers because of concerns rather than evidence of abuse, but it is also clear that much serious physical, sexual and emotional abuse goes unreported.

**3.2** The latest statistics show that in England on 31 March 1992 there were 38,600 children on registers (3.5 children per thousand population under 18). 24,500 additions were made to registers in the year ending 31 March 1992, broken down into the following categories: neglect 3,700 (15%); physical injury 7,100 (29%); sexual abuse 4,200 (17%); emotional abuse 1,700 (7%); grave concern 8,900 (36%).

**3.3** In Wales there were 2,112 children on child protection registers at 31 March 1992 (3.2 per thousand population aged under 18: this proportion varied from 4.7 per 1,000 in Dyfed to 1.0 per 1,000 in Gwynedd). Analysed by category of abuse, more than twice as many children were on registers for physical abuse alone (481) than sexual abuse alone (237). In addition 357 were categorised as 'grave concern, household contains known abuser', and a further 605 'grave concern, other'.

**3.4** For the first time since collection of national data began in 1989, the 1992 figures for total numbers on registers and the number registered in the year showed a fall of 6,700 (15%). In October 1991 a revised version of *Working together*, the inter-agency guide to co-operation for protection of children, was issued[2]. It withdrew 'grave concern' as a category for registration on child protection registers; this category had accounted for approximately 50% of registrations. Children already registered as 'grave concern' were to be re-allocated at the next review. In fact by 31 March 1992, numbers registered as 'grave concern' had fallen from 47% of all registrations to 34%, but this made virtually no difference to numbers allocated under other categories.. It seems at least questionable whether the proposal to end use of the category has reduced the need for child protection, which previous trends suggested was steadily increasing. Rates for registration of girls are slightly higher than for boys (2.3 per 1,000 compared with 2.1 per 1,000). By age, the highest rate for registrations is for under one year-olds - 5.1 per 1,000.

**3.5** According to Home Office figures, in England in 1991 72 children under five were killed by someone known to them and two by strangers[3].

**3.6** The NSPCC has also published detailed studies based on the work of the Society's child protection teams in some areas[4]. ChildLine publishes analyses of the calls it receives from children: of the 68,958 children counselled between 1 April 1991 and 31 March 1992, 15% called about sexual abuse, 14% about physical abuse. In 88% of cases the perpetrator of abuse comes from within the child's family circle. Four times as many girls as boys call ChildLine. The majority of children counselled (66%) are between 12 and 15[5]. Interim statistics from ChildLine Scotland's free help-line for children in care showed that of 300 children counselled in the first six months, 21% were calling about physical abuse, 19% about sexual abuse and 11% about bullying. While some callers may not have been abused in care, this illustrates the importance of confidential advice and counselling for those in care.

> *'In the care sector there should be counselling sessions, time given to individuals to off-load stress and put it in a bin. Young people need to off-load instead of society making them suppress it and telling them to get on with life because you are an adult now. You need a chance to off-load it rather than turn to violence or drugs or wrecking cars or getting pregnant or into prostitution. All these negative areas derive from being hurt and hateful inside, you should be able to use it all in a direct positive manner.'*
> (18 year-old, Merseyside)

**3.7** There has been no comprehensive attempt to measure the extent of all forms of violence experienced by children in the UK, either in the home or in institutions. John and Elizabeth Newson's studies of child-rearing, carried out by interviewing parents over 40 years, have provided information on rates of physical punishment of children. A 1985 study found over two thirds of a large sample of mothers admitting to smacking their baby before the age of one; earlier studies found that 22% of seven year olds had already been hit with an implement, and another 53% threatened with an implement[6]. In other countries, studies which have included interviewing children as well as parents have found consistent under-reporting by parents of violence to their children.

**3.8** The Department of Health has commissioned a large-scale 'Family Life Study' which aims to:
- obtain information on punitive and non-punitive control strategies used by parents, and on the nature of parental authority over children;
- identify variables associated with high levels of physical punishment of children;
- investigate children's concepts of parental control strategies, and in particular of physical punishment'.

Results should be available in 1994. This study has included limited interviewing of children as well as parents[7].

**3.9** A study of the prevalence of sexual abuse in a sample of 16 to 21 year-olds concluded that one in two girls and one in four boys will experience some form of sexual abuse before their eighteenth birthday. In the survey of 1,244 young people, 59% of young women and 27% of young men reported at least one sexually intrusive experience before they were 18 years old. Sexual abuse was defined broadly to include 'flashing', being touched, being pressured to have sex and attempted and actual assaults/rapes. Almost a third of the incidents occurred before the age of 12. If 'flashing', abuse attempts which were successfully resisted and 'less serious' forms of abuse by peers are excluded, the prevalence figures are one in five for women and one in 14 for men[8].

**3.10** In Finland, a valuable indication of levels of violence including sexual abuse experienced by children was provided by asking 15 year-olds in school to fill in a detailed questionnaire in confidence. Such research would be of value

in monitoring implementation of Article 19 in the UK[9].

## ACTION REQUIRED FOR COMPLIANCE

**Compliance with Article 19, the right to protection from all forms of physical or mental violence, requires that there is further monitoring of the extent to which children are now protected. There should be research at regular intervals involving interviewing a representative sample of children in various age groups, and parents of very young children, concerning their experience of all forms of violence from adults and from peers, in their homes and in other settings.**

# 4 Upholding children's rights to physical and personal integrity

## 4.1 'Reasonable chastisement'

**4.1.1** The first and most urgent task must be to ensure that legislation throughout the UK no longer tolerates physical or mental violence to children. Article 19 insists that children must be protected from '*all forms of physical or mental violence*'.

**4.1.2** The protection provided to children by the law on assault and the law on cruelty is qualified by the common law concept of 'reasonable chastisement', which provides parents and other carers with a defence. This allows treatment and punishment of children involving physical and mental violence, in breach of Article 19. Courts are currently left to determine what constitutes 'reasonable'. In the case of adults, assaults without consent, however trivial, are technically offences. When marital rape was declared illegal by the courts earlier in the 1990s, it left physical punishment of children as the only physical assault tolerated under the law.

**4.1.3** Thus current legislation, far from providing '*special care and protection*' for children, affords them less protection from violence than adults. Within the laws against cruelty to children in force for England and Wales, Scotland and N Ireland, there are specific provisions confirming the common law defence of 'reasonable chastisement'[10]. Courts' interpretation of 'reasonable' chastisement varies widely, but very recently parents who have beaten their children with belts and canes causing serious bruising have been acquitted of assault or cruelty. In 1990 Scotland's then most senior judge commented in a case in which a nine year-old girl was bruised by a belting by her mother: 'It is evident that [the child] richly deserved punishment and that the mother's intention was to inflict on her the punishment she deserved'[11]. At Brighton Crown Court in October 1991, a mother who had beaten her 11 year-old daughter with a garden cane and an electrical flex was cleared of assault and cruelty. In March 1993, North Avon magistrates acquitted a father who admitted using a belt on his five and eight year-old sons (although a clinical medical officer testified that she had only seen such injuries twice in 10 years). In April 1993 at Southampton Crown Court a mother was cleared on appeal against her conviction for assault (she had slippered her eight year-old daughter causing heavy bruising). The judge commented: 'In the words of one of my colleagues, if a parent cannot slipper a child, the world is going potty'[12].

*'Parents shouldn't have the right to hit children, it just makes children grow up to be violent. Hitting children should be banned.'*
(13 year-old Lincolnshire)

**4.1.4** In five other European countries (Sweden, Finland, Denmark, Norway and Austria) there has been law reform to ensure that children's physical integrity is fully protected. In Sweden, family law now reads: 'Children are entitled to care, security and a good upbringing. Children are to be treated with respect for their person and individuality and may not be subjected to corporal punishment or any other humiliating treatment'[13]. Research indicates that these legal reforms,

coupled with information campaigns encouraging positive discipline, quickly transform attitudes and practice.

*'Schools should teach from day one the kind of opinion that children should be appreciated and not beaten.'*
(14 year-old, N Ireland)

**4.1.5** Two recommendations from the Council of Europe Committee of Ministers have proposed ending all physical punishment of children in member-states, including the UK. A 1985 recommendation proposed that member-states should 'review their legislation on the power to punish children in order to limit or indeed prohibit corporal punishment, even if violation of such a prohibition does not necessarily entail a criminal penalty'. The explanatory memorandum to the recommendation stated: 'It is the very assumption that corporal punishment of children is legitimate that opens the way to all kinds of excesses and makes the traces or symptoms of such punishment acceptable to third parties'[14]. A further recommendation from the Committee of Ministers in 1990 stated: 'The importance should be emphasised of the general condemnation of corporal punishment and other forms of degrading treatment as a means of education, and of the need for violence-free education'[15].

*'I think hitting a child makes more bitterness between parents and children, I think there are other more suitable forms of punishment.'*
(15 year-old, N Ireland)

**4.1.6** A recent proposal to limit the defence of 'reasonable chastisement' came from the governmental Scottish Law Commission in its 1992 report on family law[16]. The Commission proposed that striking a child with any kind of implement, or in a way which causes or could cause injury, or pain or discomfort lasting more than a very short time, should become a criminal offence. The Commission proposed, however, that what it termed 'safe, disciplinary smacking' should remain untouched by the law. Considering Article 19 of the UN Convention, the Commission argued: 'It is by no means clear that an ordinary smack, which causes no injury, would come within the category of violence, abuse or maltreatment... The question of when physical contact, even physical contact intended to cause temporary pain, becomes physical violence is, in our view, a question of degree'.

**4.1.7** This view seeks to make a special case for mild inter-personal violence when directed at children. But the Convention emphasises children's need for '*special care and assistance*'. There is no question of the application of the law on assault to other forms of inter-personal violence being limited by some arbitrary definition of 'acceptable' violence. Implementing Article 19 implies extending to children at least equal protection from inter-personal violence. Implementation of the Scottish Law Commission's proposal would do much to limit more extreme forms of violence to children which are currently legal. But it would maintain a disrespectful inequality of protection for children, and fail to implement Article 19.

**4.1.8** Article 5 of the Convention requires the state to respect the responsibilities, rights and duties of parents and others responsible for the child '*to provide, in a manner consistent with the evolving capacities of the child, appropriate direction and guidance in the exercise by the child of the rights...*' in the Convention. Article 19 indicates that '*direction and guidance*' must not involve any form of mental or physical violence.

Compliance with Article 19 requires that:

● primary legislation should be used to remove or substantially amend the common law defence of 'reasonable chastisement' and the statutory confirmation of it in the law on child cruelty, to ensure that any punishment involving physical or mental violence is unlawful. The concept of 'reasonable chastisement' is not compatible with the Convention's emphasis on parental responsibility for the welfare of the child, and should be replaced by parental duties to guide and safeguard their children according to the child's evolving capacity;

● the law on cruelty should also be amended to remove the current implied justification of 'necessary' suffering or injury to health caused by assault, ill-treatment or neglect of children.

## 4.2 Children witnessing violence in the home

**4.2.1** There is growing evidence of the affect on children of witnessing violence - generally against their mother - in the home, whether or not they too are victims of violence (and research suggests that in a majority of cases men who beat their wives also physically abuse children in the home). One recent study of couples found that 90% had a child aged under five while the violence was taking place. Effects on the child can include increased levels of anxiety and sadness, psychosomatic illnesses such as headaches, abdominal complaints and asthma, and lower ratings in social competence, especially for boys[17].

**4.2.2** A study of refuges found that children make up two thirds of the refuge population, and that more than 15,000 children pass through Women's Aid refuges in England every year[18]. Few refuges can currently afford to employ a child care worker, although the Women's Aid Federation has been campaigning for years to raise awareness of the crucial role played by these workers in helping children to come to terms with their experiences. Children in refuges in England and Wales should come within the definition of children 'in need' in the Children Act 1989, and thus receive appropriate services from local authorities. The Children's Legal Centre made detailed recommendations to help protect children from the effects of witnessing domestic violence in a 1992 memorandum to the House of Commons Home Affairs Committee[19].

Compliance with Article 19 requires that:

● all those involved in child protection and responding to violence in the home receive training on the effects of such violence on children;

● children in refuges be recognised as children 'in need' under the Children Act 1989, and under the Act and similar legislation in other jurisdictions receive appropriate support from local authorities. All refuges which may take children should have appropriately trained child care workers, and the Government should ensure that sufficient resources

are available.

## 4.3 Protection of children outside the home

**4.3.1** Outside the home, there is variable and generally inadequate legal protection of children from '*all forms of physical or mental violence*'. Many of the scandals involving institutional abuse of children which have been publicised in the last few years have included violent and/or humiliating sanctions or treatment. The current situation fails to satisfy Article 19 and discriminates between children in different categories of institution and quasi-institutional care.

*Protection from physical punishment in schools*
**4.3.2** Only in the case of school pupils has primary legislation been used to limit physical punishment. Since 1987, physical punishment has effectively been abolished in all state-supported education throughout the UK by removing teachers' defence of 'reasonable chastisement' in any civil, but not criminal action taken against them for assault. The legislation specifically avoids making 'reasonable' corporal punishment by teachers a criminal offence, although such actions directed at an adult would be criminal assaults[20]. The legislation does not protect children in private schools whose fees are being paid by their parents and not the state. The Education Act 1993 included a further limitation on any corporal punishment used in schools, that it must not be 'inhuman or degrading'[21]. This followed a judgment of the European Court of Human Rights which found that a particular instance in which a seven year-old boy had been hit three times with a rubber-soled gym shoe by his head teacher in a private boarding school did not constitute a breach of Article 3 of the European Convention on Human Rights (which bars 'inhuman or degrading treatment or punishment'). The judges' decision was by the narrow margin of five votes to four and the judgment emphasised that 'the Court did not wish to be taken as approving in any way corporal punishment as part of the disciplinary regime of a school'[22].

**4.3.3** During the passage of the Education Bill in 1993, an amendment was moved seeking to extend abolition of corporal punishment to all pupils. This was resisted by the Government and when taken to a vote in the House of Lords was rejected by a small margin. The implications of the UN Convention were specifically raised during debate in the House of Lords, but the Minister responded that 'In the Government's view, as regards the use of corporal punishment in schools the [UN] Convention does not impose any obligations which go beyond those imposed by the European Convention [of Human Rights]'[23].

**4.3.4** Article 28(2) of the Convention insists: '*States Parties shall take all appropriate measures to ensure that school discipline is administered in a manner consistent with the child's human dignity and in conformity with the present Convention*' (our emphasis). This means in conformity with Article 19 - without any form of physical or mental violence. It is clear that this is a higher and additional standard of protection to that provided by Article 37 of the UN Convention which echoes Article 3 of the European Convention on Human Rights and Article 7 of the International Covenant on Civil and Political Rights, in outlawing '*inhuman or degrading treatment or punishment*'.

*Protection from physical punishment in child care and daycare*

**4.3.5** Physical punishment of children is prohibited in regulations applying to local authority community homes and voluntary and private (registered) homes in England and Wales[24]. It is also prohibited in regulations applying to residential care homes in England and Wales[25]. In Scotland it is prohibited in children's homes and certain other residential establishments[26]. In N Ireland, relevant regulations do not as yet prohibit physical punishment, but legislation is currently under review, and reforms similar to those under the Children Act applying in England and Wales are expected.

**4.3.6** The regulations covering foster-care arranged by local authorities and voluntary organisations in England and Wales require a written agreement from foster-carers that they will not use corporal punishment on any child placed with them[27]. There are as yet no controls on corporal punishment or other humiliating sanctions in foster-care in Scotland or N Ireland, but current reviews have proposed similar legislation to that applying in England and Wales.

**4.3.7** Guidance issued under the Children Act indicates that physical punishment should not be used in any group daycare setting, including childminding in England and Wales (and similar guidance has been issued under the Act to cover Scotland)[28]. Guidance also indicates that physical punishment should not be used in private foster-care in England and Wales[29]. In N Ireland there are as yet no controls on sanctions in daycare settings, and no controls in N Ireland or Scotland on sanctions in private foster-care.

**4.3.8** The ability of guidance to protect children was challenged by a court in 1993. Sutton magistrates ruled that Sutton Council was wrong to refuse registration to a childminder who declined to give an undertaking that she would not smack a minded child[30]. The decision is being appealed, but emphasises the need for clear legislation.

### ACTION REQUIRED FOR COMPLIANCE

**Compliance with Article 19 requires that:**

- **the defence of 'reasonable chastisement' should be removed or substantially amended. This would ensure consistent protection of children from physical punishment in all settings. In the short term, private school pupils should be protected from institutional physical punishment by amendment of education legislation; in the child care system and daycare settings, consistent regulations should replace guidance.**

- **in Scotland and N Ireland current reviews of children's law should enable appropriate reforms to be included.**

*Protection from other sanctions involving violence*

**4.3.9** The only legislation in the UK which protects children from undesirable sanctions other than physical punishment is that applying to local authority, voluntary and private children's homes in England and Wales, issued under the Children Act[31]. The regulations prohibit:

- any form of corporal punishment;
- any deprivation of food or drink;
- restriction on visits or communication with parents, friends etc;

- any requirement to wear distinctive or inappropriate clothes;
- intentional deprivation of sleep;
- use or withholding of medication or medical or dental treatment.

**4.3.10** Behaviour modification techniques involving forms of humiliation and deprivation of basic rights have been used in some institutions for children, including psychiatric units, private health institutions and special schools[32].

**4.3.11** The Convention demands consistent protection of all children from '*all forms of physical or mental violence*' (Article 2 and 19). It also demands consistent standards for institutions, services and facilities responsible for the care or protection of children (Article 3.2). Proper legislative safeguards against inappropriate sanctions are required in all residential and non-residential institutions which include children throughout the UK.

### ACTION REQUIRED FOR COMPLIANCE

**Compliance with Article 19 requires that regulations applying to all day and residential institutions including all schools, and to other formal placements for children must include a list of prohibited sanctions (similar to that in regulation 8 of the Children's Homes Regulations issued under the Children Act for England and Wales) which may involve physical or mental violence, in addition to a general prohibition of inhuman or degrading treatment or punishment (also Articles 2 and 3.2).**

*Protection from bullying*

**4.3.12** Bullying is a form of violence which we now know affects many children in schools and other institutional settings. Recently there has been growing public debate and concern at levels of bullying in schools, and the Government has commissioned major research. In 1990 ChildLine, the national help-line for children, opened a special 'bullying line'. Over a three-month period 2,054 children were counselled. An analysis of the calls showed that children found a wide range of behaviour to be bullying, from teasing to serious physical harm. Nearly a quarter of the children reported bullying involving violent assault. Others reported thefts of money or possessions, or extortion. A report concluded: 'Children frequently doubt adults' ability to stop the bullying, and with good reason: many adults do not know what to do when faced with a child being bullied'[33].

> '*Every young person at some point gets abused by other people whether it's by adults or people of their own age and there's no support mechanism for them to deal with it in schools and it's just seen as something that happens like falling over and banging your head. It's not seen as a form of abuse or a big problem.*'
> (15 year-old, N Ireland)

**4.3.13** Bullying in other institutions has not been documented to the same degree, and further research is required in child care, health and penal institutions. In young offender institutions, bullying has been reported to be a dominant feature of young inmates' lives[34].

**4.3.14** There is as yet no legislation to ensure effective action to prevent and respond to bullying in any institutions, although the Government has distributed advice to schools on challenging bullying, and has emphasised that it attaches importance to 'the eradication of bullying, wherever and whenever it occurs'[35].

> *'I think bullying can have long term effects and when you reach a certain age it's no longer physical but more mental.'*
> (17 year-old, Shropshire)

(See also **UK Agenda Report 7 on education,** page 168 and **9 on youth justice,** page 220).

### ACTION REQUIRED FOR COMPLIANCE

**Compliance with Article 19 requires that:**

● **further research is undertaken to monitor levels of bullying in all institutions which include children;**

● **legislation should oblige responsible authorities for all schools and other institutional settings including children to develop detailed policies to prevent and respond to bullying (also Article 3.2).**

*Protection from potential abusers*

**4.3.15** Much physical, sexual and emotional abuse of children is perpetrated by adults employed to care for or treat them. There are particular concerns over arrangements to protect disabled children. Over the last 10 years there have been attempts to improve arrangements designed to prevent potential abusers gaining access to children through employment or voluntary work. These have included arrangements for checking on possible criminal backgrounds of those who apply to work with children, as well as proper recruitment procedures.

**4.3.16** Most recently, following the conviction of a residential care worker for numerous sexual and other offences against children in a local authority children's home, the Department of Health set up a Committee of Inquiry chaired by Norman Warner to consider recruitment of staff for children's homes[36].

**4.3.17** The Convention demands appropriate legislative and administrative action to protect children from all forms of physical or mental violence (Article 19). It also demands that all institutions, services and facilities for the care and treatment of children conform to consistent standards (Article 3.2)

**4.3.18** None of the current arrangements for vetting those applying for work with children is mandatory. The arrangements are set out in circular, not legislation, and they vary widely from one jurisdiction to another within the UK. Evaluations of vetting procedures have shown that police checks must not be regarded as a panacea, and that other recruitment and employment procedures may be more significant for child protection. It has been proposed that vetting - a time-consuming and therefore expensive process even when all criminal records are in centralised computer systems - should be limited to those who will have 'substantial unsupervised' access to children. But the present inconsistency of checking procedures is illogical and dangerous. For example a recent circular issued by the Department of Health emphasised that criminal record checks should be carried out on all childminders and on staff working in local authority day nurseries, but that there should not be checks in relation to staff of private or voluntary playgroups, day nurseries, out of school clubs or holiday play-

schemes (although access to children is just as substantial and no more supervised in these settings)[37].

**4.3.19** There is further dangerous inconsistency in arrangements for reporting concerns about those already working with children. Regulations applying to children's homes in England and Wales place an obligation on the appropriate authority to report to the Secretary of State 'any conduct on the part of a member of staff of the home which is or may be such, in the opinion of the responsible authority, that he is not, or as the case may be would not be, a suitable person to be employed in work involving children'. But there is no similar duty in relation to carers working in other child care institutions or quasi-institutional settings such as foster-care, or daycare (it is however the case that any incidents of suspected or actual abuse do come within the remit of child protection procedures and should be dealt with under the procedures). Local education authorities and other education employers, and proprietors of independent schools are required to make misconduct reports.

> *'My foster father would come home drunk and pretend to be all affectionate which he was never like in the day and try to kiss me, but it didn't go any further than that. He give me a love bite once but it wasn't anything really bad. I could deal with it.'*
> (18 year-old, Merseyside)

**4.3.20** Regulations issued under the Children Act enable individuals in England and Wales to be disqualified from private fostering, from being involved in any way in a voluntary or private children's home, providing daycare or working as a childminder[38]. But strangely these provisions on disqualification do not apply to children's homes, foster-care or daycare provided by or paid for by local authorities.

### ACTION REQUIRED FOR COMPLIANCE

**Compliance with Article 19 requires that:**

● **all employers - local authority, health authority, voluntary and private - of those whose work involves substantial unsupervised contact with children should be required to follow statutory codes of practice on recruitment, induction and supervision of such employees. The codes would include appropriate mandatory arrangements for police checks;**

● **all such employers should be under consistent legal duties to report any conduct suggesting that an employee is not or may not be a suitable person to be employed in work involving children (also Article 3.2).**

*Inspection*

**4.3.21** Arrangements for inspection of institutions where children and young people spend significant periods of their lives vary widely between different services (health, education, social services, penal) and according to their status (maintained, voluntary, private). Some institutions are inspected by local authority appointed inspectors, some by government inspectors, others by quasi-independent inspectors, eg Her Majesty's Inspectors of Schools and the new 'registered inspectors', and some by all three. In the case of some institutions (eg local authority children's homes in England and Wales) there is no statutory duty to inspect.

**4.3.22** The Government cannot fully implement Article 3.2 of the Convention unless there are consistent arrangements for inspection of all the settings where children may spend significant periods. Current arrangements for inspection vary in frequency (in some cases not specified at all); whether reports are publicly available; whether they specify what aspects of the institution and of the children should be inspected; whether inspectors are required to see and talk to children.

### ACTION REQUIRED FOR COMPLIANCE

**Compliance with Article 19 requires that arrangements for inspection of all institutions and quasi-institutional settings (eg foster-care and daycare settings) for children should be rationalised to ensure that there are clear and consistent powers and duties on central and local government to arrange appropriate inspections at regular prescribed intervals. The primary purpose must be to safeguard and promote the welfare of children. Children must have an opportunity to speak in private to inspectors (also Article 3.2).**

*Reviewing care and treatment*
**4.3.23** Another essential safeguard for children living away from home is regular review of their care and treatment. Article 25 specifically underlines *'the right of the child who has been placed by the competent authorities for the purposes of care, protection, or treatment of his or her physical or mental health, to a periodic review of the treatment provided to the child and all other circumstances relevant to his or her placement'*.

**4.3.24** Current arrangements for regular review of children's care and treatment are extraordinarily inconsistent both between jurisdictions within the UK, and between different services and institutions within each jurisdiction.

**4.3.25** Children and young people living at home with parents or guardians are not subject to any compulsory review by outside authorities, unless they are in care to a local authority, or in Scotland are under the supervision of a children's hearing. There is no statutory framework for developmental checks, or for visits from health visitors.

**4.3.26** Arrangements for formal review of children placed away from home vary widely (for a detailed analysis of the arrangements see a detailed report on child protection published in 1993, *One scandal too many*[39]).

### ACTION REQUIRED FOR COMPLIANCE

Compliance with Article 19 requires that arrangements for formal review of placement and treatment of children, involving the children themselves and similar in frequency and scope to those required under the Review of Children's Cases Regulations 1991, issued under the Children Act 1989 for England and Wales, should extend to all children being accommodated in institutional or quasi-institutional settings throughout the UK (also Articles 3.2 and 25).

## 4.4 Children involved in prosecution of abusers

**4.4.1** While there have been recent changes (in particular in the Criminal Justice Act 1991) to improve the position of child victims and child witnesses giving evidence, there remain concerns that children's evidence is given insufficient weight, and that the court experience is unnecessarily threatening to the child (as it often is to other victims of violent crime including rape). There are also unacceptable delays in hearing cases, and a lack of counselling and support in the period before the hearing. All this conflicts with the obligation to make the child's best interests a primary consideration (Article 3.1).

**4.4.2** The Convention emphasises that the best interests of the child must be a primary consideration in all matters concerning them, and that affected children's views must be heard and taken seriously: this should apply to all decision-making relating to prosecution of abusers.

### ACTION REQUIRED FOR COMPLIANCE

Compliance with Article 3.1, the duty to ensure that 'best interests' of the child are always a primary consideration and Article 12, the right of the child to express a view, requires that:

● authorities involved in making decisions concerning prosecution for offences of child abuse should be bound by the 'best interests' principle (police, prosecuting authorities, courts), and by the requirements of Article 12 to ensure proper consideration of the child's views;

● arrangements for child victims and witnesses to take part in criminal proceedings should be subject to the requirements of the same Articles.

# 5 Child abuse and child protection procedures

## 5.1 Definition of child abuse

**5.1.1** It is important to note that the current definition of 'child abuse' in common usage and in most child protection policies and practice in the UK is not based on the child's right to protection from '*all forms of physical or mental violence*' but condones quite a high level of violence to children, because of the defence of 'reasonable chastisement' referred to above. If one looks at the parallel issue of protection of women from domestic violence, there is no similar concept of 'acceptable' violence to wives or partners. It is important that child protection, like protection of women from violence, should be based on the right of all people to physical and personal integrity. Revising the definition of child abuse aims to challenge the acceptability of any violence to children: it does not imply more formal interventions or prosecutions, as such actions are very unlikely to be in the best interests of the children concerned.

**5.1.2** There is no statutory definition of child abuse. The Children Act, in defining grounds for investigation and intervention in families, refers to 'significant harm'; 'harm' is further defined as 'ill-treatment or the impairment of health or development'; 'ill-treatment' includes 'sexual abuse and forms of ill-treatment which are not physical'; 'development' means 'physical, intellectual, emotional, social or behavioural development'; and 'health' means 'physical or mental health' (section 31 (9)). The Act also states that 'where the question of whether harm suffered by a child is significant turns on the child's health or development, his health or development shall be compared with that which could reasonably be expected of a similar child' (section 31(10)). Guidance issued jointly by the relevant government departments on child protection in England and Wales provides no further definition. It appears that local Area Child Protection Committees are currently left to determine their own definitions beyond the statutory ones.

> '*Most people don't realise what abuse is. People who realise what abuse is least are people who have been abused, because parents or whoever is abusing you, don't want you to know about it.*'
> (16 year-old, N East)

**5.1.3** There is concern that current interpretations of 'significant harm' and of authorities' duties to investigate are not providing adequate protection for many children from physical violence and from neglect which may involve mental violence. There is no systematic monitoring of children referred to statutory agencies following allegations of physical harm and injury. Many cases appear to be 'filtered out' without children and/or families receiving necessary support, which in some cases could avoid the need for formal and potentially damaging interventions[40]. (See also **UK Agenda Report 2 on care of children,** page 24).

> '*I was abused by my dad from about the age of eight and the only reason it stopped was because one day he kicked me about so much that the social services got involved but they only checked my face and my outside injuries, they didn't check anywhere else.*'
> (16 year-old, N East)

### ACTION REQUIRED FOR COMPLIANCE

**Compliance with Article 19 requires that:**

- official guidance should ensure that the definition of child abuse used in child protection policy and practice does not suggest that any form of physical or mental violence to children is acceptable. This does not imply that there should be more formal intervention, but that preventive work is based on the child's right to physical and personal integrity;

- there should be systematic local monitoring of action taken following allegations of physical or mental violence to children, to ensure that protection is effective and that the Convention's principles are consistently respected, including the 'best interests' principle and the right of children to express views, have them taken seriously, and be heard in all administrative and judicial procedures.

## 5.2 Child protection procedures

**5.2.1** While there have been major judicial inquiries and reports about child protection procedures (for example Cleveland and Orkney), there has been no comprehensive review of procedures in recent years. Ratification of the Convention provides further pressure for a full review to ensure that the procedures respect the principles and standards in the Convention, and that intervention does not further abuse children. In particular, monitoring is required to ensure that there is no discrimination in the administration of the procedures (Article 2), that children's views are ascertained and taken seriously at all stages and that their right to be heard in any administrative and judicial proceedings is respected (Article 12). In addition, it is important that there should be monitoring to determine children's views of the appropriateness and effectiveness of interventions following allegations of child abuse. It is significant that more than half the children who phone ChildLine in confidence about sexual abuse have not told anyone else: it seems they do not see child protection services as approachable. (See also **UK Agenda Report 1 on personal freedoms,** page 14 for implications of Article 16 for children's right to confidentiality).

**5.2.2** Child protection responsibilities and procedures also need to be reviewed in the light of recent and forthcoming changes in local government and health service administration in all jurisdictions.

### ACTION REQUIRED FOR COMPLIANCE

**Compliance with Article 12, the right of the child to express a view and Article 19 requires that:**

- children's views of the appropriateness and effectiveness of interventions following allegations of abuse should be systematically ascertained by monitoring and research;

- there should be co-ordinated reviews of child protection procedures throughout the UK, taking as their starting point the basic principles in the Convention.

## 5.3 Child protection services

**5.3.1** There is as yet no statutory basis for the maintenance of child protection registers, or for reviewing children placed on registers. There is continuing evidence that in some local authority areas children who are on child protection registers have no designated social worker. In the Children Act Report 1992 the Department of Health acknowledged that failure to allocate a key social worker to children on the register 'not only prevents progress in carrying out the child protection plan but reduces opportunities for full parental participation and for the views of the child to be taken into account in any decision about his or her future'[41]. At 30 June 1992 the total number of reported unallocated child protection cases in 104 authorities was 1,110 or 3.2% of the total on the Register (the report notes that in Wales there were currently no unallocated cases). In the London Borough of Lambeth 140 children on the register were not allocated, out of a total of 914. 23.7% of the unallocated cases had been unallocated for over three months.

## ACTION REQUIRED FOR COMPLIANCE

**Compliance with Article 19 requires that arrangements for placing children on child protection registers and for regular review of their protection should become statutory throughout the UK, so that any failure to make appropriate arrangements can be challenged. Resource allocation must be adequate to ensure effective child protection.**

# 6 Educational measures to protect children's physical and personal integrity

**6.1** Current social attitudes condone quite high levels of physical and mental violence to children in child-rearing, child care and education. Legislative changes as outlined above are essential to implement the Convention's principles and standards, and to provide a clear basis for child protection, prevention of all forms of violence and for information programmes on positive child-rearing and caring without violence or humiliation.

**6.2** The Government has as yet provided no advice for parents discouraging physical punishment and humiliation of children. Under the Children Act (for England and Wales) the Department of Health has issued some positive guidance to other carers, including those working in children's homes, foster-care and daycare[42].

> *'They put us into a home where the foster mother was having an affair with the lodger and the foster father was trying to commit suicide all the time. They starved us as well, the only meal we ever got while I was there was stew, baked beans or steam pudding and we always chose the steam pudding because it was more filling. My weight must have dropped dramatically but it was never reported.'*
> (18 year-old, Merseyside)

**6.3** Most recently in 1993 further guidance was issued on permissible forms of control in residential care[43]. The introduction recognised that there had not been enough positive advice on control of 'often volatile young people'; it also noted 'increasing concern by the Government and the wider public that we may have gone too far in stressing the rights of children at the expense of upholding the rights and responsibilities of parents and professionals in supervising them'. But the other, unmentioned, context was the continuing series of scandals involving ill-treatment and abuse of children in a wide variety of institutions, and particular cases in which inappropriate restraint had caused serious injury.

> *'I never got hit about to any great extent, just thrown about or sat on but some were not so lucky. I saw one member of staff run across the room and knee one gut in the nose, bang, just because he was throwing a tantrum.'*
> (18 year-old, S Wales)

## ACTION REQUIRED FOR COMPLIANCE

**Compliance with Article 19 requires that:**

● **appropriate government departments and other agencies (eg the Health Education Authority and similar agencies in Wales, Scotland and N Ireland), local authorities and health authorities should promote and provide information to the public, including in particular parents and those working with them, on respecting children's right to physical and personal integrity, discouraging physical punishment and other humiliating treatment of children. Such information programmes should promote positive forms of discipline which do not involve violence or humiliation;**

- such information should be promoted as part of family life education within the National Curriculum; encouragement of non-violent conflict resolution should also be an explicit part of the National Curriculum;

- guidance should be issued to appropriate institutions and carers on responding to challenging behaviour, and on the minimum use of force in restraining children who are a danger to themselves or others.

# 7 Traditional practices prejudicial to health

**7.1** Traditional practices can involve physical and/or mental violence to children, and hence threaten their physical or personal integrity. The Convention requires states to ensure protection from '*all forms of physical or mental violence*' while children are in the care of parents and others (Article 19); it also explicitly insists that states take '*all effective and appropriate measures with a view to abolishing traditional practices prejudicial to the health of children*' (Article 24.3). This provision was included in the Convention because of concern over the particular issue of genital mutilation of girls and young women. This has been practised at different times in many cultures and countries. It remains common in parts of Africa, Asia and the Middle East. Article 2 emphasises that there must be no discrimination in implementation of rights; thus traditional practices which involve physical or mental violence or are prejudicial to health of children cannot be justified by reference to culture, race, or religion.

**7.2** In the UK the Prohibition of Female Circumcision Act 1985 has not been effective in ending the practice within certain communities in the UK, and by November 1992 there had been no prosecutions under it[44]. It is welcome that guidance on child protection and on private foster-care issued under the Children Act alerts relevant carers and professionals to the issue. During 1993 the General Medical Council struck off the register and fined a doctor who had offered 'circumcision' to a journalist posing as a potential patient.

**7.3** Male circumcision for non-medical reasons is a declining but still common traditional practice. While it is not in any sense comparable with genital mutilation of girls and young women, it does involve an invasion of the boy's physical integrity, normally carried out before he can give an informed consent. This and some other traditional practices are clearly related to reinforcement of cultural identity as well as religious ritual. In some cases male circumcision is still carried out by adults with no medical training, and it is often carried out without anaesthesia. It has led to infection, injury and mutilation for a significant number of children.

**7.4** Other traditional practices include piercing of ears and/or nose, scarring, scratching, coin-rubbing and so on, without the informed consent of children.

## ACTION REQUIRED FOR COMPLIANCE

**Compliance with Article 24.3, the duty to take measures to abolish traditional practices prejudicial to health, requires that:**

- **there should be a comprehensive review in all communities of any traditional practices which threaten the physical integrity of children and/or are prejudicial to their health, in the light of the Convention's principles;**

- **educational campaigns are required within communities to emphasise the child's right to physical integrity in relation to any traditional practices which involve physical or mental violence or may be prejudicial to health.**

# 8  Rehabilitation of victims

**8.1**  Much violence suffered by children in the UK remains currently lawful, and there is therefore no provision for rehabilitation or support.  Where child abuse is acknowledged and action taken to remove and/or prosecute abusers, child victims often receive little appropriate support.  In particular where there is a prosecution, therapy and support may be withheld until after the court case - often months or years after the event.

> *'For children who have been abused there should be a lot more help to get them through it, you need counselling, it's important to let everything out.'*
> (17 year-old, London)

**8.2**  Article 39 obliges the Government to *'take all appropriate measures to promote physical and psychological recovery and social reintegration of a child victim of any form of neglect, exploitation or abuse; torture or any other form of cruel, inhuman or degrading treatment or punishment...'*.

## ACTION REQUIRED FOR COMPLIANCE

**Compliance with Article 39, the duty to provide rehabilitative care for victims of maltreatment, requires that all victims of abuse should be offered appropriate assessment to determine what measures are needed to promote recovery and social reintegration.  Monitoring should ensure that therapy and other forms of support proposed by assessments are made available to victims.**

# Summary of action required for compliance

**1**  Compliance with Article 3.1, the duty to ensure that 'best interests' of the child are always a primary consideration and Article 12, the right of the child to express a view, requires that:

● authorities involved in making decisions concerning prosecution for offences of child abuse should be bound by the 'best interests' principle (police, prosecuting authorities, courts), and by the requirements of Article 12 to ensure proper consideration of the child's views;

● arrangements for child victims and witnesses to take part in criminal proceedings should be subject to the requirements of the same Articles.

**2**  Compliance with Article 12, the right of the child to express a view and Article 19, the right to protection from all forms of physical or mental violence, requires that:

● children's views of the appropriateness and effectiveness of interventions following allegations of abuse should be systematically ascertained by monitoring and research;

● there should be co-ordinated reviews of child protection procedures throughout the UK, taking as their starting point the basic principles in the Convention.

**3**  Compliance with Article 19, the right to protection from all forms of physical or mental violence, requires that:

● primary legislation should be used to remove or substantially amend the common law defence of 'reasonable chastisement' and the statutory confirmation of it in the law on child cruelty, to ensure that any punishment involving physical or mental violence is unlawful.  The concept of 'reasonable chastisement' is not compatible with the Convention's emphasis on parental responsibility for the welfare of the child, and should be replaced by parental duties to guide and safeguard their children according to the child's evolving capacity.  In the short term, private school pupils could be protected from institutional physical punishment by amendment of education legislation; in the child care system and daycare settings, consistent regulations should replace guidance;

● the law on cruelty should also be amended to remove the current implied justification of 'necessary' suffering or injury to health caused by assault, ill-treatment or neglect of children;

● in Scotland and N Ireland current reviews of children's law should enable appropriate reforms to be included;

● regulations applying to all day and residential institutions including all schools, and to other formal placements for children must include a list of prohibited sanctions (similar to that in regulation 8 of the Children's Homes Regulations issued under the Children Act for England and Wales) which may involve physical or mental violence, in addition to a general prohibition of inhuman or degrading treatment or punishment (also Articles 2 and 3.2);

● legislation should oblige responsible authorities for all schools and other institutional settings including children to develop detailed policies to prevent and respond to bullying (also Article 3.2);

- arrangements for formal review of placement and treatment of children, involving the children themselves and similar in frequency and scope to those required under the Review of Children's Cases Regulations 1991, issued under the Children Act 1989 for England and Wales, should extend to all children being accommodated in institutional or quasi-institutional settings throughout the UK (also Articles 3.2 and 25);

- arrangements for placing children on child protection registers and for regular review of their protection should become statutory throughout the UK, so that any failure to make appropriate arrangements can be challenged. Resource allocation must be adequate to ensure effective child protection;

- official guidance should ensure that the definition of child abuse used in child protection policy and practice does not suggest that any form of physical or mental violence to children is acceptable. This does not imply that there should be more formal intervention, but that preventive work is based on the child's right to physical and personal integrity;

- guidance should be issued to appropriate institutions and carers on responding to challenging behaviour, and on the minimum use of force in restraining children who are a danger to themselves or others;

- all employers - local authority, health authority, voluntary and private - of those whose work involves substantial unsupervised contact with children should be required to follow statutory codes of practice on recruitment, induction and supervision of such employees. The codes would include appropriate mandatory arrangements for police checks;

- all such employers should be under consistent legal duties to report any conduct suggesting that an employee is not or may not be a suitable person to be employed in work involving children (also Article 3.2);

- arrangements for inspection of all institutions and quasi-institutional settings (eg foster-care and daycare settings) for children should be rationalised to ensure that there are clear and consistent powers and duties on central and local government to arrange appropriate inspections at regular prescribed intervals. The primary purpose must be to safeguard and promote the welfare of children. Children must have an opportunity to speak in private to inspectors (also Article 3.2);

- appropriate government departments and other agencies (eg the Health Education Authority and similar agencies in Wales, Scotland and N Ireland), local authorities and health authorities should promote and provide information to the public, including in particular parents and those working with them, on respecting children's right to physical and personal integrity, discouraging physical punishment and other humiliating treatment of children. Such information programmes should promote positive forms of discipline which do not involve violence or humiliation;

- such information should be promoted as part of family life education within the National Curriculum; encouragement of non-violent conflict resolution should also be an explicit part of the National Curriculum;

- all those involved in child protection and responding to violence in the home receive training on the effects of such violence on children;

- children in refuges be recognised as children 'in need' under the Children Act 1989, and under the Act and similar legislation in other jurisdictions receive appropriate support from local authorities. All refuges which may take children should have appropriately trained child care workers, and the Government should ensure that sufficient resources are available;

- there should be systematic local monitoring of action taken following allegations of physical or mental violence to children, to ensure that protection is effective and that the Convention's principles are consistently respected, including the 'best interests' principle and the right of children to express views, have them taken seriously, and be heard in all administrative and judicial procedures;

- there is further monitoring of the extent to which children are now protected. There should be research at regular intervals involving interviewing a representative sample of children in various age groups, and parents of very young children, concerning their experience of all forms of violence from adults and from peers, in their homes and in other settings;

- further research is undertaken to monitor levels of bullying in all institutions which include children.

4 Compliance with Article 24.3, the duty to take measures to abolish traditional practices prejudicial to health, requires that:

- there should be a comprehensive review in all communities of any traditional practices which threaten the physical integrity of children and/or are prejudicial to their health, in the light of the Convention's principles;

- educational campaigns are required within communities to emphasise the child's right to physical integrity in relation to any traditional practices which involve physical or mental violence or may be prejudicial to health.

5 Compliance with Article 39, the duty to provide rehabilitative care for victims of maltreatment, requires that all victims of abuse should be offered appropriate assessment to determine what measures are needed to promote recovery and social reintegration. Monitoring should ensure that therapy and other forms of support proposed by assessments are made available to victims.

# References

1. *Inquiry into the removal of children from Orkney in February 1991*, HMSO, London (1992)

2. *Working together under the Children Act 1989: guide to arrangements for inter-agency co-operation for the protection of children*, Department of Health, HMSO, London (1991)

3. *Homicide data*, personal communication from the Home Office, S1 Division (1993)

4. *Child abuse trends in England and Wales 1988-90*, Creighton S, NSPCC (1992)

5. *ChildLine Annual Report 1992*, Second Floor, Royal Mail Building, Studd Street, London N1 0BR

6. *The extent of parental physical punishment in the UK*, Newson J & E, Approach Ltd, London (1990)

7. Further information from Dr Marjorie Smith, Thomas Coram Research Unit, 27/28 Woburn Square, London WC1H 0AA

8. *An exploratory study of the prevalence of sexual abuse in a sample of 16-21 year-olds*, Kelly L et al, Child Abuse Studies Unit, Polytechnic of North London (1991)

9. Heikki Sariola, Central Union for Child Welfare, Helsinki (1988)

10. Section 1(7) Children and Young Persons Act 1933 (England and Wales); section 12(7) Children and Young Persons (Scotland) Act 1937 (Scotland); section 20(6) Children and Young Persons (Northern Ireland) Act 1950

11. B v Harris (1990) SLT 208.

12. 'Caning mother cleared', *Daily Mail* (4 October 1991); 'Father: why I beat my sons', *North Avon Evening Post* (19 March 1993)

13. *Parenthood and Guardianship Code*, Sweden

14. *Violence in the family*, Recommendation R(85)4, adopted by the Council of Europe Committee of Ministers (26 March 1985)

15. *Social measures concerning violence in the family*, Recommendation R(90)2, adopted by the Council of Europe Committee of Ministers (15 January 1990)

16. *Report on family law*, Scottish Law Commission, HMSO, Edinburgh (1992)

17. *Children of battered women*, Jaffe P, Wolfe D, Wilson S, Sage (1990); *Private violence and public policy*, Pahl J, Routledge and Kegan Paul (1985)

18. *Women's Aid refuges: adult reflections on the experience of childhood in a refuge*, Saunders A, MA dissertation, Department of Social Work, University of Sussex (1993)

19. *Domestic violence*, House of Commons Home Affairs Committee Session 1992-93, Third Report, Volume II, Appendix 2: Memorandum by the Children's Legal Centre, HMSO (1993)

20. Education (No 2) Act 1986, section 47 (England and Wales); section 48 (Scotland); Education (Corporal Punishment) (Northern Ireland) Order 1987

21. Education Act 1993, section 293 (England and Wales); section 294 (Scotland)

22. Costello-Roberts v UK, European Court of Human Rights, Strasbourg (March 25 1993)

23. House of Lords Hansard (July 6 1993) col 1355

24. The Children's Homes Regulations 1991, issued under the Children Act 1989

25. The Residential Care Homes (Amendment) Regulations 1988

26. The Social Work (Residential Establishments - Child Care) (Scotland) Regulations 1987

27. The Foster Placement (Children) Regulations 1991

28. England and Wales: The Children Act 1989 Guidance and Regulations: Volume 2 *Family support, day care and educational provision for young children*, Department of Health, HMSO (1991); Scotland: *Regulation and Review of Childminding, Daycare and education services for children under eight*, Scottish Office (June 1991)

29. The Children Act 1989 Guidance and Regulations: Volume 8, *Private fostering and miscellaneous*, Department of Health, HMSO (1991)

30. Sutton Family Proceedings Court (8 July 1993)

31. Children's Homes Regulations 1991, SI 1991 No 1506, regulation 8

32. *One scandal too many: the case for comprehensive protection of children in all settings*, Gulbenkian Foundation (1993): provides a detailed summary of current law and guidance on child protection

33. *Bullying: the child's view*, by Jean La Fontaine, Gulbenkian Foundation (1991)

34. *Regimes in young offender institutions*, NACRO Briefing (November 1991)

35. Eric Forth, Junior Education Minister, (18 May 1992); *Action against bullying, a support pack for schools*, prepared by the Scottish Council for Research in Education under contract from the Scottish Office Education Department (1992): circulated to all schools

36. *Choosing with care, report of the committee of inquiry into the selection, development and management of staff in children's homes*, chaired by Norman Warner, HMSO (1992)

37. *The Children Act and daycare for young children registration*, Circular LAC(93)1, Department of Health (January 1993)

38. Disqualification for Caring for Children Regulations 1991

39. see reference 32

40. eg see *Family participation and patterns of intervention in child protection in Gwent*, Denman G and Thorpe D H, Department of Applied Social Science, Lancaster University (1993); *Making a case in child protection*, Wattam C, Longmans (1992)

41. *The Children Act Report 1992*, Department of Health and Welsh Office (1992)

42. *Children Act Guidance and Regulations*, volumes 2,3,4, and 8, Department of Health, HMSO (1991)

43. *Guidance on permissible forms of control in children's residential care*, Department of Health (April 1993)

44. House of Commons Hansard, column 461 (23 November 1992)

# UK Agenda for Children

# 4

## An adequate standard of living

# Contents

*The unreferenced quotations in this report are comments made during a consultation exercise undertaken by the Children's Rights Development Unit with groups of young people throughout the UK.*

# 1 Introduction

**1.1** Article 27 asserts the '*right of every child to a standard of living adequate for the child's physical, mental, spiritual, moral and social development*'. The wording of Article 27 makes clear that poverty can no longer be considered as an absolute concept measuring minimum standards based on biological needs for food, water and shelter, but must take account of the needs of the child relative to standards which are considered to be acceptable within that society. The extent to which a child's development is affected by their standard of living will be informed not only by income levels, but also the relationship between income and the cost of living, the climate, the built environment, social expectations, availability of transport, housing costs, and social support networks. The requirements to fulfil the right to an adequate standard of living will be unique to each country. Poverty takes on a different meaning in an industrialised country such as the UK compared with its implications in many developing countries. An evaluation of compliance with Article 27 requires an analysis of the experience of children which takes as its starting point the interaction between family income, family needs and the fulfilment of all the social rights in the Convention. It must also be considered in the context of Article 4 which states that governments must '*undertake all appropriate legislative, administrative, and other measures for the implementation of the rights [in the Convention]*'; in respect of economic, social and cultural rights they must '*undertake measures to the maximum extent of their available resources*'.

**1.2** This report demonstrates that poverty in terms of low income does exist in the UK. A series of indicators are then looked at against which '*a standard of living adequate for the child's physical, mental, spiritual, moral and social development*' can be tested in the context of that poverty. The paper then assesses the extent to which each indicator is met. Each of the indicators represents standards which are embodied in the Convention and are significant factors in contributing to a child's overall well-being and development. Failure to meet any or all of these standards provides an indication that the child's proper development is likely to be adversely affected. The indicators which are used are as follows:

- the ability to afford the basic necessities including a diet necessary for healthy development, the cost of fuel and water supply (Article 27.1 and 2, Article 26);
- access to adequate housing (Article 27.3);
- access to health care and to an environment which is not detrimental to health (Article 24);
- access to family life (Article 9);
- freedom from discriminatory factors inhibiting access to an adequate standard of living (Article 2);
- an environment in which safe play and recreational opportunities exist (Article 31);
- opportunities to participate in social activities accepted as part of childhood - opportunities for citizenship (Article 27.1).

# 2 Relevant articles in the Convention

## 2.1 General principles

**Article 2:** all rights in the Convention must apply without discrimination of any kind irrespective of race, colour, language, religion, national, ethnic or social origin, disability or other status.

**Article 3:** the duty in all actions to consider the best interests of the child.

**Article 12:** the right to express an opinion and to have that opinion taken into account in any matter or procedure affecting the child.

## 2.2 Articles relevant to the right to an adequate standard of living

**Article 9:** the right to live with one's family unless this is not in the child's best interests and, where separation does take place, the right to maintain contact with both parents on a regular basis.

**Article 24:** the right to the highest level of health possible and to access to health care services.

**Article 26:** the right to benefit from social security.

**Article 27:** the right to a standard of living adequate for the child's physical, mental, spiritual, moral and social development.

**Article 28:** the right to education, including vocational education, on the basis of equality of opportunity.

**Article 30:** the right of minority groups to enjoy their own culture, language and religion. (Article 30 is not addressed in the report but has general relevance to all services and institutions.)

**Article 31:** the right to play, rest, leisure, recreation and participation in cultural and leisure activities.

*For the full wording of the articles, see the UN Convention on the Rights of the Child, page 311.*

# 3 Does poverty exist?

**3.1** The social security system in the UK is designed to ensure that every member of society is protected against both loss of income and extra needs whether through old age, disability, illness, unemployment or single parenthood. There are a complex range of inter-related benefits some of which exist to compensate for loss of earnings, some in partial recognition of particular costs such as those associated with disability or children, and others designed to prevent parents and children falling below a minimum prescribed income level whether in or out of work. There are two ways in which money is targeted specifically at children - through means-tested allowances and child benefit, a universal benefit paid to parents for each child. In common with most of European states, the UK has ceased to make any provision for children through the tax system, preferring instead to redistribute this money into child benefit. In theory, therefore, the structures exist to provide every child, whether or not the parents are working, with an adequate standard of living to ensure their proper development.

**3.2** The UK Government would probably argue that the social security system does protect children from poverty. Certainly, Government ministers have been at pains to deny that poverty exists. In 1989 the then Secretary of State for Social Security claimed that economic successes meant that poverty no longer existed in our society.

**3.3** With this denial goes a refusal to establish a 'minimum income standard' against which to assess people's income and the levels of state benefits. This approach has been adopted in a number of Western countries and both the House of Commons Social Security Select Committee and the Social Security Advisory Committee (SSAC), a body established to advise the Government on social security policy, have argued for the setting of such a standard[1].

**3.4** Similarly, there is no agreed definition of poverty in this country. Two possible approaches are either to use the level of income provided through income support, the so-called safety net benefit for people unable to work and without any form of social insurance, or to define the poverty line as 50% of average full-time income after housing costs, a measure widely used in many European countries. If one takes either of these measures, it is clear that poverty has grown significantly in recent years. A study carried out for the Commission of European Communities in 1989 estimated the incidence of poverty in the 12 member states over the period 1957-85, using the yardstick of 50% of average disposable income as the definition of poverty[2]. They found that the largest increase in the incidence of poverty was in the UK where the percentage of children living in poverty had increased from 9% in 1980 to 18% in 1985. One in five of Europe's poor live in the UK.

**3.5** By 1988/89 there were between 11 and 12 million people - around a fifth of the population - living in poverty, including just under a quarter of all children[3]. This figure represents a two and a half-fold increase in the past 10 years and reveals that children are disproportionately represented amongst the poor. Government figures published in July 1993 reveal clearly that there has been a further widening of the gap between rich and poor in the UK over the past 14 years[4].

Using as the definition of poverty those living on less than half the average income, there are now 13.5 million people including 3.9 million children living in poverty. This compares with 1.4 million children in 1979 and is now one in three of all children. The figures show that the poorest 10% of the population suffered a real drop of 14% in their living standards at a time when average incomes went up by 36% and top incomes by 62% after housing costs.

**3.6** Poverty is not evenly distributed within the UK. N Ireland consistently emerges as one of the poorest areas using indicators of unemployment, low wages and reliance on income support. Scotland and Wales follow closely behind. It is estimated that in the mid 1980s a quarter of rural households lived in or on the margins of poverty and it is rural areas that have the lowest rates of pay, with Dyfed in Wales at the bottom of the league followed by the Borders in Scotland. However, these figures mask considerable differences within regions. The south-east of England, whilst faring well in the regional figures, has pockets of some of the worst deprivation in the UK.

**3.7** The growth in poverty can be traced to three underlying factors:

- the growing levels of unemployment. Unemployment has increased from 1.4 million in 1979 to over three million in 1993 and the numbers of people who are long-term unemployed (defined as out of work for over one year), has increased as a proportion of the whole from 26% in 1979 to 33% in 1992[5]. Unemployment among minority ethnic groups is significantly higher than the national rate. In 1989/91 the white unemployment rate was 7% compared with 13% amongst minority ethnic groups. Child poverty is closely linked with both the extent and duration of unemployment;

- the increase in the incidence of low pay. If one uses the standard of 70% of average income after housing costs as the threshold of low pay (this approximates to the Council of Europe 'decency threshold' of 68%), it emerges that nearly 3.5 million children in 1991 were living in households where the head was in full-time low paid employment. Of these, nearly 1.5 million children were living in poverty, using the standard of income below half the national average. These figures represent a substantial rise over the past 14 years. Between 1979 and 1991 the numbers of employees on low pay rose from 7.8 million to 10 million. The reasons for this link to the considerable shift in the labour market during the 1980s, towards the creation of part-time, temporary and seasonal employment as well as home working, all of which lead to unstable and insecure incomes for employees. These changes coincided with a Government policy of deregulation of the labour market with the abolition of minimum rates of pay for some of the lowest paid occupations, the restriction of the rights and powers of trade unions and limitations on the right to seek redress against unfair dismissal. The combined impact of job insecurity, low pay and high levels of unemployment have a demonstrable impact on the extent of child poverty;

- the rise in the numbers of lone-parent families. There were over one million lone-parent families in the UK by 1990, up from 850,000 in 1981. The number of dependent children has gone up to 2.2 million[6]. There is a high correlation between child poverty and lone-parenthood. In 1992, 72% of all lone-parents were dependent on income support. They face considerable difficulties in moving into the labour market because of a combination of high unemployment, low pay and lack of affordable child care. They are therefore trapped into continued dependency on benefits, often for many years with no routes open to them to lift themselves out of poverty.

**3.8** It is evident then that not only are there very substantial numbers of children living in poverty but that the numbers have escalated rapidly in recent years. This pattern contrasts sharply with most of European countries where not only is there less child poverty, but there has been no rise in child poverty during the 1980s. A report produced for UNICEF in 1993 *The index of social health* seeks to monitor, over a 20 year period, the social wellbeing of children in industrial countries through a set of international indicators relating to children's health, education, emotional stress and economic welfare[7]. The report demonstrates that of the 10 countries studied, only in the UK and US did children end the period with lower levels of social health on every count than they started with. In the UK, charting progress on an index of 0-100, the score was 20 points lower than in 1970. The existence of state benefits and other welfare provision has failed to protect many children and their parents from the worst effects of rapid economic and social changes. The rest of this report seeks to demonstrate the ways in which families on low incomes, whether in or out of work, are unlikely to meet the indicators set out in paragraph 1.2 and how this denies many children the right to '*a standard of living adequate for [their] physical, mental, spiritual, moral and social development*'.

# 4 Ability to afford basic necessities
## Articles 27.1 and 26

## 4.1 Social security benefit levels

**4.1.1** In 1991, 2.3 million children were living in families dependent on income support. If parents who are out of work are to provide adequately for their children they need an income which is sufficient to purchase the basic daily necessities of life - food, heating, clothes, water. There is a body of evidence drawn from a considerable number of surveys that the experience of living on benefit means that many parents are unable to provide for their children a '*standard of living adequate for the child's physical, mental, spiritual, moral and social development*'. *Hardship Britain*, a report based on research carried out by Bradford University and Family Service Units, documents the difficult choices faced by claimants in budgeting their money: ' ... a majority of the claimants interviewed confirmed that the exercise of their budgeting discretion often extended no further than deciding what to do without this week'[8]. 85 out of 91 people interviewed in Bradford stated that they regularly cut down on food or fuel and over two-thirds of claimants in both surveys regularly ran out of money before the next payment was due.

**4.1.2** These findings confirm those of other studies. A survey of families living on benefit in the north-east of England revealed that two-thirds of the families interviewed did not feel they were coping financially and on average the expenditure of the families exceeded their income by nearly £9 per week[9]. Further research commissioned by the Government identified difficulties faced by families in meeting the basic costs of clothing, fuel and housekeeping needs[10]. Families with children commented on problems buying beds and bedding, washing machines, nappies and baby clothes. 27% of families lacked adequate bedding, 14% lacked floor covering in their living area and 17% did not even have enough beds for each member of the family. Research published by Child Poverty Action Group in 1993 analysed the costs of a child by estimating the weekly expense of a modest but adequate diet and a low cost budget[11]. The items and services included in each budget were chosen by a group of experts and also informed by what people actually spend their money on. The research findings demonstrated that even the low cost budget which represented a very minimal standard of living was, for a family with two children, 30% higher than the rate of income support. A family with two children would have needed £34 in addition to their income support in order to achieve a low cost budget.

**4.1.3** All the available research points to a similar picture of families dependent on state benefits, struggling to survive in the face of immense difficulty and oppressed by their inability to meet the most basic needs of their children. Many families are living in these circumstances for years, dependent on benefit levels that are too low, with continued levels of high unemployment offering no hope of life improving and, for many parents, lack of affordable child care coupled with low pay, means that even if jobs were available it would not be possible to take advantage of them. In this situation, it is not within parents '*abilities and financial capacities*' to carry out their '*primary responsibility to secure ... the conditions of living necessary for the child's development*' as described in Article 27.2. It is therefore necessary for the Government to '*take appropriate measures to assist parents and others responsible for the child to implement this right and ... in case of need provide material assistance and support programmes, particularly with regard to nutrition and clothing*' (Article 27.3). The social security system is clearly intended to achieve this but the evidence demonstrates that for many children living on benefit, the reality is a level of deprivation which denies them the opportunity for proper development which should be their right under Article 27.

### ACTION REQUIRED FOR COMPLIANCE

**Compliance with Article 27 in the context of the obligations imposed by Article 4 requires a fundamental examination of the principles which underpin the social security system and a review of its operation in the context of changing patterns of employment and family life. There is a need to address the adequacy of benefit levels and for independent research to establish a level of weekly benefit that would enable children and their parents to participate fully in society. However, the role of social security benefits in protecting family income should not be addressed in isolation from policies which give parents more opportunities to earn adequate incomes through paid employment.**

## 4.2 Debt

**4.2.1** The problem of debt grew dramatically during the 1980s. In 1989 there were 2.8 million households with arrears compared with 1.3 million in 1981, and 530,000 households in multiple debt compared with 130,000 in 1981. In 1991, 68,540 homes were repossessed, an increase from 3,480 in 1980[12][13]. This increase is an inevitable consequence of Government policy over this period. Whereas those claiming income support receive help with the costs of a mortgage, those in employment do not. Many working families on low incomes were faced during the 1980s with massive increases in interest repayments on their mortgages and were unable to meet them out of wages which were already stretched to the limit. The Government commitment to expanding home ownership at a time of high interest rates, rising unemployment and a growth in the numbers of families working in low paid and unstable employment contributed heavily to the increase in families in arrears with repayments and at risk of losing their homes. Families on a low income with children are among those most likely to fall into debt. Lone-parents are particularly at risk with on average three times the number of problems with debt as single people without children. The majority of debts that are incurred by families on low income arise not as a consequence of consumerism but rather through the daily difficulties of stretching a limited income to pay for the basic necessities of life - rent, fuel, mortgages and loans for such items as clothing and household goods.

**4.2.2** Once a debt exists poor families are often faced with cutting back on food and other daily living expenses in order to repay it. The impact on children is considerable. Not only are they likely to be denied some of the material necessities for an '*adequate standard of living*', but are also

likely to be living in an extremely stressful environment harmful to their development. A survey by the National Children's Home of 347 families on low incomes identified that of those with debts, 71% were depressed, 40% felt that they could not cope, 21% felt that their relationship with their partner was being damaged[14]: 'The experience of debt magnifies and reinforces the experience of poverty - the watchfulness and anxiety over money, the calculation and moving around of limited funds"[15]. Inevitably, stress experienced by parents is communicated to children and is detrimental to their welfare.

> '*We have to lock the door, turn off the lights and pretend we are not in every time we see the rentman or the milkman.*'
> (18 year-old, N Ireland)

**4.2.3** The costs of heating represent serious problems for many families on benefit. A survey by Family Service Units of 45 families on income support revealed that many could not afford to turn their heating systems on for fear of the cost[16]. In 1991/92 nearly 40,000 households had their gas or electricity supplies disconnected because they could not afford the bills[17]. Many others are having deductions made each week from their benefit to pay for arrears of fuel. Many more households with pre-payment meters effectively disconnect themselves when they are short of money. There is a consistent body of evidence from Family Expenditure Surveys as well as the General Household Survey that low-income households are less likely to live in accommodation that has adequate and efficient heating systems, and therefore their heating costs are likely to be high[18]. This situation is compounded in N Ireland where the costs of fuel are higher than on the mainland but there is no matching increase in benefit levels. For families with children, particularly young children, the problems associated with providing adequate heating give serious cause for concern. In this context the introduction by the Government of VAT on domestic fuel initially at 8% and increasing to 17.5% in 1995 is extremely worrying and will create greater hardship for poor families. The proposal cannot be reconciled with a commitment to promoting the best interests of poor children as it will undoubtedly heighten the difficulties many parents face in providing their children with a standard of living adequate for their needs.

**4.2.4** Many of these problems have been compounded by the switch from grants to loans by the Department of Social Security (DSS). Until 1988, families dependent on social security were able to apply for grants to cover additional costs on top of day-to-day living expenses, such as clothing, exceptionally high fuel bills, furniture and bedding. In 1988, these grants were abolished and replaced with the Social Fund which comprised community care grants for those moving out of institutional care and for families under stress and loans in other circumstances. Under this new system, families in need of a lump sum of money to purchase essential items may be able to borrow it from the DSS which it then deducts on a weekly basis from their benefit. Unlike the previous system for which the budget was demand-led, the Social Fund is cash-limited regardless of the level of demand.

> '*I need a loan for a cooker, something really essential and the social turn around and say we don't have any money for it and you think, what are you supposed to do? You can't live out of the chippy - it's a very expensive thing to do.*'
> (19 year-old, N Ireland)

**4.2.5** The outcome of this system is that many families are paying back loans which reduces their weekly income to a level which renders it almost impossible for them to manage. A recent major Government-commissioned survey of the Social Fund concluded that the system is not working[19]. The survey looked at 1,724 people of whom 80% were on income support and found that the scheme fails to achieve its prime objective, of ensuring that help is targeted on families in greatest need. It found that the Social Fund left major problems of unmet need and that repayment of loans was leading to hardship and debt for many families. The implications of this in respect of Article 27 are that many children's basic material needs are not being met, either because the family are refused a payment from the Social Fund or because once a payment has been made that family's income is reduced so much by the repayments that they are unable to afford basic necessities. The families interviewed identified major problems with paying electricity and gas bills, the cost of an adequate diet, and clothes for children.

**4.2.6** Families turn to the Social Fund for help because income support levels are not adequate for all the expenses of day-to-day living and certainly not for items of capital expenditure. Their problems are compounded by then having to repay the loan, thus further reducing their available income. There is now substantial evidence of the hardship caused to children by the loan system. The major child welfare agencies and national advice services have repeatedly expressed their concerns to the Government about the damaging consequences of a system which demonstrably fails to meet need and which forces families into debt when they are already in poverty and unable to afford basic necessities.

*'The place we moved into had no bed, no curtains, knives or forks or anything like that and when I rang up they said you are not entitled to any grant only a crisis loan which somehow you have to pay back.'*
(18 year-old, Oxfordshire)

**ACTION REQUIRED FOR COMPLIANCE**

Compliance with Article 27.3, the obligation to *'take appropriate measures to assist parents and others responsible for the child'* to implement the right to an adequate standard of living, requires that:

- **the discretionary part of the Social Fund should be abolished and replaced with a new system of legal entitlement based on grants with no cash limit and an independent right of appeal;**

- **the proposals for introducing VAT on fuel which are likely to cause increased hardship to children living in poverty, should be withdrawn;**

- **housing benefit, a system of help with rents for those on low incomes, should be extended to help with mortgage repayments.**

## 4.3 Children with disabilities

**4.3.1** Article 2 requires that all the rights in the Convention apply without discrimination to all children; thus disabled children have equal rights to an adequate standard of living. Furthermore, Article 23 states that disabled children have a right to *'enjoy a full and decent life, in conditions which ensure dignity, promote self-reliance and facilitate the child's active participation in the community'*. Provision of benefits to disabled children and their families need to be considered in the light of these obligations.

**4.3.2** The most recent study conducted by the Office of Population and Census Surveys in 1989 indicated that there are 360,000 disabled children under 16 living in England, Wales and Scotland[20]. The research looked at the financial circumstances of such families and found that the average income of families with a disabled child was 78% of the average equivalent income of families without a disabled child. Within those figures single parents had the lowest equivalent resources to spend of all family types. Parents of disabled children were less likely to be in paid employment - 75% as compared with 89% in the population as a whole. When they were employed, their rates of pay are likely to be lower. They are less likely to own their own home, 52% compared with 65% in the population as a whole. The survey also reveals that most families incur extra costs as a consequence of having a disabled child. These costs obviously varied according to the severity of the disability; on average, families were spending £6.54 extra per week. The impact of these costs meant that 28% of families had less than half the average available resources compared with 15% of families in the general population.

**4.3.3** It is clear then that in many families where there is a disabled child the fact of the disability both increases the costs for the family and can reduce the likelihood of the parents being in paid employment. The results from the survey show that the benefits available were insufficient to meet the basic costs incurred by many poorer families. The families questioned described the additional costs associated with their child's disability as including fuel, clothing, travel, laundry, and food. A third of parents felt that there were items they needed for their child which they were unable to afford. The financial hardship experienced by poorer families with a disabled child is clearly not adequate in line with the standards embodied in Articles 23 and 27.

**4.3.4** Since the OPCS surveys were undertaken in the late 1980s, there have been significant changes in the benefits available to families with a disabled child. Of particular significance was the abolition in 1988 of weekly additional payments which had been available to income support claimants, to cover extra heating, laundry and dietary costs associated with disability or ill-health. In their place is a weekly disabled child premium paid to families with a disabled child. To date there has been no research on the impact of these changes and, furthermore there has been no research which examines the child's experience of hardship or deprivation associated with disability and poverty.

**4.3.5** The quality of life of disabled children is obviously heavily influenced by their family's level of income but also of critical importance are the range of support services available to them and their families. Assistance with transport and its associated costs, the availability of integrated play and social activities, physical access to buildings, respite care and help with aids and adaptations to the home are all essential components of the support necessary to ensure that disabled children are not denied the same opportunities as other children to achieve a standard of living necessary for their proper development. In the last few years in England and Wales the NHS and Community Care Act 1990 and the Children Act 1989 have introduced positive changes which may improve the status of disabled children and the methods of providing services to them; both will need to be monitored carefully to assess their impact.

**The ability to assess compliance with Articles 23 and 27 in respect of disabled children requires research into the experience of disabled children and their families of the quality and availability of help and support offered. Without this research, it is not possible to evaluate whether the provision that is now available is adequate to ensure compliance with the right of disabled children to an adequate standard of living which ensures their active participation in the community.**

**There is an urgent need for research into the impact of the 1988 disability benefits changes and in particular a review of disability benefits which assesses the adequacy of disability child premium, in order to ascertain whether children living in families dependent on such benefits are able to achieve a standard of living adequate for their proper development. There is also a need for research which examines the views of children themselves and the adequacy of their standard of living.**

## 4.4 16 and 17 year-olds and income support

**4.4.1** In 1988 the Government introduced legislation which withdrew entitlement to income support for most 16 and 17 year-olds. In return, every young person was promised that if they were neither staying on at school nor able to find employment, they would be guaranteed a place on a youth training scheme and payment of a training allowance. In exceptional circumstances, a severe hardship payment would be made to the young person. In practice, the withdrawal of benefit has had devastating consequences for substantial numbers of young people who have been denied the right to a standard of living adequate for their *'physical, mental, moral and social development' (Article 27)* and denied *'the right to benefit from social security'* (Article 26).

**4.4.2** Many young people are unable to obtain youth training places. Youthaid, an organisation committed to promoting opportunities for young people, produces quarterly estimates of the numbers of young people not in work, education or training. In October 1992 it estimated that there were 124,000 young people in this situation of whom three quarters were unable to claim any benefits[21]. Department of Employment statistics for last year indicate that these figures are an underestimate and the Labour Force Survey in the summer of 1992 found that an average of 195,000 16 and 17 year-olds were without work, representing an unemployment rate of around 24%. Many young people, for example those with special needs, young pregnant women and those with emotional and behavioural difficulties, are not able to take advantage of schemes that are available because the schemes are not tailored to their particular circumstances. There is, then considerable evidence that the guarantee offered by the Government has not been met for all young people requiring training. Meanwhile, these young people are left without an income of any kind in clear breach of Article 26; many of them, unable to be supported by their families, do not have an adequate standard of living in breach of Article 27.

**4.4.3** The Government takes the view that young people should remain at home until such time as their income enables them to live independently. But the reality for many young people is that their parents cannot afford to keep them at home if they have no income with which to support themselves, many have left home after suffering physical or sexual abuse and others have no home to go to having spent their childhood in care. There is a system of severe hardship payments available to a young person if he or she is unable to obtain a training place and has no income. But these payments are discretionary, there are no clear guidelines as to who is eligible and severe hardship is not defined in the social security regulations. They are difficult to claim, requiring an application to three different offices, and there is no right of appeal when a claim is turned down.

**4.4.4** Severe hardship payments were designed as a stopgap for small numbers of young people temporarily without a training place but because of the failure of the training guarantee, they are now being used as the only source of income for growing numbers of young people. The number of applications has increased from just under 18,000 in 1989 to nearly 77,000 for the first nine months of 1992[22]. There is also evidence from a range of organisations working with young people that many who need help are not getting it. The problems range from a lack of information, misleading advice from officials, the complexity of the system, attitudes of DSS staff, and the lack of advocacy available. The problems are compounded by the short period for which these payments are awarded - only up to six to eight weeks at a time after which the young person has to re-apply. The outcome of these difficulties is that there are considerable numbers of young people who are left without an income at all - an estimated 76,700 in April 1993[23]. This failure to address the scale of need raises fundamental questions about whether the current system can be said to be achieving the right embodied in Article 26 to ensure that all young people are able to *'benefit from social security ... taking into account the resources and circumstances of the child'*.

**4.4.5** Even where a young person can claim income support or a severe hardship allowance, the levels at which it is paid to 16 and 17 year-olds is substantially lower than that paid to older claimants. For a young person living away from home the entitlement is only three-quarters of the rate paid to claimants aged over 25. Again, evidence from organisations advising young people in this field, documents the hardship being caused by the inadequacy of the levels of payment. The Coalition on Young People and Social Security (COYPSS), a coalition of 30 national organisations concerned about Government policy in this field, has repeatedly made representations both through individual organisations and as a coalition, about the hardship being caused to young people by the inadequacy of the benefit rates. The National Children's Home in a recent survey of 120 young people, of whom the majority were on income support, found that almost all were worried about money and depressed and anxious[24]. One in three had only eaten one meal in the past 24 hours and almost all were eating a diet which failed to meet the World Health Organisation criteria for a healthy diet. The Social Security Advisory Committee, an official body established to advise the Government on social security policy has stated: 'It cannot be right to reduce the benefit due to this group if the rate is based on basic "needs". We can see no sensible reason for this and have received no evidence to justify it. Food, clothing and housing are no cheaper for a person aged (under 25) than for someone aged 25 years or over"[25].

*'How can someone who is 17 or 24 need less money for their home than someone who is over 25?. The amount of money you need is the same, you can't spend less money because you are younger, you need a certain amount of money to survive. That's one of the main problems of the benefit system.'*
(17 year-old, Merseyside)

*'I get £29.50 a week. I pay £4 to top up the rent, £5 for bills, £5.70 for a bus pass and £15 for food. This left me as a total cabbage in my own flat with no money and nothing to do. Obviously I was not going to go without food, so I ended up getting behind on the other bills and eventually my electricity got cut off.'*
(16 year-old, Newcastle)

**4.4.6** Current Government policy for 16 and 17 year-olds is clearly failing to achieve a standard of living adequate for their proper development. Many young people are without an income at all, and those that can obtain benefit, particularly if they are living away from home, are receiving a weekly income that is so low that, in the words of one advice worker, 'Not one [young] person I have worked with living on ... income support has been able to avoid either falling into debt, turning to petty crime, or starving'. The consistency and scale of the evidence makes a powerful case for the need for changes in legislation if the Government is to comply with the rights set out in Articles 26 and 27.

### ACTION REQUIRED FOR COMPLIANCE

**Compliance with Article 26 requires that all unemployed 16 and 17 year-olds should be entitled to income support if they cannot find work or a suitable training place, and that benefit levels for 16 and 17 year-olds living independently should be paid at the same level as those paid to claimants aged over 25.**

## 4.5 Maintenance of Children

**4.5.1** Article 27.4 states that appropriate measures should be taken to recover *'maintenance for the child from the parents and other persons having responsibility for the child'*. The Government recently introduced legislation, the Child Support Act 1991, designed to increase the effectiveness of recovery of maintenance from absent parents. It sets up a new agency responsible for the collection and pursuit of maintenance. The principle of encouraging parental responsibility for children is clearly consistent with Article 27 and certainly there was concern at the low numbers of absent parents who were paying maintenance prior to the introduction of the new legislation. However, there are certain aspects of the new Act which give rise for concern with regard to the implementation of Article 2 (non-discrimination) and Article 3 (the duty to consider the child's best interests). In particular, its primary objective is to reduce expenditure on income support paid to lone mothers by increasing absent parents' contributions. Mothers on benefit and their children do not gain at all from the payment of maintenance as it is deducted pound for pound from her benefit. The principles underlying the legislation are about saving money and not the welfare of children and this is evidenced in some of the ways that maintenance is being pursued under the Act.

**4.5.2** Under the Act, single parents (usually women) who are in receipt of income support are required to name the father of their child in order that he can be pursued for maintenance. Failure to provide the father's name without 'good cause' may result in a penalty of a 20% deduction from the mother's benefit for 6 months followed by a 10% deduction for a further 12 months. It is important to bear in mind that this represents a reduction on a level of benefit designed to act as a minimum income. The mother will be defined as having good cause for refusal only if she can show that by giving the name of the father, she or any child living with her would suffer harm or undue distress. The regulations state that a reduction in benefit can be reviewed where it can be shown that the welfare of the child will be affected by continuing the deduction.

**4.5.3** There has been considerable concern voiced by a wide range of organisations working with families that this power to reduce benefit will have seriously detrimental consequences for children. Article 2 states that all children should have equal access to all the rights in the Convention without discrimination based on the *'status, activities, expressed opinions or beliefs of the child's parents'*. Yet this power will mean that children in families where the mother decides that she cannot reveal the father's identity to the authorities will suffer a significant reduction in an already poverty level income. These children will be denied an adequate income over a substantial period of time for their *'physical, mental, spiritual, moral and social development'*, and are being indirectly discriminated against on the basis of their mother's actions. They are in effect being punished for their mother's "failure" to name the father.

**4.5.4** Article 3 states that *'in all actions concerning children, whether undertaken by public or private social welfare institutions, courts of law, administrative authorities or legislative bodies, the best interests of the child shall be a primary consideration'*. The policy of threatening a deduction in benefit as a penalty for failure to disclose information is difficult to reconcile with pursuing a policy of the best interests of the child. Many women have very real reasons to keep information about former partners to themselves - fear of violence, abuse, intrusion, anger and revenge. There is no doubt that the threat or fear of violence is likely to have a damaging effect on children. Whilst in principle these fears should be considered as good cause for refusal, there is a growing body of evidence that women are being pressurised to give the names of their children's father. The National Association of Citizen's Advice Bureaux document regular examples of women refusing to claim benefit rather than give the father's name, with the consequence that they and their children are forced into living on an income below the poverty level[26]. Many women also report being misinformed and confused about what rights they have to withhold information about the father. Other women describe being harassed into providing the information. The increased financial hardship it imposes on the family coupled with stress and anxiety imposed on the mother appear to be directly counter to the child's welfare.

**4.5.5.** There are also growing concerns about the impact of the Child Support Act on children living in second families. The formula for determining maintenance from absent fathers is, in many instances, reducing the income of the second family to the level of income support. In other words, the consequence of the legislation is to force two families to live at income support level, instead of one - the lone-parent who is dependent on benefit and the second family whose earned income is reduced to benefit levels. In so doing, the legislation is directly contributing to the growth of child poverty. Whilst the policy of requiring absent parents to support their children is an appropriate one, it is not appropriate that policies introduced to achieve this objective do so at the cost of creating further child poverty and in so doing denying increased numbers of children the right to an adequate standard of living necessary for their proper development. The Child Support Act, through the pressures it brings to bear on lone mothers and the formula for recouping maintenance from absent fathers with the consequent impact on children, is failing to comply with the principles embodied in Articles 2,3 and 27. A commitment to ensuring that '*In all actions undertaken by ... administrative authorities ... the best interests of the child shall be a primary consideration*' as required by Article 3, would appear in this instance to have been subsumed to the interests of the Government in reducing the social security budget through increased maintenance contributions.

## ACTION REQUIRED FOR COMPLIANCE

**Compliance with Article 27 together with Article 3, the obligation to consider the best interests of the child, requires legislation which takes as its starting point the welfare of children. Meanwhile, greater compliance could be achieved by repealing the statutory obligation on mothers to name the father of their child and with it the power to penalise claimants for failure to comply. It is essential that the impact of the new legislation is carefully monitored to assess its implications for the welfare of children, particularly those living in second families, with a view to amending the maintenance formula if evidence of hardship is identified.**

# 5 Access to adequate housing
## Articles 27.1 and 3

## 5.1 Homelessness families

**5.1.1** Access to adequate housing is a prerequisite for the healthy development of a child. Without it, a child's right of access to education, health and health care, and social development are at risk of being seriously undermined. In the last decade in the UK we have witnessed a clear Government policy directed towards increasing home ownership coupled with a restrictions on local authorities developing and improving their provision of low-cost rented accommodation. This has been reinforced by new legislation enabling local authority tenants to purchase their homes. During the 1980s the amount of new housing to rent being built by local authorities dropped by over 80% at a time when very many properties were being sold to tenants and depleting the stock available to rent[27]. For those able to afford to buy their own homes, this legislation has been of considerable attraction. However, the implications for many low-income families and those where the parents are unemployed, the consequences have been disastrous.

**5.1.2** The problem has been compounded by the recession coupled with a period of high interest rates leading to a massive rise in the number of home owners in arrears with their mortgages and repossessions. In 1992, 68,540 homes were repossessed[28]. As a result of these Government policies there has been a dramatic increase in the number of homeless people in the UK. In 1991, about 420,000 adults and children were accepted as homeless by local authorities in England alone[29]. The official figures on homelessness have tripled since 1978. Within these figures there is also evidence that minority ethnic families are disproportionately at risk of becoming homeless. An Association of Metropolitan Authorities' working party observed in 1990 that whilst there is a dearth of information and research into homelessness amongst black and other minority ethnic communities, in London, they are three to four times as likely to become statutorily homeless as white householders[30].

**5.1.3** Local authorities which have a duty to house families with children who are unintentionally homeless have in recent years relied increasingly heavily on the use of bed and breakfast accommodation for placing homeless families. This development was an inevitable outcome of the combined pressure caused by the loss of their own housing stock through sales to tenants and the moratorium on new building at a time of rising homelessness. Although this trend is now beginning to reverse with an increasing number of families placed in other forms of temporary accommodation, such as private sector leasing, there were still, in June 1992, 11,080 homeless people in bed and breakfast accommodation in London alone. A survey in London showed that 93% of the hotels used failed to meet minimum acceptable standards set by the London local authorities[31].

**5.1.4** Bed and breakfast accommodation is a totally inappropriate environment for children to be living in. A survey of mothers and children living in bed and breakfast accommodation in 1988 documents a depressing picture[32]:

● inadequate diet: because of lack of cooking facilities, over

33% of families did not prepare cooked meals and instead relied on take-away meals and cafes. Some women did not even have facilities for making hot drinks. The majority were unhappy about the diet they were able to provide for their children;

- low birth weight babies: of all babies born to homeless families in London about a quarter have a low birth weight as compared with a national average for all babies of 7%;

- children with higher than average rates of sickness and infections compounded by difficulties in accessing health care: many families found that general practitioners were reluctant to accept them as patients, health visitors are often not informed when a family moves into a hotel and are therefore unable to offer a service, and because of the concentration of hotels in certain geographical locations, the rise in homelessness has placed enormous burdens on the primary health care services in those areas;

- substantial numbers of children not enrolled at school and those that were displayed disproportionate levels of absenteeism, poor performance and low self esteem;

- high risks of accidents for children: falling in cramped rooms, falling down stairs, burns on unguarded heaters and gas rings;

- totally inadequate access to play space or opportunities: none of the hotels in the survey had any provision for children and mothers were faced with the dilemma of allowing their children out into the dangerous territory of the hotel or 'imprisoning' them in the hotel room for hours on end.

5.1.5 Children placed in these hotels, often for as long as two years, experience a quality of life which is inimical to the rights embodied in Article 27. Furthermore, the requirement in 27.3 to provide in cases of need *'material assistance and support programmes, particularly with regard to nutrition, clothing and housing'* is not being met to a standard which could conceivably be considered as adequate. It is clearly not acceptable that children should be growing up in these conditions. The Department of Environment itself in the Code of Guidance to local authorities on Part 3 of the Housing Act 1985 says that bed and breakfast accommodation should only be used for very short periods of time and only in exceptional circumstances. Many children living in this form of accommodation are suffering serious damage to their physical and mental health, to their education and to their self respect.

5.1.6 The high costs to local authorities of bed and breakfast accommodation coupled with increasing recognition of the problems it can create for families with children has led to the search for cheaper and more appropriate alternatives. One major new development has been to house families temporarily in accommodation leased on a short-term basis from the private sector. Whilst this is a welcome development as an improvement over bed and breakfast accommodation, it is still far from satisfactory as a long-term arrangement for homeless families. Recent research on families' experience of private sector leasing highlights problems of dislocation: the properties are often a long way from the families' previous home; poor state of repair with inadequate furnishings and disconnected gas and electricity supplies, social isolation, difficulties in getting children into local schools and lack of notice about being moved into new

accommodation[33]. Two overwhelming themes that emerged from the research were the lack of information about the accommodation and the area into which families were being moved and difficulties in accessing services and support networks in an unfamiliar place[34].

5.1.7 Clearly, these problems have significant implications for children. One of the features of homelessness is the lack of security it brings, with families being housed first in bed and breakfast, then often placed temporarily in different private sector leasing accommodation. This leads to a loss of friendships and disrupted education, compounded if children are unable to obtain a place in a new school for some months. The poor quality of much of the accommodation described in the survey (para 4.6) was felt to be contributing to health problems by up to a fifth of the families interviewed. The financial hardship faced by parents who had to buy the most basic furniture and fittings was considerable and often meant children having to manage without such items as cots or pushchairs. Children living in these circumstances are not being provided with the *'conditions of living necessary for [their] development'* as required in Article 27.2, nor are their best interests being considered (Article 3).

5.1.8 Despite the now well-known adverse consequences to children of living in temporary accommodation, the Government announced in October 1993 that it would be undertaking a review of homelessness legislation which would, amongst other things reconsider the existing right of homeless single mothers to permanent housing when homeless. Instead, the possibility of offering such mothers indefinite hostel or bed and breakfast accommodation would be considered. This proposed change is apparently rooted in belief, despite any evidence to this effect, that young women deliberately get pregnant in order to obtain housing, and is intended to discourage this behaviour.

## ACTION REQUIRED FOR COMPLIANCE

**Compliance with Article 27.3 requires greater investment in the provision of good quality, low-cost rented accommodation which will ensure access to permanent homes without which children will continue to suffer from poor physical and psychological health, disrupted education, insecurity and loss of friendships that are an inevitable consequence of homelessness.**

**Compliance with Article 27.1 requires that:**

- **the existing right to permanent housing for homeless families in priority need is retained;**

- **minimum environmental health standards are drawn up for bed and breakfast hotels and they should be inspected at least every six months. Families should be informed of these standards and given information about how to complain in the event of a breach of standards;**

- **health authorities ensure that in areas where high concentrations of homeless families are accommodated, they direct resources to meet the needs of these families - extra health visitors and locally based outreach services such as antenatal and baby clinics. Measures also need to be taken to ensure that homeless families are able to register with local GPs and do not have to rely on use of casualty departments.**

Compliance with Article 27.3, the obligation to provide material assistance with regard to housing coupled with Article 3.3, ensuring that such provision conforms with adequate standards requires that:

● minimum standards are established for the provision of private sector leased property and regularly monitored;

● families moving into private sector leased property are given detailed information by the placing authority about the property (who owns it, who to contact for repairs, how the heating works) and about local services and how to access them.

## 5.2 Homeless 16 and 17 year-olds

**5.2.1** Shelter, an organisation campaigning against homelessness, estimates that in 1992 there were up to 150,000 young people homeless in the UK, a figure which represents a significant increase in recent years. The growth in homelessness has arisen as a consequence of benefit and legislative changes which have affected young people - the withdrawal of income support from 16 and 17 year-olds, changes to the rules on payment of board and lodging allowances for income support claimants which no longer make provision for the costs of meals and fuel, the effective exclusion of young people from any rights to accommodation under the statutory provisions for homelessness and a diminishing supply of both public sector and privately rented accommodation. Home ownership, the only other route to accommodation, is out of the question for most young people. As already noted above, many young people leave home because their parents cannot afford to keep them without any income, others have been physically or sexually abused at home, others are leaving care and have no homes to go to. Research undertaken in Wales in which 115 young homeless people were interviewed concludes that the interaction of the benefit changes with the reduction in supply of low cost accommodation has made a significant contribution to the growth in homelessness amongst young people[35].

*'You go up and tell them you are homeless and they say to you, go back to your parents and make it up with them but sometimes it's really bad and you can't, so you are left high and dry and that is why there are so many young people out on the streets.'*
(17 year-old, N Ireland)

**5.2.2** Once homeless young people are intensely vulnerable and many of their rights are fundamentally at risk. Homeless young people are at greater risk of sexual exploitation and abuse from which they are entitled to protection under Article 34. The Children's Society refuge for young homeless teenagers report that 7% of young women who stayed there had been raped while homeless and there is evidence of growing numbers of young men and women in prostitution as the only source of income available to them[36]. There has been a growth in the numbers of young people begging on the streets as the only means of survival open to them. Young homeless teenagers are more likely than other young people to have drug problems, as the combination of depression and easy access makes them more vulnerable to drug abuse. They are not being afforded the protection *'from the illicit use of narcotic drugs and psychotropic substances'* which Article 33 requires. Homelessness is invariably accompanied by health problems. In a study by the Central London Social Security Adviser's Forum of young homeless people, more than a third reported being ill in a four week period, many reported depression and two had attempted suicide[37]. Many homeless young people find that doctors are unwilling to accept them on their books. These factors are far from consistent with *'the right of the child to the enjoyment of the highest attainable standard of health and to facilities for the treatment of illness and rehabilitation of health'* as described in Article 24.1

**5.2.3** There has been a widespread and concerted campaign by most of the major child welfare, housing and advice organisations about the detrimental impact that the withdrawal of income support has caused in relation to young people's access to housing. The Coalition on Young People and Social Security argues that until benefit is restored to young people who are unable to find work or training, there will be a growing population of young people on the streets denied the right to a basic minimum standard of living, denied the right to protection from abuse, exploitation, violence and drugs, and denied the basic civil liberties of privacy and effective participation in decisions that affect their lives.

**5.2.4** Whilst the withdrawal of income support has exacerbated the problems of homelessness, there are also difficulties for young people because of the lack of low cost accommodation and the support needed by many vulnerable young people in order to cope with independent living. Local authorities in England and Wales have duties under section 20 of the Children Act 1989 to provide accommodation to children 'in need', where the child's welfare will be prejudiced without such provision. This requirement is consistent with the obligation on the Government in Article 27.3 to *'take appropriate measures ... in case of need [to] provide material assistance ... and housing'*. However, the evidence to date indicates that local authorities are experiencing real difficulties in fulfilling their obligations under section 20. Recent research among the 32 London authorities reveals that 77% did not have sufficient accommodation to meet the needs of 16 and 17 year-olds, 87% were not publicising services for 16 and 17 year-olds and 94% did not have enough information on the housing needs of care leavers[38]. The picture that emerges is that local authorities faced with scarce resources are not prioritising homeless young people. Over half the authorities had no policies or procedures to assess children in need under section 20 and just under half failed to carry out automatic assessments of young homeless people. Meanwhile, the numbers of homeless 16 and 17 year-olds continues to rise.

**ACTION REQUIRED FOR COMPLIANCE**

See following section for details.

## 5.3 Housing standards

**5.3.1** In the UK children who live in poor housing conditions consistently suffer more ill-health than others[39]. Damp housing conditions are known to be a threat to children's health both in childhood and later on in adult life and are linked in particular to diseases of the respiratory system. A study of over 1,100 children in Glasgow, Edinburgh and London found that those living in damp conditions are more likely to suffer respiratory problems such as wheezing, sore throats and runny noses, as well as headaches and fever[40].

Household pests are also a major problem in many housing developments and infestations of, for example, cockroaches and mice can pose serious health problems for children.

5.3.2 The Audit Commission has identified close links between poor standards of housing and bronchitis, pneumonia, hypothermia, accidents, infections and stress[41]. The English House Conditions Survey for 1991 published by the Department of Environment found over 1.3 million unfit homes in England. Although there was a decrease in the overall numbers of unfit properties between 1986 and 1991 the numbers with inadequate ventilation and kitchen facilities increased. The worst conditions are found in privately rented accommodation of which 20% were in poor condition[42]. In 1991, 83,075 council houses in Scotland were affected by "rising or penetrating dampness". One in 14 occupied local authority and housing association properties were also classified as unfit. Other evidence shows that houses in multiple occupation are in the worst state[43]. A Department of Environment survey of multi-occupied dwellings showed that 38% lacked satisfactory fire escapes, 16% were overcrowded and 33% needed major repairs[44].

5.3.3 There are no figures available to indicate how many children are living in homes which are in poor conditions but it is evident that there are substantial numbers living in large poorly-maintained council estates and substandard private accommodation. Low-income families with dependent children tend to live in multiply deprived areas with older multi-occupied properties which are more likely to be unfit, needing repair, cold, damp, mouldy and expensive to heat[45]. The 1986 English House Conditions Survey concluded that: 'Single parent families with one or two children ... were the groups most likely to have experienced some deterioration in their housing conditions. In particular, households with one or two children occupied in 1981 substantially less than their expected share of dwellings which were unfit or in "serious" disrepair, but by 1986 this position had reversed"[46]. In the *Hardship Britain* survey more than a third of families interviewed found it impossible to keep their homes warm and dry and over a quarter of the council tenants reported problems with damp[47]. The number of households in the UK unable to keep their homes warm has risen from 5.5 million in 1981 to 7 million in 1991 due to the combined effects of more widespread poverty, increased numbers of households and inadequate investment in energy efficiency improvements[48]. These problems are likely to be exacerbated by the proposed introduction of VAT on fuel (see para 3.6). The Family Service Units survey identified considerable problems amongst the families they interviewed of disrepair, overcrowding and inadequate heating[49].

5.3.4 The adverse effects of living in poor housing conditions on children's health are now well documented. They are linked with more frequent accidents, acute infections such as gastroenteritis, slower growth, loss in psychological well-being and possibly higher infant mortality[50]. Many children throughout the UK, in both public and private sector housing, are still living in conditions which fail to provide them with a physical environment which ensures the protection of their right to a standard of living adequate for their proper physical and mental development. The combined impact of poor quality and often overcrowded accommodation and inadequate incomes to enable families to keep their homes warm is causing serious hardship to many children.

## 5.4 Lack of sites for Gypsies and Travellers

5.4.1 It is estimated by the Department of Environment that there are about 12,000 Gypsy and Traveller families in England and Wales although these figures are generally recognised to be an under-estimate of the true population[51]. In recent years the population of Travellers has escalated in response to the lack of available low-cost housing and employment opportunities.

5.4.2 The Caravan Sites Act 1968 was introduced to provide Gypsies and Travellers with adequate permanent legal sites by imposing a duty on local authorities to provide sites with sufficient accommodation for all Gypsies and Travellers 'residing in or resorting to their areas'. 25 years later it is thought that at least one third of all Gypsies and Travellers are still living in unofficial sites which may lack basic facilities such as water, sanitation, electricity and refuse disposal. Even on official sites there are grave difficulties in accessing health care, education and welfare services. Not all local authorities have responded positively to their obligations under the Act and many provide no sites at all. Of those that do, many provide sites in locations that fail even minimum standards of health and safety. Research undertaken in 1988 found that basic amenities were lacking on many sites and 60% of Gypsy and Traveller mothers had problems caring for their children because of 'dirt, fast traffic, rats, lack of safe play areas, difficulty drying clothes, overcrowding, mud, dogs, broken glass, the site getting used up with toilet holes, lack of education, noises from factories, smells from nearby sewage works'[52]. Other research has identified sites located on former refuse tips or with dangerous levels of carbon and soil lead[53].

5.4.3 The lack of adequate available sites coupled with the evident poor standards on many that do exist represents a clear breach of the Government's responsibilities under a number of Articles of the Convention. Article 27.3 establishes the responsibility of governments to provide '*material assistance and support programmes, particularly with regard to nutrition, clothing and housing*'. In this instance, the

Gypsy and Traveller families are accepting the primary responsibility for securing *the conditions of living necessary for the child's development* consistent with Article 27.2 but are hampered in the fulfilment of their responsibility by the failure of local authorities to provide sufficient and appropriate sites. Article 3.3 clearly imposes a duty to ensure that *facilities responsible for the care and protection of children shall conform with the standards established by competent authorities in the areas of safety, health ... '*. Liverpool City Council (which, as an authority with direct responsibility for ensuring provision of services to Gypsies and Travellers should be recognised as a *competent authority'*), has established a Charter for Travellers including minimum standards for Gypsy and Traveller sites. These include the requirement that sites must not be located in a position likely to endanger the health of Gypsies and Travellers and that sites must be provided with adequate space and basic facilities such as water, sanitation, refuse disposal and, if practicable, electricity. It is clear that many Gypsies and Travellers on both official and unofficial sites lack access to such basic standards and, in consequence, their children are being denied their rights to adequate protection under Article 3.3.

> *'After a few days we get a court order to move out, we get no peace and so we move on ten miles down the road. If we stay too long in one place a bunch of guys get together to come along and throw stones through our windows.'*
> (15 year-old, South Wales)

**5.4.4** Despite the already serious problems facing many Gypsy and Traveller families, the Government is now (1994) proposing to introduce new legislation removing the obligation on local authorities to provide sites and imposing tough new measures to evict Gypsies and Travellers from unauthorised stopping places. It has already withdrawn the 100% subsidy that was available to local authorities for the costs of establishing sites. The proposed changes will further undermine the opportunities for Gypsy and Traveller children to achieve an adequate standard of living. Evictions can result in loss of schooling, loss of access to health care and welfare services, and insecurity and anxiety for children. A number of organisations working with Gypsy and Traveller families have expressed extreme concern at the implications of the proposals. The Save the Children Fund comments: 'The criminalisation of Gypsies and Travellers stopping without the landowners permission coupled with the tough new measures to evict people from unauthorized stopping places will be devastating to families and to children in particular ... Evictions have many potentially adverse consequences for children ... serious health risks may be involved if, for example, clean water and other amenities are not available ... Families could be moved several times a month which we consider cruel, inhuman and degrading treatment for any child and family"[54]. These proposals are clearly not consistent with the requirement in Article 3.1 to ensure that in all actions *'the best interests of the child shall be a primary consideration'*.

**5.4.5** The Government proposes two alternatives to the provision of local authority sites. First, it proposes that there should be expanded development of private sites. But this is not a realistic option for most Gypsy and Traveller families. Save the Children argue that most Gypsies and Travellers lack the capital sums necessary to buy land and obtaining planning permission will be difficult in view of local prejudice and opposition to such sites[55]. Second, it proposes that

Gypsy and Traveller families have the option to present themselves as homeless to the local authority. However, given the overwhelming difficulties local authorities already have in housing increased numbers of homeless families, this does not appear to be a realistic option at the present time. Furthermore, most Gypsies and Travellers want to continue their lifestyle and would not consider the option of permanent housing as acceptable. The right of children to enjoy their own culture as expressed in this lifestyle is clearly protected by Article 30. The proposals seek to restrict access to sites without offering adequate substitutes. In so doing they are threatening to undermine the rights of Gypsy and Traveller children to a secure environment consistent with their developmental needs.

## ACTION REQUIRED FOR COMPLIANCE

**Compliance with Article 27.1 and 3, the right to a safe environment in which the health, educational and social needs of Gypsy and Traveller children are met requires that:**

- **the duty on local authorities to provide sites under the Caravan Sites Act 1968 is retained;**

- **there is consideration of a range of options to encourage the development of more and better quality sites, including the exploration of alternative financing for local authority and private sites such as housing associations, upgrading existing sites, providing Gypsies and Travellers with accessible information on planning procedures to help them make private site applications more successful and the introduction of short term licences;**

- **there is wider consultation with Gypsy and Traveller families about site provision: they are best able to identify the variety and quality of sites needed to ensure their children's well being.**

# 6 Access to health care and the best possible health

**Article 24**

## 6.1 Material deprivation and health

**6.1.1** The National Health Service Act 1946 introduced universal health care services which were free at the point of delivery. In theory, therefore, all children in the UK have access to health care. However, Article 27 (the right to a standard of living adequate for a child's development) together with Article 6 (the right to life) and Articles 24 & 2 (the right of **all** children to enjoy the '*highest attainable standard of health*') places a clear obligation on the Government not just to provide health care for all but also to develop policies which tackle the underlying structural factors which form a barrier to children's health.

**6.1.2** There is a well-established link between material deprivation and ill-health. In the UK as a whole there has been a significant decline in infant mortality but the difference in rates between rich and poor has grown wider. A recent analysis of all births within marriage and births jointly registered outside marriage shows that 12 in a 1,000 babies in Social Class 5 died within the first year compared with six in 1,000 amongst babies in Social Class 1. Thus, if babies in families with unskilled occupations had the same risk of infant death as those in professional classes, 508 babies lives would have been saved in 1988-90[56]. The House of Commons health committee recognised these inequalities in 1991, stating: 'Without reductions in the persistent social and geographical inequalities in health, a proportion of the population will remain vulnerable during pregnancy ... Further significant improvements in relation to pregnancy outcome depend on improving social conditions such as alleviating poverty, poor housing, and inadequate diet'.

**6.1.3** Poverty not only increases the risk of mortality but also of poorer health and high levels of disability. *Hardship Britain* found that over 70% of families interviewed by Family Service Units reported ill-health or disability amongst their children and of those interviewed in Bradford, over two-thirds of 91 households described long-term illness or disability[57]. Amongst children asthma, bronchitis, bed-wetting and eczema were the most common complaints, but also evident were kidney disease, depression, sickle cell anaemia, learning difficulties, growth problems and severe behavioural difficulties.

**6.1.4** The problems of ill-health, often triggered by an interaction of factors - low income, stress, poor housing and unemployment - were compounded by the inability to afford the costs incurred by illness. *Hardship Britain* documents clearly the stress and anxiety created within families faced with the need for special diets or extra heating, clothing or bedding for warmth[58]. The very poverty which contributes to poor health in children in turn prohibits access to the resources needed to alleviate it.

**6.1.5** Poor children, then, suffer disproportionately from ill health. Article 4 stresses governments' obligations to undertake such measures as are necessary for the full implementation of the rights in the Convention '*to the maximum extent of their available resources*'. In a wealthy industrialised society such as the UK, it cannot be argued that there are insufficient resources to devote to the improvement of standards of health for all children. The failure to implement strategies to narrow the growing gap emerging between poor and rich children in child mortality statistics and to challenge the marked inequalities in health represents a failure to promote the rights of **all** children required by Articles 2 and 24. The Government did acknowledge in its Green Paper *The Health of the Nation* differences in infant and peri-natal mortality rates but failed to set standards or targets for their reduction in the White Paper that followed it[59]. The Welsh Office have however set targets for improving the health of children from disadvantaged groups. (See also **UK Agenda Report 5 on health,** page 96).

### ACTION REQUIRED FOR COMPLIANCE

Compliance with Article 24 and Article 2 requires that:

- **targets should be set throughout the UK (as they have been in Wales) for reducing inequalities in health of children and in particular, seek to reduce inequalities in infant and peri-natal mortality rates and the numbers of low-birth weight babies.**

## 6.2 Diet

**6.2.1** A survey by the National Children's Home in 1991 which looked at 354 families with children on low incomes found that one in five parents and one in ten children had gone hungry in the previous month because they did not have enough money to buy food[60]. In the *Hardship Britain* survey 85% of those interviewed stated that they regularly cut down on food; parents were particularly concerned that they could not afford to pay for a healthy diet for their children[61].

*'I think kids who are poor should get more food and clothing.'* (8 year-old, N Ireland)

**6.2.2** The Government has refused to provide a breakdown of the proportion of the weekly benefit that is expected to be spent on any particular item. It argues that such decisions are a matter for the individual claimant to determine. However, under the supplementary benefit regulations which existed until 1988, there was a presumption that a 'normal' diet for an adult costed around 40% of the single person's weekly entitlement and for a child around 30%[62]. There were several attempts during the 1980s to cost diets offering nutritional standards established by the National Advisory Council on Nutrition Education and to compare these costs with the element available in benefit rates to pay for food.

**6.2.3** These studies indicate consistently that the benefit levels only provide between 40-50% of the money necessary if a family is to eat a diet of the standard recommended for adequate health. What emerges is a clear picture of parents forced into feeding their children high fat, unhealthy and monotonous diets because the foods recommended as essential for healthy eating are beyond their means. The benefit levels have not improved in relation to the cost of living since these studies were undertaken.

**6.2.4** Children in families on income support are entitled to free school-meals, milk and vitamins. However, since 1988 children in other families with a low income have no such entitlement[63]. In 1980 the Government abolished the nutritional standards for school-meals which ensured that school-age children were offered at least one nutritional meal a day. There has therefore been a cut in the numbers of children entitled to free meals and a removal of the standards for the quality of meals provided. The public service union NUPE estimates that in 1980 40% of a child's daily nutritional requirements were met at school compared with 25% in 1993. Further, between 1979 and 1990 the number of children eating a school-lunch fell from 4.9 million to 2.8 million; a drop of 27%[64]. These changes have contributed to the difficulties for many poor children in achieving an adequate diet necessary for their proper development.

## ACTION REQUIRED FOR COMPLIANCE

**Compliance with Article 24 requires:**

● **the compulsory provision of school-meals of agreed nutritional standards (also required for Article 3.3) for children who want them;**

● **the provision of free school-meals to be extended once more to all children in families on a low income.**

## 6.3  Access to a clean water supply

**6.3.1**  The ability to afford to pay for a water supply and the right of access to that supply are a prerequisite to the achievement of a standard of living adequate for a child's healthy development. Article 24.2(c) imposes on governments the obligation to '*combat disease and malnutrition through ... the provision of adequate nutritious foods and drinking water*'. Article 3.3 states that '*institutions, services and facilities responsible for the care or protection of children shall conform with the standards established by competent authorities particularly in the areas of safety, health ...*'. The Housing Act 1985 establishes standards with regard to water supply, stating that a house without an adequate supply of wholesome water is not fit for human habitation and is a statutory nuisance because of health risks.

**6.3.2**  Access to a clean water supply has been largely taken for granted in the UK in the latter part of this century for almost the whole population. Most of the diseases associated with lack of sanitation and contaminated water have been virtually eliminated. However, since 1988 when water supplies were privatised, there has been a substantial increase in the number of households which have had their water supply disconnected for non-payment. In 1992, 21,000 households were disconnected, representing a 177% increase over the previous year[65]. Water prices over the past five years have increased over 50% with inadequate compensatory increases in state benefits. Many families are faced with disconnection simply because they cannot afford to pay for water. The increases in charges have been accompanied by a more rigorous policy of debt recovery on the part of the water companies and the combined effect has been a worrying growth in families without access to a water supply of their own. There are few public water supplies available, so once disconnected, a family becomes entirely dependent on the goodwill of neighbours.

**6.3.3**  One of the growing concerns arising from these developments has been the rise in hepatitis and dysentery in many cities where the highest rates of disconnection are occurring. Since 1988 there has been a threefold increase in

their incidence. Children are now being placed at risk of illnesses which had been largely eradicated. In Birmingham, one of the largest authorities in the country, public health officials have established a direct link between cuts in water supplies and outbreaks of dysentery and hepatitis. A city council official commented: 'Outbreaks of hepatitis A occur when sewage cannot be washed away, when people cannot wash their hands after going to the toilet and especially when there are children in the home. Disconnecting the water supply takes us right back to the 19th century'[66]. Furthermore, the risk does not rest only with those families who experience disconnections. In the densely-populated areas of inner cities the diseases, once established, can spread within the local community.

**6.3.4**  Legislation establishes the standard that a water supply is a basic necessity for all households. The National Association of Citizens Advice Bureaux comments: 'Water is an essential service and availability of supply must not rest with the consumer's ability to pay. Water disconnection is a punitive measure which exacerbates hardship as well as causing severe health risks'[67]. There are now a number of local councils who have responsibility for environmental health arguing that water companies should not be allowed to disconnect the water supply to a household for non-payment. Indeed a Bill was presented, albeit unsuccessfully, in Parliament in 1992 to render it unlawful for water companies to use this sanction. A further Bill is being presented in 1994. There are other methods which can be used for recovery of payment of arrears by the water companies.

**6.3.5**  The Convention clearly establishes that access to a clean water supply is integral to a minimum standard of living adequate for a child's healthy development. It is ironic that following the World Summit for Children in 1990, when the goal of safe water and sanitation for all children by the end of the century was agreed, the UK should be witnessing a re-emergence of children denied that right.

## ACTION REQUIRED FOR COMPLIANCE

**Compliance with Articles 27, 24.2(c) and 3.3 requires that water companies are prohibited from disconnecting water supply for non-payment and required to pursue other methods of recovering their debts.**

# 7 Access to education
## Article 28

**7.1** Article 28 states that children have a *'right to education ... on the basis of equality of opportunity'*. Clearly, if this Article is to be complied with, it is necessary to ensure that children's access to education is not hindered as a consequence of their standard of living. There is a wide body of evidence which demonstrates that there is a close relationship between educational attainment and multiple deprivation. The material conditions of living in poverty - overcrowding, inadequate diet, poor housing and ill health - all play a contributory part in adversely affecting children's capacity to benefit fully from their education. Research studies over the past 20 years have documented the correlation between poor quality housing and poor educational attainment[68]. Homelessness has an even more dramatic impact: disrupted schooling arising from frequent moves, having to wait for a place at a school, nowhere in temporary accommodation for doing homework, loss of friendships, low self-esteem, stigma associated with the status of homelessness and low expectations from teachers, all play a part. As discussed above, children in poor families are at greater risk of ill-health which in turn means higher levels of absenteeism and loss of education. Moreover, children in low-income families often do not have an adequate diet and arrive at school hungry impairing their capacity to learn. The disadvantage experienced by children in deprived areas is compounded by a comparative lack of wider cultural and educational experiences. Parents on low incomes are less able to complement the education their child is receiving in school. Lack of money, lack of books and other educational resources in the home, combined with stress leading to physical and mental ill-health all diminish the capacity to provide the support that many other children have access to.

**7.2** In addition to the impact of multiple deprivation on educational attainment, a recent HMI report observes that there is also concern that the quality of teaching in inner-city schools is less good[69]. Contributory factors to this lower quality are likely to be inadequate resources, higher turnover of staff and employment of more inexperienced teachers. Whilst it cannot be argued that all children from multiply deprived backgrounds fail to achieve their potential nor that all schools in deprived areas fail to achieve good results, the HMI report refers to the 'stubborn 30% statistic syndrome' - by which is meant the persistent under-achievement amongst around one third of pupils in deprived inner-city areas. It is serious cause for concern that children's right to education on the basis of equality of opportunity required by Article 28, is being undermined by the impact of poverty within the family, compounded by an impoverished environment and poorer schools.

### ACTION REQUIRED FOR COMPLIANCE
**Compliance with Article 2 in the exercise of Article 28 and the right to education on the basis of equality of opportunity requires an overall review of early childhood care and education services in the UK, leading to a comprehensive, integrated national policy for the development of high quality and affordable early childhood services.**

# 8 Access to family life
## Articles 7 and 9

## 8.1 Poor children and public care

**8.1.1** Article 7 identifies the right of children *'as far as possible ... to know and be cared for by his or her parents'*. This principle is reinforced in Article 9 which stresses that *'a child shall not be separated from his or her family against their will except when ... such separation is necessary for the best interests of the child'*. It is worrying therefore to discover the demonstrable link between material deprivation and the likelihood of a child not being cared for at home but, rather, being received into public care.

**8.1.2** Research undertaken by Bebington and Miles indicates that deprivation is a common factor among all types of children who enter care[70]. They show that a child between the ages of five and nine years in a white family with two parents with three or less children in owner-occupied housing and not dependent on state benefits stands a 1:7,000 chance of being in local authority care. This contrasts sharply with a mixed-race child of similar age in a one-parent family in privately rented accommodation with three or more siblings and dependency on state benefits. The second child stands a 1:10 chance of being received into care. A study in 1989 of over 200 placement decisions 'reinforced the message that children in need were not characteristically children whose parents were abusive or neglectful. It showed a preponderance of admissions due to material crises (homelessness, debt) or behavioural problems, with parents motivated by their children's welfare'[71].

**8.1.3** The extent to which poverty and housing problems influence the likelihood of a child coming into public care raises serious questions about whether current Government policies are adequately promoting children's rights to family life. Clearly, care in itself is a necessary resource for children unable to live with their families. However, for many children, it implies the loss of many rights embodied in the Convention. As documented in **UK Agenda Report** 2 care for many children is associated not only with the loss of family life but serious neglect of educational opportunities; as they leave care, they face very high risks of homelessness, unemployment, social isolation, mental illness and prison. A quarter of the prison population were in care as children. In many cases the material deprivation which inhibited the child's right to adequate *"physical, mental, spiritual, moral and social development"* and which contributed to the initial family breakdown sets up a pattern of future loss of the right to an adequate standard of living.

**8.1.4** The Bebington and Miles research also observes that it is not only poverty that increases the likelihood of children needing to be looked after away from home but also lack of social supports[72]. The Government has recognised the need for support for families in section 17 of the Children Act which imposes in England and Wales a duty on local authorities to 'promote and safeguard the welfare of children who are in need ... by providing a range and level of services appropriate to those children'. Initial research on the interpretation of 'in need' was undertaken a year after the implementation of the Act by the Social Services

Inspectorate. It observed that: 'There was a group [of families] who failed to secure a high rating, including, perhaps most worryingly, given research findings on the link between material deprivation and reception into care, families on income support and family credit, one-parent families, unemployed families ... There would seem to be a conflict between some of these figures and the intentions of the Act to make family support systems the cornerstone of local authority child care systems and to encourage a broad definition of need"[73].

**8.1.5** There are further concerns that the levels of funding available to local authorities to provide effective parental support are inadequate and that as a result, some authorities are approaching the definition of 'in need' in a minimalist way, restricting access to services to those children at risk of harm. This trend provoked the comment that 'the effect of the new provision to assess children in need is to narrow and stigmatise provision ... the entitlement to family support services under [the Children Act] is narrower than under previous legislation'[74]. The Department of Health has funded research into the implementation of Section 17 of the Children Act which should provide a much clearer picture of how far the legislation is achieving its objectives and those of Article 27.

**8.1.6** Children who experience loss of family life as a direct consequence of material deprivation are not being provided with an adequate standard of living consistent with Article 27 - the very necessity for their removal from home is testimony to that failure. Approximately 60,000 children were in care in England and Wales in October 1991[75]. Of these, it is likely that a significant proportion could have remained at home had the necessary housing and social support been available.

### ACTION REQUIRED FOR COMPLIANCE

**Compliance with Article 9, the right to family life requires that:**

- **a broad range of properly resourced support services is offered by local authorities and that the resource implications this entails are acknowledged by the Government in its allocation of funding to local authorities;**

- **social services provision is non-stigmatising, well-publicised and based on a comprehensive assessment of local need;**

- **assessment of need must take account of the views of parents and children from all sections of the community.**

## 8.2  Contact with non-resident parents

**8.2.1** The new powers under the Child Support Act for recovery of maintenance from non-resident parents (usually the mother, and therefore referred to as such in this report) gives rise to some concerns with regard to the duty to promote the best interests of the child in Article 3 together with Article 9, the right of the child to maintain contact with both parents following separation unless this is not in the child's best interests. The rigid formula applied for calculating levels of maintenance for which absent parents are liable takes no account of the costs associated with travel to and actual contact with the child. Where the absent parent lives at some distance from the child, the costs of travel

combined with a maintenance obligation may well mean that for some parents continued contact becomes severely restricted, if not impossible. In this context, neither the child's best interests nor their right to contact are being considered above the right of the state to recoup money. The standard of living being imposed on the father by the maintenance contributions is restricting the child's right to maintain contact.

### ACTION REQUIRED FOR COMPLIANCE

**Compliance with Articles 3 and 9 requires that the formula for calculating maintenance should be adjusted to take account of the costs a parent is likely to incur in maintaining a level of contact with their child consistent with the child's best interests.**

# 9 Opportunities to play in a safe environment

## Article 31

**9.1** Article 31 states that children have a right to '*rest and leisure, to engage in play and recreational activities appropriate to the age of the child and to participate freely in cultural life and the arts*'. It is widely acknowledged within UK society that recreational activity plays an important part in children's development. However, for some children, the combined effects of low income, poor housing and a barren and neglected environment means that opportunities for safe play are heavily restricted. Their standard of living is insufficient to provide the necessary opportunities for social development that play offers. In some inner-city areas, these experiences are compounded by fear of racism which can also deprive children of the opportunities to play. (See also **UK Agenda Report 8 on play and leisure,** page 177).

**9.2** Families dependent on state benefits identify as one of their most insistent concerns the inability to provide opportunities for their children that they feel are necessary to their development and well-being. It is accepted in the UK today that the responsibilities of parenthood go well beyond the basic provision of food and shelter. Parents also expect to provide toys, leisure activities, outings, participation in out-of-school activities, and holidays. But for many families on benefit and on low wages these are beyond their reach. In consequence, children in poor families have more restricted lives than their peers and are excluded from participating in many of the activities widely accepted as intrinsic to social development in the UK in the 1990s.

**9.3** Children's self-confidence and self-esteem is inevitably heavily influenced by the value they see placed on them by society. If society, as is the case in the UK, places value on material possessions, holidays, trips to parks, zoos, cinemas, theatres, concerts, fairs and leisure centres and then excludes some children from participation by denying them a level of income that makes it possible, they may grow up with a diminished sense of their own value. These barriers to participation have two serious implications: they can lead to children being marginalised and isolated from the mainstream culture of our society and they isolate many children from a level of social interaction with their peers which is vital to their social development and education.

**9.4** Many families living in poverty are also living in environments which lack play facilities or even safe play areas. Parents are faced with the choice of restricting children in the home - itself often overcrowded - or letting them play unsupervised in the locality with all the associated risks. Thus the same children who lack the resources to pay for any social activity are also often deprived of opportunities for safe play in their immediate environment: they are thus doubly deprived.

> '*Hoods go around stealing cars doing skids and turning handbrakes and all because they have no money.*'
> (10 year-old, N Ireland)

**9.5** Children in deprived environments are far more likely to suffer accidents than children in more materially advantaged areas. For example, Scotland has the second worst accident rate in Europe and the rate is highest of all in large housing estates. In 1988, 3.9% of boys and 2.1% of girls living on the Easterhouse estate in Glasgow were injured so seriously that they were detained in hospital. This was double the rate in Glasgow as a whole[76]. A study reported in the *British Medical Journal* in 1990 confirms the link between accidents and social deprivation, revealing that child deaths from head injuries were 16 times more frequent in deprived areas and that children from social class 5 were six times as likely to die from burns than children from social class 1.

**9.6** The reasons for these disparities are rooted in poverty. In deprived areas, housing is less safe and more likely to be overcrowded. Overcrowding increases the risks of children being within reach of fires, chip pans, knives and dangerous substances such as bleach. Poor parents are less likely to be able to afford fire guards, stair gates or playpens. There are more likely to be abandoned flats which themselves are hazardous. There are no gardens offering opportunities for safe play. Children play on the streets where they are at risk from traffic and dogs. On one estate in Glasgow a child is run over every four days[77]. Many deprived areas suffer a lack of playgrounds, limited play schemes and community buildings. There also tends to be a higher level of violence in areas of high unemployment with more fights and muggings.

**9.7** Children play creatively on their own but they need space which is free from danger both inside and outside their home. The implementation of Article 31, the right to play, is hampered for many poor children by the paucity of their environment. A fundamental indicator against which to test the adequacy of the standard of living children that experience must be whether the environment they inhabit is appropriate for their social development. Play is integral to social development and hence where safe opportunities for play are denied children are also being denied their rights under Article 27 to an adequate standard of living.

## ACTION REQUIRED FOR COMPLIANCE

**Compliance with Article 31 for children living in deprived environments requires that local authorities give a high priority to the development of safe play areas. A co-ordinated approach between social services, education, planning, environmental health, leisure, housing and transport departments is essential if there is to be a genuine commitment to the creation of safe and attractive play opportunities for all children. Changes to the physical environment will be necessary in many areas and there will need to be good quality, low cost, supervised activities both out of school and in the holidays.**

# 10 Freedom from discrimination
## Article 2

9.1 Article 2 states that the rights in the Convention must be available without discrimination of any kind. However it is clear that there are certain structural factors in the UK, which serve to discriminate against groups of children as a result of their race or status or disability and which result in those children suffering disproportionately from the consequences of poverty.

## 10.1 Refugees

10.1.1 Article 22 states that refugee children '*shall receive appropriate protection and humanitarian assistance in the enjoyment of the applicable rights set forth in the present Convention.*' Article 2.2 states that all the rights in the Convention must apply without discrimination on the basis of the status of a child's parents. The current regulations that prescribe that people seeking asylum in the UK shall only receive 90% of the basic income support level of benefit appears to breach of these Articles. It is a clear example of discrimination which necessarily affects children in refugee families.

10.1.2 The difficulties are further compounded by the fact that refugee families usually arrive in this country with no belongings, few clothes, little money and no knowledge of where or how to access help. This means that they have no resources on which to draw in order to supplement their restricted income. They are often faced with having to set up home from scratch with no furniture, bedding and cooking equipment. Help from the Department of Social Security is limited as it will usually only offer loans, and repayment for families on a reduced level of social security is extremely difficult. The consequences for children in such families can be that they suffer serious deprivation as their parents struggle to make an income already inadequate for day-to-day living extend to provide the essentials for setting up a home.

10.1.3 Further discrimination against refugees has been introduced in the homelessness provisions of the Asylum and Immigration Appeals Act 1993. These new measures mean that local authorities are no longer required to offer accommodation to homeless asylum seekers and their children whilst any housing, however temporary or inadequate is available to them. Families will have to be actually on the street before they can obtain help, with all the consequent distress and anxiety for the children involved. This legislation represents a clear breach of Article 2 by discriminating against refugee children in their rights of access to accommodation as compared with other children in similar circumstances. It also represents a breach of the requirement in Article 27.3 '*in case of need [to] provide material assistance and support programmes, particularly with regard to nutrition, clothing and housing*'. As argued earlier in this report, access to adequate housing is essential to the provision of an adequate standard of living.

### ACTION REQUIRED FOR COMPLIANCE

**Compliance with Articles 2 and 27.3 requires that:**
- **the provisions in the Asylum and Immigration Appeals Act 1993, which deny refugee children equal rights to help with housing, are repealed;**
- **income support for refugees is paid at the same level as to other claimants.**

## 10.2 Racism and discrimination

10.2.1 There are deep structural inequalities in our society. A recent report published by the Runnymede Trust and Child Poverty Action Group, *Poverty in black and white*[78], comments: 'To be born into an ethnic minority in Britain, particularly a minority whose origins are in Bangladesh, the Caribbean or Pakistan, is to face a much higher risk of leading a life marked by low income, repeated unemployment, poor health and housing, working for low wages with few employment rights and being forced to rely on social security benefits than someone who is white'.

10.2.2 In the UK, ethnic origin and poverty are closely linked and children growing up in minority ethnic families are less likely than white children to achieve a standard of living adequate to their development consistent with Article 27. There are a number of complex and inter-related factors which serve as an impediment to their chances of benefiting from all the rights in the Convention without discrimination on grounds of race and social origin. *Poverty in black and white* identifies a number of key strands which link ethnic origin and poverty:

- immigration policy which denies access to social security and housing for an increasing number of people from abroad;
- growing unemployment which has disproportionately affected areas where most people from minority ethnic communities live;
- the social security system operates in both directly and indirectly discriminatory ways. Its reliance on contributions for many benefits excludes those with interrupted work patterns amongst whom people from minority ethnic groups are heavily represented, the residence tests exclude many people from minority ethnic groups, and there is growing evidence that administrative procedures within the social security system can serve to exclude black claimants from benefits to which they are entitled[79];
- widespread, persistent racism which continues to pervade our society and hinders access to jobs, housing and education.

10.2.3 There is a lack of official data on the relationship between low income, reliance on state benefits and ethnicity but there is evidence from national and local surveys of the extent of poverty amongst many minority ethnic communities. For example, a survey in the London Borough of Islington found that 40% of people from minority ethnic groups were living on or close to poverty levels compared with 30% of the total population[80]. In looking at social and material deprivation including diet, clothing, housing, lack of family activities recreation and education, they also revealed that minority ethnic families are likely to experience high levels of deprivation.

10.2.4 Whilst the causes of these structural inequalities are complex, much of the problem is rooted in aspects of public policy, or in social attitudes which could be influenced by changes in public policy.

Compliance with Article 27 without discrimination (Article 2) requires:

- **research and statistics which allow analysis of data by ethnic origin:** only with detailed information about the relationship between low income, dependency on state benefits and ethnicity will it be possible to begin to implement policies necessary to achieve change. The 1991 Census information is useful but other sources such as the *Family expenditure survey, Households below average income, The new earnings survey* and the *Social security statistics* should also provide a breakdown by ethnic origin.

- **urgent action to improve take-up of benefits by people from minority ethnic communities and to ensure that discrimination which is sometimes experienced in gaining access to benefits is challenged.** This will necessitate improved interpreting services, more information published in appropriate languages, and more training for staff to help them encourage claimants whose first language is not English.

# 11 The opportunity to participate in society

**11.1** As central to children's wellbeing as the material provision of housing, clothing and an adequate diet is the right to participate in social activities accepted as part of the daily routine of childhood – those activities which contribute to the right of citizenship. Fulfilment of the right of every child to a standard of living for '*mental, spiritual, moral and social development*' requires that children are provided, through their families, with sufficient resources to feel themselves to be part of society. Citizenship is about membership of a community and this is understood in terms of participation in that community. Ruth Lister, in her pamphlet on citizenship and the poor, argues that participation is an expression both of the formal political, legal and social rights and duties of citizenship and the social and economic conditions under which they are exercised[81]. Poor children are increasingly denied full citizenship through their exclusion from social rights. This report has demonstrated their lack of adequate health care, diet, benefit levels, a growing problem of homelessness and also the relationship between deprivation and reception into public care.

> '*Each generation has to achieve more than their parents, but we are not going to because there are no jobs for us so it's pretty pointless.*'
> (17 year-old, Shropshire)

**11.2** The Convention as a whole recognises children's rights to social and civil citizenship. Yet one of the most powerful messages that emerges from recent research into poverty is the experience of exclusion, lack of choice and isolation which it imposes. A recent report by the Archbishop of Canterbury comments that: 'Poverty is not just about shortage of money. It is about rights and relationships, about how people are treated and how they regard themselves, about powerlessness, exclusion and loss of dignity'[82]. A survey of poor families in the North East of England concludes: 'The picture that emerges ... is one of constant restriction in almost every aspect of people's activities ... The lives of these families and perhaps most seriously the lives of children within them, are marked by the unrelieved struggle to manage with dreary diets and drab clothing. They also suffer what amounts to cultural imprisonment in their homes in our society in which getting out with money to spend on recreation and leisure is normal at every other income level'[83].

**11.3** *Hardship Britain* documents the lives of a number of families living on state benefits. What emerges is the sense of powerlessness, guilt, stigma and loss of self-esteem experienced by the members of those families. Parents felt keenly that lack of money was preventing them from fulfilling their role adequately. Parents are for the most part the most effective and committed advocates promoting their children's rights and certainly most parents fight to ensure that their children's standard of living is adequate for their development in line with their obligations under Article 27.2. However, they cannot achieve this in isolation.

**11.4** The Convention, both in the Preamble and in Articles 18.2 and 27.3, makes explicit that, whilst the primary responsibility for childrearing rests with parents, the state has a duty to support parents in that role. Clearly the current benefit system, together with the Children Act in England and Wales (and comparable legislation in Scotland and N Ireland), and education and health legislation, are intended to fulfil that role. However, during the 1980s, there has been a growing trend in tax and child care policy towards the affirmation of parenthood as a consumer choice. Parents are increasingly expected to carry the burden of costs of children without state support. Not only has there been a massive failure to tackle the growth of poverty, but there has been an explicit and growing view amongst some Government ministers that the poor are to blame for their poverty.

**11.5** This view seeks to construct a close link in the public mind between claiming benefits and fraud, and represents an attempt, whether deliberate or otherwise, to link poverty and dependency on state benefits with laziness, dishonesty and an unwillingness to accept one's responsibilities. Lone-parents have been particularly singled out for criticism by the Government.

**11.6** Some members of the Government, academics and journalists also argue that the poor are poor, not because of lack of jobs or opportunities, but because of their unwillingness to work or train, their disassociation from the mainstream culture and values of our society; that there is in society an 'underclass' unable to participate in or benefit from the opportunities available to them. This view is effectively summarised in the following extract: 'The underclass spawns illegitimate children without a care for tomorrow ... Its able bodied youth see no point in working and feel no compunction either. They reject society while feeding off it ... No amount of income redistribution or social engineering can solve the problem ... They exist as active social outcasts wedded to an anti-social system'[84].

**11.7** Yet there is little empirical evidence of the existence of an underclass. Studies of people on benefit reveal that they share the same culture and aspirations as the rest of the population, the only key distinguishing feature being their lack of money to enable them to fulfil their aspirations.

> *'There is a stereotype that all homeless young people are new-age travellers, people think you are a parasite, but most of us just want to be doing something. They want a chance to get a bit of self respect.'*
> (17 year-old, Oxfordshire)

**11.8** In these ways the poor, adults and children alike, are socially marginalised and denied the acceptance that goes with citizenship. The consequences of this marginalisation of children are incompatible with the commitment in the Preamble to the Convention that States Parties consider *'the child should be prepared to live an individual life in society and brought up in the spirit of the ideals proclaimed in the Charter of the UN and in particular, in the spirit of peace, dignity, tolerance, freedom, equality and solidarity'*. Nor is it consistent with the supportive role required of the Government in Article 27.3 to take *'appropriate measures to assist parents'* to assure the *'conditions of living necessary for the child's development'* (Article 27.2).

**11.9** By casting the poor as 'guilty', the **physical exclusion** from participation forced on poor children by their poverty, is compounded by a **social exclusion** created by social attitudes of condemnation and blame. Such exclusion is inimical to the promotion of the child's development necessary for compliance with Article 27, runs counter to the anti-discrimination requirement in Article 2, and indeed breaches the spirit of the Convention as a whole. Children have a right to participate as members of society and Government policy needs to be rooted in a fundamental commitment to the promotion of that right.

# Summary of action required for compliance

1 Compliance with Article 27 in the context of the obligations imposed by Article 4 requires a fundamental examination of the principles which underpin the social security system and a review of its operation in the context of changing patterns of employment and family life. There is a need to address the adequacy of benefit levels and for independent research to establish a level of weekly benefit that would enable children and their parents to participate fully in society. However, the role of social security benefits in protecting family income should not be addressed in isolation from policies which give parents more opportunities to earn adequate incomes through paid employment.

2 Compliance with Article 27.3, the obligation to '*take appropriate measures to assist parents and others responsible for the child*' to implement the right to an adequate standard of living, requires that:

- the discretionary part of the Social Fund should be abolished and replaced with a new system of legal entitlement based on grants with no cash limit and an independent right of appeal;

- the proposals for introducing VAT on fuel which are likely to cause increased hardship to children living in poverty, should be withdrawn;

- housing benefit, a system of help with rents for those on low incomes, should be extended to help with mortgage repayments.

3 Compliance with Article 27.4, the duty to secure the recovery of maintenance together with Article 3, the obligation to consider the best interests of the child requires legislation which takes as its starting point the welfare of children. Meanwhile, greater compliance could be achieved by repealing the statutory obligation on mothers under the Child Support Act to name the father of their child and with it the power to penalise claimants for failure to comply. It is essential that the impact of the new legislation is carefully monitored to assess its implications for the welfare of children, particularly those living in second families, with a view to amending the maintenance formula if evidence of hardship is identified.

4 Compliance with Article 27.1 and .3, the rights of children and young people to an adequate standard of living, including access to appropriate housing, requires:

- the right to an income which enables young people to have access to accommodation: without an income, young people who are unable to live at home cannot obtain housing;

- the right to housing when homeless: at present, the Housing Act 1985 which places on local authorities a duty to provide accommodation for homeless people effectively excludes young single people as they are not treated as being in priority need;

- advice and practical help from local authorities or other agencies about the different housing options, as well as support in sustaining independent living;

- greater investment in the provision of good quality, low cost rented accommodation which will ensure access to permanent homes without which children will continue to suffer from poor physical and psychological health, disrupted education, insecurity and loss of friendships that are an inevitable consequence of homelessness;

- that the existing right to permanent housing for homeless families in priority need is retained;

- minimum environmental health standards to be drawn up for bed and breakfast hotels and they should be inspected at least every six months. Families should be informed of these standards and given information about how to complain in the event of a breach of standards;

- that health authorities ensure that in areas where high concentrations of homeless families are accommodated, they direct resources to meet the needs of these families - extra health visitors and locally based outreach services such as antenatal and baby clinics. Measures also need to be taken to ensure that homeless families are able to register with local GPs and do not have to rely on use of casualty departments;

- minimum standards to be established for the provision of private sector leased property and regularly monitored;

- families moving into private sector leased property to be given detailed information by the placing authority about the property (who owns it, who to contact for repairs, how the heating works) and about local services and how to access them;

- that the duty on local authorities to provide sites under the Caravan Sites Act 1968 is retained;

- consideration is given to a range of options to encourage the development of more and better quality sites, including the exploration of alternative financing for local authority and private sites such as housing associations, upgrading existing sites, providing Gypsies and Travellers with accessible information on planning procedures to help them make private site applications more successful and the introduction of short term licences;

- wider consultation with Gypsy and Traveller families about site provision: they are best able to identify the variety and quality of sites needed to ensure their children's well being.

5 Compliance with Article 27 without discrimination (Article 2) requires:

- research and statistics which allow analysis of data by ethnic origin: only with detailed information about the relationship between low income, dependency on state benefits and ethnicity will it be possible to begin to implement policies necessary to achieve change. The 1991 Census information is useful but other sources such as the *Family expenditure survey*, *Households below average income*, *The new earnings survey* and the *Social security statistics* should also provide a breakdown by ethnic origin;

- urgent action to improve take-up of benefits by people from minority ethnic communities and to ensure that discrimination which is sometimes experienced in gaining access to benefits is challenged. This will necessitate improved interpreting services, more information published in appropriate languages, and more training for staff to help them encourage claimants whose first language is not English;

- the provisions in the Asylum and Immigration Appeals Act 1993, which deny refugee children equal rights to help with housing, are repealed;

● income support for refugees is paid at the same level as to other claimants.

**6** The ability to assess compliance with Articles 23 and 27 in respect of disabled children requires research into the experience of disabled children and their families of the quality and availability of help and support offered. Without this research, it is not possible to evaluate whether the provision that is now available is adequate to ensure that compliance with the right of disabled children to an adequate standard of living which ensures their active participation in the community. There is an urgent need for research into the impact of the 1988 disability benefits changes and in particular a review of disability benefits which assesses the adequacy of disability child premium, in order to ascertain whether children living in families dependent on such benefits are able to achieve a standard of living adequate for their proper development. There is also a need for research which examines the views of children themselves and the adequacy of their standard of living.

**7** Compliance with Articles 27, 24.2(c) and 3.3 requires that water companies are prohibited from disconnecting water supply for non-payment and required to pursue other methods of recovering their debts.

**8** Compliance with Article 24 and Article 2 requires that:

● targets should be set throughout the UK (as they have been in Wales) for reducing inequalities in health of children and in particular, seek to reduce inequalities in infant and peri-natal mortality rates and the numbers of low-birth weight babies;

● there should be compulsory provision of school-meals of agreed nutritional standards (also required for Article 3.3) for children who want them;

● the provision of free school-meals should be extended once more to all children in families on a low income.

**9** Compliance with Article 9, the right to family life requires that:

● a broad range of properly resourced support services is offered by local authorities and that the resource implications this entails are acknowledged by the Government in its allocation of funding to local authorities;

● social services provision is non-stigmatising, well-publicised and based on a comprehensive assessment of local need;

● assessment of need must take account of the views of parents and children from all sections of the community;

● the formula for calculating maintenance should be adjusted to take account of the costs a parent is likely to incur in maintaining a level of contact with their child consistent with the child's best interests.

**10** Compliance with Article 26 requires that all unemployed 16 and 17 year-olds should be entitled to income support if they cannot find work or a suitable training place, and that benefit levels for 16 and 17 year-olds living independently should be paid at the same level as those paid to claimants aged over 25.

**11** Compliance with Article 2 in the exercise of Article 28 and the right to education on the basis of equality of opportunity requires an overall review of early childhood care and education services in the UK, leading to a comprehensive, integrated national policy for the development of high quality and affordable early childhood services.

**12** Compliance with Article 31 for children living in deprived environments requires that local authorities give a high priority to the development of safe play areas. A co-ordinated approach between social services, education, planning, environmental health, leisure, housing and transport departments is essential if there is to be a genuine commitment to the creation of safe and attractive play opportunities for all children. Changes to the physical environment will be necessary in many areas and there will need to be good quality, low cost, supervised activities both out of school and in the holidays.

# References

1. *The justice gap*, The Commission for Social Justice (1993)
2. *Child poverty and deprivation in industrialised countries: recent trends and policy options*, Cornia G A, Innocenti Occasional Papers, UNICEF, International Child Development Centre (1990)
3. *Poverty: the facts*, Oppenheim C, Child Poverty Action Group, London (1993)
4. *Households below average income 1979-1990/91*, HMSO (1993)
5. *Poverty and inequality in the UK: the effects on children*, Kumar V, National Children's Bureau (1993)
6. *Population trends*, Office of Population and Census Surveys (1993)
7. *The index of social health: monitoring the social well-being of children in industrial countries; a report for UNICEF*, Miringoff M and Opdycke S, Fordham Institute for Innovation in Social Policy (1993)
8. *Hardship Britain: being poor in the 1990s*, Cohen R, Coxall J, Craig G and Sadiq-Sangster A, Child Poverty Action Group, London (1992)
9. *Living on the edge: a study of the living standards of families on benefit in Tyne and Wear*, Bradshaw J and Holmes H, Child Poverty Action Group, London (1989)
10. *Evaluating the social fund*, Huby M and Dix G, Department of Social Security, Research Report No 9, HMSO (1992)
11. *The cost of a child: living standards for the 1990s*, Oldfield N and Yu A, Child Poverty Action Group, London (1993)
12. *Credit and debt in Britain: the PSI report*, Berthoud R and Kempson E, Policy Studies Institute (1992)
13. see reference 1
14. *Deep in debt: a survey of problems faced by low income families*, National Children's Home (1992)
15. *Consuming credit: debt and poverty in the UK*, Ford J, Child Poverty Action Group, London (1991)
16. *Just About surviving: life on income support, quality of life and the impact of local services*, Family Services Unit (1991)
17. see reference 3
18. *Of little benefit: a study of the adequacy of income support rates*, Stitt S, Campaign Against Poverty (1991)
19. see reference
20. *OPCS surveys of disability in Great Britain: the financial circumstances of families with disabled children living in private households*, Smyth M and Robus N, HMSO (1989)
21. *Four years severe hardship: young people and the benefits gap*, Maclagan I, Youthaid, Coalition on Young People and Social Security (COYPSS) and Barnardos (1993)
22. see reference 21
23. *Working brief*, Issue 45, Youthaid (June 1993)
24. *A lost generation: a survey of the problems faced by vulnerable young people living on their own*, NCH (1993)
25. *Social Security Advisory Committee: eighth report*, HMSO (1992)
26. *Social policy bulletin*, National Association of Citizens Advice Bureaux (April 1993)
27. *Prescription for poor health: the crisis for homeless families*, Conway J, London Food Commission, Maternity Alliance, Shelter Housing Aid Centres and Shelter (1988)
28. see reference 1
29. *Homes cost less than homelessness*, Burrows L and Walenkowicz P, Shelter (1992)
30. *Homelessness: report of local authority housing and racial equality working party*, Association of Metropolitan Authorities (1990)
31. see reference 29
32. see reference 27
33. *The experiences of homeless families in private sector leased temporary accommodation*, Edwards R and Tritter J, Social Sciences Research Centre, South Bank University (1993)
34. *The experience of homeless families in private sector leased temporary accommodation: a report for the London Homelessness Forum*, Edwards R and Trotter J, South Bank University (1993)
35. *Young and homeless in Wales*, Hutson S and Liddiard M, Occasional Paper No 26, University College of Swansea (1991)
36. *Young homelessness: a national scandal*, Young Homelessness Group (1992)
37. *One day I'll have my own place to stay*, Central London Social Security Adviser's Forum (1989)
38. *Housing our children: the Children Act 1989*, Centrepoint (1993)
39. *Inequalities in health: the health divide*, Whitehead M, Penguin (1988)
40. 'Damp housing, mould growth and symptomatic health state', Platt S D et al, *British Medical Journal*, (24 June 1989) vol 298, pp1673-8
41. *Healthy housing: the role of the environmental health services*, Audit Commission, HMSO (1991)
42. *English house condition survey: 1991 - preliminary report on unfit dwellings*, Department of the Environment, HMSO (1993)
43. see reference 41
44. reported in 'Health visitors and homeless families', Drennan V and Stean J, *Health Visitor*, no 59 (1986) pp340-342
45. see reference 5
46. *English house conditions survey 1986*, DoE (1988)
47. see reference 8
48. *Ten years cold - lessons from a decade of fuel poverty*, Boardman B, Neighbourhood Energy Action (1991)
49. see reference 16
50. see reference 5
51. *Traveller mothers and babies: who cares for their health?*, Durward L, Maternity Alliance (1990)
52. *Health and health care among Travellers*, Pahl J and Vaile M, Journal of Social Policy, 17, 2, pp195-214 (1988)
53. see reference 52
54. *Response to the Government consultation paper: Gypsy sites and illegal camping, reform of the Caravan Sites Act 1968*, The Save the Children Fund (1992)
55. see reference 54
56. see reference 3
57. see reference 8
58. see reference 8
59. *The health of the nation*, Department of Health, HMSO (1992)
60. *Poverty and nutrition survey*, National Children's Home (1991)
61. see reference 8
62. see reference 18

63. *Health services management welfare food scheme,* Department of Health, HC(89)13 (1989)

64. *School meals factfile No 1,* NUPE (1992)

65. *Public utilities information bulletin,* Public Utilities Access Forum (April 1993)

66. see reference 65

67. *High and dry; CAB evidence on water charges, debt and disconnections, submission to OFWAT,* NACAB (1992)

68. see reference 5

69. *Education in England 1990/91; the annual report of HM Senior Chief Inspector of Schools,* Department of Education (1992)

70. 'The background of children who enter local authority care', Bebington A and Miles J, *The British Journal of Social Work,* vol 19, no 5 (1989)

71. *Child care now,* Rowe J, Hundelby M and Garnett L, British Agencies for Adoption & Fostering (1989)

72. see reference 70

73. *Capitalising on the act: a working party report on the implementation of the Children Act 1989 in London,* Social Services Inspectorate, London Region, (1992)

74. *The Children Act 1989 and family support: principles into practice, Chapter 9: local authorities' practices on children in need,* ed. Gibbons J, HMSO (1993)

75. *Children Act Report 1992,* Department of Health and Welsh Office, HMSO (1992)

76. 'It's no accident', Holman B, *Poverty,* no 80, Child Poverty Action Group, London (1991)

77. see reference 76

78. *Poverty in black and white: deprivation and ethnic minorities,* Amin K and Oppenheim C, Child Poverty Action Group and Runnymede Trust (1992)

79. *Barriers to benefit: black claimants and social security,* National Association of Citizens Advice Bureaux (1991)

80. *Islington: poverty in the 1980s,* Islington Council Anti-Poverty Strategy, Briefing no 3, Islington Council (1990)

81. *The exclusive society: citizenship and the poor,* Lister R, Child Poverty Action Group, London (1990)

82. *Faith in the city: call for action by church and nation,* vol 15, Part 1, Church House (1985)

83. see reference 9

84. *Sunday Times* (26 November 1989)

## UK Agenda for Children

Health
and
health care
services

# Contents

> *The unreferenced quotations in this report are comments made during a consultation exercise undertaken by the Children's Rights Development Unit with groups of young people throughout the UK.*

# 1 Introduction

**1.1** The UN Convention on the Rights of the Child provides a set of principles and standards on which to base services for health care and the promotion of health. Article 24.1, the right to the '*highest attainable standard of health*', gives important emphasis to the positive concept of health as 'a state of complete physical, mental and social well-being and not merely the absence of disease or infirmity' as defined by the World Health Organisation (WHO)[1]. Given this widely accepted definition, it is clear that the state of health of a country's children cannot be measured simply by reference to mortality and morbidity rates but must also take into account general well-being. Attempts to develop indicators of positive health, in particular people's own perception of their health or ill-health, are still in the very early stages and resources need to be developed further.

**1.2** As well as ensuring rights to health Article 24.1 emphasises that '*States Parties shall strive to ensure that no child is deprived of his or her right of access to ... health care services*'. A policy of universal health care services, free of charge at the point of delivery, was first introduced in the UK in 1948, but from the early days free services have been gradually eroded with, for example, the introduction of charges for prescriptions, dental and eyesight checks and chiropody services[2]. Limited resources must always mean 'rationing' of services and there is continued debate on how that rationing should occur. Implementation of Article 24.1 clearly implies that rationing of services should not allow children and young people to be deprived of their right to health care services, but this report describes the considerable evidence that for many children and young people in the UK access is restricted.

**1.3** This report in the **UK Agenda** looks at the rights of children and young people in relation to some aspects of health and health care services. Failures in the Government's social, economic and environment policies to promote the best possible health for all the UK's children and young people are discussed fully in other reports in the **UK Agenda**. For discussion of rights relevant to the care of children see **UK Agenda Report 2 on the care of children,** page 19; non-accidental injury, genital mutilation and other traditional practices prejudicial to health see **UK Agenda Report 3 on physical integrity,** page 51; inequalities in health see **UK Agenda Report 4 on standard of living,** page 67; environmental factors affecting health, including accident prevention and safety policies see **UK Agenda Reports 6 on the environment,** page 127 and **8 on play and leisure,** page 177; and the specific problems faced by young refugees see **UK Agenda Report 11 on nationality and immigration,** page 243.

# 2 Relevant articles in the Convention

## 2.1 Underlying principles

**Article 2:** all rights in the Convention must apply without discrimination of any kind irrespective of race, colour, language, religion, national, ethnic or social origin, disability or other status.

**Article 3.1:** the duty in all actions to consider the best interests of the child.

**Article 12:** the right to express an opinion and to have that opinion taken into account in any matter or procedure affecting the child.

## 2.2 Articles relevant to health and health care services

**Article 3.2:** the duty to ensure children the care and protection necessary for their well-being.

**Article 3.3:** the duty to ensure that services and facilities are provided to an agreed standard.

**Article 5:** the duty of the Government to respect the rights and responsibilities of parents to provide guidance and direction to children which is appropriate to the evolving capacity of the child.

**Article 6:** the right to life and development.

**Article 9:** the right when separated from family to maintain contact with both parents on a regular basis.

**Article 23:** the right of disabled children to special care.

**Article 24:** the right to highest level of health possible and to access to health services.

**Article 24.2(a):** the duty to diminish infant and child mortality.

**Article 24.2(b):** the duty to provide medical assistance and health care to all children with emphasis on the development of primary health care.

**Article 24.2(c):** the duty to ensure the provision of adequate nutritious foods and clean drinking water, and to consider the dangers and risks of environmental pollution.

**Article 24.2(d):** the duty to provide appropriate pre- and post-natal care for mothers.

**Article 24.2(e):** the duty to ensure that parents and children have information and are supported in the use of basic knowledge relating to child health and nutrition, breast-feeding, hygiene and environmental sanitation and accident prevention.

**Article 24.2(f):** the duty to develop preventive health care, guidance for parents, and family planning education and services.

**Article 25:** the right of children placed in the care of the State to periodic review of treatment.

**Article 28:** the right to education on the basis of equality of opportunity.

**Article 30:** the right of children from minority communities to enjoy their own culture and practise their own language and religion.

**Article 31:** the right to play.

**Article 33:** the right to protection from the use of narcotic and psychotropic drugs.

*For the full wording of the articles, see the UN Convention on the Rights of the Child, page 311.*

# 3 The right to health

## 3.1 The State's role in promoting health
(Article 24.1)

**3.1.1** The role of the State in promoting Article 24.1, the right to health for all children and young people, is complex. Social, economic and environmental factors all have a major impact on health and Government policy and planning in these areas has often failed to acknowledge this. The result has been a failure to introduce policies which will ensure each child the opportunity to attain the best possible health. Promoting health also requires the provision of 'preventive' health care services designed to provide health information and identify potential health problems as early as possible; offering suitable care and advice. The National Health Service is responsible for ensuring the provision of a range of services to meet this need but this report shows that frequently the standards set by the Convention for preventive health services are not met.

**3.1.2** Article 6 describes the *'inherent right to life'* of every child, and although there is no such right in UK law the European Convention on Human Rights guarantees that: 'Everyone's right to life shall be protected by law' (Article 2.1). The European Commission of Human Rights has confirmed that this duty obliges the State not merely to refrain from taking life, 'but, further, to take appropriate steps to safeguard life'[3]. The fact that UK legislation provides no *'right to life'* nor places any duty on the State to ensure *'to the maximum extent possible the survival and development of the child'* or *'the highest attainable standard of health'* means that there is no legal basis from which to develop criteria for measuring the extent of implementation of these rights.

### ACTION REQUIRED FOR COMPLIANCE

**Compliance with Articles 6, the right to life and the duty to ensure, to the maximum extent possible the survival and development of the child and Article 24, the right to health and health care services, requires that health legislation throughout the UK should include duties to ensure, to the maximum extent possible, the survival and development of the child and a right of access to appropriate health care services. This would provide a clear and enforceable framework for full implementation of the basic health rights in the Convention.**

## 3.2 Rights for all (Article 2)

**3.2.1** Ill-health amongst children, as reported by parents, increased between 1979 and 1990. Results from the OPCS General Household Survey suggest an increase in reported 'long-standing illness' in children from birth to four years old from 8% in 1979 to 14% in 1990 amongst boys, and from 6% - 12% amongst girls. Among 5 to 15 year-olds the reported increases were from 14% - 20% for boys, and 10% - 17% for girls. Reports of chronic illnesses which restrict activity in some way also increased from 2% - 4% overall for 0 to 4 year-olds and from 6% - 8% overall for 5 - 15 year-olds. Again, significantly fewer girls than boys appear to have illnesses[4].

**3.2.2** Article 2 states that governments have a duty to *'respect and ensure the rights set forth in the present Convention to each child within their jurisdiction ... '.* This principle must therefore apply to both Article 6, the duty to *'ensure to the maximum extent possible the survival and development of the child'* and to Article 24.1, the right of children and young people to the *'enjoyment of the highest attainable standard of health'.* Yet in the UK today there are major variations in the life expectancy and general health of children and young people.

**3.2.3** Several major reports published recently analyze links between poverty and deprivation and children's health. The most recent review, *Children, teenagers and health - the key data,* confirmed earlier evidence that children living in poor families have higher rates than other children of infant and child mortality and are more likely to be diagnosed as suffering from infectious diseases, slow growth, dental disease, respiratory problems, accidents, and behavioural and emotional disorders[5][6][7][8].

**3.2.4** There are distinct regional differences in England relating to infant and childhood mortality. The UK figure for infant mortality, of 7.5 per 1000 live births, hides variation from 6.8 in the South West health region to 9.9 in the West Midlands. Within regions there are also wide variations between districts. In Wales, in 1990, the rate was 6.9, in Scotland 7.7 and in N Ireland 7.5 but these figures also hide wide variations. Regional differences reflect in part patterns of poverty and deprivation[9].

**3.2.5** Perinatal and infant mortality rates vary with ethnicity. The death rate amongst babies of mothers born in Pakistan is nearly twice that of mothers born in the UK. Infants of women born in the Caribbean also have a high mortality rate whilst those of others born in Bangladesh seem to have a lower risk[10]. The reasons for this diversity are complex and not fully understood but cannot be explained solely by reference to relative socio-economic position.

**3.2.6** Regional differences occur with other health problems, for example in Scotland dental health tends to be poorer than elsewhere in UK and there is concern about the trend that sees dental health as separate from other areas of health services. Community dentists are often more child-centred than private ones and there are fears that increased privatisation of the service, being encouraged by the Government, may result in families in deprived areas not attending the dentist.

**3.2.7** Children and young people in Traveller families may also be disadvantaged in health terms. Still births and perinatal and infant mortality rates are higher than national rates and birth weights tend to be lower[11]. Traveller mothers and babies need guaranteed minimum standards of care and sites should be provided with adequate space and basic facilities such as water, sanitation, refuse disposal and, if practicable, electricity[12].

**3.2.8** Poor housing conditions also have an impact on health. The inadequacy of the physical environment leads to high rates of illness or accidents through, for example, faulty electrical wiring, burns, diseases spread by pests, damp, unprotected stairwells, and inadequate sanitation. A study of housing in London, Glasgow and Edinburgh showed that children living in damp and mouldy homes were more prone to wheezing, sore throats, runny noses, coughs, headaches and fever[13]. Homeless families living in bed and breakfast and temporary accommodation are likely to suffer even more. Between 1979 and 1990 the number of people accepted as homeless by local authorities (a conservative estimate of the real numbers) rose from 7,232 to 169,526[14]. Homelessness, especially if children are living in bed and breakfast hotels, has a major effect on their diets and causes disruption and unhappiness which can affect their mental as well as physical health[15].

**3.2.9** Ill health is a major problem for homeless young people living on the streets. More than a third of the young people in one study of homelessness reported being ill in a four-week period, and many reported depression. For some young people the combination of homelessness and the prejudice they face can result in serious depression and other forms of mental distress[16].

**3.2.10** Although in Wales targets have been set to reduce inequalities in health the same is not true for the rest of the UK and the absence of any legislative duties in line with the Convention undermines full implementation of Articles 2 and 24.1 and the rights of **all** children and young people to enjoy '*the highest attainable standard of health*'.

### ACTION REQUIRED FOR COMPLIANCE

**See UK Agenda Report 4 on standard of living for action required to meet the Government's obligations to ensure an adequate standard of living (Article 27) to promote the best possible health.**

## 3.3 The right to be protected
(Article 3.2)

**3.3.1** Article 3.2 places a duty on the Government to '*ensure the child such protection and care as is necessary for his or her well-being,...* ' but the evidence is that the health of many children and young people in the UK is not being properly protected. The Government could do considerably more to ensure that all children and young people are able to grow up in a safer, healthier environment. **UK Agenda Report 6 on the environment and 8 on play and leisure** look in detail at accidents and accident prevention policies, the importance of planning in creating safe surroundings and the dangers of environmental pollution. This report discusses smoking, tobacco and drugs.

*Smoking*
**3.3.2** One of the major threats to the health of children and young people in the UK is their increasing use of cigarettes. Although smoking levels amongst adults continue to fall, numbers amongst teenagers, especially girls, are increasing[17]. It is estimated that about 450 children start smoking every day and that one in four 15 year-olds are regular smokers[18]. Over 500,000 young people in Britain, between 11 and 15 years old, are smokers[19]. In Scotland 90% of teenagers who smoke even three or four cigarettes find themselves trapped in a career of regular smoking which typically lasts for 30 or 40 years. Repeated surveys have shown that 1.5 million cigarettes a week are smoked by Scottish school children between 12 and 15 years, and that most of these have been bought openly from shop keepers[20].

**3.3.3** In recognition of these problems the Government has set targets to reduce the prevalence of smoking among 11-15 year-olds by at least a third (to less than 6%) between 1988 and 1994[21]. Its strategy to achieve this target includes a high level of taxation on tobacco (to keep prices high) and the continuation of existing national programmes on teenage smoking. Existing programmes have not been effective and despite high rates of awareness amongst young people of anti-smoking messages in the press and on television, there has been little change in behaviour. The present voluntary agreements between the Government and the tobacco industry, which are supposed to protect children from exposure to tobacco promotion, are ineffective.

**3.3.4** Also, despite legislation, cigarettes are still readily available to children and young people. The Children and Young Persons (Protection from Tobacco) Act 1991 increases the penalties for those who sell cigarettes to children under 16. It also makes illegal the sale of unpackaged cigarettes often sold as 'singles', and dictates that retail outlets must display a warning statement that it is illegal to sell tobacco products to anyone under 16. But a recent survey showed that only 15% of children had been refused cigarettes in a shop the last time they tried to buy them[22]. In failing to find out and address the reasons why young people take up smoking and in failing to control the sale of tobacco sales to children and young people the Government is also failing in its duty under Article 3.2 to protect their well-being.

**3.3.5** The smoking habits of adults affect the health of children and young people. Passive smoking is increasingly recognised as a serious threat to children's health and the Chief Medical Officer of Health's report for 1991 shows that the majority of young people smoking have parents or siblings who also smoke. There is evidence that smoking during pregnancy increases the risk of miscarriage, premature labour, higher perinatal mortality and allergies in infancy, and that its effects may extend beyond infancy[23].

> '*Parents should not be allowed to smoke, I hate it when my mammy blows smoke into my mouth.*'
> (6 year-old N Ireland)

**3.3.6** As one of its health targets *The health of the nation* proposes that at least one third of women smokers will stop smoking at the start of their pregnancy by the year 2000. But anti-smoking strategies do not appear to take account of the reasons why many women, especially those with low incomes and in other very difficult circumstances, continue to smoke. The evidence suggests that some women may find it easier to stop smoking if some of the material stresses associated with caring for children were relieved.

**3.3.7** Another factor that undermines the Government's anti-smoking strategy is its refusal to ban tobacco advertising despite strong evidence that children and young people are highly susceptible to such advertising and that a ban can be effective in reducing levels of smoking. Research demonstrates that children are aware of, and very susceptible to, cigarette advertising, that it encourages children to start smoking and those who already smoke to continue doing so. There is compelling evidence from New Zealand, Norway and Canada that a ban on advertising leads to a reduction in smoking and tobacco consumption[24]. Although in *The health of the nation* the Government proposes to review the effect of voluntary codes, particularly on children, and to consider what further steps are necessary if they are failing, it has, to date, refused to introduce a ban. In failing to do this the Government is not taking adequate measures to implement Article 17(e) and protect children and young people from '*information and material injurious to his or her well-being..*' or Article 3.1, to consider the '*best interests*' of the child '*in all actions taken by public or private social welfare institutions, courts, administrative authorities or legislative bodies*'.

## ACTION REQUIRED FOR COMPLIANCE

**Compliance with Article 3.2, the duty to ensure children adequate protection to safe-guard their right to health from the dangers of smoking, requires that:**

- **research into the reasons why pregnant women, parents, children and young people continue to smoke, despite the fact that they are well versed in the risks to their health and the health of others, should have a higher priority in Government strategies; information gleaned from existing studies should be used as a basis for anti-smoking campaigns;**

- **the increasing evidence about the dangers of passive smoking and its effects on the health of children should be more widely publicised, especially to adults who have regular contact with children;**

- **children and young people should be involved in the design of anti-smoking programmes aimed at their peers (also Article 12);**

- **there should be a complete ban on the advertising of all tobacco products (also Articles 17(e) and 24.1);**

- **there should be stricter enforcement of the laws relating to the sale of cigarettes to children and young people (also Articles 24.1 and 24.2(e)).**

*Alcohol*

> '*I don't think there should be an age limit at all, if your parents let you drink, like when you have wine with your dinner, then you grow up respecting alcohol and not abusing it when you are older.*'
> (15 year-old, N Ireland)

**3.3.8** Alongside smoking, the misuse of alcohol is one of the major health threats to children and young people in the UK. In today's society alcohol is available from a variety of sources and the use of alcohol is widely considered to be a social necessity. With increasing availability and a drop in the 'real price' of alcohol, consumption is rising and so are the social costs of alcohol misuse. Alcohol is a major contributor to health problems, family breakdown and law and order problems.

**3.3.9** Most children have tried alcoholic drinks before they enter their teens. The age at which drinking starts is decreasing and the amounts consumed are increasing[25]. Young people may be particularly susceptible to the detrimental effects of consuming alcohol and to long-term health risks. Alcohol affects them more quickly as they are lighter in weight then the average adult. When drinking without supervision they can be exposed to the dangers of experimentation with potentially harmful consequences[26]. For example:

- about 1,000 children under 15 are admitted to hospital each year with acute alcohol poisoning[27]. Some of these are experimenting with alcohol and some are children who have gained access to bottles accidentally. Few parents take as much trouble to keep alcohol out of the reach of children as they do medicines. The most common problems faced by children drinking excess alcohol are cuts, fractures, head injuries and hypothermia. Many need emergency treatment and intensive care;

- alcohol consumption is also a major contributor to road accidents. As young people's tolerance to alcohol is generally lower than adults, drinking begins to affect their judgement and reactions before they reach the legal limit and this, combined with their relative inexperience as drivers, adds to the danger[28]. 30% of young people aged 16-19 years killed in road accidents in the UK have blood alcohol concentrations over the legal limit[29];

- convictions for drunkenness amongst young people have shown a dramatic rise[30]. The rate of findings of guilt or cautions for drunkenness reaches its peak at about 18[31]. Amongst 17 year-olds the rate is slightly lower but still higher than for those over 21. There is also a strong link between intoxication and certain crimes of violence and disorder in which young men, in particular, are implicated;

- for a minority of young people, drinking to excess is an established habit and causes significant and sometimes very serious problems[32].

**3.3.10** Many children are also affected by adults, in particular their parents, drinking excessively. Children of problem drinkers may develop social, educational, emotional and relationship problems[33] [34]. Children and young people experiencing problems because of a parent's or guardian's use of alcohol or because of their own use, need help and support. Many organisations specialising in alcohol problems tend to develop with only the adult problem drinker in mind. With the required funding, many of these organisations could ensure that services exist to which these children could refer themselves or be referred.

## ACTION REQUIRED FOR COMPLIANCE

**Compliance with Article 3.2, the duty to ensure that children have adequate protection to safeguard their right to health from the dangers of alcohol, requires that:**

- **schools should be encouraged to provide alcohol education programmes which emphasise informed decision-making and life skills and enable young people to make positive and healthy choices about their behaviour;**

- **children and young people should be involved in the design of alcohol education programmes aimed at their peers;**

- **there should be stricter enforcement of the laws relating to the sale of alcohol to young people;**

- **services should be provided for children and young people seeking help or information with regard to their own use of alcohol or because of problems experienced as a result of the drinking problems of a close person.**

*The illicit use of drugs*

**3.3.11** In addition to its responsibilities under Article 3.2, the duty to ensure the protection of children and young people, Article 33 places a duty on the Government to '*take all appropriate measures, including legislative, administrative, social and educational measures, to protect children from the illicit use of narcotic drugs and psychotropic substances ... and to prevent the use of children in the illicit production and trafficking of such substances*'. Within the Government the Home Office, the Department for Education and the Department of Health are all involved in tackling drug abuse amongst young people but there is little evidence of a co-ordinated strategy between these departments[35].

**3.3.12** Between 1989 and 1992 the numbers of young people admitting to having used illegal drugs almost doubled from 15% - 29%. The relatively stable youth drug use patterns of the mid 1980s have changed dramatically in the early 1990s with the increased use of established drugs such as cannabis, solvents, amphetamines and magic mushrooms and an upsurge in the use of ecstasy and LSD[36]. A more widespread problem than hard drug use is solvent abuse. Between 1988 and 1990, 398 people, most of them in their teens, died from causes related to solvent abuse; mostly from spraying butane down their throats. The main users are between eight and 17 years old[37].

**3.3.13** Other surveys have shown similar results relating to increased drug use. In 1992 it was estimated that approximately one in seven school leavers had tried cannabis and one in 12 had tried solvents. About 5-7% of 15 and 16 year-olds are estimated to have tried hallucinogenic and stimulant drugs whilst 1% have tried cocaine or heroin. However, these averages cover wide differences in different areas and schools. One study in England showed that, amongst children of the same age and sex, the proportion of children admitting to having been offered heroine ranged from less than 7% in one school to over 30% in another. Similarly, in Scotland, in one school 57% of children admitted to having used illegal drugs whilst in another only 8% did[38]. In 1992 71% of 16 year-olds in co-educational schools in Greater Manchester and Merseyside had been offered illicit drugs of whom 47% had tried them. Between a quarter and a third of the young people surveyed were described as 'drugs users' rather that 'triers'. An important finding was the close link between alcohol consumption and drug use and 'weekly drinkers' were far more likely to have been in situations where drugs were on offer than less regular drinkers. 40% of the weekly drinkers had used a drug in the last month whilst only 4% of non-drinkers had. Young people in schools in relatively well off suburban areas were less likely to have been offered or tried these drugs[39].

**3.3.14** Although ecstasy is not widely believed to be addictive there have been deaths associated with its use. Seven deaths involving the use of ecstasy, reported in 1992, were caused by a combination of the drug and the rave environment in which it tends to be used. The problems can also be compounded by the fact that drinks are not always available or are very expensive. In some clubs water in the washroom taps is disconnected, people are searched for drinks on their way in and high prices are charged for drinks of water at the bar. There are also potential dangers arising from sales of polluted drugs. Cases of dog worming tablets and heroin being sold as ecstasy have been reported[40].

**3.3.15** Despite recent wide publicity given to changing patterns and increasing drug and solvent use amongst young people there is little evidence that this is being matched by increases in suitable services. In most parts of the country there are virtually no services for young drug users. Most established services tend to provide for young people on an ad hoc basis, or as an add-on to adult services[41]. Considerable resources were put into drug prevention and support programmes in the 1980s but the services established were primarily directed towards long term opiate users and injectors, mostly over 20 years old. Drug services for adults mushroomed during the 1980s as a result of heroin 'epidemics' and fears about the spread of HIV infection. These programmes tended to have a 'non-medical' approach with flexibility and innovation. This type of approach must continue if new programmes to face new problems are to be effective. Recent increases in the numbers of young people using drugs and in the variety of drugs they are using suggests that the drug services of the future must be flexible and those involved have knowledge about a wider range of drug related problems[42].

> '*You should have the right to take risks but based on accurate information of those risks.*'
> (17 year-old Shropshire)

**3.3.16** In schools the new wave of drug use amongst young people is coinciding with a considerably reduced commitment to drug education. Specific funding, within the Education Support Grant from central Government to local education authorities, for health education co-ordinators, was abolished in March 1993. The funding of the posts was put at the discretion of the local authorities[43]. Over the same time Government policy has been to de-prioritise spending on health education in favour of education reforms and measures to reduce truancy. One researcher commenting on the abolition of ring-fenced money for health education coordinators described that decision as 'a further sign of a government totally out of touch with the realities of contemporary youth'[44].

**3.3.17** Drug education in schools is also being affected by devolution of power and budgeting to individual schools resulting, in many areas, in advisory teachers having to sell their services to individual schools. It has also suffered as a result of the pressures of the National Curriculum. Drug education is one of nine elements in the non-statutory guidance to schools on health education. Pressure to concentrate on the National Curriculum, and on examination results, has helped to push drug education down the agenda to the extent that it may not be dealt with as a topic on its own but dissipated across the statutory curriculum.

**3.3.18** There appear to be fears in some schools that highlighting drugs in the health education curriculum could conflict with attempts to create a 'drug free' image in order to attract pupils and therefore funding. This fear may have contributed to the rapid increase in the numbers of young people being excluded from school because of drug use. One factor underlying this increase is thought to be the need to present an 'attractive face' in school league tables. Drug agencies have had increasing numbers of calls from young people excluded from school for drug use or for being with others using drugs and not reporting it. Stamping down on any hint of drug use on their premises is one way schools hope to send a strong 'no drugs' message to students and prevent the development of more serious incidents[45].

> *'We don't receive drug education in school, we get it from Brookside.'*
> (14 year-old, Manchester)

**3.3.19** Where there is drugs education in schools it often takes the form of one-off assemblies held by visiting Drugs Services. However, in a more progressive manner one school in East Anglia developed close links with the local NHS Community Alcohol and Drugs Service. This resulted in an informal, confidential drop-in service in the school and close links between the teachers of social and personal education and the Service. Issues raised by the young people in the confidential sessions centred on substance-related harm, including information in particular about poppers, cannabis, alcohol and nicotine; relationships and sexual health, in particular HIV and AIDS. Anecdotal evidence suggested that information from the Service had also been passed around among friends[46]. Schools need co-ordinated drugs policies worked out with the students, the staff, local drug education and support agencies and the local police[47].

> *'They might do it in the fourth or fifth year but we need it now in the first year because somebody may come up to you and say do you want this and you would not have a clue about what it is, we don't even know what they look like.'*
> (11 year-old, Lincolnshire)

**3.3.20** Boredom, low self esteem and lack of positive routine all contribute to drug taking. The way forward in protecting children and young people from the illicit use of solvents, drugs and psychotropic substances is to adopt a long-term strategy of both prevention and harm reduction. Services need to be flexible, non-discriminatory, responsive and sensitive to the young person's needs. Treatment must involve offering drug users opportunities to overcome their fears, to gain in confidence, to learn trust and to recognise their full potential. Self-help groups, organised and run by users can help this process[48].

> *'If you are depressed at home you think oh well drugs will make me happy, it's a release from hassles that may be happening at home, in school or whatever.'*
> (17 year-old, N Ireland)

**ACTION REQUIRED FOR COMPLIANCE**

Compliance with Article 33, the duty to protect children and young people from the misuse of solvents, narcotics and psychotropic substances, requires that:

● in order for children and young people to have confidence in drugs services the rules of confidentiality should be clear from the outset and the circumstances under which confidentiality may be broken, if there are any, should be explained. Young people should be able to use the services knowing that they are safe from unwarranted intervention into their lives;

● resources should be concentrated in work aimed at stopping the move by individual young people from non-addictive to addictive substances in the early stages before full blown addictions are developed;

● there should be more broad-based community programmes aimed at tackling the root causes of solvent abuse;

● schools should provide more education relating to

solvent and drug abuse and should be encouraged to provide informal, confidential advice and drop-in centres, staffed by skilled workers from outside the school, to advise and answer the questions of their pupils.

## 3.4 Reducing infant and child mortality
(Article 24.2(a))

**3.4.1** Article 24.2(a) places on the State a duty to take appropriate measures to reduce infant and child mortality. Although the likelihood of a baby dying has dropped significantly over the last 15 years (the UK infant mortality rate - deaths of infants under one year-old per 1,000 live births - dropped from 17.9 in 1971 to 7.5 in 1991), UK infant mortality rates have declined more slowly than in some other countries. They are still high compared with France, Italy, Sweden, Hong Kong and Japan[49]. Also, the decrease has been much less amongst babies from inner-city, deprived areas than for babies in more affluent areas[50]. Infant and child mortality rates show marked differences based on income and social class. In the UK children of unskilled workers are twice as likely to die before their first birthday than those with parents who are professionals[51]. Increased income inequality in the UK in the 1980s has been accompanied by a widening in social class differences in infant mortality: the ratio between social classes V and I increased from 1.8 in 1978 to 2.0 in 1990[52]. The differences are even greater for children born outside marriage. Perinatal mortality rates are also higher amongst babies from some minority ethnic groups, in particular those born to Pakistani mothers[53].

**3.4.2** Acknowledgment of socio-economic differences in infant and perinatal mortality was made in the Green Paper *The health of the nation* but the Government has not set standards or targets for reductions in infant mortality rates in the White Paper for England which followed it. In Wales there is discussion of improving social support for 'high risk' women[54].

**3.4.3** One significant positive move was the setting up of the *Confidential Enquiry into Stillbirths and Deaths in Infancy (CESDI)* in 1991 to investigate the underlying reasons for regional and population group differences in perinatal and infant mortality rates. It cannot, however, as now set up, investigate the role of socioeconomic factors.

**ACTION REQUIRED FOR COMPLIANCE**

Compliance with Article 6, the right to life and 24.2(a), the duty to diminish infant and child mortality, requires that:

● the Government commissions necessary research to seek to determine the reasons behind current differences in perinatal and infant mortality rates between socio-economic groups, regions and ethnic groups, where these reasons are not known;

● in addition to continuing to seek overall reductions in infant mortality rates throughout the UK, the consistent differences between population groups must be addressed (also Article 2).

## 3.5 Provision of adequate nutritious food (Article 24.2(c))

**3.5.1** Article 24.2(c) makes it the responsibility of the Government to combat disease and malnutrition *'through the provision of adequate nutritious food ...'* and Article 27.3 states that the Government must take appropriate measures to assist parents and others responsible for the child by, in cases of need, providing material assistance and support programmes with regard to nutrition. Article 24.2(e) says it must also ensure that children and their parents have information about child health and nutrition and *'are supported in the basic use of [this] knowledge'*. Evidence suggests, however, that for many children and young people, the Government is failing in these duties.

*New-born babies*

**3.5.2** One important factor in the high incidence of perinatal mortality and morbidity amongst babies born to women with low incomes is thought to be the nutritional status of the mother. Research comparing the pregnancies of women living in an affluent area of inner London, with women living in a deprived area of inner London has found that women in the deprived area, who had smaller babies, also had considerably poorer diets, often because they could not afford to follow accepted dietary advice[55]. Evidence also shows that the incomes of women dependent on means-tested benefits are insufficient to meet the costs of a healthy diet for women who are pregnant[56]. Lone mothers are more likely to be living on low incomes and may be particularly at risk. Although free vitamins may be available for some the overall quality of their diet, including the calorific value, proportions of fat and sugar and amount of dietary fibre, is not improved by them.

*Babies and infants*

**3.5.3** It is widely acknowledged that breastfeeding is the best way to feed new-born babies and infants. But there are wide differences in the proportion of babies from different socio-economic groups who are breastfed. Babies born into disadvantaged families are less likely to be breastfed than their better-off peers despite the fact that many women are aware that breast-feeding is better for their babies. More than four times as many infants are breastfed at six weeks in social class I than in social class V[57]. Breast-feeding rates in Scotland are about three-quarters those in England and Wales.

**3.5.4** Article 24.2(e) makes it the duty of the Government to ensure that parents are given basic information and *'supported in the use of basic knowledge of ... the advantages of breastfeeding ...'*. One reason women do not breastfeed is the negative attitude often encountered when breast-feeding outside the home. Mothers often feel intimidated and victimised when feeding in public places. Others include lack of support and appropriate information both for women who wish to breastfeed and for the wider public.

**3.5.5** During the late 1980s a number of health authorities developed infant feeding policies which positively discouraged the use of leaflets provided by companies producing formula baby milks. In 1990 the Department of Health issued guidance that no sample of or advertising for first milk should be given to women leaving hospital but that follow-on milks could. Many mothers, therefore, still leave hospital not only with leaflets but also free formula milk. At clinics leaflets advertising baby milks are freely available and magazines aimed at mothers of young babies contain many baby milk advertisements. So, whilst receiving information from nurses and midwives about the positive advantages of breastfeeding, women are also given tacit encouragement to use formula milks.

**3.5.6** The Government has set up a national working group to help identify and implement action to increase the proportion of infants who are breastfed both at birth and at six weeks[58]. Also UNICEF has recently introduced the 'baby-friendly' initiative. The objectives of this programme are to encourage hospitals and maternity facilities adopt their 'Ten Steps to Successful Breastfeeding'. The programme gives hospitals assessment criteria to ensure that they are doing everything they possibly can to encourage breastfeeding amongst women in their care[59].

*Children's eating habits*

**3.5.7** Despite vigorous nutrition education over the last 15 years the eating habits of children and young people, whose diets were already deficient in the important nutrients, deteriorated during the 1980s[60]. Improvements in dental health of children observed in the 1970s and early 1980s appeared to have levelled off by the mid to late 1980s and there is also evidence to suggest that obesity among children may have increased[61]. A recent report by the National Food Alliance shows clear evidence of the strong influence on children's diets of food advertising which concentrates on products high in fat and sugar and with a low nutrient density[62].

**3.5.8** Many families on a low income have difficulty in buying sufficient food to feed their children in accordance with nutritional standards approved by the Government[63]. In one study, one in 10 children had gone without a meal at some time during the previous month because of lack of money, and very few of the children, whose families were mainly living on income support, ate fruit and/or vegetables on a regular basis[64]. Fruit and vegetables are important components of a diet to promote health and prevent ill-health.

**3.5.9** Children in families on income support are entitled to free school meals, milk and vitamins. However, children in other families with a low income have no such entitlement[65]. Good quality school meals are not only an important source of nutrition for children from families with a low income, they are an important nutrition education tool. Improving the nutritional quality of school meals, and making them attractive to children and young people, improves the nutritional quality of the food eaten outside the school[66]. Government policy since 1980, which has abolished price controls and nutritional standards for school meals, removed statutory provision except for children on income support, and reduced eligibility for free school meals, has resulted in a decline in the school meals service - both in the number of children and young people eating school meals and in the quality of the meals provided. In 1992 a coalition of expert groups and individuals formed the *School Meals Campaign* which published nutritional guidelines for school meals agreed by a group of some of the UK's leading nutrition, child health and catering experts. Article 3.3 states that *'institutions, services and facilities responsible for the care or protection of children shall conform with the standards established by competent authorities, particularly [in relation to] health ...'*.

Clearly, these standards have been set by '*competent authorities*' but the Government has consistently refused to introduce compulsory nutritional standards for school meals.

**Compliance with Articles 24.2(c) and 27.3, the right to an adequate nutritious diet, requires that:**

- **means tested benefit levels should be adequate to ensure that all families are able to afford diets for their children which meet appropriate nutritional standards;**

- **the Government should actively promote, through bodies responsible for health education, health authorities and trusts and health professionals, the advantages to children of breastfeeding, and provide active support for mothers who breastfeed (also Article 24.2(e));**

- **education legislation should be amended to ensure that school meals of agreed nutritional standards are available in all maintained schools for children and young people who want them. The free provision of such meals should be extended once more to all children and young people in families with a low income.**

- **planning requirements should ensure that all new public buildings provide suitable facilities for breast-feeding mothers. Guidelines should be issued by the Department of the Environment to encourage those managing existing public buildings to make suitable provision (also Article 24.2(e);**

- **purchasers of health care should ensure adequate provision of enough, appropriately trained staff to support women in breastfeeding, especially in the early days and when at home;**

## 3.6 Provision of clean drinking water and a safe environment
(Article 24.2(c))

3.6.1 Article 24.2.(c) states that States must take appropriate measures to combat disease and malnutrition through the provision of clean drinking water and take account of the dangers of environmental pollution. These issues are discussed fully in **UK Agenda Reports 6 on the environment**, page139 **and 4 on standard of living,** page 82.

# 4 Preventive health services

## 4.1 The right to express an opinion
(Article 12)

4.1.1 Article 12, the right of children and young people to express their own opinions and to have those views '*given due weight in accordance with the age and maturity of the child*' has implications for the planning, provision and administration of all health services. It must also include the right of children to comment on services and if necessary complain about them.

4.1.2 There is little information or guidance on how to include the views of children and young people in any aspect of health services relating to them and much of the research conducted into 'consumer' views of care of children in hospital focuses exclusively on parents, with few direct interviews with children themselves. One researcher felt the need to point out 'of course, the real patients on a children's ward are the children themselves. A true patient satisfaction survey would have had to interview them'[67].

**Compliance with Article 12, the right of children and young people to be heard in planning health services which affect them, requires that their views are heard and they should be identified as specific groups within Department of Health guidance documents. Guidance on consulting with children and young people should be published and made widely available.**

## 4.2 Health information and support
(Article 24.2(e))

4.2.1 Children and young people and their parents need usable and accessible information in order to promote their own good health. Article 24.2(e) commits States Parties to ensuring that parents and children '*are informed, have access to education and are supported in the use of basic knowledge of child health and nutrition, the advantages of breastfeeding, hygiene and environmental sanitation and the prevention of accidents*'. The aim of health promotion activities, therefore, should be to support children and young people so that they are able to make informed choices about their own health and health needs. To meet the standards in the Convention, in particular Article 12, health promotion must address problems children and young people themselves define as important. It must involve effective participation of children and young people in problem-solving and decision-making and must be supported by public policy. In Scotland young people are particularly concerned about receiving more and better advice on contraception, HIV and drug issues. The Health Education Board for Scotland (HEBS), in its most recent plan, identifies several health education programmes, including community and schools programmes[68]. It is not clear to what extent HEBS will be consulting with young people on the issues which concern them, and the ways in which health education programmes could best be targeted.

> '*They explain it to you weird and use those big doctor words. They also ask you personal questions like how long have you been with your boyfriend and have you slept with him.*'
> (16 year-old, South Wales)

**4.2.2** Although there are separate, centralised, Government-funded bodies responsible for health education in England, Scotland, Wales and N Ireland, most local areas have health promotion or health education departments. One of their functions is to produce information about health promotion locally. Successful health promotion depends on co-ordination and multi-disciplinary teamwork but at present this approach is not universal. New alliances between health promotion departments and schools, for example, are emerging but to grow these must be properly funded and encouraged.

**4.2.3** Much health information is directed at encouraging children and young people to adopt healthy lifestyles, or urging them and their parents or carers to adopt safety measures. However, this information is not always appropriate, and there is often insufficient support available for parents to follow advice. For example:

- much information is directed at white British families without financial problems and fails to take account of the circumstances in which people with different cultural backgrounds or low incomes may live;

- educational information about food and nutrition is often provided free to schools by the food industry which has a vested interest in promoting its own products and does not necessarily give unbiased information;

- very little information for pregnant women and new mothers is produced for young mothers and most materials are unsuitable for these young women - both in the information provided and the format in which it is presented;

- whilst most people are aware of the basic principles of hygiene and sanitation, families living in bed and breakfast hotels and young people living on the streets often have difficulty practising even the most basic hygiene;

- many people in disadvantaged areas, where accident rates to children are relatively high, know the potential dangers and understand the basic principles of safe behaviour and the need for safety equipment, but do not have the money to buy it;

- there is a lack of health promotion material for young people who are HIV positive. These young people may also be isolated from contact with mainstream health promotion services. Young gay men may be particularly at risk and particularly isolated. HIV prevention is almost exclusively targeted at the 'assumed to be negative' population;

- there is very little guidance for parents regarding HIV/AIDS and nothing coming from the Government.

**4.2.4** Article 30 highlights the right of children and young people '*to use his or her own language*'. This is of importance in Wales, for example, and means that health care staff who are not Welsh speaking may need extra training so that they are able to communicate with children whose first language is Welsh. Many children and their families in Wales have difficulty in getting services such as speech therapy and health visiting in the medium of the Welsh language. They are often under pressure to accept services in English to the extent that there has been pressure on some families to change the home language from Welsh to English. Compliance with the Convention requires that provision and design of appropriate services in Wales, through the medium of the Welsh

language, must be actively promoted, encouraged and facilitated.

**4.2.5** There is little health information throughout the UK for those who do not speak or read English. General practitioners setting contracts for care are now reminded in guidance from the Department of Health of the importance of providing interpretation services, leaflets and appropriate language facilities. Community nurses also have to take into account cultural beliefs when discussing care and provision for children and their families[69]. There is also similar guidance in *The welfare of children and young people in hospital* for those purchasing and providing hospital services[70].

**4.2.6** Despite guidance, practice and provision vary widely. Some hospitals have very good teams specialising in local community languages while others have no provision at all. A study by Action for Sick Children *Health for all our children* of 22 multi-racial health districts in the Midlands found that only 9 of the 17 districts who responded provided an interpreting service. When paid interpreting services do exist parents are not always informed about them. Hospital staff may not be aware of the availability of the service, and inadequate and uncertain funding may result in insufficient interpreters being employed. Also, problems can arise where provision is ad hoc and supplied by volunteers. Untrained support workers may cause distress unknowingly, for example if they try to save parents from the pain and shock of serious information by not telling them the whole truth[71]. Children are still sometimes used by health professionals as interpreters for other family members. This may keep children away from school, raise issues of confidentiality and accuracy and cause them embarrassment.

### ACTION REQUIRED FOR COMPLIANCE

**Compliance with Article 24.2(e), the right of children and young people and their parents and carers, to information about health and to support in the use of that information, requires that:**

- **children and young people should be involved in the design and implementation of health promotion programmes, which should include issues identified as important by them (also Article 12);**

- **health education and promotion programmes should take account of different communication needs of different groups of children and young people. In Wales health information should always be available in a bilingual format (also Articles 30 and 17(d));**

- **safety information and advice should be drawn up in conjunction with the people whom it is designed to help to ensure that it is useful and relevant to their way of life and to their social and economic circumstances;**

- **the Nutrition Task Force set up by the Department of Health as part of its Health of the Nation initiative should develop guidelines for the production of health information for schools by industries with vested interests;**

- **the information needs of children and young people who are HIV positive or affected by HIV/AIDS should be seen as a priority by those health promotion units not already doing so.**

## 4.3 Development of preventive health care services (Article 24.2(f))

**4.3.1** In pursuing full implementation of Article 24.1, the right to '*the enjoyment of the highest attainable standard of health*', Article 24.2(f) states that the Government must take appropriate measures to '*develop preventive health care [and] guidance for parents*'. In the UK this provision takes the form of immunisation programmes and health surveillance.

### Immunisation

**4.3.2** On the whole immunisation programmes in the UK have been successful but there are still some groups of children who consistently miss out. In 1990 uptake of immunisation, in England and Wales, against diphtheria, polio and tetanus was 93%, for measles, mumps and rubella 90%, and for whooping cough 88%. However, these averages mask the fact that in some districts rates are as low as 61%. These were more deprived inner city districts which tend to have more highly mobile populations, more families in temporary accommodation and often inadequately resourced primary care services[72].

**4.3.3** The Department of Health guidelines discuss immunisation policy for the administration of BCG vaccine to prevent tuberculosis[73]. However, despite this, and the rising rates of tuberculosis in some inner city areas, there seems to be a reluctance by some purchaser and provider units to comply[74].

### Health surveillance

**4.3.4** One of the foundations of preventive health care for children in the UK is Child Health Surveillance (CHS) which involves individual screening, assessment and health promotion. It is designed to monitor the physical, social and emotional health and development of children, to promote health and prevent disease by, for example, health education and, where necessary, intervention can be offered and arranged[75]. Government guidelines to purchasers (commissioners) of health care, Family Health Service Authorities (FHSAs) and Directly Managed Units (DMUs) in May 1992 recommend a 'core programme' for CHS of medical examinations, health education and identification of children who may be defined as 'in need' under section 17 of the Children Act 1989. Specific payments for CHS are available to GPs as part of their NHS contract.

**4.3.5** Guidelines and standards for CHS are relatively new and there has been little monitoring of the way in which it is conducted or evaluation of its effectiveness as a tool for improving the overall health of children in the UK. This is important because whilst there are clear benefits from early detection of health problems, health screening may subject children to more routine intrusive examinations than they would have at any other age and might be construed as a breach of the child's rights to physical integrity[76]. It is, therefore, particularly important to differentiate between avoidable intrusions into the child's life and necessary monitoring to detect potential health problems which can be prevented.

**4.3.6** Recent monitoring of implementation of section 17 of the Children Act 1989 amongst local authorities, shows wide variations in the definition of 'in need', often depending on availability of resources rather than actual need. In a study of 60 local authorities only 23 identified children with special

health needs as a group automatically requiring extra services. 19 acknowledged the special needs of children and young people involved in drug and solvent abuse and only 21 defined children at risk of HIV/AIDS in their group with priority needs[77]. The implication of this is that health professionals involved in CHS and in identifying children 'in need' may be working to different standards and definitions depending on the resources available to the local authority. If this is the case children with similar health status will be receiving differing amounts of support and services, depending on where they live. This would be in contravention of Article 2 and the right not be discriminated against on any grounds.

### The school health service

**4.3.7** As children enter school the school health service becomes involved in preventive health care. School nurses, where they are appointed, are involved health promotion and screening children for health problems. In 1976 the Court Report and its subsequent review recommended that every school should have a named nurse[78]. However, over recent years there have been major cuts in the school nursing services. In a survey carried out by the Royal College of Nursing (RCN) in 1992, 61% of the nurses responding said there had been cuts in services or changes which affected the quality of care being delivered by them. In some areas school nurses were being appointed on reduced hours or lower grades and there was no training available for some new school nurses[79].

**4.3.8** School nurses can play an important part in providing a school health profile as well as carrying out individual health care interviews with children and young people. In the RCN survey only half of the school nurses were involved in school health profiling while 80% were involved in health care interviews. The report recommended that the school nursing service be increased and case loads reduced.

**4.3.9** School nurses can play an important part in supporting disabled children and their teachers. Article 23 states that assistance for disabled children should be provided in a manner conducive to the child's achieving the fullest possible social integration and individual development. Evidence suggests that some teachers are unaware of the role of the school nurse and - as a result - do not use her for information about children with disabilities[80].

### The child's involvement

**4.3.10** Opportunities exist, in line with Article 12, the right of children and young people to express their views on any matter concerning them, for involving children in decisions about their own health care from an early age but these are not generally exploited. For example, in CHS there is no notion of the young child as an active participant in the process. The guidelines do not mention the right of children to express their own views about their health, or to have access to their own records. Similarly in the guidelines for training doctors to carry out CHS there is no mention of training in respect of eliciting the views of young children about their own health and health care[81]. The guidelines only stress the value of parent-held medical records. At present the involvement of children in health surveillance is as passive recipients. Steps should be taken to involve them more actively. Health professionals should be supplying children with comprehensive, comprehensible information as well as involving them in decisions about their own individual health needs.

**4.3.11** Hand-held records could be particularly valuable for children and young people in care, who tend to move between placements and often GPs. They would form a consistent, continuous record and help carers in their responsibilities towards the young person as well as promoting the participation of children and young people in their own health care.

## ACTION REQUIRED FOR COMPLIANCE

**Compliance with Article 24.2(f), the continued development of effective preventive health services and guidance for parents, requires that:**

● **Child Health Surveillance should only be carried out in the best interests of the child and should not impinge on the rights of the child to physical integrity and privacy. There should be regular monitoring of CHS programmes to ensure that they are always carried out to a high standard and that there is consistency throughout the country; regular monitoring of the programme is needed to ensure consistency and effectiveness;**

● **screening programmes, according to age, should be standardised across the country. This should be a Department of Health initiative and should be research-based;**

● **the important role of the school health service in providing a range of preventive health care services, with appropriate medical back-up, must be recognised by the Government and suitable guidelines issued. Guidelines should take account of the detailed consultation report on the school health service published by the British Paediatric Association**[82]**;**

● **the extension of patient held records to school-age children should be encouraged in all health districts and ways of involving young children in their health records should be explored. The training for all professionals involved in Child Health Surveillance (CHS) should ensure that they understand the importance of involving children in their own health and health care from an early age (also Article 12).**

## 4.4 Developing family planning education and services (Article 24.2(f))

**4.4.1** Appropriate, effective contraceptive and family planning information and sex education is vital to the health of children and young people. Article 24.2(f) requires governments to '*develop preventive health care, guidance for parents and family planning education and services*'. Effective family planning services for parents are vital for the health of their children but the fact that 20% of known conceptions, to women of all ages, end in abortion suggests that family planning services and advice may be inadequate. 31% of mothers of six month old babies say the pregnancy was not intended. Sterilisation is now the method of contraception for 25% of couples, but free sterilisation is no longer available in all health districts[83].

**4.4.2** Current family planning and contraceptive services and facilities do not appear to meet the needs of young people. The UK has a very high rate of teenage pregnancies compared with other European countries. The Chief Medical Officer of Health for England's report for 1990 showed that one in 15 young women between the ages of 15 and 19 became pregnant. The number of conceptions amongst girls aged 13 and 15 went up by 40% between 1980 and 1990 and had reached 10.1 per thousand girls in 1990. Amongst 15 to 19 year-olds the conception rate had increased by 17%. One in 54 young women between the ages of 14 and 19 had an abortion in 1990.

**4.4.3** Teenage mothers often have less appropriate information and social and economic support available to them than other mothers and there are few services designed specifically to meet their needs. This may be an important factor in the high rate of infant mortality and small-for-date babies born to these young women. *Children, teenagers and health - the key data* shows that babies born to teenage mothers are twice as likely to die in infancy as those born to women aged 25-29. In 1992 the Government acknowledged the problem of high conception rates amongst young women between the ages of 15 and 19 and in *The health of the nation* announced its target to halve the rate of conception amongst young women under 16 between 1989 and the year 2000.

**4.4.4** Countries with the lowest teenage pregnancy rates are those which have more liberal attitudes to sex, easily accessible contraceptive services for young people, and effective programmes of sex education[84]. Family planning services in the UK span primary health care and hospital and community services, and guidelines issued in January 1992 by the NHS Management Executive give advice on targeting services, information about services, sex education, and the particular needs of young people. GPs are advised to set up drop-in clinics for young people. The guidance also suggests that in organising contraceptive services for young people it might be helpful to make separate, less formal arrangements than for older age groups. It advises that staff working with young people should be experienced in dealing with young people and their problems[85].

*'My experience of going to the family planning clinic was that it was cold and unfriendly. The staff just made me feel like I shouldn't be there. When I went back for a new supply of pills I asked for condoms, because of AIDS, and they said to me "What do you want them for? You're on the pill".'*
(16 year-old, Lincolnshire)

**4.4.5** Until recently only 56% of health authorities provided a youth advisory service and 84% of these were scheduled only once a week. Some clinics refused to see those under 16 unless they were accompanied by a parent, even when there was a request for emergency contraception. Failure to publicise services as confidential deters many younger teenagers from seeking help until they have taken a risk[86]. However, in England, as part of the commitment to reduce teenage pregnancies made in *The health of the nation*, more resources have been put into contraceptive services for young people. In N Ireland, however, where the targets do not have the same status, there is little provision and little evidence of impending improvements.

**4.4.6** In direct conflict with the recent Government commitment to reduce teenage pregnancies, and the comment of one minister that an important factor in the high level of teenage pregnancies '... must be our British reluctance to talk about sex' is the recent legislation and guidance on sex education in schools[87]. To be effective sex education must start at a very early age. Many children begin their active sex lives in their early teens and most young people do not use condoms the first time they have sexual intercourse[88]. Many continue to take risks with their sexual behaviour and many are generally misinformed about AIDS[89]. Calls to Childline from children about HIV and AIDS doubled in 1991 and they received over 4,000 calls from teenage girls who were having unprotected and unsafe sex[90]. One recent study has shown that about 30% of young people now have sex before the age of 16, and they continue to put themselves at risk of HIV[91]. Many young people feel that sex education in schools is too little too late.

> *'Our school has a condom machine but no sex education.'*
> (13 year-old, London)

**4.4.7** The Education Act 1993 diminishes the rights of children in England and Wales to receive sex education, apart from basic information about human development and reproduction. These restrictions are in conflict with Article 24.2(f)'s particular emphasis on developing preventative health care and family planning education. They also are in direct conflict with the Government's own health targets raises particular concerns over the lack of co-ordination in policy for children, and lack of consideration for the implications of the Convention. (See **UK Agenda Report 1 on personal freedoms,** page 9 for a detailed discussion of the law relating to sex education.)

**4.4.8** Experience in other countries shows that sex and HIV/ AIDS education do not promote earlier or increased sexual activity in young people, a widely held belief in the UK which has a powerful effect on Government policy towards sex education. In contrast, evidence shows that sex and AIDS education may lead to an increased use of safer sex practices and in some cases to later introduction to sexual activity[92]. Evidence from the UK shows similar results. A recent major survey of the sexual experiences of 19,000 people, carried out in 1990-91, found that those reporting formal teaching as their main source of information had the lowest rate of sexual activity under 16[93]. In the same study 70% of 16-24 year-olds felt that they did not know enough about sex when they had their first sexual experience.

**4.4.9** Careful training of teachers is required if there is to be good quality sex education about HIV/AIDS. Misunderstandings about the nature and transmission of HIV and AIDS results in those who are HIV positive being stigmatised if their condition is known. A recent survey showed that one fifth of 11 to 13 year-olds believe they would treat classmates who are HIV positive differently and most of them would avoid any physical contact[94]. The needs of children who are HIV positive, or are affected by HIV in family members, are generally neglected by mainstream health prevention programmes. The open discussion of HIV in the classroom may confuse or distress child who has been told not to discuss it with anyone but their parent. Teachers should be trained and resources made available to ensure that these situations are approached sensitively, and recognition of these children's needs should be built into HIV education.

## ACTION REQUIRED FOR COMPLIANCE

Compliance with Article 24.2(f), the duty to provide family planning education and services, requires that:

● sex education in school, linked to the National Curriculum, should be available to all children and young people, and taught at an age when it will be of use to them and in a manner sensitive to their needs. Governors should not be responsible for deciding whether or not a school provides sex education. There should be special training for staff involved and parents should not have the right to withdraw their children. If parental right of withdrawal from sex education stands, then at the very least arrangements should be made to monitor the numbers and reasons for such withdrawal, with a view to reviewing the provision (also Articles 2, 3, and 13);

● teaching about HIV/AIDS and other sexually transmitted diseases, must be re-instated as a key part of any curricular activity about sex or health education;

● in planning contraceptive services for young people there should be confidential consultation with those for whom the service is provided. Their views should be a major factor in the design of services (also Article 12);

● in N Ireland contraceptive service for young people must be made more widely available (also Article 2);

● research should be carried out into why young people continue to practice unsafe sex in spite of the known health risks.

# 5 Children and young people affected by medical conditions

**5.1** The previous section of this report looked in detail at the implementation of Article 24.1 and the duty on the Government to '*recognize the right of the child to the highest attainable standard of health*' for all children and young people. There are, however, many children and young people whose general state of health is affected by long-term medical conditions and for whom extra facilities and services are required if they are to reach their 'highest attainable standard of health'.

## 5.2 Facilities for the treatment of mental illness (Article 24.1)

**5.2.1** In the late 1980s severe mental illness was estimated to affect 250,000 (2%) children under 16 in the UK[95]. Approximately 10,000 were thought to be suffering from psychotic illness, usually following the onset of puberty[96]. In all, two million children were estimated to be suffering mental ill-health, half of whom had moderate to severe problems. The reported incidence of children's mental health problems is also increasing. The incidence of depression, suicide, and attempted suicide in children, and a number of other problems such as eating disorders including both anorexia and obesity, have all increased[97][98]. Higher numbers of young men are committing suicide but there is little investigation into the reasons why[99]. In the last 40 years suicide rates amongst people under 25 have increased steadily[100]. Yet studies show that GPs identify psychiatric disturbances in only 2% of children attending surgeries when up to 23% are believed to be affected[101].

> '*For children who have been abused there should be a lot more help to get them through it, you need counselling, it's important to let everything out.*'
> (17 year-old, London)

**5.2.2** The provision of services for these children and young people is inadequate and they are disadvantaged in medical terms because mental health budgets are disproportionately small compared with resources allocated for physical health and because less than 5% of the total mental health budget is spent on units for children and young people, in spite of the fact that they form 20-25% of the population[102].

> '*In the care sector there should be counselling sessions, time given to individuals to off-load the stress and put it in a bin. Young people need to off-load instead of society making them suppress it and telling them to get on with life because you are an adult now. You need a chance to off load it rather than turn to violence or drugs or wrecking cars or getting pregnant or into prostitution. All these negative areas derive from being hurt and hateful inside, you should be able to use it all in a direct positive manner.*'
> (18 year-old, Merseyside)

**5.2.3** The rights of many young people diagnosed as suffering from mental illness and accepted into residential psychiatric care are not adequately respected. The Mental Health Act 1983 only gives protection in respect of treatment and compulsory detention to those who are formally 'sectioned' and since most young people are admitted into mental health institutions informally they are not protected

by the Act. Other childcare systems, such as the juvenile justice and social services are governed by legislation which sets out a series of procedures designed to give bench-marks for decision-making and to provide safeguards for the rights of parents and children. The same is not true of the psychiatric system, where such procedures are operated at the discretion of individual health authorities and professionals working in the field. In the absence of any legislative procedures which define the kind of behaviour requiring psychiatric admission, there is likely to be considerable variation between professionals in how they reach a decision.

**5.2.4** Department of Health statistics in 1986 indicated that more than 90% of young people were admitted to psychiatric care informally, by a parent or care authority. Informal patients do not have the same rights of appeal as a 'sectioned' person but, following the Gillick judgement, young people cannot be detained in hospital as informal patients against their will if they are judged to have 'sufficient understanding'. However, it is likely that many young people admitted into psychiatric care do not know this.

**5.2.5** Research by the Children's Society in 1991 found inadequate provision of services and lack of protection for young people diagnosed as having mental health problems[103]. It found:

- a lack of comprehensive data collection concerning young people's admissions to residential psychiatric care;
- unclear procedures for gaining access to information about psychiatric admissions amongst young people;
- lack of formal policies and guidelines setting out who should receive care and safeguarding the rights of parents and young people;
- lack of information about the extent of provision for residential psychiatric care;
- medical definitions of behavioural and emotional difficulties covering a wide range of conditions, from defiance and disobedience to sexual misconduct and delinquency;
- some young people finding themselves in residential psychiatric care due to lack of resources within social services or educational provision;
- some young people being discharged to residential special schools because mainstream schools were reluctant to accept those who have been in psychiatric care;
- some young people being admitted to adult psychiatric provision because no other residential places are available;
- admission to residential psychiatric care not always meeting the young person's other social and educational needs.

### ACTION REQUIRED FOR COMPLIANCE

**Compliance with Article 24.1, the right to the 'highest attainable standard of health' and the provision of appropriate 'facilities for the treatment of illness and rehabilitation of health' for children and young people diagnosed as suffering from mental ill health, requires that:**

- **better data collection systems relating to mental-ill health amongst young people must be instituted;**
- **the Department of Health should issue guidance**

which sets out criteria for admission to psychiatric care and provide safeguards for the rights of these young people. These should be as vigourous as those for other forms of residential care;

● the practice of placing young people in adult or non-psychiatric provision because of insufficient psychiatric resources needs to be addressed;

● the remit of the Mental Health Act Commission should be extended to cover children and young people admitted informally for treatment of mental illness.

## 5.3 Facilities and care for disabled children (Articles 24.1 and 23.3)

**5.3.1** In addition to the right to enjoy the '*highest attainable standard of health*' and access to health care services (Article 24.1) disabled children have should have access to services '*in a manner conducive to the child's achieving the fullest possible social integration and individual development ...*' (Article 23.3).

**5.3.2** The ability of disabled children to make full use of health care services is often restricted by physical and social barriers. In recognition of this there are new Government guidelines which discuss access for disabled children[104]. *The welfare of children and young people in hospital* also recognises that a child with disabilities who has to be admitted to hospital is more disadvantaged than others and need extra support and services. However, there is little monitoring of the implementation of either of these guidance documents and no record of how improvements are being implemented or whether sufficient resources are available.

**5.3.3** Services for children with disability span health, education and social services. It is essential that at senior management and service delivery level services are planned jointly by these agencies in co-ordination with parents and disability groups. But there is often a lack of appropriate co-ordination and services to achieve this. For example:

● there are major problems in obtaining specialist services for childhood disability as resources tend to be concentrated on overall provision aimed at adults. Specialist paediatric services in the community tend not to be available;

● there is a major problem of rehabilitation after brain injury, both from head injuries and a wide range of other illnesses. A smooth transition from highly specialised acute units through to a community-based service is required and does not exist;

● lack of paediatric intensive care and fully supported paediatric neurosurgery limits the preventive role that acute services can provide for neurodisability. The health service should improve these services as well as services for children who are damaged as a result of such illness;

● there are several groups of conditions which constitute major chronic problems of childhood disability and require high quality multi-disciplinary services. But there is frequently a lack of integrated services at the point of delivery hampered by the lack of funding and training for all disciplines;

● lack of sufficient and appropriate respite care for disabled children sometimes means that the only place to go is a hospital, which is not suitable;

● monitoring and research into the effects of illness and disability within the family have tended to concentrate on medical and psychological issues which are of interest to clinicians. There is very little information or monitoring concerning quality of life issues which affect children.

**5.3.4** Despite these difficulties there are some existing integrated multidisciplinary community services for childhood disability which are a major resource and should be strengthened and expanded but disabled children have even greater difficulties at the point of transition to adult services which are often very poorly integrated.

### ACTION REQUIRED FOR COMPLIANCE

**Compliance with Articles 23 and 24.1, the right of children and young people with disabilities and learning difficulties to have the opportunity to enjoy the highest attainable standard of health and access to integrated health services, requires that:**

● **the principle of integrated services for disabled children should be built into health legislation and reflected in training and service provision;**

● **information about services must be made available in a way that is relevant and useful to disabled children and young people;**

● **implementation of section 17 of the Children Act should be carefully monitored to ensure that the needs of disabled children who suffer health disadvantage are met adequately.**

## 5.4 Facilities and care for those affected by inherited blood disorders (Article 24.1)

**5.4.1** The life chances of children and young people from some ethnic groups are particularly threatened by two major blood diseases - sickle cell anaemia and thalassaemia. Sickle cell anaemia primarily affects children and young people with Afro-Caribbean origins but some people from Mediterranean and Arabian communities may also suffer. Thalassaemia tends to be found in people with Mediterranean origins or whose origins are in the Indian sub-continent and the Middle East. Both conditions can be very debilitating, with painful symptoms, and fatal. Sickle 'crisis' is often related to cold or damp conditions, so affected children and young people who live in poor housing conditions are particularly at risk[105].

**5.4.2** Screening for carrier status of these conditions is possible before conception, during early pregnancy - followed by the offer of an abortion - or soon after birth. If a baby is found to carry either trait or is born with the disease, counselling for the child and the family are essential.

**5.4.3** As yet there is no co-ordinated policy for screening, genetic counselling advice, treatment, and information about the care and management of sickle cell disorders and thalassaemia, even though the incidence is probably higher than for some other conditions, such as phenylketonuria, where screening is well established[106]. Nationally, there are only 23 specialist centres to provide the counselling, information, support and advice needed. A study undertaken in January 1992 found that only 20 health authorities had specialist counsellors in post; in most of these areas the provision did not meet the need[107].

**5.4.4** Some children and young people with sickle cell anaemia or thalassaemia experience inadequate or inappropriate services. Lack of suitable services means that many of those affected have to attend attending accident and emergency departments at times of crisis. Widespread ignorance and lack of understanding in these departments about the nature of the pain result in the administration of inappropriate pain relief or in some circumstances, denial of pain relief. This happens in particular to teenage boys as stereotyping often results in their sense of judgement being questioned[108].

### ACTION REQUIRED FOR COMPLIANCE

**Compliance with Article 24.1, the right to the highest attainable standard of health for children and young people affected by inherited blood disorders, requires that:**

● **there must be universal policies to provide appropriate screening for haemaglobinopathies through the provision of more specialist centres;**

● **staff in accident and emergency departments should be given information and training to ensure that appropriate treatment and respect are offered (also Article 2).**

## 5.5 Facilities for intensive specialist care
(Article 6)

**5.5.1** Article 6 states that all children have the right to life and the Government has a duty to ensure '*to the maximum extent possible the survival and development of the child*'. Two per cent of new-born babies now receive intensive care, primarily because they are born prematurely. Evidence suggests that, because of higher levels of expertise and better resourcing, babies born before 28 weeks' gestation are most likely to survive if they are cared for in specialist neo-natal units rather than in units at general hospitals. There is also evidence, cited by the Audit Commission in its report *Children first* that the survival rate of children over four weeks of age, who require intensive care, may be up to four times greater in specialist units than in local district hospitals[109]. But there are differences in availability of both intensive care cots and appropriate specialist nursing and, in many areas, provision still falls well below the levels recommended by the British Paediatric Association and the British Association of Perinatal Medicine. A recent survey by the British Paediatric Association found that every children's intensive care unit in the UK reported having refused admission to critically ill children in the period 1991 -1992. The reason most commonly given for refusing admission was a shortage of both beds and nursing staff[110].

### ACTION REQUIRED FOR COMPLIANCE

**Compliance with Articles 6 and 24.1, the duty to ensure to the maximum extent possible the survival and development of the child, requires that babies needing specialised treatment throughout the UK have sufficiently local access to appropriately staffed and equipped children's intensive care units.**

## 5.6 Facilities and care for those affected by HIV/AIDS (Article 24.1)

**5.6.1** HIV and AIDS are an increasing threat to children and young people in the UK. A small but growing number of babies have acquired HIV from their mothers during pregnancy or childbirth. The instance of HIV among women in Britain grew by nearly 25% in 1991; 412 new reported cases brought the total to 2,079[111]. Anonymous testing in UK ante-natal clinics showed that 80% of HIV positive women were unaware that they were positive[112]. In *Children first* the Audit Commission cited studies in Europe suggest that the transmission rate from mother to baby during pregnancy is about one in seven, or 14%. There is also a group of older children who have been infected through blood products and some young people are becoming infected through unprotected sex and the shared use of needles for injected drugs[113].

**5.6.2** In addition to those children and young people who are HIV positive there is a growing number who are directly affected by the presence of HIV or AIDS in close family members, in particular their parents. Ensuring opportunities for all these children to enjoy the '*highest attainable standard of health*' (Article 24.1) requires specialised support and services. Planning without strategic reference to children's rights is a particular problem in relation to services for HIV/AIDS. Whilst Department of Health guidance exists for local authorities there is little guidance for those directly involved in health care services where the information needs may be different[114]. Much of the regular contact with children and families affected by HIV/AIDS takes place in hospitals or adult HIV or drugs agencies. Within the National Health Service discussion of services for children and young people who are HIV positive or are affected by HIV/AIDS tend to focus on the health rights of children only within medical services. It is important to try to develop and maintain a general children's rights perspective in the provision of services.

**5.6.3** A particular feature of HIV/AIDS is its unpredictable effects on more than one generation of a family. Service delivery to children and adults can be fragmented. The development of integrated family services such as family clinics, should be promoted to rectify this. Parents with AIDS often want to continue to care for their children, but need support to do so. At present there is insufficient support, and a particular shortage of day care facilities[115]. There is also an increasing need for supplementary care leading to permanent alternative care for children in families affected but the structures are not, as yet, in place to deal with this.

**5.6.4** The relatively small numbers of HIV positive children and the intense academic and media spotlight on them can lead to conflicts about confidentiality and informed consent. Safeguards should be in place to ensure that medical and research interventions are really in the best interests of the child concerned, and are not excessive or intrusive. There also needs to be some discussion about children's rights in the context of private and alternative therapies connected with HIV. There is little discussion and no guidance on this important issue. Whilst children should have access to the full range of health care available, alternative therapies are usually developed for adults and with their needs in mind.

**5.6.5** HIV positive children, particularly those in the older age group, may be living in vulnerable and isolated situations. It is not clear that their own health rights are being respected; for example, their access to ordinary health services such as dentistry, health promotion information, or to appropriate and useful information about HIV and its effects. There is considerable scope for bringing services for children and young people affected by HIV more into the mainstream of childcare provision; in particular, local authorities should be guided to include HIV positive children and those affected by HIV within their 'in need' categorisation under section 17 of the Children Act. Continued steps need to be taken to ensure that gaining access to children's services is not in itself stigmatising, by for example, more systematic funding of voluntary sector projects.

**5.6.6** The incidence of HIV/AIDS varies widely across the UK and there are four broad areas where HIV has distinctive effects; some inner London boroughs, other urban centres, the Lothian region of Scotland and non-urban areas of the UK as a whole. Each of these areas need a distinctive approach. Provision of information, advice, counselling and treatment also needs to take account of the particular linguistic and cultural characteristics of affected children and families but the pattern of service planning and provision does not reflect this at present.

**ACTION REQUIRED FOR COMPLIANCE**

**Compliance with Article 24.1, the duty to ensure access to medical treatment and the opportunity to reach the 'highest attainable standard of health' for children and young people affected by HIV/AIDS or who are HIV positive, requires that:**

- **the Government should take steps to promote a children's rights perspective in all care programmes for children affected by HIV/AIDS or who are HIV positive and should develop detailed guidance aimed at health authorities in line with that provided for local authorities;**

- **the same quality standards should be applied across the board where children are receiving this kind of service and in planning health services for all. Attention needs to be paid to geographical inequalities in the needs associated with HIV/AIDS across the UK;**

- **integrated family services such as family clinics should be developed to support these children and greater resources must be devoted to meeting the increasing need for supplementary care leading to permanent alternative care for children in families affected;**

- **services and information must take account of individual cultural and linguistic needs.**

## 5.7 Facilities and care for asthma sufferers (Article 24.1)

**5.7.1** The incidence of asthma amongst children and young people has increased rapidly in recent years and there is evidence which suggests that many of those affected may be inadvertently being denied their rights to appropriate medical treatment and, therefore, to their opportunities to achieve the 'highest attainable standard of health' (Article 24.1).

**5.7.2** A recent survey published by the National Asthma Campaign found that:

- one in four secondary school pupils did not have access to their own inhalers and, in the majority of these cases, inhalers were kept in locked cupboards;

- managing pupils asthma was a particular concern of 75% of school staff;

- only 7% of school staff claimed they knew a lot about asthma and 74% felt they wanted to know more[116].

See **UK Agenda Report 6 on the environment,** page 140 which contains a detailed discussion of the effects of environmental pollution on children's health, including the dramatic rise in the incidence of childhood asthma in recent years.

**ACTION REQUIRED FOR COMPLIANCE**

**Compliance with Article 24.1 to ensure the opportunity to reach the 'highest attainable standard of health' and have access to medical treatment for children and young people with asthma, requires that there should be better training available to school staff on the day to day care of children's health and that teachers and ancillary staff should liaise closely with school nurses.**

# 6 Care and treatment of illness

## 6.1 Background

**6.1.1** Children and young people have an independent right to *'facilities for the treatment of illness and rehabilitation of health'* and Article 24.1 states that States Parties shall strive to ensure that no child is deprived of his or her right of access to such health care services. To achieve this the Government must provide the *'necessary medical assistance and health care'* (Article 24.2(b)). States Parties also have a duty, under Article 3.3, to *'ensure that institutions, services and facilities responsible for the care or protection of children conform with standards established by competent authorities...'*. Those providing health care services have a duty to ensure that other related Articles are fully implemented (see para 2.2).

**6.1.2** According to the Audit Commission report *Children first* young people under 18 (about 1.27 million) are admitted to hospital in England and Wales each year. This represents about 16% of all in-patient admissions. The average length of stay is about two days[117]. For many children their first contact with a hospital is in the accident and emergency department. About one child in four attends an accident and emergency department in any one year. In the UK the aim of the health care services for most children and young people who are ill or require long-term care and support is for them to spend as short a time as possible in hospital and, where possible, to be cared for in their own home. This is in line with Article 24.2(b) and the Convention's emphasis on primary health care and prevention and Article 9, on minimum separation of children from parents. Good primary care can reduce the need for secondary care and there is evidence that secondary care is increasingly provided at home[118].

## 6.2 The welfare principle in health care provision (Article 3.1)

**6.2.1** One of the underlying principles of the Convention, Article 3.1, is the duty on all those taking decisions which affect children and young people to make *'the best interests of the child ... a primary consideration'*. Efficient, effective and child-centred services for sick children and young people depend as much on having a clear and consistent strategy for purchasing services as on having a strategy for delivering them. It is the role of purchasers of health care services to ensure that a comprehensive range of child-centred services is provided and properly co-ordinated.

**6.2.2** It is widely accepted that the best possible health care for children and young people involves well co-ordinated services between hospital, community and general practice. Co-ordination is important because it can help ensure that children and their families understand the role of the different services involved, know how to make the best use of available services, receive consistent information and experience continuity of care and services. Those involved in identifying need, planning provision, and placing contracts for children's health services are encouraged in *The welfare of children and young people in hospital* to provide a comprehensive, co-ordinated range of health services for children and young people. However the effects of competition between Directly Managed Units (DMUs) and Trusts for business may compromise the goal of co-ordinated services and one way of ensuring the well-being of children is to nominate key workers for individual children. Debates about the ways in which 'seamless' services are best provided must be informed by Article 3.1 and the need to ensure that *'the best interests of the child shall be a primary consideration'*.

**6.2.3** The welfare principle was an important consideration informing guidelines produced for the care of children in hospital by the National Association for the Welfare of Children in Hospital[119]. It also underpins *The welfare of children and young people in hospital*. Subsequent guidelines have also been produced by the Joint Working Party on Medical Services for children, which discussed purchasing responsibilities for staffing in the combined service in their unpublished report *Health for school children* and the Faculty of Public Health Medicine and the British Paediatric Association in their joint report *Together for tomorrow's children*.

**6.2.4** There is, therefore, no lack of guidance promoting the welfare principle in health care but the fact that it is guidance not legislation means there is no legal obligation for those providing health services to apply it. Although many purchasers acknowledge the existence of the guidance there is often no assessment of the extent to which standards are currently being met. Nor are there plans to monitor this in the future. Purchasing contracts may be drawn up by people who know very little about children and children's health. Few purchasing authorities have either clear strategies for children's services or plans to develop such strategies. Some purchasers do not classify children's services as a separate entity but include them under contracts for adult services, particularly for surgery. Another problem is that very few purchasers or providers are developing information systems which will allow them to draw up needs-based service plans. The Audit Commission found that, in general, child-focused quality specifications are rare. Whilst hospital managers are expected to audit their services the confidential nature of the audits mean that staff may not have access to them. The information will be made public only if the audit raises serious cause for concern. In monitoring contracts for their co-ordinated services for children and young people some purchasing authorities will find themselves unable to enforce required standards because they have not specified the information they will need in order to do so.

### ACTION REQUIRED FOR COMPLIANCE

**Compliance with Article 3.1, the duty to take account of the best interests of children, requires that:**

- **the welfare principle should be written into health service legislation;**

- **purchasing authorities should ensure that each provider from whom they purchase services has a written policy for the care of children and young people, and that the policy covers the principles set out in the Department of Health guidelines, *The welfare of children and young people in hospital*. Appropriate monitoring procedures should be in place. This includes monitoring the views of the children and young people as part of the process (also Article 12);**

- **all purchasing authorities should designate a senior officer, experienced in children's issues, to be responsible for purchasing all services for children.**

They should procure a child health service co-ordinated between primary and secondary care;

- when plans to reorganise services are being drawn up a primary consideration must always be the best interests of affected children and potential effects on their health rights (Articles 3, 6, 24);

- in meeting the needs of chronically ill children and young people, it may be necessary to appoint a 'key worker' for each child, responsible for ensuring co-ordination of agencies outside the NHS as well as those within it (also Articles 24.1 and 23).

## 6.3 Access to health care services
(Article 24.1)

**6.3.1** Article 24.1 places a duty on the Government to '*strive to ensure that no child is deprived of his or her right to ... health care services*'. Yet there are identifiable groups of children and young people and individuals who are have less access to health services than others. These include children whose health tends to be the worst. In general, poor families with high risk of poor health tend to be concentrated in those areas where many services, including health, education and social services, are under pressure. In the primary health care service there is no obligation on GPs or dental practitioners to accept any patient entitled to NHS treatment who does not require emergency care. The problems of access faced by different groups of children and young people vary. For example:

- many homeless or highly mobile families have problems registering with a GP and so continuity of care may be difficult; often records do not follow patients quickly enough to ensure suitable preventive care and many families depend on the accident and emergency departments of local hospitals for their primary health care[120]. Current reviews of hospital services recommend the closure of a number of district hospitals that provide accident and emergency services, which may well reduce some children's access to primary health care still further;

- children and young people looked after in the care system often have very interrupted health care. Equally those who are assessed as having health care requirements which are identified once they are being 'looked after' may find that the resources are available whilst they are being looked after, but no further help is given when they are return to their homes;

- the mobility, homelessness and poverty of young people living on the streets restricts their access to medical services and counselling which are available to the rest of the population[121];

- families living in rural areas have problems with access, especially if they do not have their own transport. In Scotland, one of the greatest concerns in relation to equal access to health services is for children and families in rural or isolated areas. In some areas, there is a clear lack of development of services, and this requires to be addressed by health boards whose areas include rural communities;

- Travelling families may be being moved on continually from one health district to another. The threat of enforced mobility puts an extra stress on pregnant women and those with new born babies. Evidence suggests that many GPs are unaware of the cultural issues involved and see Travellers as awkward patients who will not always make appropriate use of available services. Many have no access to previous health records, and this makes both consultation and continuity of care difficult[122];

- services for young mothers are inadequate and often inappropriate;

- some parents do not take their children for treatment or preventive services. This may be because, for example, parents without officially recognised immigration status fear that confidentiality may not be respected and that by visiting a doctor they may be reported to the immigration authorities;

- refugee children experience problems because of the lack of a health history as well as lack of resources to ensure adequate training for health professionals relating to the particular mental and physical health difficulties they may encounter;

- children and young people caring for their parents or other family members who are ill or disabled often have difficulty in communicating with and commanding the respect of health professionals. Parental ill-health and disadvantage also mitigate against children receiving appropriate services.

**6.3.2** For many children and young people from black and minority ethnic groups access to health care services is restricted because those services are inappropriate, hostile and do not meet their social and cultural needs. In the past the health services have failed many of these children and young people by taking a 'colour blind' approach to care and service delivery. The National Children Bureau's report *Charting child health services* shows that children from black and minority ethnic families have also been shown to suffer both direct and indirect racism within the NHS[123].

**6.3.3** Staff attitudes have an important impact on the use these families make of services. The research by Action for Sick Children published in *Health for all our children* found some parents felt that it was assumed by staff that they would not understand the information they were given. Some of the parents felt invisible, ignored and marginalised or - at worst - treated with contempt and condescension by hospital staff.

**6.3.4** Despite guidance in *The welfare of children and young people in hospital* that purchasers of health care and provider units need to be sensitive to the individual needs of children and families from minority groups of different ethnic, religious or cultural backgrounds there are many problems and evidence of non-compliance with the guidance. Action for Sick Children found that hospitals do not always ensure that they have culturally appropriate play and recreation facilities, washing facilities, food, education and respect for privacy. The report also highlights the lack of play and play equipment to reflecting the racial and cultural experience of children from black and minority ethnic families.

**6.3.5** There is often no recognition of the fact that young people from black and minority ethnic families may have differing needs from the indigenous white population. The visiting needs of families may differ and there may be a need for religious leaders to make visits and provide specialist services. Children from black and minority ethnic communities admitted to adult wards may be doubly disadvantaged. They are not only isolated from other children, but tend not to receive services which give any respect to their religion, culture and traditions.

**6.3.6** The Chief Medical Officer of Health, in his 1991 report on the state of public health, acknowledged that discrimination against people from black and minority ethnic groups exists both in the provision of services which are inappropriate or insensitive and through staff applying racist stereotypes. In March 1993 the Department of Health set up a new task force to improve the health of people from British black and minority ethnic communities. Its aim is to examine and record action at all levels to ensure the wide application of current best practice in the provision of health services for people from black and minority ethnic communities[124].

**6.3.7** In order for purchasing authorities to purchase services which fully meet the needs of their local population, the needs of black and minority ethnic children and young people in the community must be assessed accurately and then incorporated into service planning. However, care needs to be taken over how research is undertaken and interpreted, or further discrimination can occur. A recent review of the way in which ethnicity and race are included in health research has shown an inconsistency in the use of terms and the way in which they are included. There was a poor level of understanding amongst researchers of the underlying issues, inappropriate interpretation of results, and insufficient discussion of the importance of the results for the implications for services and for health. People from different black and minority groups were often grouped together inappropriately, resulting in the obscuring of information which might otherwise be important[125].

**6.3.8** When planning services which will enable and encourage access by children and young people from all the cultural and ethnic groups in a community, health authorities should look more closely at the need for advocates, link workers, translators and interpreters. One study of health advocacy in the inner London borough of Hackney showed that when women from local minority ethnic groups had advocates working with them prior to the birth of their baby and during post-natal care, the outcome of their pregnancy was better than that of women from similar ethnic groups who had no such support[126].

### ACTION REQUIRED FOR COMPLIANCE

**Compliance with Article 24.1, the right of access to health care services, in line with Article 2, the duty to ensure rights for all, requires that:**

- **purchasing authorities should be required to have written policies and targets to ensure access to services for all children and young people. Specific attention needs to be given to access to services for those who are disadvantaged;**

- **there must be careful monitoring of current changes in the structure of the health service to ensure that access to services for all children and young people is guaranteed;**

- **health authorities developing a framework to improve their services for children and young people from black and minority ethnic groups should look at their equal opportunities policy and acknowledge that equity should be an objective in purchasing services. Attempts should be made to ensure that the workforce, at all levels of planning,**

**management and care giving, is representative of the community served. All managers and staff should be trained in anti-racist practice as well as being given information about the culture, traditions, religions, language and lifestyles of people in the local population;**

- **purchasers and providers of health care must develop links with local communities to seek advice on the appropriateness and effectiveness of services required to meet particular needs;**

- **advocates, link workers and interpreters should have clear job descriptions, training, and proper determination of grades and salaries, and health service users should have direct access to their services (also Articles 30 and 17(d)).**

## 6.4 The right to be informed and express a view (Article 12)

**6.4.1** Article 12 insists that children and young people have the right to express their views freely in all matters affecting them, '*the views of the child being given due weight in accordance with age and maturity*'. It also states that children have a specific right to be heard in '*any judicial and administrative proceedings affecting the child*'.

**6.4.2** UK law is consistent with Article 12, to some extent, in relation to children's and young people's independent rights to consent and refuse consent to treatment, but the recognition is neither complete, nor consistent between England and Wales, Scotland and N Ireland.

> '*My pet hate is when doctors talk over my head to my parents. I'm the patient regardless of my age and they should talk directly to me.*'
> (15 year-old London)

**6.4.3** Throughout the UK the law gives young people aged 16 and over an independent right to consent to medical treatment. The Family Law Reform Act 1969, the Age of Majority Act (NI) 1969 and the Age of Legal Capacity (Scotland) Act 1991 all state that the consent of a young person of 16 or over for any surgical, medical or dental treatment, is adequate for the treatment to go ahead without necessarily obtaining the consent of their parents or carers. For those under 16 the situation is different. In Scottish law, under the 1991 Act, any child has the legal capacity to give his or her own consent to any medical procedure, if the medical practitioner considers the child to be capable of understanding the nature and possible consequences of the procedure. In England, Wales and N Ireland, the effect of the House of Lords decision in the Gillick case is that they have an independent right to consent if judged to have sufficient understanding. The judgment stated: 'The parental right to determine whether or not their minor child below the age of 16 years will have medical treatment terminates if and when the child achieves a sufficient understanding and intelligence to enable him or her to fully understand what is proposed'.

**6.4.4** However, a ruling from the Appeal Court in 1992, in the case of Re W (concerning a young woman suffering from anorexia nervosa) sought to distinguish between consent and refusal to consent to treatment[128]. As a result a competent child under the age of 18 who refuses treatment which a doctor considers necessary could be required to have that treatment against his/her will if any person with parental responsibility consents to that treatment. The judgment suggested that children and young people could be overruled if their decision would have 'irreparable consequences'. In the case of Re W the Master of the Rolls also commented on the rights of children and young people under 16. If the child refuses consent but the parents give consent, the decision should be left to the doctor.

**6.4.5** The Gillick judgment recognised children's growing right to self-determination by proposing that individual children and young people are assessed as to their competence to make decisions for themselves. The Re W ruling, although from a lower court, has put in question this principle of individual competence by suggesting that those with parental responsibility can overrule the child's **refusal** of treatment. The Department of Health acknowledged in 1993 that following Re W there is 'some confusion in respect of the capacity of competent children to make decisions for themselves', and that it should set out guidance on the legal position. As the Re W ruling does not apply in Scotland there is currently no authoritative legal ruling and the situation is unclear.

**6.4.6** Implementing Article 12 fully means that in assessing a child's competence to be involved in decisions about their medical care, his or her own views on competence must be considered. Children learn to care for themselves when encouraged to make choices from an early age, but competence develops unevenly depending on children's abilities, experience, confidence, and relationships with their parents. The ability of children to make decisions about their own treatment depends not only on their capacity, but also on how much they are informed and respected by adults involved. Research has shown that most 14 year-olds have the same level of competence as most adults to make decisions such as consent to treatment[129]. In one transplant unit a nursing sister who worked very closely with children said she felt that five year-old children, who had experienced serious chronic illness, were able to grasp the main issues and make informed decisions. The few children who seemed unable to understand the implications of treatment were those whose parents had not discussed with them how ill they were[130].

> *'When I was younger and had my first operation I don't remember my parents consulting me about whether I wanted the operation or not. My parents made all the decisions then but they have always tried to be honest with me and explained in detail why the operation was needed. When I was younger I took their advice and didn't argue. I know the operations I have had have always been necessary for my health and I accepted that they had to be done without really questioning why. However when I was 12 my consultant explained about the leg lengthening to me and I refused immediately. Later I discussed it with my mum and she said something as drastic as leg lengthening would have to be my decision but she would help whatever I decided. I thought it over and decided that I wasn't going to go through all that pain and discomfort just so that society in general would feel better about my size. I have not regretted my decision. Society in general should change to accept people of all types and respect everyone's right to make their own decisions once they have all the facts be they adults or children. If parents and professionals listen to children then they will know that they are ready to make decisions for themselves whether they are 7 or 17.'*
> (15 year-old, London)

**6.4.7** In order to make informed choices, children and young people may want or need access to their medical records. The Access to Health Records Act 1990 provides that, in general, anyone can have access to their medical records if they apply in writing. It also allows for restricted access by parents to their child's records if the child has asked specifically for confidentiality to be observed and the medical professional involved has agreed to this.

**6.4.8** Although access to medical records is important, children and young people need information about their care and treatment that they can understand. However, a recent study by Action for Sick Children of parents' experiences with hospitals showed clearly that parents do not receive adequate information about the care and services available to their children in hospital[131]. If parents are not receiving adequate information it is almost certain that children are not receiving it either. Often, when information is available, it is inappropriate and given in such a way that it is meaningless to the parents or child.

**6.4.9** Complaints procedures in the NHS have recently come under review, providing an ideal opportunity to ensure that there is adequate provision for children's and young people's complaints. For these procedures to be effective they must be widely publicised and easy to use[132].

## ACTION REQUIRED FOR COMPLIANCE

**Compliance with Article 12, the right participate in decisions about health and health care, requires that:**

- **the principle in Article 12 that children have a right to state their views and have them taken seriously, and to be heard in any judicial or administrative proceedings concerning them should be built into health legislation;**

- **there must be wide ranging consultation and debate with a view to statutory clarification of the rights of children and young people in relation to consent and refusal of medical treatment. Included within this debate must be an understanding of the rights of the child to confidentiality about their medical consultation being independent of their 'Gillick competence';**

- **there should be careful monitoring of guidance related to consultation with children and young people and the provision of appropriate information. Monitoring and research should canvass the views and ideas of children and young people themselves;**

- **the current review of complaints procedures should look specifically at the avenues for complaint by children and young people and, in conjunction with them, should draw up new, effective procedures, accessible to all children.**

## 6.5 The right to agreed standards of health care (Article 3.3)

**6.5.1** Article 3.3 states that institutions, services and facilities provided for the care of children must conform with standards established by competent authorities. Yet, despite the existence of wide-ranging guidelines with the potential for improving the rights of children and young people in the health services there is consistent evidence that these guidelines are not widely implemented or used as a basis for setting standards. The recent Audit Commission study *Children first* identified as the main problem the fact that clinicians, managers and other staff do not pay sufficient attention to the needs of children and their families. This underlines the need for consistent respect throughout the health service for the best interests principle in Article 3. The Audit Commission found that there were few written policies, no management focus, and poor communication between staff and parents. The response of the Government to the findings of the Audit Commission report gives major cause for concern. There is no commitment to supporting health authorities in improving provision or to increase monitoring or scrutiny of the use of guidelines[133].

**6.5.2** Examples of non-compliance with standards, indicating non-compliance with Article 3.3, identified by the Audit Commission and in other surveys, include the following:

- despite guidance that accident and emergency departments need specialist paediatric areas with staff with experience and knowledge of children and child health and special waiting facilities, a 1992 study of 174 hospitals found that 55% of out-patient departments and 43% of accident and emergency departments were caring for children in non-specialist paediatric areas[134]. This confirmed the findings of an earlier report from the British Paediatric Association and the British Association of Paediatric Surgeons[135];

- evidence from the British Paediatric Association in 1990, the National Confidential Enquiry into Peri-operative Deaths in 1989 and the Audit Commission in 1993 found that guidelines for staffing levels for paediatrician, surgeons, anaesthetists, nurses and play specialists are not being followed[136];

- the need for adequate paediatric community nursing care after early discharge from hospital has never been properly addressed. In 1959 the Platt Report, *The welfare of children in hospital*, recommended a rapid expansion in the community home nursing service. This did not happen and in 1976 the Court Report, *Fit for the future*, criticised the fact that Platt's recommendations had been ignored. Similar recommendations were also made in the Government guidance, *The welfare of children and young people in hospital* in 1991 and also by the Audit Commission in 1993. In recent years there has been an increase from the very low provision but still only one third of health authorities in England and Wales have a paediatric community nursing service[137]. The Audit Commission also found that the number of schemes involving children's nurses working in the community is very low and that adequate support is not always available. Another report *Bridging the gap* by Caring for Children in the Health Services and Action for Sick Children also found that even when schemes do exist there are often only one or two nurses available in each district[138]. As a result, some children remain in hospital unnecessarily whilst others are sent home without appropriate nursing care;

- despite guidance that where possible separate accommodation should be provided for adolescents, and children should not be treated on adult wards, only one in 10 of the hospitals visited by the Audit Commission had separate wards for adolescents, and 25% of all children under 16 are still being placed in adult wards. This is a particular problem in some surgical specialities,

for example ophthalmology and ear, nose and throat. The more recent study published by the British Paediatric Association *Care of critically ill children* found that in adult intensive care units looking after children only 2% of the nurses were qualified in the care of children and less than 1% had training in children's intensive care. Seven per cent of the adult units admitting children had no nurses with children's training;

- although there are guidelines aimed at ensuring a 'seamless' service between hospital and community care, there are many examples of confusion and lack of support and co-operation between professionals involved. Many of the problems are highlighted in *Bridging the gap* which describes discussions with sick children and their parents about their experiences of health care;

- there is evidence that financial restraints cause problems between local authorities and health authorities in the care of children[139]. This undermines the effectiveness of guidance designed to ensure the co-ordination of services by professionals in different parts of the NHS and in other statutory and voluntary agencies;

- *The welfare of children and young people in hospital* advises that all hospitals should aim to achieve improvements in the health and well-being of the children they serve, with the least possible stress and disruption to the children and their families. The full effect of treatment on the children (the outcomes) should be monitored to ensure that effective care is provided consistently, that shortcomings can be rectified, and that changing needs are catered for. However, the Audit Commission found that the outcomes of treating and caring for children were not monitored routinely, making it difficult to assess the effectiveness of those treatments;

- the Audit Commission found little attempt to comply with Government advice to ensure that information systems distinguish children and young people from other patients in order that the quality and outcome of their care and treatment can be evaluated against the relevant contractual requirements;

- guidelines say that purchasers of health care services should ensure that the quality standards in their specifications cover play provision, including the employment of qualified play staff[140]. *The welfare of children and young people in hospital* also states that hospitals should ensure that staff are not expected to do work which would be done more appropriately by people with other qualifications. Current provision of play staff is poor: the Audit Commission found that 30% of 34 wards surveyed had less than the equivalent of a half-time post allocated to a trained play staff member;

- one essential pre-requisite of quality care for children and young people with disabilities and learning difficulties is the collection of information for planning services. Special Conditions Registers (SCRs) - linked to the health surveillance register of all children - have been piloted in different parts of the country. Studies of these registers have emphasised the need for them to be comparable. But effective co-ordination is lacking among and between district health authorities developing the registers, the social services departments currently setting up registers of disabled children, and the general practitioners currently computerising their practice registers. A national policy on health information systems for children with special needs is needed urgently. Without this potential contribution to the continuity of care for individual children, and to planning and monitoring services at regional and national level, a valuable way of looking at the causes and treatment of unusual conditions will be lost[141];

● survival rates for most forms of childhood cancer are significantly higher if they are treated at paediatric oncology centres[142]. However, in a sample reported by the Audit Commission of 3,000 children diagnosed as having cancer between 1981 and 1984, 25% were not treated at such a centre.

6.5.3 If standards for health care are to be set and maintained monitoring is crucial. In the past, monitoring of NHS provision has been on the basis of 'inputs'; for example, the number of people seen, the number of treatments given and hours spent in consultation. More recently, however, there have been moves to monitor 'outcomes' including the effects of treatments and interventions. This latter type of monitoring in more in line with the spirit of the Convention.

6.5.4 In designing monitoring systems it is important that there is co-ordination nationally of both measurement and technique, so that realistic comparisons can be made. This will also allow for careful monitoring of the implementation of the Convention throughout the UK.

6.5.5 In Scotland the Clinical Resource and Audit Group (CRAG) has developed medical auditing. According to the Government's *Framework for action* CRAG will be extending its work to develop guidelines to help health service providers to establish local standards[143]. The Scottish Health Management Efficiency Group (SCOTMEG) has also played a role in looking at improved patient care. The Government has said CRAG and SCOTMEG will continue to look at how standards may be set and monitored. *Framework for action* says their priorities will be: mental illness; old age; maternity services; and accident and emergency services. In view of the Government's commitment to the Convention, it seems appropriate that it should ask CRAG and SCOTMEG to prioritise setting standards for children's health services.

### ACTION REQUIRED FOR COMPLIANCE

**Compliance with Article 3.3, the duty to ensure that standards of provision and care within the NHS meet those agreed by 'competent authorities', requires that:**

● **purchasers and providers should be under a legal obligation to provide care, services and facilities which meet agreed, basic standards;**

● **all staff involved in the care and treatment of children and young people should know what agreements and standards for best practice exist between the purchaser of care and the provider unit, and they should be given a copy of those that relate to their area of work;**

● **purchasers of health care should monitor the outcomes of treatment, especially on the quality of life of children and young people, to ensure that the best possible treatment is being offered, and that children and their parents are able to make informed choices as to the type of treatment they require ( also Articles 6, 12, 13);**

● **those purchasing health care should ensure that the most up-to-date information is included and that**

**there are procedures in each contract to monitor compliance. Data collection for monitoring the effectiveness of children health services should be standardised;**

● **in Scotland the Clinical Resource and Audit Group and the Scottish Health Management Efficiency Group should be asked to identify ways in which standards may be set and monitored in relation to services for children and young people and should see this as a priority.**

## 6.6 The right of children not to be separated from their parents or carers (Article 9)

*Children in hospital*

6.6.1 Article 9 stresses the right of children and young people not to be separated from their parents against their wishes or unless separation is necessary for the child's best interests, and Article 18.2 states that their parents have a right to '*appropriate assistance*' with their child-rearing responsibilities. *The welfare of children and young people in hospital* reinforces this, stating that one of the 'Cardinal Principles' is that 'Families with children have easy access to hospital facilities for children without needing to travel significantly further than to any other similar amenities' and that parents, carers and members of the immediate family should not be seen as visitors but should be encouraged and assisted to be with their child at all times unless that is against the interests of the child.

6.6.2 Although most hospitals provide some facilities for parents to stay overnight, these are often far from ideal. The Audit Commission in *Children first* found that in one hospital only 39% of parents were able to stay within 'dressing gown distance' of the ward. One third of wards surveyed had no facilities for parents to wash or shower, and there was no monitoring of parents' views of the facilities. These problems tended to be more acute for parents of children who were staying on adult wards.

6.6.3 *The welfare of children and young people in hospital* also states that no charge should be made to parents who are staying with their children in hospital. However, some hospitals do charge parents to stay. One example is Harefield hospital in Middlesex which allows parents of children undergoing major surgery to stay free in a flat by the children's ward in the post operative period, but does not provide free accommodation while the child is recovering. Parents and carers can stay in a hostel in the grounds for £15. Also, car parking fees are charged in many hospitals so it can be very expensive for someone who wants to stay all day with their child.

6.6.4 The question of whether charges should be made for services such as meals is left to each hospital, but the guidance suggests that parents and carers, whether or not they stay overnight, should be offered the benefit of any subsidised canteen meals. The importance for NHS trusts, in an internal market, to raise funds through surpluses may affect the provision of free or subsidised facilities. This should be carefully monitored and guidelines strengthened to ensure support for parents (Article 18.2) in caring for their sick children.

**6.6.5** For employed parents and carers there is no statutory right to time-off to be with a sick child and there have been cases reported of parents losing their job over having a child in hospital[144]. The UK Government blocked a EU directive which would have allowed for up to three months paid or unpaid leave in member countries, and said such arrangements had to be voluntary[145].

**6.6.6** For parents and carers with low incomes the cost of travel to visit their children in hospital may also lead to enforced separation. A survey in 1992 by Action for Sick Children of several hundred parents of children and young people in hospital revealed that 25% could not afford to visit the hospital as often as they wanted, 15% suffered financially as a result of visiting and 5% got into debt[146]. Families on income support can apply to the DSS Social Fund for a discretionary grant to cover their visiting costs, but many are refused and offered a loan instead. No help is available for other families on low incomes[147]. Centralisation of services for specialist care increases travelling distances for many people. A recent report recommending the amalgamation and closure of specialised units specifically refers to the 'financial burden on families of visiting costs' which will result. It recommends that these costs should be met in the negotiated contract for care between purchaser and provider[148].

**6.6.7** A Travel Cost scheme does exist to allow one parent to accompany a child to hospital for treatment however this does not cover the costs of visiting a child in hospital. *The welfare of children and young people in hospital* states that hospitals should ensure that the travel cost schemes are publicised and that families are advised about benefits that might be available to them. Extra support should be given to families in particularly difficult circumstances. At present the scheme is inadequate because it only covers the cost of one escort for the patient. There should be provision made to pay the costs of two escorts when there is a life-threatening condition, for example, if a child is having an out-patient appointment where both parents may have to be there to consider taking life-threatening decisions.

*Parents in hospital*
**6.6.8** Many children and young people have parents who are admitted to hospital for variable lengths of time. Earlier NHS guidelines advised hospitals to adopt a general policy of allowing children to visit their parents and other close relatives frequently and regularly if the patient wanted this[149]. However, this guidance was superceded by *The welfare of children and young people in hospital* which make no mention of the issue.

**ACTION REQUIRED FOR COMPLIANCE**

Compliance with Article 9, the right for children not to be separated from their parents or carers unless it is in their own best interests, requires that:

- **health care services must, wherever possible, be within easy travelling distance of children's homes; clinics must be timed so that working parents can bring their children; support must be available for parents with other children who need to be looked after; and there must be provision for parents with disabilities;**

- **financial assistance for travelling costs to escort or visit children in hospital should be reviewed in the light of Government guidance which recognises the importance of parents being with their children. A visiting costs scheme should be established to provide assistance to parents facing financial hardship as a result of visiting and the travel costs scheme should be broadened to allow for both parents to accompany a child to hospital;**

- **hospitals must ensure that there are subsidised meals in the canteen as well as access to ward kitchens for making tea and coffee on the ward for parents of sick children. Also, there should be no parking fees for parents or other similar additional costs.**

## 6.7 The right to education (Article 28)

**6.7.1** Articles 28 states that all children and young people have a right to education. Approximately 6% of children of compulsory school age enter hospital as in-patients each year. At present the provision of education for children in hospital or sick at home is patchy and variable. It can take from three days to three weeks before a child in hospital receives the services of a teacher. Few local education authorities (LEAs) have written policies referring to home tuition; standards of services vary; and many LEAs provide insufficient hours per child per week. The Government's own Her Majesty's Inspectorate (HMI) report, published in 1989, described some of the shortcomings. Qualifications vary, and teachers are often expected to work in noisy wards, with little storage space and meagre resources. They are isolated from other teachers and have little opportunity of updating their knowledge. The maximum number of hours offered per week was 10[150].

> *'I have had three operations since the age of seven, two on my legs which meant being in a hip-spike plaster for six weeks each time and my last operation which was my biggest, on my neck to fuse my skull and first two vertebrae together. The result of this was that I was in a halo plaster for six months and off school for a year.'*
> (15 year-old, London)

**6.7.2** Despite the fact that *The welfare of children and young people in hospital* gives clear advice about the provision of education for all sick children and young people the provision in law is inadequate. The Education Act 1993 places a duty on LEAs in England and Wales, from September 1994, to provide education to children unable to attend school. Section 298 of the Act says: 'Each local education authority shall make arrangements for provision of suitable full-time or part-time education at school or otherwise than at school for those children of compulsory school age who, by reason of illness, exclusion from school or otherwise, may not for any period receive suitable education unless such arrangements are made for them'. The Act does not apply to Scotland and N Ireland.

**6.7.3** In its present form the implementation of the legislation depends on the local education authority and the resources they are prepared to devote to education for these children. The ad hoc nature of provision is unacceptable and clear guidelines must be drawn up. The most important criteria for the children are flexibility and continuity. A major concern is that local authorities do not appear to be being given any extra resource to provide new services under the Act. The Education Reform Act 1988 puts hospitals under no obligation to provide the National Curriculum[151].

## ACTION REQUIRED FOR COMPLIANCE

Compliance with Article 28, the right to education, requires that:

● education legislation in Scotland and N Ireland should be amended to safeguard the right to education for children and young people unable to attend school;

● regulations issued under the Education Act 1993 must clarify details of the rights to education for children and young people unable to attend school for medical reasons;

● funding of education for sick children may need special protection to ensure that there is clear responsibility for provision on education or health services;

● purchasers commissioning health care for children at home should ensure that local authorities are involved in providing education for those children. Increasing attention should be paid to home tuition as the trend towards shorter stays in hospital grows. Linking home teachers with hospital teachers, enabling them to share resources or work with the same child whether in hospital or at home, should form part of the process;

● children and young people in hospital should be consulted about when a teacher comes to work with them and about how much tuition they should be given (also Article 12).

## 6.8  Review of treatment (Article 25)

6.8.1 Article 25 recognises the right of children to have any treatment or placement reviewed regularly. While there are detailed arrangements under the Children Act for social services departments in England and Wales to review regularly children who are being looked after or accommodated by them, there are no such arrangements for regular review of children in NHS or private hospitals.

6.8.2 The Children Act 1989 makes it the duty of English and Welsh health authorities to notify the local social services department of all children and young people in England and Wales who are in NHS or private hospital or institutional care for more than three months. The social services department then has an obligation under the Act to ensure that the child's welfare is being adequately safeguarded and promoted. But the obligation does not specify any duty to visit or review children regularly. At present there is no such provision in N Ireland but it would be in keeping with Article 25 if the draft Children (NI) Order 1993 were to include duties to ensure regular review of children in NHS and private health institutions.

## ACTION REQUIRED FOR COMPLIANCE

Compliance with Article 25 without discrimination requires that there should be legislative duties to ensure regular review of children in NHS and private health institutions, similar in form and frequency to those applying to children being looked after or accommodated by social services departments in England and Wales.

# Summary of action required for compliance

1 Compliance with Articles 6, the right to life and the duty to ensure, to the maximum extent possible the survival and development of the child and Article 24, the right to health and health care services, requires that health legislation throughout the UK should include duties to ensure, to the maximum extent possible, the survival and development of the child and a right of access to appropriate health care services. This would provide a clear and enforceable framework for full implementation of the basic health rights in the Convention.

**Underlying principles**

2 Compliance with Article 2, the duty to ensure rights for all with no discrimination and Article 24.1, the right of access to health care services, requires that:

● purchasing authorities should have written policies and targets to ensure access to services for all children and young people. Specific attention needs to be given to access to services for those who are disadvantaged;

● there must be careful monitoring of current changes in the structure of the health service to ensure that access to services for all children and young people is guaranteed;

● health authorities developing a framework to improve their services for children and young people from black and minority ethnic groups should look at their equal opportunities policy and acknowledge that equity should be an objective in purchasing services. Attempts should be made to ensure that the workforce, at all levels of planning, management and care giving, is representative of the community served. All managers and staff should be trained in anti-racist practice as well as being given information about the culture, traditions, religions, language and lifestyles of people in the local population;

● purchasers and providers of health care must develop links with local communities to seek advice on the appropriateness and effectiveness of services required to meet particular needs;

● advocates, link workers and interpreters should have clear job descriptions, training, and proper determination of grades and salaries, and health service users should have direct access to their services (also Articles 30 and 17(d));

● Government guidelines to health authorities on meeting the spiritual needs of patients and staff should be followed more closely and there should be careful monitoring on progress in implementing these guidelines[153] (also Article 14).

3 Compliance with Article 3.1, the duty to take account of the best interests of children and young people in the purchasing of health services, requires that:

● the welfare principle should be written into health service legislation;

● purchasing authorities should ensure that each provider from whom they purchase services has a written policy for the care of children and young people, and that the policy covers the principles set out in the Department of Health guidelines, *The welfare of children and young people in hospital.* Appropriate monitoring procedures should be in place. This includes monitoring the views of the children and young people as part of the process (also Article 12);

● all purchasing authorities should designate a senior officer, experienced in children's issues, to be responsible for purchasing all services for children. They should procure a child health service co-ordinated between primary and secondary care;

● when plans to reorganise services are being drawn up a primary consideration must always be the best interests of affected children and potential effects on their health rights;

● in meeting the needs of chronically ill children and young people, it may be necessary to appoint a 'key worker' for each child, responsible for ensuring co-ordination of agencies outside the NHS as well as those within it (also Articles 24.1 and 23).

4 Compliance with Article 12, the right to participate in decisions about health and health care, requires that:

● the principle in Article 12 that children have a right to state their views and have them taken seriously, and to be heard in any judicial or administrative proceedings concerning them should be built into health legislation;

● there must be wide ranging consultation and debate with a view to statutory clarification of the rights of children and young people in relation to consent and refusal of medical treatment. Included within this debate must be an understanding of the rights of the child to confidentiality about their medical consultation being independent of their 'Gillick competence';

● there should be careful monitoring of guidance related to consultation with children and young people and the provision of appropriate information. Monitoring and research should canvass the views and ideas of children and young people themselves;

● the current review of complaints procedures should look specifically at the avenues for complaint by children and young people and, in conjunction with them, should draw up new, effective procedures, accessible to all children;

● children and young people should be identified as specific groups within Department of Health guidance documents and their views on issues covered should be sought. Guidance on consulting with children and young people should be published and made widely available;

● the extension of patient held records to school-age children should be encouraged in all health districts and ways of involving young children in their health records should be explored. The training for all professionals involved in Child Health Surveillance (CHS) should ensure that they understand the importance of involving children in their own health and health care from an early age (also Article 24.2(f));

● in planning contraceptive services for young people there should be confidential consultation with those for whom the service is provided. Their views should be a major factor in the design of services (also Article 24.2(f));

● children and young people should be involved in the design and implementation of health promotion programmes, which should include issues identified as important by them (also Article 24.2(e));

● children and young people in hospital should be consulted about when a teacher comes to work with them and about how much tuition they should be given (also Article 28).

**Rights to health and development**

5 Compliance with Article 6, the right to life and 24.2(a), the duty to diminish infant and child mortality, requires that:

● the Government commissions necessary research to seek to determine the reasons behind current differences in perinatal and infant mortality rates between socio-economic groups, regions and ethnic groups, where these reasons are not known;

● in addition to continuing to seek overall reductions in infant mortality rates throughout the UK, the consistent differences between population groups must be addressed (also Article 2);

● babies needing specialised treatment throughout the UK have sufficiently local access to appropriately staffed and equipped children's intensive care units.

6 Compliance with Articles 24.2(c) and 27.3, the right to an adequate nutritious diet, requires that:

● means tested benefit levels should be adequate to ensure that all families are able to afford diets for their children which meet appropriate nutritional standards;

● the Government should actively promote, through bodies responsible for health education, health authorities and trusts and health professionals, the advantages to children of breastfeeding, and provide active support for mothers who breastfeed (also Article 24.2(e));

● education legislation should be amended to ensure that school meals of agreed nutritional standards are available in all maintained schools for children and young people who want them. The free provision of such meals should be extended once more to all children and young people in families with a low income.

● planning requirements should ensure that all new public buildings provide suitable facilities for breast-feeding mothers. Guidelines should be issued by the Department of the Environment to encourage those managing existing public buildings to make suitable provision (also Article 24.2(e);

● purchasers of health care should ensure adequate provision of enough, appropriately trained staff to support women in breastfeeding, especially in the early days and when at home.

7 Compliance with Article 24.2(e), the right of children and young people and their parents and carers, to information about health and to support in the use of that information, requires that:

● health education and promotion programmes should take account of different communication needs of different groups of children and young people. In Wales health information should always be available in a bilingual format (also Articles 30 and 17(d));

● safety information and advice should be drawn up in conjunction with the people whom it is designed to help to ensure that it is useful and relevant to their way of life and to their social and economic circumstances;

● the Nutrition Task Force set up by the Department of Health as part of its Health of the Nation initiative should develop guidelines for the production of health information for schools by industries with vested interests;

● the information needs of local children and young people who are HIV positive or affected by HIV/AIDS should be seen as a priority by those health promotion units not already doing so.

**8** Compliance with Article 24.2(f), and the continued development of effective preventive health services and guidance for parents, requires that:

● Child Health Surveillance should only be carried out in the best interests of the child and should not impinge on the rights of the child to physical integrity and privacy. There should be regular monitoring of CHS programmes to ensure that they are always carried out to a high standard and that there is consistency throughout the country; regular monitoring of the programme is needed to ensure consistency and effectiveness;

● screening programmes, according to age, should be standardised across the country. This should be a Department of Health initiative and should be research-based;

● more research into the role being played by health professionals in identifying children defined as 'in need' under section 17 of the Children Act should be undertaken;

● the important role of the school health service in providing a range of preventive health care services, with appropriate medical back-up, must be recognised by the Government and suitable guidelines issued. Guidelines should take account of the detailed consultation report on the school health service published by the British Paediatric Association[154].

**9** Compliance with Article 24.2(f), the duty to provide family planning education and services, requires that:

● sex education in school, linked to the National Curriculum, should be available to all children and young people, and taught at an age when it will be of use to them and in a manner sensitive to their needs. Governors should not be responsible for deciding whether or not a school provides sex education. There should be special training for staff involved and parents should not have the right to withdraw their children. If parental right of withdrawal from sex education stands, then at the very least arrangements should be made to monitor the numbers and reasons for such withdrawal, with a view to reviewing the provision (also Articles 2, 3, and 13);

● teaching about HIV/AIDS and other sexually transmitted diseases, must be re-instated as a key part of any curricular activity about sex or health education;

● in N Ireland contraceptive service for young people must be made more widely available (also Article 2);

● research should be carried out into why young people continue to practice unsafe sex in spite of the known health risks.

**10** Compliance with Article 3.2, the duty to ensure children adequate protection to safe-guard their right to health from the dangers of smoking and alcohol, requires that:

● research into the reasons why pregnant women, parents, children and young people continue to smoke, despite the fact that they are well versed in the risks to their health and the health of others, should have a higher priority in Government strategies; information gleaned from existing studies should be used as a basis for anti-smoking campaigns;

● the increasing evidence about the dangers of passive smoking and its effects on the health of children should be more widely publicised, especially to adults who have regular contact with children;

● children and young people should be involved in the design of anti-smoking and anti-drinking programmes aimed at their peers (also Article 12);

● there should be a complete ban on the advertising of all tobacco products (also Articles 17(e) and 24.1);

● there should be stricter enforcement of the laws relating to the sale of cigarettes and alcohol to children and young people (also Articles 24.1 and 24.2(e));

● schools should be encouraged to provide anti-smoking and alcohol education programmes which emphasise informed decision-making and life skills and enable young people to make positive and healthy choices about their behaviour;

● services should be provided for children and young people seeking help or information with regard to their own use of tobacco or alcohol or because of problems experienced as a result of the smoking and drinking problems of a close person.

**11** Compliance with Article 33, the duty to protect children and young people from the misuse of solvents, narcotics and psychotropic substances, requires that:

● in order for children and young people to have confidence in drugs services the rules of confidentiality should be clear from the outset and the circumstances under which confidentiality may be broken, if there are any, should be explained. Young people should be able to use the services knowing that they are safe from unwarranted intervention into their lives;

● resources should be concentrated in work aimed at stopping the move by individual young people from non-addictive to addictive substances in the early stages before full blown addictions are developed;

● there should be more broad-based community programmes aimed at tackling the root causes of solvent abuse;

● schools should provide more education relating to solvent and drug abuse and should be encouraged to provide informal, confidential advice and drop-in centres, staffed by skilled workers from outside the school, to advise and answer the questions of their pupils.

**Rights to care and treatment**

**12** Compliance with Articles 23 and 24.1, the right of children and young people with disabilities and learning difficulties to have the opportunity to enjoy the highest attainable standard of health and access to integrated health services, requires that:

● the principle of integrated services for disabled children should be built into health legislation and reflected in training and service provision;

● information about services must be made available in a way that is relevant and useful to disabled children and young people;

- implementation of section 17 of the Children Act should be carefully monitored to ensure that the needs of disabled children who suffer health disadvantage are met adequately.

**13** Compliance with Article 24.1, the right to the 'highest attainable standard of health' and the provision of appropriate 'facilities for the treatment of illness and rehabilitation of health' for children and young people with medical conditions, requires that:

*Mental health*

- better data collection systems relating to mental-ill health amongst young people must be instituted;
- the Department of Health should issue guidance which sets out criteria for admission to psychiatric care and provide safeguards for the rights of these young people. These should be as vigourous as those for other forms of residential care;
- the practice of placing young people in adult or non-psychiatric provision because of insufficient psychiatric resources needs to be addressed;
- the remit of the Mental Health Act Commission should be extended to cover children and young people admitted informally for treatment of mental illness.

*Inherited blood disorders*

- there must be universal policies to provide appropriate screening for haemaglobinopathies through the provision of more specialist centres;
- staff in accident and emergency departments should be given information and training to ensure that appropriate treatment and respect are offered (also Article 2).

*HIV/AIDS*

- the Government should take steps to promote a children's rights perspective in all care programmes for children affected by HIV/AIDS or who are HIV positive and should develop detailed guidance aimed at health authorities in line with that provided for local authorities;
- the same quality standards should be applied across the board where children are receiving this kind of service and in planning health services for all. Attention needs to be paid to geographical inequalities in the needs associated with HIV/AIDS across the UK;
- integrated family services such as family clinics should be developed to support these children and greater resources must be devoted to meeting the increasing need for supplementary care leading to permanent alternative care for children in families affected;
- services and information must take account of individual cultural and linguistic needs.

**14** Compliance with Article 3.3, the duty to ensure that standards of provision and care within the NHS meet those agreed by 'competent authorities', requires that:

- purchasers and providers should be under a legal obligation to provide care, services and facilities which meet agreed, basic standards;
- all staff involved in the care and treatment of children and young people should know what agreements and

standards for best practice exist between the purchaser of care and the provider unit, and they should be given a copy of those that relate to their area of work;

- purchasers of health care should monitor the outcomes of treatment, especially on the quality of life of children and young people, to ensure that the best possible treatment is being offered, and that children and their parents are able to make informed choices as to the type of treatment they require ( also Articles 6, 12, 13);
- those purchasing health care should ensure that the most up-to-date information is included and that there are procedures in each contract to monitor compliance. Data collection for monitoring the effectiveness of children health services should be standardised;
- in Scotland the Clinical Resource and Audit Group and the Scottish Health Management Efficiency Group should be asked to identify ways in which standards may be set and monitored in relation to services for children and young people and should see this as a priority.

**Other rights of those affected by ill health**
**15** Compliance with Article 9, the right for children not to be separated from their parents or carers unless it is in their own best interests, requires that:

- health care services must, wherever possible, be within easy travelling distance of children's homes; clinics must be timed so that working parents can bring their children; support must be available for parents with other children who need to be looked after; and there must be provision for parents with disabilities;
- financial assistance for travelling costs to escort or visit children in hospital should be reviewed in the light of Government guidance which recognises the importance of parents being with their children. A visiting costs scheme should be established to provide assistance to parents facing financial hardship as a result of visiting and the travel costs scheme should be broadened to allow for both parents to accompany a child to hospital;
- hospitals must ensure that there are subsidised meals in the canteen as well as access to ward kitchens for making tea and coffee on the ward for parents of sick children. Also, there should be no parking fees for parents or other similar additional costs.

**16** Compliance with Article 25 without discrimination requires that there should be legislative duties to ensure regular review of children in NHS and private health institutions, similar in form and frequency to those applying to children being looked after or accommodated by social services departments in England and Wales.

**17** Compliance with Article 28, the right to education for children and young people who are unable to attend school for medical reasons, requires that:

- education legislation in Scotland and N Ireland should be amended to safeguard the right to education for children and young people unable to attend school;
- regulations issued under the Education Act 1993 must clarify details of the rights to education for children and young people unable to attend school for medical reasons;
- funding of education for sick children may need special protection to ensure that there is clear responsibility for provision on education or health services;

● purchasers commissioning health care for children at home should ensure that local authorities are involved in providing education for those children. Increasing attention should be paid to home tuition as the trend towards shorter stays in hospital grows. Linking home teachers with hospital teachers, enabling them to share resources or work with the same child whether in hospital or at home, should form part of the process.

# References

1. *Constitution of the World Health Organisation*, WHO, New York (1946)
2. *National Health Service Act 1946*, HMSO, London
3. European Commission of Human Rights, Application No 7154\75, Association X v UK. Strasbourg: Decision of the Commission (12 July 1978)
4. *OPCS General Household Surveys 1989, 1990*, preliminary results, reported in reference
5. *Children, teenagers and health - the key data*, Woodroofe C et al, Open University Press, Buckingham (1993)
6. *Poverty and inequality in the UK: the effects on children*, Kumar V, National Children's Bureau, London (1993)
7. *Poverty can seriously damage your health*, Cole-Hamilton I, Child Poverty Action Group, London (1991)
8. Communication from Eastern Health and Social Services Board, Directorate of Nursing to CRDU (1993)
9. *Public health - common data set 1991 England and Wales*, Compiled by Institute of Public Health, University of Surrey, Department of Health (1992)
10. *Mortality statistics 1990*, OPCS, London (1992)
11. 'The health needs of Travellers' children', Bannom M, *Medical Monitor* (28 Feb 1992) pp70-71
12. 'Traveller mothers and babies', Durward L, *Maternity Alliance*, London (1990)
13. 'Damp housing, mould growth and symptomatic health state', Platt S et al *British Medical Journal*, 298 (1989) pp1673-1678
14. Department of the Environment, Scottish Office and Welsh Office statistics quoted in *Give us a chance: children, poverty and the Health of the Nation*, Health Visitors Association, Child Poverty Action Group and Save the Children, London (1992)
15. *Prescription for poor health - the crisis for homeless families*, Conway J (ed), The London Food Commission, Maternity Alliance, SHAC and Shelter, London (1988)
16. *Young homelessness, a national scandal*, Gosling J, Young Homelessness Group, London (1992)
17. *On the state of public health for the year 1991, the annual report of the Chief Medical Officer of the Department of Health*, HMSO, London (1992)
18. *Smoking and young people*, Royal College of Physicians, London (1992)
19. 'Young people, tobacco and 1992', Amos A, *Health Education Journal*, 50 (1992) p26-30
20. *Health in Scotland (1991)*, Report of the Chief Medical Officer for Health, HMSO (1992)
21. *The health of the nation*, Department of Health, HMSO, London (1992)
22. *Government clamp down on illegal sales of cigarettes to children*, Department of Health Press Release (1993) H93/569
23. 'Children's health', Kurtz Z, *Children Now*, National Children's Bureau, London (1993) p13
24. *The effect of tobacco advertising on tobacco consumption - a discussion document reviewing the evidence*, Smee C, Economics and Operational Research Division, Department of Health, London (1993)
25. *Young people and alcohol*, British Medical Association, London (1986)
26. *The new drinkers: teenage use and abuse of alcohol*, Smart

R, Addiction Research Foundation, Toronto (1976)

27. 'Children intoxicated by alcohol in Nottingham and Glasgow', Beatties J et al, *British Medical Journal*, 292 (1986)

28. *The facts about drinking and driving*, Transport and Road Research Laboratory, Crowthorne (1986)

29. *Transport and road research laboratory statistics*, Crowthorne (1986)

30. *UK statistical handbook 1984*, Brewer's Society, Brewer's Publications Ltd (1985)

31. *Young people and alcohol*, Home Office Standing Conference on Crime Prevention, HMSO, London (1987)

32. *Adolescent drinking*, Marsh A et al, OPCS, HMSO, London (1986)

33. *Counselling for alcohol problems*, Velleman R, Sage Publications, London (1992)

34. *Alcohol and the family*, Velleman R, Institute of Alcohol Studies, London (1992)

35. 'School drug plague hits crisis level', Hurgill B and Taylor D, *Observer*, London (26 September 1993)

36. *National audit of drug misuse in Britain - 1992*, Institute for the Study of Drug Dependency, London (1993)

37. 'Fuel of forgotten deaths', Russell J, *New Scientist*, London (6 February 1993) pp21-23

38. studies referred to in reference 36

39. 'Alcohol and drug use amongst North West youth', *University of Manchester Communications*, Manchester (8 October 1993)

40. '"Heatstroke" cause of ecstasy deaths', *Druglink*, Institute for the Study of Drug Dependency, London (September/October 1992) p5

41. *Drug misuse and caring for children*, Northern Drugs Services Child Care Group Working Party, Grimsby (1991)

42. 'The post-heroin generation', Measham F et al, *Druglink*, Institute for the Study of Drug Dependency, London (May/June 1993) pp16-17

43. 'Drug education funding axed', *Druglink*, Institute for the Study of Drug Dependency, London (September/October 1992) p4

44. see reference 42

45. 'Drugs slip down education agenda', *Druglink* (July/August 1992) p7

46. 'The drug agency goes to school', Berry P and McKenna G, *Druglink*, Institute for the Study of Drug Dependency, London (May/June 1993) pp14-15

47. 'A guide to working with schools', Burgess R, *Druglink*, Institute for the Study of Drug Dependency, London (January/February 1992) pp19-20

48. 'The bootstrap solution', Wilson T and Stewart D, *Druglink* (November/December 1992) pp15-16

49. *The state of the world's children*, UNICEF, Oxford University Press (1991)

50. *Urban trends*, Policy Studies Institute, London (1992)

51. 'Influence on birth weight on differences in infant mortality by social class and legitimacy', Leon D, *British Medical Journal*, 303 (1991) p964-67

52. see reference 6

53. 'Pregnancy, birth and maternity care', Parsons L, *"Race" and health in contemporary Britain*, Ahmad W (ed), Open University Press, Milton Keynes (forthcoming). Also see reference 5

54. *Protocol for investment in health gain - maternal and early child health*, Welsh Office, NHS Directorate (1991)

55. 'A comparison of food intake during pregnancy and birth weight in high and low socio-economic groups', Doyle W, *Human Nutrition: Applied Nutrition*, vol 36A (1982) pp95-106

56. *Poverty and pregnancy*, Durward L, Maternity Alliance, London (1988)

57. *Present day practice in infant feeding*, Reports on health and social subjects No 9, HMSO, London (1998)

58. see reference 21

59. *Baby-friendly hospital initiative - a summary*, UK Committee of UNICEF London (1992)

60. *The nutritional case for school meals*, White J et al, School Meals Campaign, London (1992)

61. see reference 6

62. *Children - advertisers dream, nutrition nightmare*, Dibb S, National Food Alliance, London (1993)

63. *Dietary reference values*, Department of Health, HMSO, London (1991)

64. *Poverty and nutrition survey*, National Children's Homes, London (1991)

65. *Health services management welfare food scheme*, Department of Health, HC(89)13 (1989)

66. 'A study of the eating habits of 11- and 12-year old children before and one year after the start of a healthy eating campaign in Northumberland', Hackett et al, *Journal of Human Nutrition and Dietetics*, no 3 (1990) pp323-332

67. 'Standard setting - taking the first steps', Bain G, *Papers for the Society of Paediatric Nursing 7th annual residential conference*, Royal College of Nursing, London (1992)

68. *Strategic plan: 1992-1997*, Health Education Board for Scotland (1992)

69. *The extension of the hospital and community health services elements of the GP fund hold*ing scheme from 1 April 1993 - supplementary guidance NHS Management Executive HSG (92)53 (1992)

70. *The welfare of children and young people in hospital*, NHS Management Executive, HSG(91)1 Department of Health, London (1991)

71. *Health for all our children: achieving appropriate health care for black and minority ethnic children and their families*, Slater M, Action for Sick Children, London (1993)

72. see reference 5

73. *Immunisation against infectious diseases*, Department of Health, HMSO, London (1992)

74. see reference 5

75. *Health for all children - report of the joint working party on child health surveillance*, D Hall (ed), 2nd edition, Oxford Medical Publications (1991)

76. 'Rights of children and young people', P. Alderson in *The welfare of citizens - developing new social rights*, Coote A (ed), Institute for Public Policy Research, London (1992) pp153-187

77. *National monitoring of the Children Act*, Aldgate J et al, Oxford University/NCVCCO (1992)

78. *Fit for the future (The Court report)*, Department of Health and Social Security, HMSO, London (1976)

79. *Survey of school nursing*, Royal College of Nursing, London (1992)

80. 'What teachers think', Rogers J, *Primary Health Care* vol 2, no 10 (1992) pp12-14

81. *Training and accreditation of general practitioners in child health surveillance*, British Paediatric Association, General Medical Services Council and Royal College of General Practitioners, RCGP, London (1991)

82. *Health services for school age children - consultation report of the joint working party*, British Paediatric Association, London (1993)

83. see reference 5

84. 'Teenage pregnancy in industrialised countries', Jones E et al, Yale University Press 1986, in *Primary Health Care*, vol 2, no 10 (1992) pp16-17

85. Family planning services for young people, Department of Health and Social Security, HC(86)1 (1986)

86. 'Teenage girls still wary of clinics, claims Brook annual report', *Young People Now* (5 November 1992)

87. *Health minister condemns 'appalling national failing'*, Department of Health press release, H93/657 (24 March 1993)

88. *The socio-sexual lifestyles of young people in England*, South Western Regional Health Authority (1991)

89. *HIV - AIDS: Who's telling the children?* Barnardos, Ilford (1992)

90. 'Childline HIV enquiries double' *Social Work Today* (26 November 1992) p26

91. 'Sexual lifestyles and HIV risk', Johnson A et al, *Nature*, 360 (1992) p410-412

92. *Does sex education lead to earlier or increased sexual activity in youth?* Baldo M et al, Global Programme on AIDS, Geneva, PO- DO2-3444 (1993)

93. *National sexual lifestyles survey*, Wellings K, paper presented to the Sex Education Forum (July 1993)

94. see reference 89

95. *The prevalence of disability among children*, Bone M and Melzer H, Office of Population Census and Surveys, HMSO, London (1989)

96. 'Isle of Wight revisited - 25 years of social psychiatric epidemiology', Ritter M, *Journal of American Academy of Child and Adolescent Psychiatry*, 28 (1989) pp633-653

97. 'Behavioural and intellectual development', Graham P, in Alberman E & Peckham C (eds) *Childhood Epidemiology: British Medical Bulletin*, vol 42, no 2 (1986) pp155-62

98. see reference 20

99. 'By their own hand', Hawton K, *British Medical Journal*, 304 (1992) p1001

100. see reference

101. 'Mental illness in the young' in *Mental illness: the fundamental facts'*, Mental Health Foundation, London (1993)

102. Communication from Royal College of Psychiatrists to Children's Rights Development Unit (1993)

103. *Psychiatric admissions - a report on young people entering psychiatric care*, Malek M, The Children's Society, London (1991)

104. *Health services for people with learning disabilities (mental handicap)* NHS Management Executive, London (1992) - NHS(92)42

105. see reference 17

106. see reference 71 p10

107. Personal communication from research study, Anionwu E, reported in reference 71 p17

108. see reference 71 p18

109. *Children first - a study of hospital services*, Audit Commission, HMSO, London (1993) p5

110. *The care of critically ill children - report of the multidisciplinary working party on paediatric intensive care convened by the British Paediatric Association*, British Paediatric Association, London (1993)

111. 'Positive thinking', Rickford F, *Social Work Today* (14 May 1992)

112. 'Demanding the best - training staff to work with children who are HIV positive', Murray N, *Community Care* (15 October 1992) pp18-19

113. *AIDS and HIV infection in the United Kingdom*, Communicable Disease Surveillance Centre, 2 (1992) p200

114. *Children and HIV -guidance for local authorities*, Department of Health, HMSO, London (1992)

115. 'Aids mothers fear for children', *Social Work Today* (2 April 1992)

116. *Schools need extra lessons in asthma care*, press release, National Asthma Campaign, London (1994)

117. 'Statistics on children in hospital', *Keypoints 5*, Action for Sick Children, London (1993)

118. 'Paediatric home care in the UK', Tatman M and Woodroffe C, *Archives of Disease in Childhood*, 69 (1993) pp 677-680

119. *The NAWCH Charter*, National Association for the Welfare of Children in Hospital, London (1984)

120. 'How do we value our children? as reflected by children's health, health care and policy' Kurtz Z and Tomlinson J, *Children and Society*, vol 5, no 3 (1991) pp207-224

121. *Young homelessness, a national scandal*, Gosling J, Young Homelessness Group, London (1992)

122. see reference 11

123. *Charting child health services*, National Children's Bureau, London (1990)

124. *Department of Health press release*, H93/661 (24 March 1993)

125. 'Race and ethnicity in health records', Sheldon T and Parker H, *Journal of Public Health Medicine* vol 14 no 2 (1992) pp104-110

126. 'Improving obstetric outcomes in ethnic minorities: an evaluation of health advocacy in Hackney', Parsons L and Day S, *Journal of Public Health Medicine* vol 14 no 2 (1992) pp183-191

128. see *Re W [A Minor: Consent to Medical Treatment]* (1993) 1 FLR 1

129. 'The competency of children and adolescents to make informed treatment decisions', Wiethorn L & Campbell S, *Child Development*, 53 (1982) pp1589-1598

130. see reference 76

131. 'Finding out what parents want', Shelley P, *Cascade* (July 1992) pp4-5

132. *Family health service complaints - NHS (service, committees and tribunal) regulations 1992*, NHS Management Executive HSG(92)17

133. *Minister responds to report on childrens health services*, Press Release, H93/527, Department of Health, London (1993)

134. *A survey to identify progress made towards meeting the requirements of ENB Circular 1988/53/RMHLV - Suppression of students gaining nursing experience in children's wards*, English National Board for Nursing, Midwifery and Health Visiting (1992)

135. *Children's attendance at accident and emergency departments - a report by the Joint Accident Committee of the BPA and BAPS*, British Paediatric Association and British Association of Paediatric Surgeons, London (1987)

136. *The report of the National Confidential Enquiry into Peri-operative Deaths 1989*, Campling E et al, HMSO, London (1991)

137. *Directory of paediatric community nursing services*, Royal College of Nursing of the United Kingdom, London (1993)

138. *Bridging the gap*, Thornes R, Caring for Children in the Health Services and Action for Sick Children, London (1993)

139. 'Hospital chiefs warned Camden of court action', Limehan T, *Social Work Today* (3 September 1992)

140. *'Quality management for children: play in hospital*', Hogg C, Play in Hospital Liaison Committee, c/o Save the Children, London (1990)

141. 'A special conditions register', Woodruff C and Abra A, *Archives of Disease in Childhood*, vol 66 (1991) pp927-930

142. *Access to and availability of specialist services*, Clinical Standards Advisory Groups Reports, HMSO, London (1993)

143. *The National Health Service in Scotland: framework for action*, Scottish Office (1991)

144. 'Leave for family reasons', *Cascade*, Action for Sick Children, London (8 April 1993) p3

145. *Proposal for a Council Directive on parental leave and leave for family reason*s, Commission of the European Communities, CDM(83)686 final

146. *The cost of visiting children in hospital*, Goulding J, Action for Sick Children, London (1992)

147. *Hospital travel costs scheme - a guide for the NHS*, NHS Management Executive, London (1991) HC(91)19

148. *Report of an independent review of specialist services in London, - review of specialist children's services,* Department of Health and London Implementation Group, HMSO, London (1993)

149. *Visiting patients by children*, Department of Health and Social Security and Welsh Office, H.M.(71)50 (1971)

150. *Home and hospital education services*, Education Observed 11, HMI Report, Department of Education and Science, London (1989)

151. 'Education for children in hospital', *Keypoints 3*, Action for Sick Children, London (1991)

153. *Meeting the spiritual needs of patients and staff*, NHS Management Executive, London (1992) - HSG(92)2

154. *Health services for school age children - consultation report of the joint working party*, British Paediatric Association, London (1993)

# UK Agenda for Children

6 Environment

# Contents

*The unreferenced quotations in this report are comments made during a consultation exercise undertaken by the Children's Rights Development Unit with groups of young people throughout the UK.*

**Acknowledgement**
Much of the information in this report is drawn from *Children and the Environment*, by Martin Rosenbaum (National Children's Bureau, 1993).

# 1 Introduction

**1.1** Physical surroundings have a major impact on the health and development of children who are significantly affected by housing policy, access to public facilities and services, town and country planning, transport policies and environmental pollution. This report uses the term 'environment' to describe a wide range of features in the physical surroundings of children, including their home environment, the built environment and the wider, open environment.

**1.2** Primary responsibility for policy relating to the physical environment in which children and young people live lies with the Department of the Environment (DoE) in each jurisdiction, although Department of Transport also has a crucial role. Current policy stems from the World Health Organisation (WHO) 'Health for All' policy and targets adopted by the 32 Member States of the European Region of the WHO in 1984. In 1989, 29 European countries, including the UK, met specifically to discuss the implications of the 'Health for All' targets for environmental policy and adopted the *European Charter on Environment and Health*[1]. From this, a new framework for UK policy in relation to the environment was developed and published in 1990 in the White Paper *This common inheritance*[2]. It covered a wide range of issues and promised regular, statistical updating of the information it contained. An update to the White Paper was published in 1992[3].

**1.3** 1992 was also the year of the Earth Summit in Brazil and a commitment from the Government to implement *Agenda 21* by adopting 'national sustainability strategies', increasing the participation of children and young people in matters of environmental policy, and producing periodic national implementation reports. The UK Government is committed to producing a report covering progress towards sustainable development in the UK, the first sections of which were published in January 1994. In addition to these reporting duties the DoE publishes an annual report which describes recent and future policy development and includes its future expenditure plans[4]. The Department of Transport publishes a similar report[5].

# 2 Relevant articles in the Convention

## 2.1 Underlying principles

**Article 2:** rights in the Convention must apply without discrimination of any kind irrespective of race, colour, language, religion, national, ethnic or social origin, disability or other status.

**Article 3.1:** the duty in all actions to consider the best interests of the child.

**Article 12:** the right to express an opinion and to have that opinion taken into account in any matter or procedure affecting the child.

## 2.2 Articles relevant to environmental issues

**Article 3.2:** the duty to ensure the protection and care necessary for the well-being of the child.

**Article 6:** the right to life and development.

**Article 18.2:** the duty to support parents and carers in bringing up their children.

**Article 23:** the right of disabled children to special care, education and training to ensure the fullest possible social integration.

**Article 24:** the right to highest level of health possible.

**Article 24.2(a):** the duty to diminish infant and child mortality.

**Article 24.2(c):** the duty to ensure the provision of adequate nutritious foods and clean drinking water, and to consider the dangers and risks of environmental pollution.

**Article 24.2(e):** the duty to ensure that parents and children have information and are supported in the use of basic knowledge relating to child health and nutrition, breast-feeding, hygiene and environmental sanitation and accident prevention.

**Article 24.2(f):** the duty to develop preventive health care, guidance for parents, and family planning education and services.

**Article 27:** the right to a standard of living adequate for the child's physical, mental, spiritual, moral and social development.

**Article 29.1(e):** the duty to ensure that education encourages respect for the natural environment.

**Article 30:** the right of children from minority communities to enjoy their own culture and practise their own language and religion. (Article 30 is not addressed in this report but has general relevance to all services and institutions).

**Article 31:** the right to play, rest, leisure, recreation and participation in cultural and artistic activities.

*For the full wording of the articles, see the UN Convention on the Rights of the Child, page 311*

# 3 Children and the environment

## 3.1 Consultation and participation
(Article 12)

**3.1.1** Underpinning all the rights in the Convention is Article 12, the right of every child *'who is capable of forming his or her own views .... to express those views freely in all matters affecting the child'*. Yet despite the considerable interest shown by children and young people in environmental issues there are few opportunities for them to be actively involved in planning and policy formulation. Article 12 is about ownership of ideas and plans. If participation is authentic and opinions are genuinely listened to, then children and young people are more likely to respect and use services and resources.

**3.1.2** Levels of understanding amongst children and young people about the environment are high, particularly among those who are able to grasp the more complex inter-relationships between human behaviour and its long-term effects[6]. Although concern is higher about wider environmental issues, it is the more localised issues which young people feel they can actually do something about. Transport and mobility, including the cost of travel are important to them, as are homelessness, safety and the cleanliness of the locality. There is also concern that priorities for funding chosen by some adults do not meet the real needs of the local community.

> *'When he hung up the hanging baskets I thought "what's that got to do with it?". We need something done for the environment and young people. Spending money on hanging baskets is a waste of time. If you had a hostel the money spent on those hanging baskets could have bought - God knows what'.*
> (15 year-old, Manchester)

> *'I was thinking about the lighting on that building. Have you seen it at night, shining up all the statues? If you put the money spent on that light alone, it could light up a couple of alleys and that could maybe save a couple of rapes from happening'.*
> (14 year-old, Manchester)

**3.1.3** Despite this interest and knowledge, examples of involving children and young people in local planning are relatively rare, although they are becoming more common[7]. Under the requirements of the Children Act 1989 in England and Wales, local authorities are required to seek the views of children and young people when making decisions about their care. In the same way, children and young people could be actively consulted about other local authority activities which affect them, including planning applications, development plans, design and planning of parks, playgrounds and leisure facilities and the design of traffic systems. *Agenda 21* stresses the importance of involving children and young people in discussing environmental policy: 'Governments ... should take measures to establish procedures allowing for consultation and possible participation of youth of both genders, by 1993, in decision-making processes with regard to the environment, involving youth at local, national and regional levels'[8].

**3.1.4** Involving children and young people in policy and planning relating to the wider environment is also important

and there are a number of projects involving them in data collection and research. These include the 'Ozone Project' and 'National River Watch' which receive funding from the Department of the Environment[9]. However, there is little evidence of serious involvement of young people in actually planning policy. In 1991 a British Youth Council conference developed a *Youth environment charter* but its recommendations have not been taken up by policy makers[10].

### ACTION REQUIRED FOR COMPLIANCE

**Compliance with Article 12, the right to express views on environmental matters, requires that:**

- **consultation with children and young people from all sectors of the community should take place at the beginning, and throughout service planning and development. It should be implicit in all local environment statements, strategies and policies. Neighbourhood forums or councils made up of children, adults and professionals, should be developed;**

- **those involved in producing local development plans should appoint officers with specific responsibility for consulting children and young people and promoting their interests in the planning process.**

## 3.2 Education (Article 29.1(e))

**3.2.1** Article 29.1(e) states that *'States Parties agree that the education of the child shall be directed to: ... the development of respect for the natural environment.'* In formal education, environmental education is one of five cross-curricular themes recognised by the Department of the Environment and the National Curriculum Council as an essential part of every pupil's curriculum. Environmental issues are also discussed as part of the science and geography curriculum. However a survey carried out in 1991 among a random sample of schools found that in reality environmental education had a low priority[11]:

- 66% of primary schools and 80% of secondary schools did not have an agreed policy for environmental education;

- even fewer schools in the independent sector had such a policy;

- 46% of schools with no policy had no intention of developing one;

- environmental education has the lowest priority amongst cross-curricular themes;

- a significant proportion of secondary schools offer little or no field work out of school.

**3.2.2** At a conference of young people in Birmingham in 1992, the following statement was formulated by those discussing environmental issues.

> *'We the Young People [of Birmingham] who are concerned about the environment think that our National Government should readily bring environmental issues into our schools so that we can broaden our knowledge of the environment and the issues in the world today. Environmental issues should be in the National Curriculum, not really be taught in the areas of science and technology. Our community should make a formal request to the schools and the schools governing body, for environmental issues to be part of the curriculum. Our*

*schools should start up a recycling point, and should also do projects that combine with the environment.'[12]*

**3.2.3** Full implementation of the Convention requires that Article 12, the right to be consulted, is read in conjunction with Article 29.1(e), the right to environmental education. There are some excellent examples of work in schools which combine environmental education and participation. In one, a 'Safe School' project in a primary school in Glasgow, the work led to an understanding of why strict rules applied to dangerous places, eg stairways. The project involved children, parents, governors, teachers, the Parent Teachers Association, the local education authority and local health board. One aim was to help children understand the risks outside school by learning how to look at their environment[13]. The project was not just about reducing injury; it also provided a place where children could learn and play in safety, respecting each other and adults around them to 'buy in' to a good environment. *Learning through Landscapes*, a scheme for involving children and young people in the design of their school environment, is another important initiative which could be widely expanded to increase compliance with both Articles 12 and 29.1(e)[14].

**3.2.4** Pressure from young people on local councils can have an effect, such as one group based in a youth club who had organised its own 'clean up' campaign:

*'We designed and did a clean up campaign round our area. We got 15 children and 20 adults, we designed the posters and stuck them in pubs and schools, and a lot of people joined in. We got a newspaper reporter round and that went in a local newspaper. Each day we made a diary. We got a video camera. The Council thought they would have to do something and it was putting them in a bad light. We got the community services helping us.'*
(16 year-old, Manchester)

**ACTION REQUIRED FOR COMPLIANCE**

**Compliance with Article 29.1(e), the duty to provide education which promotes respect for the natural environment, requires that:**

● **education on the environment should form a key part of the National Curriculum;**

● **inspectors for environmental education should be appointed by local authorities in England, Wales and Scotland and by the relevant bodies in N Ireland. They would support the development of the subject both in the school and by helping to create links with local organisations;**

● **innovative projects designed to combine education with participation should be widely encouraged and adequately resourced. All schools should be encouraged to involved pupils in drawing up environmental policies and action plans.**

# 4 The right to adequate housing

**4.1** Children and young people have the right to a standard of living adequate for their '*physical, mental, spiritual, moral and social development*' (Article 27.1) and the Government has a duty, in the case of need, to '*provide material assistance and support programmes, particularly with regard to .... housing*' (Article 27.3).

## 4.2 Housing standards (Article 27.3)

**4.2.1** In the UK, poor housing conditions contribute to consistently higher levels of physical and mental ill-health:

● damp housing conditions are a threat to children's health and are linked in particular to diseases of the respiratory system[15]. In 1992, in London alone, 87,400 of the 799,100 families with children under 16 (11%) considered they suffered from serious damp in their home. Families with children were more likely than other households to experience such problems[16];

● many families live in tower blocks which are often unsuitable for children with the constant danger that a child might suffer a fatal fall. The need to keep young children under close supervision means they go out less, have less stimulation, mix less with other children and their development may be hindered[17]. In 1992 the *London housing survey* showed that, in the capital, 32,300 (4%) families with children under 16 years old, including 49,200 children, were living in flats where the lowest level of their accommodation was above the fourth floor. This was an increase from the previous survey in 1987. 85% of these families were council or housing association tenants;

● in N Ireland, there is a very high incidence of respiratory disease and damp housing is a contributory factor. The problem is compounded by the fact that fuel costs in N Ireland are higher than on the mainland with no proportionate increase in benefit levels;

● bed and breakfast hotels, in which many homeless families are given temporary accommodation, are often overcrowded, insanitary and lacking in basic amenities. Children living in these hotels are more likely to suffer from infectious diseases, infestations, injuries, poor nutrition, behavioural problems and impaired development[18]. The number of people accepted as homeless by local authorities and therefore faced with such housing conditions, has risen dramatically over the past decade increasing from 7,232 in 1979 to 169,526 in 1990[19]. In June 1993 an estimated 3,215 families with children were living in bed and breakfast hotels in London alone[20]. The problem is even more acute in isolated rural areas where homelessness trebled between 1989 and 1992, and rural homelessness in general grew faster than urban homelessness[21];

● homeless families are increasingly housed in temporary accommodation in privately rented properties. Many of these are substandard with the accommodation often in a poor state of repair and lacking amenities. Furnishing is usually very poor and lack of storage space means that stairways and landings are often blocked creating a major fire hazard[22][23];

● in many substandard housing developments, inadequate heating, ventilation, lighting and cooking facilities, household pests, poor escape routes, general disrepair and lead in paint all create health hazards[24] [25].

**4.2.2** Many children living in these poor housing conditions are not achieving a standard of living adequate for their proper development as required by Article 27.1. Furthermore, Article 24.1 states that all children have the right to '*the enjoyment of the highest attainable standard of health*'. Yet for many children who are living in inadequate accommodation which is contributing to their ill health, this right is not being respected. These include those in families with a lone parent or low income families with one child, who are more likely to be living in privately rented accommodation which usually represents the worst housing conditions. In 1991 although on average only 4% of families with children lived in privately rented homes, amongst those with the lowest incomes 10% of two parent, one-child families and 7% of lone parent families lived in this type of accommodation[26]. Families with unemployed heads and from black and minority ethnic groups are also disproportionately represented amongst those in poor and temporary housing[27]. (See **UK Agenda Report 4 on standard of living,** page 76 for a detailed discussion of Article 27 and housing and homelessness).

**4.2.3** Data from the Department of the Environment highlights Government failure to comply fully with Article 27.3 and '*in the case of need provide material assistance and support programmes, particularly with regard to ... housing*'. The English House Conditions Survey for 1991 found over 1.3 million unfit homes in England. Although there was a decrease in the overall number of unfit properties between 1986 and 1991, the number with poor ventilation and inadequate kitchen facilities increased. The worst conditions were found in privately rented properties of which 20% were in poor condition. One in 14 occupied local authority and housing association properties were also classified as unfit[28]. In N Ireland the recently completed Housing Conditions survey found the worst conditions to be in privately rented properties of which 28% were found to be in poor condition. In the public sector only one in 50 occupied Housing Executive and housing association dwelling were unfit. In Scotland public housing is in a deteriorating state and dampness is a particularly widespread problem.

**4.2.4** The responsibility for inspecting the condition of housing falls to local authority environmental health services which have powers to enforce standards of fitness. There are an estimated 290,000 houses in multiple occupation (HMOs) in England, of which an estimated 180,000 need attention. In 1991-92 enforcement action was taken by local authorities on only 4,800 such properties. The lack of pro-active strategies to deal with the worst houses in the HMO sector is caused by the complexity of such premises and the lack of resources available to fund such programmes. Environmental health officers face conflicting calls on their limited resources and responsibilities are increasing rapidly. Many local authorities have limited policies on the improvement of housing stock, and many have no co-ordinated strategy to implement such policies. Local authority housing environmental health officers have no statutory right to require repair works to be carried out or to insist on improvements.

## 4.3 Availability of housing (Article 27.3)

**4.3.1** Between 1985 and 1992 only 28,000 new units of social housing were built each year in England and Wales. During the same period the numbers of homeless households living in temporary accommodation increased from 13,000 to 60,000. This problem has been particularly bad in the south of England. The 'Right to Buy' programme, allowing residents in social housing to buy their properties for reduced prices, resulted in a drop in social housing stock of more than a million homes. But by the end of the 1980s, the recession meant that many home owners were no longer able to afford their mortgages. In 1991 12% of homeless households in England were people who were in mortgage arrears[29]. The Audit Commission calculates that the gap between the need for and supply of social housing will not be eliminated even if local authorities spend the maximum they are allowed to by central Government.

**4.3.2** The annual cost of keeping a family in a council house is about £7,000 compared with £13,150 for bed and breakfast accommodation and £11,000 for temporary accommodation rented from the private sector[30]. Yet local authorities are restricted by Government regulations in their building activities and are unable to use assets gained from the sale of housing during the 1980s. Housing associations, which are expected to be the main providers of social housing, cannot meet current need. Lack of housing finance has also contributed to the growing number of families with children being housed in high rise blocks of flats. With increasing recognition during the 1980s of the inappropriateness of high rise accommodation for young children, many local authorities have had policies of not placing children above the 4th or 5th floor in any tower block. But lack of availability of family-sized council housing has made this increasingly difficult to maintain and a number of councils have abandoned the policy[31].

**4.3.3** Taking the implementation of Article 12 seriously and involving young people in trying to solve some of their own housing problems has proved an invaluable experience for some young homeless people in Oxford. Their self build co-op, Oxford Young Self Builders, is planning to build a community of 13 houses with funding from the Housing Corporation. The impetus came from the young people themselves[32]: 'Until you've got your own front door other people will keep holding you back.' ... 'I think being in this group has made people realise how much more powerful you can be as part of a group.' ... 'Confidence is the main word - helping you face society with a sense of purpose. I don't want to be just a someone bludging off the social.' This type of initiative, if properly funded, is one way of implementing Article 12, the right to be heard, in relation to housing. The Rural Development Commission is also helping to fund projects with young homeless people which include providing short-term accommodation, on-site counselling services and training facilities.

**4.3.4** Children in rural areas may also be at risk of homelessness. Many rural authorities are more restrictive in interpreting relevant parts of the homelessness legislation. For example many will not accept young single people or those living in mobile homes. Rural authorities are also more likely to classify particular families as intentionally homeless including those previously living in tied accommodation, those losing short-term lets and those in rent arrears[33].

Homelessness and poor housing are issues of major concern to many children throughout the UK:

> 'There should be more accommodation for people in general anyway. There shouldn't be homeless people. If homeless people haven't got a house they can't get a job so they can't improve. They won't employ you if you're on the street'.
> (16 year-old, South Wales)

> 'They should be putting more money into the homeless. It's like building all these houses that no-one can afford unless they're rich anyway. They should be putting money in to house the homeless... You see people on the streets and it's not giving our city a good name'.
> (15 year-old, Manchester)

## 4.4 Accidents in the home
(Articles 6 and 24.2(e))

**4.4.1** Accidents to children in their homes are the largest single cause of death and injury for children from aged one to four[34]. Government statistics indicate that the numbers of children injured by burns and scalds, falls, 'foreign objects' and swallowing or inhaling poisonous substances has increased over the last five years[35] [36]. There was also an increase in the number of children dying or being injured in uncontrolled fires, the most common cause of accidental death in children within the home.

**4.4.2** Children in families with low incomes are particularly at risk. Often their parents cannot afford to buy safety equipment. For many people, accident prevention is limited by lack of money as well as the poor design of the environment. Maintaining safety is a question of cost as well as behaviour. Until 1988 it was possible for families receiving benefit to claim one-off payments to buy safety equipment such as fireguards and stair gates. It was also possible to claim additional money to buy household equipment, when without it there would have been serious risk to health and safety. Since the introduction of the Social Fund in 1988, these payments no longer exist and the only way to get the money required for safety equipment is to apply for a discretionary loan. Repayments for these loans are deducted from regular income support payments and considerable hardship faces families who borrow money in this way. The Government is failing in its duties to provide parents and carers with 'appropriate assistance ... in the performance of their child-rearing responsibilities' (Article 18.2), and whilst informing parents and children about accident prevention is not ensuring that they are 'supported in the use of' this knowledge (Article 24.2e).

### ACTION REQUIRED FOR COMPLIANCE

**Compliance with Article 27.3, the duty to provide assistance and housing programmes for those in need, requires that:**

- the Government must allow local authorities the freedom to use financial reserves from the sale of houses to invest in new social housing. Housing legislation and standards should explicitly reflect the needs of children and young people, and authorities responsible for housing should be ensured adequate finances to build new family housing particularly in areas where there is insufficient suitable housing;

- housing regulations should ensure compulsory, wide ranging safety design features for low cost, social housing, and the 'housing fitness standard' should include safety design features;

- environmental health officers should be given powers to deal with substandard housing conditions in local authority housing; home safety should become a statutory function for local authorities and be funded by central Government. Local authorities could then more actively promote home safety issues, including those relating specifically to children;

- there should be national child safety guidelines for temporary accommodation which set enforceable standards. Meanwhile authorities with responsibility for housing should prioritise improving the condition of temporary accommodation given to families with children and, as a matter of urgency, develop standards and rigorously monitor their implementation.

**Compliance with Article 3.2, the duty to ensure the necessary care and protection for the well-being of the child, Article 6, the right to life and to maximum potential development and Article 24.2(e), the duty to support parents and carers in the use of accident prevention knowledge, requires that the Government should make the fitting of smoke detectors mandatory in all new living accommodation. Families with low incomes should be able to obtain financial assistance to ensure safety equipment is installed in their homes and that dangerous equipment can be replaced; and the Department of Social Security should reconsider the Social Fund criteria to make safety equipment, such as fireguards and stair gates, eligible for grants (also Article 18.2).**

**For further action required relating to housing policy see UK Agenda Report 4 on standard of living, page 76.**

# 5 The accessibility and safety of public places

## 5.1 Accessibility (Articles 3.1 and 23)

**5.1.1** Article 3.1 states that '*in all actions concerning children whether undertaken by ...administrative authorities or legislative bodies, the best interests of the child shall be a primary consideration*'. Article 18.2 commits the Government to support parents through '*appropriate assistance...and ensure the development of institutions, facilities and services for the care of children*'. Yet, much of our built environment remains hostile and unfriendly to families with children.

**5.1.2** In the UK, there are numerous examples of public buildings such as shopping centres and transport stations which are not designed to meet the needs of children and their carers[37] [38]. Planning regulations currently ensure access and the provision of certain facilities for people with disabilities in new buildings. However, these regulations do not apply to existing buildings and the requirements of people with disabilities are not necessarily synonymous with those of children. For example, many families use double pushchairs, which are wider than wheelchairs and spaces which accommodate wheelchairs will not necessarily accommodate a double pushchair.

**5.1.3** Article 31 states that children have a right to '*engage in play and recreational activities appropriate to [their] age*'. For many children, their local environment is increasingly inaccessible to them as an arena with opportunities for play. Children under 10 usually play within a few hundred yards of their homes[39]. Even if children live in houses with their own gardens they often choose to play in more public areas and in urban areas this often means playing in the street[40]. However, housing estates are often dissected by busy major roads subjecting residents not only to air pollution but also to dangerous road crossings, subways with inherent dangers of personal assault, and footbridges impossible to cross with prams, pushchairs and bikes. A report from National Association for the Care and Resettlement of Offenders in 1988 concluded that most planners had failed to plan for children and were principally concerned with protecting the environment from children and young people rather than including them in it[41]. For many children, outdoor activities are restricted because of parents' fears of abduction and molestation. Many children also have fears about their local environment.

> '*You've got to make sure that the area you're in is going to be safe so that kids can go out, can walk, can get the bus, without getting mugged or being afraid that you might*'.
> (13 year-old, Manchester)

> '*I came up from Blackpool with my friend and I had to walk to the bus stop on my own from Oxford Street station and the lighting is not that good and I was really scared. Around our area the lighting isn't that good, there are dark streets and dark alleyways where horrible things can happen. It's to do with safety yet again*'.
> (15 year-old, Manchester)

**5.1.4** In rural areas the countryside does not necessarily represent an accessible environment for children either. Most land is privately owned and increasing mechanisation and intensive farming leads to a greater possibility of accidents. Problems of access to the countryside can be created by loss of public footpaths and the need to keep children safe from farm machinery and pesticide stores[42]. In N Ireland access to the countryside may be particularly restricted. Unlike the rest of the UK there are no National Parks and 'protected' areas are much smaller. This difference has been attributed to lack of resources[43].

**5.1.5** All these restrictions on the activities of children and young people can inhibit their growing independence as well as their physical activities. If Articles 3.2 and 31 are to be fully implemented and they are to benefit from their rights to protection, health, development and leisure, the Government must devise strategies to enable children and young people to enjoy and play in the surroundings in which they live, with minimum fears of danger.

**5.1.6** Article 23.3 states that assistance for children with disabilities must help them in achieving the '*fullest possible social integration and individual development ...*'. Suitable facilities are often particularly limited for children with disabilities, especially for those living in isolated rural communities, on run-down housing estates and in generally deprived areas[44].

**5.1.7** Most mainstream schools are in old buildings and are inaccessible for children and young people with mobility disabilities. Because there is no national monitoring of accessibility of school premises, it is not possible to determine the extent of the problem. Article 23.3 states that disabled children have the right to receive education '*in a manner conducive to the child's achieving the fullest possible social integration*' but for many this right is denied because of the physical properties of the school buildings. Improvements in the built environment to increase physical accessibility must also be accompanied by improvements to meet the needs of those who have sensory impairments. Standards should be set for the introduction of loop systems and minicom telephones for the deaf, good contrast marking for those with poor sight and aids for those with no sight.

**5.1.8** Building regulations require new public buildings to have some provision for access and sanitary facilities for people with mobility, sight or hearing difficulties[45]. However, these regulations make scant provision for up-grading existing buildings and do not make it compulsory to install facilities where there were none before, even if alterations are being made. Any alterations have only to ensure that new facilities are no worse than those previously existing. At present the Department of the Environment is investigating methods of improving old buildings.

**5.1.9** Article 3.1 places a duty on all those involved in actions or decisions which affect children to ensure that the '*best interests*' of those children are a primary consideration. The responsibility, under the Planning and Compensation Act 1991, for overseeing planning and development in their localities lies with local authorities who are obliged to prepare co-ordinated development plans (Unitary Development Plans - UDPs) which include the need for an Environmental Assessment, public consultation and notification of plans to local people. However planning regulations make no specific reference to children's needs. For example there are no legal requirements to provide playgrounds, safe play areas or out-of-school care facilities. With the current climate of local authority cuts, much provision is under threat, including grant aid to voluntary organisations providing such services.

**5.1.10** One way of ensuring that Article 3.1 is implemented in planning decisions and that the '*best interests*' of children are a '*primary consideration*', would be for UDPs to include compulsory assessment of the impact of the development on children, in the same way as they are expected to include an environmental assessment. These assessments would need to differentiate between the needs of children and young people of different ages and also make specific reference to the needs of those with disabilities and learning difficulties. UDPs also provide an opportunity for local authorities to publicise and clarify their plans relating to all aspects of provision for children and young people. This could include, for example, day care provision for children and young people, nursery schools, play and recreation facilities and general facilities for young people. The UDP could also define standards (in line with Article 3.3) and planning criteria which should include the specific needs of children and young people.

**5.1.11** Many of these policies rely on adequate finance and other resources being available. For some urban regeneration programmes, money is available directly from the Department of the Environment through the City Challenge programme. To qualify for these grants, coalitions of public, private and, where appropriate, voluntary sector organisations bid for funds for specific projects. Bids must meet certain criteria and identify strategic objectives[46]. The criteria make no mention of the needs of specific population groups, referring generally to the needs of disadvantaged groups, and fail to address the specific needs of children.

### ACTION REQUIRED FOR COMPLIANCE

**Compliance with Article 18.2, the duty to provide appropriate support for parents and carers in their child-rearing responsibilities requires that:**

- **planning regulations should be amended to ensure that applications for planning permission for new buildings show that, where appropriate, they include safety features and access and facilities for children in prams and double pushchairs as well as for children with disabilities. Building regulations should be amended accordingly;**

- **where possible these features should also be incorporated into existing buildings through rolling programmes in consultation with children and young people and their representative organisations. When buildings are being modified the opportunity should be taken to make them more child friendly.**

**Compliance with Article 23.3 and the right to the fullest possible integration for disabled children requires that the Government makes a commitment to improve access and facilities for these children and young people in existing buildings and developments. Consideration should be given to the allocation of central grant allocation for this purpose and a time scale should be identified. Central Government funding should be available for this.**

**Compliance with Article 3.1, the duty to consider the best interests of the child in all matters that affect them, requires that:**

- **the Planning and Compensation Act 1991 should be amended to include the need for 'Child Impact Statements' in all Unitary Development Plans and child impact assessment for all planning applications; Development Plans should include details of proposed provision of all services relevant to children and young people within the locality;**

- **City Challenge applications should be required to include details of how the interests of children and young people have been considered and this should be taken into account in assessment of applications.**

**Action required in relation to the provision of accessible, safe play space is described in UK Agenda Report 8 on play and leisure activities, page 177.**

## 5.2 Safety (Articles 3.2 and 24.2(e)

**5.2.1** Article 3.2 makes clear that every child has the right to '*such protection and care as is necessary for his or her well-being, ...*' and the State has a duty to ensure this protection through '*all appropriate legislative and administrative measures*'. However evidence suggests that is not always the case. This report looks primarily at safety in areas where children live and play. Safety issues related to pre-school care facilities and schools are discussed in **UK Agenda Reports 2 on the care of children,** page 26 and **7 on education,** page 170.

**5.2.2** Most accidents to children and young people outside the home happen during play and leisure activities. Accidents are the largest single cause of death for children aged 1- 14 and result in about 2 million attending accident and emergency departments every year in the UK[47][48]. After road accidents and house fires, drowning is the third most common cause of accidental death in children in Britain. In 1988 and 1989, 300 children in the UK drowned or nearly drowned[49]. Also in 1991 there were approximately 84,000 accidents to children riding bicycles not including motorised vehicles on public highways. For many children, the surroundings outside their home present many dangers and there is little or no safe outdoor place to play[50]. Most places, facilities and services in the UK used by the general public are designed by adults for adults with little or no consideration given to the needs of children. (Road accidents are discussed in section 6.2 of this report). ·

**5.2.3** Accidents happen amongst all groups of children and young people but are consistently most common among children from low income families and those living in deprived areas.[51] One study in the north of England showed that children in deprived areas were 15 times more likely to die from head injuries than those in well-off areas[52]. Traveller children are particularly prone to accidents because of the unsafe surroundings in which families are often forced to live, and children from some black and minority ethnic groups are more likely to be involved in household accidents than white children although social disadvantage seems to be a more important factor than ethnicity in this[53]. Twice as many boys as girls die from accidents[54][55]. Boys are injured more frequently than girls in almost all accident types in which the child is an active participant. Girls tend to be injured more in passive situations such as car passenger injuries[56].

**5.2.4** Article 24.2(e) states that not only do children and their parents have a right to information about accident prevention but they also have the right to be '*supported in the use of [this] basic knowledge*'. Government strategy[57][58][59][60] concentrates on educating the public to adopt safer behaviour but there is less discussion of legislation and policy to remove the causes of accidents or to ensure that parents and carers have sufficient resources to make their homes and neighbourhoods safer[61]. Despite setting targets to reduce accidents to children and young people in England and Wales, over the next ten years, so far there has been no extra central Government funding to support new initiatives. In Wales targets have been set to reduce differences in accident rates between rich and poor children. There been no such commitment in the other jurisdictions. Nor is there any attempt to promote strategies aimed at reducing differences in accident rates between boys and girls. In Scotland, which has a worse record for accident prevention than England and Wales no official targets for accident reduction have been identified[62].

**5.2.5** Despite the formal protection of legislation and Government guidelines for safety many accidents occur in parks and playgrounds and during sporting and other leisure activities[63]. In 1991 40,700 children were involved in accidents in playgrounds[64]. Outdoor play facilities in both urban and rural areas are often badly maintained, vandalised, in poor condition and sometimes dangerous. A survey in 1991 of nearly 900 children's play areas found only one that was considered fault free[65]. At the same time, in both urban and rural areas, there are fewer and fewer open spaces in which children and young people can play freely. Although British Standards exist for outdoor play equipment which give methods of testing, specifications for construction and performance and codes of practice for installation and maintenance, these standards are not mandatory[66]. Accidents in play areas still happen because of poorly designed equipment, poor siting and layout, inadequate maintenance, incorrect installation, lack of age-appropriate facilities and inappropriate use of equipment.

**5.2.6** Developing and monitoring the success of accident prevention strategies can only be effective if accurate information about the nature and types of accidents is available. However much of the information collected and the way in which it is presented is inadequate. For example, since 1985 data on household and leisure accidents has not included any information relating specifically to young people between 15 and 18[67]. Also there is no information about the social or psychological background of the child and no monitoring of the long term effects of accidents on children and young people.

**5.2.7** In failing to develop specific policies aimed at reducing accidents amongst high risk groups of children and young people the Government is failing in its duties to '*ensure the child such protection and care as is necessary for his or her well-being*' (Article 3.2), to '*ensure to the maximum extent possible the survival and development of the child*' (Article 6.2) and to take appropriate measures to '*diminish infant and child mortality*' (Article 24.2.a) amongst **all** groups of children and young people (Article 2).

## ACTION REQUIRED FOR COMPLIANCE

**Compliance with Article 3.2, the duty to provide the necessary '*protection and care*' for the well-being of children, requires that:**

● **accident prevention programmes must be altered to ensure they meet the needs and circumstances of different groups of people. They must include more effective, legally enforceable, controls over the planning and construction of the environment in which the child is growing up. Wider ranging laws and regulations should be introduced to enforce safety behaviour by those responsible for creating hazards (also Article 24.2(e));**

● **official targets should be set for accident reduction in Scotland in line with those for the other jurisdictions;**

● **British Standards for outdoor play equipment in public playgrounds should be made mandatory. There should be guidelines on the health and safety of children in the 'outdoors' and training for staff;**

● **education for child cyclists should have a higher priority and the use of cycle helmets at all times should be encouraged. More resources should be invested in safe cycle paths and routes used by children and young people by ensuring better lighting and fewer hidden areas.**

# 6 Transport and transport policy

## 6.1 Independence and mobility
(Articles 3.1 and 6.2)

**6.1.1** The opportunity to gain independence during childhood is an important aspect of the maturation of children and becoming independently mobile is an important element in this[68]. If the Government's responsibility to '*ensure to the maximum extent possible the ... development of the child*' (Article 6.2), is to be implemented fully, planning and transport policy must allow for the independent mobility needs of children and young people. A recent study has shown how in the past 20 years children's independent mobility has declined dramatically as car use has nearly doubled and roads have become increasingly dangerous[69]. Children have less physical activity and are less fit as a result with potentially harmful effects on their long term health reducing their opportunities for '*the enjoyment of the highest attainable standard of health*' (Article 24.1).

**6.1.2** Much transport planning and policy is based on the development of private road transport so the needs of those who use other methods of transport tend to be overlooked. For example, young people aged 11-15 are the least likely to depend on the car for transport. They are more likely to walk, ride a bicycle or use a local bus service. International comparisons suggest that if cycling was safer and more convenient children and young people would choose to cycle more often. The Policy Studies Institute research shows that although the majority of 5-11 year-olds own bicycles, very few are allowed to use them on public roads. In countries where there are better facilities for bicycles a higher proportion of young people cycle than in the UK. For children and young people, therefore, little attention is paid either to their '*best interests*' (Article 3.1) or to their preferences (Article 12) in transport planning and policy.

**6.1.3** For most families transport and mobility is a crucial part of their daily lives and important for the development of their children. For well-off families, a car ensures this freedom. In 1990, among better-off families with professional or managerial heads, more than 95% had their own private transport, of whom more than half owned two or more vehicles[70]. But for those with low incomes the use of public transport is essential. Families least likely to have their own private transport are lone-parent families and those with four or more children. In 1991 two out of three lone-parent families had no transport of their own, nor did three out of ten large families[71]. In N Ireland where unemployment is high and incomes relatively low public transport can be particularly important in allowing children and young people freedom to travel around. Provision is very poor and significant improvements are required.

**6.1.4** In order to ensure that all families have access to transport and parents are given '*appropriate assistance ... in their child-rearing responsibilities*' (Article 18.2) public transport systems must be accessible and flexible enough to meet the needs of those families least likely to have their own cars. However, using public transport in the UK is often inconvenient and stressful for adults transporting small children. Parents with children are often unhappy with transport services. Trains, coaches, buses, and stations were all thought to cater badly or poorly for adults travelling with young children[72].

**6.1.5** Mobility is fundamental to the pursuit of most other activities and for those with disabilities it is a major factor in their ability to acquire any level of independence. Public transport is largely inaccessible to disabled children. At present neither bus nor train services accommodate their needs adequately and there is no legal obligation on the providers of services to address this issue. The Department of Transport is, however, piloting a number of schemes to improve public transport facilities, one of which is the 'kneeling bus'. These schemes need support and encouragement[73].

> '*Transport is not accessible for disabled people at all, especially trains. I had to lift Jim out of the wheelchair and onto the seats, because wheelchairs do not fit through them doors, on the trains, this is going first class now. ... There was a stage when Jim was going on the train and he had to be put in the corridor because they wouldn't allow the chair to be along the aisle of the train*'.
> (17 year-old, N Ireland)

> '*The buses are no good for the disabled and it's embarrassing being carried around like a little baby - shoved in a car and then shoved back out again*'.
> (18 year-old, Shropshire)

**6.1.6** If Article 23 is to be fully implemented and children and young people with disabilities and learning difficulties to have the opportunity to lead '*a full and decent life in conditions which ensure dignity, promote self reliance, and facilitate the child's active participation in the community*', provision of adequate, appropriate transportation is essential.

### ACTION REQUIRED FOR COMPLIANCE

**Compliance with Article 6.2, the right to maximum development and Article 23, the right for disabled children to active participation in the community, requires that:**

● **the Department of Transport, in conjunction with the Department of the Environment should develop a co-ordinated transport policy which takes account of the needs of all children and young people as well as adults. It should allocate public spending carefully to children's preferred modes of travel; ensure that adequate transport is available for those with disabilities; ensure that independent means of travel are safe and convenient;**

● **at the earliest possible opportunity all transport facilities and stations should be altered to ensure that the basic needs of children and young people travelling with or without accompanying adults are met (also Article 18.2);**

● **pilot schemes trailed by the Disability Unit of the Department of Transport which are found to be successful for improving access to transport for children and young people should receive appropriate resources to enable them to be brought into use as soon as possible and as widely as possible.**

## 6.2 Safety on the roads
(Articles 3.2 and 6)

**6.2.1** Road accidents are the main cause of accidental death to school-age children in the UK and in 1991 were the cause of 61% of accidental deaths among children aged 5-16[74]. Whilst the Government cannot be expected to take responsibility for eliminating this threat to children and young people, it does have a duty to *'ensure to the maximum extent possible the survival and development of the child'* (Article 6.2). However, current policies do not do all they can to reduce road accidents.

**6.2.2** The Government road accident statistics show that in 1991 over 44,500 children under 16 were involved in reported road accidents. Of these 383 were killed and nearly 7,723 seriously injured. 60% of children killed and 63% of those seriously injured in road accidents were pedestrians. In 1991 nearly 8,200 casualties to cyclists under 16 years of age were reported, of which 50 were fatal. Of those killed about 75% had head injuries[75]. Given that there is substantial under-reporting of slight and serious injuries published records are likely to be under-estimates[76].

**6.2.3** Although the numbers of road accidents involving children is declining, amongst child pedestrians under 10 the death rate is three times as high in the UK as it is in Sweden. For 10-14 year olds it is one of the highest in Europe[77]. There are also large social class differences and the chance of a child with unskilled parents being killed as a pedestrian is four times greater than the child of professional parents. If they are unemployed, the difference is seven times as great. Amongst families with unemployed heads, children aged 1-4 are 12 times as likely to be killed as those with parents in professional families[78]. Children with hearing disabilities are over 30 times more likely to be knocked down than children with good hearing and boys are eight times more likely to be injured than girls[79].

**6.2.4** The journey to and from school is one of the most dangerous times for children. Nearly all children travel to school so there is an obligation to make the journey as safe as possible. In 1991 the Royal Society for the Prevention of Accidents (RoSPA) recorded that, on their journey to school, 44 children were killed, 38 of whom were pedestrians. Over 8,000 were injured: 1,200 on bicycles, 5,000 as pedestrians, 1,250 in cars, taxis and minibuses and 450 in public service vehicles[80]. Twice as many accidents happen to children on the way home from school compared with going to school. The needs of school aged children are not adequately catered for after school hours, a time when accidents can occur. One possible solution to this could be the greater use of school premises out of school hours[81].

**6.2.5** Two major road safety problems are drivers exceeding speed limits and young drivers who drive recklessly. Excess speed causes one in three fatal road accidents. The seriousness of injuries to pedestrians depends strongly on the speed of the car. Drivers under the influence of alcohol are also a major problem. Other dangers on the road include parked cars blocking the view for crossing, and debris associated with road works and housing repairs.

**6.2.6** Policies adopted by the Government to help reduce road accidents to children and young people include tightening up seat belt legislation, giving local authorities more freedom to set variable speed limits, pilot schemes for variable speed limits outside schools, the use of cameras to spot cars going too fast and educating drivers about the potential dangers of their driving habits[82]. Many people consider UK legislation covering road accidents too lenient and some support proposals such as those in Denmark where it is a prisonable offence for a driver making a near-side turn to collide with a cyclist as a result of not checking for the presence of the cyclist. Whilst such measures may seem severe, the attitude of motorists to vulnerable road users has to change in the UK if roads are to become safer. Encouraging the use of safety equipment such as seat belts and child restraints in cars, a major part of accident prevention strategy, is of little benefit to many people with low incomes for whom buying the necessary equipment is often considered a luxury well beyond their means.

**6.2.7** UK transport policies are widely criticised because of lack of commitment to reduce road traffic. Research in New Zealand has shown that discouraging the use of private vehicles, promoting cycling and encouraging the use of rail, river and sea transport for freight can reduce significantly child pedestrian mortality. But despite the fact that a strong correlation has been found between traffic volume and child pedestrian mortality the Government predicts that road traffic will double between 1990 and 2025[83]. The Countryside Commission believes that current transport and planning policies could result in a fourfold increase in rural traffic and recommends that ways of discouraging car use should be sought[84].

**6.2.8** A recent report commissioned by the Department of the Environment and the Department of Transport shows that where traffic calming and reduction measures have been introduced successfully in other countries, more people have used bicycles and accidents to pedestrians have been reduced. The report concludes that there should be a focus of development in urban areas and that existing neighbourhoods, towns and city centres should be maintained and revitalised. Rail transport should be improved and other possibilities for non-car transport should be investigated and expanded[85]. However, despite this advice, and concern from the Department of the Environment about air pollution and damage to the countryside, the Department of Transport gives no indication of a commitment to reducing the number of cars on the roads. On the contrary it is committed to a £24 billion road building programme over the next ten years, and is rumoured to be planning a network of 12-lane motorways[86].

**6.2.9** In failing to address the problems caused by increased traffic volume the Government is failing in its duties to ensure *'such protection and care as is necessary for [the child's] well-being'* (Article 3.2); to give proper consideration to *'the dangers and risks of environmental pollution'*, (Article 24.2(c)), to protect the *'inherent right to life'* of all children and young people (Article 6.1) and of supporting parents and children *'in use of basic knowledge in … the prevention of accidents'* (Article 24.2(e)).

**6.2.10** As children's play and out of school activities tend to happen near home, the needs of children and other pedestrians in residential areas should take priority over cars. Cordoned-off play streets may not necessarily be the answer because they prioritise children over all others. However, 'home zones' in residential areas, which have strict restrictions on speed limits, give pedestrians priority, and ensure that all those children who want to can walk or cycle to school, are a more probable solution[87].

**Compliance with Article 3.2, the duty to provide adequate care and protection for the well-being of children and Article 6, the right to life, requires that:**

- **safety on the roads is enhanced by the widespread introduction of traffic calming measures. Driver education campaigns about the risks of speed should be intensified and greater penalties for drivers breaking speed restrictions introduced;**

- **consideration should be given to legislation which places a legal liability on drivers to prove they were not negligent where pedestrians or cyclists are knocked down by motor vehicles in residential areas or 'home zones';**

- **new facilities should be located within walking or cycling distance of as many people as possible. The location of new schools in particular should take into account the ability of children to travel to them safely and independently (also Article 3.1);**

- **indicators for road safety should include use of the open environment by children and young people. For example the proportion of children of specified ages allowed to cross roads on their own and coming home from school on their own and cycle on main roads could be monitored;**

- **initiatives from the Department of the Environment to reduce dependence on cars should be a major priority. This must involve more investment in public transport, better arrangements for cyclists and pedestrians, less road building and improved approaches to town planning.**

# 7 Environmental pollution and child health

## 7.1 Pollution and health (Article 24.2(c))

**7.1.1** Children tend to be more susceptible to the health effects of pollution than adults. They are small, growing and biologically less prepared for many hazards. They are likely to absorb more of a harmful substance than adults in relation to body size, given the same exposure. Their immature body systems generally combat toxicants less effectively than those of adults. Pollution which affects the process of development can cause permanent damage. In 1991 the British Medical Association identified children as a 'high-risk sub-section of the population, ... who experience toxic effects at lower level of exposure than the general population ... and may require special protective measures'[88]. Because of this, extra vigilance is required if Articles 3.2, the duty to ensure '*the protection and care*' of children and 24.1, the right to '*the enjoyment of the highest attainable standard of health*' are to be fully implemented in the UK. However, evidence suggests that this vigilance is lacking in Government policy, and children are at risk from pollutants through their diets, the water they drink, the air they breathe and the land on which they move about.

*Food and water*
**7.1.2** Article 24.2(c) states that the Government must ensure the provision of '*adequate nutritious foods and clean drinking water, taking into account the dangers and risks of environmental pollution*'. However, the presence of pesticide residues in the diets of children has been of concern in the UK for some time[89] [90]. Children ingest pesticides in food and water and a major new report in the USA has expressed grave concern about the ways in which these are monitored and controlled[91]. Problems in the USA are no greater than those in the UK and the findings of the report are equally valid here. Where regulations do exist they are not properly monitored and are often flouted[92] [93].

**7.1.3** Tap water is a major source of lead intake for large numbers of UK children[94]. It is estimated by the Water Research Centre that the lead level in the tap water of 310,000 households in England and Wales (3% of the total) exceeds the UK regulatory limit of 50 micrograms per litre; and that the proposed new World Health Organisation limit of 10 micrograms per litre is exceeded in 1.9 million households (21%)[95]. There have been many other surveys which found lead in drinking water to be well above the legal limit[96]. Lead is a poison which damages the brain and nervous system. Children are especially vulnerable. Even exposure to low levels has been linked to reduced intelligence, and there is evidence that the development of children in the UK has been affected[97] [98] [99]. Bottle fed babies may be particularly at risk[100].

**7.1.4** Lead enters drinking water mainly through lead plumbing, particularly in areas with soft water which dissolves the lead more easily. These include large parts of the Midlands, the South West, Merseyside and Scotland. To eliminate lead in drinking water it is necessary to remove all lead plumbing especially in areas of soft water. At present the cost of doing this generally falls on the owner of the house and many people cannot afford it. Although it is possible to receive grants from local authorities, very few are currently awarded[101]. Water authorities in some areas have been removing their own lead piping and adding chemicals to water to reduce the amount of lead dissolved from pipes[102].

7.1.5 Nitrates and pesticide residues in water also give cause for concern. Nitrates have been linked to 'blue baby syndrome' and stomach cancer. The health effects of long-term low-level exposure to pesticides are uncertain. In 1992 a survey found that up to 3.5 million people were at risk of receiving water supplies with levels of nitrates above the legal limits and that 14.5 million people were receiving water which breached the standards for pesticides. Pressures on the Government to delay implementing European Union (EU) standards and negotiate for them to be reduced have resulted in EU leaders accepting a request from the UK Government to dilute requirements[103].

## ACTION REQUIRED FOR COMPLIANCE

**Compliance with Article 24.2(c), to ensure the provision of adequate nutritious food and clean water, requires that:**

- **the Ministry of Agriculture, Fisheries and Food consider the conclusions of the recent USA report on pesticides in the diets of children and, as a matter of urgency, implement its main recommendations;**

- **the Department of the Environment institutes a publicly-funded rolling programme of removing lead pipes entirely from the water distribution system in homes, schools, hospitals and other buildings. Grants should be available for households to do the work;**

- **in the meantime publicity campaigns targeted at those most at risk should give information about how to minimise the risks of lead pollution in tap water;**

- **the Government return to its programme of maintaining safety levels for nitrate and pesticide contamination of water in line with original EU directives.**

*Air pollution*
7.1.6 Article 24.2(c) states that in its attempts to *'combat disease'* and ensure the *'highest attainable standard of health'*, the Government must take into consideration *'the dangers and risks of environmental pollution'*. Air pollution in the UK is a serious problem. International studies have shown links between respiratory disease and levels of air pollution. Evidence suggests that air pollution in the UK, mainly from cars, is in part responsible for an increase in asthma amongst children[104]. The health effects on children may well be greater where there are industrial or waste disposal plants which contribute substantially to local air pollution. The chief airborne pollutants in the UK which can affect the health of children are nitrogen dioxide, ground level ozone and sulphur dioxide.

7.1.7 Nitrogen dioxide has been linked by numerous international studies to respiratory illness, particularly among children, including asthma[105]. The Department of the Environment estimates that in 1991, the UK produced 2.75 million tons of nitrogen oxides of which 51% came from road

transport and 26% from power stations. Emissions rose steadily during the 1980s. The growth is entirely accounted for by road transport emissions which increased from 810,000 tons in 1981 to 1.4 million in 1991, an increase of 73%. In 1991 in central London nitrogen dioxide levels were found to be 'poor' or 'very poor' (by Government standards) on 32 days. This was an increase from 27 days in 1990[106]. Monitoring in London and Manchester has consistently recorded levels above EU guide values in recent years, and similar problems are experienced by other large cities.

7.1.8 All new cars manufactured or imported into the UK must now be fitted with catalytic converters which reduce emissions of carbon monoxide, nitrogen oxides and hydrocarbons. The use of catalytic converters, whilst helpful, is not a complete solution. Their efficiency is limited in the low speed, stop-start driving conditions of many cities. The growth in road traffic is likely to outweigh the consequent reduction in emissions over the next 20-30 years. According to Greenpeace calculations based on official figures, nitrogen dioxide levels in the year 2000 may only be 5% less than in the early 80s and will then rise[107].

7.1.9 Ground level ozone formed by reactions between hydrocarbons and nitrogen oxides emitted in car fumes may also cause health problems. High levels of ozone can increase susceptibility to infectious and respiratory diseases and irritate the eyes, nose, throat and respiratory system. Several studies in the USA have linked increasing levels of ozone to poor lung function in children affecting their ability to take deep breaths[108]. Other studies have also linked ozone with asthma in 8-15 year olds[109]. In 1990-91 World Health Organisation guidelines were exceeded on several days at each of 18 sites in the UK's national ozone monitoring network[110].

7.1.10 Sulphur dioxide can cause temporary respiratory problems and long term exposure can lead to an increase in the incidence of respiratory illness. There is also a strong association between the frequency of chronic cough and bronchitis and levels of sulphur dioxide and smoke[111]. Studies in North America and Europe show that, at levels found in some British cities, a mixture of sulphur dioxide and smoke pollution can impair the lung function of school age children[112]. The UK's worst levels are in Belfast and certain mining areas in the north of England. In 1991 there were 44 days when air levels were 'poor' or 'very poor' according to Government standards. This was an increase from 28 days in 1990[113].

7.1.11 Children can also be affected by pesticides by direct contact through spray drift and playing in or near treated fields. Spray drift means that pesticides sometimes reach nearby roads, footpaths, public spaces, gardens or homes[114].

*Indoor air quality*
7.1.12 Children's health is known to be affected by inhaling cigarette smoke from others in the same room. A 1990 study of children aged 11-15 showed that 33% of children in England reported that their mother smoked and 36% that their father smoked. In Wales the figures were 35 and 38% respectively and in Scotland both were 39%[115]. The Royal College of Physicians suggests that children of parents who smoke inhale the same amount of nicotine as if they themselves smoked 60-150 cigarettes a year. The children of smokers are more likely to suffer respiratory diseases such as

bronchitis, pneumonia, asthma, and ear, nose and throat problems. They are also more likely to be shorter and suffer from chronic lung disease and cancer as adults. Parental smoking is thought to be responsible for at least 17,000 admissions to hospital each year of children under five. Children of smokers are more often absent from school and their education may be affected[116]. (For a detailed discussion and recommendations on the effects of smoking on health see **UK Agenda Report 5 on health and health care services,** page 97).

*Land pollution*
**7.1.13** In recent years there have been a number of reported incidents of children found living or playing in areas made potentially dangerous by past pollution. These include landfill sites, private tips and closed-down industries which had potentially harmful products on their sites. It is estimated that there are 100,000 such sites in the UK. Contaminated land poses a direct threat to children's health through the possibilities of physical contact with or ingestion of soil, and through pollution of water sources. Many of the pollutants found are poisonous or suspected of causing cancer. Some of these chemicals can pass through the skin[117]. Old household appliances are often dumped without consideration of safety and children have been known to die trapped in abandoned fridges and freezers.

**7.1.14** At present there is little monitoring of old landfill sites and dumping grounds. It is Government policy to refer people who want to find out about contaminated land to their local authority. The Environmental Protection Act 1990, section 143 gives the Secretary of State for the Environment the power to compel local authorities to compile registers of land likely to be contaminated. However, these powers have never been implemented and, according to Friends of the Earth, in 1993 one in three local authorities had no information on contaminated land and only 16% had undertaken a local survey. In N Ireland, the Act does not apply but equivalent legislation is in the course of preparation.

*Polluted beaches*
**7.1.15** Over 300 million gallons of raw or virtually untreated sewage are discharged around the UK coastline every day[118]. As a result children swimming in the sea at many of Britain's beaches can face health problems. Children who have swum in polluted sea are more likely to suffer from vomiting, diarrhoea, itchy skin, fever, lack of energy and loss of appetite[119]. Some children have been affected even more seriously by swimming in areas where there is untreated sewage[120]. The worst affected region is northwest England where in 1992 two out of every three beaches did not comply with EU bathing water regulations. In Wales 24% of beaches did not comply and in Scotland 35% did not. In northwest England there were 16 beaches which did not comply with the standards in any year between 1988 and 1992[121].

**7.1.16** The UK Government does not take the whole EU directive into account when assessing compliance and it would appear from National Rivers Authority data that there are beaches which meet the Government's criteria but not the original EU directive. The Government has recently negotiated less stringent implementation rules with the EU. On publication of a recent ruling by the European Court of Justice on the failure of the Government to clean up two popular beaches in northwest England, the Secretary of State

for the Environment is quoted in the press as having dismissed the EU directive as 'not properly written' and 'old hat'. He is reported to have added 'I am rather pleased with our beaches and am happy with the progress we are making'[122]. In N Ireland and northwest England there is also concern about contamination from the Sellafield nuclear reprocessing plant.

*Stratospheric ozone*
**7.1.17** The depletion of the ozone layer due to particular chemicals allows through more ultra-violet radiation which can cause skin cancer. Children are particularly vulnerable to this. The UK is party to the Montreal protocol, an international agreement on the phasing out of the chemicals involved, but there is concern over the long timetable the phasing-out of some chemicals.

### ACTION REQUIRED FOR COMPLIANCE

**Compliance with Article 24.2(c), the duty to take into account *'the dangers and risks of environmental pollution'* whilst implementing Article 24.1, the right to *'the highest attainable standard of health'*, requires that:**

● **the UK Government reverse its current position and press the EU to adopt directives which cover all major forms of air pollution, not only those covered at present;**

● **the UK Government should meet all World Health Organisation guidelines as well as EU directives, and the air quality information system should inform the public when WHO guidelines have been exceeded;**

● **the Secretary of State for the Environment should use his power under section 143 of the Environmental Protection Act 1990 to compel local authorities to create registers of contaminated land. The N Ireland Department of the Environment should take into account the failures of the 1990 Act and ensure these are not repeated in legislation for N Ireland. Laws relating to the disposal of old domestic appliances should be rigorously enforced;**

● **local authorities should instigate programmes to identify and clean up contaminated sites and the costs of these programmes should be met, where possible, by those responsible for the contamination. Where the polluter cannot be identified or is unable to pay the cost should be borne by a levy on the polluting industry;**

● **measures should be introduced to ensure that owners of polluted sites make the land safe and remove all contamination before leaving;**

● **the Department of the Environment should ensure better monitoring of spray drift incidents and enforcement of measures designed to prevent them;**

● **the UK should help ensure the phasing out of all ozone depleting chemicals as quickly as possible.**

## 7.2 Monitoring pollution and its effects
(Articles 3.2 and 24.2(c))

**7.2.1** Protecting children and young people from the dangers of environmental pollution as required by Articles 3.2 and 24.2(c) is only possible if current monitoring of levels and effects on children and young people is improved. Monitoring networks could include facilities at schools which enable the school community, especially children, to be involved. The main problems include the lack of adequate information to determine 'safe levels' of intake for children and young people and methods of determining actual levels of intake.

*'Safe' levels of use*

**7.2.2** There is evidence to suggest that UK limits for some environmental pollutants are too high in respect of children, for example lead and pesticide residues[123][124]. There is a lack of information specifically relating to children, who may be affected differently from adults because of their body size and metabolism. The recent USA report on children's health and pesticides (see para 7.1.2) recommends a fundamental change in the approach to setting 'safe levels of intake' and measuring intake levels. In the UK there has as yet been no action by the Government to clarify risks to children.

**7.2.3** The Department of the Environment has, however, recently set up an expert panel on air quality standards which will look at levels of sulphur dioxide, ground level ozone, benzene, carbon monoxide and acid aerosols[125]. It has also agreed to support a new 'Institute of Environment and Health' to act as a focal point on research into links between environmental quality and health[126]. To comply with Article 3.1, and ensure that the *'best interests'* of children are a *'primary consideration'*, and to ensure the implementation of Articles 3.2 to ensure *'protection and care'* of children and Article 24.2(c) *'taking into consideration the dangers and risks of environmental pollution'* in implementing their right to the *'highest attainable standard of health'* (Article 24.1), both these organisations should ensure that they look specifically at the effects of air pollutants on children and young people of all ages.

*Assessing intakes*

**7.2.4** Strategies to protect children and young people from the dangers of pollutants must be based on detailed knowledge of current levels of intake. In its 1992 statistical report on the environment the Department of the Environment discussed lead pollution[127]. Whilst acknowledging that low levels of exposure to lead may have an adverse effect on children's intellectual and behavioural development, and giving a 'provisional tolerable weekly intake', it gave no information about actual levels of lead intake in children. Age/sex intake tables were given only for people over 18 and intake levels for the population were calculated from diet surveys based on average family intakes. The National Food Survey, on which the data is based, does not collect information on food intakes of individual family members and so there are no lead intake estimates for children. Information on blood lead levels is based on results from adults only. In addition, the report only publishes average intake figures and does not give ranges. Average intakes figure are of little use in assessing whether or not some individuals are exceeding recommended limits - ranges and numbers within different levels of intake must also be published. This situation is true for intakes of all potentially harmful pollutants.

**7.2.5** There is therefore little data on which to make accurate assessments of lead intakes of children or of the real effect of those intakes on their health and development. Despite recommendations in the USA of blood tests for every child

during the first year of life, there is little or no public discussion of the issue by the UK Government. Educational materials for the public are very limited.

**ACTION REQUIRED FOR COMPLIANCE**

**Compliance with Article 3.2, the duty to provide appropriate care and protection for the well-being of children and 24.2(c), the duty to take into account *'the dangers and risks of environmental pollution'* whilst implementing Article 24.1, the right to *'the highest attainable standard of health'*, requires that:**

● **the new Government panel on air quality standards and the Institute of Environment and Health should set up expert panels to look specifically at how pollution levels affect children of different age groups and in different circumstances. These panels should set targets for air quality specifically geared to the special vulnerability of children. The panels should make their findings public at regular intervals in the statistical updates to *This common inheritance*;**

● **total exposure to toxic chemicals, from both dietary and non-dietary sources, must be considered when 'safe' levels and actual levels of intake are being considered. Intake data and methodologies should be standardised to enable comparative information and trends to be identified;**

● **the foods most frequently eaten by children and infants should be identified and quantified to ensure that precise information is available about potential intakes of toxic substances. Comprehensive data sets should be established which actually sample the levels of toxic chemicals in these foods;**

● **monitoring networks should be extended so that more local data is available, and children and young people are involved in data collection.**

## 7.3 Controlling the use of toxic substances (Articles 3.2 and 24.2(c))

**7.3.1** In signing *Agenda 21* the Government reinforced its commitment to two important principles for the care and protection of children and young people and the implementation of Article 3.2. It pledged to ensure: 'Preventive measures to protect the environment in the absence of scientific certainty (the precautionary approach)' and to apply the 'polluter pays' principle[128]. However, the Government now appears to be considering policies contrary to these commitments.

**7.3.2** Breaches of the 'precautionary' approach are particularly evident in the use of pesticides. One pesticide which it is strongly suggested has affected the sight of new-born babies is still in use, and the Government is reported to have said it wants further evidence before it will take stronger action[129].

**7.3.3** The Government and water companies have pledged that all UK water supplies will comply with European Union (EU) limits by 1995. However the Director General of Water Services recently urged the Government to negotiate for a change in European water quality standards and in particular the time limits for implementation, on the basis increases in bills[130]. Friends of the Earth argue that, since the standards were agreed in 1980 for compliance by 1985, potential price rises are not a result of the need to implement 'new' standards but of Government attempts to delay meeting the early standards. The result is that consumers either subsidise those who pollute the water to ensure the profits of privatised water companies, or drink sub-standard water which may affect the health of children in particular[131]. Making water consumers pay directly for reducing pollution levels in their supply contradicts the 'polluter pays' principle agreed in both the *European Charter* and *Agenda 21*.

7.3.4 Another example is the evidence that the Government, in conjunction with the property and insurance industries, is resisting moves to implement the 'polluter pays' principle with regard to cleaning up contaminated land. The Government's Advisory Committee on Business and the Environment has objected to the public being given rights to challenge companies who are polluting the environment[132].

## ACTION REQUIRED FOR COMPLIANCE

**Compliance with Article 3.2, the duty to provide appropriate care and protection for the well-being of children and 24.2(c), the duty to take into account *'the dangers and risks of environmental pollution'* whilst implementing Article 24.1, the right to *'the highest attainable standard of health'*, requires that:**

- **the Government strictly enforces the 'polluter pays' principle;**

- **the Government adopts the precautionary principle agreed in Agenda 21 and bans substances where there is evidence questioning their safety pending proof of their innocence.**

# Summary of action required for compliance

1 Compliance with Article 3.2, the duty to provide adequate care and protection for the well-being of children and Article 6, the right to life, requires that:

- the Government should make the fitting of smoke detectors mandatory in all new living accommodation. Families with low incomes should be able to obtain financial assistance to ensure safety equipment is installed in their homes and that dangerous equipment can be replaced; and the Department of Social Security should reconsider the Social Fund criteria to make safety equipment, such as fireguards and stair gates, eligible for grants (also Articles 6, 18.2 and 24.2(e));

- accident prevention programmes must be altered to ensure they meet the needs and circumstances of different groups of people. They must include more effective, legally enforceable, controls over the planning and construction of the environment in which the child is growing up. Wider ranging laws and regulations should be introduced to enforce safety behaviour by those responsible for creating hazards (also Article 24.2(e));

- official targets should be set for accident reduction in Scotland in line with those for the other jurisdictions;

- British Standards for outdoor play equipment in public playgrounds should be made mandatory. There should be guidelines on the health and safety of children in the 'outdoors' and training for staff;

- initiatives from the Department of the Environment to reduce dependence on cars should be a major priority. This must involve more investment in public transport, better arrangements for cyclists and pedestrians, less road building and improved approaches to town planning;

- safety on the roads should be enhanced by the widespread introduction of traffic calming measures. Driver education campaigns about the risks of speed should be intensified and greater penalties for drivers breaking speed restrictions introduced;

- consideration should be given to legislation which places a legal liability on drivers to prove they were not negligent where pedestrians or cyclists are knocked down by motor vehicles in residential areas or 'home zones';

- education for child cyclists should have a higher priority and the use of cycle helmets at all times should be encouraged. More resources should be invested in safe cycle paths and routes used by children and young people by ensuring better lighting and fewer hidden areas;

- new facilities should be located within walking or cycling distance of as many people as possible. The location of new schools in particular should take into account the ability of children to travel to them safely and independently (also Article 3.1);

- indicators for road safety should include use of the open environment by children and young people. For example the proportion of children of specified ages allowed to cross roads on their own and coming home from school on their own and cycle on main roads could be monitored;

2 Compliance with Article 3.2, the duty to provide

appropriate care and protection for the well-being of children and 24.2(c), the duty to take into account 'the dangers and risks of environmental pollution' whilst implementing Article 24.1, the right to 'the highest attainable standard of health', requires that:

- the UK Government reverse its current position and press the EU to adopt directives which cover all major forms of air pollution, not only those covered at present;

- the UK Government should meet all World Health Organisation guidelines as well as EU directives, and the air quality information system should inform the public when WHO guidelines have been exceeded;

- the Government should strictly enforces the 'polluter pays' principle;

- the Government should adopt the precautionary principle agreed in Agenda 21 and bans substances where there is evidence questioning their safety pending proof of their innocence;

- the Secretary of State for the Environment should use his power under section 143 of the Environmental Protection Act 1990 to compel local authorities to create registers of contaminated land. The N Ireland Department of the Environment should take into account the failures of the 1990 Act and ensure these are not repeated in legislation for N Ireland. Laws relating to the disposal of old domestic appliances should be rigorously enforced;

- measures should be introduced to ensure that owners of polluted sites make the land safe and remove all contamination before leaving;

- the Department of the Environment should ensure better monitoring of spray drift incidents and enforcement of measures designed to prevent them;

- the UK should help ensure the phasing out of all ozone depleting chemicals as quickly as possible;

- total exposure to toxic chemicals, from both dietary and non-dietary sources, must be considered when 'safe' levels and actual levels of intake are being considered. Intake data and methodologies should be standardised to enable comparative information and trends to be identified;

- the foods most frequently eaten by children and infants should be identified and quantified to ensure that precise information is available about potential intakes of toxic substances. Comprehensive data sets should be established which actually sample the levels of toxic chemicals in these foods;

- monitoring networks should be extended so that more local data is available, and children and young people are involved in data collection;

- local authorities should instigate programmes to identify and clean up contaminated sites and the costs of these programmes should be met, where possible, by those responsible for the contamination. Where the polluter cannot be identified or is unable to pay the cost should be borne by a levy on the polluting industry;

- the new Government panel on air quality standards and the Institute of Environment and Health should set up expert panels to look specifically at how pollution levels affect children of different age groups and in different circumstances. These panels should set targets for air quality specifically geared to the special vulnerability of children. The panels should make their findings public at regular intervals in the statistical updates to *This common inheritance*.

**3** Compliance with Article 12, the right to express views on environmental matters, requires that:

- consultation with children and young people from all sectors of the community should take place at the beginning, and throughout service planning and development. It should be implicit in all local environment statements, strategies and policies. Neighbourhood forums or councils made up of children, adults and professionals, should be developed;

- those involved in producing local development plans should appoint officers with specific responsibility for consulting children and young people and promoting their interests in the planning process.

**4** Compliance with Article 24.1, the right to the enjoyment of the highest attainable standard of health and Article 6.2, the right to maximum development, requires that:

- the Department of Transport, in conjunction with the Department of the Environment should develop a co-ordinated transport policy which takes account of the needs of all children and young people as well as adults. It should allocate public spending carefully to children's preferred modes of travel; ensure that adequate transport is available for those with disabilities; ensure that independent means of travel are safe and convenient;

- pilot schemes trailed by the Disability Unit of the Department of Transport which are found to be successful for improving access to transport for children and young people should receive appropriate resources to enable them to be brought into use as soon as possible and as widely as possible (also Article 23);

- at the earliest possible opportunity all transport facilities and stations should be altered to ensure that the basic needs of children and young people travelling with or without accompanying adults are met (also Article 18.2);

**5** Compliance with Article 24.2(c), to ensure the provision of adequate nutritious food and clean water, requires that:

- the Ministry of Agriculture, Fisheries and Food consider the conclusions of the recent USA report on pesticides in the diets of children and, as a matter of urgency, implement its main recommendations;

- the Department of the Environment institutes a publicly-funded rolling programme of removing lead pipes entirely from the water distribution system in homes, schools, hospitals and other buildings. Grants should be available for households to do the work;

- in the meantime publicity campaigns targeted at those most at risk should give information about how to minimise the risks of lead pollution in tap water;

- the Government return to its programme of maintaining safety levels for nitrate and pesticide contamination of water in line with original EU directives.

**6** Compliance with Article 27.3, the duty to provide assistance and housing programmes for those in need, requires that:

- the Government must allow local authorities the freedom

to use financial reserves from the sale of houses to invest in new social housing. Housing legislation and standards should explicitly reflect the needs of children and young people, and authorities responsible for housing should be ensured adequate finances to build new family housing particularly in areas where there is insufficient suitable housing;

- housing regulations should ensure compulsory, wide ranging safety design features for low cost, social housing, and the 'housing fitness standard' should include safety design features;

- there should be national child safety guidelines for temporary accommodation which set enforceable standards. Meanwhile authorities with responsibility for housing should prioritise improving the condition of temporary accommodation given to families with children and, as a matter of urgency, develop standards and rigorously monitor their implementation;

- environmental health officers should be given powers to deal with substandard housing conditions in local authority housing; home safety should become a statutory function for local authorities and be funded by central Government. Local authorities could then more actively promote home safety issues, including those relating specifically to children.

7 Compliance with Article 29.1(e), the duty to provide education which promotes respect for the natural environment, requires that:

- education on the environment should form a key part of the National Curriculum;

- inspectors for environmental education should be appointed by local authorities in England, Wales and Scotland and by the relevant bodies in N Ireland. They would support the development of the subject both in the school and by helping to create links with local organisations;

- innovative projects designed to combine education with participation should be widely encouraged and adequately resourced. All schools should be encouraged to involved pupils in drawing up environmental policies and action plans.

# References

1. *Environment and health: the European charter and commentary*, World Health Organisation Regional Publications, European Series No.35, WHO, Copenhagen (1990)
2. *This common inheritance*, Cmnd 1200, HMSO, London (1990)
3. *The UK environment*, Brown A, Department of the Environment, HMSO, London (1992)
4. *Annual report 1993 - the Government's expenditure plans for 1993-94 to 1995-96*, Department of the Environment, HMSO, London (1993)
5. *The Government's expenditure plans for transport 1993-94, 1995-96*, Department of Transport, HMSO, London (1993)
6. *Young eyes*, Henley Centre, London (1992)
7. *How local authorities can assist in putting children higher on the environmental agenda*, Agyeman J, (presentation by T Hams at National Children's Bureau conference - Children and the Environment), London (1993)
8. *Earth summit '92 - the united conference on environment and development*, section 111B, Regency Press Corporation, London (1992)
9. These projects are organised by *Watch*, (the junior club of the Royal Society for Nature Conservation), Lincoln
10. *Youth environment charter*, British Youth Council, London (1991)
11. *Environmental education in England - report of survey*, The Royal Society for the Protection of Birds, Sandy, Beds (1992)
12. *Birmingham young people's conference*, Birmingham City Council, 21 Nov 1992
13. *Safe schools are no accident*, Child Accident Prevention Trust, London (1993)
14. *Learning through Landscapes*, Winchester, SO23 9DL
15. 'Damp housing, mould growth and symptomatic health state', Platt S D et al, *British Medical Journal*, vol 298 (1989) pp 1673-8
16. *Findings from the London housing survey 1992*, London Research Centre, London (forthcoming)
17. *National tower blocks directory*, Clark S, National Tower Blocks Network London (1992)
18. *Prescription for poor health*, Conway J, The London Food Commission, Shelter, SHAC and Maternity Alliance (1988)
19. *Give us a chance: children, poverty and 'The health of the nation'*, Health Visitors Association, Child Poverty Action Group and Save the Children, London (1992)
20. *Bed and breakfast exchange briefing*, London (1993)
21. *Homelessness in rural areas: summary of research findings*, Research Report number 12, Rural Development Commission, Salisbury (1992)
22. *Safe and houses? - guidelines for the safety of children in temporary accommodation*, Child Accident Prevention Trust, London, (1991)
23. *Accidents and the safety of children in temporary accommodation: suggested approaches to preventive work*, Child Accident Prevention Trust/ Save the Children, London (1993)
24. *Healthy housing: the role of the environmental health services*, Audit Commission, HMSO, London (1991)
25. *Healthy housing: a practical guide*, Ranson R, E&FN

Spon, WHO (1991)

26. *Family spending: a report on the 1991 Family Expenditure Survey*, Government Statistical Service, HMSO, London (1992) Table 111

27. *Poverty in black and white*, Child Poverty Action Group, London (1992)

28. *English house condition survey:1991 - preliminary report on unfit dwellings*, Department of the Environment, HMSO, London (1993)

29. *Developing local authority housing strategies*, Audit Commission, HMSO, London (1992)

30. *Homes cost less than homelessness*, Shelter, London (1992)

31. see reference 16

32. 'Building a brighter future', Burke T, *Young People Now* (May 1993) p30

33. see reference 21

34. *Home safety*, Fact sheet, Child Accident Prevention Trust, London (July 1990)

35. *Home accident surveillance system*, Department of Trade and Industry, HMSO, London (1987-1991)

36. *Home accident admissions to Northern Ireland hospitals 1982-1991*, Royal Society for the Prevention of Accidents & Northern Ireland Home Accident Prevention Council, Belfast (1992)

37. *Thinking of small children: access, provision and play*, Jaspert J et al, Women's Design Service and London Borough of Camden (1988)

38. 'Good practice for child friendly facilities in public places', Notes from *Children and the environment conference*, National Children's Bureau, London (11 March 1993)

39. *Children's range behaviour*, C. Parkinson, Birmingham Play Board (1987)

40. *Mean streets - the crisis on our doorsteps*, National Playing Fields Association, London (1989)

41. *A review of play and recreational needs of young people growing up on housing estates*, National Association for the Care and Resettlement of Offenders, London (1988)

42. *The child in the country*, C. Ward, Bedford Square Press (1988)

43. *Social attitudes in Northern Ireland: the second report*, Stringer P and Robinson G (eds), Blackstaff Press Ltd (1992) Chapter 2

44. *Children and the environment*, Rosenbaum M, National Children's Bureau, London (1993)

45. *Part M of the Building Regulations (1991)*, for England and Wales, Part R of the Northern Ireland regulations and *Part T of the Building Standards (Scotland) Regulations (1990)*, for Scotland.

46. *City challenge: bidding guidance 1993-94*, Department of the Environment, London (February 1992)

47. *Road accidents Great Britain 1991*, Department of Transport, HMSO, London (1992)

48. *Basic principles of child accident prevention*, Child Accident Prevention Trust London (1989)

49. Sibert J, *British Medical Journal*, vol 304 (1992) pp1143-1146 [in *Child Safety Review*, CAPT, London, (June 1992) p8]

50. 'Safety as a social value: a community approach', H. Roberts et al, in *Private risks and public dangers*, Scott S et al (ed), Avebury, Aldershot (1992) pp184-200

51. (a) 'Preventing accidental injuries to children', Levene S, *Paediatric Nursing* vol 4 no 9 (1992) pp12-14
    (b) *Epidemiology of childhood Accidents - first report of April 1993*, Child Accident Prevention Project, Belfast (1993)

52. 'Causes of fatal childhood accidents involving head injury in the Northern Region 1979-86', Sharples P et al, *British Medical Journal*, vol 301 (1990) pp1193-1197

53. *On the state of public health for the year 1991, the annual report of the Chief Medical Officer of the Department of Health*, HMSO, London (1992)

54. 'Accidents in schools', Jackson H, *Child Safety Review*, CAPT, London (December 1992) p4

55. *Home and leisure accident research: 1990 data*, Consumer Safety Unit, Department of Trade and Industry, London (1992)

56. see reference 51(a)

57. *The health of the nation*, Department of Health, HMSO, London (1992)

58. *Protocol for investment in health gain - injuries*, Welsh Health Planning Forum, Welsh Office/NHS Directorate (1992)

59. *A regional strategy, 1992-1997*, Department of Health and Social Services, N. Ireland (1992)

60. *Scotland's health: a challenge to us all*, HMSO (1992)

61. 'The health of the nation', Pankhurst L, *Child Safety Review*, Child Accident Prevention Trust, London (Dec 1992) p5

62. *Health in Scotland - 1992*, Chief Medical Officer of Health, HMSO (1992)

63. Legislation includes the *Health and Safety at Work Act 1974*, Sections 3 and 4 place a clear duty on playground providers to ensure, as far as reasonably practicable the health and safety of those using the facilities. The *Occupiers' Liability Acts 1957 and 1984* allows damages to be paid to people injured using the facilities. Section 2(3)a emphasises the special care required to ensure the safety of children. There is also a limited duty to ensure the safety of trespassers. For example, if something on site is likely to attract children and then be a danger to them eg broken glass hidden under sand the owner is responsible.

64. see reference 55

65. *Danger - children at play*, Birmingham Townswomen's Guild (1991)

66. *Play equipment intended for permanent installation outdoors*, British Standards Institute, Milton Keynes, BS5696. Parts 1 and 2 (1986). Further amendments (1990)

67. see reference 55

68. *Children, transport and the quality of life*, Policy Studies Institute, London (1993)

69. *One false move... a study of children's independent mobility*, M. Hillman et al, Policy Studies Institute, London (1990)

70. *General household survey - 1990*, Office of Population Census and Surveys, HMSO, London (1992) Table 3.22

71. see reference 26, Table 3

72. *Going places with children - a survey of the facilities for babies and children while travelling on public transport*, Fyfe G, Scottish Consumer Council, Glasgow (1993)

73. *Disability Unit annual report 1992/1993*, Department of Transport, London (1993)

74. see reference 47

75. *Child pedal cycle accidents*, Fact sheet, Child Accident Prevention Trust, London (Dec 1988)

76. *Cycling: towards health and safety*, British Medical Association, Oxford University Press (1992)

77. *Cutting pedestrian casualties: cost effective ways of making walking safer*, Preston B, Transport and Health Study Group, Transport 2000, London (1992)

78. *Occupational mortality England and Wales - childhood supplement*, OPCS, HMSO, London (1988)

79. *Children and roads: a safer way*, Department of Transport, London (1990)

80. *Care on the road*, Royal Society for the Prevention of Accidents (1993)

81. 'Into European time,' *Child Safety Review*, CAPT, London (Dec 1992) p3

82. 'Safety on the roads', S. Hook, *Play it safe newsletter*, CAPT, London (December 1992) p3

83. *British Medical Journal*, vol 305, 1 August 1992, [in *Transport Retort*, Transport 2000, London (Sept-Oct 1992)]

84. *Trends in transport in the countryside*, Countryside Commission, Manchester (1992)

85. *Reducing transport emissions through planning*, Department of the Environment and Department of Transport, HMSO, London (1993)

86. 'Asthma study may lead to curb on cars', Lean G, *Observer*, London (27 July 1993) p7

87. 'Why boys and girls stay in to play', Wheway R, *Guardian*, London (12 August 1992)

88. *Hazardous waste and human health*, British Medical Association, Oxford University Press (1991) pp87-88

89. 'Pesticide Residues', *Which?*, Consumer's Association, London (October 1990)

90. *Pesticides, chemicals and health*, British Medical Association, London (1992)

91. *Pesticides in the diets of infants and children*, National Research Council, National Academic Press, Washington DC (1993)

92. 'MAFF tests miss pesticide contamination', *Living Earth & The Food Magazine*, The Food Commission, London (May/July 1993)

93. 'Dodgy residues found in 10% of UK lettuces', *SAFE Alliance press release*, Sustainable Agriculture Food and Environment, London (29 July 1993)

94. 'The continuing hazard of lead in drinking water', Russell Jones R, *The Lancet*, London (16 September 1989)

95. Economics of lead pipe replacement, Water Research Centre (1992)

96. see reference 44

97. *The lead scandal*, Wilson D, Heinemann, London (1983) p30

98. 'Influence of blood lead on the ability and attainment of children in Edinburgh', Fulton M et al, *The Lancet*, London (30 May 1987)

99. 'A retrospective analysis of blood lead in mentally retarded children', Moore M et al, *The Lancet*, London (2 April 1977)

100. 'The Sensitivity of Children to Lead', Davis M and Grant L, in *Similarities and differences between children and adults: implications for risk assessment*, Guzelian P et al (eds), Washington DC USA International Life Sciences Institute (1992)

101. see reference 44

102. 'Limit on lead in drinking water could cost billions', Watts F, *Independent*, London (29 September 1992) p8

103. *Millions supplied with polluted drinking water - 'customers champion' ties to sell them short*, Press release, Friends of the Earth, London (13 July 1993)

104. *Air pollution and child health*, Read C, Greenpeace UK, London (1991)

105. see reference 44

106. *Digest of environmental protection and water statistics, No 15, 1992*, Department of the Environment, HMSO, London (1993)

107. *Gasping for change*, Greenpeace UK (1992)

108. 'Effects of ambient ozone on respiratory function in active normal children', Spektor D et al, in *American Review of Respiratory Disease* vol.137 (February 1988) pp313-320

109. see reference 104

110. *Air quality in the UK: a summary of results from instrumented air monitoring networks in 1990-91*, Warren Spring Laboratory, Stevenage (1992)

111. 'Effects of ambient sulphur oxides and suspended particulates on respiratory health of pre-adolescent children', Ware C et al, *American Review of Respiratory Disease*, vol.133 (May 1986) pp834-842

112. see reference 104

113. see reference 106

114. see reference 44

115. *Smoking among secondary school children in 1990*, Lader D and Matheson J, HMSO, London (1990)

116. *Smoking and the young*, Royal College of Physicians, London (1992)

117. *Buyer beware! a guide to finding out about contaminated land*, Friends of the Earth, London (1993)

118. *Bathing water*, Briefing sheet, Friends of the Earth, London (1991)

119. 'Symptomatology of children in contact with sea water contaminated with sewage', Alexander L et al, *Journal of Epidemiology and Community Health*, vol 46 (1992) pp340-344

120. see reference 44

121. see reference 106, Table 4.1

122. "Britain condemned over dirty beaches", Palmer J, *The Guardian*, (15 July 1993) p4

123. *Lead in food: progress report*, Food Surveillance Paper no. 27, Ministry of Agriculture Fisheries and Food, HMSO, London (1989)

124. Pesticide fears grow as number of babies born blind doubles', Boulton A, *The Observer*, (31 January 1993) p3

125. see reference 57 p29

126. 'Government to support Institute for Environment and Health', *Department of the Environment news release*, London (27 July 1993)

127. see reference 106

128. Think globally, act locally - putting the '92 Earth Summit into practice, Department of the Environment, London (1992)

129. see reference 3

130. *Paying for quality, the political perspective*, OFWAT, Birmingham (1993)

131. see reference 103

132. *Report on the financial sector working party on environmental liability*, Advisory Committee on Business and the Environment, Section 201, p21, Department of Trade and Industry/Department of the Environment, HMSO (1993)

UK Agenda for Children

7 Education

# Contents

*The unreferenced quotations in this report are comments made during a consultation exercise undertaken by the Children's Rights Development Unit with groups of young people throughout the UK.*

# 1 Introduction

**1.1** An initial glance at the requirements in the Convention with regard to education could lead to the conclusion that current legislation in the UK more than satisfies the minimum standards it establishes as the right of all children. In the UK all children have a right to full-time education from the beginning of the term following their fifth birthday up to the age of 19. In N Ireland, many children are obliged to begin school at four as the Education Reform (N Ireland) Order 1989 requires children born on or before 1 July to start school in September of the year in which they become 5. Our legislation therefore well exceeds the more limited expectations contained in Article 28.

**1.2** However, it is necessary to take a much broader view of the Convention if proper consideration is to be given to the standards it is setting for children in an industrialised society. It is necessary to address not only the statutory provision of education and the basic rights to that educational service but also the equality of access to it, the rights of children to be heard in the education system, the quality of the experience of school for all children and respect within the school system for children's civil rights. If children's rights in relation to education are to be progressed in the UK, it is necessary to move beyond the traditional yardsticks of literacy levels and attendance rates, important though these are, and develop more sophisticated measures to evaluate the extent to which our educational provision complies with all the principles embodied in the Convention.

**1.3** Government policy on education has over the past decade been dominated by concerns with parental choice, the National Curriculum, and the encouragement of greater managerial and financial independence for schools. It has sought to diminish the role of local authorities in planning and managing the delivery of education and to devolve that responsibility down to the individual school. This process of devolution, together with the right of parents to choose schools for their children, have created a market in education in which schools are in competition with each other. These policies, however, whilst concerned with the rights of parents, have singularly failed to address the rights of children although they have major implications for them. The Convention offers an opportunity to construct a principled framework within which to develop the education service and this report undertakes an examination of the implications of existing Government policy within that framework.

# 2 Relevant articles in the Convention

## 2.1 General principles

**Article 2:** all rights in the Convention must apply without discrimination of any kind irrespective of race, colour, language, religion, national, ethnic or social origin, disability or other status.

**Article 3:** the duty in all actions to consider the best interests of the child.

**Article 12:** the right to express an opinion and to have that opinion taken into account in any matter or procedure affecting the child.

## 2.2 Articles relevant to education

**Article 19:** the right to protection from all forms of violence, injury, abuse, neglect or exploitation.

**Article 22:** the right of refugee children to appropriate protection and assistance in pursuit of the rights in the Convention.

**Article 23:** the right of disabled children to special care, education and training to ensure the fullest possible social integration.

**Article 28:** the right to education, including vocational education, on the basis of equality of opportunity.

**Article 29:** the duty of the government to direct education at developing the child's fullest personality and talents and promoting respects for human rights.

**Article 30:** the rights of children from minority communities to enjoy their own culture, language and practise their own religion and culture.

**Article 37:** the duty of the government to prohibit torture, cruel treatment or punishment.

*For the full wording of the articles, see the UN Convention on the Rights of the Child, see page 311.*

# 3 Access to education

## Article 28

### 3.1 Admissions procedures

**3.1.1** Article 28 affirms children's rights to education *'on the basis of equal opportunity'*. This requirement is underpinned by Article 2 which stresses that all the rights in the Convention must apply *'without discrimination of any kind irrespective of the child's or his or her parent's or legal guardian's race, colour, sex, language, religion. political or other opinion, national, ethnic or social origin, property, disability, birth or other status'*. These principles are consistent with the provisions in the Race Relations Act 1976 which make it unlawful to discriminate against someone either directly or indirectly in the field of education. (This legislation does not apply in N Ireland). Section 17 of the Act states that educational establishments may not discriminate on the grounds of race in the terms on which they offer admission, refuse applications, or in the way access is offered. Despite this legislative protection, some of the procedures adopted by schools on admissions can serve either explicitly or implicitly to discriminate against certain groups of children.

**3.1.2** The Commission for Racial Equality's (CRE) report *Secondary school admissions*, published in 1992, which investigated the admissions policy in Hertfordshire County Council indicates how easily policies can be indirectly discriminatory unless positive measures are taken to tackle them[1]. The report found that published criteria for admission were having a sibling already at the school, nearness to the school and other reasons given for wanting a place. But in practice, the likelihood of obtaining a place rested heavily on the written application from parents and the number of reasons it contained for wanting a child to attend that particular school. This system meant that it was more difficult for Asian children to obtain a place because their parents were less likely to be aware of the informal criteria for admission and because, for many families whose first language is not English, it is more difficult to produce a written application. It is unlikely that Hertfordshire is alone in operating such policies and there is, therefore, a need for scrutiny by all LEAs and schools of their admissions policies. The existence of discriminatory barriers to obtaining school places is clearly at odds with the principles embodied in Article 2 and Article 28.

**3.1.3** There are numerous other ways in which admissions procedures can discriminate against children from minority ethnic communities. The CRE points to the commonly used practice of giving preference to siblings in school admissions policies which can serve to perpetuate a pool within a community which has access while excluding those who have more recently arrived in an area[2]. It also expresses concern about certain rules requiring uniforms which are unacceptable to particular racial groups, schools which require applications a year in advance of admission, requirements to apply in person and requirements that parents demonstrate a commitment to the school. Many of these practices are not introduced with intent to discriminate but may have the consequence of excluding certain groups of pupils. The growing number of schools which have grant maintained status and which are independent of the local authority means that it is of even greater importance that all schools are required to operate admissions policies that are non-discriminatory and ensure that all children have equal opportunities to schools.

**3.1.4** The disproportionate numbers of Afro-Caribbean boys who are excluded from school indicates that there is a problem of discrimination against this group of pupils. There is often a tendency to stereotype them as troublesome. Organisations such as the CRE have expressed concerns that, with the growing emphasis on schools competing with each other for pupils, they will become more reluctant to accept children who are perceived as more disruptive or demanding. There is a danger that many children from black and minority ethnic communities may find it increasingly difficult to obtain school places. It is imperative therefore that measures are taken to ensure that admissions policies specifically address the need not to allow discriminatory practices to develop. Failure to do so would deny both the right to equality of opportunity and the right not to be discriminated against on grounds of race. Any policies which did so would be in breach both of the Race Relations Act 1976 and Articles 2 and 28 of the Convention.

**3.1.5** There are also problems for many Gypsy and Traveller children in gaining access to education. The National Gypsy Council has expressed concern that many head-teachers and local education authorities are reluctant to accept Traveller children particularly when there is a real possibility that the child will be moved within a short period of time[3]. They advocate strongly that Gypsy and Traveller children should be educated within the framework of mainstream education. Segregated provision isolates them from opportunities for social education and denies children, both from the Traveller and the settled community, the opportunity to learn from each others' way of life. Traveller children need access to a broad-based curriculum and a variety of teachers with different expertise and skills. This can only be achieved through admission to mainstream schools. Compliance with Articles 2 and 28 requires that Traveller children have access education on the same basis as other children.

**3.1.6** Schools are required to undertake ethnic monitoring of **admissions** at the entry ages of five and 11 years. However they do not have to monitor **applications** for admission. The collection of this data would provide extremely useful material with which to analyse the extent of any discrimination ensuing from admission policies and give guidance to the need for changes in policy to overcome that discrimination.

### ACTION REQUIRED FOR COMPLIANCE

**Compliance with Article 2, the right not to be discriminated against, requires that:**

● **education authorities, governing bodies, the Funding Agency for Schools and headteachers are encouraged to ensure that all admission procedures are actively scrutinised to ensure that they do not discriminate against any group of children, that they comply with the requirements of the Race Relations Act 1976 and the CRE Code of Practice on the Elimination of Racial Discrimination in Education;**

● **local education authorities and grant maintained schools develop clear guidelines on admission**

**policies.** Schools should be required to publish their admission criteria in an accessible form and in relevant community languages;

● all schools, including grant maintained schools, undertake ethnic monitoring of applications for admission and analyse the data with a view to changing any practices which discriminate against any groups of children.

## 3.2 Exclusions

*Growth in the number of exclusions*

**3.2.1** Article 28.1(a) and (b) states that the Government must '*recognise the right of the child to education and with a view to achieving this, and on the basis of equality of opportunity … make primary education compulsory and available free to all [and] encourage the development of different forms of secondary education [making] them free and accessible to all*'. Article 28.1(e) goes on to state that they must '*take measures to encourage regular attendance at schools and the reduction of drop out rates*'. The Education Act 1944 gives all children between the ages of five and 19 the right to education, but there has been growing concern over the past couple of years over the substantial rise in the numbers of children being excluded from school and therefore failing to receive an adequate education. In 1992 the National Union of Teachers undertook a survey of 26 authorities in England and Wales which revealed that there had been a 20% increase in the numbers of children excluded. They estimate that if this increased level is reflected in all other authorities then there are an estimated 25,000 children being excluded from school each year. The Department for Education (DFE) published the results of the National Exclusions Reporting System, a two-year survey of school exclusions, in April 1993[4]. The analysis of returns from local authorities over the period 1990-92 shows there were 6,743 permanent exclusions; 2,910 in the first year and 3,833 in the second. These figures demonstrate the substantial rise which has taken place over the last 12 months. The DFE survey also reveals that there were often lengthy delays in securing alternative provision for excluded pupils either by admission to another school or otherwise. The actual situation is worse than the figures reveal because numbers of parents are encouraged to remove their children voluntarily. Also worrying is the growing number of primary school children being excluded.

**3.2.2** There are many complex reasons for the growth in the problem. The National Union of Teachers argues that two primary causes can be identified[5]. First, the Union expresses concern about the level of resources available to schools for support services for children with special needs, such as psychological services, and also points to the difficulties of working with increased class sizes which give teachers less time to deal with the needs of individual pupils. Secondly, it points to the Government policy requiring the production and publication of league tables of school performance: the Union considers that this puts pressure on schools to improve the appearance of their results and that this makes the presence of children with behavioural problems or special needs less attractive. It encourages schools to exclude them in order to make the school more 'marketable' to parents. This approach is not consistent with Article 3 and the requirement to consider the best interests of the child, nor is it consistent with the right of all children to full-time education on the basis of equality of opportunity.

*'I left care and went home and as soon as that happened, social services wanted nothing to do with me and education wanted nothing to do with me. The pair of them thought: good he's off our hands, pass the buck to someone else. It was brilliant living at home again and I wanted to go to a normal school again but once you have got the reputation of being chucked out of school a lot of schools won't accept you.'*
(14 year-old, North East)

**3.2.3** The Advisory Centre for Education (ACE), an independent organisation which advises parents, reports a substantial increase over the period 1988-91 in inquiries about children excluded from school[6]. ACE points to a number of concerns raised by parents about the ways in which exclusions are handled, such as injustice in the way children involved in the same incidents are treated differently and long delays in finding alternative school-placements after an exclusion, with all the consequent implications for loss of education, particularly for those in crucial exam years.

**3.2.4** The Government, in response to concerns over this issue, introduced provisions in the Education Act 1993 which abolish the category of indefinite exclusions in England and Wales. This change represents a considerable improvement over the previous position where children could be excluded indefinitely without any right of appeal, a situation which breached both Article 28.1 and Article 12.2 and the right of the child to be heard in any judicial or administrative proceedings. However, there are still no criteria set out in legislation which must be satisfied before a child can be excluded, although draft guidance issued for consultation early in 1994 does include such criteria. Given the serious nature of a decision to exclude, together with evidence from the DFE's survey of wide and inexplicable differences in the patterns of exclusions amongst schools, the application of statutory criteria would be of considerable benefit to parents, pupils and headteachers. Such an approach would be consistent with the requirement to protect the right of the child to education and to ensure that decisions made on exclusions were rigorous in challenging any potential discrimination when excluding a child from school.

*'Catholic schools especially don't like kids in care; you must stop with your family no matter what happens. I got expelled by getting into a fight with a girl who lived at home. It was exactly the same situation: she was in a fight and got excluded, they had a meeting and she was back in school the following day; they had a meeting about me and you can guess the rest.'*
(16 year-old, North East)

**3.2.5** In Scotland, although indefinite exclusions are still possible, schools are only allowed to exclude pupils where **either** it is considered that the pupil's parents are failing to comply or allowing pupils to fail to comply with school rules **or** the school considers that the pupil's continued presence would be detrimental to discipline or the educational well-being of pupils.

**3.2.6** However, despite the restrictions that apply in Scotland, there is evidence from a recent survey of discipline in Scottish schools that exclusions are used regularly as a short-term punishment. These findings are consistent with the concerns expressed by the Scottish Child Law Centre over the use of exclusions and highlight the need for further research into the application of the law[7].

*Rights of appeal against exclusions*

**3.2.7** Parents, but not children under 18, do have a right of appeal but only where an exclusion is permanent. Compliance with Article 12.2 which states that children must *'be provided with the opportunity to be heard in any judicial or administrative proceedings affecting the child, either directly or through a representative or an appropriate body'* would necessitate that this right should be extended to children. Children can be excluded without having any opportunity whatever to defend themselves or to challenge the decision. It is also important to recognise formally that the child's perspective will not necessarily coincide with the parents' views or wishes. It is of the greatest importance that children should be given a right to be heard when a decision of such significance is being made and should also have access to independent advocacy.

> *'If a child becomes too much for a school and it comes to a decision to expel, then there should be a meeting, so they know why it is occurring and then be part of the decision if they want to go to another school or whatever, instead of being just left on the streets.'*
> (18 year-old, London)

*Evidence of race discrimination in exclusions*

**3.2.8** The evidence on patterns of exclusion also reveal other worrying trends. The DFE survey shows that Afro-Caribbean pupils are disproportionately represented amongst the pupils excluded: 8.5% of the total, four times their proportion in the school population. The Commission for Racial Equality documents evidence of widespread racism and harassment amongst pupils in schools and a formal investigation by the Commission in Birmingham in 1985 found that children from minority ethnic communities were four times more likely to be suspended for the same offence as other children[8]. Since that time, considerable efforts have been made by Birmingham Education Authority to tackle discrimination but even so the figure has only been reduced to a likelihood three times as high. A report published in 1992 by Wolverhampton Race Equality Council found that between 1986-90 pupils from minority groups comprised 40.8% of the total of those excluded. The percentage of the local population aged 0-15 years from ethnic minorities is 26%. Nottinghamshire Education Authority produced a report on exclusions in the year 1990/91 which reveals that Afro-Caribbean boys are excluded at five times the rate of other children[9]. These figures are deeply disturbing and raise concerns not only that such pupils are being denied their right to education under Article 28 but are also being discriminated against in breach of Article 2.

> *'They would rather pick on a black person so you end up getting blamed a lot. By the time I got to my third year I was expelled. My mother and I fought for eight months to get me back into school, because you don't learn anything in a centre.'*
> (18 year-old, London)

**3.2.9** At present, schools are not required to monitor exclusions according to ethnicity. It is important that such a requirement is introduced in order that systematic evidence is available to analyse the problem and introduce necessary changes to overcome discrimination against this group of pupils.

*Exclusions of children with special needs*

**3.2.10** A further concern highlighted by the rise in reported exclusions is the high proportion of children with special needs included in the figures. Pupils with statements of special educational needs represented 15% of the total in the second year of the DFE survey although they represent only 2% of the whole school population[10]. It was the view of many parents in the ACE survey that schools were unable to cope with their children because there was insufficient support in the classroom to deal with their educational needs[11]. Many children with special needs do create additional pressures on teachers in the classroom. Schools are widely reporting cuts in the specialist services that they need if they are to teach such children effectively. Without these services the behaviour of children with special needs often deteriorates, leading to the increased likelihood of exclusion. As such, they are being denied the right to education. Providing such children with equal opportunity of access to education in line with Article 28 does necessarily depend on the provision of the support services to ensure that their educational needs are met.

*Education for excluded pupils*

**3.2.11** Once a child is excluded, their access to education can be seriously eroded. Many children fail to obtain another school for several months. Home tuition is only part-time at best and there are considerable variations in its provision. The Education Act 1993 introduces new Pupil Referral Units for excluded children. It will be important to monitor the resources, use and effectiveness of these units. There is also a need for research into the outcome of exclusion in terms of alternative educational provision and attainment.

> *'Your reputation follows you around. They made me out to be this big thing who came into classes and disrupted them, yet I was asking them for education because I was worried about missing out so much that I just wouldn't be able to catch up. Now there is some light at the end of the tunnel but I think three years is a long time for someone to sort me out a stable education.'*
> (14 year-old, North East)

*Children excluded because of lack of provision*

**3.2.12** There are also a small number of children who are excluded from school simply because no places are available. In the London Borough of Tower Hamlets, for example, there were in early 1993 100 children out of school and who had been on a waiting list for a place for up to six months. In other authorities, schools have had to operate on a part-time basis during the course of the 1992/93 academic year because the authority lacked the funding to keep the schools open. These are problems which to date have only affected a small number of children, but it is a new and disturbing development which needs careful monitoring as it is clearly in breach of the Government's obligation under Article 28.1.

*Children excluded from education rights*

**3.2.13** Children and young people detained in prisons and young offender institutions, and those detained under the Mental Health Act have no rights to education (Education Act 1994, section 116) although many are under school-leaving age. Under the Convention, education should be available to all without discrimination.

## ACTION REQUIRED FOR COMPLIANCE

**Compliance with Article 28, the right to education on the basis of equality of opportunity, consistent with Article 2, the right not to be discriminated against, requires that:**

- legislative criteria to limit school exclusions are introduced throughout the UK which place an obligation on schools to take all reasonable steps to prevent the exclusion and to satisfy themselves that, unless excluded, the pupil's behaviour is likely to be seriously detrimental to the education or welfare of the pupil or other pupils, or to the welfare of the staff;

- research into exclusions in Scottish schools should be carried out with a view to identifying the effectiveness of the legislation and the need for further guidelines to schools on its implementation;

- ethnic monitoring of school exclusions should be introduced as a requirement for all schools. The data gathered should then be used to develop policies to tackle any identified discrimination;

- all unmet need for support services for children with special needs is recorded and built into the planning process for the development of services;

- monitoring of the new pupil referral units is undertaken with reference to the resources available for their development, levels of use, effectiveness and the experience of children using them;

- children and young people detained in penal establishments or under the Mental Health Act should retain basic rights to full-time education.

Compliance with Article 12, the right to be heard in administrative or judicial proceedings, requires that:

- children, in addition to parents, have a right of appeal against exclusions;

- children have a right to be present at the hearing and to independent advocacy to help them present their case.

## 3.3 Racism in schools

3.3.1 Education in the UK is provided, in principle, on an equal basis for all children and the Race Relations Act 1976 renders it unlawful in England, Wales and Scotland (although not in N Ireland) for any child to be discriminated against on grounds of race. However, we live in a society in which racism, including race discrimination, is widespread. Children are particularly vulnerable to its consequences and its presence can have a significant effect on the opportunities children have to benefit from the education system. The Convention, in addition to defining freedom from discrimination as a right (Article 2), links the principle with the right to an identity (Article 8), to be free from abuse and harassment (Articles 16 and 19) and to have one's culture and language and religion respected (Article 30). These principles must be translated into policies which are effectively implemented, monitored and evaluated. Furthermore, necessary resources must be committed to rectifying any failings in policy.

> 'I went to school until I was 15. Every time I travelled around and we stopped I would have to go to a different school. It was horrible, they didn't accept you and just called me names.[12]'

3.3.2 We know at present that this does not happen anywhere near adequately. The recent HMI report *Education*

*in England 1990-1991* observes that progress in schools on equal opportunities is patchy with too wide a divide between policies and actual practice[13]. It also observes that there was 'substantial under-achievement by some groups of ethnic minority pupils ... Of particular concern was the lack of success of black British (Caribbean) boys and pupils of Bangladeshi origin'. A recent survey based on extensive interviews with children over two years reveals that race issues and racism are significant features of the culture of children in predominantly white primary schools[14]. Racism impinges on the curriculum content, the attitudes of many of the staff, bullying and name calling in the playground, low educational expectations for black pupils an racial stereotyping in many presumptions about behaviour of black children. The accumulative effect of the experience of racism is inevitably detrimental to a child's capacity to take maximum advantage of the educational system. This is evidenced in the consistently poorer academic achievements attained by students from some minority ethnic groups. It is compounded by the lack of black role models in the teaching profession. Recent DFE figures indicate that only 3.3% of teachers are from minority ethnic communities as compared with 8.5% of pupils.

> 'My experience in school was that if you are black then they don't give a damn about you. If you get caught talking then you are straight out of the door. White kids will get away with it and so you have to sit in silence because you know that as soon as you open your mouth you will be out of the door.'
> (17 year-old, London)

3.3.3 One of the difficulties we face in assessing the extent to which children from minority ethnic communities experience disadvantage and discrimination is the lack of information. For example, as stated above, whilst schools are required to collect ethnic data on pupils or entry at five and 11 years, there is no requirement to monitor applications to schools. Nor is there any requirement to monitor suspensions, exclusions, drop-out rates, success and failure rates. Without this information we are not able to assess the extent of our compliance with Article 2 or to develop appropriate policies for tackling discrimination.

### ACTION REQUIRED FOR COMPLIANCE

Compliance with Article 2, the right not to be discriminated against, requires that:

- the provisions of the Race Relations Act 1976 are extended to N Ireland;

- schools collect ethnic data on the origins of pupils at key stages - including applications and admissions, exclusions and suspensions, truancy rates, setting and banding assessments including attainments, examination entries and results, and school leaver destinations. This information should be used by inspectors of schools to assess evidence of race discrimination and to ensure that appropriate action is taken to tackle it. There is also a need for research into low attainment among specific groups.

## 3.4 Children looked after by the local authority

3.4.1 There is growing evidence that children who have been looked after by the local authority are leaving school with extremely poor and often no academic qualifications. In response to the evident failure on the part of many local authorities to take this issue sufficiently seriously, a campaign has recently been launched by children looked after by the local authority which sets out a charter of rights to education for children in care. This campaign is being co-ordinated through the Who Cares? Trust, an organisation committed to widening the scope of services to young people looked after by local authorities. The concerns derive from evidence that as many as 75% of such children leave school with no qualifications at all, compared with 11% in the whole school-leaving population[15]. More than half those who left care in 1992 are either unemployed or, of those that are employed, often in badly paid and unskilled jobs. Up to one-third are living on the streets and a fifth are likely to end up in prison. These findings are consistent with a small-scale survey of young people in care in Scotland carried out by the Children's Rights Development Unit in 1993. Of 22 young people interviewed, 13 commented that they had attended school less often after going into care and many identified disruption and negative attitudes of teachers as contributory factors to their deteriorating education.

*'You get picked on by teachers for not wearing the correct uniform and they will suspend you or expel you much quicker. The teachers also become more nosey when you are in care. Since I went into care I have been kicked out of school four times and now I'm permanently excluded.[16]'*

**3.4.2** These figures are extremely disturbing and would appear to indicate that, whilst these children may have formal rights to education in line with Article 28, their access to an education which offers them equal life chances is seriously restricted. Article 2, in listing those groups of children who must not experience discrimination, adds *'or other status'*. This was intended to extend the scope of the Article as widely as possible and certainly includes children whose status is defined as being accommodated by or in the care of the local authority.

**3.4.3** The underlying reasons for these poor results are complex. Very often, there has been a problem with education prior to the child being looked after by the local authority but the problems are then compounded by the removal from home. Research undertaken by the National Foundation for Educational Research reveals a number of interlinking problems which result in poor achievement[17]. The child's education was frequently disrupted by the removal from home. Social workers and other professionals tended to have very low expectations of children in their care and therefore expected low achievement from them, which meant that less emphasis was placed on education than perhaps should have been. Often no-one takes responsibility for the child's education; for example, visiting the school, attending parents' evenings, checking work, listening to problems associated with school or homework. There was a lack of support for carers, especially those looking after children with special needs, and residential homes were often not able to provide quiet space for or help with homework. Far too little attention was generally given by social workers to education as of critical importance to children in care. School often tended to be seen as a means of containing the child rather than offering something of value in its own right.

*'You are expected to be a bad influence and a terror but kids are in care for lots of reasons - not because they have done crimes or been kicked out of school and, if they have, in a lot of cases it's been because of serious problems at home. But*

*they expect you to be bad and so you think okay I will.'*
(15 year-old, North East)

**3.4.4** The research also highlights a need for much better liaison between social services and education departments to ensure that the child is not 'lost' in the system with no-one following through their school career. Manchester City Council commented that: 'It is often assumed that the education service as a whole ... operates in a somewhat benign fashion so as to be automatically inclusive, supportive and responsive to children irrespective of their backgrounds or circumstances. It is also assumed that with the full weight of statute behind every child's educational entitlement equal and appropriate access to the wider education service is assured ... to many children the education world is beneficent only in theory. In reality it often constitutes failure, authority, remoteness, domestic pressure, legal problems, regulations, delays and incomprehensible bureaucracy. Nowhere is this more true than for children and families who come into contact with the social services department'.

**3.4.5** In response to these concerns, the Council have established a major new service to redress the problems of inequality of access experienced by young people they are looking after. They have created a team of 35 teachers, integrated within the social services department, whose objective is to ensure that young people looked after by the local authority do not lose out educationally for avoidable reasons. It also provides a source of educational advice, support and advocacy to the social services department. Since its inception in 1990, it has produced dramatic results. By supporting foster carers, the number of breakdowns in placements has gone down, reducing the demand for residential placements.

## ACTION REQUIRED FOR COMPLIANCE

**Compliance with Article 28, the right to education on the basis of equality of opportunity, consistent with Article 2, the right not to be discriminated against, requires that:**

- **all staff working with children and young people looked after by the local authority - social workers, foster carers, residential staff - receive training on the importance of education in the lives of those young people;**

- **both initial and in-service teacher education includes information about the general circumstances of children looked after by the local authority in order that teachers can become more sensitive to the implications for those children and be more aware of their needs in relation to education;**

- **social services and education departments review and evaluate their arrangements for liaison and collaboration over education provision for children looked after by the local authority. Where possible, specialist services designed to provide educational support to young people looked after, foster carers and other professionals in social services departments should be established. Reviews should always address the education of the child concerned;**

- **individual case files should have a separate section on education.**

## 3.5 Poverty

**3.5.1** Whilst free education is available for all children in the UK, there is evidence of a growing pattern of charging for certain services and of direct requests to parents for contributions to the school. A survey of 2,000 schools undertaken by the National Confederation of Parent Teacher Associations (NCPTA) revealed that between 1985 and 1990 there had been a threefold increase in the number of schools making direct requests for financial help with equipment, books or teaching materials[18]. The incidence of such requests had risen from 15% to 50%. Some schools are raising money from parents to resource basic repairs and decorations to the school. This increase in the expectations being made of parents coincides with a substantial growth in the numbers of families living in poverty and therefore unable to afford the contributions being requested.

**3.5.2** This trend has a number of consequences for children living in poor families. It creates a widening disparity between schools based in more affluent areas and those in poor or deprived parts of the community. Schools whose intake is predominantly middle class are generally able to raise the money necessary for basic equipment the local authority is no longer able to provide. However, in poor areas where there are high numbers of families living on benefit or on low incomes, it is not possible to raise comparable sums of money: so these schools and their pupils are losing out. This pattern is leading to a growing disparity between schools in breach of Article 2 and the equal rights of all children, and can lead to a deterioration in the quality both of education being provided and the physical environment of the schools.

**3.5.3** Children are also being asked increasingly for contributions towards school activities. There is evidence that some grant-maintained schools are asking parents to contribute to the costs of teachers' salaries. A school in Cheltenham recently asked all parents to donate £210 to save a teaching post. Family Service Units in its response to the Education White Paper *Choice and diversity* comments that its research has shown that charges for school trips cause serious hardship for parents on income support[19]. It observes that: 'Although these charge are in theory "voluntary", nearly all felt they had to pay, either because they did not realise they could be exempted or because they did not want their child to be singled out'.

**3.5.4** Many parents were faced with the choice of cutting back on basic expenses for other necessities in order to pay, or denying their child the opportunity to go. These additional costs can place very real strains on a limited family budget and force some children to withdraw from school activities. The increasing numbers of children apparently faced with this dilemma would appear to be in breach of Article 28 and the right of all children '*to education ... on the basis of equal opportunity*'. The NCPTA survey indicated that the policies of charging for out of school activities and visits have resulted in these activities being reduced in 30% of primary schools and 22% of secondary schools. These financial demands on parents are clearly resulting, in many instances, either in the individual child withdrawing from the activity, or the school itself withdrawing. The outcome is that children's education is being restricted because neither the school nor the parents can afford certain activities which have traditionally been taken for granted as part of the curriculum.

---

**ACTION REQUIRED FOR COMPLIANCE**

**Compliance with Article 28, the right to education on the basis of equality of opportunity, consistent with Article 2, the right not to be discriminated against, requires that school activities which are undertaken during the school day are provided free of charge and that resources are made available to subsidise those children who cannot afford to undertake out of school activities.**

---

## 3.6 Truancy

**3.6.1** Article 28.1(e) states that the Government must: '*Take measures to encourage regular attendance at school and the reduction of drop-out rates*'. There is a general recognition amongst all those involved in education that the problem of children absent from school is growing. In particular, children in primary schools are increasingly likely to truant. In response to these concerns the Government has introduced a requirement on schools to provide truancy rates which are then published in national league tables. This policy is intended to give parents access to information in order that they can make informed decisions about choice of school. It is also intended to exert pressure on schools to tackle unacceptable truancy rates. In addition, the Government has also advocated a network of truancy watch schemes in which members of the public take responsibility for looking out for children out of school.

**3.6.2** However, neither of these strategies address the real nature of the problem of truancy:

● the figures that are produced on truancy levels are misleading and inaccurate. Schools are required to report authorised and unauthorised absences. Only unauthorised absence constitutes truancy. As schools apply widely differing definitions to these terms, the figures become meaningless. Furthermore, as the figures are published and schools are competing for pupils, it is in their interests to keep their figures as low as possible and conceal the extent of the problem. This militates against the development of effective and open strategies for examining the cause of truancy within the school;

● such research as is available indicates that the primary cause of truancy is the school curriculum. Children will not attend those lessons which they see as irrelevant or badly taught. They are increasingly disaffected with their lack of opportunities for participation and the inappropriateness of much of the National Curriculum. Strategies for tackling high levels of absence therefore need to start by listening to children to determine what they consider needs to change in order to improve attendance rates.

*'If I had an alternative to going to school I might have done it, but I didn't go to school because it did my head in having people telling me what to do. By the time I was 14 or 15 I'd already decided who I was and so I was not concerned about their attitude, because I was never going to come into contact with them ever again. It was false for me to stay there and say "Yes sir, no sir", when I had no respect for those people.'* (18 year-old, Oxfordshire)

**3.6.3** Effective strategies for tackling truancy must start by listening to children as well as parents and teachers; their perceptions of the causes of truancy should be the basis for developing policies to increase attendance rates.

**ACTION REQUIRED FOR COMPLIANCE**

**Compliance with Article 28.1(e) requires that schools should develop strategies for encouraging attendance in consultation with pupils reflecting the individual needs of each school.**

## 3.7 Early years education

**3.7.1** Whilst Article 28 only specifies a requirement to provide education for all children from primary school age upwards, it does also assert the importance of education on the basis of equality of opportunity. Article 29.1(a) also requires that education must be directed to: *'The development of the child's personality, talents and mental and physical abilities to the fullest'*. Research evidence both from the UK and the United States demonstrates that investment in early years education is one of the most effective means of providing all children with a firm foundation for future attainment. The disadvantage experienced by children growing up in impoverished and deprived backgrounds is considerably diminished by the experience of high quality pre-school education[20]. Despite this evidence, provision of pre-school education in the UK is patchy and inadequate. 50% of three and four year-olds currently attend school although there is wide variation in provision, ranging from under 20% in some authorities to over 80% in others. However, many of these children are in reception classes of ordinary schools, rather than nursery classes, which is not necessarily the most appropriate form of provision for this age group. Only one-third of children in Wales and Scotland are in nursery schools and one-quarter in England. Investment in such provision would directly improve the potential and opportunities of the substantial number of children in the UK currently deprived of early years educational provision[21] [22]. Government arguments that UK provision for three to four year-olds compares well with the rest of Europe are misleading; most of our provision is in playgroups, which are under-resourced and offering very short hours, and reception classes, which are often inappropriate for four year-olds.

**ACTION REQUIRED FOR COMPLIANCE**

**Compliance with Article 28, the right to education on the basis of equality of opportunity, consistent with Article 2, the right not to be discriminated against, requires an overall review of early childhood care and education services in the UK, leading to a comprehensive, integrated national policy for the development of high quality and affordable early childhood services.**

## 3.8 Services for children with special educational needs

**3.8.1** Article 23.1 states that disabled children have a right to *'enjoy a full and decent life, in conditions which ensure dignity, promote self-reliance, and facilitate the child's active participation in the community'*. Article 23.2 goes on to recognise the right of a disabled child to *'special care ... and assistance ... which is appropriate to the child's condition'*. In particular, disabled children must be provided with *'assistance designed to ensure*

*that the disabled child has effective access to and receives education'*. Article 28 points to the importance of equality of access for all children to education and the need for secondary education to be accessible and available to every child. In England and Wales the Education Act 1981, as amended by the Education Act 1993 (and comparable legislation in Scotland and N Ireland), makes provision for the education of children with special educational needs. This legislation expanded the definition of children with special educational needs and abolished the previous categories of specific handicap. Prior to the legislation only about 2% of children were receiving special education, almost all of them in special schools. Since the 1981 Act a further 18% are identified as likely to have special needs. The legislation, therefore, identified a substantial number of children requiring help who had previously gone unrecognised. Another central feature of the legislation was the introduction of a requirement on local authorities to draw up statements assessing the educational needs of children with physical disabilities or learning difficulties.

**3.8.2** However, since the introduction of the Act, there have been concerns that the actual provision for children with special needs is less than effective. The Audit Commission/ HMI report published in 1992 documents very considerable waiting times before many children are statemented, leaving them meanwhile without vital services that they require[23]. They found that some pupils were having to wait for up to three years for a statement and the average wait was 12-months. Without the provision of a statement, these children are not receiving the specialist help that they require and consequently are being denied the right to an effective education. The Spastics Society argues that many children who are not provided with appropriate support services fall into a cycle of truancy, low self-esteem and poor achievement which can then spiral into crime. The Society considers that there is a crisis in the provision of special education as a result of failings in local authority assessment procedures and inadequate resourcing[24]. It is estimated that the special educational needs of as many as one million children are not being met and as many as 90% of LEAs have difficulties in carrying out their responsibilities under the 1981 Act because of shortage of funding[25]. Government figures indicate that whilst the numbers of statements has risen since 1988, the amount of money available has not, so that less resources are available for each child.

**3.8.3** Some of these difficulties have been addressed in the Education Act 1993 both by the introduction of a six-month deadline on the production of statements and a Code of Practice which provides guidelines to tackle the problems of vaguely worded statements which fail to specify exactly what support is needed and how it will be provided. However, without the resources to back up these requirements it is likely that little will change. Without the provision of the services to meet children's special needs, their educational opportunities are diminished. As such their rights to equality of access to the benefits of education, as required under Article 28, are not being met, nor their rights to *'effective access to education'* (Article 23).

**3.8.4** For the 18% of children with special needs but without statements the position is even more worrying. These children are not protected by legislation which gives them any formal rights to special provision and there is a growing body of evidence from around the country that the support services that do exist are being seriously eroded as local authorities face increasing pressure on their budgets. This evidence is echoed by Her Majesty's Inspectorate of Schools which in 1990 commented, 'Sadly, less able pupils are much more likely to experience the shabby and shoddy than the more able ... a worrying persistent feature of UK education at all levels'[26].

**3.8.5** There are concerns that, whilst the levels of support for children with special needs in mainstream schools, is currently inadequate, it will be further undermined as a consequence of the Education Act 1993. This legislation, which establishes a considerably diminished role for local education authorities, will reduce the capacity for the development and maintenance of wide-ranging support services to provide for children with special educational needs in the mainstream sector. It is proposed that 85% of the education budget is devolved to school level and, as an LEA does so, it will be increasingly limited in its ability to resource provision such as specialist teaching, psychological services or advice about technological aids. Some LEAs have already stated that extra staffing available to support the work of schools in providing for children with special needs will be cut once the budgets are devolved[27].

**3.8.6** One of the problems facing parents and children in gaining access to the educational services they require is a lack of information about their rights, who to go to for help and knowledge of what services were available. The Education Act 1981 does impose a duty on health authorities to notify parents of children under five of relevant voluntary organisations which might help them and also to notify the education authority of children under five who might have special educational needs. The guidance to the Children Act stresses that there is also a need for social services departments to work directly with education and health authorities in the provision of information and to develop a collaborative approach to ensuring that parents have the information that they need[28].

**3.8.7** However, a survey undertaken in 1992 by the Spastics Society revealed a picture of parents confused by the complexity of procedures and lacking vital information that they needed[29]. For example, of 240 families responding to the survey, 40% had not been told that they had a right to an assessment of their child's needs. Of those who had been told, a quarter were not informed until the child was over five. This is of particular concern given the severity of the disabilities of the children in the study and the importance of obtaining early help. Research in Scotland published in 1989 revealed similar problems with parents left uninformed about procedures and their implications as well as their legal rights[30]. If disabled children are to be offered education on the basis of equality of opportunity, it is imperative that their families have full information about their rights and where to go for help as early as possible in their child's life.

**3.8.8** There is also concern that those acting on behalf of children cannot obtain appropriate legal assistance to help them pursue their rights. Very few lawyers have expertise in relation to law on education.

**ACTION REQUIRED FOR COMPLIANCE**
**Compliance with Article 23, the rights of disabled children to effective access to education on the basis of equality of opportunity, requires that:**

- LEAs and governing bodies duty to 'use their best endeavours to secure' appropriate provision for children with special educational needs who are not statemented should be amended to require them to provide whatever provision is needed for a particular child. This must be reinforced by appropriate levels of resourcing from central government ring-fenced in the budgets to individual schools;

- local education authorities, in conjunction with health authorities and trusts and social services, provide accessible information about all the services that are available, who provides them and the rights available to children and parents under the law. All information provided must also be made available in relevant community languages;

- in order to increase access to the law in pursuing rights, the Law Society should consider post qualifying legal education courses on education law with particular reference to special educational needs.

## 3.9 Integrated Education

*Children with special needs*
**3.9.1** Section 2 of the Education Act 1981 in England and Wales (although not in Scotland) sets out a qualified duty on LEAs to place children with special educational needs in ordinary schools wherever possible. This requirement is consistent with the principle embodied in Article 28 that all children should have equal access to education and the requirement in Article 23 that disabled children should be able to receive education *'in a manner conducive to the fullest possible social integration and individual development'*. However, the full implementation of section 2 has been substantially undermined by the condition placed upon it that decisions about the placement of a child in a mainstream school have to be compatible with the 'efficient use of resources'.

> *'I am in an integrated school now but it would have been better right from the start because you still get people who look down on you or treat you differently. The access could also be better.'*
> (18 year-old, Shropshire)

**3.9.2** This section has been consistently used by many LEAs to defend the continued use of special-school placements and there has, in practice, been very little progress towards integration. Analysis of Department of Education and Science (DES) returns shows that there was only a 4% decrease in segregation between 1982-89[31]. The Council for Disabled Children, in its response in 1992 to the Government's proposals for education comments that: 'The 1981 Act's broadly integrationist intent was marred by the condition of the efficient use of resources'[32]. Research in Scotland, where the legislation omits a specific commitment to meeting pupil's needs in a mainstream setting, has indicated that 'for the majority of pupils, recording [statementing] appears to be equated with segregated provision'[33]. Continued placement of children in segregated schools marginalises children with special needs and perpetuates much of the ignorance, fear and prejudice which surrounds disability in our society. If children with special educational needs are to be able to enjoy *'active participation in the community'* (Article 23.1) they need to be offered opportunities which promote disability as normal and enable them to lead lives which are as 'ordinary' as possible. Integrated schools are a vital component of such a process.

> *'In school we would all be put together and I would be doing work that I had done years ago because very often it would be out of my age range.'*
> (18 year-old, Shropshire)

**3.9.3** The Audit Commission/HMI report published in 1992 shows that the costs of good integration and special school provision are broadly similar and yet it continues to be argued by many LEAs that it is not cost effective to educate children with some special needs in mainstream schools[34]. No additional funding was provided by central government to implement the 1981 Education Act and lack of resources is often cited as the reason behind lack of progress towards integration. However, it can be argued that the resources are available but that they are locked into the segregated sector. The funding for integration could be financed by making a gradual transfer of resources and skills from the segregated sector to facilitate a more diverse provision within mainstream education[35].

**3.9.4** The Special Educational Consortium, which was convened to lobby on the Education Act 1993 during its passage through Parliament and includes a wide range of organisations in the field of disability and special needs, has also expressed concern that integration has not developed in line with the spirit and intent of the 1981 Act. It argues that there are significant numbers of parents who would ideally like integrated placements for their child but who opt for a special-school placement because of concerns about levels of support available to them in mainstream schools. Research carried out between 1983-86 found that in cases where the parent insisted on mainstream placements and the local authority was not in agreement, the children were not given adequate resources to enable the placement to succeed[36]. Because such high levels of resources are tied up in segregated provision, there is often inadequate money available to develop good integrated placements. Meanwhile those children continue to be denied access to schools which offer them the same opportunities as those available to other children to an integrated education: this perpetuates practices at odds with the spirit of the 1981 Act as well as in breach of Articles 23 and 28.

**3.9.5** The concerns outlined above with regard to the implications of the Education Act 1993 are of equal relevance for the future of integration as a realistic choice for children with special needs. In view of the worries already expressed by parents about the lack of support available in mainstream schools, the Council for Disabled Children argues that fears about the future vulnerability of these services now constitute a significant barrier to integration.

**3.9.6** Article 23.1 states that a disabled child should *'enjoy a full and decent life in conditions which ... facilitate the child's active participation in the community'* and 23.3 goes on to stress the right of the disabled child to education *'conducive to ... achieving the fullest possible social integration'*. Clearly if these principles are to be achieved, it is vital that disabled children are given the opportunity to enter mainstream education. Segregating children does effectively marginalise and exclude them. It defines them through their disability first and not as children first.

**3.9.7** Effective integration depends upon teachers having the

necessary training to work with children with special needs. It is also enhanced by the presence of disabled teachers in schools. It requires that all teachers are equipped with the skills to manage a class of children with differing needs and abilities. Clearly mainstream teachers need specialist help but their capacity to integrate a wide ability range would benefit considerably from appropriate training. Without specialised training, the quality of teaching will be diminished, the stress on the teacher greater and the likelihood of children's special needs being met will be substantially reduced. At present the provision of such training is inadequate. Compliance with the provision of education on the basis of *'equality of opportunity'* (Article 28.1) and *'effective access to education'* (Article 23.3) will necessitate appropriate support and training for teachers in order to maximise their skills and expertise in providing integrated education.

## ACTION REQUIRED FOR COMPLIANCE

**Compliance with Articles 23.1 and 2 together with Article 2, the right not to be discriminated against, requires that:**

- **LEAs and schools should have a duty to make provision for the fullest possible integration of children with special needs. There should be a target period within which to plan for full integration and make the changes necessary to achieve it;**
- **both initial and advanced in-service teacher education should be available for teachers to enhance their capacity to offer effective access to education for children with special needs in an integrated setting. Governors and non-teaching assistants should also receive training on services for children with special needs.**

*Children in N Ireland*

**3.9.8** In N Ireland, the majority of schools are segregated on religious lines, with most children attending either Protestant or Catholic schools. This separation of children within the education system contributes to the perpetuation of prejudice and social conflict in N Ireland and represents a breach of the right under Article 14 to *'freedom of thought, conscience and religion'*. It also inhibits the duty under Article 29 to prepare the child *'for responsible life in a free society, in the spirit of understanding, peace, tolerance, equality of sexes, and friendship among all peoples, ethnic, national and religious groups and persons of indigenous origin'*. A survey in 1968 conducted for the *Belfast Telegraph* recorded as many as 65% of young people wanting integration at primary level and 75% at secondary level[37].

> *'Through the land, schools should be mixed because if we're divided from the Protestants it produces divisions. We grow up with the divisions and it breeds discrimination and prejudice.'*
> (13 year-old, N Ireland)

**3.9.9** Reform in this field has been assisted by the Education Reform (NI) Order 1989 which allows integrated schools to receive Government funding and existing segregated schools to become integrated if more than 50% of the parents vote for the change. However, comparatively little progress has been made to date - only 2% of schools are currently integrated, despite 30% of parents expressing a preference for such schools - and many of those who apply to integrated schools are turned away because of lack of places[38].

> *'Something that needs to be examined is the whole issue of integrated schools; there are about twenty integrated schools in N Ireland but there should be far more, so people have the opportunity of at least being open- minded and not pushed into a situation where it leaves the way open for minds to be poisoned against one community or the other.'*
> (17 year-old, N Ireland)

### ACTION REQUIRED FOR COMPLIANCE

**Compliance with Article 14, the right to freedom of religion, and Article 29, the responsibility to promote tolerance and peace, requires that immediate steps are taken to remedy the failure to provide all children in N Ireland with the opportunity to attend an integrated school**

## 3.10 Funding and equity

**3.10.1** The Education Reform Act 1988 introduced a new status for schools: they can apply for grant-maintained status and operate independently of the local authority and are funded through a share of the local authority budget calculated on a percentage based formula. It was the expressed intention of Parliament in introducing this new status that the financial effect of opting out of local authority control would be broadly neutral. Their funding allocation should be no more generous than if they had remained with their local education authority[39].

**3.10.2** In practice, since the legislation was introduced, there is a growing body of evidence that grant-maintained schools are being disproportionately generously funded. A report prepared for the Association of County Councils demonstrated that on the existing funding formula, the entire education budget of a local authority could have been lost when just over half its schools had opted out. The study also demonstrated that the allocation of education authority central service costs pro rata to pupil numbers benefited secondary schools because the latter required a much higher level of central support. Article 28 requires that education is provided on *'the basis of equal opportunity'*. A funding formula which discriminates in favour of certain types of schools without reference to the educational needs of the children in those schools is clearly in breach of this principle.

**3.10 3** The Association of Metropolitan Authorities has accumulated a body of evidence which demonstrates the inequity of the current arrangement[40]. Amongst the many authorities which have expressed concern are Wandsworth Education Authority which reports that its 1992/93 budget would have an overspend of £1 million pounds because of over-funding of grant-maintained schools and Brent Education Authority which estimated that the overfunding of its two grant maintained schools in 1992/93 was £¼ million. Other authorities have observed that the formula includes a proportion of the education authority budget which is for special needs provision and support services irrespective of whether that school draws on those services. In so doing, the allocation to grant-maintained schools can effectively discriminate against other schools by cutting the funding for services on which they rely. The consequence of the present system is that children in grant-maintained schools are benefiting to the detriment of other children. This process is

inequitable and unjust. All children within the state education system should be entitled to provision of education based on need and not on the status of institution which they attend. The current arrangements fail to achieve this objective and thereby contravene Article 28.1 as well as Article 2, the right of all children to equal access to all the rights in the Convention.

### ACTION REQUIRED FOR COMPLIANCE

**Compliance with Article 28, the provision of education on the basis of equal opportunity requires that regulations governing funding to grant-maintained schools should be amended to ensure equity with LEA maintained schools in order that the resourcing of children's education is not influenced by the status of school they attend**

## 3.11 Refugees

**3.11.1** Article 22 states that the Government shall *'take appropriate measures to ensure that a child who is a refugee ... shall receive appropriate protection and humanitarian assistance in the enjoyment of applicable rights set forth in the present Convention'*. Refugee children in school require special help if they are to benefit from the educational system. They arrive in this country often frightened and shocked by their experiences, isolated from their language and culture, unfamiliar with the new environment in which they find themselves. Education is vital to them if they are to survive the trauma of being both displaced and dispossessed. At present, for many children in this situation, schools are not able to respond adequately and as such they are failing to meet the requirements embodied in Article 22. One of the most pressing needs for refugee children is the provision of appropriate language teaching. However, there is inadequate funding in many authorities for teaching English and, until recently, the special funding for such provision available under section 11 of the Local Government Act 1966 was only available for individuals from the New Commonwealth and Pakistan. This restriction has now been amended, but unless the level of funding available under the scheme is increased to reflect its wider remit, the change will result in little practical benefit for children in need of special help (see also para 17). Current Government proposals are to reduce the subsidy under this provision from 75% to 54%.

> *'We had difficulties with English and in dealing with a different culture.'*
> (17 year-old, Oxfordshire)

**3.11.2** Isolation is a serious problem for many refugee children and can profoundly inhibit their capacity to benefit from the social and cultural aspects of education. Without the opportunity to understand and be made to feel a part of the local community, it is hard for many refugee children to overcome the barriers of linguistic and cultural difference. Teachers need to be provided with training in awareness of the experience of refugees. Schools need to know more about the languages and culture of refugee children in order to be able to respond appropriately to the situation in which the children find themselves. Unless schools are able to better understand the experience of refugee children, those children will continue to be marginalised and unable to benefit from the education system on the basis of equality of opportunity. Children also need well-prepared induction programmes to facilitate their introduction into a school. All these services require additional resources. In addition, there are considerable difficulties facing parents of refugee children in understanding the education system and how to get help and advice on finding a school place, the requirements of the law with regard to education and the rights they and their children have in education law. Without this information, it is often difficult for parents to access the services they need for their children.

**3.11.3** At present, with very limited authority budgets, it is proving very difficult for them to make the necessary provision of language teaching, counselling and support and teacher training available to comply with the rights of refugee children as required in Article 22. There is provision under section 210(2)(c) of the Education Act 1988 for the Government to make grants for the education of people who are resident 'in a camp or other accommodation or establishment provided for refugees or other displaced persons'. One of the difficulties with this provision is that most refugees are not housed in camps or similar establishments. This means that whilst the legislation was designed in recognition of the special needs of refugees with regard to education, in practice very few are able to benefit from that provision. There were attempts to amend the legislation during the passage of the Education Act 1993 through Parliament in order to reflect better the actual situation in which most refugees are living. But the Government has been unwilling to introduce any change. Without the availability of more resources to provide support services to refugee children, they will continue to be denied full access to the education system.

**ACTION REQUIRED FOR COMPLIANCE**

Compliance with Article 22, the rights of refugee children to the provision of adequately resourced support, requires that:

● the budget under the Local Government Act 1966, section 11 is increased in line with the additional costs associated with the rights of refugee children to specialist help;

● the Education Act 1988, section 210 is amended to ensure that the grants available under the section are extended to cover all refugees irrespective of their housing arrangements;

● local education authorities and schools develop comprehensive programmes of support for refugee parents and pupils, training for teachers, induction for pupils, and language tuition in order that refugee children are able to benefit from the education system as quickly and as constructively as possible.

# 4 Consultation, participation and respect for the child
## Articles 3 and 12

## 4.1 Background

**4.1.1** There is no tradition in the UK of acknowledging the civil and political rights of children in the processes of education. Children have no formal rights to any control over or participation in matters concerning their education. The focus of politicians in addressing issues of access to information and choice has been exclusively on the parents. It is parents and not children who are defined as the 'consumers' of education; the child is seen as the 'product' in the process. Both from the perspective of the importance of respecting children's basic civil rights and also the value for children of acquiring the skills and understanding necessary to participate in a democratic society, a commitment to children's rights to participation is of vital importance. Education legislation, as it currently stands, contains no principled framework within which to promote the rights of the child and lacks any commitment to promoting the best interests of the child. (See also **UK Agenda Report 1 on personal freedoms,** page 9 for a discussion of children's civil rights in schools.)

## 4.2 The welfare principle

**4.2.1** Article 3.1 imposes a duty to ensure that '*in all actions concerning children, whether undertaken by public or private social welfare institutions, courts of law, administrative authorities or legislative bodies, the best interests of the child shall be a primary consideration*'. The local education authority in this context is certainly an administrative authority, as will be the Funding Agency for Schools being established under the Education Act 1993. In Article 3.2 there is a duty on governments '*to ensure such protection and care as is necessary for his or her well being ... and, to this end ... shall take all appropriate legislative and administrative measures*'. At present there is no such principle embodied in education law. The Education Act 1944, section 1, requires that the Secretary of State for Education must 'promote the education of the people of England and Wales and the progressive development of institutions devoted to that purpose'. The legislation goes on to state that local education authorities must make available schools 'sufficient in number, character and equipment to afford for all pupils opportunities for education offering such variety of instruction and training as may be desirable in view of their different ages, abilities and aptitudes' (section 8 of the 1944 Act). However there is no obligation when making decisions concerning either individual children or the broad provision of education to address the best interests of the child as a guiding principle.

**4.2.2** The importance of a best interests principle has been widely recognised in child welfare legislation. The Children Act 1989 in England and Wales (and the draft Children (NI) Order) places courts under a duty, when considering any issue relating to a child's upbringing, to give 'paramount consideration' to the welfare of the child. A comparable principle exists in the Social Work (Scotland) Act 1968. Similarly, the Children Act, section 17, requires local authority social services departments in England and Wales 'to safeguard and promote the welfare of children in their area who are in need'. (Similar provisions apply in N Ireland and in Scotland there is a general welfare duty placed on local authorities in relation to all children in their area.) This principle is central to the philosophy of the legislation and to its recognition that children and their interests must come before other considerations. However, no comparable provision exists in education legislation. LEAs, governors and head teachers are under no duty when making decisions to respect to this principle.

**4.2.3** What happens to children in school is of vital significance to them both during the period that they attend and for their future life opportunities. It is imperative that decisions that are made throughout a child's education are prompted by the requirement to promote their best interests in relation to that education. This is of particular significance in the context of the diminishing role of education authorities and the greater powers now vested in governing bodies. These bodies have very considerable responsibility for the control of finances, staffing, discipline, special education, pupil intake and aspects of the curriculum. It is of critical importance, therefore, that legislation provides a principled framework within which those responsibilities are carried out.

**4.2.4** In many authorities and schools the introduction of a welfare principle into legislation would merely be a confirmation of good practice already in operation. However, even in such schools, it would be valuable to have an explicit requirement against which to evaluate the policy and administration of the school and the basis on which decisions affecting individual children are made. The application of the best interests principle has relevance to decisions about every aspect of education provision. It needs to be acknowledged, for example, in the allocation of budgets, the implementation of school rules, policies on school exclusions, staffing issues, provision of special needs education, policies on integration, admission procedures and criteria, staffing and organisation of playgrounds.

> 'One of the most important aspects of a child's life in this country is education and school. Yet in the very place which is supposed to promote positive learning, and give the children a wide education on all different aspects of life, little is done to treat the children as individual, thinking, human beings. Indeed, the prevelant attitude in many schools goes directly against the spirit of the Convention and it is for this reason that I think that education and school life in general is an area that needs a great deal of thought and consideration if the Convention is to be comprehensively and successfully applied.'
> (17 year-old, North East)

**4.2.5** LEAs, governing bodies and head teachers are often faced with balancing the needs of the individual child against those of the rest of the children in a class or in the school as a whole. They have responsibilities to all the children within a school or local authority area. It is therefore necessary that the welfare of the child is seen to be the 'primary' and not the 'paramount' consideration as is the case for court hearings under the Children Act.

**ACTION REQUIRED FOR COMPLIANCE**

**Compliance with Article 3.1 requires that education law throughout the UK is amended to incorporate a principle stating that it shall be the duty of the Secretary of State and of funding authorities, local education authorities, governing bodies of all schools in the exercise of any of their functions to ensure in any decision concerning a child that the welfare of the child shall be a primary consideration.**

## 4.3 Decisions affecting an individual child

**4.3.1** Article 12 states that the Government must 'assure to the child who is capable of forming his or her own views the right to express those views freely in all matters affecting the child, the views of the child being given due weight in accordance with the age and maturity of the child'. But, at present, children have no rights in law to be consulted or to be taken account of in any matter concerning their individual rights within the education system.

**4.3.2** There is a duty in the Children Act 1989 in England and Wales (and in the Draft Children (NI) Order) for courts and social services to ascertain and give due consideration to the views of children when making decisions concerning their welfare. It is a principle now well-established in the field of child care. A similar principle is placed on social work departments under the Social Work (Scotland) Act 1968 but does not extend to court decision-making. Government ministers have suggested that the introduction of the requirement to ascertain the wishes and feelings of children into education law is unnecessary because it is covered by the Children Act. However, the provisions under the Children Act do not extend to LEAs, governing bodies and head teachers making decisions in relation to children's education. Children have no right to be consulted over school choice, school suspensions or exclusions or to be heard in appeals over these matters. Disabled children have no formal right to be consulted over whether or not they attend a special school or are able to enter mainstream education nor about the process of assessment and statementing. Nor is there any formal requirement to hear the views of an individual child concerning any issue relating to their education such as religion or sex education or problems in school, such as bullying and harassment. The extent to which space is created to listen to children and to respond to issues raised is a matter entirely for the individual school head and governors. This lack of rights represents a clear breach of Article 12.2 which states that 'the child shall ... be provided the opportunity to be heard in any judicial and administrative proceedings affecting the child, either directly or through a representative or an appropriate body, in a manner consistent with the procedural rules of national law'.

> 'I was never given a choice of what school I wished to attend, ideally I would have much preferred to attend an integrated school with able-bodied people but that was never discussed or put down as a possibility because most of the time it's automatically assumed that you must attend a school that is distinctly set aside for disabled people and I think that is wrong.'
> (18 year-old, N Ireland)

**4.3.3** The Children Act does contain a requirement that where a pupil is under an education supervision order, his or her wishes and feelings must be ascertained and given due consideration. Similarly, some independent schools with less than 50 boarders and non-maintained special schools are under a duty to 'ascertain so far as is reasonably practicable the wishes and feelings' of a child before making any decision in respect of that child. The Education Act 1993 limited it to those schools which accommodate children for most of the year. In other words, there is already provision that a small minority of children in the context of their education have a right to be consulted. If the principle is considered to be of sufficient significance to be included in the Children Act for these children there is an equally strong case to be made for this right to be extended to all children. It is entirely anomalous that children should only be afforded the right to be consulted if their individual circumstances or the educational institution they attend happens to fall within the framework of the Children Act.

**4.3.4** Schools are not required to introduce formal complaints procedures and children therefore have no access to a publicised or clearly defined route through which to air any grievance or injustice they have experienced. The Children Act imposes a statutory requirement on all social services departments to establish complaints procedures to which children have access. Such a provision is integral to any meaningful process of listening to children and giving due consideration to their views. Whilst it is always preferable for decisions to be made through discussion and negotiation, the right to be heard is an empty protection if it is not backed up by the opportunity to challenge any breach of that and other rights. The introduction of a right for children to have their views and feelings considered in the context of their education also needs to be backed up by the provision of statutory complaints procedures, with an independent element. Only by so doing will children's right to be given an opportunity to express their views in line with Article 12 begin to have any effective impact.

**4.3.5** Prior to the introduction of the complaints procedures under the Children Act, there was a great deal of concern expressed that children would abuse the right to complain and social services would be flooded by scores of frivolous and malicious complaints. Similar concerns were expressed when attempts were made to introduce amendments to the Education Act 1993 for a statutory complaints procedure. In fact, initial research undertaken by the organisation, Voice for the Child in Care, indicates that over 80% of complaints by children have been upheld and there was, in those cases, serious justification for the complaint[41]. There is no reason to believe that the experience in education would be any different. A joint complaints procedure for children in the health, education and social work departments in Lothian was introduced in 1992 with access to an independent adjudicator in the event of a failure to resolve the problem internally. Certainly there is no evidence to date that the scheme has been abused or overburdened.

**4.3.6** Article 12 underpins the entire philosophy of the Convention. Its implementation is far from being achieved within our education system at present. Whilst there are many examples of good practice, these alone are not sufficient. Article 2 requires that all children have equal access to all the rights in the Convention. Only by the introduction of a formal requirement to consult children on matters of concern to them would we begin to move towards the introduction of comprehensive structures designed to respect this right for all children.

**ACTION REQUIRED FOR COMPLIANCE**

**Compliance with Article 12, the right of children both**

to express their views and have them taken seriously within the education system and be heard in judicial or administrative proceedings that affect them, requires:

● **legislation introducing a duty on schools and local authorities to establish formal procedures for both ascertaining and giving due consideration to the views of individual children on matters affecting them and enabling them to make complaints when they are dissatisfied with either the process or outcome of any decision made in respect of them.**

● **legislation to ensure the child has a right to be heard in decision-making and appeals concerned with school choice, exclusions from school, special needs assessment and making of statements (or records in Scotland) of special educational needs.**

## 4.4 Participation in the running of schools

**4.4.1** Article 12 requires that children are able to express their views and have them taken seriously in **all** matters affecting them. This means not just decisions affecting them as individuals but also decisions which affect them as a body. At present, children have no formal rights to participate in matters of school policy or administration. There is no requirement to involve children in decisions on, for example, school uniform, curriculum, arrangements for school meals, supervision in the playground or discipline. Very few schools have school councils which provide an institutionalised structure within which to consult children and to hear their views and ensure that they are taken account of in developing policy.

**4.4.2** Yet the Elton inquiry, *Discipline in schools* stated: 'Headteachers and teachers should recognise the importance of ascertaining pupils' views ... encourage active participation of pupils in shaping and reviewing schools behaviour policy ... LEAs should regularly evaluate [behaviour] policies in relation to ... the perception of ... pupils'[42]. The White Paper on education *Choice and diversity* also acknowledged the value of listening to children: 'Listening to their views, both through their parents and directly, can help schools in improving standards of their service'[43].

> *'Some schools have school councils with representatives from the student body, but more often than not these appear to be mere tokens, rarely being consulted and only on trivial matters. The fact is that every effort should be made to consult the pupils of the school on each issue that concerns them. This would obviously take a great deal of work on the part of the staff, as well as the pupils, and I am aware of the pressures of time, but I do believe that in the long run it would be worthwhile, with the pupils responding to the responsibility that they had been given.'*
> (17 year-old, North East)

**4.4.3** Learning to participate in a democratic society is a fundamental objective of education. One of the key principles of our democratic society is that people have an opportunity to express their views - through the freedom of the press, through the courts, tribunals and complaints procedures and through informal systems which operate in many of our institutions. Children are people too and as such should be afforded respect for their views. The only means of ensuring that these rights are properly respected is to incorporate them into our legislation. Without this safeguard there can be no assurance that the right will be upheld in compliance with Article 12 and no redress for children whose rights in this respect are ignored.

**4.4.4** This principle has not been translated into education legislation. Indeed, the right of under 18 year-olds to become pupil governors was abolished by the Government in the Education Act 1988. The Government had the opportunity of introducing these principles during the passage through Parliament of the Education Act 1993: but amendments drafted to introduce a right for children to be consulted on matters of concern to them were opposed by the Government.

## ACTION REQUIRED FOR COMPLIANCE

**Compliance with Article 12 requires that:**

- **schools and local authorities introduce procedures for ensuring that children are provided with the opportunity to express their views on matters of concern to them in the running of schools and that their views are given due weight in accordance with their age and maturity;**

- **both initial and in-service teacher education is founded on principles of respect for children and greater democracy within schools.**

# 5 Curriculum
## Article 29

## 5.1 Human rights and democracy

**5.1.1** Article 29.1(b) stresses that education of children must be directed to '*the development of respect for human rights and fundamental freedoms and the principles enshrined in the UN Charter of the United Nations*'. However, there is no obligation in education legislation to promote human rights, and it is not included in any of the statutory orders issued for the National Curriculum. The National Curriculum, introduced by the Education Reform Act 1988 (Education Reform (NI) Order 1989 in N Ireland), applies in England and Wales and N Ireland but it has no equivalent in Scotland, although there are the Scottish '5-14' guidelines which are intended to standardise provision. One of the cross-curricular themes identified by the National Curriculum Council (NCC) is 'Education for citizenship' but these themes are not compulsory parts of the curriculum and their implementation in schools varies enormously. Research carried out by the Institute of Education shows that only a quarter of schools surveyed had a policy on the 'Education for Citizenship' theme[44].

**5.1.2** When the Education Reform Act 1988 was being debated in Parliament, there were pressures on the Government to introduce amendments to make human rights a required subject under the National Curriculum but they were consistently opposed. Without legislation, the incorporation of human rights curriculum supported by a school environment which is respectful of children, will continue to take place on an ad hoc basis. Furthermore, the reliance on cross-curricular themes, in which concepts of rights and citizenship are segregated out from the curriculum as a whole, marginalises the issues. Schools need to develop a whole school approach to the subject which incorporates the issues throughout both the curriculum and day to day practice of the school.

## ACTION REQUIRED FOR COMPLIANCE

**Compliance with Article 29.1(b), the duty to direct education to promoting respect for human rights and freedom, requires that the National Curriculum fully incorporates perspectives on human rights and democracy as an integral component.**

## 5.2 Multi-culturalism and anti-racism

**5.2.1** Closely linked with the concept of education for citizenship are the issues of multi-cultural and anti-racist education. Article 29.1(c) and (d) stress the importance of '*the development of respect for a child's parents, his or her own cultural identity, language and values, for the national values of the country in which the child is living, the country from which he or she may originate, and for civilisations different from his or her own*' and further that education should prepare a child for '*responsible life in a free society, in the spirit of understanding, peace, tolerance, equality of sexes, and friendship among all peoples ethnic, national, and religious groups and persons of indigenous origin*'.

**5.2.2** The National Curriculum documents do give an initial impression of addressing issues of equality. The curriculum as defined by the Education Act 1988 is required to:

a) promote the spiritual, moral, cultural, mental and physical development of pupils at the school and of society;

b) prepare such pupils for the opportunities, responsibilities and experience of adult life[45].

The NCC guidance to schools advises that 'a commitment to providing equal opportunities for all pupils should permeate every aspect of the curriculum'.

**5.2.3** However, detailed examination reveals that very low priority is given to issues of equality generally[46]. There is a lack of clarity about the use and meaning of the terms 'equal opportunities' and 'minority ethnic groups' and no references to racism. There has been very little representation on the working groups of members from minority ethnic communities and there is concern that, whilst lip service has been paid to equal opportunities within the National Curriculum, in practice children are unlikely to receive the type of education in which they are properly integrated.

**5.2.4** The implementation of Article 29 needs to be achieved through the incorporation into the curriculum within schools of an explicit commitment to anti-racism and multi-culturalism. It is the view of a number of organisations working in this field that the National Curriculum now taught in all maintained schools is failing to achieve these objectives. It has been argued by Professor Sally Tomlinson, chair of the Advisory Centre for Education that: 'Multicultural issues are being excluded from all aspects of the National Curriculum at a time when it has never been more important to encourage young people to understand and value our ethnic diversity'[47]. She argues that there were advances made up to the mid 1980s in raising awareness of multi-cultural and anti-racist issues culminating in the publication of the Swann Report in 1985[48]. This report set out the curriculum changes needed to provide a multi-cultural and international education for all.

**5.2.5** Since then there has been strong resistance by the Government to the inclusion within the National Curriculum of a multi-cultural dimension. A working group established by the NCC to produce what would have been non-statutory guidelines on the multi-cultural content of the National Curriculum had its recommendations ignored by the Government. During the past few years, consultation documents produced by the subject working groups on the National Curriculum have largely ignored the issue. The mathematics working group explicitly reported that it had included no multi-cultural aspects in any of their attainment targets, the English working group had its original proposals for 'informed discussion of the multi-cultural nature of British society' watered down to exclude non-European literature and the History working group experienced direct political intervention leaving them concerned that 'school history will be used as propaganda'.

**5.2.6** The Commission for Racial Equality (CRE) expressed concern that the development of multi-cultural education has not been properly monitored and there is no legislative framework for it. There is no legal requirement within the curriculum for the *'development of respect for the child's parents, his or her cultural identity, language and values, for the national values of the country in which the child is living, the country from which he or she may originate, and for civilisation different from*

*his or her own*' (Article 29.1(c)). The development of such provision rests with individual local authorities and individual schools at present. The likelihood of more schools opting out of local authority control over the next few years highlights the need for legislation, requiring schools to promote these issues.

**5.2.7** In order to be effective, multicultural education must take place in the context of an active commitment to anti-racism. If schools are to comply with the requirement to ensure that the education of children promotes respect for others, they will need to ensure that they have effective equal opportunities and anti-bullying policies which are regularly monitored and evaluated, that issues such as name calling and racial and sexual harassment are dealt with speedily and seriously. It is also important that teachers are trained in a way which is appropriate for a multi-racial and multi-cultural society[49]. This will necessitate, for example, some understanding of the social conventions of various minority ethnic groups and the ability to avoid stereotyping children on the basis of ethnicity.

**ACTION REQUIRED FOR COMPLIANCE**

**Compliance with Article 29.1(b) and (d) requires that both initial and in-service teacher education are explicitly designed to equip teachers to undertake their duties without racially discriminating and in a way that meets the demands of schools in a multi-racial and multi-lingual society. There should be clear guidelines within schools on the disciplinary procedures to be taken in the event of discrimination.**

## 5.3 English as a second language

**5.3.1** For the many children in school for whom English is not their first language, access to the education system is dependent on the provision of the teaching of English as a second language. This has been long accepted as an essential part of schooling and is usually eligible for special funding by the Home Office under section 11 of the Local Government Act 1966 (see para 12.1). The legislation, originally restricted to people from New Commonwealth countries, has been amended to extend its provisions to other countries but this change is not being backed up by any increase in funding available to develop the necessary resources. It is important that the needs of these children are recognised as of equal significance in the allocation of resources for special needs education. Failure to do so represents both a breach of their rights not to be discriminated against (Article 2) and their rights to education on the basis of equal opportunity.

**5.3.2** The CRE has also expressed concern over the practical organisation of the teaching of English as a second language. In some schools, pupils may be withdrawn from school and placed in separate units or classes which can seriously disadvantage them and may constitute unlawful discrimination[50]. The CRE strongly recommends that classroom-based integrated language support is the most appropriate method of teaching pupils for whom English is a second language. The Swann Report also argued for integrated provision, stating 'we are wholly in favour of a move away from English as a second language provision being made on a withdrawal basis'[51]. Clearly, a commitment to *'the development of the child's personality, talents and mental and physical abilities to their fullest potential'* (Article 29.1(a)) would require that children are offered a setting for learning which strives to achieve that optimum potential. Research into the teaching of English as a second language demonstrates fairly conclusively that pupils benefit most from learning a second language alongside first language speakers in an ordinary mainstream setting[52].

**Compliance with Article 2 in respect of both Articles 28.1 and 29.1(a), education on the basis of equality of opportunity which promotes the talents and abilities of all children, requires that all schools work progressively towards the provision of integrated teaching of English as a second language. (See also action required for compliance under section on refugees)**

## 5.4 Language diversity

**5.4.1** Article 29.1(c) stresses that education should seek to develop respect for the child's '*own cultural identity, language and values*'. This objective is reinforced by Article 30 and the right of a child to '*use his or her own language*'. This Article is of critical importance in Wales where Welsh is the indigenous and historic language of the country. It continues to be spoken by a substantial minority of the population and is still the main language of communication for a majority of children and families across a large part of the land area of Wales. The Government does recognise Welsh as an official language and there has been considerable advance in recent years in the provision of education through the Welsh language at primary and secondary level. These advances have been strengthened by the Education Reform Act 1988 which provided that Welsh be taught as a core subject in all schools in Wales unless exempted by the Secretary of State. Recognition has been further acknowledged in the Welsh Language Act 1993 which provides that the Welsh language in Wales should be treated on a basis of equality with English. This is to be achieved through the establishing of Welsh language schemes approved by a statutory Welsh Language Board and which will set out the services which public bodies will provide through the medium of Welsh.

**5.4.2** However, to date, in too many parts of Wales there remains an apparent reluctance to plan properly for the known growth in demand for education through the Welsh language. This has led to children and families facing difficulties in gaining access to primary education and in ensuring a smooth transfer from primary to secondary level. Furthermore, there are concerns that the Education Act 1993, which encourages schools to opt out of local authority control, will render Welsh medium schools more vulnerable. Whilst the Welsh Language Board will be empowered to require all schools to submit a Welsh language scheme, it is not yet clear whether this Board will have the powers to secure change by requiring the provision of adequate Welsh medium education.

**5.4.3** There are no legal obligations to provide education in the languages spoken in a child's home, other than Welsh and Gaelic where it is spoken in Scotland, when this is not English. Under the National Curriculum minority ethnic languages can be taught but the CRE and community groups are concerned that these languages 'may be regarded as second class compared with European languages and that there are few resources or incentives for their inclusion in mainstream teaching'[53]. A European Commission Directive on the education of children of migrant workers, which is binding on the UK, insists that states must take appropriate steps to promote the teaching of mother tongues and cultures of the country of origin and to ensure that this provision is co-ordinated within ordinary education[54]. The DES response to the Directive was that insufficient ethnic and linguistic data are available about children in schools to monitor implementation effectively.

**Compliance with Articles 29.1(c) and 30, promoting respect for a child's own language, requires that:**

- **monitoring of the provision of Welsh medium education following the implementation of the Education Act 1993 is undertaken to assess its adequacy;**
- **research is undertaken to enable effective planning for the development of community languages within schools.**

## 5.5 Religious education

**5.5.1** There is discrimination in the current policy in respect of religious schools: some established religious groups have been permitted to establish and receive substantial funding for voluntary aided schools but others have not, to date, been able to do so. There are large numbers of voluntary aided Church of England, Catholic and some Jewish schools but applications from Muslim parents for voluntary aided status funding have failed. This means that children from certain religions can pursue their faith in a relevant school environment but others cannot. This situation would appear to be in breach of Article 2 in denying equal rights for all children to '*freedom of thought, conscience and religion*' as required in Article 14. The Swann Report *Education for all* on the education of minority ethnic children recommended that it was time to reconsider the role of the Church in education and the legal provisions in the Education Act 1944 on religion in schools[55]. The report recommended that the provisions of the Act in relation to voluntary schools should be reviewed 'to see whether alterations are required in a society that was now very different'. It would seem that the thinking behind this recommendation is that religious schools of any denomination might be considered inappropriate in a multi-racial society.

> '*If you don't find out about other religions, then you only get one view of how the world should be.*'
> (13 year-old, London)

**5.5.2** The CRE has recommended that there should be a wide-ranging public debate on the future of religious schools but that the debate should address the role of all religious schools and not just minority-faith ones[56]. The Commission also recommends that so long as existing arrangements for granting voluntary status are in force, an application from a minority faith school should be given exactly the same consideration as any other application. Failure to do so is certainly in breach of Article 2.

See **UK Agenda Report 1 on personal freedoms,** page 11 for an analysis of children's rights to exercise a personal choice of religion.

**Compliance with Article 2, the equal rights of all**

children in respect of access to religious schooling, requires that there should be no discrimination on grounds of religion in considering applications to voluntary aided status, or in the provision of state resources for education.

# 6 Protection and safety for children in schools
## Articles 19 and 37

## 6.1 Bullying

**6.1.1** Article 19 states that children have the right to be protected '*from all forms of physical and mental violence, injury or abuse ... while in the care of ... any person who has care of the child*'. This Article clearly applies to abuse perpetrated by other children as well as adults and is therefore of relevance to children in school, in the care of teachers, who experience bullying by other children. There is a clear obligation on the relevant authorities, within the terms of this Article, to take appropriate measures to tackle bullying in schools. Bullying is a term which can be used to cover a very wide range of behaviours but can generally be defined as long-standing violence, physical or psychological, conducted by an individual or group and directed against an individual who is not able to defend him or herself in the situation.

> '*Every young person at some point gets abused by other people whether it's by adults or people of their own age and there's no support mechanism for them to deal with it in schools, and it's just seen as something that happens like falling over and banging your head. It's not seen as a form of abuse or a big problem.*'
> (15 year-old, Merseyside)

**6.1.2** Substantial evidence exists to show that bullying in schools is widespread and is experienced by a significant proportion of pupils. The Bullying Project based at Sheffield University, undertaking research into bullying in 24 schools in Sheffield, discovered that on average 27% of primary-age pupils and 10% of secondary-age pupils were bullied more than once or twice during the term prior to the survey being conducted and of these children 10% and 4% respectively report being bullied once or several times a week[57]. Equally worrying is the evidence that about half the pupils did not report the bullying. These figures indicate not only that disturbingly high numbers of children face bullying as a regular feature of their school life but also that 50% have no confidence that school staff will take action on their behalf. In Scotland research published in 1990 revealed that, of nearly 1,000 children interviewed, 50% stated that they had been bullied once or twice during their school careers. The research also mirrors the English evidence in that around half the children had informed no-one.

**6.1.3** Figures from the Sheffield survey show that the majority of bullying takes place in school playgrounds. School lunch breaks are generally overseen by lunch-time supervisors who have little training for the task. Improving their training and status and enhancing the quality of the physical environment of the playground can reduce bullying.

**6.1.4** Further research by the Sheffield Bullying Project into the particular experiences of children with special needs reveals that they are significantly more at risk of bullying than other children. A sample of children in mainstream schools which had integrated resources for children with special needs were asked whether there was anyone at school who ever bullied or was nasty to them. 65% of the children with special needs said yes compared with 30% of mainstream children[58]. It was also evident from the research that teachers tend to underestimate the extent of bullying experienced by children with special needs.

**6.1.5** There have also been a number of investigations into racist name-calling and bullying: one study in three schools in Manchester revealed that almost two-thirds of children from minority ethnic communities had been teased and bullied[59]. Again this research indicates that few children complained to teachers, taking the view that their responses were unlikely to be effective. Teachers were viewed as unwilling to listen and unlikely to act.

**6.1.6** It is clear then that for all these children, the right to protection from all forms of violence contained in Article 19 is far from being respected. In addition, bullying often takes the form of attack on a child's language or culture, thus denying them the right (Article 30) to have their culture respected and to be able to use their own language. Article 16 states that '*No child shall be subjected to arbitrary or unlawful interference with his or her privacy, family ... nor to unlawful attacks on his or her honour and reputation. The child has the right to protection against such interference or attacks*'. Bullying often takes the form of sexual harassment or attacks on a child's family or status, and unless effectively challenged represents a breach of the child's right to personal integrity (Article 16). Bullying can also constitute a breach of the child's right to freedom of expression (Article 13); for example, where a child is being harassed about their sexuality, their style of dress, or their views. (See **UK Agenda Report 3 on physical integrity,** page 51 for a more detailed discussion of children and violence.)

**Compliance with Article 19, the right to protection from all forms of violence, requires that:**

- **all schools adopt a whole school behaviour policy which addresses the physical environment and staffing of playgrounds and classrooms and which is developed in consultation with the pupils and all other members of the school community;**
- **legislation should oblige responsible authorities for all schools to develop detailed policies to prevent and respond to bullying;**
- **governors and all staff supervising playgrounds should receive training or anti-bullying strategies.**

## 6.2 School discipline

**6.2.1** Article 28(2) stresses that appropriate measures must be taken to ensure that '*school discipline is administered in a manner consistent with the child's human dignity and in conformity with the ... Convention*'. This is reinforced by Article 19 which requires protection from '*all forms of physical or mental violence*' and Article 37 which requires that '*no child shall be subjected to torture or other cruel, inhuman or degrading treatment or punishment*' and goes on to add that no child should be '*deprived of his or her liberty unlawfully or arbitrarily*'.

**6.2.2** Progress has been made towards implementation of these Articles with the abolition of corporal punishment in all state-supported education. But it remains legal to hit children in schools where parents are paying for their

education. A recent judgement by the European Court on this issue found that the assault of the child in that particular case did not reach the level of severity necessary to breach Article 3 of the European Convention on Human Rights which states that no-one shall be subjected to inhuman or degrading treatment or punishment[60]. Nevertheless, the judges stressed that their conclusion should not in any way be interpreted as an endorsement of physical punishment in schools. (See **UK Agenda Report 3 on physical integrity** for a more detailed discussion.)

**6.2.3** The continued use of violence against children in this way represents a fundamental lack of respect for their physical integrity. The defence of the Government that parents should have the choice of allowing their children to be beaten reveals a worrying failure to acknowledge the independent rights of the child. Defending physical assaults on children on the basis of freedom of choice for the parent perpetuates the traditional view of children as the property of their parents and does little to encourage confidence that the Government is seriously committed to the promotion of children's rights consistent with the ratification of the Convention.

**6.2.4** Although corporal punishment is outlawed in state schools and the provisions in the Education (No 2) Act 1986 expressly apply to all assaults there is evidence of violations of the legislation. EPOCH, an organisation campaigning for the abolition of all physical punishment of children receives regular complaints of violations such as pulling hair, banging heads together, hitting with books. Many children complain of teachers using sarcasm, mockery and humiliation. Arbitrary and unlawful restriction of liberty also takes place, for example, with children in some special schools contained in purpose-built 'time out' rooms or even cupboards. It is ironic that, whilst the law continues to allow children in the private school sector to be subjected to physical punishment, it is in a small number of independent schools that children are offered the greatest protection from humiliating treatment. Under the Children Act 1989 in England and Wales boarding-schools with less than 51 pupils which accommodate some children during most of the year are obliged to register as children's homes and as such are covered by regulations which list prohibited sanctions.

> '*In our school there is a teacher who if you do something wrong she makes you kneel with two biros underneath your knees which is very sore and in front of the whole class.*'
> (14 year-old, N Ireland)

**6.2.5** It is discriminatory that children have different protection purely on the basis that the school they attend falls within the remit of different sets of regulations or legislation. There is an urgent need for all children to be afforded the same levels of protection. Early in 1994 the DFE issued detailed draft guidance which does emphasise the importance of positive discipline and states that punishments should not be humiliating. But such basic principles should be in regulations rather than guidance. Failure to make such provision presents a breach not only of Articles 19, 28 and 37 but is also in breach of Article 2 in that the rights to protection are not being applied consistently to all children.

**Compliance with Articles 19, 28 and 37, the right of children to be protected from all forms of violence, requires that:**

- the law applying to all institutional settings for children should consistently prohibit punishment and treatment which may involve physical or mental violence; in particular the abolition of corporal punishment should be extended to cover all pupils;

- similar regulations to those currently applying to children's homes in England and Wales which provide a list of unacceptable sanctions should cover all residential settings for children; appropriately amended regulations should apply to day settings;

- guidance to school staff on the appropriate use of physical restraint should be issued following consultation with all relevant staff and children;

- initial teacher education should incorporate the principles of respect for children's personal and physical integrity.

## 6.3 Health and safety in schools

**6.3.1** Article 3.3 states that '*institutions, services and facilities responsible for the care or protection of children shall conform with the standards established by competent authorities, particularly in the ares of safety, health ... '*. In line with these requirements there are explicit obligations and liabilities on local education authorities (LEAs) and individual schools to maintain the standards of school buildings and protect the health and safety of their pupils. The Occupier's Liability Act 1957 requires that the LEAs exercise a 'common duty of care' which is defined as a duty to ensure that any visitor can be reasonably safe in the building. In this context a visitor would include a pupil. The Health and Safety at Work etc Act 1974 aims to protect the health, safety and welfare of employees and others in the workplace. Again 'others' would include pupils. Pupils are also protected by the duties resting with teachers to take reasonable care for their safety.

**6.3.2** However, despite the formal protection afforded by the legislation, there is considerable evidence to show that in practice, many schools provide a far from adequate standard of health and safety for children. A recent HMI report revealed that 40% of secondary schools were sub-standard[61]. An HMI report on physical education in secondary schools commented that many playing fields were in a very poor and sometimes dangerous state[62]. The Inspectorate would certainly fall within the definition of a '*competent authority*' as described by Article 3 and it is clear that, if such authorities are expressing high levels of concern about the physical environment of many schools, then there is reason to believe that those standards are not consistent with the requirements of that Article. Further evidence can be found in a survey on the state of schools undertaken by the National Confederation of Parent Teacher Associations[63]. Of the 2,000 schools which took part in the survey, 30% stated that the condition of the buildings and decoration overall had deteriorated. Hundreds of schools reported leaking roofs, rotten windows, peeling plaster, dangerous electrics, poor ground maintenance and pot holes in drives and paths. 44% of schools had not been decorated internally for five years or more and 23% for more than 12 years. They observe that, despite increased levels of capital investment, little improvement in the state of schools has taken place in the past five years.

**6.3.3** These results confirm the findings of HMI that there is widespread evidence of inadequate standards of repair. They are worrying both in terms of the potential risks and health hazards they pose for children but also because of the detrimental effect that such an environment has on their education. The National Audit Office in 1991 stated: 'Her Majesty's Inspectorate has commented in its reports over the last decade on the adverse effects on the quality of education caused by buildings which are unsuitable for current educational demands, and badly maintained accommodation'[64].

**6.3.4** If these problems are to be tackled, greater investment will be needed to maintain the physical fabric of schools. Concerns have been expressed that this will become more difficult as a result of the devolving of budgets under the local management of schools. Whereas responsibility for maintenance previously lay exclusively with the LEA now, where the school manages its own budget, it takes on certain limited responsibility for many internal repairs. There are clearly advantages in this division of responsibility which enables school governors to undertake routine repair work quickly. However, where they are under severe financial pressure, there is a worry that repairs will take a lower priority than other financial demands and that the standard of repair in schools will deteriorate still further.

### ACTION REQUIRED FOR COMPLIANCE

**Compliance with Article 3.3 requires that additional central government funds should be made available to invest in the infra-structure of schools to bring them up to a standard of repair and decoration necessary both to ensure the health and safety of all pupils and that the physical environment of schools is not detrimental to their educational opportunities.**

# Summary of action required for compliance

1 Compliance with Article 3.1, the duty to consider the best interests of the child, requires that education law throughout the UK is amended to incorporate a principle stating that it shall be the duty of the Secretary of State and of funding authorities, local education authorities, governing bodies of all schools in the exercise of any of their functions to ensure in any decision concerning a child that the welfare of the child shall be a primary consideration.

2 Compliance with Article 3.3, the duty to provide services and facilities of an agreed standard, requires that additional central government funds should be made available to invest in the infra-structure of schools to bring them up to a standard of repair and decoration necessary both to ensure the health and safety of all pupils and that the physical environment of schools is not detrimental to their educational opportunities.

3 Compliance with Article 12, the right of children both to express their views and have them taken seriously within the education system and to be heard in administrative or judicial proceedings, requires:

● that children, in addition to parents, have a right of appeal against exclusions;

● that children have a right to be present at the hearing and to independent advocacy to help them present their case;

● legislation introducing a duty on schools and local authorities to establish formal procedures for both ascertaining and giving due consideration to the views of individual children on matters affecting them and enabling them to make complaints when they are dissatisfied with either the process or outcome of any decision made in respect of them;

● legislation to ensure the child has a right to be heard in decision-making and appeals concerned with school choice, exclusions from school, special needs assessment and making of statements (or records in Scotland) of special educational needs;

● the introduction by schools and local authorities of procedures for ensuring that children are provided with the opportunity to express their views on matters of concern to them in the running of schools and that their views are given due weight in accordance with their age and maturity;

● both initial and in-service teacher education to be founded on principles of respect for children and greater democracy within schools.

4 Compliance with Article 14, the right to freedom of religion, and Article 29, the responsibility to promote tolerance and peace, requires that immediate steps are taken to remedy the failure to provide all children in N Ireland with the opportunity to attend an integrated school

5 Compliance with Article 19, the right of children to be protected from all forms of violence, together with Articles 28 and 37, requires that:

● all schools adopt a whole school behaviour policy which addresses the physical environment and staffing of playgrounds and classrooms and which is developed in consultation with the pupils and all other members of the school community;

● legislation should oblige responsible authorities for all schools to develop detailed policies to prevent and respond to bullying;

● governors and all staff supervising playgrounds should receive training or anti-bullying strategies;

● the law applying to all institutional settings for children should consistently prohibit punishment and treatment which may involve physical or mental violence; in particular the abolition of corporal punishment should be extended to cover all pupils;

● similar regulations to those currently applying to children's homes in England and Wales which provide a list of unacceptable sanctions should cover all residential settings for children; appropriately amended regulations should apply to day settings;

● guidance to school staff on the appropriate use of physical restraint should be issued following consultation with all relevant staff and children;

● initial teacher education should incorporate the principles of respect for children's personal and physical integrity.

6 Compliance with Article 22, the rights of refugee children to the provision of adequately resourced support, requires that:

● the budget under the Local Government Act 1966, section 11 is increased in line with the additional costs associated with the rights of refugee children to specialist help;

● the Education Act 1988, section 210 is amended to ensure that the grants available under the section are extended to cover all refugees irrespective of their housing arrangements;

● local education authorities and schools develop comprehensive programmes of support for refugee parents and pupils, training for teachers, induction for pupils, and language tuition in order that refugee children are able to benefit from the education system as quickly and as constructively as possible.

7 Compliance with Article 23, the rights of disabled children to effective access to education on the basis of equality of opportunity, requires that:

● LEAs and governing bodies duty to 'use their best endeavours to secure' appropriate provision for children with special educational needs who are not statemented should be amended to require them to provide whatever provision is needed for a particular child. This must be reinforced by appropriate levels of resourcing from central government ring-fenced in the budgets to individual schools;

● local education authorities, in conjunction with health authorities and trusts and social services, provide accessible information about all the services that are available, who provides them and the rights available to children and parents under the law. All information provided must also be made available in relevant community languages;

● in order to increase access to the law in pursuing rights, the Law Society should consider post qualifying legal education courses on education law with particular reference to special educational needs;

LEAs and schools should have a duty to make provision for the fullest possible integration of children with special needs. There should be a target period within which to plan for full integration and make the changes necessary to achieve it;

- both initial and advanced in-service teacher education should be available for teachers to enhance their capacity to offer effective access to education for children with special needs in an integrated setting. Governors and non-teaching assistants should also receive training on services for children with special needs.

8 Compliance with Article 28, the right to education on the basis of equality of opportunity, consistent with Article 2, the right not to be discriminated against, requires that:

- education authorities, governing bodies, the Funding Agency for Schools and headteachers are encouraged to ensure that all admission procedures are actively scrutinised to ensure that they do not discriminate against any group of children, that they comply with the requirements of the Race Relations Act 1976 and the CRE Code of Practice on the Elimination of Racial Discrimination in Education;

- local education authorities and grant maintained schools develop clear guidelines on admission policies. Schools should be required to publish their admission criteria in an accessible form and in relevant community languages;

- all schools, including grant maintained schools, undertake ethnic monitoring of applications for admission and analyse the data with a view to changing any practices which discriminate against any groups of children;

- legislative criteria to limit school exclusions are introduced throughout the UK which place an obligation on schools to take all reasonable steps to prevent the exclusion and to satisfy themselves that, unless excluded, the pupil's behaviour is likely to be seriously detrimental to the education or welfare of the pupil or other pupils, or to the welfare of the staff;

- research into exclusions in Scottish schools should be carried out with a view to identifying the effectiveness of the legislation and the need for further guidelines to schools on its implementation;

- ethnic monitoring of school exclusions should be introduced as a requirement for all schools. The data gathered should then be used to develop policies to tackle any identified discrimination;

- all unmet need for support services for children with special needs is recorded and built into the planning process for the development of services;

- monitoring of the new pupil referral units is undertaken with reference to the resources available for their development, levels of use, effectiveness and the experience of children using them;

- children and young people detained in penal establishments or under the Mental Health Act should retain basic rights to full-time education;

- the provisions of the Race Relations Act 1976 are extended to N Ireland;

- schools collect ethnic data on the origins of pupils at key stages - including applications and admissions,

exclusions and suspensions, truancy rates, setting and banding assessments including attainments, examination entries and results, and school leaver destinations. This information should be used by inspectors of schools to assess evidence of race discrimination and to ensure that appropriate action is taken to tackle it. There is also a need for research into low attainment among specific groups;

- all staff working with children and young people looked after by the local authority - social workers, foster carers, residential staff - receive training on the importance of education in the lives of those young people;

- both initial and in-service teacher education includes information about the general circumstances of children looked after by the local authority in order that teachers can become more sensitive to the implications for those children and be more aware of their needs in relation to education;

- social services and education departments review and evaluate their arrangements for liaison and collaboration over education provision for children looked after by the local authority. Where possible, specialist services designed to provide educational support to young people looked after, foster carers and other professionals in social services departments should be established. Reviews should always address the education of the child concerned;

- individual case files should have a separate section on education;

- school activities which are undertaken during the school day are provided free of charge and that resources are made available to subsidise those children who cannot afford to undertake out of school activities;

- an overall review of early childhood care and education services in the UK is undertaken, leading to a comprehensive, integrated national policy for the development of high quality and affordable early childhood services;

- all schools work progressively towards the provision of integrated teaching of English as a second language;

- there should be no discrimination on grounds of religion in considering applications to voluntary aided status, or in the provision of state resources for education;

- schools develop strategies for encouraging attendance in consultation with pupils reflecting the individual needs of each school;

- regulations governing funding to grant-maintained schools should be amended to ensure equity with LEA maintained schools in order that the resourcing of children's education is not influenced by the status of school they attend.

9 Compliance with Article 29, the duty in education to promote the child's personality and talents and respect for human rights, requires that:

- the National Curriculum fully incorporates perspectives on human rights and democracy as an integral component;

- both initial and in-service teacher education are explicitly designed to equip teachers to undertake their duties without racially discriminating and in a way that meets the demands of schools in a multi-racial and multi-lingual society. There should be clear guidelines within schools on the disciplinary procedures to be taken in the event of discrimination;

● monitoring of the provision of Welsh medium education following the implementation of the Education Act 1993 is undertaken to assess its adequacy;

● research is undertaken to enable effective planning for the development of community languages within schools.

# References

1. *Secondary school admissions: report of a formal investigation into Hertfordshire County Council*, CRE (1992)
2. *Draft circular on admission arrangements*, CRE (1993)
3. *Working across boundaries, working across cultures: forum report*, Preston Community Project, The Save the Children Fund (1990)
4. *National school reporting survey*, DFE (1993)
5. *NUT survey on pupil exclusions: information from LEAs*, National Union of Teachers (1992)
6. *Fair play*, Bulletin no 53, ACE (May/June 1993)
7. *Discipline in Scottish Secondary Schools: A Survey*, Johnstone and Munn, SCRE (1992)
8. *Birmingham Education Authority and schools: referral and suspension of pupils*, CRE (1985)
9. *Pupil exclusion from Nottingham secondary schools*, Nottingham County Council (1991)
10. see reference 5
11. see reference 6
12. *Travellers and school: travellers in Lewisham talk of their experiences of school*, Dowber H, Lewisham Bridge Publications (1992)
13. *Education in England and Wales: the annual report of the HM Senior Inspector of Schools*, HM Inspectorate, DFE (1992)
14. *Racism in children's lives: a study of mainly white primary schools*, Troyna B and Hatcher R, National Children's Bureau (1992)
15. *Leaving care and after*, Garnett L, National Children's Bureau (1992)
16. *Not just a name: the views of young people in residential and foster care*, Fletcher B, National Consumer Council (1993)
17. *Changing schools? Changing people?: a study of the education of children in care*, Fletcher-Campbell F and Hall C, NFER (1990)
18. *The state of schools in England and Wales*, NCPTA (1991)
19. *Education White Paper: choice and diversity, a new framework for schools: A response from the Family Service Units*, FSU (1992)
20. *Learning before school*, Sylva K & Moss P, (contains a summary of recent research evidence), National Commission on Education (1992)
21. *Becoming a breadwinner: policies to assist lone parents with childcare*, Holterman S, Day Care Trust (1993)
22. *Investing in your children: costing and education - daycare service*, Holterman S, National Children's Bureau (1992)
23. *Getting in on the Act - provision for pupils with special educational needs: the national picture*, Audit Commission/HMI (1992)
24. *'Call to protect special needs'*, *Social Work Today* (28 January 1993)
25. *'1m special needs pupils 'failed' by hard-up councils'*, *Guardian* (29 March 1993)
26. *Standards in education 1988-1989: the annual report of the HM Senior Chief Inspector of Schools*, HM Inspectorate, DFE (1990)
27. see reference 25
28. *The Children Act Guidance and regulations: vol 6: children with disabilities*, HMSO (1991)
29. *A hard Act to follow: a study of the experience of parents and children under the 1981 Education Act*, The Spastics Society (1992)

30. *Children with special educational needs: policy and provision,* Thomson, Riddell and Dyer, (1989)

31. *Integration statistics - LEAs reveal local variations,* Swann W, CSIE (1989)

32. *Special educational consortium: a response to the Government's current proposals for education,* Council for Disabled Children (1992)

33. see reference 30

34. see reference 23

35. *The integration of statemented children in mainstream schools,* Stone K, Social Work Monographs (1991)

36. *The implementation of the 1981 Education Act: policy and provision for special education needs,* Evans J, Goucher B, Welton J and Wedell K, Social Services Research No 3 (1987)

37. 'Clear call for end to religious separation in schools', *Belfast Telegraph* (October 1968)

38. *Peace making, discrimination and the rights of children to attend integrated schools in N Ireland,* Irwin C, submission to the UN Committee on the Rights of the Child (1993)

39. *Hansard,* col 490, (17 July 1988)

40. *Funding of grant-maintained schools,* AMA Briefing to the 3rd Standing Committee on Statutory Instruments, AMA (13 May 1993)

41. *An evaluation of the independent person service in London,* A Voice for the Child in Care (1992)

42. *Discipline in schools: report of the Committee of Enquiry chaired by Lord Elton,* HMSO (1989)

43. *Choice and diversity: a new framework for schools,* DFE (1992)

44. *Cross curricular work in secondary schools: summary of results of a survey carried out in 1992,* Rowe G, Institute of Education (1992)

45. *The Education Reform Act 1988: the school curriculum and assessment,* Circular no 5/89, HMSO (1989)

46. 'Equal opportunity issues in the context of the National Curriculum: a black perspective', Shah S, *Gender and education,* vol 2, no 3 (1990)

47. 'A nationalistic curriculum for white superiority', Tomlinson S, *ACE Bulletin,* no 51, ACE (Jan/Feb 1993)

48. *Education for all: the report of the Committee of Inquiry into the education of children of all ethnic minority groups,* Swann Report, DES (1985)

49. *Commission for Racial Equality response to the DES consultation on proposals for reform of initial teacher training,* CRE (1992)

50. *Teaching English as a second language: report of a formal investigation into Calderdale LEA,* CRE (1986)

51. see reference 48

52. see reference 49

53. *CRE submission to the National Commission on Education,* CRE (1992)

54. *The education of migrant workers,* European Commission Directive 77/486/EEC (1977)

55. see reference 48

56. *Schools of faith: religious schools in a multicultural society,* CRE (1990)

57. 'Bullying in UK schools: the DES Sheffield Bullying Project', Sharp S and Smith P K, *Early Child Development and Care,* vol 77, pp47-55

58. 'Bullying and children with special needs in schools', Nabuzoka D, Whitney I, Smith P K and Thompson D, to appear in *Understanding and managing bullying,* Tatum D (ed), Heinemann

59. *Racism in schools: new research evidence,* Kelly E and Cohn T, Trentham Books (1988)

60. Costello-Roberts v UK, European Court of Human Rights, Strasbourg (1993)

61. *HMI Annual Report,* HMSO (1990)

62. *A survey of work in physical education in secondary schools,* HMI/DES (1990)

63. see reference 18

64. *Repairs and maintenance of school buildings,* National Audit Office (1991)

# UK Agenda for Children

## 8 Play and leisure

# Contents

*The unreferenced quotations in this report are comments made during a consultation exercise undertaken by the Children's Rights Development Unit with groups of young people throughout the UK.*

**Acknowledgement**
The sections in this report relating to play were compiled by Jan Cosgrove, 'Fair Play for Children'.

# 1 Introduction

## 1.1 Background

**1.1.1** In the UK the responsibility for ensuring the provision of facilities and services for play, leisure, art and culture is, in general, delegated by the Government to other bodies including Arts Councils, Sports Councils, play bodies and local authorities. Much provision also comes through the voluntary and private sector.

**1.1.2** This report looks primarily at Article 31 which recognises that children and young people have the right to rest and leisure, to play and recreational activities and to be actively involved in cultural life and the arts. The UK Government has no co-ordinated policies and strategies aimed at encouraging the provision of services and facilities; the provision which does exist is often not '*appropriate*', and does not ensure '*equal opportunities*' for **all** children and young people.

**1.1.3** Article 31 upholds the right to '*engage in play ... '*. In the UK this right, in particular, has never been consistently supported by the Government. Play is fundamental to development. It is the way in which children and young people explore and learn about their physical, social, cultural, creative and spiritual environment. It is created and organised by children themselves. In this it is different from formal education, organised recreation and leisure activities which are adult-initiated and lead.

**1.1.4** Responsibility for ensuring play opportunities, whether through provision of facilities and services or through creating safe environments for free play, are spread between government departments, with none taking a lead role or responsibility for policy co-ordination and development. As a result, provision is ad hoc and underfunded.

**1.1.5** The central issue for younger children is safety. Whilst playing with friends is their main pastime they have major concerns over safety. These worries include danger from vehicles (particularly stolen ones), kidnappers, adults following them, bullying and unsafe play areas, spoilt by, for example, broken glass and rubbish. Many children are playing in an atmosphere of fear and stress.

**1.1.6** For young people, frustration at the lack of consultation is of major concern and results in the widespread provision of services of little interest to them. Many want cafe-style places to go and be with their friends, away from adult supervision. Lack of money and restriction of movement by parents are also issues of concern as is fear of violence, particularly from other young people. Many of these problems are experienced even more strongly by young people in isolated areas, disabled young people and young carers.

**1.1.7** In addition to analysing Article 31, this report also looks specifically at the implementation of Article 17 and the rights of children and young people in relation to information produced and disseminated by the mass media. It shows, in particular, the failure of the Government to ensure and promote the availability of information and resources through the public library system; its failure to promote and support the production of materials which meet the needs of children and young people for whom written English is not a primary means of communication; and it also highlights the Government's role in protecting children and young people from information which may be damaging or harmful to them.

## 1.2 The importance of play and leisure activities

> '*You cannot stop children from playing. They'd do it anyway. And if they stopped children from playing, I'd write a letter to the Prime Minister and I'd say - you can't stop play, it's too important. Instead of making less play schemes, you should make more and make more easy areas for kids to play. If they do not play, they won't learn easily*'[1].

**1.2.1** All children and young people have the right to develop to their full potential and to enjoy the '*highest attainable standard of health*' (Article 6.2 and Article 24.1) and studies over many decades have shown that play is of crucial importance to the development of educational, social, physical and creative abilities in later years. Department of Health guidance to the Children Act 1989 (volume 2) recognises the importance of play and leisure activities in the development of children. It says that 'Children's need for good quality play opportunities changes as they grow up, but they need such opportunities throughout childhood in order to reach and maintain their optimum development and well-being. Under-fives develop knowledge of themselves and their world through play ... For school-aged children play is a means whereby they can develop a broader range of interests, complementary to subjects learnt during school time, and a positive use of leisure time'. Play and leisure activities involve communicating and co-operating with others, and children and young people are able to develop the skills necessary for this. They can learn how to work together and with adults in the neighbourhoods where they live. Many organisations which are controlled by adults and work on behalf of children can contribute to this educative process but the scope for child-led initiatives is enormous.

**1.2.2** Play and recreational activities are important in promoting physical health and fitness. National surveys show that the UK population is becoming increasingly unfit and that health is suffering as a result[2][3]. The enjoyment of physical activity develops from an early age through play and leisure activities. Those who take up exercise and sports in childhood are more likely to carry on in adulthood. But in the 1990s children are living increasingly isolated existences with less physical activity than ever. Many are taken to and from school by their parents in cars and are often driven to sporting and other leisure activities; and they can spend hours watching television, videos and playing computer games.

**1.2.3** Encouraging an interest and participation in different types of arts brings benefits in terms of children's development and learning. One example of this is the use of theatre in education. An interest in theatre and the impact of the growth of theatre in youth work during the 1980s provided important opportunities for previously disadvantaged young people to develop their skills and talents. It provided the main impetus for work which involved the experiences of people from many different ethnic groups and those with disabilities. Many successful actors with disabilities and from black and minority ethnic groups started out in community-based youth theatre projects. Many of these actors had few training opportunities and, in the case of disabled actors, many were actively denied training by drama schools[4].

**1.2.4** The full implementation of Article 31 is therefore fundamental to the attainment of both Article 6.2, the maximum potential development of the child and to Article 24.1, the *'highest attainable standard of health'*. In not recognising this in policy and resource allocation the Government is failing in its duties to ensure full implementation of the Convention.

**1.2.5** One of the principle Articles underlying the Convention is Article 12 which upholds the rights of children to express their views freely in any matters which affect them and have those views given *'due weight in accordance with the age and maturity of the child.'* In order to obtain full benefit from their rights to be consulted, children need to gain skills in decision-making and expressing their opinions. Play and leisure activities offer children and young people opportunities to discover and learn in their own way. The exploratory nature of play provides a foundation for acquiring the skills and confidence children need if they are to grow into adults capable of playing a full part in society.

**1.2.6** Article 13 describes, in more detail, the right to express views and feelings *'through any ... media of the child's choice'* and also the right to seek and receive information. For many young people being involved in artistic and cultural activities gives them the opportunity and means to express themselves and communicate a wide range of thoughts, feelings and emotions arising from their own experience. For example, theatre companies involved in successful youth work in the 1980s offered opportunities for young people to question and explore ideas of interest to them many of which involved questions about race, gender, sexuality, disability and class[5]. For those who experience discrimination and alienation, involvement in the arts offers opportunities to express themselves fully without the fear and restrictions they often face, and provides a creative way of teaching and learning about the importance of respecting the individual beliefs and behaviours of others.

**1.2.7** In order for children and young people to be able to express their views much depends on the attitudes of the adults they are involved with. Often an adult will help a child or young person to think through what it is they want and how they could go about making their views known to adults. If implementation of Article 13 is to have any meaning adults need to create appropriate structures and opportunities for children and young people to become involved. Only when young people are exposed to a varied range of choices - backed up by improved facilities - will they be able to decide what they want to do and what they want to say through the medium of the arts.

## 1.3 Structures for play and leisure activities

*'You need a seesaw and you need a big aeroplane and you*

*need a wee rubber duck for your bath. You need somewhere to play'.*
(7 year-old, N Ireland)

**1.3.1** In England responsibility for play falls within the brief of the Department of National Heritage which has delegated some responsibility to the Sports Council, which funds the National Play Information Centre and oversees the programme for education and training set up by the now disbanded National Children's Play and Recreation Unit. The Department of the Environment also has had some involvement through its funding of urban programmes, many of which have provided play facilities. In Scotland the Scottish Office has overall responsibility and gives funding to the National Centre for Play; the N Ireland Youth Council supports PlayBoard and the Welsh Office funds Play Wales.

**1.3.2** At present the structure of local government in the UK is under review and sweeping changes are to be introduced. This could provide an important opportunity for the development of co-ordinated services throughout the unitary authorities but there is concern that this opportunity will not be used and in some areas re-organisation may threaten co-ordinated play and leisure policies. No clear information is available to forecast what scale of provision is required for children's play and leisure and there is a need for much basic research in these fields[6].

**1.3.3** In order to rectify some of the problems created by lack of commitment and co-ordination for children's play the National Voluntary Council for Children's Play was established. It published its own Charter for Children's Play in 1992[7]. In Scotland, Children in Scotland has also published a Charter for Play, as have play organisations in N Ireland and Wales. These Charters are based on the UN Convention, setting out broad objectives and standards.

**1.3.4** The Department of National Heritage has overall responsibility for the arts, and for museums and galleries, libraries, film, sports, broadcasting and the press. However, many of these responsibilities are delegated to 'arms length' organisations such as the Arts Council of Great Britain (which has sub-committees for Scotland and Wales), the Arts Council for N Ireland, the UK wide Museums and Galleries Commission, the Sports Council of Great Britain; and the Sports Councils of Scotland, Wales and N Ireland. The Welsh, Scottish and N Ireland Offices are also involved in their own right. Current re-organisation within the Arts Council of Great Britain will reform it into separate, autonomous bodies in England, Scotland and Wales, probably in April 1994. The Sports Council is also undergoing reorganisation and its future role is still unclear.

**1.3.5** Local government sets policy for its youth provision and in this is guided by a youth service curriculum which was introduced in the late 1980s but with no additional funding to ensure its use[8]. Most provision is targeted at the 13-18 age range although it is often used by younger children. In N Ireland the service aims to provide for all those from 5-25. In many areas of the UK the services tends to rely on the traditional youth club model. Local authorities wanting to develop alternative strategies are often restricted in developing such provision by lack of funding.

# 2 Relevant articles in the Convention

## 2.1 General principles

**Article 2:** all rights in the Convention must apply without discrimination of any kind irrespective of race, colour, language, religion, national, ethnic or social origin, disability or other status.

**Article 3.1:** the duty in all actions to consider the best interests of the child.

**Article 12:** the right to express an opinion and to have that opinion taken into account in any matter or procedure affecting the child.

## 2.2 Articles relevant to play and leisure

**Article 31:** the right to rest and leisure, to engage in play and recreational activities appropriate to age and take part in cultural life and the arts. The Government must promote this right and encourage the provision of '*appropriate and equal opportunities for cultural, artistic, recreational and leisure activity*'.

**Article 3.2:** the duty of the Government to provide the necessary care and protection for the child's well-being and introduce appropriate legislative and administrative procedures to achieve this end.

**Article 3.3:** the duty of the Government to ensure that the standards of services provided for the care and protection of children are adequate, particularly in relation to safety, health, staffing and supervision.

**Article 13:** the right to freedom of expression and to information.

**Article 17:** the duty of the Government to ensure that children have access to information and material from a diversity of sources and to:

● encourage the mass media to disseminate information and material of social and cultural benefit to the child;

● encourage the production and dissemination of children's books;

● encourage the media to provide for the linguistic needs of the child who belongs to a minority group or who is indigenous;

● encourage the development of appropriate guidelines for the protection of the child from information and material injurious to his or her well-being.

**Article 18:** the duty of the Government to recognise that both parents have joint primary responsibility for bringing up their children and to support them in this task.

**Article 23:** the right of disabled children to special care, education and training to ensure the fullest possible social integration.

**Article 30:** the right of children from minority communities to enjoy their own culture and practise their own language and religion.

*For the full wording of the articles, see the UN Convention on the Rights of the Child, see page 311.*

# 3 The right to rest and leisure
## Article 31.1

**3.1** Children and young people have the right to rest and leisure (Article 31) and the Government has a duty to ensure that, if necessary, parents and carers are given adequate assistance to ensure this right (Article 18.2).

**3.2** The main structure imposed on children and young people in the UK is compulsory, formal primary and secondary education. The education system has long recognised the necessity and importance of 'breaks' but recently there is a trend towards telescoping the school day with an earlier start and end. The effect of this is to reduce the number and length of rest and leisure breaks. The reasons for these changes seem to be more connected with increased benefits to the school of reducing costs rather than children and young people. Article 3.1 requires that '*in all actions concerning children the ... best interests of the child shall be a primary consideration*'. Thus, decisions to alter the timing of the school day should look closely at the effects of this on the time available during the day for children to have adequate rest between work periods. For many children, often under pressure to achieve, school homework, private tuition and supplementary schooling also impinge on their leisure time. Once again, careful attention needs to be paid to whether decisions are being made which respect the child's best interests or only those of parents and institutions. The lack of leisure opportunities for young children is compounded in N Ireland where many children are required to start formal schooling at four.

### ACTION REQUIRED FOR COMPLIANCE

**Compliance with Article 12, Article 3.1 and Article 31.1 requires that:**

● **all authorities and schools considering changes to the length and structure of the school day ensure that the children affected are consulted, that their welfare is a primary consideration and that adequate break times for rest are time-tabled in. Current and new arrangements should be regularly reviewed for the same reasons;**

● **in N Ireland parents of children under the age of five should have the right to choose whether or not their child enters formal schooling and play should form a major part of the early years curriculum.**

# 4 Promoting and encouraging facilities for play and leisure activities

**Article 31.2**

## 4.1 Inadequate policy co-ordination and development

**4.1.1** Article 31.2 places a duty on the Government to *'promote the right of the child to participate fully in cultural and artistic life and ... encourage the provision of appropriate and equal opportunities for cultural, artistic, recreational and leisure activity'*. One element in ensuring the full implementation of this right must be co-ordinated policy development at both national and local level. However, it is clear that there is no commitment to this at Government level and little at local level:

- the Arts Council and Sports Council, the two Government bodies concerned with adult leisure and recreation, are given substantial resources annually by the Government for their work but in neither case do they have any policy which accepts the premise of Article 31.2's *'appropriate and equal opportunities'* for access to their programmes by children. Although both state their recognition of the importance of such work with children and young people, no quantifiable budgets for programmes are identified;

- within the arts there is no one body with a real overview of the arts needs of young people. The youth arts which grew during the 1980s came from three distinct disciplines; theatre, community arts and the youth service. As a result provision is piecemeal and ad hoc. In the late 1980s there was wider recognition of the need for more co-ordinated arts policies at local level but there are major funding problems;

- the overall national provision of arts facilities for young people shows wide variations from county to county, depending on local structures, history and politics[9]. Provision related to a broad cross section of young people has never been high on the agenda of most established arts organisations and until very recently the world of youth work has paid very little attention to the development of youth arts[10]. Amongst adults responsible for providing services for young people there are low expectations about what is possible, lack of confidence and inexperience in certain fields and inadequate training;

- in England there is no national policy or framework for play and play-work and the Government has recently abolished the only publicly funded national play co-ordinating body. Despite extensive lobbying from all those involved in the field the Government disbanded the National Children's Play and Recreation Unit in 1993. In Scotland and N Ireland any expansion in activities over the last few years has come from the voluntary sector and there appear to be no Government strategy or development plans for play;

- at local government level there is no specific department with responsibility for overseeing services for children and young people. Different needs are addressed by different departments including education, social services and leisure, but the overall needs of children and young people are never assessed. As more services are contracted out to a variety of service providers there is more fragmentation and even less opportunity for a holistic approach;

- there is no consistent approach to play policy within local government. Some local authorities approach play provision on an ad hoc basis, whilst others develop policies through a community development approach involving parents and organisations. Few involve children and young people. Policy on school-age play and care provision has been, and remains, without clear government guidelines or legislation;

- the same lack of perception as to the importance of play is found in local authority planning departments. As a result most planning decisions over two or more decades have paid minimal attention to the specific needs of children and young people and there is no legislative framework to enable councillors to demand review and change in respect of planning applications where play needs have been ignored or under-considered;

- for the youth service, the other major provider for leisure activities for young people, a national curriculum was proposed in 1990 drawn up by the National Youth Bureau[11]. However, since this was discussed there have been massive cuts to the youth services and its proposals have not been given realistic support.

**4.1.2** In 1991 an Arts Council discussion document proposed a shift of resources to youth arts workers, companies and projects which attract young people and a re-think on the part of the youth service away from conventional youth clubs to flexible youth arts teams[12]. In the long term it proposed a national youth arts policy based on a regional youth arts audit of need and provision and involving innovative youth arts projects developed strategically in areas of greatest need with new qualifying courses for youth arts workers. This document was, in part, included in the Arts Council policy document, *A creative future*, which gives some ideas and principles for developing youth arts. However, the future and status of the document remains uncertain as major changes in the structure of the Council are to be introduced in 1994[13].

**4.1.3** An arts policy for all, including appropriate and equal opportunities for children and young people, in line with Article 31.2, would ensure that every young person has easy access to properly funded youth arts projects where their experience and skills are valued and developed. They should be able to see performance in a wide variety of art forms in their neighbourhoods and should feel that their local arts centres are accessible, reflect their experience and interest and are stretching and challenging. Children and young people should be encouraged to take part in the development and organisation of youth arts at every level. The aim of the youth service should be to see that arts methods become an important part of practice, to initiate new arts projects and to help them flourish. Organisations and public authorities should adopt practical policies for youth arts[14].

**4.1.4** The Sports Council has also started developing a policy for sports provision for children and young people. Its policy document *Young people and sport* is a step in the right direction and was drawn up after wide consultation including with young people[15]. Full implementation of its ideas will be important in implementing Article 31 and must be given full Government support. An important initiative from the Sports Council, providing a model for the potential success of projects based on adequate funding, forward planning and working in partnership is the 'Champion Coaching' scheme, initially funded by the Government and run by the National Coaching Federation; it provides quality schemes for young people around the country.

## ACTION REQUIRED FOR COMPLIANCE

**Full implementation of Article 31.2 promoting and encouraging play and leisure opportunities for all, through co-ordinated planning and policy development, requires that:**

**at government level:**

● **the Department of National Heritage should formally be given the responsibility for ensuring the implementation of Article 31 throughout the UK and should liaise with relevant departments and organisations in each jurisdiction. It should initiate an urgent examination of children's and young people's leisure and play and consideration should be given to establishing a legislative duty on local government to provide children's and youth service encompassing all these aspects. In N Ireland, the Department of Education should assume a lead role in co-ordinating both policy and provision across agency boundaries;**

● **the Government should, after consultation, publish Charters covering the rights to play and to leisure facilities for all children and young people, describing what children and young people and their parents have the right to expect by way of provision in their own localities, related to age;**

● **the Department of National Heritage should establish a research panel to commission and fund research which will identify, for example, the range, forms and distribution of play provision throughout the UK. It should also set up a Governmental inter-departmental forum to ensure that all Government programmes take account of the play and leisure needs of children and young people;**

● **the Department of National Heritage should appoint officers for children's play and leisure provision with designated responsibility and consider setting up an expert advisory group to advise ministers;**

● **the arts and sports councils in each jurisdiction should be requested to undertake, and publicise widely, detailed reviews of their policies and programmes with specific reference to Article 31 and develop targets for service provision and budget allocation which should be systematically monitored;**

**at local level:**

● **corporate strategies by local authorities must recognise play and leisure activities as crucial in the development of children. Plans must be explicit in all children's services and a multi-disciplinary**

understanding of the many elements of play and leisure must be achieved. They must also reflect the importance of access for disabled children including, for example, physical access, availability of different forms of communication and transport;

● **every local authority leisure and amenities department should appoint designated teams to oversee the provision of services for children and young people throughout the authority's responsibilities. These teams should develop and publish a co-ordinated, comprehensive child and youth policy relating to the provision of play and leisure activities. The teams should have advisory groups and networks drawn from the local population of children and young people;**

● **youth services should develop regional arts plans and youth arts budgets, buy in the skills of freelance artists, set up indigenous youth arts projects and pressurise arts funders for better provision. All Regional Arts Boards should have specific youth officer posts, have a youth arts policy and make youth arts a budgetary priority.**

## 4.2 Inadequate funding

*'There's cuts going on everywhere, like through the Government. Like in the youth service, where are the kids supposed to go to if the youth club gets closed down? ... There's no other youth club in the area, where are they going to go? What are they going to do? They're going to turn to violence. They're going to turn to crime.'*
(17 year-old, N Ireland)

4.2.1 Although it is impossible to estimate the proportion of Government expenditure on arts and leisure activities devoted specifically to play and leisure activities for children and young people it is clearly not related to the 20% of the population they represent. In 1992/3 the combined Government expenditure on the arts and sports councils was £280 million. At the same time the National Children's Play and Recreation Unit (NCPRU) received only £800,000. Although the sports and arts councils do allocate some of their budgets to facilities for children and young people a recent report by the National Playing Fields Association estimated that the Department of National Heritage spends 3p on the needs of children compared with £100 for adult leisure[16].

4.2.2 A positive commitment to implementing Article 31, and to *'encourage the provision of ... cultural, artistic, recreational and leisure activity'* would involve ensuring that current provision is not eroded through lack of resources. However, severe financial cut-backs are a major problem for those involved in developing services and facilities:

● funding for the only central body to co-ordinate and promote high quality play provision has recently been drastically cut. The £800,000 given to the Sports Council in 1992/93, ring-fenced to fund the NCPRU, has been cut and in 1993-94 only £300,000 is being allocated to play-related functions;

● in the past much play provision for children has been funded through the Urban Programme which gave money, via local authorities, to many small local initiatives. This scheme has now been replaced by the

City Challenge scheme with a different funding basis and as a result many small play projects have lost their funding base;

● a recent survey of play projects in N Ireland conducted by PlayRight showed that over 80% of respondents faced funding difficulties. They tended to rely on volunteers or short-term employment schemes which meant frequent changes of staff;

● throughout the UK the youth service has suffered major cuts in resources. Until the early 1990s, the Government allowed an identifiable Grant Related Expenditure Assessment in the Rate Support Grant for youth services. On average, this amounted to approximately 1% of overall education budgets but there were wide variations between authorities. Despite this funding the youth service suffered cuts during the 1980s. The Community and Youth Workers Union estimated that between 1979 and 1983 there were 12.3% cuts in real terms across the country, and that this was never restored. In the early 1990s there have been more cuts. Two-thirds of local education authorities have cut youth service funding since 1990/91[17]. The Government-funded National Youth Agency estimates that, on local authority's own assessments, in 1993-94 alone, youth service budgets have decreased in 62% of local authorities, remained static in 24% and grown in only 14%[18]. This is considered to be an underestimate of the cuts as inflation is not taken into account. These cuts come on top of similar cuts in recent years[19]. Capping by central Government of local authority expenditure or the threat of this has affected the youth service disproportionately[20];

● facilities for young people to become involved in the arts have been drastically cut in recent years. At a time when there is increasing interest in theatre in schools, financial cutbacks have led many small theatre companies which have been working in schools to disband or forced to reduce their activities. They are declining so rapidly that there is concern that they may disappear altogether[21]. Resources and funding for community based and touring youth theatre projects are currently inadequate. There is no clear funding structure, and provision depends on the personality and commitment of individual youth services and regional arts associations officers;

● public money to support the arts for young people from the Arts Council is distributed between different art forms, but since many projects which interest young people cover a number of art forms, finding funding can be a problem. The result is that fundraisers for youth arts spend a considerable amount of time trying to raise money from different public and charitable sources, when they could be concentrating on developing art work with young people. Projects which are jointly funded can run into problems if one of the funding bodies has to reduce its share[22]. Whilst local authorities do provide some support for youth arts there is little monitoring of the effectiveness of these subsidies in improving access to the arts and culture for their local populations[23];

● museum education services, which promote museums and art galleries to children and young people and help ensure that their needs are adequately catered for, are under threat. There is no coherent framework underpinning the funding of museum education services. Many are largely self-financed and charge or expect donations; others receive local authority support and some are funded out of the museum's or gallery's own

budget[24]. In some areas, where museum entry is free to the public, school parties have to pay, thus making children the only paying customers[25];

● local government collects and spends hundreds of millions of pounds on leisure each year. There are no reliable and extensive statistics to show how much of this benefits children and young people, but research in the late 1980s by Fair Play For Children suggested a minimal proportion of funding was going to children's and young people's needs - anything from under 1% to just under 7% in areas where between 20-25 per cent of the population is under 18[26].

4.2.3 Income generated by the forthcoming National Lottery and given to the Arts Council, the Sports Council and charities could be an important impetus to improving facilities for the recreational activities of children and young people. The money is to be used for 'additional expenditure', not existing revenue costs and new services for children and young people could form part of the objectives of the different boards[27].

---

**ACTION REQUIRED FOR COMPLIANCE**

**Compliance with Article 31.2, the duty to encourage the provision of facilities and services for play and leisure, and ensure adequate funding for this, requires that:**

● **structured play and leisure opportunities must be sufficiently resourced to ensure that there is age-appropriate provision, equality of access for children and young people from rural areas, those with disabilities and learning difficulties, those who do not speak English and those from all ethnic and cultural groups;**

● **urgent attention should be directed at the imbalance of resources between facilities for adults and those for children and young people. There should be consultation with all concerned, including local authorities, the arts and sports councils, cultural, recreational, youth and play bodies;**

● **in N Ireland, a funding framework for play should be established which recognises the Department of Education as having a lead responsibility;**

● **the Government should direct the National Lottery boards to include within their objectives the enhancement of the quality of life of children through improvements in facilities for play and leisure activities. Funding must cover not only initial costs but also costs involved in running and maintaining programmes over a period of time.**

---

## 4.3 Decreasing support from the education system

4.3.1 An important process in being able to '*engage in ... recreational activities ... and participate fully in cultural and artistic life*' (Article 31.2) is learning about what possibilities exist and how to make the best use of them. Introduction to different types of artistic and cultural opportunities through school activities is the only way in which large numbers of children and young people will have this chance. The Education Reform Act 1988 introduced major changes to the management and funding of schools and there are a number of examples of how the provision of play, recreational and sporting, artistic and cultural activities for children and young people has suffered:

- in N Ireland the school starting-age is four. This is the lowest in the UK and a survey in 1991 found that three of the 138 primary schools surveyed admitted children in the two months before their fourth birthday[28]. In the rest of the UK compulsory schooling starts at five, the youngest in Europe. The structured play curriculum for children under seven does attempt to introduce the concept of learning through play. With new testing arrangements at seven and increasing pressures, play is not given a high priority and is treated as peripheral to learning. In some areas there has also been a rapid increase in the number of pre-school 'schools' offering formal education to young children and reducing their opportunities for play;

- education departments no longer have direct responsibility for the use of school premises out of school hours. This is having a major impact on the availability and use of school premises for out of school recreational activities. As schools 'opt-out' of local authority control or become more financially independent as a result of Local Management of Schools (LMS), they can make charges for the use of their premises which are beyond the means of many of the youth and children's groups which previously had access to them via the local authority. At the same time, some school playing-field sites are being sold to raise funds;

- until recently, a significant number of education services provided by local authority museums were funded directly or indirectly by local education authorities. The combined effects of the Government's education reforms and financial pressures on local authorities have effected the museums education services. These include: cuts in staff seconded to museums from the local education authorities, including teachers; loss of loan services; introduction of or increases in charges for all schools services; increased charges for non-local authority schools; frozen or cut education posts and the non-renewal of short-term posts; charging schools for or ending authority provision of in-service training courses; dissolution of separate education departments within museums; loss of free mailing services to schools. The reduction and eventual abolition of local education authority museum education services means the disappearance of a vital framework of assistance and a communication network. The effects will be felt most strongly among smaller museums especially those in rural areas. Aware of growing concern about the demise of the museum education service, the Department of National Heritage has recently announced a review which will take two years to complete;

- with the introduction of LMS museums and galleries are having to sell their services to individual schools. The result is that there has been an accelerated decline in the number of visits made by schools. Visits by children in primary schools often rely on parents and other volunteers to act as guides and helpers which, unless suitable material is available, may not allow for appropriate follow-up and discussion. Changes in the funding system also mean that the cost of transport to museums or galleries is the decisive factor for many schools. Those in rural areas are likely to find their access to museums particularly restricted both by

transport costs and by attempts made by some local authority museums to increase charges to schools outside their own boundaries;

- since the implementation of the Education Reform Act the provision of teaching and support for children and young people wanting to learn a musical instrument in school has been changing rapidly. The instrumental music services offer support, advice, in-service training for teachers and lend instruments to schools. Whilst a few local education authorities increased their funding in this area, between 1989/90-1990/91, 34% cut back. Between 1990/91-1991/92, 38% had made cuts. 21 made cuts both years running and two closed their services entirely. The most common result of these cuts were reductions in the numbers of staff involved[29]. Also nearly a third of local education authorities have introduced (or re-introduced) charges for tuition. A 1991 study found that nearly a third of those taking part predicted that LMS would damage the instrumental music services. Fears included: an uneven spread of provision with rural schools and those in deprived areas missing out; fragmentation of provision; a depletion in the overall instrumental music budget and, in some cases, the complete closure of the service;

- in further education colleges pressures from 'market forces' are threatening the provision of recreational facilities such as gymnasiums and sports halls. Examples exist of gymnasiums being converted into classrooms with no alternative accommodation being proposed. This is a direct result of the need for colleges to increase their student numbers in order to increase their incomes from the Further Education Funding Council;

- demands of the National Curriculum are having an effect on the amount of physical education in schools. Despite being part of the National Curriculum, it takes a decreasing part of the school week. According to a 1992 survey reported by the National Association of Head Teachers, 56% of primary schools cannot find the time to develop the physical education curriculum[30];

- physical education in schools is also undermined by the fact that many primary school teachers do not have the generic or sporting skills required; secondary schools tend to teach sports in six-week modules which do not equip children and young people for future involvement. There is also concern about the loss of school playing fields nationwide. Schools are driven by 'unit of resource' implications which dictate that playing fields might be an expensive luxury.

## ACTION REQUIRED FOR COMPLIANCE

- **Compliance with Article 31, the duty to promote the full participation of children and young people in play, recreation, cultural life and the arts requires that:**

- **the principle of equal opportunities for cultural, artistic, recreational and leisure activities should be reflected in education legislation, in arrangements for the whole curriculum and in funding policies and practice both between and within institutions;**

- **partnerships should be set up between local education authorities, schools, play and recreation units and departments, social services, health services and community organisations. New** strategies and ventures can be initiated within each agency to ensure co-ordinated provision for children and young people.

● decisions about the use and sale of land, the use of premises and equipment should consider the best interests of affected children and young people and also the need to encourage recreational activities. A 'best interests' principle in planning law and regulations would ensure this happens.

● time spent in school in enjoying recreational, cultural and artistic activities, for all children and young people, should be preserved.

● the proposed Department of National Heritage review of museum education services and any other reviews of relevant services should seek the views of children and young people.

## 4.4 Environmental restrictions

**4.4.1** Most of the time children and young people spend playing they are not in organised facilities and services, but in and around their homes, on their own or with friends and with little or no input by adults. Children and young people and their families need to feel safe in their local environment. If full implementation of Article 31 is to be achieved the Government and local authorities must do what they can to ensure this safety. Frequently children's rights to play and leisure activities are restricted by dangers inherent in the social and physical environment.

*'Kids can't play where I live; needles everywhere, stolen cars; no one cares.'*
(14 year-old, Manchester)

**4.4.2** A report published by the Policy Studies Institute in 1991 provided dramatic evidence of the growing restrictions on children's freedom of movement in recent years. In 1971, 80% of seven and eight year-olds were allowed to go to school on their own; by 1990 this figure had fallen to 9%. Based on research into 5-11 year-olds in five areas, the report showed that, although the majority of children owned bicycles, hardly any were allowed on public roads and only 4% of journeys were made by bicycle. The reasons given were parents' concerns over traffic and fears of molestation. As a result parents increasingly escort their children to and from school and other activities and so there are even more cars on the roads[31]. In N Ireland other fears exist. In an area of south Belfast, where the local community have been campaigning for play facilities for many years, a large public park with two fully equipped play areas is not accessible to the local children because it is perceived as being in an 'unsafe area' across the sectarian divide.

**4.4.3** 'Stranger danger' is a fear expressed by children as well as parents. In a radio interview one young person commented:

*'If the 'latch-key' groups were closed down, it wouldn't be very good because if you send your children home by themselves, when they are passing the gate, someone may jump out and kidnap them and no one might see'*[32].

For children in bed and breakfast accommodation this fear is compounded by other problems and for children in travelling families, forced to camp in dangerous places, safety is also a major issue.

**4.4.4** Many physical factors affect children's play including inadequate housing and gardens, over-crowding, fear of racism and racist attacks, risks from traffic and lack of provision of suitable space. These problems are exacerbated by insufficient low-cost, quality day-care; lack of provision before and after school for children whose parents work; not enough well located play centres; the lack of targeted play-schemes; poor access to safe outdoor open spaces, quality playgrounds and recreational development schemes; and lack of sufficient equipped outdoor recreation spaces for older children[33]. Many local authorities see children's play provision as the provision of a play area with safer surfacing and a fence to keep dogs away. However, children should be able to feel that they can play freely and safely in many parts of their neighbourhood and should learn to be aware of and respect potential dangers.

**4.4.5** The Department of the Environment (DoE),which has overall responsibility for planning, has no direct responsibility for play although its urban programme has, in the past, funded a substantial number of play projects. It does, however, provide guidance for local planners on space, equipment and safety in housing estates and says that 'facilities for children's play and youth activities should be treated as a basic need on all estates with a significant population of young people'[34]. Other DoE guidance notes for local planners and developers provides a summary of the National Playing Fields Association's minimum standard for out-door playing space[35]. However, this guidance does not address the specific needs of children and young people of different ages and is not mandatory.

**4.4.6** Other methods of improving the safety of local neighbourhoods include adopting 'play friendly' strategies such as 'Home Streets' and 'Home Zones', where residents can petition for priority to be taken away from road traffic and shared with pedestrians. In existing developments, initiatives such as traffic calming measures, can be combined with the creation of dedicated play spaces. Major improvements could be made by such measures coupled with other initiatives, such as improvements to school playground environments, based on examples pioneered by Learning Through Landscapes which show the community-enhancing potential of such measures[36].

**4.4.7** The nature of play and its importance to children should make it one of the major considerations and fundamental concerns of the planning process and should be provided for in planning legislation. Various yardsticks and standards have been formulated from within the voluntary sector in the past 30 years, including those promoted by 'Fair Play for Children' and more recently the 'Six Acre Standard' promoted by the National Playing Fields Association[37]. These standards look at the planning process for an area and suggest the amount and type of provision that is required. In March 1993 a Private Member's Bill was presented to the House of Commons to secure the provision of adequate playing space in new residential developments[38]. The Bill, which has not reached the statute books, is based on the Six Acre Standard and which describes ways in which housing developments could provide play and recreational facilities for children and young people of different ages and with different needs.

(See **UK Agenda Report 6 on the environment,** page 134 for a more detailed discussion of safety and accident prevention.)

Compliance with Article 3.2, the duty to provide protection and care of children whilst promoting their rights to play and leisure activities (Article 31) requires that:

- the Government should legislate for the provision of adequate, appropriate and accessible play and recreation space for children of all ages in every neighbourhood;

- the Government should introduce legislation to enable residents of defined classes of residential road to petition their local highways authorities, with appeal to the Secretary of State, for change of priority from road traffic to shared priority with pedestrians, with adequate resourcing of traffic-calming measures, and the legislative framework to empower local authorities to make and enforce the appropriate very low-speed restrictions for such areas, to be known as 'Home Streets' or 'Home Zones';

- all local authorities should monitor the number of developments which provide a play environment as part of the initial build.

# 5 Providing 'appropriate' services and facilities

## Articles 31.1 and 2

## 5.1 Consulting with children and young people

5.1.1 The key way to find out what are '*appropriate*' facilities for play and leisure activities for children and young people must be to consult them about their needs and interests in line with Article 12 of the Convention. One of the recurring themes from the National Children's Play and Recreation Unit's Children Today projects of the early 1990s was the importance of consulting with children and their parents and carers when planning future provision and when delivering current services to ensure that needs can be met effectively[39]. Yet it is almost unknown for local authorities to consult children in any meaningful way about what they want from play and leisure facilities.

5.1.2 The participation of children in the provision and development of play opportunities and environments is an important part of their empowerment. There is a need for this at all levels; for example, local play organisations, after-school clubs, schools, play forums, within local authority play services, landscape design and development work. Advisory forums of children and young people need to have influence and resources. One successful example of participation by young people in the design of their facilities is the adventure playground. In many areas children and young people have worked with adults to obtain land and establish playgrounds. They use it. They benefit from it. The entire process, especially of obtaining permissions and resources, is a learning process. And the existence of the playground symbolises the right of children to leisure, recreation and cultural activities and to be involved.

5.1.3 Soliciting and taking account of the views of children on the planning, availability, design, content, structure, organisation and running of play and leisure facilities should form an integral part of all facilities. It should be standard practice that children and young people are consulted about both facilities and opportunities. Local authorities should make information accessible and available to children and should disseminate it on a pro-active basis. When consulting with children and young people over planning and provision of facilities and services, the purpose and scope of the consultation must be clearly defined and the use made of the findings openly discussed. At the same time evaluation of projects and services should automatically include the views of children and young people who are users and also of those who do not use the facilities to establish why they do not. All children and young people should be able to get up-to-date information about services and play facilities.

In order to ensure full participation of children and young people (Article 12) in discussion about provision for their play and leisure activities (Article 31):

- children and young people should be actively consulted and involved in deciding the location and nature of designated play spaces provided by local authorities. Children's and youth forums should be established and targets set for increasing this involvement. These targets should be monitored regularly;

- all services and facilities providing play and leisure activities should have formal evaluation policies which involve consulting with children and young people who use their services and, where appropriate, those who do not use their services but could be expected to.

## 5.2 Young people's cultural interests

**5.2.1** Ensuring appropriate provision of leisure activities (Article 31.2) and listening to what children and young people have to say (Article 12) must involve recognising activities in which they themselves choose to become involved. For a majority of young people the institutionalised arts have no place in their lives. Many have a negative view and the arts are seen as remote and institutional, the preserve of art galleries, museums and concert halls and of little interest or relevance to them[40]. At the same time many traditional sports clubs are folding as fewer young people have the interest and skills needed to join.

**5.2.2** There are many activities and resources devoted to adult leisure, recreation, culture and the arts, in which young people have the right to be involved (Article 31) and which exist on public subsidies. However, in 1987 a survey showed that, over the previous month, only 7% of the 16-19 year-olds surveyed had been to the theatre, 1% to see dance, 0% to the opera and 3% to a live jazz or soul concert[41].

> '*We were discussing museums. They're getting beyond a joke. I've been there about 16 times. We'd like to change the content of that. People have been there so many times. We were discussing fashion and peer attitudes and we can't really do it; and things like children's rights. It would be great to have a museum on that ...*'
> (13 year-old, Manchester)

**5.2.3** There are youth arts groups which enable some young people to be involved in challenging programmes. However, these reach only a minority. In order to join, it is often necessary to have already acquired a certain level of skill; there is a need to cater for the majority of young people who do not have these skills. The main focus for youth work, in whatever setting, tends to be sport, outdoor education and the more traditional, club-style activities and many young people have had no introduction to the possibilities for art and other cultural activities. In the past, the absence of young people in subsidised art projects has been interpreted as lack of interest in the arts generally, but talking with young people showed that the problem was actually lack of appropriate provision.

**5.2.4** Ensuring the provision of '*appropriate cultural and artistic activity*' (Article 31.2) for all young people requires the workers in the field to find ways of identifying young people who have had no previous interest in the arts and developing imaginative ways of showing them the possibilities for enjoyment and expression which could exist for them. A range of work needs to tap into young people's interests and to offer them possibilities they never imagined. Current provision often does not do this.

> '*My area has six or seven youth clubs and they all offer the same thing, so we're not getting anything out of it. I don't go to the youth club because it's boring. The adults provide what they think the children want and they haven't asked, and when the adults complain that the children aren't coming to the youth clubs, it's "they don't want to go".*'
> (14 year-old, Manchester)

**5.2.5** Although they may not be interested in mainstream adult arts, many young people are involved in a wide variety of pursuits. Much of their cultural activity is not organised and controlled by institutions but develops in an organic way from the lives and influences of the current generation. Informal activities such as skate-boarding and ball games with their own philosophies and sub-cultures have emerged, and a considerable industry has grown around other cultural activities. These are often different in nature from 'main stream' arts provision and include, for example, both new and traditional forms of music and dance; playground games and rhymes; graffiti and spray painting; cinema, television and videos; and style and culture. Music is one of the most popular of the youth arts. Many young people are involved in this often self-taught, self-managed performance. Often though, young people's own chosen cultural activities are disliked and prohibited by adults.

> '*They tried to get a rave organised. One bloke heard about it and went round all the parents claiming that everybody would be coming round robbing their houses, even though the aerodrome was a couple of miles away - five miles from the town.*'
> (17 year-old, Lincolnshire)

**5.2.6** Young people create their own forms of expression through shared cultural interests, clothes and experimental life-styles. They demonstrate, through what they say and do, that they would welcome more chances to dance, write, perform, paint and work co-operatively using media like video, photography and tape-recording[42]. However, few projects provide these types of facilities; there is a need for both more opportunities for young people to make their own art and for greater adult assistance.

**5.2.7** At the moment cultural production amongst young people is held back by their lack of access to and control of a wide range of resources[43]. Successful youth arts projects need audiences and ways of taking their results to others. These include videos, theatre presentations, music performances, events, tapes, books, magazines, exhibitions and poetry, and expertise and facilities need to be available to allow this[44].

### ACTION REQUIRED FOR COMPLIANCE

**Compliance with Article 12, the duty to listen to young people's views in promoting the right to appropriate leisure facilities requires that:**

- **policy for young people should consider ways of encouraging and developing self-selected leisure activities which tend to be based on informality, privacy, personal choice and power over and access to usable cultural commodities and resources. This means working closely with young people in a way that gives them some control over the use and availability of resources;**

- planners and policy makers must recognise that supporting and encouraging young people's cultural choices may need new, indirect, less structured, democratic ways and they must set up the appropriate structures. Although some expertise is useful and links should be made between youth workers and local artists the most important skills are advising, enabling and facilitating;

- the Government should establish permanent monitoring machinery to advise and assess need amongst children and young people for leisure facilities, and to what extent they have access, on the basis of 'appropriate and equal opportunities', to cultural, artistic, and recreational activities, so that appropriate response to their needs can be formulated within various areas of Government policy.

## 5.3 Age appropriate provision

**5.3.1** Article 31 states that children and young people have the right to 'engage in play and recreational activity appropriate to the age of the child'. As children and young people mature, it is more likely that they themselves will want to participate in activities which are increasingly 'adult' in their structures, rules and skills requirements. But the attitude that young people do not need to indulge in free play is misguided and results in inappropriate play provision.

*'When you are older I think you need to play more than when you are young. Because when you are older you have more things pressing on you. And playing - you just muck about and do whatever you like and there is no worries or anything'[45].*

**5.3.2** Article 31.1 stresses the right of the child to 'participate freely in cultural life and the arts'. Children and young people of all ages - pre-school, in school or in work training - have the right to activities appropriate to their ages and in each community setting this should be a part of the infrastructure. In the UK there is no recognition of the need for continuity and progression in services from early childhood through to adulthood. Most providers of recreational and leisure services for children and young people maintain rigid structural and professional divisions between services for pre-school, school-age and youth provision.

### ACTION REQUIRED FOR COMPLIANCE

**Compliance with Article 31.1, the right to appropriate play provision for all children requires that planners should look at ways of developing age-appropriate services and continuity between services.**

## 5.4 Equal opportunities in play and leisure provision

**5.4.1** 'Equal opportunities' in the context of Article 31.2 means that **all** children and young people should have access to a wide variety of play, recreational, artistic and cultural activities. This commits all who work for and with children in their leisure and play environments to ensuring children have equal opportunity to use the community's facilities and resources.

**5.4.2** It is clear, however, that for many children and young people access to facilities and services can be limited. Specific groups of children and young people affected include:

*8-12 year-olds*

**5.4.3** A legal framework for the provision of daycare services for some children under eight years-old exists under the Children Act in England and Wales and the youth service is directed towards the needs of young people over 13. In general, provision for children from 8-12 is haphazard, depending on the area, local authority and voluntary sector initiatives. The clear need for this type of provision is illustrated in the latest General Household Survey which shows that only 57% of mothers with 5-8 year-old children have substitute childcare arrangements. But throughout the UK services and facilities for these children are even more fragmented than for others.

*'Youth provision? What youth provision? There's nothing at all. You can go to the pictures. Recently there's been a music hall and they've started putting on groups playing but that's about it. When I was 7 or 8, not all that years ago, you're walking around seeing kids playing in the middle of the road, kicking a football about because there's nothing else to do, there's nothing provided for the lower age group ... There's things like superbowl but they put them on the other side of town where you can't get to them - and the prices ...'*
(17 year-old, Shrewsbury)

**5.4.4** In N Ireland there is little provision for children aged 5-10. Less than 1% of these children have specifically funded, after-school play provision. Although the youth service caters for children of this age, its funding is based on the numbers of those in the higher age groups. In some areas provision is aided by the free use of school premises allowed by the local education and library boards and assistance may be available for hiring premises. These are useful initiatives and if extended throughout N Ireland would promote better provision for out of school facilities for younger children.

**5.4.5** In the past 20 years, throughout the UK, most provision has developed within the summer holiday period in the form of short-term play schemes, often run by voluntary groups and local authorities. In one area younger children at a large secondary school expressed their view that accessible leisure facilities for them in the area were non-existent. They were too young for the youth club, and were intimidated both within and outside the school by older children. As a result, community leaders worked closely with a group of children who were supported by the school in setting up a small community cafe. The children played the main role in deciding the scope and nature of the project. It succeeded because their commitment was supported by the combined efforts of school and community, and because they were in control[46].

**5.4.6** Until the recent commitment by the Department of Employment to out-of-school provision in England and Wales, Government involvement in services for 8-12 year-olds has been restricted mainly to Urban Programme funding for summer and other holiday schemes in the inner cities and other designated areas. In recent years, with changes in government priorities, this resourcing has diminished and major cuts have been made. In one city local authorities once receiving support for about 200 summer schemes have had to replace that support from their own budgets as well as restricting some schemes and closing others[47]. In N Ireland, Government funding for services for children from 5-10 was to have been delivered through education and library boards at local level. This has not happened and no funding has been made available for play services for these children.

### Young carers

**5.4.7** An estimated 10,000 children and young people are the main carers in home where a parent is disabled or ill. There are also an unknown number of children living with an elderly relative, or providing emotional or practical stability in a family which experiences mental distress. The lack of support for these young people means that their opportunities for leisure activities may be virtually non-existent. In the words of one young carer:

*'The worst thing is being trapped on your own in the house with the person you're caring for, not being able to go out, not being able to have a social life, friends. If you've not got friends you've got no one to break down and say, "What am I going to do?". You need friends.'*
(18 year-old, Liverpool)

The actual number of young carers is not known and is hard to establish as many fear that by identifying themselves they are putting themselves and any brothers and sisters at risk of being separated. Those who have been able to take part in activities organised specifically for them, with other young carers have valued it:

*'They take us away for weekends. We've been to Pleasure Island. They've been really good. And you meet all the other young carers. It's a friendly atmosphere ... We went away for a weekend to a cottage which was foul; the cottage was foul but the atmosphere was really good. We just had a laugh ... You can just be yourself. You don't have to pretend to be anything else. If you don't want to talk about your dependants and you do get upset, everybody else will know just what you're feeling.'*
(18 year-old, Liverpool)

**5.4.8** The Children Act 1989 places a duty on local authorities in England and Wales to provide support and services to children 'in need' but, with the exception of those with disabilities, does not give a clear definition of 'in need'. Given the circumstances of many young carers and the restrictions placed on their potential health and development, it would seem appropriate to define them as 'in need'.

### Young lesbians and gay men

**5.4.9** Young lesbians and gay men have the right to information relevant to them. They need to know of their history and culture as much as any other group of children and young people. In all areas of work concerning the arts, acknowledgment of the contribution by people who are gay, lesbian or bisexual is important. Silence on the subject denies these young people the positive encouragement they may need to fully appreciate and develop their own talents.

*'Then there is the gay plague bit, portraying gay men as very promiscuous and only interested in sex, and not in having stable relationships; which for some is true, but no more than the heterosexuals, and this has relied on a very stereotyped image of the gay community, which has done nothing to help people.'*
(17 year-old, Scotland)

### Children facing discrimination and sectarianism

**5.4.10** Toys and other play materials reflect the values and attitudes of the society in which they are used and often reflect the inherent racism in white British society. Most widely available resources portray a positive image of white people, whilst either ignoring the existence of people from black or minority ethnic groups or portraying them in a negative way. Resources, toys and other playthings should foster the intellectual, social, physical and emotional development of **all** children with positive images of themselves and their communities as well as others different from themselves. Packaging of play equipment is important and manufacturers have an important role to play in presenting images which all children can relate to[48]. Many child care situations in the UK, whether largely white or consisting of children from a variety of racial groups, communities and cultures, ignore the importance of having resources which reflect all groups and communities positively and as such fail to acknowledge and respect the cultural, religious and linguistic needs of all children as required by Articles 30, 17, and 29.

**5.4.11** In N Ireland, sectarianism and the provision of segregated facilities and services can prevent children from being given the opportunity to develop to their full potential. All those involved in play must take positive steps to counter-balance the effects of societal racism and sectarianism by valuing all cultures equally through the resources used with young children. Whilst the provision of good resources alone cannot counter these powerful and damaging influences, it is an important step in offering a basic framework for working towards a non-racist, non-sectarian society.

*'There's also things in the summer; like, there's a summer school; they're also divided as well because there are summer schools which will include mostly Catholics and then there's one for five weeks, which in our time it was a separate thing. There was the three weeks when the Catholics went to summer scheme and then the Protestants went to the five weeks "sportunity". Even that's a summer thing and we're all divided as well. Its just the way it is.'*
(17 year-old, N Ireland)

### Disabled children and young people

**5.4.12** At present the extent to which disabled children can use mainstream play facilities is very limited and poor funding adds to problems of unsuitable premises and amenities, access, unsuitable equipment and the need for additional and trained help. Families including children with special needs are often reluctant to approach mainstream groups as they are not sure about how they and their children will be received[49]. The need for integrated activities for children with disabilities and learning difficulties is of particular importance as in many areas there are so few other opportunities for them to play and associate with their peers in groups and clubs or integrated schools.

*'None of the nightclubs around here are accessible and only a few of the pubs. I can get to the community centre pub but somebody needs to open the doors for me and feed me the drink because pubs never have straws there ... Sometimes, in the toilets, the taps are at the wrong height or you have to climb on something to see yourself in the mirror.'*
(18 year-old, Shrewsbury)

**5.4.13** All the available evidence points to the fact that for children and young people with disabilities and learning difficulties, equality of opportunity with others in play and leisure activities does not exist. For example:

● there is little participation in the youth service network by young people with disabilities and learning difficulties and although the vast majority of local authorities have equal opportunities policies which include sections on disability it is not clear how the implementation of these policies is being monitored. Also, few local authorities research the needs of young people with disabilities and learning difficulties and then try to provide a service in response[50];

● very few children's play facilities cater for children with disabilities. Disabled children often receive segregated play and recreation opportunities less frequently and of poorer quality than their peers;

● most drama schools will not audition disabled candidates[51];

● problems for disabled people wanting to be involved in sports activities include lack of suitable provision in special schools. One survey found that children in special schools had one physical education lesson a week whilst those in mainstream schools tended to have more. Little use is made of local authority leisure services by many special schools. Inaccessibility often compounded by unhelpful attitudes can inhibit the use and development of sports and leisure facilities for disabled children[52].

**5.4.14** Article 23.3 states that assistance to children and young people with disabilities and learning difficulties, and their families, should be designed to ensure that *'the disabled child has access to ... recreation opportunities in a manner conducive to the child's achieving the fullest possible social integration ... '.* In 1991 the HMI found that although most of the youth work investigated was said by staff to be integrated, offering equal opportunities for all, the young people with disabilities and learning difficulties were often there but with little or no opportunities to take part[53]. Children with disabilities and learning difficulties using mainstream services are often neglected or left out of activities because of lack of staff understanding, knowledge and awareness. In one survey 63% of all physical education teachers felt unable to cope with children with special needs[54]. This neglect can permanently damage their potential to develop physically and emotionally via the medium of physical activity.

**5.4.15** Increasing integration can take different forms. For example, it is possible to expand, adapt and integrate mainstream provision into specialist schemes and increase outreach work and development. The use of a variety of art forms in local communities has received growing recognition as an important way of raising issues and of supporting local people. In particular, the capacity of drama to highlight the issue of children's disability has been shown to be very effective in stimulating discussion within communities in non-threatening ways. Despite this, youth arts has, up until now, largely ignored young people with disabilities and learning difficulties.

*Children and young people in low-income families*
**5.4.16** Children and young people in families with low incomes may also have fewer opportunities to exercise their right to play and leisure activities. For example:

● much of young people's popular culture is provided by

the commercial sector and is therefore limited to those who can afford it;

● the effects of cut backs in funding for play provision and the youth service are worst for children in deprived areas who are likely to have less access to safe play areas and who are far more likely than others to be involved in accidents;

● many children are restricted from joining groups and organisations because of the cost of, for example, uniforms and other items of equipment. For those with low incomes the costs of kit, travel and equipment may well be a deterrent to sports activities. Similarly, those interested in arts activities may be inhibited by costs of, for example, ballet equipment or musical instruments;

● young people wishing to train seriously for careers in dance and drama can often only do so if their parents can afford private schools and colleges. This type of training is provided mostly by independent schools and colleges which operate without core funding and are dependent on the fees of their students to cover their costs. Students are dependent on discretionary grants from local authorities to pay their fees[55]. As a result there is discrimination against young people from families with low incomes who cannot afford the fees in areas where no such grants are available.

(See **UK Agenda Report 4 on poverty**, page 67, for a more detailed discussion.)

*Children and young people living in rural areas*
**5.4.17** Rural isolation is a problem for many children and young people. In some villages there is no common public land for children to play on and the thin scatter of rural populations makes it difficult for children to meet others of similar ages and interests. Public transport is infrequent or non-existent and parents worry if their children go out on bicycles[56]. A 1991 study showed that in rural areas there is a severe lack of child care and related services and also a lack of meeting places and recreational facilities[57]. Many villages have only small, old village halls. These are often unsuitable, unsafe and too expensive to hire. Children must rely on parents to provide transport to nearby towns. The countryside does not necessarily represent an accessible environment for children either. Most land is privately owned and increasing mechanisation and intensive farming leads to a greater possibility of accidents and injury. Problems of access to the countryside can be created by loss of public footpaths and the need to keep children safe from farm machinery and pesticide stores[58]. In N Ireland, where there is a large rural population, accidents on farms and country roads, where the few speed limits are hard to enforce, are particularly high. In all areas of the UK opportunities for children and young people in rural areas to be involved in the arts are restricted by centralised provision and lack of transport.

**ACTION REQUIRED FOR COMPLIANCE**

**Compliance with Article 31.2, the duty to promote and encourage equal opportunities in the provision of play and leisure facilities requires that:**

● **all governing bodies of sports, arts, cultural and recreational pursuits should adopt or amend equal opportunity policies or statements in line with Article 31, and to keep them under constant review. Consideration should be given to adopting a policy** on equal opportunities, in whose formulation and monitoring all users, workers (paid and voluntary) and management should participate;

● play and leisure service providers must show a commitment to equal opportunities by challenging racism, sectarianism, sexism and discrimination against those with disabilities and learning difficulties, both in policy and practice, which needs to be closely monitored by independent evaluators and users;

● local authorities and service providers must ensure that there is careful monitoring of resources used in all facilities to ensure that they do not promote racist and sectarian views and attitudes in any way and that they promote acceptance and understanding;

● young carers should be included in the 'in need' definition adopted by all local authorities under the Children Act 1989. Steps must be taken to collect information about young carers and offer appropriate action to support them in line with their wishes and feelings.

● the indicators of good practice for local authority provision of leisure facilities which provide for the needs of people with disabilities and learning difficulties, published by the British Sports Association for the Disabled, should be included in all relevant local authority contract specifications. Adequate funding should be available to ensure this. Local play and youth services need to develop a more active encouragement of and commitment to integrated activities;

● regional sports councils need to ensure they have a flexible approach to funding in areas where they have discretion and should foster good working relationships with local authorities and local groups for children and young people with disabilities and learning difficulties and their carers. The role of Sports Development Officer should be recognised and appropriately funded and Disability Officers, such as those in Leicestershire, Northamptonshire and Nottinghamshire should be appointed;

● in both rural and urban areas, where no public play space exists, opportunities to purchase common land for play should be pursued. Existing play space should be protected in local plans and up-graded as part of a district play policy. More resources are needed to meet play needs and support for networking is especially important. Links between play workers and artists and sports workers can enhance everyone's work with beneficial results for the children. There needs to be an increase in funding given to establishing multi-purpose facilities in villages which can be used by children;

● in rural areas and other areas not well served with museums and galleries loans services should be developed in conjunction with schools and youth services. Education departments in museums and galleries in these areas should be adequately financed to ensure they are able to offer appropriate, peripatetic services and training for those using loaned materials.

# 6 Safety and standards
## Article 3.2 and 3.3

**6.1** The Convention states that the Government must *'ensure the child such protection and care as is necessary for his or her well-being'* (Article 3.2) and that *'institutions, services and facilities responsible for the care or protection of children shall conform with the standards established by competent authorities, particularly in the areas of safety, health, in the number and suitability of their staff as well as competent supervision'* (Article 3.3).

**6.2** Most accidents to children and young people outside the home happen during play and leisure activities. In 1990 approximately 1.2 million children under 15 were taken to accident and emergency departments as a result of accidents during their leisure activities[59]. For many children the area around their home presents many dangers and there is little or no safe outdoor place to play. The most widespread form of recreational provision are constructed unsupervised playgrounds and play areas which exist throughout the UK in villages, suburbs, towns and cities. In general these playgrounds are provided and managed by local authorities who have in-house maintenance and inspection teams. Safety inspections are also often required by insurance companies as a condition of cover. Evidence of inspection quality and training is required.

**6.3** Over the past 20 years there have been advances in the safety of these play areas and concern for standards has led to partial adoption of British Standards by the industry. Government guidelines on safety exist but these are not enforceable in law and a large number of play areas still lack impact-absorbing surfaces, and standards of both equipment and maintenance fall short of the safety needs of children[60] [61]. Attempts to introduce legislation to enforce standards through Private Members Bills have failed. There remains a need to ensure that current health and safety legislation is strictly enforced.

**6.4** Nevertheless outdoor play facilities in both urban and rural areas are often badly maintained, vandalised, in poor condition and sometimes dangerous. A survey in 1991 of nearly 900 children's play areas found only one that was considered fault free. Bad maintenance, litter and dog fouling as well as close proximity to roads with no warning signs were major problems[62]. Other surveys have shown similar results[63].

**6.5** In England and Wales the Children Act's registration requirements cover all activities of more than two hours, for children aged under eight including, for example, playgroups and holiday schemes, but also child-minding and supervised activities such as football, ballet, horse-riding and other activities. This has created a tremendous pressure on local social services departments to such an extent that the Department of Health, responsible for oversight of this legislation, is now consulting on the idea that some of these may be removed from registration. Registration under the Children Act costs money. For facilities for school-age children which are to be open more than two hours a day the initial fee is £100 with an annual cost of £75. There is concern in the voluntary sector that this fee is beyond the reach of many small providers and that, as a result, provision will suffer.

**6.6** Recent research has shown that standards of safety and staff training in many of the rapidly expanding number of centres offering young people outdoor pursuits are totally inadequate and that there is no intention at present to develop and introduce mandatory standards for this. Many centres hold no accident records and so were unable to take part in the study. Just under half the centres in the study sought no first aid qualifications amongst their staff[64].

## ACTION REQUIRED FOR COMPLIANCE

**Compliance with Article 3.3, the need to ensure standards for safety and health, in the provision of facilities and services for play and leisure activities requires that:**

- **service providers should ensure that staff and volunteers working with children have appropriate training, knowledge and experience for the duties and responsibilities expected of them;**

- **local authorities need to ensure procedures adopted by social services departments for registering and inspecting are appropriate for each type of play services. They should ensure that professionally trained play staff are involved in these inspection procedures;**

- **parents and others who are concerned should have a right of access to information about the ownership, responsibility and safety provisions of playgrounds. Children should be able to obtain speedy redress for accidents and injuries where there is liability on the part of the owner;**

- **health and safety legislation covering the safety of children and young people using play areas, including school playgrounds, should be enforced more rigorously by regular inspections and reports. Adequate funding should be made available for this to happen.**

# 7 Information and the mass media
## Article 17

**7.1** Article 17 stresses the rights of children and young people in relation to the mass media and its importance in promoting '*social, spiritual and moral well-being and physical and mental health*'. In ratifying the Convention the Government has accepted its duty to ensure that '*the child has access to information and material from a diversity of national and international sources*' and to encourage the mass media to '*disseminate information and material of social and cultural benefit to the child*'. It is also required to ensure all children and young people the right to freedom of expression (Article 13). This right includes '*freedom to seek, receive and impart information and ideas of all kinds ...*' through any '*media of the child's choice*'.

**7.2** Articles 17 and 13 have implications for the policies of broadcasting companies, newspapers and magazines and publishers towards dissemination of information aimed specifically at young people. In particular, Article 17 requires that we examine the provision of materials for black and other minority ethnic children to ensure that '*the mass media have particular regard to the linguistic needs of the child who belongs to a minority group ...* '(Article 17(d)), and also for the many children with visual or hearing impairments who may be unable to use written materials or enjoy television or radio programmes. Radio can be an important source of entertainment and information for those with visual impairments. Cut-backs in radio broadcasts designed for children and young people, resulting from the decision to close the BBC's Radio 5, have major implications. The use and enjoyment children and young people who are hearing impaired get from television is often limited because there are no signing translators to 'dub' programmes. A major improvement could be achieved for these children if signing were to be a required procedure for information and education programmes.

**7.3** Full implementation of Article 17, together with Article 2, necessitates that measures are introduced to ensure the availability of access to the mass media for all children regardless of disability or race, language, culture or religion. It also requires that the mass media is representative of all children in its coverage of mainstream news, current affairs and in the general output. Full implementation of Article 13 also has implications for the mass media. Ensuring the right to '*impart information and ideas ... through any other media of the child's choice*' means that public service broadcasting should offer regular opportunities for children and young people to be involved.

**7.4** Public libraries provide a uniquely objective source of information for young people, enabling them to discover the power of access that information skills can provide. Books and stories make a significant contribution to the intellectual and emotional development of the child; they are important in supporting language development especially in the pre-school years; reading plays a part in shaping children's attitudes to each other and books are essential to educational development.

**7.5** The Government appears to recognise the importance of libraries and in 1991 published guidelines for library services: they should be tailored to the needs of local groups, should support local education provision, ensure physical access for all and act as a focal point for cultural activities[65]. But, although overall spending on the service has remained static in real terms there have been a number of detrimental changes. For example:

● the purchasing power of UK library book funds declined by 16.5% between 1980/81 and 1990/91[66];

● there has been a gradual decline in the number of professional librarians employed by public libraries from 8,384 in 1982 to 7,477 in 1992, a decline of over 10% in 10 years, and this has affected in particular children's librarians[67];

● in 1979 there were 119 public libraries in the UK which opened in the evenings and all day on Saturday. In 1993 the latest estimate suggests that there are 49 of which 36 are in Scotland, 13 in England and Wales and none in N Ireland. This particularly affects children and young people who are often likely to be at school during library opening hours;

● in 1993/4, 75% of public library authorities are expecting to make cuts, many in their opening hours.

**7.6** In remote rural areas the use of mobile resources is an important way of supporting local communities. They enable rural people to know who can help them, and they can bring information of direct benefit to children including, for example, facilities such as junior youth clubs and holiday play opportunities. In addition they can act as a meeting point for children living on isolated farms and settlements, a regular opportunity to talk and play. There are also obvious educational benefits arising from the information brought by mobile services.

**7.7** School libraries can also play an important role but their services are often of poor quality and may be under threat from devolved budget holding (LMS). HMI reports in 1990 and 1991 documented the inadequacies[68].

● 43% of the secondary schools investigated has 'less than satisfactory' staffing levels in their libraries;

● 22% had less than the recommended number of books per pupil;

● the average spent per pupil on new books each year was less than £1 in 26% of schools;

● over half the primary schools were found to have unsatisfactory staffing arrangements;

● none has what was considered to be 'very good' quality stock.

By the end of 1993 it is expected that at least 28 of the school library services provided by local education authorities will have had all or part of their budgets delegated to schools. There is considerable concern about the future of school library services, given the financial constraints experienced by many schools.

**7.8** There are marked disparities in the level and quality of library provision for children and young people within the UK. The Library Association has produced two sets of guidelines setting out good practice for children's services within public libraries and for school libraries. Full implementation of these guidelines would make a significant contribution to meeting the standards required by a number of the articles in the Convention relating to information and cultural activities[69] [70].

**7.9** Reading Article 17(c), which requires the Government to 'encourage the production and dissemination of children's books', in conjunction with Article 29(c), the need for education to engender respect for a child's 'own cultural identity, language and values ...' and for those of people from 'civilisations different from his or her own' shows a clear obligation to ensure the provision of a wide range of anti-racist books and resources written by authors from many ethnic and cultural backgrounds for children and young people from different countries and in different languages.

**7.10** From a very early age, young children learn social attitudes from adults close to them and from their surroundings. Books support, inform, confirm and challenge these observations. Parents and carers in the black and minority ethnic communities have campaigned for many years for books which show positive images of their children, families communities and countries. Despite over 30 years of campaigning for non-racist children's books there is still relatively little, and much of what does exist is of poor quality and often reinforces racism. Similarly, information books about other countries often reinforce racist attitudes[71] [72].

**7.11** At present, a large proportion of non-racist children's books and resources are published by small independent publishers and it appears that most mainstream publishers in the UK do not have anti-racist policies which cover their whole publications list. There is a tendency for those publishers which do produce good, anti-racist materials to ghettoise these publications into 'multi-cultural titles' lists, giving rise to a situation where some publishers produce excellent, anti-racist materials alongside offensive materials, all in the same catalogue. At the same time many of the anti-racist books which do exist are only available from specialist bookshops and mail order. Many publishers still have back lists of titles which were once considered acceptable but are now widely seen as tokenistic and/or offensive. These books, which often show stereotypical facial features, are constantly reprinted whilst other excellent titles have gone out of print and new titles are not published. One major failing of publishers is that many books with excellent anti-racist texts are let down by stereotypical illustrations.

**7.12** Article 17(d) states that the Government must 'encourage the mass media to have particular regard to the linguistic needs of the child who belongs to a minority group or who is indigenous'. In the UK this has significance for children and young people arriving from other countries who do not speak or have English as a first language, those in N Ireland or Wales who speak or read Irish or Welsh and for those unable to read because of poor or no sight. For those whose first language is not English there should be the provision of mother-tongue programmes on local radio stations to serve local minority groups. This should form part of Government guidelines on public service broadcasting.

**7.13** In Wales, where the Welsh language is recognised as an official language, although there have been some advances in recent years, there is still a reluctance to plan properly for the growth in demand for education through the Welsh language. In N Ireland, despite the growth of Irish language schools and play-schemes, there is no recognition of Irish as an official language and inadequate finance and media time is given to its development[73].

**7.14** The Voluntary Braille Transcribers Group is involved in the provision of braille books for blind children in integrated schools but in recent years, as a result of Government financial cutbacks, braille production in the UK has been considerably reduced. Blind children have never had access to the same scope of resources as sighted children because of the expense of producing braille books. Teachers are becoming increasingly dependent on voluntary groups since the introduction and promotion of integrated schools, because the children now need the same materials as their sighted peers. As increasing integration occurs and schools for children with visual impairments are reduced or closed there must be sufficient funds provided to enable blind children to have equal access to resources as other children. Funding must also take account of the need for 'talking books' and audio-tapes of children's books in school and public libraries.

**7.15** Article 17(e) puts a duty on the Government to protect children and young people by encouraging the '*development of appropriate guidelines for the protection of the child from information and material injurious to his or her well-being ... '*.

**7.16** There has been considerable discussion recently about the role of television and videos in promoting an unacceptable level of violence in society. There is a strongly emerging view that the increased use of television, video and computer games by children and young people is contributing to increased levels of violence and intolerance in our society[74]. However, there is as yet little conclusive evidence about the relationship between the media and patterns of behaviour. The responsibility for introducing appropriate guidelines to protect children from materials which are '*injurious to his or her well-being*' has to be balanced against the child's right to freedom of expression and the role of parents in the upbringing of children (Article 13 and Article 18). Many children have strong views on the issue of censorship, its appropriateness and implications for their lives. It would be a valuable exercise to consult widely with young people on their views of the role that television plays in their lives and its impact or otherwise on their behaviour.

> '*I think in America you get a recommended age for films and then you decide, rather than tell people what they can or can't see. Because if you tell young people they can't see a film, the more determined they will be to see it anyway.*'
> (12 year-old, Shropshire)

## ACTION REQUIRED FOR COMPLIANCE

**Compliance with Article 17, the best interests principle in Article 3 requires that:**

- libraries must ensure that changes in policy such as reducing hours or stock do not adversely affect children's rights;

- the Library Association guidelines for services for children and young people should be adopted and implemented by all public library services. All schools should adopt and implement the Library Association's guidelines for school libraries.

**Compliance with Article 17(d) and Article 29(c), the duty to ensure the provision of books and materials which meet the needs of children and young people from minority and indigenous groups requires that the use of agreed guidelines for monitoring children's books and resources to ensure that they help develop awareness of a positive identity of all children from black and minority ethnic groups.**

**Compliance with Article 17(c) requires that the Government and local education authorities in Wales and N Ireland should promote and facilitate the provision of educational books and resources in the Welsh and Irish language. The Department of National Heritage and the Department of Education in N Ireland should fund monitoring projects to encourage the widespread use of anti-racist children's books.**

**Compliance with Article 17(d), the obligation to ensure the provision of materials for all children and young people requires that partnerships should be established between voluntary organisations, schools, children and their families to ensure and encourage the provision of these resources.**

**Compliance with Article 17(e), the obligation to develop guidelines for protecting children from harmful materials requires that:**

- further research is undertaken into the effects of television, video and computer games on the mental and physical development of children. The Department of National Heritage should commission an investigation at the earliest possible opportunity;

- guidelines for protecting children and young people from harm through the media should be drawn up in conjunction with children and young people themselves.

# Summary of action required for compliance

**1  Full implementation of Article 31, to ensure the rights of children and young people to rest and leisure, to engage in play and recreational activities appropriate to their age and to participate freely in cultural life and the arts, requires the following action;**

## 1a  At government level:
*Policy development*

● the Department of National Heritage should formally be given the responsibility for ensuring the implementation of Article 31 throughout the UK and should liaise with relevant departments and organisations in each jurisdiction. It should initiate an urgent examination of children's and young people's leisure and play and consideration should be given to establishing a legislative duty on local government to provide children's and youth service encompassing all these aspects. In N Ireland, the Department of Education should assume a lead role in co-ordinating both policy and provision across agency boundaries;

● the Government should, after consultation, publish Charters covering the rights to play and to leisure facilities for all children and young people, describing what children and young people and their parents have the right to expect by way of provision in their own localities, related to age;

● the Department of National Heritage should establish a research panel to commission and fund research which will identify, for example, the range, forms and distribution of play provision throughout the UK. It should also set up a Governmental inter-departmental forum to ensure that all Government programmes take account of the play and leisure needs of children and young people;

● the Department of National Heritage should appoint officers for children's play and leisure provision with designated responsibility and consider setting up an expert advisory group to advise ministers;

● the arts and sports councils in each jurisdiction should be requested to undertake, and publicise widely, detailed reviews of their policies and programmes with specific reference to Article 31 and develop targets for service provision and budget allocation which should be systematically monitored;

● the proposed Department of National Heritage review of museum education services and any other reviews of relevant services should seek the views of children and young people;

● the Government should establish permanent monitoring machinery to advise and assess need amongst children and young people for leisure facilities, and to what extent they have access, on the basis of 'appropriate and equal opportunities', to cultural, artistic, and recreational activities, so that appropriate response to their needs can be formulated within various areas of Government policy;

● all governing bodies of sports, arts, cultural and recreational pursuits should be encouraged, through education, legislative requirements on statutory funding agencies etc to adopt or amend equal opportunity policies or statements in line with Article 31, and to keep them under constant review. Consideration should be given to adopting a policy on equal opportunities in whose formulation and monitoring all users, workers (paid and voluntary) and management should participate;

*Resource allocation*

● urgent attention should be directed at the imbalance of resources between facilities for adults and those for children and young people. There should be consultation with all concerned, including local authorities, the arts and sports councils, cultural, recreational, youth and play bodies;

● in N Ireland, a funding framework for play should be established which recognises the Department of Education as having a lead responsibility;

● the Government should direct the National Lottery boards to include, within their objectives, the enhancement of the quality of life of children through improvements in facilities for play and leisure activities. Funding must cover not only initial costs but also those involved in running and maintaining programmes over a period of time; a specialist group should be responsible for disbursement;

*Legislative change*

● the principle of equal opportunities for cultural, artistic, recreational and leisure activities should be reflected in education legislation, in arrangements for the whole curriculum and in funding policies and practice both between and within institutions;

● the Government should legislate for the provision of adequate, appropriate and accessible play and recreation space for children of all ages in every neighbourhood;

● in N Ireland, parents of children under the age of five should have the right to choose whether or not their child enters formal schooling and play should form a major part of the early years curriculum;

● the Government should introduce legislation to enable residents of defined classes of residential road to petition their local highways authorities, with appeal to the Secretary of State, for change of priority from road traffic to shared priority with pedestrians, with adequate resourcing of traffic-calming measures, and the legislative framework to empower local authorities to make and enforce the appropriate very low speed restrictions for such areas, to be known as 'Home Streets' or 'Home Zones'.

## 1b  By regional bodies:

● regional sports councils need to ensure they have a flexible approach to funding in areas where they have discretion and should foster good working relationships with local authorities and local groups for children and young people with disabilities and learning difficulties and their carers. The role of Sports Development Officer should be recognised and appropriately funded and Disability Officers, such as those in Leicestershire, Northamptonshire and Nottinghamshire should be appointed;

● all regional arts boards should have specific youth officer posts, have a youth arts policy and make youth arts a budgetary priority.

## 1c  By local authorities:

*Policy development*

- corporate strategies by local authorities must recognise play and leisure activities as crucial in the development of children.  Plans must be explicit in all children's services and a multi-disciplinary understanding of the many elements of play and leisure must be achieved.  They must also reflect the importance of access for disabled children including, for example, physical access, availability of different forms of communication and transport;

- every local authority leisure and amenities department should appoint designated teams to oversee the provision of services for children and young people throughout the authority's responsibilities.  These teams should develop and publish a co-ordinated, comprehensive child and youth policy, relating to the provision of play and leisure activities.  The teams should have advisory groups and networks drawn from the local population of children and young people;

- partnerships should be set up between local education authorities, schools, play and recreation units and departments, social services, health services and community organisations.  New strategies and ventures can be initiated within each agency to ensure co-ordinated provision for children and young people;

- all services and facilities providing play and leisure activities should have formal evaluation policies which involve consulting with children and young people who use their services and, where appropriate, those who do not but could be expected to;

- policy for young people should consider ways of encouraging and developing self selected leisure activities which tend to be based on informality, privacy, personal choice and power over and access to usable cultural commodities and resources.  This means working closely with young people in a way that gives them some control over the use and availability of resources;

- planners and policy makers must recognise that supporting and encouraging young people's cultural choices may need new, indirect, less structured, democratic ways and set up appropriate structures.  Although some expertise is useful and links should be made between youth workers and local artists the most important skills are advising, enabling and facilitating;

- local planners should look at ways of developing age-appropriate services and continuity between services;

- young carers should be included in the 'in need' definition adopted by all local authorities under the Children Act 1989.  Steps must be taken to collect information about young carers and offer appropriate action to support them in line with their wishes and feelings;

- local authorities need to ensure procedures adopted by social services departments for registering and inspecting are appropriate for each type of play services.  They should ensure that professionally trained play staff are involved in these inspection procedures;

- youth services should develop regional arts plans and youth arts budgets, buy in the skills of freelance artists, set up indigenous youth arts projects and pressurise arts funders for better provision;

*Resource allocation*

- structured play and leisure opportunities must be sufficiently resourced to ensure that there is age-appropriate provision, equality of access for children and young people from rural areas, those with disabilities and learning difficulties, those who do not speak English and those from all ethnic and cultural groups;

- health and safety legislation covering the safety of children and young people using play areas, including school playgrounds, should be enforced more rigorously by regular inspections and reports.  Adequate funding should be made available for this to happen;

*Planning departments*

- all local authorities should monitor the number of developments which provide a play environment as part of the initial build;

- children and young people should be actively consulted and involved in deciding the location and nature of designated play spaces provided by local authorities.  Children's and youth forums should be established and targets set for increasing this involvement.  These targets should be monitored regularly;

- in both rural and urban areas, where no public play space exists, opportunities to purchase common land for play should be pursued.  Existing play space should be protected in local plans and up-graded as part of a district play policy.  More resources are needed to meet play needs and support for networking is especially important.  Links between play workers and artists and sports workers can enhance everyone's work with beneficial results for the children.  There needs to be an increase in funding given to establishing multi-purpose facilities in villages which can be used by children;

*Service provision*

- play and leisure service providers must show a commitment to equal opportunities by challenging racism, sectarianism, sexism and discrimination against those with disabilities and learning difficulties, both in policy and practice which needs to be closely monitored by independent evaluators and users;

- local authorities and service providers must ensure that there is careful monitoring of resources used in all facilities to ensure that they do not promote racist and sectarian views and attitudes in any way and that they promote acceptance and understanding;

- the indicators of good practice for local authority provision of leisure facilities which provide for the needs of people with disabilities and learning difficulties, published by the British Sports Association for the Disabled should be included in all relevant local authority contract specifications.  Adequate funding should be available to ensure this.  Local play and youth services need to develop a more active encouragement of and commitment to integrated activities;

- in rural areas and other areas not well served with museums and galleries, loans services should be developed in conjunction with schools and youth services.  Education departments in museums and galleries in these areas should be adequately financed to ensure they are able to offer appropriate, peripatetic services and training for those using loaned materials;

● service providers should ensure that staff and volunteers working with children have appropriate training, knowledge and experience for the duties and responsibilities expected of them;

● parents and others who are concerned should have a right of access to information about the ownership, responsibility and safety provisions of playgrounds. Children should be able to obtain speedy redress for accidents and injuries where there is liability on the part of the owner.

## 1d By schools:

● decisions about the use and sale of land, the use of premises and equipment should consider the best interests of affected children and young people and also the need to encourage recreational activities. A 'best interests' principle in planning law and regulations would ensure this happens;

● time spent in school in enjoying recreational, cultural and artistic activities, for all children and young people, should be preserved;

● all authorities and schools that are considering changes to the length and structure of the school day ensure that the children affected are consulted, that their welfare is a primary consideration and that adequate break times for rest are time-tabled in. Current and new arrangements should be regularly reviewed for the same reasons.

2 Full implementation of Article 17 to ensure the wide dissemination of information, available to all children whilst protecting them from harm requires the following action:

● libraries must consider the effects of their policies on reducing hours and stock on children and young people when making changes;

● the Library Association guidelines for services for children and young people should be adopted and implemented by all public library services. All schools should adopt and implement the Library Association's guidelines for school libraries;

● the use of agreed guidelines for monitoring children's books and resources to ensure that they help develop awareness of a positive identity of all children from black and minority ethnic groups;

● the Department of National Heritage and the Department of Education in N Ireland should fund monitoring projects to ensure the widespread use of anti-racist children's books;

● further research is required into the effects of television, video and computer games on the mental and physical development of children. The Department of National Heritage should commission an investigation at the earliest possible opportunity;

● guidelines for protecting children and young people from harm through the media should be drawn up in conjunction with children and young people themselves.

# References

1. Quotes from a *BBC Radio 5* broadcast of interviews with children about play, from the Bedford Hill Latchkey Group (12 August 1992)

2. *Allied Dunbar national fitness survey*, Allied Dunbar, Health Education Authority and the Sports Council, Allied Dunbar, London (1992)

3. Studies conducted for the Chest Heart and Stroke Association in Northern Ireland have shown similar results

4. *Arts review*, p7 (December 1992)

5. *Youth arts: discussion document*, Feldberg R, National Arts and Media Strategy, The Arts Council of Great Britain, London (1991)

6. *A review of national support for children's play and recreation*, Torkildsen G, National Playing Fields Association, London (1993)

7. *A charter for children's play*, National Voluntary Council for Children's Play, London (1992)

8. *Danger or opportunity: towards a core curriculum for the youth service?*, National Youth Bureau, Leicester (1990)

9. see reference 5

10. *Intention to reality - developing youth arts policy*, Chamberlain D, Youth Clubs UK, Leicester (1991)

11. see reference 8

12. see reference 5

13. *A creative future - the way forward for the arts, crafts and media in England*, The Arts Council of Great Britain, HMSO (1993)

14. see reference 10.

15. *Young people and sport - policy and framework for action*, Sports Council, London (1993)

16. Statement at the launch of the *National Playing Fields Association report*, Laing C, reference (6 July 1993)

17. *Youth work and community work into the 21st century*, Policy Statement, Community Youth Workers Union, Birmingham (1992)

18. *Youth service budgets 1993-94: part 2*, National Youth Agency, Leicester (1993)

19. *Youth services funding and expenditure 1988-92*, National Youth Agency, Leicester (1992)

20. see reference 17

21. 'Too many final curtain calls', Beckett F, *Guardian Education*, p6 (30 March 93)

22. see reference 5

23. *Local authorities, entertainment and the arts*, Audit Commission, London (1991)

24. *Responding to change: museum education services at the crossroads*, Museums Association Annual Report 1992/93, The Museums Association, London (1993)

25. 'Museums and the contract culture', Hebditch M, *Museums Journal*, pp32-34 (December 1992)

26. *Response to sample survey of local authority leisure departments 1989-90*, Fair Play for Children, Bognor Regis (1989-90)

27. see reference 6

28. *Four year olds in primary school - issues and concerns*, an internal report for Northern Ireland Pre-school Playgroups Association, NIPPA, Belfast (1992)

29. *When every note counts - the schools instrumental music service in the 1990s*, Sharp C, National Foundation for Educational Research, Slough (1991)

30. reported in reference 6

31. *One false move ... a study of children's independent mobility*, Hillman M et al, Policy Studies Institute, London (1990)

32. see reference 1

33. see reference 6

34. 'Servicing the Community', *Handbook of estate improvement*, Department of the Environment, HMSO

35. *Planning policy guidance 17*, Department of the Environment/Welsh Office, HMSO

36. *Learning through landscapes*, Winchester, SO23 9DL

37. *The six acre standard*, National Playing Fields Association, London (1993)

38. Children's Playing Space Bill, *Hansard*, col 787-788, House of Commons (23 March 1993)

39. *Children today - a national overview*, National Children's Play and Recreation Unit, London (1992)

40. *Moving culture - an enquiry into the cultural activities of young people*, Willis P and team, Calouste Gulbenkian Foundation, London (1990)

41. OPCS in reference 5

42. see reference 10

43. see reference 40

44. see reference 10

45. see reference 1

46. *Children and neighbourhoods*, Henderson P, Community Development Foundation, Leeds (1993)

47. *Monitoring of the effects of local authority expenditure restrictions 1992-93*, Fair Play for Children, Bognor Regis (1993)

48. *Guidelines for the evaluation and selection of toys and other resources for children*, Working Group Against Racism in Children's Resources, London (1991)

49. *Ordinary, everyday families - action for families and their young children with special needs, disabilities and learning difficulties*, Cameron J and Sturge-Moore L, Under Fives Project, MENCAP, London (1990)

50. *Youth work with young people with disabilities*, HMI, Department of Education and Science, London (1991)

51. see reference 5

52. *Sport for all - a report on sports opportunities for disabled people in Greater London*, Greater London Association for Disabled People (GLAD), London (1987)

53. see reference 50

54. British Association of Advisors and Lecturers in PT and Standing Conference on Physical Education (1990)

55. *The impact of the decline in discretionary grants on vocational training in dance and drama*, The Arts Council of Great Britain, London (1993)

56. *Children today - in Devon*, National Children's Play and Recreation Unit, London (1992)

57. *Survey of rural services*, Lievesley, Keith and Maynard Warwick, Rural Development Commission (1991)

58. *The child in the country*, Ward C, Bedford Square Press 1988

59. *Home and leisure accident research*, Department of Trade and Industry, HMSO (1992)

60. *Play equipment intended for permanent installation outdoors*, British Standards Institution BS5696, Parts 1 and 2, Milton Keynes BSI (1986, further amendments 1990), and *Methods of test of impact absorbing surfaces*, British Standards Insitution BS7188

61. *Playground safety guidelines*, Welsh Office, National Children's Play and Recreation Unit and Department of Education and Science, NCPRU (1992)

62. *Danger - children at play*, Birmingham Townswomen's Guild (1991)

63. *Children and the environment*, Rosenbaum M, National Children's Bureau, London (1993)

64. *Managing a safer product - activity holiday centres*, SaiL, Safety in Leisure Research Unit, Swansea Institute of Higher Education (1993)

65. *Setting objectives for public library services*, Office of Arts and Libraries, HMSO (1992)

66. *Public libraries and their book funds: a report from the National Book Committee*, Book Trust, London (1992)

67. *LISU annual library statistics 1993*, Sumison J et al, Library and Information Statistics Unit, London (1993)

68. *A survey of secondary school libraries in six local education authorities*, Department of Education and Science, London (1990); *Library provision and use in 42 primary schools*, Department of Education and Science, London (1991)

69. *Children and young people - library association guidelines for public library services*, The Library Association, Library Association Publishing, London (1991)

70. *Learning resources in schools: library association guidelines for school libraries*, Kinnell M (ed), Library Association Publishing Ltd, London (1992)

71. *Guidelines for the selection and evaluation of child development books*, The Working Group Against Racism in Children's Resources, London (1991)

72. *Guidelines and selected titles - 100 picture books*, Working Group Against Racism in Children's Resources, London (1993)

73. *Charter for children's play*, PlayRight, Belfast (1992)

74. *Children's spirituality and violent entertainment today*, Stutz E, Play for Life, Norwich (1992)

# UK Agenda for Children

**9** Youth justice

# Contents

> *The unreferenced quotations in this report are comments made during a consultation exercise undertaken by the Children's Rights Development Unit with groups of young people throughout the UK.*

**Acknowledgement**
This report is drawn from a paper produced by NCH Action for Children and the National Association for the Care and Resettlement of Offenders

# Introduction

## 1.1 The policy framework

**1.1.1** During the late 1980s Home Office statistics indicate that the level of juvenile crime fell substantially. This was brought about by a new approach to dealing with young offenders which was initially developed by practitioners and subsequently endorsed by policy-makers in legislation and guidance. Until recently, therefore, it is true to say that there existed a consensus about good practice in youth justice, the main components of which reflect the importance of achieving an approach which strikes an appropriate balance between the **welfare** of a young person, as a minor, and their right to **justice**. This approach has been reflected in policy throughout the UK in recent years and found expression in England and Wales in the Criminal Justice Act 1991. However, since the implementation of the Act on 1 October 1992 the UK has experienced a major public debate on law and order which has produced a considerable backlash against current responses to juvenile offenders.

**1.1.2** Primary responsibility in England and Wales for providing services to the juvenile court has rested with local authority social services departments in recent years. This is consistent with their wider responsibilities for the protection and welfare of children and young people and ensures that these general considerations are not overlooked in the criminal process. The probation service role has become more prominent as a result of the Criminal Justice Act 1991. The Act aligned the criminal law with the civil law by bringing 17 year-olds within the remit of the juvenile court, which was re-named the Youth Court. The new Youth Court has access to a range of community sentences for 16 and 17 year-olds which are specifically provided by probation services. These are the probation order (to which may be added a range of requirements), the community service order and the combination order which contains elements of both probation and community service.

**1.1.3** The change of emphasis from local authorities to probation has worried some commentators who believe it challenges the principle that young people who offend are young people first and offenders second. They fear that young people who offend will in future be dealt with by the probation service as offenders while other young people in difficulties will be dealt with by local authorities as being in need of care or protection.

**1.1.4** The currently shared responsibilities of local probation services and social services departments are mirrored at national level by the respective roles of the Home Office and the Department of Health which are generally responsible for criminal justice and child welfare matters respectively. However, it is important to remember that the UK has no Ministry of Justice. There is an additional government department, the Lord Chancellor's Department, involved in the administration of the criminal justice system. In Wales, N Ireland and Scotland these responsibilities are carried out by the Welsh Office, the DHSS(NI) and Scottish Office.

## 1.2 Principles of good practice

**1.2.1** In recent years there has been a well-established consensus on good practice which has been grounded in principles consistent with the Convention: (Article 40.3(b) the need to divert young people from crime, (Article 37(b)) the use of imprisonment as a measure of last resort, (Article 40.4) the need for minimum but appropriate intervention. Policies based on these principles have according to the Home Office between 1981-1991 in England and Wales seen:

- 'criminal' care orders fall in use from approximately 10,000 to 300, prior to its abolition;
- use of custodial sentences for young people under 17 fall from 7,900 to 1,700;
- level of prosecutions of juveniles fall by approximately two-thirds;
- proportion of juveniles in the population who were either cautioned or prosecuted for an offence fall by 37%.

**1.2.2** Notwithstanding this record and the Government's responsibilities to pursue policies underpinned by the Convention, these principles are now threatened by a major shift in Government policy in England and Wales towards a tougher and more punitive response to teenage crime which will threaten continued good practice with young offenders. These proposals will:

- deal with young offenders primarily as offenders;
- re-introduce secure institutional responses for children as young as 12 years of age;
- locate these institutions outside the wider framework of services for young people;
- overturn the principle of minimum intervention with a response which is based on heavy, early intervention.

**1.2.3** In Scotland the recently published White Paper *Scotland's children: proposals for child care policy and law*, has re-affirmed the importance in Scotland of the primarily welfare approach to young offenders[1]. However, perhaps partly as a result of well-publicised serious offences in England, the White Paper is concerned that the children's hearings should have more powers to 'know more quickly or more frequently how well [the child] is responding to the supervision of the social work department, so that they can consider whether any further action is needed'. New powers to prescribe a review date will be given to hearings and in addition the Government will carry out a review of secure accommodation in Scotland.

**1.2.4** In Scotland, the relevant legislation is the Criminal Procedure (Scotland) Act 1975 and the Social Work (Scotland) Act 1968. Young offenders under 16, unless they commit very serious offences, are referred to a children's hearing if, in the opinion of the Reporter to the Children's Panel, he or she requires compulsory measures of care. Even in the case of serious offences, the opinion of crown counsel or agreement of Lord Advocate would be required for a child to stand trial in a criminal (sheriff) court. The system allows the hearings to explore a young person's whole circumstances and background before deciding what disposal to make. The hearings are panels of trained lay people, and the procedures and settings are less formal than a court setting, which helps the young person and their family discuss solutions with the panel.

**1.2.5** In N Ireland, youth justice is inextricably linked with strategies employed by the police and security forces for dealing with violence arising from the political conflict. (For a more detailed analysis of these issues, see **UK Agenda Report 12 on violent conflict in N Ireland,** page 259).

# 2 Relevant articles in the Convention

## 2.1 General principles

**Article 2:** all rights in the Convention must apply without discrimination of any kind irrespective of race, colour, language, religion, national, ethnic or social origin, disability or other status.

**Article 3:** the duty in all actions to consider the best interests of the child.

**Article 12:** the right to express an opinion and to have that opinion taken seriously in any matter or procedure affecting the child.

## 2.2 Articles relevant to youth justice

**Article 19:** the right to protection from all forms of violence.

**Article 24:** the right to the best possible health and access to health care.

**Article 25:** the right to periodic reviews of placements.

**Article 30:** the right of minority.groups to enjoy their own culture, language and religion. ( Article 30 is not addressed in this report but has general relevance to all services and institutions).

**Article 37(a):** the right not to be subjected to cruel, inhuman, or degrading treatment.

**Article 37(b):** the duty of the Government to ensure that detention or imprisonment is used only as a measure of last resort and for the shortest appropriate time.

**Article 37(c):** the right when deprived of liberty to be separated from adults and to maintain contact with family.

**Article 40.2(b)(ii):** the right of the child to be informed of charges against him or her.

**Article 40.2(b)(iii):** the right of a child accused of an offence to have the matter dealt with without delay.

**Article 40.2(b)(iv):** the right to an interpreter where necessary.

**Article 40.3(a):** the duty of the Government to establish a minimum age of criminal responsibility.

**Article 40.3(b):** the duty of the Government to provide alternatives to judicial proceedings wherever possible.

**Article 40.4:** the duty of the Government to provide alternatives to institutional care.

*For the full wording of the articles see the UN Convention on the Rights of the Child, page 311.*

# 3 Treatment of young people in custody

## Article 37(a)

**3.1** Article 37(a) requires that no young person '*shall be subjected to torture or other cruel, inhuman or degrading treatment or punishment*'. This right to protection is re-affirmed in both Article 37(c), which asserts the right to '*be treated with humanity and respect for the inherent dignity of the person*' and Article 40.1 which states that young people accused of breaking the law must be treated '*in a manner consistent with the promotion of the child's sense of dignity and worth*'. There is considerable evidence to suggest that the treatment of young people in custody in England and Wales contravenes Articles 37(a) and (c) of the Convention. Successive reports in recent years of Parliamentary Select Committees and official inquiries have concluded that the overall prison population should be reduced, conditions improved and regimes expanded. The problems of the general prison system were outlined most clearly in the comprehensive *Woolf Inquiry into prison disturbances* in 1990[2]. These included the over-emphasis on security and control at the expense of justice and purposeful activity, management problems and industrial relations strife, the confused and sometimes contradictory regulations governing the operation of prisons, and the constant pressure on resources and staffing levels.

> '*I was remanded for two days and locked up for 23 hours a day, it is wrong to remand 15 year-olds into a prison or police cell.*'
> (15 year-old, South Wales)

**3.2** The evidence suggests that life in a young offender institution is little different from that in an adult prison. According to Circular Instruction 40/88 the main purpose of custody in a young offender institution is to: ' ... ensure that the whole of the sentence, from the time an inmate is received into custody to the completion of the period of supervision after release, should be to prepare the offender for re-settlement in the community. The regimes should build on existing experience in youth custody centres and detention centres, co-ordinating and developing for offenders positive regime activities designed to promote self-discipline and a sense of responsibility. The personal development of the offender will be achieved through purposeful activity and positive relationships'. Yet in the view of the independent inquiry set up by the Howard League for Penal Reform into the suicides of four boys at Feltham Young Offender Institution between August 1991 and March 1992 the regime at Feltham 'does not come close to this description'[3]. The report documents, amongst other failures, a lack of meaningful activity for prisoners, widespread bullying, poor basic living conditions, limited work opportunities and very low pay rates, boredom, poor staffing levels and low morale.

**3.3** After the inquest of one of the boys (Jeffrey Horler), Joe Whitty, the Governor of Feltham, recognised the inadequacy of penal custody for juveniles: 'I personally wish to say how abhorrent it is to have to deal with children - because that is what Jeffrey was, a child - in a penal setting and under the conditions in which I have to run Feltham for want of staff. It says nothing to the credit of the Home Office, local authorities, or of society in general that we are still dealing with children in this way. It should be totally unacceptable in this age and it indicates that we are bankrupt of ideas and compassion in dealing with these admittedly very difficult, but nevertheless, very young and very vulnerable children.' Whilst the problems which have been exposed at Feltham are especially acute, there is evidence to suggest that its impoverished regime and poor standards are reproduced in prisons for young offenders.

> '*I got there and they said put this uniform on and I said no chance, so they told me, put it on or we will put you in it. The attitude was bad, it was all yes sir or no sir; there was no respect, it was all based on fear and so it all goes wrong.*'
> (18 year-old, South Wales)

**3.4** The enduring nature of these problems indicate that the prison service has failed to create an approach to the treatment of juveniles which distinguishes between them and older prisoners. Despite its faults, the previous 'borstal' system at least recognised the different physical, emotional and developmental needs of young people. The disappearance of this system, together with the failure of the 'short, sharp shock' detention centre experiment, has left young offenders' institutions without a clear sense of direction.

**3.5** There has also been considerable concern expressed recently about the treatment of young people in local authority 'secure accommodation' (lock-ups in the child care system). Particular attention has focused on the Aycliffe Centre in Durham, with allegations being made that restraint techniques employed by some care staff have resulted in children having bones broken or fractured. A review of the Centre carried out in 1993 by the local social service department revealed that there had been unacceptable practices throughout the Centre and that staff were inadequately qualified, experienced and supervised[4].

**3.6** However, children who are locked up in secure accommodation within the care system are at least protected in law from inhuman or degrading treatment by safeguards such as regulations prohibiting specific measures of control, or requirements for regular inspection and approval by the Secretary of State (the inspectors pay particular regard to the use of solitary confinement, which can only be used under strictly defined terms). The two youth treatment centres run by the Department of Health are also supposed to be governed by these safeguards (although they are not legally bound to do so). However, children whose liberty is restricted in schools or health units have considerably fewer protections. For example, the locked accommodation does not have to be inspected or approved and there are very few regulations governing treatment. No measures of control are banned in health units (whether State or private); corporal punishment is outlawed for all pupils in schools save those in independent schools whose fees are not paid by the State but otherwise there are no regulations on permissable measures of controls in schools.

---

### ACTION REQUIRED FOR COMPLIANCE

**Compliance with Article 37(a), the right of young people not to be subjected to cruel or inhuman treatment, requires that:**

- **the Government urgently reviews current facilities and regimes in young offender institutions;**

- a specific plan with a short-term timetable is published for the achievement of the standards set out by the Home Office in Circular Instruction 40/88. In particular, the review should seek to end the practice of locking inmates in dormitories or cells for long periods without meaningful activity, and should protect vulnerable inmates from bullying and intimidation by other inmates;

- Regulation 8 of the Children's Homes Regulations 1991, which specifies permissable measures of control, and Regulation 3 of the Children (Secure Accommodation ) Regulations 1991, which requires approval of the Secretary of State for secure accommodation, should apply to youth treatment centres, schools and health units which restrict the liberty of children.

# 4 Imprisonment as a measure of last resort
## Article 37(b)

## 4.1 Remands

**4.1.1** Article 37(b) states that '*arrest, detention or imprisonment shall ... be used only as a measure of last resort and for the shortest appropriate period of time*'. This applies to all under 18 year-olds (Article 1). Under the Criminal Justice Act 1991 the practice of remanding unconvicted juveniles (those under 17) to prison custody will be abolished. The Government currently expects to implement this provision in 1995-96 when more secure accommodation has been built to cater for those currently remanded in prison establishments. Although 17 year-olds appear before the youth court as minors, they will not be protected by this legislation at the remand stage.

**4.1.2** However, under existing transitional arrangements, boys aged 15 and 16 may be remanded in prison custody and are frequently held in remand wings of adult prisons. The criteria for such decisions, such as a history of absconding or likelihood of interference with witnesses, are vaguely worded and difficult to interpret. Approximately 40% of those juveniles remanded in custody are subsequently acquitted, or given a non-custodial penalty, which suggests that some remanded young people are not imprisoned '*as a measure of last resort*' but unnecessarily and even, in some circumstances, in order to circumvent laws which forbid a custodial sentence on conviction.

**4.1.3** When juveniles are denied bail they should be remanded to local authority accommodation. The local authority may, if it believes it to be necessary, apply to the court for a secure accommodation order so that the child can be locked up.. The local authority bears the cost of this decision. In 1995-6, when juvenile remands to prison custody are abolished, courts will instead be given the power to remand 15-16 year-olds, both male and female, directly to secure accommodation without a local authority application. In addition there are new proposals to toughen the laws on granting bail which could lead to more young people being remanded to custody or into security when that provision comes in. It is widely expected that the overall number of young people locked up when still unconvicted will rise significantly.

**4.1.4** There is much which can be done to reduce the level of remands in prison custody and secure accommodation and the length of time spent on remand. Both have risen substantially since the introduction of transitional arrangements in October 1992. Measures to reverse these trends include bail information, bail support and remand fostering schemes, as well as local inter-agency agreements to reduce delays in bringing cases to trial. Though there is encouraging evidence of the effectiveness of these measures, there is no obligation on any agency to provide them, no clear definition or guidance to assist in their establishment and no central mechanism to provide funding for their development. Without the necessary commitment to institute strategies for the reduction of remands, the Government is failing in its obligations under Article 37(b) to use '*detention or imprisonment only as a measure of last resort and for the shortest* *appropriate period of time'.*

> *'I have been on remand for two months and nothing has happened. It's doing my head in.'*
> (15 year-old, South Wales)

## 4.2 Sentencing

**4.2.1** Comparisons with the rest of Europe indicate that Britain already has a severe sentencing policy towards young people. Although the comparisons are difficult to make because of some variations in the way data is collected, the latest Council of Europe figures demonstrate that the countries of the United Kingdom lock up a vastly greater proportion of young people than virtually any other state in Europe. For example, France, which defines 'young prisoners' at the same age (21), and which has a similar overall use of custody, has, as a proportion of its population, only half the number of young prisoners as the UK. In most countries the proportion of the prison population who are young prisoners is only one quarter that of the UK. In sheer numbers, the difference is even greater, given that most of these countries make less use of custody for all age groups[5].

**4.2.2** Under the Scottish children's hearing system young offenders under 16 do not appear before a criminal court but attend a hearing where a panel of lay members decides, after discussion with family, social workers, teachers and the child, on a disposal based on the welfare of the child. This is clearly in keeping with the aims of Article 40 and Article 3. The White Paper *Scotland's children* re-affirms the commitment to community based disposals and alternatives to custody, but does nevertheless contain indications of an apparent tightening up on young offenders comparable with the proposals being put forward for England and Wales[6]. The Paper suggests children on supervision because of offending behaviour require more careful review and possibly more stringent conditions.

**4.2.3** Evidence from the N Ireland Office reveals discouraging trends towards custodial sentencing for young offenders. During a period when the juvenile population fell by over 14%, the number of children committed to training schools for offending behaviour proportionally increased from 11.9% in 1982 to 21.1% in 1991. There is also evidence to suggest that juveniles charged with a similar offence tend to be given harsher treatment than adults. Indeed, juveniles are more than 1.5 times more likely to receive immediate custody than adults.

**4.2.4** These statistics suggest that the UK has not tended to use imprisonment and detention *'as a last resort'* as required by Article 37(b). The Criminal Justice Act 1991 sought to address this problem by tightening the criteria for custodial sentences for all offenders. This was in line with the Act's new sentencing philosophy, matching sentences to the seriousness of the offence rather than to the offender's previous record. Section 1(2) provides that a court 'shall not pass a custodial sentence on an offender unless it is of the opinion:

a) that the offence, or the combination of the offence and one other offence associated with it, was so serious that only such a sentence can be justified for the offence; or

b) where the offence is a violent or sexual offence, that only such a sentence would be adequate to protect the public from serious harm from him'.

**4.2.5** The intention of the Act was to try to ensure that prison places were more appropriately targeted at the serious or violent offender, with petty offenders maintained within the community as far as possible. This would have ensured that prison for young people would be used *'as a last resort'*. The legislation does not apply in N Ireland, where there are concerns that juveniles in the training school system for care or control reasons can too readily be made subject to a training school order on the finding of guilt for a criminal offence. The full range of options are often not considered for such young people as court reports are prepared by agencies other than the Probation Board.

**4.2.6** However, in May 1993 the Government bowed to pressure from magistrates, judges, politicians, and the media and announced its intention to alter these criteria (especially section 1(2)(a) and section 29) to give sentencers wider discretion and to ensure that previous convictions could be taken fully into account (rather than in the limited circumstances set out in the 1991 Act). This was duly achieved under the Criminal Justice Act which was implemented in August 1993.

**4.2.7** This major change to the Criminal Justice Act 1991, which had undergone lengthy consultation before it became law and had only been in force for six months, (together with proposals in the Criminal Justice and Public Order Bill 1993, see para 4.2.8) will doubtless lead to more young offenders, who have committed frequent but not necessarily serious offences, being locked up. The National Association for the Care and Resettlement of Offenders consider that these changes will have particular impact on young offenders rendering them less well protected against inappropriate custodial sentences than at any time since 1982[7].

**4.2.8** The Government has (in 1993) introduced the Criminal Justice Bill and Public Order Bill which provides for the secure detention of persistent offenders aged between 12-14 years, doubles the existing maximum sentence length for 15-17 year-olds from one to two years and extends the · powers of courts to order young people aged 10-13 to be detained for long periods. These measures will clearly serve to increase both the number of young people sentenced to some form of custodial detention and the length of time they are detained. They suggest that the existing predisposition of the UK towards custody for children and young people will increase and that it will be even less true in future that young people are imprisoned only *'as a measure of last resort and for the shortest appropriate period of time'*.

**4.2.9** Article 37(b) is not satisfactorily implemented for children whose liberty is restricted outside the penal system, for the following reasons:

● *The scope of the law*
Section 25 of the Children Act 1989 provides that all children who are looked after by local authority social services departments, or who are accommodated by a local authority or health authority or private health unit, may not be locked up at all unless certain criteria are met and may not be locked up for more than 72 hours in a month without a full court hearing.

However, this creates a serious ambiguity about children who are not protected by section 25, such as children in care of parents or private foster parents, children in day schools or day health units or children in independent schools. The regulations issued under section 25 expressly prohibit the restriction of children's liberty in private and voluntary children's homes (although the current (1994) Criminal Justice and Public Order Bill proposes to repeal this), but there is no prohibition for children otherwise outside the scope of section 25.

Clearly those who are responsible for children, particularly younger ones, should and do have power to restrain them when this is immediately and obviously necessary - for example, stopping a child running into a busy road. This is implicit in statute and common law. But anything beyond these common sense short-term measures should either be banned or strictly regulated.

● *The definition of restriction of liberty*
Section 25 of the Children Act 1989 defines restriction of liberty by means other that placing in 'accommodation provided for the purpose of restricting liberty'. This is an unsatisfactory definition as it does not cover restriction of liberty by means other than placing in 'accommodation' - for example, through the use of handcuffs or tying children to chairs and beds, or through tranquillising drugs.

In practice, children can be detained and treated in psychiatric units against their will without any legal safeguards coming into play. This can occur because their parents have consented on their behalf. The children are then defined as 'informal patients' and are subject neither to the Children Act nor the Mental Health Act 1983 (which provides rights of appeal against compulsory detention or treatment). Until 1992 only children under 16 deemed to have insufficient understanding to consent could be detained in this way. However, a Court of Appeal case ruled in 1992 that, if any child under 18 refused medical treatment, parents had the right to consent on his or her behalf. (See **UK Agenda Report 5 on health**, page 113 for a more detailed discussion of this case.)

● *The grounds for restricting liberty*
The grounds for restricting liberty under section 25 are that it must appear that:

a)(i) [the child] has a history of absconding and is likely to abscond from any other description of accommodation, and

(ii) if he absconds, he is likely to suffer significant harm, or

b)that if he is kept in accommodation of any other description he is likely to injure or himself or other people'.

Although, on the face of it, these might appear to be sensible grounds the evidence of considerable geographical variations in the use of secure accommodation strongly suggests that much of it is used unnecessarily. The latest statistics on local authority use of secure accommodation show dramatic variations; some locking up no children within the specified year, some over 20. These variations do not correspond to population size, socio-economic deprivation or use of prison custody. The only relevant factor seems to be whether an authority manages a unit or not; of the top 15 users of secure placements in 1992/93, 11 managed their own secure units. One other likely cause of this variation is that some local authorities place insufficient weight on providing alternatives to a locked placement. The need

to lock up children who are a danger only to themselves is particularly hard to understand, except in terms of poor resources. But research also shows that the reasons why children in care run away or act aggressively almost always relates to the quality of care they are receiving.

## ACTION REQUIRED FOR COMPLIANCE

**Compliance with Article 37(b), the duty to ensure that detention or imprisonment is used only as a measure of last resort and for the shortest period to time, requires that:**

● **the principle that under 18 year-olds should only be imprisoned or detained as a measure of last resort and for the shortest appropriate period of time must be included in criminal justice legislation;**

● **the Government brings forward the target date (currently 1995/6) for ending the practice of remanding juveniles in prison service custody;**

● **the Government announces a timetable for the application of these juvenile remand agreements to 17 year-olds;**

● **the Government specifically prohibits the restriction of children's liberty in all institutions not covered by the Children (Secure Accommodation) Regulations 1991;**

● **the definition of restriction of liberty under section 25 of the Children Act 1989 should be amended to include restriction of liberty by means other than through placement in accommodation provided for that purpose;**

● **children who are detained against their will in psychiatric units should be safeguarded by the provisions of the Mental Health Act 1983, which protects adult patients who are compulsorily detained or treated;**

● **the use of tranquillising medication to control rather than treat should be outlawed;**

● **the Government establishes an independent working party, with members drawn from experts in the fields of child care and work with young offenders and with advisors from all relevant government departments and agencies to review all aspects of current arrangements for the detention of minors. This group's remit should include the development of a national policy and standards to apply to the many forms of detention for minors and the development of alternatives to custody or secure accommodation;**

● **the Government sets targets for annual reductions in the numbers of young people detained under remand or sentence in young offender institutions, remand centres, secure units, youth treatment centres and secure training centres. It should seek to achieve this by making available ring-fenced funding for community based alternatives;**

● **new legislation is introduced in N Ireland to ensure that the Probation Board is the statutory authority for preparing pre-sentence reports in all juvenile cases.**

# 4.3 Secure training centres

**4.3.1** The Government announced on 2 March 1993 its intention to introduce a new secure training order and a new institution, the secure training centre, to contain the activities of a small 'hard core' of persistent young offenders who were committing a large number of petty offences.

**4.3.2** The Criminal Justice and Public Order Bill proposes to allow courts to make a 'secure training order' for 12-14 year-olds convicted of an imprisonable offence. Such an order will allow detention in a secure training centre for between three months and a year followed by an equal period of supervision. The proposed criteria allow for orders to be made on an offender who has been convicted of three or more imprisonable offences, not necessarily on separate occasions and with no test relating to seriousness of the offence(s), and who has been found to have breached a supervision order or been convicted of an imprisonable offence while subject to a supervision order. An imprisonable offence is one punishable by imprisonment in the case of a person aged 21 or over.

**4.3.3** Thus, a young person could be imprisoned for three relatively minor offences such as shoplifting. The provisions breach the principles in Article 37 to use imprisonment *as a measure of last resort and for the shortest appropriate period of time*' and in Article 40 to seek '*alternatives to institutional care ... to ensure that children are dealt with in a manner appropriate to their well being*'.

**4.3.4** They also conflict with Article 17.1(c) of the 1986 UN Standard Minimum Rules for the Administration of Juvenile Justice (The Beijing Rules) which states that: 'Deprivation of personal liberty shall not be imposed unless the juvenile is adjudicated of a serious act involving violence against another person or of persistence in committing other serious offences and unless there is no other appropriate response'. The commission of three shoplifting offences - perhaps on one occasion - leading to a secure training order hardly fulfils the definition of 'persistence in committing other **serious** offences'. In fact, it is already possible in England and Wales to remove a persistent young offender from home for up to six months and to hold them in a secure unit, if necessary, under the supervision order with residential requirement introduced by the Children Act 1989.

**4.3.5** The Criminal Justice Bill also proposes to extend the powers of the courts to order young people aged 10-13 to be detained for long periods. The categories of offences for which 10-17 year-olds can be sentenced to long-term, indefinite detention to include: those punishable in the case of an adult with imprisonment for 14 years or more; indecent assault of a woman; in the case of a young persons causing death by dangerous driving and causing death by careless driving while under the influence of drink or drugs (clause 16). The Bill also contains new proposals regarding bail which will reverse the presumption to the right of bail for certain offenders either as a result of the type of offence they have committed or having committed the offence whilst on bail.

**4.3.6** The Government's plans have been condemned by a wide range of organisations. In March 1993, 36 agencies, including representatives from the law, child care, penal reform, child health, education and youth services, signed a published statement opposing the introduction of the new centres. There is a widespread consensus that insufficient work has been done to identify the nature and scale of the problem of persistent offending.

**4.3.7** There is also considerable concern that introducing new secure facilities will not tackle persistent offending effectively because:

● similar institutions have had an appalling record in preventing re-offending (70 to 80% of young offenders re-offend within two years of discharge) and represent a long-term danger to public safety;

● incarcerating children exposes them to significant dangers of bullying, abuse, and self-harm;

● the costs are likely to be enormous (estimated in the Bill as 'in excess of £30 million per year);

● the small number of places (around 200) will mean that children will be held a long distance from their families; there will therefore be problems in maintaining family contact and reintegration into the community;

● the centres will have a distorting and damaging effect on the existing pattern of services and facilities and inhibit any imaginative developments.

**4.3.8** Many organisations believe that a more appropriate response, consistent with the principles embodied in Articles 37 and 40, would involve:

● re-assessment of the regional variations in use of existing local authority secure accommodation and closer examination of the mixture of children who are detained in such settings for their own welfare or because of their criminal behaviour;

● an extension of community-based facilities through increasing funding for bail support, remand fostering and intensive intervention programmes to ensure that these are universally available;

● broader long-term measures to strengthen the capacity of home, school and community to 'hold on' to young people in trouble.

## ACTION REQUIRED FOR COMPLIANCE

**Compliance with Articles 37(b) and 40.4 requires that the Government withdraws proposals in the Criminal Justice and Public Order Bill 1993 to introduce secure training orders, to extend powers of courts to order young people aged 10-13 to be detained for long periods and the accompanying extension of categories of offences attracting long-term indefinite detention and reversing the presumption of bail in certain cases.**

# 5 Separation of children and adults in custody

## Article 37(c)

**5.1** Article 37(c) states that '*every child deprived of liberty shall be separated from adults unless it is considered in the child's best interests not to do so*'. The UK Government made a reservation on this article: 'Where at any time there is a lack of suitable accommodation or adequate facilities for a particular individual in any institution in which young offenders are detained, or where the mixing of adults and children is deemed to be mutually beneficial, the United Kingdom reserves the right not to apply Article 37(c) in so far as those provisions require children who are detained to be accommodated separately from adults'.

> '*It is such a bad environment to put someone so young and so vulnerable and put them into that situation. It is madness, it's no surprise to me that there are so many suicides in prison because I know I wanted to myself. Locking young people up in adult prisons does not work; it didn't work for me and it didn't work for anybody else I know.*'
> (18 year-old, South Wales)

**5.2** The basis for the Government's reservation was set out by the then Foreign Minister, Mark Lennox-Boyd, in a response to a Parliamentary Question from Roger Sims (Hansard, 21 March 1991): 'In some respects our legislation is more sophisticated than that contained in the Convention and one area is that of juvenile custody. In England and Wales experience has shown that the mixing of adult and juvenile girls in custody can be mutually beneficial and 17 year-old males are as a matter of course held with 18-20 year olds as young adult offenders. We will therefore be making a reservation to cover this aspect.'

**5.3** Despite this stated position, Home Office circular *Regimes in young offender institutions* strongly upholds the principle of age segregation. Indeed, in its reply to a House of Commons Home Affairs Committee report in 1987, the Government said: 'Separation of juveniles from young adult offenders is achieved only to a limited degree in youth custody centres ... The Government readily recognises the desirability of separating young adults from juvenile offenders but there are practical restraints on achieving this completely in the present system'[8].

**5.4** Outlining the Government's proposal for a new unified custodial sentence for young offenders to replace the existing detention centre and youth custody centre orders, the response continued: 'It is intended, so far as possible, that all young offenders will be held in young offender institutions. The new provisions in the Bill require juveniles to be held in young offender establishments save, exceptionally, on the direction of the Secretary of State for temporary purposes. Within the young offender estate, juveniles and short sentenced young offenders will be held in separate establishments (or in discrete wings of young offender establishments) from long sentenced young adult offenders, with only limited sharing of facilities under supervision'.

**5.5** Subsequently, it was announced that separate accommodation would be provided, either in separate institutions or in separate units within the same institution, for juvenile offenders under 17, young adult offenders aged 17-20 serving short sentences and young adult offenders serving longer sentences.

**5.6** In practice, this has never been fully achieved. Male juveniles are routinely held with young adults (especially on remand), whilst young women are detained with both young adult and adult prisoners. In fact, given that the Home Office announced plans in January 1992 to introduce a small number of adult prisoners into young offender institutions as a stabilising factor, it is clear that the Government has no intention of achieving its previously stated policy. This is a particularly serious matter as there is much evidence that younger prisoners can become more criminally sophisticated through their association with older prisoners. In addition, they are frequently subjected to bullying, abuse and victimisation from older prisoners; this is especially prevalent in the dormitory accommodation which is a common feature of young offender institutions.

**5.7** The situation regarding female prisoners, whilst similar, is still more worrying. The threats of bullying and 'contamination' remain, but the risk is made greater because the fewer than 50 female juveniles in the prison system are held in establishments which also hold adult women. The Government has claimed that this practice (which, again, contrasts with its stated policy in 1987) is justified by the beneficial influence of older women prisoners on juvenile prisoners. However, there is only anecdotal evidence for this assertion and it is likely, in any event, that the benefits to staff of fewer control problems would be greatly outweighed by the costs to individual juvenile prisoners of bullying and abuse.

**5.8** In the response to the parliamentary question quoted in para 5.2 the Government stated that UK legislation in relation to juvenile offenders is more sophisticated than that contained in the Convention. Yet, on the evidence presented above, it is clear that the supposed benefits of age mixing are insignificant in comparison with the dangers.

**5.9** In making this reservation the Government was no doubt aware that the number of cases where suitable accommodation is not available is likely to rise. One reason for this is the falling number of juvenile offenders in custody (from around 9,000 in the early 1980s to a provisional figure of approximately 1,500 in 1990), which means that having separate juvenile institutions is no longer economically viable. Another reason is that if and when the more locally-based community prisons envisaged in the Woolf Inquiry Report are introduced it will inevitably become more difficult to ensure separate detention[9].

### ACTION REQUIRED FOR COMPLIANCE

**The Government should withdraw its reservation to Article 37(c) and announce the immediate cessation of the practice of mixing juveniles and adults in custody. This practice continues for reasons of cost-cutting and administrative convenience and cannot be justified on any other grounds.**

# 6 The right to maintain contact with family

## Article 37(c)

**6.1** Article 37(c) states that children and young people *'shall have the right to maintain contact with [their] family through correspondence and visits, save in exceptional circumstances'*. This right is re-affirmed in Article 9.3 which states that the child has a right to *'maintain personal relations and direct contact with both parents on a regular basis'*. However, one of the consequences of the fall in the number of juveniles sentenced to custody, and the number of institutions available for them, has been that the catchment areas of young offender institutions (YOI) have had to be extended radically, thus restricting the opportunities for family contact. Female juveniles are routinely held at a great distance from their families owing to the small number of women's prisons. The prison authorities are well aware of this problem, as their document on community prisons published in 1993 indicates: 'Because of the current distribution of young offender institutions within the prison estate, many young offenders at present serve their sentences a considerable distance from their home area. They are separated from their families at what is probably one of the most stressful times they have yet experienced, and additional strain is placed on what are often fragile relationships[10]'.

> *'After they moved me to Bridgend I had no contact with my family and friends. The only time I would see them is when I would steal a car and go home to visit everybody and so I would stay overnight at my mother's and the police would be around to pick me up in the morning.'*
> (18 year-old, South Wales)

**6.2** The Prison Service's Suicide Awareness Support Unit's information paper highlights the implications this separation may have: 'Social isolation is a major cause of depression in prison, and lack of family contact is often exacerbated for prisoners held in remote locations, far from their home communities[11]. A number of suicides have been associated with prisoners' concerns about broken links with their partners, parents or children'.

**6.3** The dangers are particularly clear in the case of young prisoners. Not only is their well-being in custody in jeopardy, but also the best chance of them staying away from future criminal activity may well depend on maintaining stable community links. If the provisions in the Criminal Justice Bill to introduce secure training centres for 12-14 year-old 'persistent' offenders are implemented, the difficulties associated with placement a long way from home are likely to be extreme; as only a small number of places are envisaged (around 200), centres will inevitably be located far from many of the young person's homes. Additional difficulties arise for young Irish prisoners held on the mainland whose families experience extreme problems in maintaining contact.

**6.4** The Children's Homes Regulations 1991 specifically ban as a measure of control any restrictions on visits or communication with the family. However, other institutions which restrict children's liberty are not subject to such a ban. It appears that some psychiatric units regularly restrict access to family at the outset of placement.

**6.5** Whilst prisoners in UK prisons do have the *'right to maintain contact with their families'* through correspondence and visits, these rights are seriously circumscribed by the lack of easy access to family, friends and community. There are also concerns that some young prisoners in N Ireland are held by security forces for up to 48 hours under the emergency legislation without anyone being informed of their whereabouts. Such actions are in breach of Article 9.4 and the duty on detention of a young person to *'provide the parents with the essential information concerning the whereabouts of the absent member of the family'*. In practice, therefore, juveniles in custody are often effectively denied their right to contact because of the distance from home, or through the failure to inform parents, in breach of both Article 37(c) and Article 9.3 and 4.

(See also **UK Agenda Report 13 on violent conflict: N Ireland**, page 274)

## ACTION REQUIRED FOR COMPLIANCE

**Compliance with Article 37(c) and Article 9.4, the right to maintain contact with family, requires that:**

- **there should be a legal requirement that all under 18 year-old offenders serving custodial sentences should be held in the young offender institution nearest their home area unless doing so is not in their best interests;**

- **subsequent transfers should occur only in the best interests of the young person;**

- **any young person who cannot be accommodated in a prison service establishment within 100 miles of their home address should either be transferred to local authority secure accommodation or, in suitable cases, granted temporary release;**

- **all institutions should be prohibited from using as a measure of control restrictions on visits and communication by the family of a child whose liberty is restricted.**

# 7 The right to be informed of charges

## Article 40.2(b)(ii)

**7.1** Article 40.2(b)(ii) states that a child has the right '*to be informed promptly and directly of charges against him or her*'. However, recent research has identified that a significant proportion of interviews with juveniles take place when there are little or no grounds for the 'reasonable suspicion' which is supposed to be a precondition of arrest[12]. As a result formal interviews are sometimes no more than 'fishing expeditions', often resulting in the collapse of the interrogation.

> '*And when I was arrested they never told me my rights - there or down at the police station.*'
> (16 year-old, South Wales)

**7.2** Research suggests that young people are not necessarily informed 'promptly and directly' of charges against them[13]. Indeed, the researchers had some difficulty in establishing the exact legal offence for which some of the juveniles in their sample were dealt with. As a consequence, charges are open to negotiation and change during the decision-making process.

**7.3** An analysis of the sample of 164 taped interviews suggests that a major purpose of some of the interviews appears to be not only to obtain a confession but also to decide what offence the juvenile should be charged with. In 61.5% of the cases for which taped interviews were obtained, suspects were informed at the beginning of the interview precisely what offence they were being questioned about. In the remaining 38.5 per cent of cases they were not directly told what they were accused of. In these cases interviews typically start with questions of the type: 'Do you know why you have been arrested?', 'Can you tell me about the incident that happened today?' or 'Do you know why you are here?'. The suspect is then left to give an account of what they think they may have done in their own words. At no point in these interviews are they told precisely why they are being interviewed or why they have been arrested[14]. The evidence would appear to indicate that Article 40.2(b)(ii) is not being complied with for all juveniles questioned by the police.

**7.4** When a child or young person is referred to a children's hearing in Scotland, the 'grounds for referral' are put to them. The Scottish Child Law Centre is concerned that many children being referred on offence grounds receive no legal advice before or at the hearing on the consequences of accepting such a ground. Acceptance constitutes a conviction for the purposes of the Rehabilitation of Offenders Act 1974. The Government reservation in respect of children's hearings is clearly designed to avoid legal aid having to be made available for hearings (see para 16.1.4).

## ACTION REQUIRED FOR COMPLIANCE

**Compliance with Article 40.2(b)(ii), the right to be promptly informed of charges, requires that:**

- **the guidance issued to police officers under the Police and Criminal Evidence Act 1984 is amended to ensure that children are informed as promptly as possible and again, when being interviewed in the presence of a parent, appropriate adult or lawyer, of the charges of which he/she is suspected, and of the grounds for that suspicion;**

- **guidance from the Scottish Office to social work departments and children's hearings in relation to child care policy and practice makes reference to the importance of full information and legal or other appropriate advice for a young person before they attend a hearing.**

# 8 Avoidance of delays in hearings

**Article 40.2(b)(iii)**

**8.1** A central principle of the Children Act 1989 is that: 'in any proceedings in which any question with respect to the upbringing of a child arises, the court shall have regard to the general principle that any delay in determining the question is likely to prejudice the welfare of the child'.

**8.2** Compliance with Article 40.2(b)(iii) and the requirement '*to have the matter determined without delay*' requires a similar principle being applied to criminal proceedings involving children and young people. It is also in line with Article 20 of the 1986 UN Standard Minimum Rules for the Administration of Juvenile Justice (the Beijing Rules). Delays are endemic in the criminal justice system as a whole and acute in relation to juveniles. For example, research in Derbyshire in 1991 into 60 cases involving young people found they took between 57 and 448 days to come to court. In N Ireland delays can be over two years.

> '*We were remanded for a month and now we have to wait another month; two months on remand and we will probably get remanded again because they got two murder cases on at the moment.*'
> (16 year-old, South Wales)

**8.3** The uncertainty caused can have a very detrimental effect on a young person and, as the commentary to Article 20 of the Beijing Rules suggests, make it increasingly difficult for him or her to relate the procedure and disposition to the offence. It can also contribute to the commission of offences on bail. A recent crime prevention study conducted by South Glamorgan social services department compared the levels of known juvenile crime in two areas served by different courts and concluded that there was a far greater decrease in recorded juvenile crime in the area where cases were dealt with more swiftly under the new procedures (35% compared with 11%)[15].

**8.4** The Government set up a Working Group on Pre-Trial Issues in 1990 and proposals from this group have influenced practice in some areas of the country. Nevertheless, there is still scope for considerable improvement in others and Government should encourage all areas to set up inter-agency reviews of delays and to draw up action plans in response.

## ACTION REQUIRED FOR COMPLIANCE

**Compliance with Article 40.2(b)(iii), the duty to have the matter determined without delay, requires that all area criminal justice liaison committees should be required to develop action plans which seek to reduce delays in the process of juvenile cases. There should be a time limit of 70 days upon proceedings involving a young person who is subject to a remand in custody or security requirement whilst retaining existing safeguards. Cases not brought within that period should be discontinued.**

# 9 The right to an interpreter

**Article 40.2(b)(vi)**

**9.1** Article 40.2 (b)(vi) states that a young person has the right to '*have the free assistance of an interpreter if the child cannot understand or speak the language used*'. The obligation to have an interpreter available at every stage of the criminal process is not consistently written into UK legislation applying to police investigation, arrest, detention and court proceedings. Furthermore there is no agency in the judicial process with responsibility for ensuring the availability of interpreters.

## ACTION REQUIRED FOR COMPLIANCE

**Compliance with Article 40.2(b)(vi), the right to an interpreter, requires legislation to guarantee that all young people in the criminal justice system for whom spoken English is not their first language should have free access to an interpreter/sign service at each stage of the process, from police interview to court hearing. Clear responsibility for making provision should be identified and training made available.**

# 10 The age of criminal responsibility

## Article 40.3(a)

10.1 Article 40.3(a) does not give any guidance as to what might constitute an internationally acceptable age limit below which prosecution should be impossible but it does require the establishment of such an age. However, other international instruments suggest that the limit should not be too low. Article 4.1 of the Beijing Rules states that: 'In those legal systems recognising the concept of the age of criminal responsibility for juveniles, the beginning of that age shall not be fixed at too low an age level, bearing in mind the facts of emotional, mental and intellectual maturity'. In addition, the commentary identifies 'the close relationship between the notion of responsibility for delinquent or criminal behaviour and other social rights and responsibilities (such as marital status, civil majority, etc)'.

10.2 The age of criminal responsibility is currently 10 in England, Wales and N Ireland, whereas it is eight in Scotland. The minimum age of prosecution tends to be higher in other European countries (18 in Belgium, 15 in Germany and Sweden, 13 in France, 12 in Portugal) and there is a clear trend internationally to raise the age. In England and Wales, The Children and Young Persons Act 1969 set the minimum age for prosecution at 14. However, this section of the Act was never implemented and was recently repealed by the Criminal Justice Act 1991.

10.3 The Scottish Law Commission *Report on family law* suggests that for civil proceedings there should be a presumption of maturity at 12[16]. The White Paper *Scotland's children* also proposes 12 in relation to a child's right to attend child care reviews[17]. The effect of such laws would be to accept that although children under the age of 12 should be listened to in civil proceedings in many cases there would be no question of them determining matters as they would still be regarded as unable to understand the full implications of the issues involved. The White Paper *Adoption: the future* published in 1993 proposes 12 as the age at which children should have responsibility for giving consent to adoption[18]. It does appear anomalous therefore that, in criminal law proceedings, eight year-olds in Scotland and 10 year-olds in the rest of the UK, charged with a serious offence, are deemed to be fully responsible for their actions, but in civil proceedings are not considered competent to take responsibility for decisions that affect them.

10.4 In the early part of 1993 the public and parliamentary attention which focused on 'persistent offenders' below the age of 15 led to some calls for the age of criminal responsibility to be lowered. But, in the light of the evidence presented above, such a move would be out of step with developments in other countries and with international instruments. Moreover, the international trend is increasingly to view offending by a young person within the context of his or her welfare needs and therefore to tackle juvenile offending primarily through child care rather than criminal legislation (Article 3.1).

# 11 Alternatives to judicial proceedings

## Article 40.3(b)

**11.1** Article 40.3(b) states that Government should provide *'wherever possible and desirable, measures for dealing with such children without resorting to judicial proceedings, providing that human rights and legal safeguards are fully respected'*. Certainly, until recently the benefits for young people of diversion away from the formal criminal process have increasingly been recognised throughout the UK. Government circulars in 1985 and 1990 emphasised that diverting young people at an early stage makes them less likely to re-offend than those who become involved in judicial proceedings. In Scotland the Social Work (Scotland) Act 1968, section 43(1) requires that criminal proceedings should not be taken against a child unless there are compelling reasons of public interest. The Home Office has shown that 87% of those are **not** convicted of a further offence within two years - compared with 70 to 80% who are following a custodial sentence). Informal action and police cautions have proven swift and cost-effective responses.

**11.2** There was a great increase in the use of cautioning in England and Wales during the 1980s. The proportion of males aged under 14 cautioned rose from 65% in 1980 to 89% in 1990 and the cautioning rate for females rose from 85%-96%. For 14-16 year-old young men cautions rose from 34-69% and from 58-85% for young women over the same period.

**11.3** Recent public attention has focused on the extent of cautioning for juveniles with suggestions that repeated cautions are used too frequently. But Home Office Circular 59/90 requires chief police officers to 'bear in mind the danger that inappropriate use of cautioning, especially repeat cautioning, might undermine the credibility of the police and ultimately the law'. In reality the vast majority of cautions are administered to first-time offenders. Home Office figures given in response to a Parliamentary Question (26 October 1992) showed that 73% had no previous convictions, 16% had one previous caution and only 3% had been cautioned more than twice. Within the overall figures there are, however, sharp regional differences both within and between police force areas. For example, in 1991 Avon and Somerset cautioned 77% of under 14s who came to their notice, compared to 99% in Dyfed-Powys; Durham cautioned 54% of 14-16 year-olds, compared to 88% in Kent; Durham and South Wales cautioned 11% of 17 year-olds, compared to 58% in Kent.

**11.4** Calls are currently being made for the introduction of cautions linked to community work (community plus). However, there are fears that compulsory conditions could prove more onerous than a penalty the courts would impose. Such a move would also lead to the development of an alternative sentencing system outside the courts with insufficient safeguards for the young person.

**11.5** Linking this Article to Article 2, research has also suggested that in many areas young black people are likely to receive fewer cautions than young white people, and are likely to receive fewer cautions before being taken to court. There are also substantial sex differences in cautioning rates (see also para 13.2 on discrimination). Cautioning practice also raises concerns about young people's rights to privacy. Some forces send a form containing details of the young person and the offence to a range of agencies including schools, social services and, in some cases, youth organisations and voluntary organisations.

**11.6** If *'human rights and legal safeguards are [to be] fully respected'*, as Article 40.3(b) makes clear they should be, there needs to be greater consistency in diversion policy and practice at a number of levels. Placing cautioning on a statutory basis would encourage this. However, changes outlined in the draft supplementary guidance on cautioning produced by the Home Office in 1993 suggest a more restrictive framework, in particular by advocating restricting the number of cautions for individuals to one only. This would inhibit flexibility to take the most appropriate action in each case and would not therefore allow for compliance with Article 3 and the obligation to ensure that *'in all actions concerning children, the best interests of the child shall be a primary consideration'*.

### ACTION REQUIRED FOR COMPLIANCE

**Compliance with Article 40.3(b), the duty to seek alternatives to judicial proceedings wherever possible, requires that:**

- **cautioning is placed on a statutory basis. Ring-fenced funds should be provided for organisations to develop post-cautioning support services in local areas in partnership with the local authority;**

- **measures are introduced to provide greater consistency in diversion policies which protect the legal rights of children and ensure that action is always able to be taken in the best interests of the individual child.**

# 12 Alternatives to institutional care

## Article 40.4

12.1 Article 40.4 requires that there are available a '*variety of dispositions such as care, guidance and supervision orders, counselling, probation, foster care, education and vocational training programmes and other alternatives to institutional care ... to ensure that children are dealt with in a manner appropriate to their well-being and proportionate both to their circumstances and the offence*'. However, in spite of the growth over the last decade in the availability of community-based facilities for young offenders, there are widespread fears that the priority accorded to youth justice work has steadily fallen within local authorities. This is partly due to the very effectiveness of such work during the 1980s and partly due to increasing emphasis on other departmental activities[19].

> '*If your dog whines you don't kick it because you know it's just going to whine some more and it's the same with children. Sometimes when we do things like stealing cars it's because we are trying to say something, express ourselves, because we can't always use our voice because the people who care for us very often won't listen to us, so sometimes you steal a car to get some attention because what you need is some care and understanding. Punishment is not needed because very often we do it not to be vindictive but because we don't know any better. I just needed someone to hug me and tell me they cared for me because when someone cares for you then you take the time to care about yourself, but if no-one cares about you then you think, well why the hell should I when everybody you ever known or trusted let you down?*'
> (18 year-old, South Wales)

12.2 There are also considerable fears that preventive measures intended to strengthen social support, ensure appropriate housing provision and allocation and increase employment and leisure possibilities are not sufficiently widely available. Furthermore, there is evidence of significant cuts in employment schemes for ex-offenders, drink and drug programmes, off-site school units, therapeutic communities and imaginative criminal-justice projects. The greatest attention has focused on cuts in youth service budgets; the National Youth Agency estimates that the annual budget for the service nationally has decreased by about £30 million from its 1991 figure of £240 million.

policy and provision, training and employment provision, welfare benefit entitlements and the availability of leisure facilities.

## ACTION REQUIRED FOR COMPLIANCE

**Compliance with Article 40.4, the duty to ensure a wide variety of available dispositions, requires that:**

● **a joint circular is issued from the Department of Health, the Home Office, Welsh, Scottish and N Ireland Offices and the Department for Education setting out basic minimum arrangements in local areas for inter-agency co-operation and the provision of services to young offenders;**

● **an independent working party is established by the Government into the position of young people (that is, those aged 14 and under 18) and the role of the youth service and other agencies. It should develop a co-ordinated strategy for this age group, which would include a review of current educational**

# 13 The right not to be discriminated against

## Article 2

**13.1** Article 2 states that governments must take steps to ensure that the rights in the Convention are available to all children *'without discrimination of any kind, irrespective of the child's or his or her parent's or legal guardian's race, colour, sex, language, religion, political or other opinion, national, ethnic or social origin, property, disability, birth or other status'*. It goes on to state that governments *'shall take all appropriate measures to ensure that the child is protected against all forms of discrimination or punishment on the basis of the status, activities, expressed opinions, or beliefs of the child's parents, legal guardians, or family members'*. Statistics on the impact of race and gender on the criminal justice process are limited. However, section 95 of the Criminal Justice Act 1991 imposes a duty on the Home Office to publish information to enable those engaged in the administration of criminal justice to 'avoid discriminating against any persons on the grounds of race or sex or any other improper ground'. The first two publications which meet this duty provide the most comprehensive information to date. However, no comparable requirement exists in N Ireland, although the discussion document on Criminal Justice Policy does state that 'all offenders should be treated equally without regard to differences in gender, race or religion'.

> *'An Irishman will never get a fair trial here. The English police don't like us travellers and they will try to do their worst on us.'*
> (15 year-old, South Wales)

## 13.2 Race

**13.2.1** The introduction to *Race and the criminal justice system* published by the Home Office states that: 'Both statistics and research findings provide evidence which supports the concerns which have been expressed about differential treatment of Afro-Caribbeans (that is, people of West Indian or African origin), although they do not at present show that there is any comparable cause for concern about the treatment of members of other ethnic groups'[20].

**13.2.2** The same publication provides further evidence that young people from minority ethnic communities are more likely to live in high crime areas and to be victims of crimes than whites; that they remain under-represented in nearly all the criminal justice agencies; that Afro-Caribbeans are significantly more likely to be stopped by the police and to be remanded in custody before trial; that young people from minority ethnic communities are over-represented in the prison population (Afro-Caribbeans particularly so); and that Asians and Afro-Caribbeans serve a proportionately large number of long sentences.

**13.2.3** Among young offenders the evidence is similar. The 1990 Prison Statistics show that of all those young people whose ethnic origin was recorded, people from minority ethnic communities accounted for:
- 14% of all males remanded in custody;
- 20% of all females remanded in custody;
- 10% of all males sentenced up to 18 months in custody;
- 14% of all females sentenced up to 18 months in custody;

- 18% of all males sentenced to over 18 months in custody;
- 29% of all females sentenced to over 18 months in custody;
- 14% of the total young offender prison population[21].

**13.2.4** Whilst Home Office publications are careful to point out that such differences may not necessarily be a result of discrimination, the evidence does point strongly in this direction. Recent research reveals that young black males are the group most likely to be stopped and searched[22]. Overall, Afro-Caribbean males aged 16-24 were the group most affected but the subsequent arrest rate of 8% for all groups implies no greater incidence of criminality amongst Afro-Caribbeans. Further research published by the Policy Studies Institute indicates that of the sample surveyed, 63% of all Afro-Caribbean young men were stopped in a one-year period compared with 44% of all young men[23]. Additionally, Afro-Caribbean young men had been stopped about four times in the year compared with a mean average of 2.5 times for white young men.

**13.2.5** A recent large-scale study of race and sentencing highlighted variations based on race relating to the use of community-based schemes for young people[24]. For instance, black offenders were more likely to receive a community service or attendance centre order rather than be placed on probation. Other evidence indicates that Afro-Caribbeans, and in some areas Asians as well, were prosecuted rather than given cautions for comparable offences[25].

**13.2.6** A survey conducted by the Association of Chief Officers of Probation and NACRO of 421 15-16 year-old males remanded to custody in 1992 came to particularly dramatic conclusions: 15% of those remanded were from ethnic minorities, although they only represent 5% of the general population. Afro-Caribbean and Asian young people accounted for 51% of remands from the London region and 36% from Birmingham.

**13.2.7** This broad range of research dealing with all aspects of the justice system raises serious concerns over the extent to which young black men are being discriminated against and provides disturbing evidence of the failure to comply with Article 2.

## 13.3 Gender

**13.3.1** A recent Home Office report on *Gender and the criminal justice system* shows there are significant differences in the way men and women are treated by the criminal justice system[26]. For example, women commit fewer crimes of all types, and proportionately fewer serious and violent crimes than men (although offending by women is increasing); women are more likely to be discharged by the courts than men, but less likely to receive a community service order or be fined. Among young offenders the peak age of known offending for women is 15 compared with 18 for men.

**13.3.2** Although the report qualifies these indications by suggesting that differences in the way men and women are treated by the criminal justice system do not necessarily mean that discrimination is taking place, it goes on to say that: 'If the range of non-custodial penalties is not fully available or is not fully used for female offenders, they may be more at risk of custody than men'. A recent investigation by HM Inspectorate of Probation (1991) into probation service provision for women concluded that current probation practice made this a real danger[27].

**13.3.3** The fact that woman offenders are always in a minority, that resources will not always stretch to providing separate community service arrangements for women, and that probation officers prefer not to supervise mixed community service groups (because of the very real difficulties for women offenders working in community service groups where they are in a small minority) means that community service is not being used for women in many areas. The Inspectorate Report found that only in a few areas was serious attention being given to providing facilities for female offenders.

**13.3.4** The report shows that females aged 10-16 are more likely than males to receive a discharge and less likely to be sentenced to an attendance centre order. Whilst the greater use of discharges reflects the fact that women commit fewer and less serious offences than men, the Inspectorate findings support the view that the lack of usage of attendance centres is because insufficient places are available for women.

**13.3.5** According to draft specifications published by the Government in July 1993, if secure training centres are established for those aged 12-14, it is proposed that boys and girls will be held together in each of the units planned. This has caused grave concern among both child care and criminal justice agencies. The differential levels of involvement in crime of boys and girls and the differential sentencing patterns which then apply suggest that in each 40-place unit there may be only one or two girls. This could be a very intimidating situation as well as an inappropriate and potentially dangerous one for such young girls. Such a policy would certainly be in breach of the requirement in Article 3 to consider the best interests of the child in all actions concerning them, and would potentially constitute '*cruel, inhuman and degrading treatment or punishment*' in breach of Article 37(a). It would also expose young girls to potential sexual harassment and assault in breach of their right in Article 34 to protection '*from all forms of sexual exploitation and sexual abuse*'.

**13.3.6** Concerns have also been expressed in N Ireland that there is no young offender centre for females and that they are therefore held in a women's prison where they are subject to the stringent security procedures, including strip searching, that apply to category A High Security Terrorist women prisoners. Such treatment does not apply to boys under 17 who are held in a separate young offender institution. Young girls are thus exposed to differential treatment and furthermore to treatment which is arguably in breach of Article 37 and the right not to be subjected to '*cruel, inhuman and degrading treatment*'.

**13.3.7** Another area which causes considerable concern and may indicate discriminatory practice is the use of local authority secure accommodation for 10-18 year- olds. Of the 1,409 young people admitted to secure units in 1991/92, 71% were boys and 29% were girls. The statistics also show that a higher proportion of girls are likely to be placed in security because of concern about their welfare or behaviour, rather than for reasons directly associated with offending.

**13.3.8** A substantial body of research indicates that ideological assumptions about how young women should behave tend to govern their experiences of youth justice and the child care systems. They are not judged against a yardstick of 'boys will be boys' but against a complex definition of womanhood. This definition is tied closely to a woman's role within the private sphere of the family and ideals of respectability, decency, and concepts of the 'good girl'. At the same time, fears are often expressed about girls' promiscuity, prostitution and teenage pregnancy; this may in fact result in girls being locked up in circumstances where boys might not be. As Hudson has argued: 'There is plenty of evidence that focusing on the welfare needs (real or supposed) of girls who come to the notice of the social control agencies has led to large numbers of girls and young women, without having committed any serious acts of criminal delinquency, being removed from home or being placed under the supervision of social workers because of adult disapproval of their sexual activity and general lifestyle and demeanour[28].' These practices mean that many girls are being discriminated against in breach of Article 2 in the exercise of their right to be provided on an equal basis with boys appropriate alternatives to custody.

## 13.4 Status of institutions

**13.4.1** The rights and safeguards of children whose liberty is restricted outside the penal system vary depending on their legal status and where they are placed. In para 4.2.9, various unacceptable anomalies are highlighted between children locked up in secure accommodation in the care system and those locked up in education or health institutions. In addition the Children (Secure Accommodation) Regulations provide that only children in secure accommodation in community homes must have the need for their detention regularly reviewed, must have their parents promptly informed of the detention and must have full records kept of their case; only children under 13 in community homes must have the permission of the Secretary of State before they can be locked up. None of these safeguards apply to schools and health units. In addition, children in care and children in health units have legal rights to complain but children in schools do not. These discrepancies amount to an unjustifiable discrimination between children.

### ACTION REQUIRED FOR COMPLIANCE

**Compliance with Article 2, the equal rights of all children to all the rights in the Convention, requires that:**

- **there is compulsory police and prison officer training on anti-discriminatory practice;**

- **a policy of active recruitment from the whole community into all professions within the youth justice system is pursued;**

- **the Government consults with the Equal Opportunities Commission, the Commission for Racial Equality and agencies involved in the (youth) criminal justice system, to develop a straightforward, uncomplicated and thorough complaints procedure for the investigation of complaints of unlawful discrimination under Section 95 of the Criminal Justice Act 1991;**

- **the Government announce that girls aged between 12-14 sentenced to a secure training order will be held in a local authority secure unit near to their home and not in the predominantly male secure training centres;**

- there should be a statutory duty to produce and publish information throughout the UK on the treatment of young offenders with particular reference to gender, race and religion;

- the Government should ensure consistency of safeguards against all ill-treatment or unnecessary restriction of liberty in all institutions which lawfully restrict children's liberty.

# 14 Promoting the best interests of the child

## Article 3.1

14.1 In Scotland, the Social Work (Scotland) Act 1968, section 43(1) requires that the children's hearing panel must, in making any decision in respect of the child, ensure that the decision is taken in the child's best interests. The Criminal Procedure (Scotland) Act 1975 also makes reference to the welfare principle in relation to the disposal of young offenders aged 16-17. Until the introduction of the Criminal Justice Act 1991 criminal courts dealing with 17 year-olds in England and Wales were under no obligation to consider the best interests of the child, in line with the requirement in Article 3 of the Convention, which states that '*in all actions concerning children, whether undertaken by public or private social welfare institutions, courts of law, administrative authorities or legislative bodies, the best interests of the child shall be a primary consideration*'. The 1991 Act established the new youth courts system which extended the principle up to the age of 18. The Home Office/Health/Welsh Office Circular (1992) states that: 'The existence of a separate court for dealing with young people reflects the special consideration that has to be given to them when they are involved in the criminal justice process ... This is intended to ensure that young people are dealt with in a way which has proper regard to their youthfulness. The principle set out in section 44 of the Children and Young Persons Act 1933, that all courts must have regard to the welfare of children and young people who appear before them, is accordingly extended to include 17 year-olds'.

14.2 The N Ireland Office discussion paper on Criminal Justice Policy proposes to take a similar approach. However, despite this endorsement of previous practice in the juvenile court, there are fears that the importance attached to the welfare of young people appearing before the youth courts is likely to be weakened. This is because the creation of the youth court has caused a sharp separation of criminal and welfare jurisdictions, with many of the magistrates who had experience of both kinds of cases in the former juvenile court transferring to the new family proceedings court.

14.3 There are also proposals that section 44 of the Children and Young Persons 1933 should be updated to include a more assertive statement regarding the importance of recognising the best interests of children in judicial proceedings. In fact, the Children Act 1989 in England and Wales is based on fundamental principles which could be translated to the criminal justice sphere. The child's welfare is the paramount consideration and delays should be avoided. Courts should have regard, amongst other principles, to the wishes and feelings of the child and to his or her physical emotional and educational needs, age, sex and background. And when a court is considering whether to make an order, it should only do so if it believes that doing so would be better for the child than making no order at all. Whilst the Children Act does not apply in N Ireland, the draft Children (NI) Order 1993, which is expected to be implemented in 1995, is based on similar principles.

Compliance with Article 3, the promotion of the child's best interests, requires that:

● the principle of the child's best interests being a primary consideration is extended to all legislation dealing with young offenders;

● the Department of Health, Home Office, Lord Chancellor's Department and Welsh, Scottish and N Ireland Offices develop guidance for magistrates and judges designed to emphasise the importance of, and promote good practice in, the protection of 'the best interests of the child' in criminal proceedings.

# 15 Maintaining high standards in all institutions
## Article 3.3

15.1 Article 3.3 requires governments to '*ensure that the institutions, services and facilities responsible for the care or protection of children shall conform with the standards established by competent authorities, particularly in the areas of safety, health, in the number and suitability of their staff, as well as competent supervision*'. Currently there is no set of statutory minimum standards for conditions in British prisons. There is therefore wide variation in the degree to which cell-sharing, access to work, education, exercise and decent sanitation are present. Furthermore, prisoners in UK prisons have no effective means of ensuring that the authorities comply with the requirements of the Prison Rules.

15.2 The Woolf Inquiry Report recommended a system of Accredited Standards[29]. However, the subsequent White Paper *Custody, care and justice* only promised to codify the existing regulations given in Prison Rules, the prison building regulations, and so on[30]. A Code of Standards has been drafted by the Home Office although not yet published (early 1994) but it will not provide the sort of legally actionable system of standards envisaged in the Woolf Report.

15.3 In the light of repeated criticisms in reports of HM Chief Inspector of Prisons it can be argued that standards within custodial institutions in England and Wales fall far short of '*conforming with the standards established by competent authorities*'. There is also serious concern about the conditions in which young people are held on remand in N Ireland.

## ACTION REQUIRED FOR COMPLIANCE

Compliance with Article 3.3, the maintenance of high standards for residential institutions, requires implementation of the recommendation of the Woolf Report for a system of accredited standards for prisons. In the case of young people under 18, the aim should be to develop a set of minimum standards for all forms of secure institutions, including local authority secure units, adolescent psychiatric units, youth treatment centres and (if and when they are established) secure training centres as well as young offender institutions. It should be the responsibility of the local authority and the social services inspectorate respectively to monitor standards and carry out inspections.

# 16 Right of the child to express an opinion
## Article 12

## 16.1 Effectiveness of legal representation

**16.1.1** Article 12 requires that young people have *'the right to express those views freely in all matters affecting the child, the views of the child being given due weight in accordance with the age and maturity of the child'*. The capacity to express an informed opinion depends on the young person having access to adequate information. Juveniles often lack a proper understanding of their legal rights and of the implications of the answers which they give when questioned. The right of the child to express an opinion in proceedings depends, in part, on the quality of representation they receive. Article 12.2 requires that *'the child shall in particular be provided the opportunity to be heard in any judicial and administrative proceedings affecting the child, either directly, or through a representative or an appropriate body, in a manner consistent with the procedural rules of national law'*. Furthermore, Article 40.2(b)(ii) states that children have the right to *'legal or other appropriate assistance in the preparation and presentation of [their] defence'*. Certainly this right applies in theory in England, Wales and N Ireland and all children appearing before the court have a right to legal representation.

**16.1.2** However, it is well-established that the police use a range of persuasive questioning strategies as a means of psychologically manipulating suspects. The juvenile suspects only protection against this may be the presence of a solicitor and of an appropriate adult at the police station but because of the system of adversarial justice the police often treat representatives of the child as allies in questioning, and representatives may collude in this process. Such practices are inconsistent with the right of the child to independent representation required by Article 12. Research for the Royal Commission on Criminal Justice makes particular criticism of solicitors' involvement at police stations for taking too neutral a role, failing to formulate advice properly and giving little active assistance to the suspect[31].

> *'I was young and I just didn't understand; your feet are swept away from under you and you are carried off with no power to stop it. You just feel so weak and helpless.'*
> (18 year-old, South Wales)

**16.1.3** Such criticisms mirror those relating to appropriate adults. The research for the Royal Commission indicates that although appropriate adults are not just there to observe but to advise and to ensure interviews are conducted fairly: 'by and large they leave juveniles exposed and unsupported. When parents contribute to interviews they are as likely to act for the police as for their children ... It seems remarkable that professionals ... appear either to ignore or to be unaware of their obligation to advise suspects and ensure that interviews are conducted fairly'. On this basis, juvenile suspects' rights to be heard in proceedings, especially within informal settings, are often restricted.

**16.1.4** In Scotland, where young offenders under 16 are dealt with through the children's hearings system, children do not even have a right in principle to legal representation. The Government entered a reservation in respect of the hearing system. It states: 'In Scotland there are tribunals (known as children's hearings) which consider the welfare of the child and deal with the majority of offences which a child is alleged to have committed. In some cases, mainly of a welfare nature, the child is temporarily deprived of his or her liberty for up to seven days prior to attending the hearing. The child and its family are, however, allowed access to a lawyer during this period. Although the decisions of the hearings are subject to appeal to the courts, legal representation is not permitted at the proceedings of the children's hearings themselves. Children's hearings have proved over the years to be a very effective way of dealing with the problems of children in a less formal, non-adversarial manner. Accordingly, the UK in respect of Article 37(d) reserves its right to continue its present operation of children's hearings'.

**16.1.5** Lawyers are allowed at the hearings but no legal aid is available and in fact children rarely have representation. It is the view of the Scottish Child Law Centre that children need advice on referral on offence grounds to the hearing system and should be aware of their right not to accept the grounds. In addition to the need for adequate advice both before and during the hearing, the Scottish system of safeguarders, independent people who can make an independent assessment of the child's best interests, is very under-used. Although the chair of the children's hearing should consider the need for a safeguarder in every case, the requirement that they can only be appointed where there is a conflict between parents' and children's interests means that they are used in only around 1% of cases. The result is that Scottish children are denied the guarantee of an independent assessment of their best interests.

## 16.2 Complaints procedures

**16.2.2** If children and young people are to be given effective rights to express views on all matters of concern to them (Article 12) they must have adequate information with which to form opinions and this right is affirmed in Article 13 which states that children must have the right to *'to seek, receive and impart information and ideas of all kinds, regardless of frontiers, either orally, in writing or in print'*. However, information within prisons has always been tightly controlled. There is no apparent logic to what appears in the Prison Act, the Prison Rules, Standing Orders, Circular Instructions, Headquarters Memoranda, or is transmitted by telephone or letter. Recent publication of some previously classified material, together with the production of a Prisoner's Information Pack, have helped to rectify this situation and are welcome initiatives. Yet, in practice, questions remain about how readily such information is made available within prisons. Without access to information it is not possible to challenge breaches of rights.

**16.2.3** Recent changes to the grievance procedure (abolishing the 'petitions' system) have established some important new rights for prisoners. Under the new scheme, prisoners' grievances will be considered first at the prison, and second at Prison Service Headquarters. The system seeks to encourage informal resolution at wing or landing level, and to allow for confidential access to higher adjudication. Time limits to the process are included at each stage. The Government also agreed to the setting up of a Prisons Ombudsman (Complaints Adjudicator) in Autumn

1993. In principle, these changes enhance the right of young offenders to '*be provided with the opportunity to be heard in ... administrative proceedings affecting [them]*' (Article 12.2).

**16.2.4** However, despite these changes, prisoners remain sceptical of their impact and argue that, in many cases, the paper rights they now enjoy are not respected in practice. For example, concerns have been raised that time limits are not being met; a response to a recent Parliamentary Question given by a Home Office Minister revealed, for example, that in one area - London South - no less than 61% of prisoners are still waiting for a reply from area managers after the official six-week period. Failures of this nature are particularly serious in relation to juvenile prisoners, owing to their greater vulnerability.

**ACTION REQUIRED FOR COMPLIANCE**

Compliance with Article 12, the right of children to express their views and be heard in any relevant proceedings, requires that:

● the Government withdraw the reservation in respect of the lack of independent representation in the Scottish children's hearing system (this is also required for compliance with Article 40.2(b)(ii);

● consideration is given to the need to interview subjects under 18 separately from their parents and others who might adversely affect their ability to give their own version and explanation of circumstances and events;

● all future guidance on work with young offenders (for example, cautioning circulars, guidance on remands, etc) emphasises the need to consider the views of the young person concerned;

● the Department of Health and the Home Office develop new joint guidance on the appointment, training and deployment of 'independent persons', with a short timetable for implementation. There should be a duty to appoint independent persons for all children and young people in custody or detention;

● children are provided with easily accessible relevant information and greater involvement in case reviews;

● improved monitoring of procedures is introduced, incorporating the perspectives of prisoners;

● the official British Crime Surveys of public attitudes should fix a minimum age lower than 16 or 17. This would help to provide a more representative picture of young people's experience and should inform the development of future policies aimed at supporting young people.

# 17 The right to protection from violence
## Article 19

**17.1** Article 19 states that children have the right to protection '*from all forms of physical or mental violence, injury or abuse, neglect or negligent treatment or exploitation, including sexual abuse, while in the care of ... any ... person who has care of the child*'. During the past two years much attention has been focused on poor standards of care and abuse of children within residential institutions. The report of the enquiry into the 'Pindown' regimes at four children's homes in Staffordshire criticised, in particular, the use of solitary confinement for young people[32].

> '*I never got hit about to any great extent, just thrown about or sat on but some were not so lucky. I saw one member of staff run across the room and knee one guy in the nose, bang, just because he was throwing a tantrum. You need to talk to a young person in that situation, not hit them and then expect them to behave, you need care and understanding because it is due to a lack of care and understanding that you are there and, if you get even less, it escalates because you want it even more, so you go out and steal something because you think that you are getting back at them.*'
> (18 year-old, South Wales)

**17.2** Yet, within the prison system, extreme forms of segregation in 'strip cells' still occur in conditions worse than those uncovered in the 'Pindown' scandal. Whilst detained in such a cell the prisoner will have no books, newspapers, radio or personal belongings of any kind and there is very limited contact with staff. In the view of the Howard League report into suicides in Feltham, strip cells, especially when used in relation to prisoners who injure themselves, are 'a barbaric substitute for proper observation and care' and as such their use represents a breach of Article 19, the right to protection from all forms of violence, as well as Article 37, the right not to be subjected to '*cruel, inhuman or degrading treatment*'[33].

> '*I was only just turned 15 and they remanded me into Swansea prison. It is a really bad environment for somebody so young. They don't care about you. You are just a number. I was Williams 3542 and nothing else. I could not comprehend why I was there and by the third day I was suicidal and started to bang my head against the wall and so the other person in the cell hit the alarm button. I needed someone to talk to, to listen to me and tell me why I was there and why my local authority or my mother would not take me, what I didn't need was to be stripped and locked in another cell with a camera on me.*'
> (18 year-old, South Wales)

**17.3** Another feature of prison life which is highly damaging to young people is the bullying and intimidation they are often subjected to by other prisoners. In the case of 18 year-old Lee Waite, who hanged himself in his cell at Feltham in August 1991, the Howard League report states: 'Evidence given by the pathologist at the inquest showed that Lee had clearly suffered a brutal sexual assault (possibly with a snooker cue) some hours before his death. The pathologist found bruises to the buttock and the anal passage was bruised and torn inside. The injuries would have been very painful and she would have expected Lee to scream. This attack must have taken place during evening association, but again officers on duty were not aware of the assault and no one at the inquest was able to say exactly when this attack happened'.

**17.4** The report identifies different forms of bullying including taxing (stealing of property), initiation (testing newcomers), racial harassment, tensions between young people from different areas, attacks on those charged and convicted of sexual offences, straightforward fighting. It goes on to argue: 'There is a general belief among prisoners that the officers turn a blind eye to bullying. It is part of the culture of Feltham that in order to control boys, the control and restraint techniques are threatened or used, and the officers allow boys to beat each other up'.

**17.5** Such problems are not confined to Feltham. Reports by HM Inspector of Prisons repeatedly draw attention to these problems and it is evident from these reports and from the series of suicides and attempted suicides in recent years, that prison service establishments consistently fail to protect the children in their charge from '*all forms of physical or mental violence, injury or abuse*'[34]. Moreover, there is evidence that this behaviour often occurs with the collusion of prison officers. It is therefore apparent that this grave problem is not one which the prison service can be trusted to resolve internally.

### ACTION REQUIRED FOR COMPLIANCE

**Compliance with Article 19, the right of every child to protection from violence, requires that:**

- **codes of practice or guidance should be issued to all staff working with young people on positive methods of encouraging acceptable behaviour;**

- **young offender institutions (and secure training centres if introduced) are required in relevant legislation to have a policy on protecting young people from bullying. These polices should include strategies for its prevention, support for those who are bullied, appropriate responses to those who bully and arrangements for responding to those forms of bullying that appear to involve criminal offences.**

## 18 The right to health care
### Article 24.1

**18.1** Article 24 states that children have the right to '*the enjoyment of the highest attainable standard of health and to facilities for the treatment of illness*'. It goes on to state that '*no child [shall be] deprived of his or her right of access to such health care services*'. However, despite their unique dependence on the State, prisoners are virtually the only group of people in this country denied access to the National Health Service. Convicted prisoners are also denied access to a second medical opinion, even if they are willing to pay for it.

**18.2** Abolition of the Prison Medical Service (PMS) and the bringing of prisoner's health care within the mainstream of the NHS would improve standards of health care and the calibre of prison doctors, and counter charges that the present system sometimes operates as an agent of prison discipline. It would also bring prisoners within the complaints procedures operated by the NHS. However, although the PMS has recently been renamed the Department of Health Care for Prisons, there is little indication of substantial improvements in the service offered to prisoners.

**18.3** Prisoners lack of access to the NHS is not consistent with a right to the '*highest attainable standards of care*' (Article 24.1) nor is it consistent with Article 2 and the right not to be discriminated against in respect of any rights in the Convention irrespective of status.

### ACTION REQUIRED FOR COMPLIANCE

**Compliance with Article 24.1, the right to health care, requires that the Department of Health Care for Prisons (formerly the Prison Medical Service) should no longer manage health care arrangements in young offender institutions, which should instead become the responsibility of local health authorities and be fully integrated within the NHS.**

# 19 Review of placement
## Article 25

**19.1** Article 25 requires that every child placed for the purposes of care, protection or treatment of his or her physical or mental health must have '*a periodic review of the treatment provided to the child and all other circumstances relevant to his or her placement*'. Section 25 of the Children Act 1989 requires local authorities to obtain a youth court order to hold a child in secure accommodation for more than 72 hours in any 28 day period. Such an order permits a child to be held in secure accommodation for up to three months at a first hearing and six months on renewal.

**19.2** Questions have recently been raised about the ability and willingness of courts to challenge the professional judgements of social workers who are applying for placement renewals. According to Harris and Timms: ' ... Once in secure accommodation, youngsters tend to stay there: renewal applications are normally rubber-stamped. First, however, the requirement to prove that the original criteria continue to exist is impossible to meet in many cases (one cannot, after all, easily abscond from a secure unit); secondly, some units offer 12 month treatment programmes when the maximum renewal period is six-months, so creating pressure for further renewal; and thirdly, we have observed a curious internal contradiction that, whereas a child who is not "responding" can self-evidently not be released, one who is improving sometimes also needs to stay longer in order to take more of the successful medicine'[35].

**19.3** In consequence, secure accommodation places are often oversubscribed and many children, primarily those with welfare needs, remain in security for longer than necessary. The authors go on to suggest that the six month renewal offers the worst of all possible worlds, locking into the system the child for whom the field social worker should be actively pressing for alternatives, yet destabilising the child whose stay is unavoidably long-term. They recommend instead that short-term placements should normally be of no more than one month's duration, thus restricting six month authorizations to cases where there was serious and demonstrable risk to self or others and where a named educational or treatment programme was underway.

### ACTION REQUIRED FOR COMPLIANCE
**Compliance with Article 25, the right to periodic reviews, would be enhanced by:**

- **reducing the maximum normal renewal period for a placement in secure accommodation from six months to one month;**
- **six months renewal periods being available only where there is serious and demonstrable risk to others and where a named educational or treatment programme is underway.**

# Summary of action required for compliance

**1** Compliance with Article 37(a), the right of young people not to be subjected to cruel or inhuman treatment, requires that:

- the Government urgently reviews current facilities and regimes in young offender institutions;
- a specific plan with a short-term timetable is published for the achievement of the standards set out by the Home Office in Circular Instruction 40/88. In particular, the review should seek to end the practice of locking inmates in dormitories or cells for long periods without meaningful activity, and should protect vulnerable inmates from bullying and intimidation by other inmates;
- Regulation 8 of the Children's Homes Regulations 1991, which specify permissable measures of control, and Regulation 3 of the Children (Secure Accommodation ) Regulations 1991, which requires approval of the Secretary of State for secure accommodation, should apply to youth treatment centres, schools and health units which restrict the liberty of children.

**2** Compliance with Article 37(b), the duty to ensure that detention or imprisonment is used only as a measured last resort and for the shortest period to time, requires that:

- the principle that under 18 year-olds should only be imprisoned or detained as a measure of last resort and for the shortest appropriate period of time must be included in criminal justice legislation;
- the Government brings forward the target date (currently 1995/6) for ending the practice of remanding juveniles in prison service custody;
- the Government announces a timetable for the application of these juvenile remand agreements to 17 year-olds;
- the Government specifically prohibits the restriction of children's liberty in all institutions not covered by the Children (Secure Accommodation) Regulations 1991;
- the definition of restriction of liberty under section 25 of the Children Act 1989 should be amended to include restriction of liberty by means other than through placement in accommodation provided for that purpose;
- children who are detained against their will in psychiatric units should be safeguarded by the provisions of the Mental Health Act 1983, which protects adult patients who are compulsorily detained or treated;
- the use of tranquillising medication to control rather than treat should be outlawed;
- the Government establishes an independent working party, with members drawn from experts in the fields of child care and work with young offenders and with advisors from all relevant government departments and agencies to review all aspects of current arrangements for the detention of minors. This group's remit should include the development of a national policy and standards to apply to the many forms of detention for minors and the development of alternatives to custody or secure accommodation;

- the Government sets targets for annual reductions in the numbers of young people detained under remand or sentence in young offender institutions, remand centres, secure units, youth treatment centres and secure training centres. It should seek to achieve this by making available ring-fenced funding for the development of community based alternatives;

- new legislation is introduced in N Ireland to ensure that the Probation Board is the statutory authority for preparing pre-sentence reports in all juvenile cases.

**3** Compliance with Articles 37(b), the duty to ensure that imprisonment is used only as a measure of last resort and for the shortest possible period of time, and 40.4, the duty to provide alternatives to institutional care, requires that the Government withdraws proposals in the current (1994) Criminal Justice and Public Order Bill to introduce secure training orders, to extend the powers of the courts to order young people aged 10-13 to be detained for long periods and the accompanying extension of categories of offences attracting long-term indefinite detention, and reversing the presumption of bail in certain cases.

**4** The Government should withdraw its reservation to Article 37(c) and announce the immediate cessation of the practice of mixing juveniles and adults in custody. This practice continues for reasons of cost-cutting and administrative convenience and cannot be justified on any other grounds.

**5** Compliance with Article 37(c) and Article 9, the right to maintain contact with family, requires that:

- there should be a legal requirement that all under 18 year-old offenders serving custodial sentences should be held in the young offender institution nearest their home area unless doing so is not in their best interests;

- subsequent transfers should occur only in the best interests of the young person;

- any young person who cannot be accommodated in a prison service establishment within 100 miles of their home address should either be transferred to local authority secure accommodation or, in suitable cases, granted temporary release;

- all institutions should be prohibited from using as a measure of control restrictions on visits and communication by the family of a child whose liberty is restricted.

**6** Compliance with Article 40.2(b)(ii), the right to be promptly informed of charges, requires that:

- the guidance issued to police officers under the Police and Criminal Evidence Act 1984 is amended to ensure that children are informed as promptly as possible and again, when being interviewed in the presence of a parent, appropriate adult or lawyer, of the charges of which he/she is suspected, and of the grounds for that suspicion;

- guidance from the Scottish Office to social work departments and children's hearings in relation to child care policy and practice makes reference to the importance of full information and legal or other appropriate advice for a young person before they attend a hearing.

**7** Compliance with Article 40.2(b)(iii), the duty to have the matter determined without delay, requires that all area criminal justice liaison committees should be required to develop action plans which seek to reduce delays in the process of juvenile cases. There should be a time limit of 70 days upon proceedings involving a young person who is subject to a remand in custody or security requirement whilst retaining existing safeguards. Cases not brought within that period should be discontinued.

**8** Compliance with Article 40.2(b)(vi), the right to an interpreter, requires legislation to guarantee that all young people in the criminal justice system for whom spoken English is not their first language should have free access to an interpreter/sign service at each stage of the process, from police interview to court hearing. Clear responsibility for making provision should be identified and training made available.

**9** Compliance with Article 40.3(a), the obligation to seek alternatives to judicial proceedings, requires that:

- the age of criminal responsibility should be reviewed in the light of other European developments and the Beijing Rules;

- where children are suspected of involvement in offending behaviour, inter-agency discussion (for example, by existing cautioning panels) should have the option of taking no further action, issuing a warning, offering advice and assistance, or instituting civil proceedings in the family proceedings court.

**10** Compliance with Article 40.3(b), the duty to seek alternatives to judicial proceedings wherever possible requires that:

- cautioning is placed on a statutory basis. Ring-fenced funds should be provided for organisations to develop post-cautioning support services in local areas in partnership with the local authority;

- measures are introduced to provide greater consistency in diversion policies which protect the legal rights of children and ensure that action is always able to be taken in the best interests of the individual child.

**11** Compliance with Article 40.4, the duty to ensure a wide variety of available dispositions requires that:

- a joint circular is issued from the Department of Health, the Home Office, Welsh, Scottish and N Ireland Offices and the Department for Education setting out basic minimum arrangements in local areas for inter-agency co-operation and the provision of services to young offenders;

- an independent working party is established by the Government into the position of young people (that is, those aged 14 and under 18) and the role of the youth service and other agencies. It should develop a co-ordinated strategy for this age group, which would include a review of current educational policy and provision, training and employment provision, welfare benefit entitlements and the availability of leisure facilities.

**12** Compliance with Article 2, the equal rights of all children to all the rights in the Convention requires that:

- the age of criminal responsibility should be consistent throughout the UK;

- there is compulsory police and prison officer training on anti-discriminatory practice;

- a policy of active recruitment from the whole community into all professions within the youth justice system is pursued;

- the Government consults with the Equal Opportunities Commission, the Commission for Racial Equality and agencies involved in the (youth) criminal justice system, to develop a straightforward, uncomplicated and thorough complaints procedure for the investigation of complaints of unlawful discrimination under Section 95 of the Criminal Justice Act 1991;

- the Government announce that girls aged between 12-14 sentenced to a secure training order will be held in a local authority secure unit near to their home and not in the predominantly male secure training centres;

- there should be a statutory duty to produce and publish information throughout the UK on the treatment of young offenders with particular reference to gender, race and religion;

- the Government should ensure consistency of safeguards against all ill-treatment or unnecessary restriction of liberty in all institutions which lawfully restrict children's liberty.

13 Compliance with Article 3.1, the promotion of the child's best interests, requires that:

- the principle of the child's best interests being a primary consideration is extended to all legislation dealing with young offenders;

- the Department of Health, Home Office, Lord Chancellor's Department and Welsh, Scottish and N Ireland Offices develop guidance for magistrates and judges designed to emphasise the importance of, and promote good practice in, the protection of 'the best interests of the child' in criminal proceedings.

14 Compliance with Article 3.3, the maintenance of high standards for residential institutions requires implementation of the recommendation of the Woolf Report for a system of accredited standards for prisons. In the case of young people under 18, the aim should be to develop a set of minimum standards for all forms of secure institutions, including local authority secure units, adolescent psychiatric units, youth treatment centres and (if and when they are established) secure training centres as well as young offender institutions. It should be the responsibility of the local authority and the social services inspectorate respectively to monitor standards and carry out inspections.

15 Compliance with Article 12, the right of children to express their views and be heard in any relevant proceedings requires that:

- the Government withdraw the reservation in respect of the lack of independent representation in the Scottish children's hearing system (this is also required for compliance with Article 40.2(b)(ii);

- consideration is given to the need to interview subjects under 18 separately from their parents and others who might adversely affect their ability to give their own version and explanation of circumstances and events;

- all future guidance on work with young offenders (for example, cautioning circulars, guidance on remands, etc) emphasises the need to consider the views of the young person concerned;

- the Department of Health and the Home Office develop new joint guidance on the appointment, training and deployment of 'independent persons', with a short timetable for implementation. There should be a duty to appoint independent persons for all children and young people in custody or detention;

- children are provided with easily accessible relevant information and greater involvement in case reviews;

- improved monitoring of procedures is introduced, incorporating the perspectives of prisoners;

- the official British Crime Surveys of public attitudes should fix a minimum age lower than 16 or 17. This would help to provide a more representative picture of young people's experience and should inform the development of future policies aimed at supporting young people.

16 Compliance with Article 19, the right of every child to protection from violence requires that:

- codes of practice or guidance should be issued to all staff working with young people on positive methods of encouraging acceptable behaviour;

- young offender institutions should be required in relevant legislation to have a policy on protecting young people from bullying. These polices should include strategies for its prevention, support for those who are bullied, appropriate responses to those who bully and arrangements for responding to those forms of bullying that appear to involve criminal offences.

17 Compliance with Article 24.1, the right to health care requires that the Department of Health Care for Prisons (formerly the Prison Medical Service) should no longer manage health care arrangements in young offender institutions, which should instead become the responsibility of local health authorities and be fully integrated within the NHS.

18 Compliance with Article 25, the right to periodic reviews would be enhanced by:

- reducing the maximum normal renewal period for a placement in secure accommodation from six months to one month;

- six months renewal periods being available only where there is serious and demonstrable risk to others and where a named educational or treatment programme is underway.

# References

1. *Scotland's Children: proposals for child care policy and law*, HMSO (1993)1.
2. *The Inquiry into prison disturbances*, HMSO (1991)
3. *Suicides in Feltham*, Howard League for Penal Reform (1992)
4. *Report of the SSI: enquiry into the Aycliffe Centre for Children*, Department of Health (1993)
5. *The prison population in Britain and Europe*, The Prison Reform Trust (1993)
6. *Scotland's children : proposals for child care policy and law*, Scottish Office Social Work Services Group, HMSO (1993)
7. 'Amendments to the Criminal Justice Act 1991: the implications for young offenders', *NACRO Briefing* (1993)
8. *State and use of prisons*, Home Office Affairs Select Committee report, HMSO (1987)
9. see reference 2
10. *Community prisons: a consultation paper*, HM prison Service (1993)
11. *Caring for prisoners at risk of suicide and self injury -the way forward: and information paper issued by the Suicide Awareness Support Unit*, HM Prison Service, (1992)
12. *The case for the prosecution: police suspects and the construction of criminality*, McConville et al, Routledge and Kegan Paul (1991)
13. *Comparing different juvenile cautioning systems in one police force area*, report to the Home Office Research and Planning Unit (1991)
14. *The conduct of police interviews with juveniles*, Research Study 8, Royal Commission on Criminal Justice, HMSO (1993).
15. *Crime prevention study*, South Glamorgan Social Services Department (1990)
16. *Report on family law*, Scottish Law Commission, HMSO (1992)
17. *Report on family law*, Scottish Law Commission, HMSO, (1992)
18. *Adoption: the future*, Department of Health, Welsh Office, Home Office and Lord Chancellor's Office, HMSO (1993)
19. *Recent trends in juvenile justice*, National Youth Agency (1992)
20. *Race and the criminal justice system*, HMSO (1992)
21. *Young black people in custody: a review of Home Office prison statistics*, National Association of the Care and Resettlement of Offenders Briefing, NACRO (1992)
22. *The use, effectiveness and impact of police stop and search powers*, Willis C F, Home Office (1983)
23. *Police and people in London*, Smith D J, volume 1, Policy Studies Institute Report, PSI (1983)
24. *Race and sentencing*, Hood R (in collaboration with Gracacordovil), Clarendon Press, Oxford, (1992)
25. *Submission from the Commission for Racial Equality to the Royal Commission on Criminal Justice*, CRE (1992)
26. *Gender and the criminal justice system*, Home Office, HMSO (1992)
27. *Report on women offenders and probation service provision: report of a thematic inspection*, HM Inspectorate of probation/Home office, (1991)
28. 'Justice or welfare?', Cain M (ed), *Growing Up Good*, Sage, London (1989)
29. see reference 2
30. *Custody, care and justice*, Home Office White Paper, HMSO (199?)
31. *Custodial legal advice and the right to silence*, McConville et al, Royal Commission for Social Justice (1992)
32. *The Pindown experience and the protection of children: report of the Staffordshire child care inquiry*, Levy A and Kahan B, Staffordshire County Council (1990)
33. see reference 3
34. *The report of HM Inspector of Prisons 1991-1992*, HMSO (1993)
35. 'Juvenile courts and secure accommodation', Timms N and Harris R, *The Journal of Social Welfare and Family Law*, No 1, (1993)

## UK Agenda for Children

# 10

### Child labour

# Contents

*The unreferenced quotations in this report are comments made during a consultation exercise undertaken by the Children's Rights Development Unit with groups of young people throughout the UK.*

# 1 Introduction

**1.1** Legislation on child employment grew out of the reforms introduced at the turn of the century when the horrors of child labour were exposed and there was a growing commitment to the provision of universal education. This legislation was developed in the Children and Young Persons Act 1933 and the Children and Young Persons (Scotland) Act 1937 and primary legislation in this area has not changed substantially since. It gives local authorities power to restrict employment and offer protection through registration and enforcement by the making of bye-laws. Amid concern about child employment in the early 1970s further legislation passed through Parliament which was intended to replace the variations in local bye-laws with consistent safeguards and provide greater protective powers. However this legislation, the Employment of Children Act 1973, has never been enacted because of its resource implications. In 1976 the Department of Health issued guidelines to local authorities in England and Wales to encourage them to update the existing bye-laws on child employment to bring them in line with the spirit of the 1973 Act but the response was, at best, haphazard.

**1.2** As the law currently stands, there is a clear distinction in the protection afforded to children according to their age:

- no child can work under the age of 13 years;

- children between the ages of 13-16 can work for up to two hours a day provided it is not during school hours and is not before 7am or after 7pm. There are also restrictions on work which involves lifting, carrying or moving anything heavy enough to cause injury;

- young people over the minimum school-leaving age are considered as adults in the labour market and therefore subject to no restriction or special protection. The legislation which did exist to provide a protective framework for 16-18 year-olds in the labour market was repealed by the Employment Act 1988.

**1.3** Other than the changes introduced to remove protection from 16-18 year-olds, the Government has been silent on the subject of child employment since 1976. We therefore continue to rely on legislation introduced 60 years ago when the world of work was a dramatically different place. The school-leaving age, types of work, the environment in which it is conducted, expectations of young people and their relationships with employers, are all very different from those which pertained when the current employment protection legislation was introduced in the 1920s and 1930s.

**1.4** There is growing evidence both of the inadequacies of protection for 13-16 year-olds and the risks facing 16-18 year-olds in the workplace. Despite this the Government appears to take the view that in the case of the former the legislation is adequate whilst for the latter protection is unnecessary. In consequence, many children and young people continue to participate in the labour market with little regulation, inadequate registration or enforcement of existing legislation and at great risk to their health and safety.

**1.5** Furthermore, there is a growing population of young people for whom a number of other rights are being denied - the right to an adequate standard of living (Article 27), to access to benefits (Article 26), to appropriate vocational training (Article 28), to having their best interests considered as a primary concern (Article 3), to freedom from discrimination in relation to all the rights in the Convention (Article 2). This failure has grave consequences both in terms of immediate hardship and demoralisation experienced by the young people but, even more significantly, in the long term loss of life chances that it heralds. Many young people feel that they should have more freedom to seek employment without restrictions on age, including the right to leave education and proceed to full-time employment, but with some forms of protection against exploitation. Young people over the age of 15 also feel very strongly about the exploitation of young people through low pay and in particular youth training schemes, which many dismiss as exploitation of young people by providing employers with cheap labour, with inadequate training and health and safety.

**1.6** In this context the Convention provides an invaluable framework against which to test both the principles underlying our legislation and the standards of employment protection which exist for this vulnerable group of workers.

---

In view of the different legislation affecting young people of different ages, in this report we use the terminology 'children' to describe those below the minimum school-leaving age and 'young people' to describe those above the school-leaving age. The minimum school-leaving age (MSLA) is defined as follows: in England, Wales and Scotland, a pupil who attains the age of 16 between 1 September and 31 January may leave school at the end of the Easter term. A pupil who attains the age of 16 between 1 February and 31 August may leave school on the Friday before the last Monday in May. In N Ireland, a pupil who becomes 16 between 1 September and 1 July in the following year can leave school on 30 June in that year. A pupil who becomes 16 between 2 July and 31 August in any year cannot leave school until 30 June the following year.

# 2 The UK reservation

**2.1** In evaluating the extent to which the standards established by the Convention are matched by current law, policy and practice in the UK, it is necessary to take account of the reservation entered by the UK Government when it ratified the Convention. A reservation is made when a government has identified a conflict between its national law and a provision in the Convention and is unwilling to modify the law to achieve compliance with the Convention. Where this occurs, the government can make a reservation indicating that it does not agree to be bound by certain provisions in the Convention. The Convention defines a child as a person below the age of 18 years. The Government has entered a reservation relating to employment of young people which states that:

> *'Employment legislation in the United Kingdom does not treat persons under 18, but over the school-leaving age as children, but as "young people". Accordingly the United Kingdom reserves the right to continue to apply Article 32 subject to such employment legislation'.*

**2.2** The Department of Employment takes the view in entering this reservation that 16-17 year-olds should be treated as adults and be free to negotiate their own terms and conditions of employment. Protective legislation therefore is considered unnecessary and inappropriate.

**2.3** It is important to be aware that those issues which affect children below the MSLA who are employed are **not** covered by the reservation and the UK is therefore committed to comply with the Convention's standards. The reservation only applies to issues concerning 16-17 year-olds. However, this report includes the implications of the full implementation of the Convention and other European and international instruments.

# 3 Relevant articles in the Convention

## 3.1 General principles

**Article 2:** all rights in the Convention must apply without discrimination of any kind irrespective of race, colour, language, religion, national, ethnic or social origin, disability or other status.

**Article 3:** the duty in all actions to consider the best interests of the child.

**Article 12:** the right to express an opinion and to have that opinion taken into account in any matter or procedure affecting the child.

## 3.2 Articles relevant to child employment

**Article 13:** the right of access to information.

**Article 26:** the right to benefit from social security.

**Article 28:** the right to education, including vocational education, on the basis of equality of opportunity.

**Article 31:** the right to rest, leisure and play opportunities.

**Article 32:** the right to be protected from economic exploitation.

*For the full wording of the articles, see the UN Convention on the Rights of the Child, page 311.*

# 4 A principled framework for child labour

**4.1** When the Children and Young Person's Act 1933 was introduced, the differential between the minimum school-leaving age and the age at which employment was allowed was very narrow. There was therefore a much clearer distinction between work and education. Once young people were free to leave school they were free to work subject to certain constraints on hours and types of work. Since that time, the minimum school-leaving age has been raised to 16 thus introducing a three-year period in children's lives when they are able to combine full-time education with part-time work. In the last 10 years there have been further changes in education legislation, with the development of the National Curriculum and the emphases on further and continuing education or entrance to employment through training schemes. The Children Act 1989 stresses the welfare of the child as paramount, and emphasises parental responsibility for children and the promotion of their physical, spiritual, moral and educational development. But employment legislation for children under 16 has stood still and exposes some key questions relating to the status of children in the labour market and the nature of protective legislation needed.

**4.2** Within the European Union there are moves to raise the minimum age of employment. In 1992, they published a draft *Directive on the protection of young people at work* setting out standards of protection in employment of all young people and recommending that the minimum age for employment should be 15 although it provides for specific types of employment to be undertaken on a part-time basis from the age of 13[1]. Also in 1992 the European Parliament passed a draft *Charter on the rights of the child* which recommended that the minimum age of employment for all member states should be 16. These developments have been underpinned by a belief that education is the main focus for children of this age and that there should be no presumption that they are part of the workforce. However the draft Directive also recognises that there need to be opportunities for children to obtain part-time work if they choose to do so, in order to achieve a measure of financial independence, autonomy and new skills and experience. Such an approach combines both a protective and a permissive model of participation in the labour market. It is protective in the sense that it asserts that children are not **expected** to work until they are allowed to leave school. If they do so, there is a clear statutory framework within which any employment must take place. It is permissive in that it acknowledges that there are many 13-16 year-olds wanting to obtain part-time employment. It allows for this in areas of employment considered safe and appropriate and provides measures to prevent exploitation or harm to children's education, health and development. The proposals are therefore consistent with the standards for child employment set out in Article 32.

**4.3** However, the UK Government is opposing the draft Directive. It takes the view that it is both unnecessary for children in employment below the MSLA and harmful to employment opportunities for young people. This view is not consistent with the requirements of the Convention.

# 5 Regulation of employment
## Article 32.1 and 2(b) and (c)

**5.1** Article 32 establishes the right of children to be protected from economic exploitation and work which is hazardous to their health, education and development, and also imposes a duty on the Government to take the necessary measures to ensure that that right is respected. The Employment of Children Act 1973 in England and Wales was introduced to standardise safeguards in bye-laws and to strengthen enforcement powers of local authorities in the regulation of the employment of those under the MSLA. However, it has never been implemented. In the absence of that legislation, the existing protection is based on the Children and Young Person Act 1933 (Children and Young Person's (Scotland) Act 1937) which empowers local authorities to introduce protective bye-laws but imposes no duties. In consequence, the level of regulation afforded to children in employment is inconsistent and often inadequate. Where it exists, local authorities do not have the resources to implement it. The inadequacy in the legislation is compounded by the lack of clear responsibility for the protection of children in employment. The legislation covering those under MSLA rests with the Department of Health in England and Wales, the responsibility for enforcing it with local education authorities whilst responsibility for employment of 16-17 year-olds lies with the Department of Employment.

**5.2** There are very many children below the MSLA in part-time employment. The *National child employment study* carried out in Birmingham in 1991 indicates that more than 40% of children under 16 have some form of employment[2]. The survey confirms earlier findings from research carried out in Luton, Bedfordshire and London and leads to the conclusion that, of approximately four million school children in England and Wales, between 1.75 and two million are probably working.

**5.3** The *National child employment study* indicates that there is considerable cause for concern about the degree of exploitation of child workers. The survey of 1,827 children identified the following issues of concern:

- lack of knowledge amongst many children of employment law (eg only 52% of those working knew of any restrictions);
- 576 children were employed during school term-time and 799 indicated that they were employed in school term-time and holidays;
- 74% of children were employed illegally;
- 25% of those children found working were under the age of 13 (141 children);
- 35% of children working had an accident in the preceding year of whom 27% needed medical attention.

A similar survey undertaken in Scotland, *Forgotten workforce*, revealed that of 65 children interviewed, 26 were working in prohibited environments or in illegal jobs[3].

**5.4** The evidence of so many children employed illegally in relation to the very basic controls contained in the Children and Young Person Act 1933 indicates non-compliance with Article 32.1. The standards of protection that current legislation offers are very limited and yet even these are being flagrantly disregarded.

**5.5** Not only are substantial numbers of children working illegally, but there is little or no commitment to the enforcement of that legislation that does exist to protect children as required by Article 32.2(c): the Government must *'provide for appropriate penalties or other sanctions to ensure the effective enforcement of the present article'*. This includes enforcement of the *'right to protection from work which is exploitative, hazardous or likely to interfere with education'*. Figures issued by the Government for prosecutions in England and Wales under the employment provisions of the Children and Young Persons Act 1933 show that there were only 22 convictions in 1988. The Government has quoted this figure as evidence that there is no real problem. In reality the resource problems of pursuing convictions are too great for most local authorities. Taking the figures from the *National child employment study* and extrapolating them for the secondary school population in Birmingham, it is estimated that 20,000 school children are working of whom 16,000 may be illegally employed. Yet in Birmingham there have been no convictions in the last five years. There is no reason to believe that Birmingham's record in this field is any worse than that of other authorities; in which case the adequacy of regulations and the effectiveness of penalties and sanctions for failing to comply are clearly open to question. Further research in Strathclyde shows that over 49% of children surveyed were working illegal hours[4].

**5.6** The types of employment in which children are involved have changed enormously since the existing legislation was introduced. Whilst many continue to be employed in shops, factories and cleaning work, others are undertaking jobs such as door-to-door canvassing and deliveries, where they are unsupervised and often placed in dangerous or compromising situations. *Forgotten workforce* revealed that over half of the children in the surveys undertaken were working in delivery jobs. The dangers of such work were starkly illustrated by a *Glasgow Herald* report on 3 May 1990 which told of an 18 year-old boy requiring treatment for a protruding disc caused by three years' employment as a paper boy delivering Sunday papers. Article 32.2 requires that the Government takes *'legislative, administrative, social and educational measures'* to ensure implementation. Reliance on legislation that is 60 years old and which significantly fails to address the nature of work being undertaken by young people is not consistent with an active commitment to the implementation of this Article.

**5.7** Much of the current work undertaken by children is not subject to regulation; for example, babysitting is excluded as are the increasing numbers of children who are self-employed under franchising arrangements. Similarly, there are a number of exemptions in law for people employing children in their family business. There is a body of legislation protecting children in the field of entertainment which, at present, is contained in the Children and Young Persons Act 1933, the Children and Young Persons Act 1963 and the Education Act 1944 as amended by subsequent legislation. This full range of protective legislation needs to be reviewed and rationalised in order to bring it in line with the realities of working children in the 1990s and to ensure that it fully meets the standards embodied in Article 32.

**5.8** There are two possible alternative methods of achieving the necessary protection for children. One is to extend regulation into those unprotected employment areas. The other is to raise the minimum age of work to the MSLA, with specified exemptions for certain types of work.

**5.9** As the law currently stands with 13 as the minimum working age, any form of employment which falls outside the exemptions in the Children and Young Persons Act 1933 is permissible. This means that as new types of work evolve they are not subject to regulation. So there are many children working who are not adequately protected from harm to their *'health or physical, mental, spiritual, moral or social development'* (Article 32). The hours they are working, the nature of much of that employment, the high risk of accidents and lack of effective sanctions against employers all point to a failure to comply with the basic principle of Article 3 (that the best interests of the child must be a primary consideration) and with Articles 28 and 31 (the rights to benefit from education, play and leisure). There is a presumption in law, whether intended or not, that employment for these age groups, unless specified otherwise, is acceptable. If, on the other hand, the minimum age was raised to the MSLA, no form of employment would be allowed unless there was a specific exemption in the legislation permitting it.

**5.10** This legislative change would achieve a number of objectives necessary for compliance with Article 32:

● it would be possible to control much more effectively the range of work in which children were employed. The onus would be on the employer to demonstrate that the type of work fell within the exempted categories rather than, as is the case at present, that unless the job is specifically covered by the legislation, it falls outside any regulatory control;

● the Factories and Shops Act, which was repealed in 1989 in order to remove restrictions on the employment of 16-17 year-olds, also by default removed protection from school children undertaking work experience. This protection was useful in providing a guide to good practice for teachers and others organising work experience schemes and for employers accepting school pupils for experience on their premises. New legislation should introduce measures to ensure the appropriate level of protection for children on work experience;

● it would remove the present reliance on bye-laws, which vary widely throughout the country, resulting in very uneven protection for 13-16 year-olds according to where they live. This inconsistency of approach means that children do not have equal access to the rights contained in Article 32, which represents a breach of Article 2 (the principle that **all** the rights in the Convention must apply equally to **all** children). This inequality is further exacerbated by the widely disparate approach taken by local authorities to enforcement of the regulations. Some authorities have used their powers to increase protection of children at work but many others are either unaware of their powers or unwilling or unable to use them.

**5.11** At present, responsibility for the enforcement of regulation of child employment in England, Wales and Scotland falls on local education authorities (Education Boards in N Ireland), is invariably a low priority and is, in consequence, poorly resourced. Registration and enforcement are peripheral to the authorities mainstream functions. There is an urgent need for a comprehensive review of the current legislation in order to examine the most appropriate minimum age for employment and the most competent bodies to regulate, monitor and enforce that legislation. Anti-Slavery International, after examining the current legislation in 1987, concluded 'the laws relating to the employment of children in Britain are a thorough mess. Urgent action is required to provide a body of legislation which is universally applicable throughout the country, which lays down unambiguously the conditions in which children may, or may not be employed and which is reasonably intelligible to the potential employer'[5]. Nothing has changed since that report was written. Compliance with Article 32.2(a) and (c) does require not only that adequate legislation is in place but that it is effective in achieving its objectives. At present the law is both inadequate and ineffective. Any review of the legislation must take account of the views of children and young people in line with Article 12.

## ACTION REQUIRED FOR COMPLIANCE

**Compliance with Article 32 together with Article 28, the right to education, and Article 31, the right to leisure and play, requires a broad-ranging review of children and employment to explore the following areas:**

● **the minimum age of employment and whether it is appropriate, considering European Union legislation and recommendations of the International Labour Organisation, to raise it to the minimum school-leaving age. The need for opportunities for children to engage in part-time work in exempted categories of employment must be considered. The views of children and young people must be sought as part of this review (Article 12);**

● **the adequacy or otherwise of current legislation which provides protection for children in employment and the measures which exist to impose penalties on employers for breaches of the legislation (Article 32.2(b) and (c)). Particular reference needs to be made to the position of school children on work experience;**

● **the relationship between the different departments with responsibility for children and employment (Departments of Health, Education and Employment). There needs to be a careful analysis of where responsibility does and should lie for regulating the employment of children, together with the recognition of the need for appropriate resourcing to provide effective protection (Article 3.2 and 3.3).**

# 6 Health and safety: young people in employment
## Article 32.1

**6.1** Article 32.1 stresses the right of all children and young people to be protected from work which is *'harmful to the child's health or physical development'*. The Government states that there is no justification for introducing special protection for young people on health and safety grounds and, in line with this view, removed most of the protective legislation governing 16-18 year-olds in the Employment Act 1989 and also removed protection provided by the Wages Councils under the Wages Act 1986. These measures have resulted in young people over school-leaving age being treated as adults in the labour market. The Government's reservation on Article 32 (see above) confirms its stated position that young people are in no need of special measures of protection. However, there are studies cited in the draft *Directive on the protection of young people at work* which indicate that young people are at greater risk than adults in employment. These risks are associated with:

● the lack of physical maturity of 16-18 year-olds rendering them more vulnerable to certain forms of muscular, sensory, cardio-respiratory fatigue;

● increased likelihood of accidents. There is evidence to show that young people suffer twice as many accidents during their first year at work and are more vulnerable to psychological pressure;

● specific risk factors related to particular types of work such as greater likelihood of damage to feet caused by standing for long periods, burns caused by acids in industry are more common amongst young people, and a greater quantity of toxic dust is inhaled by young people over a given period.

**6.2** This research data challenges the Government's observation that there is no need for protective legislation. At the very least, the evidence points to a need for more detailed information about the incidence of accident and disease amongst young people in employment in the UK before it is possible to state with any confidence that our current legislation adequately protects the welfare of young people at work. The removal of any entitlement to income support from this age group (see para 12.1.2) renders them more vulnerable to risk in the labour market. Without any safety net system of income maintenance, they can be forced to remain in jobs which may be harmful to their health simply because there is no alternative available means of support.

**6.3** The combined impact of current policies can mean that young people are faced with a situation in which they are entitled to no special protection in employment in recognition of their youth, inexperience and physical immaturity and, if they leave employment in order to protect themselves, they have no right to benefit. The Government has no evidence to justify its claim that the recommendations in the Directive are unnecessary. Current policy is inconsistent with the requirement to promote the best interests of all young people as required in Article 3 and is certainly not consistent with the obligation to protect young people from risks to their health and development in the labour market (Article 32).

**6.4** The *National child employment study* also highlights a disturbing level of accidents amongst children under MSLA at work. Of the 1,827 children interviewed in 1991 more than a third had an accident during the past year. There are concerns about the level of induction, training, and health and safety information provided for many children. Full compliance with Article 32 and the right of children to be protected from '*work ... which is harmful to the child's health or physical, mental, spiritual, moral or social development*' requires much more rigorous measures to prevent accidents and injury to children. The Health and Safety Inspectorate, which has responsibility for safe conditions at work, lacks the resources to provide effective monitoring. Tighter controls on health and safety are needed if we are to comply fully with Article 32.1 and ensure that children are provided with the necessary equipment, protective clothing, training and supervision to reduce their exposure to risk of accidents.

**6.5** The Government in the *Health of the nation*, a strategy for health in England establishes the prevention of accidents as a key priority area[6]. In particular, targets are established to reduce the death rate by accidents amongst children under 15 by 33% by the year 2005 from 6.7% to no more than 4.5% per 100,000. For young people between 15 and 24 years, the target is to reduce the death rate from 23.2% to 17.4% per 100,000 population. Deaths by accident amongst children and young people do occur at work. For example, between 1979 and 1989, 112 children were killed working or playing on farms. The law on health and safety in agriculture is different from most other industries; for example, a child of 13 can legally drive a tractor and operate other farm machinery. Yet despite the fact that agriculture is one of the most hazardous industries in the UK, there is currently only, on average, one inspector employed by the Health and Safety Executive to every 2,000 agricultural premises[7].

**6.6** *Health of the nation* fails to acknowledge the particular risks to which children and young people in employment are exposed and in its strategy for accident prevention makes no relevant recommendations. There is a need for a coherent inter-departmental strategy to address the risks faced by children and young people in employment.

## ACTION REQUIRED FOR COMPLIANCE

**Compliance with Article 32.1 requires the construction of a strategy which should involve the relevant government departments - Department for Education, Department of Employment and the Department of Health and the N Ireland, Scottish and Welsh Offices together with the Health and Safety Executive, relevant unions and interested organisations such as the Child Accident Prevention Trust to identify:**

● **where accidents in different types of employment are occurring, their rates and their severity;**

● **what additional information needs to be collected;**

● **whether current legislation for protecting children and young people at work throughout the UK is sufficient to comply with Article 32;**

● **the level of resourcing necessary to ensure that any legislation is properly enforced.**

**Compliance with Article 32.1 and 32.2(b) also requires Government support for the recommendations in the draft *EC directive on the protection of young people at work* and the introduction of legislation in the UK to provide the protective rights that it proposes. In particular, there should be:**

● **statutory holiday pay of at least four weeks per annum;**

● **regulation of hours of work to ensure that young people in employment or on combined work/ training or working during summer holidays should not exceed eight hours a day or 40 hours a week;**

● **measures to ensure adequate protection from occupational accidents and diseases which take account of all the available research on the vulnerability of young people in the work place.**

# 7 Ignorance of the law

### Articles 32.1 and 13

**7.1** The *National child employment study* revealed that 50% of children in the survey had no knowledge of the law in relation to their employment. If they are unaware of the existence of protective legislation, it is certainly possible that many of their parents are equally unaware and this lack of knowledge increases the likelihood of children being employed illegally. Article 13 stresses the importance of the right to receive appropriate information and certainly the capacity to make informed choices about working relies on access to information. It is also important to recognise that one of the most effective means of ensuring that children are *'protected from economic exploitation and from performing any work which is likely to be hazardous ... '* (Article 32.1) is to equip them with the information with which to protect themselves. It is therefore imperative that information about the law relating to employment and the duties of those employing children under the minimum school-leaving age is made available to children and their parents.

### ACTION REQUIRED FOR COMPLIANCE

**Compliance with Articles 13 and 32.1 requires that information is made available in all appropriate community languages and through the appropriate media to raise public awareness of the law. This should be backed up by the provision of independent advice and advocacy services for young people.**

# 8 Hours of work

### Article 32.2(b)

**8.1** Children below the MSLA are currently only allowed to work for two hours per day between the hours of 7am and 7pm and not during school hours. This is a level which, when adhered to, is consistent with the provision of *'appropriate regulation of the hours ... of employment'* (Article 32.2(b)). However, the *National child employment study* revealed that many children are employed illegally in respect both of the number of hours worked and the times at which they are working. This illegal employment places children at risk in a number of ways:

- it can mean that they are out on the streets early in the morning and late at night, at times when it is least safe to be out alone and therefore liable to harm (Article 32);

- if they are working in excess of two hours per day, it will necessarily interfere with their capacity to benefit fully from their education either because they are too tired or because they have insufficient time for homework, or both (Article 28);

- long hours of work leave very little time or energy for play, recreation and leisure, an important aspect of children's normal and healthy development (Article 31).

**8.2** In this case, it is not the legislation that is inadequate but the resources for and commitment to enforcing it. Employers are routinely breaking the law with little fear of sanction and, as pointed out above, most children have no idea what the law says in relation to child employment.

**8.3** It is imperative, in order to ensure that the rights of children to protection, education and play are adequately respected, that enforcement of the restrictions on hours of work is taken seriously and properly resourced and that these issues are properly addressed in any review of the regulation of child employment.

**8.4** Young people aged 16-17 experience a complete lack of protection from any statutory restrictions on the number of hours they can work and the times at which they can work them. This lack of protection has been brought about by the repeal of the Factories Act and the Shops Act in 1989.

### ACTION REQUIRED FOR COMPLIANCE

**Compliance with Article 32.2(b), the duty *'to provide appropriate regulation of the hours ... of employment'* could be achieved by the adoption of the recommendation in the *EC Directive on the protection of young people at work* that working time for young people, including those in combined work/training or working during summer holidays, should not exceed eight hours a day or 40 hours a week.**

# 9 Terms and conditions of employment
## Article 32.1 and 2(b)

**9.1** Article 32 explicitly states that young people have a right to be protected from economic exploitation but at present in the UK 97% of 16-17 year-olds earn less than the Council of Europe's decency threshold of earnings (£5.15 per hour in 1992)[8]. This group of workers earn less than one third of average adult wages and this gap has widened during the 1980s. The International Labour Organisation recommends that: 'Measures should be taken to ensure that the conditions in which children and young people under 18 years are employed or work, reach and are maintained at a satisfactory standard ... special attention should be given to the provision of fair remuneration and its protection.'[9] Yet real average weekly earnings of 16-17 year-olds have remained static since 1988 and have fallen in the recession of the early 1990s, and the lowest 10% of young workers have lost £5 per week in real terms since 1989.

**9.2** Clearly, young people who are training for a job will expect to be paid less than adults who are experienced. But many young people enter jobs such as shopwork, catering or repetitive assembly work where they are as productive as adults doing the same job, but are used by employers as a source of cheap labour.

> 'YTS is cheap slave labour. They just use you until you get to the right age and they have to pay you extra, then they get rid of you and get another on YTS.'
> (19 year-old, Lincolnshire)

**9.3** The effect of Government policy has been to reduce young people's pay[10]. These effects can be seen in the impact of the following measures which were introduced in the 1980s:

- in 1981, the introduction of a young worker's scheme offering a subsidy to employers if they paid low wages to young people;

- in 1986, the abolition of minimum rates of pay for young people under 21 in retailing, catering, clothing, hairdressing and other employment sections previously protected by Wages Councils;

- in 1988, the abolition of income support for 16-17 year-olds other than in very exceptional circumstances.

**9.4** The accumulative effect of these changes has been to encourage employers to pay low wages to young people who are often compelled to accept exploitative rates of pay in the absence of any alternative means of support, a problem compounded by the high levels of unemployment amongst young people. A recent report by the National Association of Citizen's Advice Bureaux highlights this problem, citing evidence of numerous cases in which young employees have had already low wages cut further by employers[11].

**9.5** In addition, the right to claim unfair dismissal only applies to employees who have been in employment for over two years. This restriction automatically excludes young people under 18 years who have necessarily been working for less than that period. The combination of the lack of protection against dismissal, the lack of protection against low wages and the absence of protection by the social security system renders young people peculiarly vulnerable to exploitation in the labour market.

## ACTION REQUIRED FOR COMPLIANCE

**Compliance with Article 32.1 and 2(b) requires that:**

- **minimum rates of pay should be re-introduced for 16-17 year-olds;**

- **the qualifying period for claiming unfair dismissal should be returned to its pre-1979 level of 6 months continuous service in order that young people are not excluded from access to this protection.**

# 10  Rest periods and paid leave
### Article 32.2(b)

**10.1** The UK is the only country in the EU without provision of statutory paid leave for employees. The *Draft directive on protection of young people at work* proposes a minimum of four weeks a year. Whilst many employees do have contractual rights to holiday pay and work breaks, many young employees are offered no such protection. The requirement in Article 32.2(b) to '*provide for appropriate regulation of ... conditions of employment*' implies the necessity for regulation in this aspect of employment. The Government's view has consistently been that 16-17 year-olds should negotiate their own conditions of employment and this should not be a matter of statutory intervention.

**10.2** However, the realities are that many young people are employed in small workplaces where there is no trade union and, as young inexperienced workers in an environment of high and growing unemployment, they are in a very weak position to bargain for even minimally appropriate conditions of employment.

> '*I can't join a trade union because I know I will lose my job over it.*'   (17 year-old, York)

The Convention clearly states that young people have a right to protection from economic exploitation and harm in the workplace. The Government's reservation on protection of young people in employment means that young people will continue to be vulnerable and at risk in the absence of any statutory obligation on employers to provide appropriate working conditions.

### ACTION REQUIRED FOR COMPLIANCE

**Compliance with Article 32.2(b) would be further promoted if the Government were to support the recommendations in the draft *EC Directive on the protection of young people at work* and introduce the necessary legislation in the UK to reflect the protective rights that it proposes. In particular, there should be statutory holiday pay of at least four weeks a year.**

# 11  The best interests of children and young people
### Article 3

**11.1** Article 3.1 requires that '*in all actions concerning children ... the best interests of the child must be a primary consideration*'. This Article has application both in relation to the impact of work on other aspects of a child's life such as education and leisure as well as the nature of the employment and the work environment.

**11.2** For children below the MSLA there is a range of legislation which has a bearing on their welfare. The Education Act 1944 (section 58) gives local education authorities in England and Wales powers to restrict the employment of children where that employment might interfere with the right to full-time education. The Act also places teachers 'in loco parentis' during the hours children are at school and imposes a duty on parents to ensure that their children receive full-time education. The Children Act 1989 in England and Wales requires a person with care of a child to do all that is reasonable in all the circumstances for the purposes of safeguarding or promoting the child's welfare.

**11.3** Clearly during school hours, therefore, both parents and teachers have responsibilities towards ensuring the child's education. Parents can be prosecuted for failure to ensure that the child receives full-time education and there is provision under the Children Act (section 36) for the courts to make education supervision orders where a child is failing to attend school. However, whilst employers can be prosecuted for illegal employment of children (although in practice very few are) they are under no duty of care whilst a child is in their employ. It would be consistent with Article 3 to require employers by statute to ensure that the best interests of a child they are employing is a primary consideration. This welfare principle should take precedence over other considerations, such as profitability or efficiency, and would encourage employers to take responsibility for the vulnerability of children in the labour market.

### ACTION REQUIRED FOR COMPLIANCE

**Compliance with Article 32.1 and Article 3 requires that employers of children should be under a duty of care and ensure that the best interests of the child is a primary consideration whilst the child is in their employ.**

# 12 Training opportunities for 16-17 year-olds
## Article 28.1(b)

## 12.1 Background

**12.1.1** Article 28.1(b) requires that the Government, on the basis of equal opportunity, shall '*encourage the development of different forms of secondary education, including general and vocational education, make them available and accessible to every child and take appropriate measures, such as the introduction of free education and offering financial assistance in case of need*'. This duty needs to be examined in the context of the range and quality of vocational provision for 16-17 year-olds in the UK today and the training opportunities which are available to them.

**12.1.2** In 1988, the Government introduced a guarantee of a suitable youth training place for every young person not in full time education or employment. At the same time they withdrew entitlement to income support for all 16-17 year-olds except in a few limited circumstances. This withdrawal of benefit entitlement is estimated to have affected 100,000 young people[12]. In place of benefit, the provision of a youth training place is accompanied by payment of an allowance. Youth training is mainly government-funded and is managed locally by Training and Enterprise Councils (TECs) and Local Enterprise Companies (LECs). In N Ireland youth training is funded through the Youth Training programme administered by the Training and Employment Agency (T&EA).

## 12.2 Inadequacy of training provision
(Articles 26 and 28.1(b))

**12.2.1** There is substantial evidence accumulated over the past few years of the failure to meet the guarantee of a training place for all young people who want or need one. Youthaid, an organisation committed to promoting better opportunities for young people to lead independent and productive lives, undertook a survey in 1992 of youth training provision[13]. In Inner London alone, career officers estimated a shortfall of 10,000 places. In 1991 the House of Commons Select Committee on Employment wrote to TECs for details of their capacity to meet the guarantees. Of 60 replying, 32 stated that they could not meet the guarantee. The Local Enterprise Councils (LECs) estimated that there were 9,746 young people in Scotland waiting without a training place and in the last week of November 1992 the English TECs estimated that there were 35,000 young people waiting for a place[14]. Youthaid produces quarterly estimates of the numbers of young people not in work, education or training. In October 1992, it estimated that there were 124,000 young people in this situation of whom three-quarters were unable to claim any benefits[15]. The Department of Employment figures for 1992 indicate that these figures are an underestimate and the Labour Force Survey in the summer of 1992 found that an average of 195,000 16-17 year-olds were unemployed, representing a rate of around 24%[16].

**12.2.2** This failure has profound consequences for many young people. Not only are they unable to gain access to appropriate training as required by Article 28, but in the absence of either work or training they are also precluded from entitlement to income support. This would appear to be a clear breach of Article 26 which states that '*every child has a right to benefit from social security, including social insurance and [the Government] shall take the necessary measures to achieve full realization of this right in accordance with national law*' (for more details on this issue, see **UK Agenda Report 4 on poverty,** page 74). By removing entitlement to benefit, the Government is operating in direct contravention of this principle. Its justification for the loss of entitlement was that the provision of training was a more desirable alternative for young people than the prospect of unemployment. This is undoubtedly the case but, as described above, there is a significant body of evidence to suggest that there is a lack of available and suitable training for all young people requiring it and that the guarantee of a place for all has not been met. Despite this and the growing problem of youth unemployment, there has been no proposal to restore benefit to 16-17 year-olds with the result that many are facing extreme hardship and there are rapidly rising numbers of homeless young people in UK cities.

*'If they give you £60 a week and you were better off than on the social then it would be worth it. I'd rather be on the streets than on a YT scheme.[17]'*

**ACTION REQUIRED FOR COMPLIANCE**

**Compliance with Article 26 requires that income support should be restored to all 16-17 year-olds who are actively seeking work or training**

## 12.3 Quality of youth training
(Article 28.1(b))

**12.3.1** In addition to the inadequacies in the extent of provision of youth training there is widespread evidence of the poor quality of much that is available. Article 28 not only asserts that young people have a right to vocational education but stresses that this must be available on the basis of equal opportunities. For many young people the low standard of training, support and supervision provided on these schemes offer them far from equal opportunities to gain skills and gain a foothold in the labour market. These concerns are expressed by young people, careers officers and TECs alike.

**12.3.2** The report *A broken promise* cites substantial evidence of young people on youth training receiving no supervision, having nothing to do and concerned about inadequate organisation or structure of courses[18]. Further concerns were identified about the failure to offer young people training which bore any relationship to their interests or aptitudes. One TEC described the problem as one of 'squeezing young people into irrelevant training simply to meet a numerical Government target'. The Edinburgh Rights Campaign has identified a 'treadmill of training' whereby employers take successive young people on youth training placements, never offering the hope of genuine employment to those who have completed their training. For many young people, this is their only chance of acquiring skills and it is failing them. This failure needs addressing as a matter of urgency if the

Government is to comply with Articles 28 and 2 and ensure that these young people are not denied fundamental rights to benefit from vocational training to equip them to participate effectively as economically active adults.

*'I was supposed to be an apprentice carpenter, but they stuck me in the canteen because they were short staffed.*[19]*'*

*'I would go to my YT in the morning and then get sent home later because no one would be there to supervise us.'*
(17 year-old, Scotland)

**12.3.3** Inevitably the failure of the guarantee has the most serious consequences for young people who already experience disadvantage in some way - those who are homeless, or have a disability, those with learning difficulties or whose first language is not English, previous offenders or pregnant young women. If the principle of equality of opportunity is to be achieved, there needs to be more investment and commitment to the development of training of high quality which provides relevant qualifications for all young people who need it. This will necessitate resourcing provision for young people of widely disparate abilities, aptitudes, motivations and life experiences. Training, for example, for young people who have extra support needs or learning difficulties, needs to be flexible and responsive to their specific capacities. Unless this is done, the UK will continue to be in breach of Article 28 (the right to vocational training on the basis of equal opportunities) and continue to fail these young people.

**ACTION REQUIRED FOR COMPLIANCE**

**Compliance with Article 28.1(b) requires that greater investment is made in high quality training leading to recognised and relevant qualifications for young people. The withdrawal of income support and the attempt to guarantee training to every young person needing a place has led to widespread incidence of hastily constructed and sometimes ill thought-out and poorly prepared training which serves little purpose other than that of achieving a numerical target.**

## 12.4 Lack of choice (Articles 2 and 3)

**12.4.1** An essential feature of training must be that it is selected by the young person because they perceive it as having intrinsic value. The process of undergoing training is an investment in the future. Indeed the Government in introducing the scheme was clear that the scheme was voluntary. John Moore, the then Secretary of State for Social Security, stated at its inception 'it will encourage - and I say encourage - not conscript, coerce or force - young people towards training ... '[20]. However, in reality many young people are forced on to schemes as the only available means of getting enough money to live on. The courses they take are often not appropriate for their needs and the drop-out rate is high. The linkage of training with the withdrawal of income support has meant the denial of any choice for many young people.

**12.4.2** The imposition of unwanted training on young people with already low self-esteem is likely to damage what motivation they have and further limit their self-confidence. Such an approach cannot be said to be in their best interests

as required by Article 3 and is discriminatory, in breach of Article 2, in that it only denies choice to those young people already substantially disadvantaged. If the Government is to make a serious commitment to promoting the rights of all young people to appropriate training, in line with its obligations under Articles 2 and 28, the current system of effectively coercing many young people into the youth training system needs to cease. This would be helped by the restoration of income support for 16-17 year-olds together with greater investment in quality training for young people.

**ACTION REQUIRED FOR COMPLIANCE**

**Compliance with Articles 2 and 3 requires a commitment to enabling young people to choose the training they undertake subject to their own interests and aptitudes. The present system operates in such a way that it is often young people who are already disadvantaged who are offered least choice and who can be forced through lack of alternative means of support into unwanted training.**

## 12.5 Racism and discrimination
(Article 2)

**12.5.1** Prior to the introduction of the TECs in 1990, information was available on a national basis of a scheme-by-scheme breakdown of the proportion of young black people provided with places. This information is no longer available and it is therefore no longer possible to identify companies who may be operating discriminatory recruitment practices. There is generally a much higher rate of unemployment amongst young black people. This problem will be compounded in the future if young black people are further discriminated against in relation to their access to training. In N Ireland, the T&EA is developing a comprehensive system of equality monitoring on the basis of community background, marital status and disability. A comparable programme needs to be set in place throughout the UK as, without this information, effective monitoring of the implementation of Article 2 is impossible to achieve. The information must be used to evaluate the extent of discrimination and to encourage the implementation of equal opportunities policies in the provision of training. Further monitoring needs to be done to ascertain the proportion of young black people who are able to find employment at the end of training.

**ACTION REQUIRED FOR COMPLIANCE**

**In order to obtain the information necessary to ensure compliance with Article 2 it is necessary to introduce comprehensive monitoring of the allocation of places within the youth training schemes, the types of placements offered, drop-out rates and employment outcomes. Without this information, it will not be possible to ascertain whether or not young black people are being discriminated against and the extent of any discrimination that is occurring. The data collected needs to be used to undertake systematic analysis of the opportunities being offered to young people from black and other minority ethnic groups and to inform the need for the introduction or re-evaluation of equal opportunities policies and their practice.**

# Summary of action required for compliance

1 Compliance with Article 32 together with Article 28 (the right to education) and Article 31 (the right to leisure and play) requires a broad-ranging review of children and employment to explore the following areas:

● the minimum age of employment and whether it is appropriate, considering European Union legislation and recommendations of the International Labour Organisation, to raise it to the minimum school-leaving age. The need for opportunities for children to engage in part-time work in exempted categories of employment must be considered. The views of children and young people must be sought as part of this review (Article 12);

● the adequacy or otherwise of current legislation which provides protection for children in employment and the measures which exist to impose penalties on employers for breaches of the legislation (Article 32.2(b) and (c)). Particular reference needs to be made to the position of school children on work experience;

● the relationship between the different departments with responsibility for children and employment (Departments of Health, Education and Employment). There needs to be a careful analysis of where responsibility does and should lie for regulating the employment of children, together with the recognition of the need for appropriate resourcing to provide effective protection (Article 3.2 and 3.3).

2 Compliance with Article 32.1 requires the construction of a strategy which should involve the relevant government departments - Department for Education, Department of Employment and the Department of Health and the NIreland, Scottish and Welsh Offices together with the Health and Safety Executive, relevant unions and interested organisations such as the Child Accident Prevention Trust to identify:

● where accidents in different types of employment are occurring, their rates and their severity;

● what additional information needs to be collected;

● whether current legislation for protecting children and young people at work throughout the UK is sufficient to comply with Article 32;

● the level of resourcing necessary to ensure that any legislation is properly enforced.

3 Compliance with Article 32.1 and 32.2(b) requires:
● statutory holiday pay of at least 4 weeks per annum;
● regulation of hours of work to ensure that young people in employment or on combined work/training or working during summer holidays should not exceed eight hours a day or 40 hours a week;
● measures to ensure adequate protection from occupational accidents and diseases which take account of all the available research on the vulnerability of young people in the work place;
● minimum rates of pay re-introduced for 16-17 year-olds;

● the qualifying period for claiming unfair dismissal returned to its pre-1979 level of 6 months continuous service in order that young people are not excluded from access to this protection;

● employers of children to be under a duty of care and ensure that the best interests of the child is a primary consideration whilst the child is in their employ;

● information to be made available in all appropriate community languages and through the appropriate media to raise public awareness of the law. This should be backed up by the provision of independent advice and advocacy services for young people.

4 Compliance with Article 26 requires that income support should be restored to all 16-17 year-olds who are actively seeking work or training.

5 Compliance with Article 28.1(b) requires that greater investment is made in high quality training leading to recognised and relevant qualifications for young people.

6 Compliance with Articles 2 and 3 requires a commitment to enabling young people to choose the training they undertake subject to their own interests and aptitudes. The present system operates in such a way that it is often young people who are already disadvantaged who are offered least choice and who can be forced through lack of alternative means of support into unwanted training.

7 In order to obtain the information necessary to ensure compliance with Article 2 it is necessary to introduce comprehensive monitoring of the allocation of places within the youth training schemes, the types of placements offered, drop-out rates and employment outcomes. Without this information, it will not be possible to ascertain whether or not young black people are being discriminated against and the extent of any discrimination that is occurring. The data collected needs to be used to undertake systematic analysis of the opportunities being offered to young people from black and other minority ethnic groups and to inform the need for the introduction or re-evaluation of equal opportunities policies and their practice.

# References

1. *Proposal for a council directive on the protection of young people at work*, Commission of the European Communities (1992)
2. *The hidden army: children at work in the 1990s: national child employment study*, Low Pay Unit and Birmingham City Council Education Department (1992)
3. *Forgotten workforce*, Lavalette, McKechnie, Hobbes, Scottish Low Pay Unit (1991)
4. see reference 3
5. Summary of conclusions from *School age workers in Britain today*, Anti-Slavery International reported in their response to the Department of Employment Consultation Document of November 1992 on the European Commission Directive on the Protection of Young People at Work (1987)
6. *Health of the nation*, HMSO (1992)
7. *Health and safety: an alternative report*, IPMS (1992)
8. *New earnings survey*, Department of Employment (1992)
9. *International Labour Organisation's Minimum Age Convention*, No 138 (1973)
10. *The New Review* (April/May 1992)
11. *Job insecurity: CAB evidence on employment problems in the recession*, NACAB (1993)
12. *Hansard*, Written answer, Column 553 (19 February 1992)
13. *A broken promise: the failure of youth training policy*, McLagan I, Youthaid and The Children's Society (1992)
14. *The work of the Employment Department group: minutes of evidence 21/10/92*, Employment Select Committee, HMSO (1992)
15. *Four years severe hardship*, Maclagan I, Coypss, Youthaid and Barnados (1993)
16. see reference 8
17. see reference 13
18. see reference 13
19. see reference 13
20. *Hansard*, Column 743 (2 November 1987)

# CHILDREN'S RIGHTS
## DEVELOPMENT UNIT

## UK Agenda for Children

HELLO

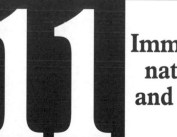

**11** Immigration, nationality and refugees

# Contents

**Acknowledgement**
This report is drawn from an original paper written by the
Children's Legal Centre

# 1 Introduction

**1.1** Immigration policy in the UK has been characterised by two significant themes - first, the need to meet the demands of the labour market and second, a determination to ensure that the social costs of immigration (such as welfare services) are kept to a minimum. Legislation dating from the beginning of the century, such as the Aliens Act 1905, has been designed to restrict the entry of 'undesirable' immigrants. Since then a series of Acts have systematically imposed ever-more restrictive rules governing entry into the UK. The consequence of these changes to immigration, nationality and asylum law is that many children are affected by the provisions in such a way as to deny them a number of the rights contained in the UN Convention.

## UK reservation to the Convention

**1.2** In ratifying the Convention the Government entered a reservation in relation to nationality and immigration:

> 'The United Kingdom reserves the right to apply such legislation, in so far as it relates to the entry into, stay in and departure from the United Kingdom of those who do not have the right under the law of the United Kingdom to enter and remain in the United Kingdom, and to the acquisition and possession of citizenship, as it may deem necessary from time to time.'

**1.3** Article 51.2 states that a 'reservation incompatible with the object and purpose of the present Convention shall not be permitted'. The reservation entered by the UK Government undermines the implementation of three basic principles in the Convention. First, UK immigration and nationality legislation does not allow decisions to take account of the best interests of the child (Article 3). Second, both the legislation itself and its implementation are discriminatory in relation to certain groups of children (Article 2). Third, the legislation does not provide for children expressing their views on decisions made about their life (Article 12). Since these three Articles underpin the implementation of every right contained in the Convention, disregard of these principles in relation to nationality and immigration law makes it impossible for the UK to comply with the 'object and purpose of the Convention'. The reservation is incompatible with the spirit of the Convention and should be withdrawn. The Children's Rights Development Unit, the Children's Legal Centre and other organisations, have made representations to this effect to both the UN Committee on the Rights of the Child and other States Parties.

**1.4** This report analyses the extent to which law, policy and practice in respect of immigration and nationality in the UK currently fail to comply with the principles and standards embodied in the Convention, without regard to the reservation.

# 2 Relevant articles in the Convention

## 2.1 Underlying principles

**Article 2:** all rights in the Convention must apply without discrimination of any kind irrespective of race, colour, language, religion, national, ethnic or social origin, disability or other status.

**Article 3:** the duty in all actions to consider the best interests of the child.

**Article 12:** the right to express an opinion and to have that opinion taken into account in any matter or procedure affecting the child.

## 2.2 Articles relevant to nationality, immigration and refugees

**Article 7:** the right to a name from birth and to be granted a nationality.

**Article 8:** the right to preserve identity including name, nationality and family relations.

**Article 9:** the right to live with one's family unless this is not in the child's best interests and, when separation does take place, the right to maintain contact with both parents on a regular basis.

**Article 10:** the right to enter the country to be reunited or maintain the child parent relationship.

**Article 16:** the right to protection from interference with privacy, family, home and correspondence.

**Article 22:** the right of refugee children to appropriate protection and assistance in the pursuit of the rights in the Convention.

**Article 39:** the duty of the Government to take measures to ensure that child-victims of armed conflict, torture, neglect or exploitation receive treatment for recovery and social integration.

*For the full wording of the articles, see the UN Convention on the Rights of the Child, page 311.*

# 3 Rights for all children without discrimination

## Article 2

**3.1** Article 2.1 states that all the rights in the Convention apply to all children *'without discrimination of any kind, irrespective of the child's or his or her parent's … race, colour, sex, language, religion, political or other opinion, national, ethnic or social origin, property, disability, birth or other status'*. Furthermore, Article 2.2 goes on to require that all appropriate measures are taken *'to ensure that the child is protected against all forms of punishment on the basis of the status, activities, expressed opinions or beliefs of the child's parents'*. This Article imposes an explicit duty on the Government, not only to protect children and young people from discrimination on any grounds, but also to ensure that all the rights in the Convention are applied to **all** children and young people within its jurisdiction. The Convention prohibits discrimination by the State.

**3.2** The nature of UK immigration and nationality laws is discriminatory. Controls introduced in 1962 were designed to restrict the entry into the UK of people from those New Commonwealth countries and colonies whose populations are mainly black. The thrust of legislation has continued in this direction. Examples of direct discrimination, in direct contravention of Article 2.2, and often on the grounds of a parent's status, are set out below.

- while non-British children who are adopted in the UK by British parents become British citizens automatically, as do children born abroad to parents who are British citizens by birth, registration or naturalisation in the UK, children who are adopted abroad by British citizens do not have this right. They must apply for leave to enter the UK;

- children whose parents are not married cannot acquire British nationality through their father. They can acquire nationality through their mother only, whereas children whose parents are married can acquire British nationality through either parent;

- while children who are UK citizens have the right of freedom of movement to work, settle or study within the European Union (EU), children who are settled in the UK but are not British nationals do not. EU citizens working in the UK have the right to be joined by their families (including married heterosexual partners, children up to the age of 21, grandparents and other dependent children, none of whom needs to be EU citizens) while those who are settled in the UK or have UK nationality have no comparable right to bring over their non-British children, spouses and other family members[1][2];

- the rules governing the admission of non-British children to join parent(s) settled in this country discriminate against children whose family is on a low income or is headed by a lone parent. Children will be admitted only if the parents are able to show that they can provide support and accommodation for the child without recourse to public funds. Public funds are defined as income support, family credit, housing benefit and housing provision (for homeless persons under Part III of the 1985 Housing Act). This is despite the fact that parents have an entitlement to these benefits. This issue is of particular significance because many people from black and other minority ethnic communities face discrimination within the labour market and are thus more likely to have low incomes. In addition, a lone parent must show that he or she has (a) 'sole responsibility' for the child or that (b) there are serious compelling family or other considerations that make the child's exclusion undesirable;

- in the past many children, mainly from Pakistan and Bangladesh, were refused entry clearance on the grounds that they were not 'related as claimed' to the sponsoring parents. Many who have subsequently been able to prove their relationship through the use of DNA testing but because they are now over 18 are unable to join their families. Moreover, the recognition of past mistakes in refusing entry clearance has not tempered the stringency with which these decisions are made. The Home Office has stated that they will admit young people only if they are unmarried and can show they have remained 'necessarily' dependent on their parents rather than dependent 'by choice'. It also appears that those who are now over 23 years of age will not be allowed entry to the UK;

- children who are in the UK with 'undocumented' parents (persons who have overstayed, entered the UK illegally, or are of other status) might not have access to provisions such as health care and benefits. Because their parents are unlikely to approach the local authority housing department, for fear of exposure (a recent court decision in respect of the London Borough of Tower Hamlets allows housing departments to investigate the immigration status of applicants), undocumented children may live in crowded and substandard private rented accommodation. They are affected adversely by the low income of their parents and the long hours they work in exploitative, insecure employment[3]. Children born in the UK might be stateless if they cannot acquire their parents' nationality. If they do qualify, they might not register for citizenship because they are not aware of their entitlement, or they are fearful of disclosing the status of their parents, or they assume (wrongly) that they have citizenship already;

- the rates of refusals for visitors from predominantly black countries are much higher than countries such as the USA, Canada and Australia. As a result, children seeking to keep in touch with family members - including parents and siblings - suffer discrimination in maintaining family life. For example, the refusal rates for Jamaican visitors have been as much as 48 times higher than for American visitors. Despite the fact that visitors from India must obtain entry clearance before arriving in the UK the refusal rates for them are still eight times higher than for American visitors;

- asylum seekers of all ages receive only 90% of the rate of income support benefit available to others;

- asylum seekers who are granted ELR (Exceptional Leave to Remain) are not allowed to apply for family reunion until four years after they are granted leave, unless compelling exceptional circumstances prevail. As a result, children outside the UK whose parents have ELR, and children with ELR themselves, suffer discrimination in relation to other children since it is recognised that being with their parents and family is the most beneficial option for children.

Compliance with Article 2, the right of all children and young people to be free from discrimination, requires that:

● children should be able to acquire nationality through their unmarried father. The requirement that parents be married in order that a father be able to transmit nationality to his child should be revoked;

● asylum seekers should receive the full rates of income support. Entitlement to income support for 16-17 year-olds should be restored, and paid at the rate payable to those aged 25 and over;

● non-EU citizens who are settled in the UK should have the same rights as EU citizens to freedom of movement, settlement and study within the EU.

# 4 The best interests of the child
## Article 3

4.1 Article 3 places a duty on all those involved in taking decisions which affect children to ensure that '*the best interests of the child shall be a primary consideration*'. But immigration law does not normally take into account the best interests of children when decisions are made which affect them; there is provision for it doing so only when compelling or compassionate circumstances warrant special consideration. Use of this provision for special circumstances is discretionary; there are no rules which give force to the best interests' principle embodied in Article 3.

4.2 The problems for children created by the failure of immigration law to respect their best interests in making decisions are illustrated in the following case concerning the deportation of a parent of children who are British citizens (born in the UK before 1983 and so without automatic entitlement to British nationality).

> *Mr Fadele came to the UK from Nigeria in 1972 as a student. He married and had three children here. When he had to leave the UK the children remained here with their mother until she was killed in a car crash in 1986. Mr Fadele made arrangements to come to the UK to care for his children. He gained permission to enter the country temporarily but, despite representations from the children's school, community organisations and social workers that the children would be at serious risk if they were to be removed to Nigeria, he was not granted permission to stay here. So they left for Nigeria, where they lived in a broken shack with 12 other relatives, and with no electricity, sanitary facilities or running water. They were unable to attend school because of language difficulties and, as a result of their lack of immunity to local conditions, contracted several serious illnesses requiring hospitalisation. It was only after an application to the European Commission of Human Rights that the UK Government agreed to allow Mr Fadele to return to live in this country[4].*

This family and others in similar circumstances are faced with a stark choice. Either the parents are forced to leave without the children, or the children are forced to leave the country in which they have grown up, in order to remain with their parents.

4.3 Under section 1(1) of the Children Act in England and Wales and under comparable legislation in Scotland, the child's welfare must be paramount in court decisions about his or her upbringing. Since decisions of the Home Office, entry clearance officers and the Immigration Appellate Authorities are subject to review by the courts it is arguable that their decisions should be subject to the requirements of the Children Act. The children's welfare was an important factor in the success of a recent appeal against the refusal of an entry clearance officer to issue a Bangladeshi mother of two with entry clearance[5]. The adjudicator recommended that the mother be granted entry clearance in spite of the fact that under immigration law she had been ineligible for settlement since she was the sponsor's second wife in a polygamous marriage. The reason given was that it 'is very important to have regard to the interests of the children. It would be extremely harsh to separate a three-year-old child from her mother'.

**4.4** Immigration detention centres where children might be detained have no special facilities or services for children. As a result, unaccompanied children at the ports of entry can be interviewed under circumstances that add needlessly to their fear and distress.

**Compliance with Article 3.1, the duty to consider the 'best interests' of the child in any decision affecting the child, requires that:**

● **the principle that children's best interests must be a 'primary consideration' in all decisions affecting them should be integrated into immigration and nationality law, policy and practice. Clear standards and guidelines regarding the application of this principle should be established for entry clearance officers, immigration officers, adjudicators and Immigration Tribunals;**

● **children should never be detained in immigration detention centres;**

● **all unaccompanied refugee children under 18 should be considered 'children in need' under section 17 of the Children Act 1989 in England and Wales and so eligible for local authority services. Similar safeguards should be included in Scottish and N Ireland legislation. At the ports of entry unaccompanied 16 and 17 year-olds should be referred to the local authority social services department;**

● **when providing care and accommodation for unaccompanied refugee children, local authorities must take careful account of the child's refugee experience. An assessment should be made by a person with expertise in the effects of the refugee experience on children. Preferably they should be from the child's background.**

# 5 The right to be consulted
## Article 12

**5.1** Article 12.1 states that children *'who are capable of forming [their] own views [have] the right to express those views freely in all matters affecting [them], the views of the child being given due weight in accordance with the age and maturity of the child'*. Article 12.2 goes on to require that children *'be provided with the opportunity to be heard in any judicial or administrative proceedings affecting (them)'*.

**5.2** In general, immigration procedures do not provide for children to be heard, either directly or through a representative, when decisions are made which affect them. This happens only if they are the subject of the proceedings. Where their views are heard it is rare that they are taken seriously. Local authority social services staff providing care for unaccompanied refugee children often lack the skills and understanding to ensure that refugee children's views and wishes are articulated clearly and that a proper assessment is made of their needs. Children are often afraid to tell the truth about their history and may not know whether their parents and other relatives are dead or alive. Placements may be inappropriate, as when - for example - a refugee child is placed in a family with insufficient regard to the child's language, culture or religion or to the carer's understanding of their experience as a refugee. In addition, unaccompanied children do not know about the society into which they have come. If they are not provided with information they will be unaware of the options available to them. In such circumstances, the expression of their wishes will be partial and uninformed.

**5.3** At entry clearance posts children aged 10 and upwards wishing to join their families in the UK may be interviewed on their own. Any statements they make which contradict other family members' statements can be used to deny the application. Entry clearance officers receive no training in interviewing children and there is no way of ensuring that the children understand fully the questions put to them.

**5.4** The right to express a view, as required by Article 12, can be exercised only if the child has access to appropriate information with which to form a view. But for many children involved in nationality and immigration proceedings, the information that they do have is unsuitable and inaccessible. For example:

● the Political Asylum Questionnaire and accompanying letter that are given to asylum seekers are available only in English whereas in some other countries they are available in the main refugee languages. This restricts a refugee child's ability to understand the process and to present the best possible case;

● interpreters who act for the Immigration and Nationality Department do not receive training in interpreting for children or for refugees. They are not necessarily professionally trained interpreters, and this has implications for the quality of interpretation;

● since bilingual teachers are not usually available in schools, children whose first language is not English and who are not yet fluent are less able to communicate and understand fully.

Compliance with Article 12, the full participation of children in immigration and nationality proceedings which affect them, requires that:

- provision for the views and wishes of affected children to be heard either directly or through representatives should be mandatory in all immigration hearings affecting the child. This should take account of the different ways children may express themselves according to age, culture, language and ability;

- whenever children are interviewed by entry clearance officers, immigration officers, or staff at the Asylum Division of the Home Office, the following should apply: the interviewing officer must be properly trained in interviewing children; the child should be accompanied by a trusted adult or representative; the surroundings should be agreeable to the child and not intimidating; where interpretation is required the interpreter should be skilled in interpreting for children and provided with clear written guidelines;

- children should be provided with written and accessible information in their own language regarding any application to the Immigration and Nationality Department.

# 6 The right to a nationality and identity

## Articles 7 and 8

**6.1** Article 7.1 stresses the right of children to a name and nationality. It states that every child '*shall have the right from birth to a name, the right to acquire a nationality and, as far as possible, the right to know and be cared for by his or her parents*'. The Article further states, in 7.2, that the Government must implement these rights '*in accordance with their national law and their obligations under international instruments, in particular where the child would otherwise be stateless*'.

**6.2** The British Nationality Act 1981 removed the automatic entitlement of children born in the UK to British nationality. Children born in the UK since 1 January 1983 are stateless if (a) neither of their married parents are settled in the UK or are British citizens **and** (b) the child cannot acquire the nationality of the parent(s). Children of parents who are not settled or British must be aged between 10 and 21 in order to register for British citizenship. This means that a child may remain stateless for the first 10 years of his or her life. It is difficult to reconcile this with the requirement in Article 7.2 to ensure the right to acquire a nationality, especially where a child would otherwise be stateless.

**6.3** Children born in the UK to 'undocumented' parents might not register for citizenship throughout their childhood due to fear of the consequences. When an individual applies for citizenship, the immigration status of his or her family will normally be investigated.

**6.4** Article 8 places a duty on the State to '*respect the right of a child to preserve his or her identity including nationality, name and family relations [and] where a child is illegally deprived of some or all elements of his or her identity, to assist in the re-establishment of that identity*'. For some children in the UK, however, this does not happen. When parents of children who are either British citizens or were born in the UK (who cannot be removed solely because of their parents' status) are deported or removed and the children leave the country with their parents, they are effectively deprived of vital aspects of their identity - home, friends, school, culture, language. Action which results in the parents leaving and the children staying is inconsistent with the right of a child to '*know and be cared for by his or her parents*' (Article 7).

Compliance with Article 7, the right to acquire a nationality, requires that:

- children who are stateless at birth, or who are born to refugee parents who cannot claim for the child the citizenship of their country of origin, should have a right to register for citizenship immediately;

- all children born in the UK since 1983 who qualify to register for citizenship should be able to do so without that having an adverse impact on their parents or other relatives.

# 7 The right to family life and family reunion

## Articles 9 and 10

**7.1** Article 9 states that children have a right '*not to be separated from [their] parents against their will, except when competent authorities ... determine ... that such separation is necessary for the best interests of the child*'. They also have the right, if separated from one or both parents, '*to maintain personal relations and direct contact with both parents on a regular basis, except if it is contrary to the child's best interests*'. Enforced separation imposed by the deportation or removal of parents constitutes a clear breach of this principle.

**7.2** The European Court of Human Rights decided in the case of Berrehab (1988 11 EHRR 322) that an infringement of a child's human right to remain in contact with both parents would occur if a parent is deported because of the breakdown of the their marriage[6]. Under British immigration rules, a spouse from abroad will be granted leave to remain for a year initially, and might be allowed to stay permanently at the end of that year. If, however, the marriage breaks down before settlement has been granted, the presence of any child of the marriage does not give the parent any claim to stay, though this might be granted if both parents are in close contact with the child. If the parent is deported but wishes to remain in contact with the child through visits to the UK, this is extremely difficult, if not impossible.

**7.3** The Home Office will not normally revoke a deportation order until the person has been out of the UK for at least three years and, even after revocation, the person still has to satisfy immigration officials that he or she complies with the criteria for entry. For visitors, for example, this means showing an intention to leave at the end of a specified period. Immigration officers generally assume that the presence of a child constitutes an incentive to remain and might, therefore, refuse the parent entry as a visitor.

**7.4** The Asylum and Immigration Appeals Act 1993 removes the right of appeal for visitors who are refused entry to the UK. As significant numbers of visitors have appealed successfully against a refusal in the past there is a risk of further wrong refusals now that this mechanism for scrutinising decisions has been abolished.

**7.5** Article 10 confirms the right to family life. Applications by parents or children to enter or leave a State for the purpose of family reunion are to be dealt with in a '*positive, expeditious and humane manner*'. Where a child has parents residing in different countries, he or she has the right to maintain direct contact with the absent parent.

**7.6** In the UK there are various rules governing family reunion for children applying to join parent(s) who are British citizens or settled in the UK. The way in which the law operates discriminates against children from some countries, particularly those in the Indian subcontinent. Children attempting to exercise the right to family reunion need to apply for entry clearance at a British embassy or high commission before travelling from abroad. Queues have been allowed to build up in most countries of the Indian subcontinent. Throughout the 1970s and 1980s the norm was a wait of over a year between application and interview. At its peak the waiting time in Bangladesh was three years. At the end of December 1991 the queues were between 3-5 months' long, but those who had applied previously and been refused permission had to wait between 6-12 months before their re-application was dealt with. Such discriminatory practice means that family applications are not dealt with in a '*humane and expeditious manner*'.

**7.7** In addition to these long delays, there are also very high refusal rates when children apply to join their parents in the UK. In 1990, the applications of 3,890 children from the subcontinent were granted on initial request. 1,150 were rejected, with 530 children appealing successfully against that refusal. This high proportion of refusals found to be wrong may reflect assumptions made by British officials that families are not related as they claim to be, as well as undue emphasis on statements made by family members which reveal alleged discrepancies and on the lack of written documentation.

**7.8** The rules about children joining lone parents state that where both parents are alive, and one parent is applying for the child to join her or him in the UK, that parent must show that he or she has had sole responsibility for the child's upbringing, or that there are compelling family or other considerations rendering the child's exclusion undesirable. It is mainly women from the Caribbean, the Philippines and West Africa who have been affected by this rule. Usually they have left their children in the care of an older relative while they have come to Britain to establish themselves. Although money is sent for the child's support, and contact is maintained, it is clearly not possible for these single mothers to prove sole responsibility. In addition, even minimal contact with the father in the child's home country can be used to refuse the child entry clearance. In practice children under 12 are normally admitted without having to prove this requirement, but the Home Office has refused to incorporate this into the rules.

**7.9** Where children are adopted abroad, by either a UK citizen or a person settled in the UK, the children do not become British citizens automatically, and their right of entry into the UK is subject to proof that (a) the parents can provide support and accommodation without recourse to public funds, (b) there has been a genuine adoption because the natural parents were unable to care for the child, and (c) the adoption was not arranged in order to facilitate the admission of the child to the UK. In some cultures the absence of formal adoption procedures may render it impossible to prove that the adoption has taken place or that the adoption process has been genuine. Furthermore, it is sometimes common practice for a childless person or couple to adopt the child of a relative who can nonetheless care for the child. Euro-centric notions of adoption can, therefore, result in discrimination against children from other cultures.

**7.10** Under the UK Immigration Rules asylum seekers have no right to family reunion, no matter how long it takes for a decision to be made on their application. Even if they are granted Exceptional Leave to Remain (ELR), on humanitarian grounds, normally they are not allowed to be joined by their immediate family for a further four years. The Secretary of State has discretion to grant permission for family reunion on compassionate grounds in exceptional circumstances, but this discretion is rarely exercised. The effect of this rule is to deprive children of their right to be cared for by both parents. When children are forced to be separated from either or both parents, they are at risk of additional pressure to that imposed by the trauma of exile.

**7.11** The harsh application of immigration rules have, in some cases, deprived children of their parent's care forever.

*Mr Turan Pekoz was an asylum seeker from Turkey. He had spent three years in Britain without a decision being taken on his case. He knew that when a decision had been reached he still could not be reunited with his family for four years. By that time some of his children would have reached the age of 18, would no longer be dependants, and would not be allowed to join him. On 12 March 1993 he became so distressed during an interview at the Immigration and Nationality Division that he set himself alight. He died four days later[7].*

The Home Office have ruled that refugees from the former Yugoslavia, who entered the country in privately- sponsored convoys, have no right to family reunion.

*Mrs Lejla Ibramovic, aged 39, was a Bosnian Muslim. She was brought into Britain in late 1992 before visa requirements were introduced to stop charitable organisations bringing refugees to the UK from the former Yugoslavia. With her were her daughter Dzenana, born in March 1992, and her son Mirza. Her husband applied for a visa to join her but was turned down, without explanation, by the British Embassy in Zagreb. During the night of 4 December 1993 Lejla Ibramovic became so distressed at the continuing separation from her husband, and the difficulties of trying to settle in the UK, that she killed herself. Her husband has now been admitted to the UK to join his children since, after their mother's death, they had become unaccompanied minors[8].*

**7.12** No statistical information is available about the number of people with ELR who have been refused family reunion, and of the resulting number of children deprived of the right to be cared for by both parents, but all refugee agencies and refugee community groups know of such cases. The Medical Foundation for the Care of Victims of Torture is currently having to provide therapeutic counselling for children suffering acute distress at being separated from one or both of their parents. They include Somali children who have been brought to the UK by young male relatives. The Government considers that these young men, some of whom are themselves only teenagers, are competent in the care of the children, and is therefore refusing permission for their parents to join them[9].

## ACTION REQUIRED FOR COMPLIANCE

**Compliance with Articles 9 and 10, the rights of all children and young people to family life, requires that:**

- **the parents of children who are UK citizens should not be deported or removed;**
- **British immigration laws should be changed, to give people settled in the UK the absolute right to be joined here by partners and children and, where appropriate, other family members. Specifically:**

  **- there should be a positive presumption that children and parents are 'related as claimed' and that children should be admitted for settlement. This presumption should be set aside only if the contrary is established to a high degree of probability;**

  **- all over-age children who have previously been denied entry clearance wrongfully and have since re-applied for entry should be allowed to come to the UK;**

  **- delays in dealing with applications should be cut, and maximum waiting times established;**

  **- the tests of 'support and accommodation without recourse to public funds' and 'sole responsibility' should be abolished;**

  **- the rule that children adopted overseas will be granted entry clearance only if there has been a genuine adoption because the natural parents are unable to care for the child should be amended to recognise that in other cultures there may be no formal adoption procedures and it may be customary for childless people to adopt children whose parents are nonetheless able to care for them;**

- **all unaccompanied refugee children, whether they have full refugee status or exceptional leave to remain, should be granted family reunion. Where parents are dead or missing, this should include siblings and members of their extended family;**

- **all refugees who have been granted exceptional leave to remain should be able to apply to bring to the UK their children who remain in their country of origin, without waiting four years or being obliged to show exceptional compassionate circumstances;**

- **asylum seekers separated from a spouse or dependent child, whose cases are still undecided after six months, should be brought into an accelerated determination procedure, in order to speed up reunion with their family[10].**

# 8 The right to privacy
## Article 16

**8.1** Article 16 requires that '*no child shall be subjected to arbitrary or unlawful interference with their privacy, family, home or correspondence, nor to unlawful attacks on his/her honour or reputation*'.

**8.2** Village visits, particularly in Bangladesh, have long been used by entry clearance officers to determine whether or not children applying to join their family are related as claimed to their sponsors in the UK. While the advent of DNA testing has resulted in a considerable reduction in the number of these village visits, occasions still arise where visits may prove to be the only option remaining to establish a claimed relationship.

**8.3** Village visits conducted by the British authorities often use methods that are highly intrusive and constitute a clear violation of a child's right to privacy, with family belongings and correspondence often examined insensitively. Attempts to prevent these 'official' invasions of privacy are viewed as admissions that a family has something to hide.

### ACTION REQUIRED FOR COMPLIANCE

**Compliance with Article 16, the right to privacy for all children, requires that village visits should be undertaken by entry clearance officers only with the consent of the family. A family's wish to maintain its private life should not be used as a ground for justifying the refusal of entry clearance.**

# 9 The rights of young refugees
## Article 22

**9.1** Article 22 states that the Government must take appropriate measures to ensure that a child who is seeking refugee status must '*receive appropriate protection and humanitarian assistance in the enjoyment of the applicable rights set forth in the present Convention and in other international instruments to which [the Government is a party]*'. In other words, young refugees, whether alone or accompanied by adults, are entitled to all the rights in the Convention as well as to rights contained in international instruments to which the UK is party. One of these places the Government under a duty to co-operate with the UN and other agencies in tracing family members.

**9.2** Refugee children are entitled to the same high level of protection as any other child deprived of his or her family; unaccompanied children, deprived of parents and country, constitute a particularly vulnerable group. There is widespread concern from both non-governmental organisations and statutory providers of services that many of the rights in the Convention are not being protected adequately in respect of refugee children. They live in a variety of settings: with compatriot families in the community, in sibling groups, in local authority accommodation. Many are not in receipt of local authority services or are provided with accommodation that is not suited to their needs.

**9.3** Statistical information about young refugees is scant. In the past only port applications for asylum were recorded, but recently the Asylum Division of the Home Office instituted a system to identify 'in-country' applications by children. However, the Social Services Inspectorate (SSI) does not monitor the numbers of unaccompanied refugee children provided with services by the local authority and there is a lack of inter-departmental co-operation by those central government departments whose policies might impinge on refugee children. All these failings result in a serious lack of accountability, inadequate implementation of child care principles espoused by the Children Act and other legislation, and no effective monitoring of the extent to which the rights of refugee children are being respected.

**9.4** Unaccompanied children are without anyone who has 'parental responsibility'. This includes children living in the community while being accommodated by the local authority. As noted previously (para 3.2), all children who arrive in England and Wales without parents - including those over 16 - should be considered as 'children in need' under section 17 of the Children Act 1989. They would thus qualify for a range of local authority services. Failure to provide support and services for refugee children represents a breach of the obligations under Article 20 to ensure that '*a child temporarily or permanently deprived of his or her family environment ... shall be entitled to special protection and assistance provided by the state*'.

**9.5** Despite a directive of January 1991 from the SSI that unaccompanied children are the responsibility of the authority to which they present themselves, some local authorities are still reluctant to accommodate unaccompanied children of any age on the grounds that, for instance, the children are the responsibility of another authority where they have stayed previously. The main reason for local authority reluctance to accommodate has been the financial burden involved. For example, £1 million was spent by Hillingdon SSD in 1991. An added complication is the fact that, in most cases, it is impossible to plan in advance for refugee children. The recent release of central government funds to local authorities caring for unaccompanied children is welcome, but this welcome is tempered because of the 'triggering threshold' which means that, in order to benefit, a local authority must already be spending considerable sums.

**9.6** At the port of entry into the UK, children aged 16 and over who are identified as unaccompanied are not referred by immigration officers to the local authority. They are left to their own resources unless they get assistance from the Refugee Arrivals Project at Heathrow. Since the definition of a child under the UN Convention is 18, it is clear that those aged 16 and 17 should be offered the same *'special safeguards and care'* (as described in the preamble to the Convention) as are younger children. It is hoped that 16 and 17 year-olds will be included in new measures announced by the Government under which immigration officers will pass details of the arrival of unaccompanied children to the local authority where the children will reside.

**9.7** Article 22 commits the Government to implementing internationally-agreed treaties and standards[11]. The guidelines of the United Nations High Commission for Refugees (UNHCR) on unaccompanied children provide for, among other things:

- the assessment of a child's ability to articulate a 'well-founded fear of persecution' by a child care expert, preferably one from the child's own background;

- the appointment of a legal guardian to 'promote a decision that will be in the minor's best interests';

- where a child cannot articulate a well-founded fear then greater regard must be given to objective factors such as the situation of the child's family, their social/ethnic/religious group, and the conditions prevailing in their country of origin;

- the liberal application of the benefit of the doubt when determining a child's status[12] [13].

**9.8** The new Immigration Rule on the determination of children's applications is a positive development and complies to some degree with these recommendations. However, there is as yet no provision for the assessment of a child's ability to articulate a 'well-founded fear of persecution' or for the liberal application of the benefit of the doubt.

**9.9** The Government is a also party to the Geneva Convention on Refugees. Until recently there have been no special procedures for the treatment of children's applications for asylum. This may be because most children are granted only Exceptional Leave to Remain, rather than full refugee status. Many of the rights that the Geneva Convention grants to full refugees are not available to those with Exceptional Leave to Remain. Children with this immigration status must wait four years to apply for family reunion (see para 7.11); their stay is insecure since they must apply for extension of Exceptional Leave to Remain after one year and again after three years; they do not qualify for UN travel documents and may be unable to leave the UK; they do not qualify for mandatory grants for tertiary education. It is hoped that the new procedures will provide for a fairer assessment of children's claims.

**9.10** It can be argued that the Immigration (Carriers Liability) Act 1987 and policies about visas prevent refugee children (both accompanied and unaccompanied) from coming to the UK and applying for asylum. Carrier Liability imposes fines on carriers who bring in persons with inadequate documentation. It is well known that refugees are often forced to travel without documents or to use forgeries. There have been cases of wrongful returns of young refugees by airlines anxious to avoid the heavy fines[14]. These practices are in breach of Article 33 of the Geneva Convention which states that no State Party will return a refugee to a territory where his or her life or liberty are threatened due to his or her race, religion, nationality, membership of a particular social group or political opinion.

**9.11** Most countries from which refugees come are listed by the UK as requiring a visa for entry. Other countries are often added to the list as soon as people start fleeing from them. It is often impossible and dangerous for refugees to acquire visas in their country of origin. This forces them to acquire visas from a neighbouring country. These are normally visitors' visas since there is no such thing as a refugee visa. As a result, when they arrive in the UK, they can be returned to that third country (under the new Immigration Rules and the Dublin Convention) if it is deemed safe for them to do so. No clear criteria have been established regarding unaccompanied children who fall in this category although the responsible Minister has said that children will not be returned unless it is established that 'there would be proper and satisfactory reception arrangements in another country'[15]. The return of children who have already been through the trauma of leaving their own country is inconsistent with an obligation to ensure that *'in all actions ... the best interests of the child shall be a primary consideration'* (Article 3).

**9.12** It can also be argued that UK regulations contravene the European Convention of Human Rights. Article 8 of this Convention states that: 'Everyone has the right to respect for his private and family life ...'. Making a child wait four years before being united with their parents is a denial of this right. Article 3 of the European Convention states that: 'No one shall be subjected to torture or to inhuman or degrading punishment or treatment'. The effect of the Immigration (Carriers Liability) Act is that refugee children can be returned to a country where they will be at risk of torture or inhuman punishment and from which they will be unable to escape.

**9.13** Children brought into the UK by ad hoc organisations, such as those operating recently in Bosnia, are not being provided with *'appropriate protection'* (Article 22). These organisations may have no child care expertise and the Government has not acted to ensure that each child is identified properly, that contact is maintained with their family, and that the situation into which the child goes meets the standards set out in the Convention. There is much that can be learnt from previous evacuations[16].

**9.14** The Refugee Council's Working Group on Unaccompanied Refugee Children and Adolescents has put forward proposals to the Department of Health and the Home Office for the establishment of a resource service which would provide expert consultation and information to local authorities and voluntary groups providing care for such children. This would contribute considerably to improved practice for refugee children and, as such, would be consistent with the requirement to promote their best interests. This proposal has not yet been implemented. Nor has there been any clear acknowledgement of the need identified by the local authority associations and the childcare professionals who support the proposal.

**9.15** The most recent legislation relating to asylum is the Asylum and Immigration Appeals Act 1993. During its passage through Parliament a number of key organisations concerned with refugee children lobbied extensively for amendments, some of which were incorporated by the House of Lords. In response, the Government has recently introduced several measures to improve the welfare of unaccompanied refugee children. These include the provision of funds to set up a panel of advisors for unaccompanied children; a new Immigration Rule on the treatment of asylum applications by children; the prioritising of children's applications; a protocol whereby immigration officers will inform social services of the arrival of a child in their area; the publication of guidance on unaccompanied children for local authorities; and the provision of some central government funding to local authorities caring for significant numbers of unaccompanied children (see para 9.5).

**9.16** Whilst these measures are welcome, the key organisations are concerned that the panel of advisors has not been given a statutory basis. It is also welcome that the Asylum Division of the Home Office has indicated a willingness to train a core group of officers in interviewing skills with children. There is also the possibility that the Asylum Division could make use of assessments of child applicants provided by independent experts to assist them in coming to a decision, and that written guidance on interpreting for children could be given to interpreters. The implementation of these measures would ensure compliance with Article 22.

**9.17** On the other hand, many provisions of the Asylum and Immigration Appeals Act are likely to worsen the position of both accompanied and unaccompanied refugee children. These include:

- all children, both dependants of applicants and child applicants themselves, can be fingerprinted as part of applying for asylum. This appears to be in breach of the right not to *'be subjected to arbitrary ... interference with his or her privacy'* (Article 16). In response to lobbying, the Government introduced an amendment to require the presence of an 'appropriate' adult when a child under 16 is fingerprinted;

- although a right of appeal has been extended to all asylum seekers, the timescale for appealing is very tight - two days only for some port applicants and 10 days for in-country applicants. Such restrictive deadlines prohibit any effective capacity to construct an appeal and limits implementation of the right to *'be provided with the opportunity to be heard in any judicial or administrative proceedings affecting the child'* (Article 12.2);

- asylum seekers will not be accepted as homeless if they have 'any accommodation, however temporary' available to them. Those accepted as homeless will be given temporary accommodation only. This includes refugees with dependent children and 16 and 17 year-olds on their own. Therefore, homeless 16 and 17 year-olds might no longer be considered vulnerable for the purposes of housing legislation. Many young refugees under 18 are currently in bed and breakfast accommodation and long-term hostels with no support. Those needing housing when leaving local authority accommodation or care might also be affected although, under section 20 of the Children Act, local authorities have a duty to provide housing for 16 and 17 year-olds whose welfare is otherwise 'likely to be seriously prejudiced'. The tightening of these rules for housing are in breach of Article 2 because families who are not refugees do not have to be 'roofless' before being accepted as homeless. The children are being discriminated against also, because of the duty in Article 27.3 to provide 'in case of need ... material assistance and support programmes, particularly with regard to nutrition, clothing and housing';

- visa requirements have been introduced for passengers in transit who are nationals of selected countries on the UK visa list. Since this amendment of the Immigration (Carriers Liability) Act 1987 will place more obstacles in the path of refugee children fleeing persecution it constitutes a breach of the duty to promote the *'best interests'* of the child (Article 3);

- a new category - claims 'without foundation' - has been created. These cases will be put on a fast-track procedure under which applicants will have no right of appeal against decisions made by special adjudicators. Claims 'without foundation' are those which it is believed do not 'raise an issue as to the UK's obligations under the Geneva Convention on Refugees who are "frivolous or vexatious"'. This means that people whose claim for asylum is based on grounds not listed in the Geneva Convention, for example people fleeing civil war and danger, could be considered 'without foundation'[17]. Many people, including child applicants who previously would have been granted Exceptional Leave to Remain because it was not safe for them to return to their country, could now be denied any status at all and be subject to removal. This provision, too, appears to take no account of the *'best interests'* of the child (Article 3).

### ACTION REQUIRED FOR COMPLIANCE

**Compliance with Article 22, the right to special protection and assistance for refugee children, requires that:**

- **all unaccompanied refugee children, whether they have full refugee status or Exceptional Leave to Remain, should be granted family reunion. Where parents are dead or missing, this should include siblings and members of their extended family;**

- **when children are being brought into the UK due to an emergency situation in their home country (as has recently occurred with children from Bosnia), the Foreign Office, the Department of Health and the Home Office should co-operate to ensure that proper documentation is obtained on the children before departure and that they receive appropriate care when in the UK. The Government should have** regard to the joint UNICEF-UNHCR statement regarding the evacuation of children from emergency situations;

- the Asylum and Immigration Appeals Act 1993, the Immigration Rules, and the Appeal Procedure Rules should be amended as follows: (a) asylum seekers should have their rights to priority housing restored; (b) all asylum seekers should have a minimum of 14 days within which to appeal against a refusal of their application for asylum; (c) the right of appeal for visitors refused entry to the UK should be restored; (d) the right to apply for judicial review in all immigration appeals should be restored; (e) refugee children should under no circumstances be fingerprinted as part of their asylum application or the application of a parent or guardian; (f) the Immigration Rules accompanying the Act should be amended in line with the criticisms of the UN High Commissioner for Refugees; (g) the category of asylum claims 'without foundation', along with fast-track procedures, should be abolished and Exceptional Leave to Remain should be granted to all asylum applicants who do not qualify for full refugee status when it is unsafe for them to return to their country of origin; (h) asylum seekers who arrive via a third country should be entitled to have their claim considered in the UK;

- the Immigration (Carriers Liability) Act 1987 should be repealed. Refugee children travelling without proper documentation should not be denied entrance to the UK. In accordance with the Geneva Convention on Refugees, they should be allowed to claim asylum;

- the Refugee Council's proposals for a resource service for those who are caring for unaccompanied refugee children should be implemented;

- the Home Office statistics on the numbers of children under 18 applying for asylum should also indicate the sex and age of the children;

- the Social Services Inspectorate should monitor the numbers of unaccompanied children in receipt of local authority services;

- when a refugee child who is the dependant of an asylum applicant becomes orphaned, the child should become the applicant. Their application would then be treated in the same way as that of an unaccompanied child, as provided for under the Immigration Rules.

# 10 The rights of child victims
## Article 39

10.1 Article 39 places a duty on the State to *'take all appropriate measures to promote the physical and psychological recovery and social integration of a child victim of any form of neglect, exploitation, or abuse; torture or any other form of cruel, inhuman or degrading treatment or punishment; or armed conflicts'*.

10.2 All refugee children are suffering from the cumulative effects of some form of violence - be it torture, imprisonment, harassment, civil war, or the loss or death of parents and other relatives. In addition, they suffer from the loss of home, friends and culture when they come to the UK. They might then encounter racist violence and discrimination for the first time. At school they might receive no support for integration, and have little or no specialist help in learning English. If parents are themselves suffering from the effects of violence and the shock of adapting to a new environment, they might be unable to offer emotional support to their children. In extreme cases the radical change in their parents' behaviour might result in children becoming disoriented and neglected. The apparent resilience of refugee children often masks their inner suffering and their real needs. For unaccompanied children, the loss of their parents imposes additional difficulties and suffering. Some children might act out their feelings in anti-social ways, leaving them even more marginalised and stigmatised. If their needs and suffering continue unrecognised, appropriate responses become more difficult to assess and provide.

10.3 With few exceptions, most local authorities do not provide the specialist treatment needed for children with a refugee background. The Medical Foundation for the Care of Victims of Torture, a voluntary organisation, provides therapeutic treatment for child and adolescent refugees. But they can see a limited number of children only. In the first half of 1993 they provided counselling to 11 unaccompanied children. According to the Foundation, a child's refugee background may seriously affect their school life if they are not provided with the opportunity to deal with the issues, and the cause of their problems is likely to go unrecognised by teachers and others involved in their case[18].

### ACTION REQUIRED FOR COMPLIANCE

Compliance with Article 39, the duty to ensure the rights of child victims, requires that:

- community health services are properly resourced to cater for the mental health needs of refugee children;
- professionals such as teachers, health workers and social workers who work with refugee children need specific training in order to be sensitive to the children's special requirements.

# Summary of action required for compliance

1 Compliance with Article 2, the right of all children and young people to be free from discrimination, requires that:

● children should be able to acquire nationality through their unmarried father. The requirement that parents be married in order that a father be able to transmit nationality to his child should be revoked (Article 7 and Article 2);

● asylum seekers should receive the full rates of income support. Entitlement to income support for 16 and 17 year-olds should be restored, and paid at the rate payable to those aged 25 and over (Article 2);

● non-EU citizens who are settled in the UK should have the same rights as EU citizens to freedom of movement, settlement and study within the EU.

2 Compliance with Article 3.1, the duty to consider the 'best interests' of the child in any decision affecting the child, requires that:

● the principle that children's best interests must be a 'primary consideration' in all decisions affecting them should be integrated into immigration and nationality law, policy and practice. Clear standards and guidelines regarding the application of this principle should be established for entry clearance officers, immigration officers, adjudicators and Immigration Tribunals;

● children should never be detained in immigration detention centres;

● all unaccompanied refugee children under 18 should be considered 'children in need' under section 17 of the Children Act 1989 in England and Wales and so eligible for local authority services. Similar safeguards should be included in Scottish and N Ireland legislation. At the ports of entry unaccompanied 16 and 17 year-olds should be referred to the local authority social services department;

● when providing care and accommodation for unaccompanied refugee children, local authorities must take careful account of the child's refugee experience. An assessment should be made by a person with expertise in the effects of the refugee experience on children. Preferably they should be from the child's background.

3 Compliance with Article 12, the right to full participation of children in immigration and nationality proceedings which affect them, requires that:

● provision for the views and wishes of affected children to be heard either directly or through representatives should be mandatory in all immigration hearings affecting the child. This should take account of the different ways children may express themselves according to age, culture, language and ability;

● whenever children are interviewed by entry clearance officers, immigration officers, or staff at the Asylum Division of the Home Office, the following should apply: the interviewing officer must be properly trained in interviewing children; the child should be accompanied by a trusted adult or representative; the surroundings should be agreeable to the child and not intimidating;

where interpretation is required the interpreter should be skilled in interpreting for children and provided with clear written guidelines;

● children should be provided with written and accessible information in their own language regarding any application to the Immigration and Nationality Department.

4 Compliance with Article 7 requires that:

● children who are stateless at birth, or who are born to refugee parents who cannot claim for the child the citizenship of their country of origin, should have a right to register for citizenship immediately;

● all children born in the UK since 1983 who qualify to register for citizenship should be able to do so without that having an adverse impact on their parents or other relatives.

5 Compliance with Articles 9 and 10, the rights of all children and young people in relation to their family life requires that:

● the parents of children who are UK citizens children should not be deported or removed;

● British immigration laws should be changed, to give people settled in the UK the absolute right to be joined here by partners and children and, where appropriate, other family members. Specifically: there should be a positive presumption that children and parents are 'related as claimed' and that children should be admitted for settlement. This presumption should be set aside only if the contrary is established to a high degree of probability; all over-age children who have previously been denied entry clearance wrongfully and have since re-applied for entry should be allowed to come to the UK; delays in dealing with applications should be cut, and maximum waiting times should be established; the tests of 'support and accommodation without recourse to public funds' and 'sole responsibility' should be abolished; the rule that children adopted overseas will be granted entry clearance only if there has been a genuine adoption because the natural parents are unable to care for the child should be amended to recognise that in other cultures there may be no formal adoption procedures and it may be customary for childless people to adopt children whose parents are able to care for them;

● all unaccompanied refugee children, whether they have full refugee status or exceptional leave to remain, should be granted family reunion. Where parents are dead or missing, this should include siblings and members of their extended family;

● all refugees who have been granted exceptional leave to remain should be able to apply to bring to the UK their children who remain in their country of origin, without waiting four years or being obliged to show exceptional compassionate circumstances;

● asylum seekers separated from a spouse or dependent child, whose cases are still undecided after six months, should be brought into an accelerated determination procedure, in order to speed up reunion with their family.

6 Compliance with Article 16, the right to privacy for all children, requires that village visits should be undertaken by entry clearance officers only with the consent of the family. A family's wish to maintain its private life should not be used as

a ground for justifying the refusal of entry clearance.

**7** Compliance with Article 22, the right to special protection and assistance for refugee children, requires that:

- all unaccompanied refugee children, whether they have full refugee status or Exceptional Leave to Remain, should be granted family reunion. Where parents are dead or missing, this should include siblings and members of their extended family;

- when children are being brought into the UK due to an emergency situation in their home country, the Foreign Office, the Department of Health and the Home Office should co-operate to ensure that proper documentation is obtained on the children before departure and that they receive appropriate care when in the UK. The Government should have regard to the joint UNICEF-UNHCR statement regarding the evacuation of children from emergency situations;

- the Asylum and Immigration Appeals Act 1993, the Immigration Rules, and the Appeal Procedure Rules should be amended as follows: (a) asylum seekers should have their rights to priority housing restored; (b) all asylum seekers should have a minimum of 14 days within which to appeal against a refusal of their application for asylum; (c) the right of appeal for visitors refused entry to the UK should be restored; (d) the right to apply for judicial review in all immigration appeals should be restored; (e) refugee children should under no circumstances be fingerprinted as part of their asylum application or the application of a parent or guardian; (f) the Immigration Rules accompanying the Act should be amended in line with the criticisms of the UN High Commissioner for Refugees; (g) the category of asylum claims 'without foundation', along with fast-track procedures, should be abolished and Exceptional Leave to Remain should be granted to all asylum applicants who do not qualify for full refugee status when it is unsafe for them to return to their country of origin; (h) asylum seekers who arrive via a third country should be entitled to have their claim considered in the UK;

- the Immigration (Carriers Liability) Act 1987 should be repealed. Refugee children travelling without proper documentation should not be denied entrance to the UK. In accordance with the Geneva Convention on Refugees, they should be allowed to claim asylum;

- the Refugee Council's proposals for a resource service for those who are caring for unaccompanied refugee children should be implemented;

- the Home Office statistics on the numbers of children under 18 applying for asylum should also indicate the sex and age of the children;

- the Social Services Inspectorate should monitor the numbers of unaccompanied children in receipt of local authority services;

- when a refugee child who is the dependant of an asylum applicant becomes orphaned, the child should become the applicant. Their application would then be treated in the same way as that of an unaccompanied child, as provided for under the Immigration Rules.

**8** Compliance with Article 39, the duty to ensure the rights of child victims, requires that:

- community health services are properly resourced to cater for the mental health needs of refugee children;

- professionals such as teachers, health workers and social workers who work with refugee children need specialist training in order to be sensitive to the children's special requirements.

# References

1. *Unequal migrants: The European Community's unequal treatment of migrants and refugees*, Centre for Research in Ethnic Relations and Joint Council for the Welfare of Immigrants, London (1989)

2. *1992 and all that: civil liberties in the balance*, Spencer M, Civil Liberties Trust, (1990)

3. *Undocumented lives: Britain's unauthorised migrant workers*, Ardill N and Cross N, The Runnymede Trust, London, (1988)

4. Application no. 13078/87

5. Abtera Khatun, TH/413/90 (12 October 1992)

6. European Court of Human Rights, Berrehab v UK (1988) 11 EHRR 322

7. *Independent* (2 and 5 April 1993)

8. *Guardian* (14 December 1993)

9. Information from The Medical Foundation for the Care of Victims of Torture, Children's Counsellor, London (1993)

10. These recommendations are based on information from *Give us a happy ending: how families are kept apart by British immigration law*, Divided Families Campaign, 131-132 Upper Street, London N1

11. *Children or Refugees? A survey of West European policies on unaccompanied refugee children*, Ayotte W and Lown J, Children's Legal Centre, London (1992)

12. *Handbook on procedures and criteria for determining refugee status under the 1951 Convention and 1967 Protocol relating to the status of refugees*, UNHCR, Geneva (1988) paragraphs 213-219.

13. *Guidelines on Refugee Children*, UNHCR, Geneva (1988)

14. *The great divide*, Children's Legal Centre, London, (1992)

15. House of Lords, *Hansard*, vol 547, no 163, col 941 (1 July 1993)

16. *Evacuation of children from conflict areas*, Everett M, Ressler, UNHCR and UNICEF

17. *Briefing on Asylum and Immigration and Appeals Bill*, Joint Council for the Welfare of Immigrants, London (1993)

18. *Integrating refugee children into schools*, Medical Foundation for the Care of Victims of Torture, London (1992)

# CHILDREN'S RIGHTS
## DEVELOPMENT UNIT

**UK Agenda for Children**

## 12 Children and violent conflict: N Ireland

# Contents

> *The unreferenced quotations in this report are comments made during a consultation exercise undertaken by the Children's Rights Development Unit with groups of young people throughout the UK.*

# 1 Introduction

**1.1** The UN Convention on the Rights of the Child obliges the UK Government to protect children in armed conflicts, to ensure their recovery from the ill effects of such conflicts, to protect their civil liberties as well as their lives, and to meet international standards of humanitarian law and juvenile justice. In particular, Article 6.1 asserts the *'inherent right to life'* of every child and Article 6.2 obliges the Government to *'ensure to the maximum extent possible the survival and development of the child'*.

**UK Agenda report 14 on international obligations (page 308) discusses the requirements of the Convention in relation to armed conflicts occurring outside the UK. This report discusses the Convention's obligations in relation to the violence in N Ireland in which children and families have suffered in a way not dissimilar to that experienced in an armed conflict. A final section (para 14) covers the Government's obligations under Article 38.3 in relation to recruitment into the armed forces. (See also UK Agenda Report 9 on youth justice, page 199, for a more detailed discussion of issues relating to young people and criminal justice)**

**1.2** Children have suffered both directly and indirectly as a result of the present conflict in N Ireland. They have been killed and injured; their parents, relatives and friends have been killed, often in their presence; they have been subject to violence and abuse from both security forces and paramilitaries, on both sides of the community divide. Their homes have been subjected to destructive searches and attacks; their civil liberties have been abused or suspended; they have been detained improperly and ill-treated in detention. They have been recruited as informers, soldiers and terrorists; subjected to illegal punishment in the form of shootings, beatings and banishment by paramilitaries; and caught up in a system of formal justice dominated by emergency provisions and special courts, and a punitive 'informal justice system', in which they have been denied due process of law. Their prospects of full health, employment and future development have been damaged. They have become ghettoised and disempowered. In N Ireland, their voice as citizens has not been heard. Elsewhere, children have become not only victims, but targets of war, against every humanitarian principle.

**1.3** Article 38.4 of the UN Convention on the Rights of the Child provides that *'in accordance with their obligations under international humanitarian law to protect the civilian population in armed conflicts, States Parties shall take all feasible measures to ensure protection and care of children who are affected by an armed conflict'*. There are conflicting messages coming from Government about the status of the political violence in N Ireland (euphemistically described as 'the Troubles'), despite more than 3,000 deaths, the heavy military and security force presence, and the 'emergency legislation' prevailing during 25 years of conflict. Hopes of peace, following the publication of a 'Joint Declaration' on 15 December 1993 by the British and Irish Governments, looked faint by the following January, and there is renewed discussion of measures such as the re-introduction of internment by the State. Technically, N Ireland is not in a situation of 'armed conflict', but rather in a long-term state of 'public emergency threatening the life of the nation', thus allowing the State to derogate from (withdraw from guaranteeing) certain rights set out in international treaties.

**1.4** Nevertheless, the violence in N Ireland has had the impact on the whole population of an armed conflict situation. There are three sides to the conflict in N Ireland, all of which are heavily armed and which have inflicted death, injury and humiliating treatment on children and young people as well as on adults; in Britain as well as in Ireland North and South. The spirit of Article 38.4 and of the whole Convention implies that the highest standards of protection should apply to children and young people affected by violent civil strife or conflict.

# 2 Background

## 2.1 Parties to the conflict

**2.1.1** There has been renewed violence in N Ireland since 1968. The nature of the conflict is disputed by the participants. The Government of Ireland Act, passed by the British Parliament in 1920, partitioned Ireland. Since then the British Government and the Republic of Ireland have had conflicting territorial claims to the area. However, they are not at war and have established a forum under the 'Anglo-Irish Agreement' to discuss matters of mutual concern in relation to the territory.

**2.1.2** On 15 December 1993, both the British and the Irish Governments agreed in a Joint Declaration that 'the most urgent and important issue facing the people of Ireland, North and South, and the British and Irish Governments together, is to remove the causes of conflict, to overcome the legacy of history and to heal the divisions which have resulted, recognising that the absence of a lasting and satisfactory settlement of relationships between the peoples of both islands has contributed to continuing tragedy and suffering'.

**2.1.3** 'Parties to the Conflict' have been defined in this report as groups holding political opinions which either explicitly support or explicitly oppose the existence of the State - whether or not they are engaged in overt acts of aggression. There are, broadly, three participant groups:

● **Nationalists:** most adults and children are not participants. They are mainly perceived as Catholic and believe that the British Government has no right to rule in Ireland and that the Irish people as a whole have a right to 'national self-determination'. Some persons perceived as Protestant also regard themselves as Nationalist. There are disputes within the Nationalist community as to the use of force to achieve these aims but the aims themselves are not in dispute. Some Nationalists (mainly middle-class) say that there is nothing which can justify the use of violence. Others (generally referred to as 'Republicans') say that there is no other way to force a British withdrawal. Few adults are active participants, and very few children and young people are. The largest Republican paramilitary group is the Irish Republican Army (IRA).

● **Unionists:** most adults and children are not participants. They are mainly perceived as Protestant and desire, and believe that they have a right, to remain British. Some people who are perceived Catholic also regard themselves as Unionist. There are disputes within the Unionist community about the use of paramilitary force but not about the right of the Unionist community to maintain the State. Some Unionists (mainly middle-class) think that the security forces are the appropriate authority to deal with State security. The police and other security force personnel are drawn almost exclusively from people perceived Protestant. Others (referred to as Loyalists) think the denial by the British government that they are fighting a war has hamstrung them in 'dealing with' the problem, and suggest that a military defeat of the IRA is the solution. Some also believe that, in the event of a betrayal by the British, the Loyalist groups will be the protection of the 'Protestant people'. The Ulster Defence Association (UDA) is the largest Loyalist paramilitary group.

● **British Government:** makes and enforces the laws of the state since Direct Rule replaced the (local) 'Stormont' Government in 1972. The Government maintains that it will remain, as long as a 'majority' of the people in N Ireland wish to be British. It does not accept the view that it has no jurisdiction in the territory and describes the conflict as caused by small groups of 'terrorists', the most threatening of which is the IRA. It is the policy of the British Government to regard paramilitary personnel as criminals and not as soldiers or as politically motivated. However, activities of these groups are considered more serious than so-called 'ordinary crime' and convictions carry tougher sentences following a different trial procedure.

## 2.2 The 'democratic deficit'

**2.2.1** N Ireland is not governed in the same way as the rest of the UK, to the detriment of democracy. Local politics are sectarian, tending to be divided along Nationalist-Unionist lines. People in N Ireland do not have the opportunity of voting for the same political parties as in Great Britain, for example, including the major parties which have a likelihood of forming Government. Many people in both main communities feel alienated from the State and from decision-making. The Opsahl Commission, an independent citizen's inquiry led by the late Professor Torkel Opsahl for 'Initiative 92', describes the situation of lack of accountable local democracy - as the 'democratic deficit'[1].

**2.2.2** The procedure for legislating for N Ireland under Direct Rule is usually by Order in Council of Parliament at Westminster for both 'transferred' matters - criminal law, housing, education, employment, social security etc - and 'excepted or reserved' matters; for example, those of national concern, law and order. Such Orders are in effect primary laws in the form of delegated legislation and, while Standing Advisory Commission on Human Rights (SACHR) admits the need for some delegated legislation, there is little allowance for effective pre-Parliamentary scrutiny. SACHR feels the lack of opportunity for detailed discussion and amendment of the proposed legislation is 'inherently unsatisfactory ... It is generally accepted that human rights are often most at risk when legislation or other governmental measures are introduced by abnormal or 'emergency' procedures'[2].

*'With any conflict you get that, it's there for the protection of the people but sometimes it's turned round into the state protecting itself, that's why it's like that over here now.'*
(18 year-old, N Ireland)

## 2.3 Abuses of human rights in N Ireland

**2.3.1** Abuses of human rights in N Ireland have been all too common and are well-documented by, for example, Amnesty International, the Committee on the Administration of Justice (CAJ), the European Commission and European Court of Human Rights, the N Ireland Human Rights Assembly held in London in April 1992, Helsinki Watch following a mission to N Ireland in 1991, and the Standing Advisory Commission on Human Rights (SACHR)[3][4][5]. Children are entitled to the same protection from abuses of their human rights as are adults but also require extra protection. The protection of everyone's human rights under the European Convention on Human Rights (ECHR), is intimately linked with the protection of the rights of children and young people under the UN Convention on the Rights of the Child.

**2.3.2** The Standing Advisory Commission on Human Rights is pressing for the incorporation of the European Convention into the domestic law of N Ireland and the formation of a Bill of Rights which would protect the human rights of all citizens, regardless of the results of political deliberations[6]. The Opsahl Commission is also of the opinion that a reform in this field is overdue and should be undertaken as soon as possible. There is widespread support for the idea of a Bill of Rights as long as certain safeguards protecting political liberties and traditional principles of the rule of law, such as the right to silence, are included[7].

**2.3.3** The CAJ has drawn up proposals for a Bill of Rights for N Ireland which incorporates international standards of human rights as well as anti-discrimination measures[8]. Brice Dickson, Professor of Law at the University of Ulster, explains that: 'The group (CAJ) believes that, unless the rights of all individuals in N Ireland are guaranteed equal protection, there is little prospect of a lasting solution being found ... A Bill of Rights, in short, is a pre-requisite to permanent peace and justice ... [It] could not only increase people's confidence in the administration of justice but also improve the content of law and make people more physically secure'[9].

## 2.4 The 'informal justice system'

**2.4.1** Due to the peculiar policing problems of certain areas within N Ireland, where the RUC are unable to police the areas 'normally', due to the risk of paramilitary attack, the paramilitary groupings on both sides have taken on this 'policing' role for themselves. Their treatment of young offenders has been described by community groups as 'inhumane and barbaric'. Whilst kneecappings (shootings of limbs) are mainly reserved for young people over the age of 17, those under 17 are frequently 'placarded' (young people accused of offending are forced to stand at public locations with a placard around their neck, giving their name and an outline of their alleged offences) and 'curfewed' (prevented from leaving their homes after a certain time in the evening), both with the threat of actual physical violence. Both the IRA, the Loyalist Ulster Volunteer Force and Ulster Freedom Fighters engage in this policing. The numbers of punishment assaults by Loyalist groups are now rivalling or outnumbering those by Republican groups. The methods employed by these groups have been termed those of the 'informal', 'summary' or 'parallel' justice system.

**2.4.2** Article 37(a) states that the Government shall ensure that 'no child shall be subjected to torture or other cruel, inhuman or degrading treatment or punishment', and Article 37(b) that the Government 'shall ensure that ... no child shall be deprived of his or her liberty unlawfully or arbitrarily'. Article 40.1 recognizes 'the right of every child alleged as, accused of, or recognized as having infringed the penal law to be treated in a manner consistent with the promotion of the child's sense of dignity and worth, which reinforces the child's respect for the human rights and fundamental freedoms of others and which takes into account the child's age and the desirability of promoting the child's

reintegration and the child's assuming a constructive role in society'. In Article 40.4, the child is guaranteed that 'a variety of dispositions, such as care, guidance and supervision orders; counselling; probation; foster care; education and vocational training programmes and other alternatives to institutional care shall be available to ensure that children are dealt with in a manner appropriate to their well-being and proportionate both to their circumstances and the offence'.

**2.4.3** Clearly the existence of what have been described as 'kangaroo courts' is a breach of the child's guaranteed rights, set out in Article 40, to the benefit of due process of law in the administration of justice - to the presumption of innocence, to the involvement of parents and legal assistance, to a fair hearing according to law by a competent, independent, impartial authority or judicial body, to the absence of duress, to conditions of equality in examining witnesses, to appeal; and, in addition, the punishments are disproportionate and breach the standards of Article 40.4.

**2.4.4** Young people who have committed crime within their areas have voluntarily handed themselves over to paramilitary groups so that certain types of punishment can be carried out. The willingness of young people to subject themselves to adult political violence, is particularly worrying. (It may also be difficult to understand unless the perceptions young people have about the legitimacy of State authority are understood.) Community groups have suggested that some young people may perceive an assault is quickly done with, compared to a term in detention; and that the monetary compensation which they are able to receive from the State for injuries can make up for the long-term effects of disability. The young people in question are in general living in a situation of poverty and deprivation.

**2.4.5** Adults in local communities will on occasion support such brutal treatment of youngsters, whether for fear of speaking out, or in desperation at the dangers to other children posed by joyriding and similar activities by local 'hoods' (alleged young offenders), or through lack of alternative policies to establish peace and good order in communities, or through a lack of understanding of the principles of justice such as those set out in the *United Nations Standard Minimum Rules for Administration of Juvenile Justice* (Beijing rules) when applied to young offenders.

# 3 Relevant articles in the Convention

## 3.1 General Principles

**Article 2:** all rights in the Convention must apply without discrimination of any kind irrespective of race, colour, language, religion, national, ethnic or social origin, disability or other status.

**Article 3:** the duty in all actions to consider the best interests of the child.

**Article 12:** the right to express an opinion and to have that opinion taken into account in any matter or procedure affecting the child.

## 3.2 Articles relevant to the violent conflict in N Ireland

**Article 6:** the right to life and development.

**Article 9:** the right to live with one's family unless this is not in the child's best interests and, when separation does take place, the right to maintain contact with both parents on a regular basis.

**Article 13:** the right to freedom of expression and to obtain and impart information.

**Article 15:** the right to freedom of association and peaceful assembly.

**Article 19:** the right to protection from all forms of violence, injury, abuse, neglect or exploitation.

**Article 29:** the duty of the government to direct education at developing the child's fullest personality and talents and promoting respects for human rights.

**Article 30:** the right of children from minority communities to enjoy their own culture and practise their own religion and culture.

**Article 31:** the right to play, rest, leisure, recreation and participation in cultural and artistic activities

**Article 37:** the duty of the Government to prohibit torture, cruel treatment or punishment, capital punishment, life imprisonment, unlawful arrest and deprivation of liberty.

**Article 38:** the duty of the Government to ensure that children under 15 do not take a direct part in hostilities or be recruited into the armed forces.

**Article 39:** the duty of the Government to take measures to ensure that child victims of armed conflict, torture, neglect or exploitation receive treatment for recovery and social re-integration.

**Article 40:** the right of children who have committed offences to respect for human rights and to benefit from all aspects of the due processes of law, including legal or other assistance in preparing and presenting their defence. Recourse to judicial proceedings and institutional placements should be avoided wherever possible and appropriate.

*For the full wording of the articles see the UN Convention on the Rights of the Child, page 311.*

# 4 Impact of the violent conflict on children
## Article 40

**4.1** Since the commencement of the present conflict in N Ireland, over 3,000 people have lost their lives due to paramilitary and security force activity. Unofficial figures indicate that since 1969 more than 400 British soldiers, 180 locally recruited soldiers, 280 police officers, and 2,000 civilians have been killed by paramilitary groups and more than 350 people have been killed by members of the security forces[10]. The UN Convention on the Rights of the Child guarantees protection from violence to children and young people under 18. In particular, Article 6 recognizes that *'every child has the inherent right to life'*. The Government *'shall ensure to the maximum extent possible the survival and development of the child'*. Many children are included within these figures, having been killed as a direct result of either paramilitary or security forces activity. They have suffered injury and loss of friends and family, and psychological trauma as a result of exposure to violence.

**4.2** There has been a growing tendency by those involved in paramilitary and/or sectarian activity to ignore the presence of children during their attacks, and to ignore - or worse, to exploit for the purposes of terror - the impact on children of witnessing such attacks. For example, explosive devices and firearms have been left in or near schools and playgrounds, placing children in danger. Homes have been firebombed, shot at or threatened, including the homes of politicians, with children present. Parents have been killed in front of their young children. In the late summer of 1993, in 13 days, 22 children lost a father or mother. During October 1993, in a traumatic series of incidents, children and young people were injured and bereaved. For instance, in the Loyalist Shankill Road, a busy shopping area, two young girls of seven and 13 were killed in an IRA bombing, and a young woman in her teens was among the victims of masked gunmen in a retaliatory massacre in the 'Rising Sun' pub in Greysteel, in a quiet country area. A girl of 11 was present in the house when gunmen killed her two older brothers on her birthday. A boy of 15 was shot dead by Loyalist paramilitaries along with the driver of his taxi.

> *'It goes from one extreme to the other; if one side attacks somebody on the other, then the side who were attacked plans retaliation and you can almost certainly guarantee that an attack will be made before the end of the evening.'*
> (17 year-old, N Ireland)

**4.3** The Centre for the Study of Conflict at the University of Ulster at Magee has found that information on the impact of the conflict in N Ireland on children is not always readily available. The violence has affected children in a number of ways[11]:

- **deaths:** data on children killed have not always been readily accessible. However, an answer to a Parliamentary Question indicated that to the end of March 1993 some 42 children under the age of 14 had been killed as a result of paramilitary actions;

- **physical injury:** numerous children have been physically injured as a result of the violent conflict in N Ireland. A recent estimate has placed the number seriously injured (requiring hospital treatment) at around 200. This includes those injured as a result of security force action;

- psychological stress: this has been one of the better researched areas[12]. The general picture to emerge is that significant numbers of children have contact with the ongoing violence. For example, one recent survey which reported data from a random sample of children selected from schools from all over the province indicated that almost 20% reported that they had been in or near a bomb explosion, 20.1% said that they had a friend or relative killed or injured, whilst 12% felt that their area was 'not safe to live in'[13]. A considerable body of research also points to the fact that some 10-12% of children in N Ireland may suffer excess levels of stress because of the continuing conflict;

- **death of a parent**: this is an area which is totally under-researched. No official statistics are available to indicate the number of children who have been bereaved because of the conflict in N Ireland. However, press reports indicate that a large proportion of the 3,000 plus people who have died have been men who were also fathers of young children. Reports also indicate that in N Ireland it is not unusual for children to be a witness to such deaths.

**4.4** The right of children and young people to life and maximum development is clearly not being respected in N Ireland, nor in Great Britain, where the deaths of two young boys by a bomb in Warrington caused an outcry. The failure of those in power to find political solutions to 'the Troubles' represents a gross betrayal of children and young people. The urgency of the need to create a lasting political settlement, so that the populace of N Ireland does not endure another 25 years like the last 25 years, has been heightened by both the upsurge in violence and the growing demand for peace. Not until recently, however, has the Government given the matter of seeking a resolution to the political violence in N Ireland priority.

### ACTION REQUIRED FOR COMPLIANCE

**Compliance with Article 6, the right to life, requires that the Government continue to treat the resolution of the violent conflict in N Ireland as a matter of priority, and the protection of all children and young people from harm, including the harm of sectarianism, as an urgent duty.**

# 5 Impact of emergency legislation on children
## Article 40

**5.1** The emergency laws applying to N Ireland - the N Ireland (Emergency Provisions) Act 1978, the N Ireland (Emergency Provisions) Act 1991 (the EPA), and the Prevention of Terrorism (Temporary Provisions) Act 1989 (the PTA) (which also operates in Great Britain) - have had a major impact on young people in N Ireland as they have allowed children and young people, as well as their parents, friends and relatives, to be 'lifted' (picked up by the security forces for screening purposes); arbitrary arrests; incarceration without access to solicitors, parents or others; long periods of interrogation; trial without juries in the 'Diplock' courts (special courts with a single judge of the Crown Court sitting without a jury); and indefinite sentences.

> *'If a peeler stops you and takes your name and address and you tell them something like New Lodge, they give you hassle and lift you.'*
> (17 year-old, N Ireland)

**5.2** Certain grave offences are designated 'scheduled' offences, which are listed in Schedule 1 of the EPA. Most of the scheduled offences are indictable, in which case they are tried before a Diplock Court.

**5.3** Article 40.2(b)(i) states that children have, as a minimum guarantee, the right *'to be presumed innocent until proven guilty according to law.'* This right is described by the Government as a fundamental principle of our criminal justice system. Yet young people arrested under emergency legislation are often reated as if they are guilty, despite the fact that some 70% are later released without charge. This constitutes a breach of Article 40.2(b)(i).

**5.4** Under section 14 of the PTA people suspected of involvement in terrorism can be detained for up to seven days without charge. Young people can be held virtually incommunicado for up to 48 hours. Helsinki Watch explains: 'Persons arrested under section 14(1) of the PTA are subject to detention and interrogation procedures far different from those authorized for arrests under the Police and Criminal Evidence (NI) Order 1989 and the EPA. Under the PTA, the arrestee can be detained for up to 48 hours after arrest and for up to an additional five days upon authorization by the Secretary of State. The power to hold and question a suspect for up to seven days raises serious human rights issues ... In 'Brogan v United Kingdom (1988)' the European Court of Human Rights ruled that a detention under the PTA that exceeded four days and six hours violated Article 5(3) of the European Convention on Human Rights. In response, the United Kingdom has 'derogated' from that section of the Convention, rather than reforming its detention practices'[14].

**5.5** These practices also breach Article 40 of the UN Convention which gives children and young people guarantees of due legal process, including the right, in Article 40.2(b)(ii), *'to be informed promptly and directly of the charges against him or her, and if appropriate through his or her parents or legal guardian, and to have legal or other appropriate assistance in* the preparation and presentation of his or her defence'; and in 40.2(b)(iii) having 'the matter determined without delay ... in a fair hearing according to law, in the presence of legal or other appropriate assistance, and ... in particular, taking into account his or her age or situation, his or her parents or legal guardians'.

**5.6** Article 40.2(b)(iv) guarantees that a child or young person is 'not to be compelled to give testimony or to confess guilt'; this implies that adverse inferences must not be drawn from their silence. Since emergency legislation makes certain offences more serious, it is important that young people are not placed in a position in which silence is incriminating. The 'right to silence' was included within the Terms of Reference of the Royal Commission on Criminal Justice, which favoured its retention. However, in N Ireland, the Police and Criminal Evidence (NI) Order 1989, the right to silence was abrogated allowing adverse inferences to be drawn from an accused's silence. This provision breaches Article 40.2(b)(iv).

**5.7** There are also concerns about the oppression of children and young people in police stations, including by their own parents or by social workers who do not understand the proper role of the 'appropriate adult'. Parents will on occasion bully a child who is in police custody, for example, and advise the young person to admit guilt. Such actions breach Article 40.2(b)(iv).

### ACTION REQUIRED FOR COMPLIANCE

**Compliance with Article 40, the right to due process of law, requires that:**

- **the Government scrutinises the emergency law as well as the criminal law for inconsistency with the Convention, and that legislation and administrative procedures be reformed in accordance with the need of children and young people for special protection and provision;**

- **the Government monitors the administration of juvenile justice to ensure that at all stages children and young people suspected or accused of an offence are treated in a way that promotes their sense of dignity and worth and is in accordance with due process of law;**

- **the length of time that children can be held and questioned under emergency legisltion should be reduced to that applying under the Police and Criminal Evidence (NI) Order 1989.**

# 6 The right to life
## Article 6

## 6.1 Duty to protect children and young people

**6.1.1** Article 6 recognizes that 'every child has the inherent right to life'. Article 38.4 states that 'in accordance with their obligations under international humanitarian law to protect the civilian population in armed conflicts', the government 'shall take all feasible measures to ensure protection and care of children who are affected by an armed conflict'. The killing and injuring of children and young people breaches Articles 6 and 38 of the UN Convention. In respect of paramilitary violence, a state is under an obligation to ensure that rights which it is obliged to guarantee under international law are not infringed by third parties (the doctrine of 'Drittwerkung' or 'Third Party Effect'). This means that the Government must take positive steps to ensure that such infringements as the violation of the right to life by paramilitary groups do not take place.

## 6.2 Use of plastic bullets

**6.2.1** Since 1971, 17 people, seven of them children, aged between 10-15 years, have been killed by rubber and plastic baton rounds in N Ireland, most deaths resulting from injuries suffered when a bullet has hit someone on the head or upper body[15]. 16 of the deaths were those of members of the minority community.

> 'They have no respect for children; the other day the two of us were walking down to his granny's and there was this Brit standing by a jeep firing plastic bullets into this crowd where there were children and I shouted at him and he just looked across at me and laughed.'
> (18 year-old, N Ireland)

**6.2.2** The use of rubber and plastic bullets as a means of maintaining public order has been controversial since they were introduced as a means of riot control. Plastic bullets, officially called baton rounds, were introduced into N Ireland in 1973, replacing rubber bullets which were withdrawn as being too dangerous. Medical evidence has, however, shown that plastic bullets cause 'more devastating skull and brain injuries'[16]. While the European Commission accepted, in 'Stewart v United Kingdom', in the light of the statistics of more than 110,000 such rounds having been fired, that the use of plastic bullets within the official rules of engagement could be an acceptable method of riot control, plastic bullets are often fired above the waist, in contravention of the government's own guidelines, and in disputed circumstances[17]. Judges, coroners and inquest juries have contradicted security force assertions that those killed were generally involved in rioting[18].

**6.2.3** While plastic bullets have not been used in Great Britain, many police forces in Great Britain have been equipped with them, and the Government seems prepared to risk their use against a civilian population. The Committee on the Administration of Justice points out that: 'While several police authorities refused to supply chief constables with the funds to buy the bullets, their wishes have been largely circumvented by a High Court ruling in 1986 supporting the Home Secretary, who announced that plastic bullets and CS gas could be issued from a central store at Home Office expense. This ruling was confirmed by the Court of Appeal in November 1987 (see 'R v Secretary of State for the Home Dept, ex parte Northumbria Police Authority' (1988) 1 All ER 556.3)[19].

Compliance with Article 6, the right to life, requires that:

● the use of plastic bullets should be discontinued immediately;

● guidelines to security forces should respect the vulnerability of the young and the highest standards of international and humanitarian law.

## 6.3 Use of lethal force

**6.3.1** The use of lethal force by the army and the RUC has also been controversial[20]. There have been allegations that a 'shoot to kill' policy exists; that there is a failure to prosecute members of the security force, or that when prosecuted, they are unjustifiably acquitted; and that there is unnecessary delay in the conduct of investigations and inquests. Such perceptions increase the alienation of sections of the Nationalist community. There is a divergence between the legal standard for the use of lethal force in the UK and international standards as set out in Article 2 of the European Convention on Human Rights and Article 6 of the UN International Convention on Civil and Political Rights, which limits the use of force to that '*which is no more than absolutely necessary*'[21]. Section 3 of the Criminal Law Act 1967 provides that any force 'reasonable in the circumstances' may be used; in practice this prevails over stricter internal army and police operating rules. The 'Yellow Card' *Instructions for Opening Fire in N Ireland* (Army Code No 70771, 1980) state that: 'You may only open fire against a person ... if he (or she) ... is committing an act likely to endanger life and there is no other way to prevent the danger'; RUC instructions are almost identical[22].

Compliance with Article 6, the right to life, requires that the defects in the law governing the use of lethal force by the security forces must be addressed and corrected, by replacing the present criterion of 'reasonable force' with that of 'minimum force which is no more than is absolutely necessary';

## 6.4 Shooting of 'joyriders'

**6.4.1** Article 6 recognises the child's inherent right to life and obliges the Government to '*ensure to the maximum extent possible the survival and development of the child*'. 'Joyriding', often done by very young children, has become a menace to the general public, threatening children and adult pedestrians, car owners, children and adults in homes trying to sleep or at risk of being damaged by cars crashing through living room windows, and safety of the children and young people stealing the cars themselves. There were 7,042 recorded incidents in 1990 rising to 8,455 in 1991 - an increase of 20%[23].

**6.4.2** Chasing stolen vehicles is dangerous and counter-productive. Policies of shooting at cars or giving chase have led to loss of life. A particular risk run by young people in N Ireland is that of being shot dead by the security forces on the grounds that they may be terrorists trying to ram a roadblock. For example, in the case of Karen Reilly and Martin Peake, teenage joyriders killed by soldiers who fired after the car as it went through an army checkpoint, eyewitness accounts implied that it was known the car was being driven by unarmed joyriders[24].

**6.4.3** The lack of access to safe play provision represents a breach of Article 31 which stresses '*the right of the child to rest and leisure, to engage in play and recreational activities appropriate to the age of the child and to participate freely in cultural life and the arts*'. Funding has been withdrawn from programmes aimed at diverting children from joyriding, such as the Auto Project in West Belfast, despite their success. The conditions leading to joyriding include high levels of deprivation, and lack of play and recreational activities. The thrill attached to joyriding can become addictive, and the threat or reality of punishment will not deter young offenders who are addicted to the 'high' of car theft. Voluntary organisations such as Voluntary Service, Belfast, Belfast Healthy Cities, Playboard and Playright emphasize the need for preventive programmes and a proper framework for funding of play projects.

Compliance with Article 6, the right to life, requires that the practice of shooting at stolen vehicles should cease immediately. The practice of chasing stolen vehicles should be replaced with alternative and more effective methods of dealing with joyriding.

Compliance with Article 31, the right to play and leisure facilities, requires that programmes aimed at preventing joyriding should be properly resourced and monitored, so that lessons can be learned from them. The roots of the problem in boredom, lack of play facilities, unemployment, and community poverty should be urgently addressed by government.

## 6.5 Children caught between paramilitaries and security forces

**6.5.1** Article 6 recognizes '*that every child has the inherent right to life*'; the Government '*shall ensure to the maximum extent possible the survival and development of the child*'. Article 36 states that the Government '*shall protect the child against all other forms of exploitation prejudicial to any aspects of the child's welfare*'. Article 37(a) states that the Government shall ensure that '*no child shall be subjected to torture or other cruel, inhuman or degrading treatment or punishment*'.

**6.5.2** In addition to deaths and injuries amongst young people, many are caught between the opposing security forces and paramilitary organisations[25]. It is not unusual for children to report harassment both verbal and physical by both members of the police and army (see para 7.1). As well as this security force harassment, other young people, particularly those engaged in petty criminal behaviour, report that members of the RUC have encouraged and pressurised them into becoming informers for the police against paramilitaries within their areas. Young people run the risk of actually being killed by members of paramilitary groups if they are found to be working for the security forces.

*'There are community policemen but you think they are always after something, they are always asking how are you, how's your brother, is he still in jail and they ask all the kids who's in the IRA or who's in the UVF or whatever.'*
(16 year-old, N Ireland)

## ACTION REQUIRED FOR COMPLIANCE

**Compliance with Article 6, the right to life, requires that security policy on intelligence be reviewed so that children are not coerced into becoming gatherers of low-level information (informers) for the security forces.**

# 7 Harassment by security forces
## Articles 2 and 16

**7.1** Article 2 debars discrimination not only on grounds of a young person's religion or political opinion but also on grounds of their parent's or legal guardian's religion or political opinion. Article 2.2 states that the Government *'shall take all appropriate measures to ensure that the child is protected against all forms of discrimination or punishment on the basis of the status, activities, expressed opinions, or beliefs of the child's parents, legal guardians, or family members'*. Harassment of a young person because of their relative's alleged or actual involvement in illegal activities is therefore a breach of that young person's human rights as guaranteed by Article 2.

**7.2** Article 16 provides that *'no child shall be subjected to arbitrary or unlawful interference with his or her privacy, family, home or correspondence, nor to unlawful attacks on his or her honour and reputation'*. Harassment by the security forces is often a daily feature of life for young people living in deprived areas, particularly for Nationalist young men, although it affects children and young people on both sides. There are persistent allegations of the use of death threats by the RUC and security forces; of harassment of families before and after fatal shootings, and of verbal abuse of young people by the security forces. Helsinki Watch found that 'harassment of children under 18 in N Ireland is endemic, is directed against children in both traditions - Nationalist and Unionist - and is in violation of international agreements and standards'[26].

*'In the hardline areas of Belfast, like the Falls and the Shankill, young people are having encounters with the police and army almost every day, I mean, it just sparks off tension.'*
(17 year-old, N Ireland)

**7.3** The experience of the Caraher family is an example. After two older brothers were shot by soldiers in December 1990 and one killed, the family experienced considerable harassment from the army; 15-year-old Phelim Caraher was photographed on the road and told the photograph would be given to the UVF (a Loyalist paramilitary group) and 16 year-old Cathal was punched on the mouth in the street[27]. Young people have been 'lifted' for screening purposes or held and then released without charge. Private homes have been invaded and damaged in security operations.

**7.4** Apart from their immediate impact on young people as a breach of Articles 16 and also 37(a) (protection from cruel, inhuman or degrading treatment), such experiences can embitter them and are counter-productive to efforts to end the violence, serving to make paramilitary alternatives appear reasonable to them.

## ACTION REQUIRED FOR COMPLIANCE

**Compliance with Articles 2, the principle of non-discrimination, and Article 16, the right to protection of privacy, requires that:**

● **the behaviour of the security forces be monitored, especially towards children and young people. Guidance to security forces should stress that young people must not be discriminated against because of family connections. The grief of bereaved families should be respected;**

- child-friendly complaints procedures be established and publicised;
- security force personnel should receive training in human rights including the rights of children.

# 8 Paramilitary abuse of children and young people
Articles 37, 38 and 15

## 8.1 Expulsions by paramilitaries

**8.1.1** Article 15 recognizes '*the rights of the child to freedom of association and to freedom of peaceful assembly*'. Article 15.2 states that '*no restrictions may be placed on the exercise of these rights other than those imposed in conformity with the law and which are necessary in a democratic society in the interests of national security or public safety, public order (ordre public), the protection of public health or morals or the protection of the rights and freedoms of others*'. Article 37(a) states that the Government shall ensure that '*no child shall be subjected to torture or other cruel, inhuman or degrading treatment or punishment*'. Article 37(b) provides that '*no child shall be deprived of his or her liberty unlawfully or arbitrarily*'.

**8.1.2** Since about April 1991, paramilitaries have engaged in expelling young people from their areas and also from the country; this is backed up with the threat of physical violence. Young people have reported that they are prevented from associating with certain people within their areas, again with a threat of physical violence. Such actions breach Articles 15 and 37.

**8.1.3** In some cases paramilitary threats have led to parents and voluntary groups seeking a place of safety order under the Children and Young Persons (NI) Act 1968 for the juvenile at risk. Professionals are caught in the dilemma of appearing to co-operate with paramilitaries to remove young people from the streets for their own safety. The young person might be found a foster home or safe house, for example with a relative, or their family may be moved. However, a young person thought to be in need of care or control may be admitted to St Patrick's or Rathgael Training Schools after a place of safety order has been obtained. A young person can be held in a secure unit for up to five weeks before the matter comes to court; this time can be extended for two further periods of five weeks to a maximum of 15 weeks. A young person who then offends, for example, on a visit home, or who is found to be 'unruly', can move across from the care to the justice side of a training school, or into a Young Offender's Centre. A young person could spend up to two years in a training school. This matter of paramilitary influence on training school admissions has been described by the Standing Advisory Commission on Human Rights (SACHR) as 'clearly unsavoury and cause for considerable concern'[28]. SACHR recommends that arrangements, possibly involving the voluntary sector, should be developed to counter the effect of paramilitary threats on such admissions.

**8.1.4** It is not clear what effect the introduction of new legislation in the form of the Children (NI) Order, due to come into force in 1995, and new criminal justice legislation, will have on the numbers of children who are admitted into care due to coming to the attention of social services because paramilitary threats have been made against them.

Compliance with Article 15, the right to freedom of association and Article 37, the prohibition of torture, cruel treatment or punishment, requires that:

● new arrangements should be sought, possibly involving the voluntary sector, to prevent children from having to come into care in circumstances where they are threatened by paramilitaries with expulsion from their communities;

● conditions be created in which the policing of children is only carried out by the statutory authorities;

● the RUC should publish statistics by age, for example, for expulsions, kneecappings, and so forth, so that the extent of abuse can be monitored.

## 8.2 Paramilitary recruitment of young people

**8.2.1** Both the security forces and paramilitary organisations recruit young people, some as informers. Young people under 18 have been used in terrorist operations. The bereavement support group LOSS has expressed concern about the numbers of 16 and 17-year-olds who have blown themselves up, either as members of, or on the fringes of, paramilitary organisations, and about the impact of bereavement on the remaining children in the family. With the upsurge in 1993 in Loyalist paramilitary violence, recruitment and volunteering of young men, including teenagers, into paramilitary groups is said to have increased dramatically. The anti-intimidation group Families Against Intimidation and Terror (FAIT), for example, has expressed concern about the extremist group Ulster Young Militants (UYM) - dubbed a junior wing of the proscribed Ulster Freedom Fighters, or UFF which it claims covertly trains boys as young as 12 to become Loyalist killers of the future, receiving training in kneecapping, bomb-making and assassination techniques. It is believed that members are encouraged to join the Army cadets and the Territorial Army to gain further training.

**8.2.2** Article 38.2 provides that the Government '*shall take al feasible measures to ensure that persons who have not attained the age of fifteen years do not take a direct part in hostilities*'. Article 31 recognizes '*the right of the child to rest and leisure, to engage in play and recreational activities appropriate to the age of the child and to participate freely in cultural life and the arts*'. Children under 15 are prohibited by humanitarian law from participation in conflict, even voluntary participation. Some children and young people in N Ireland do take not only a direct part in the conflict by, for example, volunteering to join various paramilitary organisations or their junior wings, but also an indirect part by engaging in harmful activities, such as throwing stones at the security forces, or keeping watch on targeted individuals. They do this against a background of poverty, deprivation, boredom, hopelessness, and the worst play facilities in Western Europe. The provision of adequate play and leisure facilities is an important and feasible measure which the Government ought to take in connection with its obligations under Article 38.2, providing alternative activities for children and young people, so that they do not get caught up in situations of violence.

Compliance with Article 38, the protection of children in armed conflicts, requires that:

● the Government monitors the treatment of children and young people in situations of violent conflict and takes all feasible measures to ensure their care and protection from harm;

● the Government must ensure that any collaboration between security forces and paramilitaries is vigorously opposed. The recruitment and training of young people into junior branches of the security forces should be reviewed to ensure that young people do not become involved in paramilitary activities;

● the need for adequate supervised day care, play, leisure and after-school facilities must be met and such facilities, schemes and preventive services properly resourced.

# 9 Non-discrimination
## Article 2

## 9.1 Sectarian policies and practices

**9.1.1** The N Ireland Office discussion document *Crime and the community* identifies fairness as one of the main sentencing criteria, stating that 'all offenders must be treated fairly, without regard to differences in gender, race or religion'. It also seeks views on whether there should be a similar statutory duty to publish information in N Ireland as in England and Wales. Article 2 forbids discrimination '*of any kind, irrespective of the child's or his parent's or legal guardian's … language, religion, political or other opinion, national, ethnic or social origin …* '. However, sectarianism in N Ireland is rife despite official efforts and obligations to promote fairness in the justice system as well as in the policing of N Ireland.

**9.1.2** There are concerns, for example, about the fact that the secure unit at Lisnevin is placed in a geographical area which young people from the Nationalist community perceive as threatening to themselves or which can deter their families from visiting. In the absence of a statistical analysis of young people in the justice system by sex, religion or race, it is difficult to know whether the Government is currently complying with Article 2.

## 9.2 Travellers and other minority ethnic groups

**9.2.1** Traveller children are also protected by Article 30 which provides that '*in those States in which ethnic, religious or linguistic minorities or persons of indigenous origin exist, a child belonging to such a minority or who is indigenous shall not be denied the right, in community with other members of his or her group, to enjoy his or her own culture, to profess and practice his or her own religion, or to use his or her own language*'.

**9.2.2** However, in N Ireland, there is no protection from discrimination for children of minority ethnic communities. Children of Travellers experience particular disadvantages, as do children whose first language is not English. The small size of minorities in N Ireland can mean that special protections are even more important than in the rest of the UK, but size is often used as an argument to suggest that there is little racism in N Ireland[29]. This is not the case. Racism, sectarianism, and a lack of pluralism in recognizing cultural diversity are closely related and reflected in the high degree of violence in N Irish society.

**9.2.3** There are concerns about differential treatment of minority ethnic and Traveller children and young people. Although Travellers would be more likely to be based in Nationalist areas, they are not necessarily accepted in those areas, nor do they share the politics or culture of their neighbours; some also have their own language. Anecdotal evidence suggests that Traveller children can be caught between the police and the paramilitaries, and experience harassment from both.

**9.2.4** Because the composition of the community is different from that of other communities in other parts of the UK, approaches to ensuring an end to discrimination for all children will necessarily differ. Many organisations agree that the absence of effective anti-racism legislation, backed by a separate monitoring agency, is a major concern, meaning that the guarantee to all children of their rights is unable to be supported in practice.

## 9.3 Irish language speakers

**9.3.1** The Irish language has been persistently discriminated against, or neglected by the Government, since the establishment of N Ireland. It is regarded as an important part of the Nationalist identity. It can be seen as a symbol of resistance to 'Britishness'. People experience aggravation when trying to use the Irish forms of names; for example, being more likely to be stopped by the security forces. However, the Committee on the Administration of Justice writes that: 'Irish has not only been spoken by Catholics in Ireland. Many of the settlers were Gaelic speakers from Scotland. Furthermore, at the turn of the 19th century, the revival of Irish was inspired by Belfast Protestants. And even today there are people within the Unionist community who see Irish as part of their identity, and who favour increased support for the language'[30].

**9.3.2** Legislation discriminating against Irish still exists; for example, the Administration of Justice (Language) Act (Ireland) 1737 states that all proceedings in the Court of Justice shall be in English. In 1990 the Irish language organisation Glor na nGael had its funding withdrawn until 1992, when it was restored after a campaign by civil liberties groups. Education through the medium of Irish has not received parity of support from Government in terms of the treatment of other minority languages in the UK. Children and young people should not be discriminated against or subject to special security force scrutiny on account of attending an Irish-speaking school, having an Irish name, or using the Irish version of their name.

### ACTION REQUIRED FOR COMPLIANCE

**Compliance with Article 2, concerning non-discrimination, and Article 30, the right of children to enjoy their own culture, religion, and language, requires that:**

- **a statutory duty on the N Ireland Office be introduced to collect and publish statistical analyses of children and young people within the justice system, in particular to highlight any differential treatment on grounds of gender, race or religion. All procedures should be reviewed in the light of the monitoring and all those involved in the justice system receive training designed to prevent discrimination;**

- **legislation barring discrimination on grounds of race, ethnic origin, nationality, language spoken, (and barring discrimination against Travellers), should be introduced into N Ireland as a matter of urgency. Similarly, legislation barring discrimination on grounds of religion or political opinion, should be introduced as a matter of urgency into Great Britain, so that parity of protection exists;**

- **the need for interpreters, including interpreters for deaf people, in legal processes, is fully met (also Article 40.2(b)(vi));**

- **the UK should sign the European Charter for**

Regional or Minority Languages and adopt a more positive policy towards the Irish language and culture, as it has done towards Welsh and Scots Gaelic.

# 10 The administration of juvenile justice
## Articles 37 and 40

## 10.1 Ill-treatment in detention

**10.1.1** Ill-treatment in detention of a child or a young person under 18 is a clear breach of Article 37(a), which guarantees that '*no child shall be subjected to torture or other cruel, inhuman or degrading treatment or punishment*'. It also breaches Article 37(c), which states that '*every child deprived of liberty shall be treated with humanity and respect for the inherent dignity of the human person, and in a manner which takes into account the needs of persons of his or her age*'. Paragraph 58 of the Police and Criminal Evidence (NI) Order 1989 created a new section 52(2) of the Children and Young Persons (NI) Act 1968, with a duty, where a juvenile is in police detention, to take such steps as are practicable to ascertain the identity of a person responsible for his or her welfare and to inform that person, unless it is not practicable to do so, why and where the juvenile is being detained. The *Code of practice for the detention, treatment and questioning of persons by police officers* , issued under Article 65 of the PACE Order, says that a person under the age of 17 must not be interviewed or asked to provide a written statement in the absence of an 'appropriate adult' - parent or guardian, social worker or a responsible adult over 18 who is not a police officer - unless an officer of the rank of superintendent or above considers that delay would involve an immediate risk of harm to persons or a serious loss of property.

**10.1.2** However, at present 17 year-olds do not have such safeguards. Young people in N Ireland have been ill-treated in detention. The Helsinki Watch Report *Children in N Ireland (July 1992)* describes an interview with a 17 year-old who was arrested several times during 1991, interrogated, severely beaten and abused, before being released without charge[31]. In a case reported to the N Ireland Human Rights Assembly held in London in April 1992, young men aged 17-20, were kept in Castlereagh for six days and were alleged to have been ill-treated by abuse, blows, threats and sleep deprivation[32]. The Human Rights Assembly is drawing the attention of the United Nations Human Rights Committee to conditions prevailing in detention in N Ireland, such as incommunicado detention, which allow abuses of human rights and to the lack of safeguards for individuals[33].

**10.1.3** In November 1991 the Committee for the Administration of Justice (CAJ) submitted a report to the UN Committee Against Torture expressing concern about the alarming increase in allegations of ill-treatment of detainees held in Castlereagh holding-centre and calling for an end to seven-day detentions which are in breach of the European Convention on Human Rights; the right to private consultations with legal advisors; the right of detainees to have their legal advisers present during interrogation; the scrapping of those sections of the emergency provisions which reduce the standard of admissibility of confessions; the restoration in full of the right to silence; video and audio recording of inerviews; the extension of the station visiting scheme to cover emergency detainees; and the restructuring of the police complaints system. The UN Committee expressed grave concern about the situation in Castlereagh[34].

**10.1.4** The CAJ states: 'Some communities have alleged a specific strategy by the police involving the arrest of young men as soon as they reach the age of 17. Before their 17th birthday, young people have the right to have a parent or guardian present during the detention. Families say that their sons have been warned that they will be arrested. Furthermore, a number of young men are currently awaiting trial on the basis of confessions that they allege were extracted under duress involving a significant level of psychological ill-treatment'. An example of personal abuse reported by the CAJ was that of a 17 year-old's experience of a woman police officer 'talking dirty' to him in a way that embarrassed him so much he refused to repeat it'[35]. Two of the five West Belfast teenagers known as the 'Beechmount Five' were 17 at the time of their arrest for the murder of a police officer in an IRA rocket attack on 1 May 1991. All the young people were interrogated for seven days in Castlereagh; all made statements implicating themselves in the officer's murder, and all have since repudiated the statements; and all allege physical abuse and sleep deprivation[36]. Amnesty International reported on their cases in November 1991.

**10.1.5** The young are particularly vulnerable to ill-treatment. Again, the CAJ write that: 'Communities complain that the young and politically uninvolved are increasingly targeted for arrest and detention. These observations and the allegations of ill-treatment are particularly worrisome as they combine to create a dangerously coercive mechanism. In *Coercive persuasion* Schein delineated a list of factors which make for the most submissive prisoners. Those who - being prone to social guilt, lacking a sense of commitment to some cause or group, not being sophisticated about politics, being relatively young, holding a belief in the sincerity of lenient inducements, being weakened by the removal of their usual social and psychological supports, being punished and threatened with further punishment which has been reinforced by events in society - were most likely to admit guilt regardless of the truth of those statements. When the politically uninvolved N Ireland youth is arrested and subjected to types of treatment which seem designed to break down the police's image of an hardened paramilitary, there arises the alarming possibility that he or she will fall prey to these tactics and confess irrespective of his or her actual guilt'[37].

**ACTION REQUIRED FOR COMPLIANCE**

**Compliance with Article 37, the prohibition of torture, cruel treatment or punishment, and unlawful deprivation of liberty, requires that legislative safeguards and rigorous monitoring and inspection be introduced to ensure the highest standards in the treatment of detainees, and in particular of young detainees.**

## 10.2 Wording of Cautions

**10.2.1** Article 40(2)(b)(i) provides that every child has the right 'to be presumed innocent until proved guilty according to law', and Article 40.3 obliges the Government to promote the establishment of laws and procedures 'specifically applicable to children'. The Criminal Evidence (NI) Order 1988 applies to juveniles who now receive a caution as follows: 'You do not have to say anything unless you wish to do so but I must warn you that if you fail to mention any fact which you rely on in your defence in court, your failure to take this opportunity to mention it may be treated in court as supporting any relevant evidence against you. If you do wish to say anything, what you say may be given in evidence'. This wording is unduly complicated and should be rewritten in plain English so that it can be easily understood. Inferences may be made by the court if the young person fails to supply his/her alibi evidence at the time of arrest, in custody, or in court. This applies to children from the age of 10. This has been termed 'oppressive in inferring guilt or support of other evidence simply for failing to speak' by the Committee on the Administration of Justice. The caution is couched in terms which a juvenile may not even be able to read, let alone understand it and its consequences. It thus contravenes Articles 40(2)(b)(i) and 40.3.

## 10.3 Right to silence

**10.3.1** Under Article 40.2(b)(i) 'every child alleged as or accused of having infringed the penal law has' as a minimum guarantee the right 'to be presumed innocent until proven guilty by law'; under Article 40.2(b)(iv) the right 'not to be compelled to give testimony or to confess guilt'; and under Article 40.2(b)(vii) 'the right to have his or her privacy fully respected at all stages of the proceedings'. The Criminal Evidence (NI) Order 1988 circumscribes a suspect's right to silence, permitting a court to draw adverse inferences from a suspect's refusal to answer questions during interrogation or at trial. In addition, in cases tried by the special 'Diplock' Courts, unlike in ordinary courts, confessions secured by threats or inducements can be admitted into evidence. Young detainees are particularly vulnerable to pressure, especially when they can be kept isolated, for example from a solicitor, for up to 48 hours. The Royal Commission on Criminal Justice, reporting in 1993 on the right to silence, recommended its retention; this protection against self-incrimination does not apply in N Ireland.

**ACTION REQUIRED FOR COMPLIANCE**

**Compliance with Article 40 requires that:**

- **both the language and the content of legal proceedings should take into account the vulnerability and understanding of children and young people in order to safeguard their interests;**
- **protection against self-incrimination should be ensured in both criminal and emergency legislation and the right to silence fully reinstated for children being tried in N Ireland courts.**

## 10.4 Rights of representation

**10.4.1** Article 40.2(b)(ii) provides that children and young people 'alleged as or accused of having infringed the penal law' have the right 'to be informed promptly and directly of the charges against him or her, if appropriate through his or her parents or legal guardian, and to have legal or other appropriate assistance in the preparation and presentation of his or her defence'. Some lawyers have expressed concern that young people sometimes do not receive an equal quality of legal representation or advice to that given to adults in the same circumstances. There is no independent children's law centre or central advocacy service for children and young people in N Ireland, the establishment of which would enhance the quality of legal representation of children.

Compliance with Article 40.2(b)(ii), the right to legal assistance, requires that the standard of legal representation of young people be carefully monitored with a view to seeking improvements. As a priority funding should be made available for a children's law centre.

## 10.5 Indeterminate sentences

**10.5.1** Article 3.1 states that '*in all actions concerning children, whether undertaken by public or private social welfare institutions, courts of law, administrative bodies or legislative bodies, the best interests of the child shall be a primary consideration*'. Article 40.1 recognises the right of the child to be treated in a way which '*takes into account the child's age and the desirability of promoting the child's reintegration and the child's assuming a constructive role in society*'. The Children and Young Persons (NI) Act 1968 provides that neither capital punishment nor life imprisonment without the possibility of release shall be imposed for offences committed by persons under 18. Life imprisonment can however be experienced by juveniles under 'Secretary of State's Pleasure' (SOSP) arrangements. Detention at the Secretary of State's Pleasure is automatic under section 73 of the Children and Young Persons Act 1968 for persons found guilty of a murder committed when they were under 18. It could be argued that indeterminate sentences breach Article 40.1.

**10.5.2** In 1 July 1988 there were 406 life sentence prisoners and 32 SOSP prisoners in N Ireland, around 27% of the average daily prison population (by contrast with the 6% average in the rest of the UK). Both the Bennett Report and a wide range of politicians and groups have expressed concern over the system for release of life sentence prisoners; in particular relatives of SOSP Prisoners feel that 'the normal presumptions in the criminal justice system in favour of younger offenders have not been exercised in their case'[38]. In the 'Weeks' case in the European Court of Human Rights the procedure in England and Wales for the recall of people released 'on licence' was challenged as failing to comply with Article 5(4) of the European Convention on Human Rights.

Compliance with Articles 3.1, the consideration of the child's best interests, and Article 40.1, the right to be treated in a way that takes into account the child's age and the desirability of reintegration into society, requires that the availability of indeterminate sentences for juveniles under the 'Secretary of State's Pleasure' arrangements should be reviewed. There should be moves towards determinate sentencing and an end to the mandatory life sentence for murder.
(See also **UK Agenda Report 9 on youth justice**, page 199 for a more detailed discussion on the administration of justice).

# 11 Separation from parents
## Article 9

## 11.1 Separation due to detention

**11.1.1** Article 9.4 provides that '*where ... separation results from any action initiated by [the Government] such as the detention, imprisonment, exile, deportation or death (including death arising from any cause while the person is in the custody of the State) of one or both parents or of the child [the Government] shall, upon request, provide the parents, the child, or, if appropriate, another member of the family with essential information concerning the whereabouts of the absent member(s) of the family unless the provision of the information would be detrimental to the well-being of the child*'. There are persistent allegations that the security forces have detained some parents under emergency legislation, without notifying anyone of their whereabouts for 48 hours. This is in contravention of the spirit of Article 9.4.

Compliance with Article 9.4 requires that:
● there should be statutory obligations to consider the best interests of any children affected when an adult is detained or arrested;
● the parents of any child detained should be informed immediately of the child's whereabouts and permitted to see the child, who should not be questioned without an appropriate adult being present.

## 11.2 Prisoners' families

**11.2.1** Article 9(3) provides that '*States Parties shall respect the right of the child who is separated from one or both parents to maintain personal relations and direct contact with both parents on a regular basis, except if it is contrary to the child's best interests*'. Separation due to imprisonment of the parent is not excluded. Due to the political violence, N Ireland has a disproportionately large young prison population, many of whom are parents of young children. Great stress is caused to families by current inadequate visiting arrangements, inadequate financial support for prisoners' partners, and the refusal of the Government to transfer Irish prisoners to N Ireland. The Irish Commission for Prisoners Overseas draws attention to the practice of 'ghosting' prisoners (sudden transfer to another prison), so that visiting families are obliged to search for them. The Irish Prisoners' Support Group point out that in large families it can be three or four years before children see their fathers held in prison in England. Families can be subject to the Prevention of Terrorism Act on entry into Britain, and to strip-searching on visiting prisons[39]. The Ferrers report of 23 November 1992 recommended that Irish prisoners should be entitled to transfers, and this was accepted by the Home Office; however, the problems continue.

**11.2.2** The Committee for the Transfer of Irish Prisoners states that visiting arrangements for families of Irish political prisoners serving long sentences in English jails can have 'devastating consequences on the quality of relationships that children of those prisoners can expect to have. The journey to England is an isolating, expensive, stressful one. Children have to leave the environment they are familiar with, travel long distances, stay in accommodation that is unfriendly and unwelcoming. Children travelling to England have experienced their mother being arrested under the PTA, taken away from them. They have got to prison and found that their imprisoned parent has been 'ghosted', they have been sick, frightened, bored, distressed. They miss their imprisoned parent, yet the stress of the visiting can be a quite intolerable experience ... Children are being unnecessarily punished'[40].

## ACTION REQUIRED FOR COMPLIANCE

**Compliance with Article 9 requires that:**

● **visiting facilities at all N Ireland prisons, particularly HMP Crumlin Road, should be upgraded;**

● **home leave schemes should be extended to facilitate greater contact between children and parents;**

● **financial support for prisoners' families should be improved and relate to the extra costs of prison visiting;**

● **Irish prisoners with familial links to N Ireland currently held in prisons in England and Wales should be entitled to be transferred to a prison in N Ireland;**

● **the practice of 'ghosting' prisoners should end; any transfers of prisoners should be notified to family immediately.**

# 12 Rehabilitative care of child victims
## Article 39

**12.1** Article 39 obliges the Government to '*take all appropriate measures to promote physical and psychological recovery and social reintegration of a child victim of: any form of neglect, exploitation, or abuse; torture or any other form of cruel, inhuman or degrading treatment or punishment; or armed conflicts. Such recovery and reintegration shall take place in an environment which fosters the health, self-respect and dignity of the child*'. Given the impact, detailed above, of the violence on children in N Ireland, there is clearly a need for appropriate forms of rehabilitative care. While there is no reason to believe that the State has not provided adequately for those children who have been physically injured as a result of the armed conflict in N Ireland, community groups have suggested that some young people, for example, injured joyriders, may feel stigmatised in hospital, or that cultural values of staff may mean that they are not treated very sympathetically or gently. This may prevent young people from returning for follow-up treatment.

**12.2** Research suggests that the majority of children affected by general psychological stress recover relatively quickly, especially when given adequate support by their parents and other adults in their community. Specialist services are also available for the small number who are more seriously affected.

**12.3** Despite the numbers of children who have been affected by the death of a parent, no specific research has been carried out on the impact of violent bereavement on children in N Ireland nor has any attempt been made to investigate the best way to care for such children.

**12.4** Research from other societies suggests that the death of a parent particularly in violent circumstances can have a dramatic impact on a child. Research also indicates that the surviving parent (and other significant adults) tend to deny that children suffer unduly as a result of bereavement. Such children are therefore especially in need of state support. At the moment no such support appears to be provided. A scheme is in place to support the widows of security force personnel but this makes no special provision for children. One small voluntary organisation has however begun to implement a pilot scheme to provide for the psychological needs of children bereaved as a result of the violence.

**12.5** The UK is thus failing to take all appropriate measures to promote the psychological recovery of child victims of conflict in N Ireland in relation to children who have a parent killed.

## ACTION REQUIRED FOR COMPLIANCE

**Compliance with Article 39, the right of children to rehabilitative care, requires that:**

● **the Government assess the need for rehabilitative services and provide them. To enable it to determine the size of the problem, research should be conducted to estimate the number of children who have been affected by bereavement due to the** conflict, and a review should be carried out of modern practices in other countries, in particular the USA. The State should then evaluate its own practices in the light of this information;

● the Government should provide financial help to one or more voluntary organisations who would be willing to provide appropriate support, in order to aid those who do not wish to seek State help in these circumstances.

# 13 Creating an environment for change

## 13.1 Addressing community perceptions of violence (Article 42)

**13.1.1** The government has an obligation under Article 42 '*to make the principles and provisions of the Convention widely known, by appropriate and active means, to adults and children alike*'. Knowledge of children's rights is rudimentary in some communities. Recently a multi-agency project in Londonderry has undertaken a community education programme covering a Nationalist and a Loyalist area to help both community organisations and families become more aware of children's rights as set out in the UN Convention. This model is labour-intensive; however, if successful it could be replicated in other communities.

### ACTION REQUIRED FOR COMPLIANCE

**Compliance with Article 42 requires that community perceptions of the acceptability of violence, including violent punishment by adults of children and young people be addressed. Community education programmes about the Convention, about children's rights and in particular about protection of children's physical and personal integrity should be established and adequately resourced.**

## 13.2 Tackling sectarianism
(Articles 29 and 30)

*Education*
**13.2.1** Article 29 creates a duty to educate children to respect human rights. Article 29.1(c) states that the education of the child shall be directed to '*the development of respect for the child's parents, his or her own cultural identity, language and values, for the national values of the country in which the child is living, the country in which he or she may originate, and for civilizations different from his or her own*'. Article 29.1.(d) provides for '*the preparation of the child for responsible life in a free society, in the spirit of understanding, peace, tolerance, equality of sexes, and friendship among all peoples, ethnic, national and religious groups and persons of indigenous origin*'. Since 1992, education aimed at 'mutual understanding' is one of six cross-curricular themes which is compulsory in the N Ireland Curriculum at both primary and secondary levels, at all key stages of the Curriculum. However, the Department of Education of N Ireland Inspectors' report indicates that, as yet, delivery in practice varies, and that there is room for improvement.

**13.2.2** A *Brief on integrated education* prepared for the UN and UNESCO by Colin Irwin argues that there is widespread support, including among young people, for a system of integrated (that is, denominationally mixed) education: 'The system of segregated education in Northern Ireland contributes to the perpetuation of prejudice and social conflict in Ulster while integrated education increases cross community understanding and friendship. Unfortunately, in the face of opposition from local community leaders, the churches and school boards, the N Ireland Office and Department of Education have failed to provide every child in the Province with a real option of attending an integrated school. This failure represents a breach of the human rights and fundamental freedoms of the children of Northern Ireland'[41].

> *'Something that needs to be examined is the whole issue of integrated schools. There are about twenty integrated schools in N Ireland but there should be far more, so people have the opportunity of at least being open minded and not pushed into a situation where it leaves the way open for minds to be poisoned against one community or the other.'*
> (17 year-old, N Ireland)

> *'Kids start learning young that Catholics or Protestants have horns on their head or something. Maybe if they realised that they didn't have horns on their heads then they would start to get on a bit better.'*
> (15 year-old, N Ireland)

*Status of Irish language and culture*
**13.2.3** The Committee on the Administration of Justice writes that: '23% of Protestants in Northern Ireland currently favour the teaching of Irish and Irish culture in schools, according to the report *Social Attitudes in N Ireland'*. Another indicator of the desire for more access to Irish is contained in the Opsahl Report. School children taking part in the proceedings of the Opsahl Commission requested: 'that all schools should give pupils the option to study Irish history and the Irish language ... '[42]. This approach could be helpful in encouraging cross-community understanding and in reducing prejudice and sectarianism, especially when based on ignorance of other views or traditions, or of the Irish language. Recently, for example, pubs supporting traditional Irish folk music were threatened by Loyalist paramilitaries; the threat was withdrawn after an outcry, including from prominent traditional musicians from the Protestant tradition. Children's participation in traditional Irish dance has been similarly affected by the threat of sectarian violence.

**13.2.4** Article 30 guarantees the rights of minority communities to enjoy their own culture, language and religion. This implies a pro-active approach to minority languages and cultures. The Irish-language group, Glor na Ngael points to a lack of amenities for the teaching of Irish, and a lack of Irish-language materials and media programmes. Since the question of cultural identity and national values is fundamental to the divisions in N Irish society, the full implementation of Articles 29 and 30 is crucial to the process of ending community strife and sectarianism.

### ACTION REQUIRED FOR COMPLIANCE

**Compliance with Article 29, the right to education fostering respect for one's own culture and that of others, requires that:**

● **the Department of Education for N Ireland should provide every child in N Ireland with the choice of attending an integrated school;**

● **the delivery of education for mutual understanding should continue to be monitored with a view to its improvement.**

**Compliance with Article 30, the right of children of minorities to enjoy their own culture and language, requires that the promotion of the Irish language and Irish culture should receive full support from Government, including in the development by**

Department of Education of N Ireland of materials in Irish aimed at children and young people, and funding of Irish-medium education.

## 13.3 Consulting with Children
(Article 12)

**13.3.1** Informal discussions with groups of young children indicate that they are very concerned about the violence. They reject the killings and worry about their own safety and that of other children. In deprived areas they do not feel they have safe places to play. They reject 'hoods' and 'gunmen'. They also feel at risk from accidental or deliberate injury by joyriders. Traveller children have expressed similar views about 'hoods' and 'gunmen' to both Protestant and Catholic children from North Belfast.

> *'Kidnappers make me unhappy and bombs and shootings.'*
> (6 year-old, N Ireland)

**13.3.2** Older children and young people have expressed concerns about sectarianism. While there are certain leisure activities that are integrated in terms of religious background, young people are concerned about their safety travelling to and from such activities. The Opsahl Commission, which sought the views of school students as part of its oral hearings, points to 'the growing alienation, acute sense of powerlessness, and lack of hope among young working class people, which will clearly contribute to the continuation of the violence'[43]. Listening to children and young people and taking their views on board is clearly a crucial element in supporting a sense of empowerment and optimism in young people. Article 12 requires the establishment of processes for listening to the views of children and young people and taking them seriously.

> *'Young people don't have the power; it's like the media, they don't want to know you unless you got some big name behind you like Sinn Fein or the Democratic Unionist Party. The only way you can talk on the television is when they interview you for documentaries and then they only want to know about how poor you are, and how you are oppressed by the RUC or the IRA or whatever. They don't want to see the good side, they don't want to know what you hope for.'*
> (17 year-old, N Ireland)

### ACTION REQUIRED FOR COMPLIANCE

**Compliance with Article 12, the right to express an opinion and have it taken into account, requires that:**

● **the views of children and young people should be sought by all political parties, and statutory services and given serious consideration as part of any process of finding solutions to the violent conflict in N Ireland;**

● **child-friendly mechanisms for complaints be established in all Government departments and statutory services, and by the security forces.**

# 14 UK recruitment into the armed forces

**Article 38.3**

**14.1** Under Article 38.3, the Government '*shall refrain from recruiting any person who has not attained the age of fifteen years into their armed forces. In recruiting among those persons who have attained the age of fifteen years but who have not attained the age of eighteen years*', the Government '*shall endeavour to give priority to those who are oldest*'. The minimum age for voluntary enlistment in the armed forces is 16, where parental consent is granted. The minimum age for service in the Royal Navy, Royal Marines, and Royal Air Force in N Ireland is 18. In the Army, the minimum age for service 'on the streets' in N Ireland is 18, and, if restricted to barracks, 17 .

**14.2** The minimum age for service overseas is as follows: Royal Navy - 18 (if shore- based), 16 (for surface ships); Royal Marines - 18 (if shore based), 17 (for operational tours); Army - 17 1/4; Royal Air Force - 17 . Government policy is that: 'For under 18s the age of the recruit is taken into account in determining the type of duties they are employed on. Under-18s are less likely to take part in hostilities than over-18s and they require their parents' or guardians' written consent to enlist'. Nevertheless, over 200 UK soldiers under 18 participated in the Gulf War; one died. Placing young soldiers under 18 in situations of danger contravenes the spirit of Article 38, as does placing them in a position of 'policing' civilian populations without sufficient support, such as education and training in human rights, and respect for the rights of civilian populations and for the rights of children and young people. A representative of the Ministry of Defence has assured the Children's Legal Centre that the law relating to children in armed conflicts will be properly covered in the training of UK military personnel[44].

## ACTION REQUIRED FOR COMPLIANCE

**Compliance with Article 38.3, the age limits on recruitment to the armed forces, requires that:**

- **the Government revise legislation affecting recruitment to the armed forces to discourage any recruitment of under 18 year-olds, and to ensure that where under 18 year-olds continue to be recruited, priority is given to the oldest;**

- **young soldiers in N Ireland should not be placed in dangerous situations, nor situations in which their youth and inexperience can lead to conflict with the local community. Their training should include education in human rights, and respect for the rights of civilian populations and for the rights of children and young people.**

# Summary of action required for compliance

1 Compliance with Article 2, the right not to be discriminated against, requires that:

- the behaviour of the security forces be monitored, especially towards children and young people. Guidance to security forces should stress that young people must not be discriminated against because of family connections. The grief of bereaved families should be respected;

- child-friendly complaints procedures be established and publicised;

- security force personnel should receive training in human rights including the rights of children;

- a statutory duty on the N Ireland Office be introduced to collect and publish statistical analyses of children and young people within the justice system, in particular to highlight any differential treatment on grounds of gender, race or religion. All procedures should be reviewed in the light of the monitoring and all those involved in the justice system receive training designed to prevent discrimination;

- legislation barring discrimination on grounds of race, ethnic origin, nationality, language spoken, (and barring discrimination against Travellers), should be introduced into N Ireland as a matter of urgency. Similarly, legislation barring discrimination on grounds of religion or political opinion, should be introduced as a matter of urgency into Great Britain, so that parity of protection exists;

- the need for interpreters, including interpreters for deaf people, in legal processes, is fully met (also Article 40.2(b)(vi));

- the UK should sign the European Charter for Regional or Minority Languages and adopt a more positive policy towards the Irish language and culture, as it has done towards Welsh and Scots Gaelic (also Article 30).

2 Compliance with Article 6, the right to life, requires that:

- the Government continue to treat the resolution of the violent conflict in N Ireland as a matter of priority, and the protection of all children and young people from harm, including the harm of sectarianism, as an urgent duty;

- the practice of shooting at stolen vehicles should cease immediately. The practice of chasing stolen vehicles should be replaced with alternative and more effective methods of dealing with joyriding;

- security policy on intelligence be reviewed so that children are not coerced into becoming gatherers of low-level information (informers) for the security forces.

3 Compliance with Article 9, the right to maintain contact with family, requires that:

- visiting facilities at all N Ireland prisons, particularly HMP Crumlin Road, should be upgraded;

- home leave schemes should be extended to facilitate greater contact between children and parents;

- financial support for prisoners' families should be improved and relate to the extra costs of prison visiting;

- Irish prisoners with familial links to N Ireland currently held in prisons in England and Wales should be entitled to be transferred to a prison in N Ireland;

- the practice of 'ghosting' prisoners should end; any transfers of prisoners should be notified to family immediately;

- there should be statutory obligations to consider the best interests of any children affected when an adult is detained or arrested;

- the parents of any child detained should be informed immediately of the child's whereabouts and permitted to see the child, who should not be questioned without an appropriate adult being present.

**4** Compliance with Article 12, the right to express an opinion and have it taken into account, requires that:

- the views of children and young people should be sought by all political parties, and statutory services and given serious consideration as part of any process of finding solutions to the violent conflict in N Ireland;

- child-friendly mechanisms for complaints be established in all Government departments and statutory services, and by the security forces.

**5** Compliance with Article 29, the right to education fostering respect for one's own culture and that of others, requires that:

- the Department of Education for N Ireland should provide every child in N Ireland with the choice of attending an integrated school;

- the delivery of education for mutual understanding should continue to be monitored with a view to its improvement.

**6** Compliance with Article 30, the right of children of minorities to enjoy their own culture and language, requires that the promotion of the Irish language and Irish culture should receive full support from Government, including in the development by Department of Education of N Ireland of materials in Irish aimed at children and young people, and funding of Irish-medium education.

**7** Compliance with Article 31, the right to play and leisure facilities, requires that programmes aimed at preventing joyriding should be properly resourced and monitored, so that lessons can be learned from them. The roots of the problem in boredom, lack of play facilities, unemployment, and community poverty should be urgently addressed by government.

**8** Compliance with Article 37, the prohibition of torture, cruel treatment or punishment, and Article 15, the right of freedom of association, requires that:

- new arrangements should be sought, possibly involving the voluntary sector, to prevent children from having to come into care in circumstances where they are threatened by paramilitaries with expulsion from their communities;

- conditions be created in which the policing of children is only carried out by the statutory authorities;

- the RUC should publish statistics by age, for example, for expulsions, kneecappings, and so forth, so that the extent of abuse can be monitored;

- legislative safeguards and rigorous monitoring and inspection be introduced to ensure the highest standards in the treatment of detainees, and in particular of young detainees.

**9** Compliance with Article 38, the protection of children in armed conflicts, requires that:

- the Government monitors the treatment of children and young people in situations of violent conflict and take all feasible measures to ensure their care and protection from harm;

- the Government must ensure that any collaboration between security forces and paramilitaries is vigorously opposed. The recruitment and training of young people into junior branches of the security forces should be reviewed to ensure that young people do not become involved in paramilitary activities;

- the need for adequate supervised day care, play, leisure and after-school facilities must be met and such facilities, schemes and preventive services properly resourced;

- the Government revise legislation affecting recruitment to the armed forces to discourage any recruitment of under 18 year-olds, and to ensure that where under 18 year-olds continue to be recruited, priority is given to the oldest;

- young soldiers in N Ireland should not be placed in dangerous situations, nor situations in which their youth and inexperience can lead to conflict with the local community. Their training should include education in human rights, and respect for the rights of civilian populations and for the rights of children and young people.

**10** Compliance with Article 39, the right of children to rehabilitative care, requires that:

- the Government assess the need for rehabilitative services and provide them. To enable it to determine the size of the problem, research should be conducted to estimate the number of children who have been affected by bereavement due to the conflict, and a review should be carried out of modern practices in other countries, in particular the USA. The State should then evaluate its own practices in the light of this information;

- the Government should provide financial help to one or more voluntary organisations who would be willing to provide appropriate support, in order to aid those who do not wish to seek State help in these circumstances.

**11** Compliance with Article 40, the right to due process of law, requires that:

- the Government scrutinises the emergency law as well as the criminal law for inconsistency with the Convention, and that legislation and administrative procedures be reformed in accordance with the need of children and young people for special protection and provision;

- the Government monitors the administration of juvenile justice to ensure that at all stages children and young people suspected or accused of an offence are treated in a way that promotes their sense of dignity and worth and is in accordance with due process of law;

- the length of time that children can be held and questioned under emergency legislation should be reduced to that applying under the Police and Criminal Evidence (NI) Order 1989;

- the standard of legal representation of young people be carefully monitored with a view to seeking improvements. As a priority funding should be made available for a children's law centre;

- the availability of indeterminate sentences for juveniles under the 'Secretary of State's Pleasure' arrangements should be reviewed. There should be moves towards determinate sentencing and an end to the mandatory life sentence for murder.

**12** Compliance with Article 42, the duty to promote awareness of the rights in the Convention, requires that community perceptions of the acceptability of violence, including violent punishment by adults of children and young people be addressed. Community education programmes about the Convention, about children's rights and in particular about protection of children's physical and personal integrity should be established and adequately resourced.

# References

1. *A citizen's inquiry; the Opsahl Report on Northern Ireland*, (ed) Andy Pollak, The Lilliput Press for Initiative '92 (1993)

2. 'Legislating for Northern Ireland', *Eighteenth Report of the Standing Advisory Commission on Human Rights*, Report for 1992-1993, pp 6-10, SACHR, HMSO (1 July 1993)

3. *United Kingdom: human rights concerns*, AI Index EUR 45/04/91, Amnesty International (June 1991)

4. *Broken covenants: violations of international law in Northern Ireland*, report of the Northern Ireland Human Rights Assembly, 6-8 April 1992, London, Liberty/National Council for Civil Liberties (1993)

5. *Human rights in Northern Ireland*, A Helsinki Watch Report, Human Rights Watch (October 1991). See also *Prison conditions in the United Kingdom*, a Helsinki Watch/Prison Project Report, Human Rights Watch (June 1992)

6. see reference 2

7. see reference 1

8. *Making rights count*, Committee on the Administration of Justice pamphlet no 17, CAJ (October 1990), see also *A bill of rights for Northern Ireland*, CAJ (May 1993)

9. *Civil liberties in Northern Ireland: The CAJ Handbook*, 2nd edition, p5, Brice Dickson (ed), Committee on the Administration of Justice (1993)

10. 'Legal controls on the use of lethal force: options for reform', paper by Professor Hadden T, *Eighteenth Report of the Standing Advisory Commission on Human Rights*, HMSO (March 1993)

11. *Caught in crossfire*, Cairns, Appletree Press, Belfast (1987)

12. 'Troubles, stress and psychological disorder in Northern Ireland', Wilson R and Cairns E, *The Psychologist*, vol 15, no 8, pp347-350 (1992)

13. As the violence in NorthernIreland tends to be concentrated in particular geographical locations this would lead one to predict much higher rates for such areas.

14. see reference 5

15. see reference 2, p143; see also *They shoot children - the use of rubber and plastic bullets in the North of Ireland*, Curtis L, Information on Ireland (reprinted 1989); and *Plastic bullets and the law*, CAJ pamphlet, no 15 (March 1990)

16. see reference 5

17. see reference 10

18. see reference 5

19. *Plastic bullets and the law*, CAJ pamphlet no 5 (March 1990)

20. see reference 4, Commission 1, 'The right to life'.

21. see reference 19

22. see reference 5

23. see reference 2

24. see reference 5

25. *Children in Northern Ireland: abused by security forces and paramilitaries*, Helsinki Watch, Human Rights Watch (July 1992)

26. see reference 25

27. see reference 4

28. see reference 2

29. *Racism in Northern Ireland: the need for legislation to*

*combat racial discrimination in Northern Ireland*, CAJ pamphlet no 20, (June 1992)

30. *Staid agus Stadas na Gaeilge i dTuaisceart na hEireann: the UK Government's approach to the Irish language in light of the European Charter for Regional or Minority Languages*, CAJ (1993)

31. see reference 25

32. see reference 4

33. see reference 4, Commission 2, 'Freedom from torture and cruel, inhuman and degrading treatment'.

34. *Allegations of psychological ill-treatment of detainees held under emergency legislation in Northern Ireland*, CAJ (February 1993)

35. see reference 34

36. see reference 25

37. see rference 34

38. *Life sentences and SOSP prisoners in Northern Ireland*, CAJ pamphlet, no 12 CAJ (February 1989)

39. see reference 4, Commission 5, 'The Right to Respect for Private and Family Life'

40. Letter from the Committee for the Transfer of Irish Prisoners (18 January 1994)

41. '*Peace making, discrimination and the rights of children to attend integrated schools in Northern Ireland*', a Brief made to the UN and UNESCO, Department of Social Anthropology, Irwin C J, The Queen's University of Belfast (April 1993)

42. see reference 1

43. see reference 1

44. *Childright*, no 96, Children's Legal Centre (May 1993)

# UK Agenda for Children

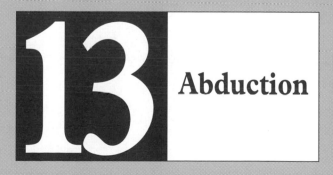

# 1 Contents

**Acknowledgement**
This report is based on a paper by the Scottish Child Law
Centre and is largely drawn from *Home and away: child
abduction in the nineties*, a report published by Reunite, the
National Council for Abducted Children on 9 March 1993.

# 1 Introduction

**1.1** Article 11 of the UN Convention obliges States Parties to take measures to combat the illicit **transfer** and **non-return** of children abroad. There are two elements to this obligation which are addressed by different categories of law.

**1.2** The illicit **transfer** of children abroad is a concern of the domestic law of the various parts of the UK. Relevant to this is the civil law which confers rights of custody or responsibility for residence, and the criminal law, which provides sanctions against those who seek to remove children wrongfully from the UK. The main piece of legislation for the civil law is the Children Act 1989 (for England and Wales) and the Law Reform (Parent and Child) (Scotland) Act 1986 for Scotland. The draft Children (NI) Order 1993 addresses these issues and is expected to be introduced in 1995. The main pieces of legislation for the criminal aspects are the Child Abduction Act 1984 and the Child Abduction (NI) Order 1985.

**1.3** The **non-return** of children abroad is the concern of international conventions through which the contracting parties seek to provide machinery for the tracing and speedy return of abducted children. The relevant conventions to which the UK is party are the *Convention on the Civil Aspects of International Child Abduction* (the Hague Convention), and the *European Convention on Recognition and Enforcement of Decisions Concerning Custody of Children* (the European Convention). Where the states concerned are parties to both conventions, the Hague Convention takes precedence. States party (at 1 August 1993) to the Hague Convention are Argentina, Australia, Austria, Belize, Burkina Faso, Canada, Denmark, Ecuador, France, Germany, Greece, Hungary, Israel, Luxembourg, Mauritius, Mexico, Monaco, Netherlands, New Zealand, Norway, Portugal, Poland, Republic of Ireland, Romania, Spain, Sweden, Switzerland, United States of America and Yugoslavia. States party to the European Convention, but not party to the Hague Convention, are Belgium and Cyprus.

**1.4** The main provisions of these conventions were incorporated into UK law by the Child Abduction and Custody Act 1985 and the Child Abduction and Custody (Parties to Conventions) Order 1986.

**1.5** This report examines how all the international conventions on child abduction are working and the extent to which they comply with the UN Convention on the Rights of the Child. It also looks at what happens when children are abducted to countries which are not party to the child abduction conventions and makes recommendations, and also addresses the question of the prevention of abduction abroad through changes to domestic law and practice and makes appropriate recommendations. The issue of abduction of children from one jurisdiction within the UK to another is also considered.

# 2 Relevant articles in the UN Convention

## 2.1 General principles

**Article 2:** all rights in the Convention must apply without discrimination of any kind irrespective of race, colour, language, religion, national, ethnic or social origin, disability or other status.

**Article 3:** the duty in all actions to consider the best interests of the child.

**Article 12:** the right to express an opinion and to have that opinion taken into account in any matter or procedure affecting the child.

## 2.2 Articles relating to implementation and dissemination

**Article 1:** a child is defined as anyone up to eighteen years of age.

**Article 4:** the duty of the Government to implement the rights in the Convention.

## 2.3 Articles relevant to abduction

**Article 9:** the right to live with one's family unless this is not in the child's best interests and, where separation does take place, the right to maintain contact with both parents on a regular basis.

**Article 10:** the right to enter the country to be reunited or to maintain the child-parent relationship.

**Article 11:** the duty of the Government to take measures to prevent kidnapping or retention of children abroad.

**Article 35:** the duty of the Government to take measures to prevent the sale, abduction and trafficking of children.

*For the full wording of the articles, see the UN Convention on the Rights of the Child, page 311.*

# 3 Current procedures following abduction

## 3.1 The Hague and European Conventions on child abduction

**3.1.1** The main difference between the two conventions lies in the fact that the Hague Convention recognises and enforces custody **rights**, whether these arise from court orders or by operation of law, whereas the European Convention recognises and enforces custody **orders**. The current trend towards reduction of the number of court orders has adversely affected the effectiveness of the European Convention.

**3.1.2** The Children Act 1989 for England and Wales aimed to prevent the making of unnecessary court orders. The same principle exists in theory in Scottish legislation (the Law Reform (Parent and Child) (Scotland) Act 1986, section 3 (2)), and it is hoped to strengthen it in future legislation (the Scottish Law Commission's Family Law Report, May 1992, Recommendation 33(a)). The implication of this is that in countries party only to the European Convention parents without custody orders will be unable to use it immediately. In order to invoke the Convention following abduction of a child, they will have to seek from a UK court an order awarding custody and declaring the removal of the child to be unlawful (European Convention, Article 12).

**3.1.3** Child abduction has traditionally been viewed as a breach of the rights of the parent rather than the child and the international conventions speak of breach of the rights of custody belonging to adults. The aim of the conventions is the prompt return of the child to the person entitled to his or her custody. The courts of the country to which the abductor has flown are generally prohibited from enquiring into the merits of the rights of custody.

**3.1.4** The **Hague** Convention (Article 12) provides that, if less than a year has elapsed from the date of the abduction, the receiving state is obliged to order the return of the child 'forthwith'. If more than a year has elapsed, they must also order the return of the child, unless it is demonstrated that the child is now settled in his or her new environment. Article 13 says that the receiving state may nevertheless refuse to return the child if:

- it is established that there is a grave risk that his or her return would expose the child to physical or psychological harm or otherwise place the child in an intolerable situation, or

- the receiving state finds that the child objects to being returned and has attained an age and a degree of maturity at which it is appropriate to take account of his or her views.

**3.1.5** The **European** Convention provides (Article 9 (3)) that:
'In no circumstances may the foreign decision be reviewed as to its substance.'
Article 10 allows refusal to return if:

- the effects of the decision are manifestly incompatible with the fundamental principles of the law regarding children and families in the state addressed;

- a change in circumstances, including the passage of time, means that the effect of the original decision is manifestly no longer in accordance with the welfare of the child.

Article 15 gives a limited right to refuse return based on the child's wishes - and related to a change in circumstances.

**3.1.6** Clearly, the UK has, in becoming party to the conventions, already displayed some commitment to combating the abduction of children abroad, as required by Articles 11 and 35 of the UN Convention.

## 3.2 Abduction to countries not party to the Hague and European Conventions

**3.2.1** Most international child abductions take place outside the scope of the Hague and European Conventions. Insofar as children abducted to the UK are concerned, British judges do not normally hesitate to return abducted children to their country of origin . The main problem concerns the removal of UK children to non-convention countries. Whereas abductions involving convention countries are dealt with by the Lord Chancellor's Department, or in Scotland by the Scottish Courts Administration, children abducted to non-convention countries fall into the province of the Foreign Office.

**3.2.2** With no conventions to rely upon, parents of these children have to seek return of their children through the courts of the country to which the child has been abducted. British legal aid is not available for foreign legal proceedings, although agreements with some countries enable litigants to apply for legal aid in the foreign country by transmitting the application. In England and Wales, it is possible to obtain legal aid in some circumstances if the child is a ward of court.

**3.2.3** The Foreign Office through its consular function can help parents recover their children, either through diplomatic or logistical help. In practice, consular help with abduction problems tends at best to be patchy. (See para 7.2.5)

# 4 Implementation and dissemination

## 4.1 Age limits (Article 1)

**4.1.1** The UN Convention applies up to the age of 18 (Article 1). The international conventions on abduction apply up to the age of 16. In England and Wales residence orders end at 16, except in exceptional cases (Children Act 1989, sections 9 (6) and (7)). The same provision is currently proposed for N Ireland. In Scotland rights of custody end at 16 and at that age children attain virtually full legal capacity and can change their own domicile. There is, therefore, no question of a breach of rights of custody over the 16-18 year-olds. Illicit transfer and non-return of this age group would be matters for the ordinary criminal law which would support the young person's rights to autonomy. There is therefore no breach of Article 1.

## 4.2 Implementation of rights (Article 4)

**4.2.1** Article 4 of the UN Convention requires governments to '*undertake all appropriate legislative, administrative, and other measures for the implementation of the rights ... in the ... Convention*'. It goes on to insist that this should be pursued '*to the maximum extent of their available resources and, where needed, within the framework of international co-operation*'. Articles 7 and 26 of the Hague Convention set out a catalogue of measures which states must take to secure the prompt return of children, including the provision of legal aid. Article 5 of the European Convention obliges the receiving state to bear all legal costs in securing the return of the child, apart from the cost of repatriation.

**4.2.2** In fact some states (including the UK - see section 11 of the Child Abduction and Custody Act 1985) limit the assistance to that provided under existing state schemes (although there is no means test). There is also a discernable imbalance in that the allegedly 'abducting' parent is not entitled to automatic, non-means-tested legal aid. This could work to the disadvantage of the child if the abducting parent is not given assistance to explore the relevance of those articles of the Convention which might justify a refusal to return the child. Moreover, the grant of legal aid under the Convention does not cover a multitude of expenses actually incurred by a parent seeking the return of a child.

**4.2.3** Appearance at court hearings may not be strictly necessary in the clearest cases. In practice, however, a faxed affidavit is not very satisfactory. The parents need to be in court. This involves the cost of travelling, accommodation and subsistence.

**4.2.4** Parents cannot recover the cost of telephone calls and letters to abducted children but they need to make such contact to retain parental bonds. Abductors tend to cease making maintenance payment when they take the child. This all happens at the point at which the infant's absence entitles the authorities to terminate child benefit. There needs to be financial provision for the fact that the cost of savings of not having a child to feed and clothe are more than cancelled out by the other irrecoverable expenses of having one's child abducted.

**4.2.5** Even if the child is returned, the fare for the journey back has to be found. This may deter the recovery of a child taken to distant countries. The fact that children under the age of five cannot travel unaccompanied compounds this problem. The actual return itself costs money. The current four-month delay for counselling on the National Health Service reported in some cases is not appropriate for a child who has been separated from his or her parent for a significant period of time. Studies indicate that some form of trauma is an almost inevitable result in children kidnapped over the age of two.

**4.2.6** The Government provides no help with any of these costs involved in child abduction. They are rarely taken into account in the calculation of income support. The problem becomes even more difficult in cases of children abducted to countries which are not party to the international conventions.

**4.2.7** Measures to achieve true implementation of the abduction obligations must recognise the actual costs incurred in obtaining return of an abducted child and the inadequacy of resources currently committed by the UK and other states. More efficient access to sources of finance abroad and a more precise assessment of the actual costs of recovery could be facilitated by the appointment of an International Children's Commissioner, with a representative in each state.

### ACTION REQUIRED FOR COMPLIANCE

**Compliance with Article 4, the duty to implement the Convention to the maximum extent possible, requires that:**

- **legal aid should be made available to parents seeking to recover children from countries where such assistance is not available or adequate;**
- **child benefit should be continued after an abduction, or at least the costs of contact with the child and his or her return must be paid by the state;**
- **an International Children's Commissioner should be appointed with a representative in each state, to represent the interests of abducted children.**

# 5 Basic principles of the Convention

## 5.1 The right not to be discriminated against (Article 2)

**5.1.1** Article 2 states that '*States Parties shall respect and ensure the rights set forth in the present Convention to each child within their jurisdiction without discrimination of any kind, irrespective of the child's or his or her parent's or legal guardian's race, colour, sex, language, religion, political or other opinion, national, ethnic or social origin, property, disability, birth or other status*'. It also obliges the Government to '*take all appropriate measures to ensure that the child is protected against all forms of discrimination or punishment on the basis of the status, activities, expressed opinions, or beliefs of the child's parents, legal guardians, or family members*'.

**5.1.2** There is a possible conflict between the requirements of Article 2 of the UN Convention and Article 10(1)(a) of the European Convention. The European Convention Article allows states to refuse to return a child if it is found that the effects of the decision are manifestly incompatible with the fundamental principles of the law relating to the family and children in the state addressed. The question arises whether these fundamental principles adequately take account of the interests of the child. If they do not, then it could be argued that children of these states are being discriminated against.

**5.1.3** Scottish children are also discriminated against in the sense that they are afforded less protection than their English counterparts due to the restricted application of the Child Abduction Act 1984 (see para 8.1.3).

### ACTION REQUIRED FOR COMPLIANCE

**Compliance with Article 2, the rights of all children to all the rights in the Convention without discrimination, requires that:**

- **interpreters, where necessary, are made available to help the independent person interact with the abducted child.**

- **Article 10(1)(a) of the European Convention is reconsidered on the basis that it may allow discrimination against children from certain countries.**

- **the application of the Child Abduction Act 1984 should be widened to Scottish children to cover cases where no court order is in existence.**

## 5.2 The best interests of the child (Article 3)

**5.2.1** Article 3 of the UN Convention states that: '*In all actions concerning children, whether undertaken by public or private social welfare institutions, courts of law, administrative authorities or legislative bodies, the best interests of the child shall be a primary consideration*'. The international conventions on child abduction operate on the presumption that the interests of the child are best served by a prompt return to facilitate the settling of disputes in the child's country of origin. The best interests of the individual child concerned are not addressed within the procedures established by the Convention. In fact, the receiving states are specifically prohibited from looking at the merits of the case. The child must be returned unless:

- there is a grave risk of physical or psychological harm, or the child would be placed in an intolerable situation (Hague Convention, Article 13);

- the child objects to being returned and has attained an age and degree of maturity at which it is appropriate to take account of its views (Hague Convention, Article 13);

- the child was abducted over a year ago and is now settled in its new environment (Hague Convention, Article 12);

- the effects of the decision are manifestly incompatible with the fundamental principles of the law regarding the family and children in the state addressed (European Convention, Article 10);

- a change of circumstances, including the passage of time, mean that the effects of the original decision are manifestly no longer in accord with the welfare of the child ( for example, taking into account the wishes of a child of appropriate age, etc) (European Convention, Article 10).

The Hague Convention aims at the making of a decision by the receiving state within six weeks of the commencement of the proceedings (Article 11).

**5.2.2** There is no doubt that the welfare of children is a main aim of the abduction conventions. It is understandable that this should create a presumption in favour of a speedy return. Time favours the abductor. The provisions of Article 12 of the Hague Convention acknowledge that the passage of time and the settling of the child in his or her new environment weakens the presumption in favour of return. Judges are understandably reluctant to disturb a child yet again. It therefore seems reasonable to discourage abductors by taking all possible measures to redress the wrong before a new status quo is established. Indeed, the Reunite report *Home and away - child abduction in the nineties* says that the 'welfare' principle can and has become a child abductors' charter.

**5.2.3** One cannot however get away from the fact that the courts in these cases apply general presumptions about the welfare of children. Apart from the exceptions outlined above, they do not address the best interests of the individual child.

**5.2.4** This appears to be a case of conflict between two worthy principles. It is submitted that 'to permit a full investigation of the circumstances of the child' - basically a redetermination of the merits of custody decisions - would tend to favour the abductor, to increase the attraction of abduction and, ultimately, to act against the interests of children generally. It is suggested that the best way to redress the balance in favour of the individual child is to make greater efforts to ensure that the children concerned are informed of their rights, in accordance with Article 42 of the UN Convention and given an opportunity to express an opinion in accordance with Article 12. This would make the exception to the speedy return principle more real and would in itself widen considerations of the welfare of the individual child.

## 5.3 The right of the child to express a view (Article 12)

**5.3.1** Article 12 of the UN Convention states that the Government must '*assure to the child who is capable of forming his or her own views the right to express those views freely in all matters affecting the child, the views of the child being given due weight in accordance with the age and maturity of the child*'. It goes on to state that '*the child shall in particular be provided the opportunity to be heard in any judicial and administrative proceedings affecting the child, either directly, or through a representative or an appropriate body, in a manner consistent with the procedural rules of national law*'.

**5.3.2** This Article obliges authorities to be pro-active in finding out the child's views and considering what weight to give them. However, apart from the exceptions outlined above, children have no absolute right to be involved in decisions about return to their country of origin. Even where the principle of Article 12 is accepted, the logistical problem arises of how one gets access to a child to ascertain whether a child has any views, and if so, what they are. There must also be a knowledgable assessment of the maturity of the child and the weight to be given to the child's views.

### ACTION REQUIRED FOR COMPLIANCE

**Compliance with Article 12, the right of children to express their views and have them taken seriously, requires that:**

- **there are arrangements for seeking and representing the abducted child's views. This could be achieved through the local offices of the International Children's Commissioner proposed above;**

- **legal aid should be provided automatically to allow independent representation of the abducted child in any country to which he or she has been taken;**

- **insofar as children abducted to the UK are concerned, an independent person should always be appointed to investigate and report on the child's circumstances, to advise the child of his or her rights, to present the child's views, and to help the child get independent legal representation if appropriate.**

# 6 A child's right to family life

## 6.1 The right not to be separated from parents (Article 9)

**6.1.1** While the international conventions are strong on returning children who have been removed in breach of custody rights, they do not normally address a situation where the child was removed by the parent with custody, thus making it practically impossible for the child to maintain contact with the other parent. Article 9.1 of the UN Convention states that the child has the right '*not [to] be separated from his or her parents against their will, except when competent authorities subject to judicial review determine, in accordance with applicable law and procedures, that such separation is necessary for the best interests of the child*'. Article 9.3 states that '*a child who is separated from one or both parents [has the right] to maintain personal relations and direct contact with both parents on a regular basis, except if it is contrary to the child's best interests*'.

**6.1.2** The Hague Convention urges states to facilitate access and the European Convention seeks to give recognition to existing rights of access. However, removal of the child to another country radically affects the potential of the non-custodial parent to maintain meaningful contact with the child. This is against not only the child's right to maintain contact but also the prevailing philosophy of continued shared parenting after divorce or separation, promoted by the Children Act 1989, and proposed for Scotland by the Scottish Law Commission (Report on family law, 1992), and for N Ireland by the draft Children (NI) Order 1993.

### ACTION REQUIRED FOR COMPLIANCE

**Compliance with Article 9.3, the right to maintain contact with both parents, requires that a protocol is added to the Hague and European Conventions to facilitate return of a child removed by the custodial parent, in order that the child may continue to have access to the non-custodial parent.**

## 6.2 The right to family reunification (Article 10)

**6.2.1** The right to leave a country is an important issue for children who have dual nationalities. Article 10.2 of the UN Convention requires that '*a child whose parents reside in different States shall have the right to maintain on a regular basis ... personal relations and direct contacts with both parents*'. There need to be procedures for the child to apply for the right to leave, with no adverse consequences. The representative of the Commissioner proposed above (para 4) in each state could advise and support children in these circumstances.

### ACTION REQUIRED FOR COMPLIANCE

**Compliance with Article 10.2, the right to family reunification, requires that procedures exist to enable children to apply for the right to leave the country. The Commissioner proposed above should be pro-active in finding and advising children and supporting them if they want to leave the country to which they have been abducted.**

# 7 The right to protection from abduction

## 7.1 The duty to combat illicit removal of children (Articles 11 and 35)

**7.1.1** Article 11 states that '*States Parties shall take measures to combat the illicit transfer and non-return of children abroad ... [and] shall promote the conclusion of bilateral or multilateral agreements or accession to existing agreements*'. Article 35 states that '*States Parties shall take all appropriate national, bilateral and multilateral measures to prevent the abduction of, the sale of or traffic in children for any purpose or in any form*'. The advantage of the multi-lateral approach to child abduction is that it establishes internationally accepted standards. Countries that subscribe to the ideals of the conventions may feel morally or diplomatically bound to accept these standards.

**7.1.2** Nevertheless, the multi-lateral approach has barely scratched the surface in terms of producing acceptable human rights standards world-wide. Not enough countries have either ratified or implemented properly the relevant treaties. The system of global treaties cannot operate without the support of bi-lateral contacts between states. Diplomatic or economic pressure applied through such contacts is often necessary to make countries see the need to adopt generally accepted standards in particular fields. This is particularly so where the country concerned feels that the international rules were made by representatives of states that do not share their social or cultural values.

## 7.2 Diplomatic steps to restrict child abduction

**7.2.1** Economic and political pressure can be applied either to ensure that multi-lateral treaties are ratified, or that bi-lateral agreements contain human rights provisions. Agreements between individual states are often simpler to negotiate because only two parties are involved. The bi-lateral approach will, however, often depend on the negotiating position of the country suggesting improvements in the other state's human rights records.

**7.2.2** Diplomatic activity is not confined to bringing recalcitrant countries into line. A significant number of countries agree with the need to reduce abductions and recover kidnapped children. However, a degree of co-ordination between legal systems is necessary in order to ensure that foreign court orders are respected and children returned to the relevant parents or access visits arranged. Moreover, governments which do not have a kidnapping problem but are keen to bring their human rights record into line with the international community, need to be kept informed of conventions which they might wish to ratify.

**7.2.3** Diplomatic activity has to operate at a number of different levels. The UK Government publicly campaigns for the global ratification of the Hague and European Conventions. Formal contacts through established groups such as the Commonwealth can provide a useful platform for the British government to bring attention to the need for action. At the same time, ordinary diplomatic exchanges may often produce a more effective means of furthering its anti-abduction policy. Countries that rely on British aid or commerce can be pressurised into improving their child abduction performance by ratifying one of the multi-lateral conventions or bi-lateral agreements dealing with the subject.

**7.2.4** The UK Government's activity in the area of child abduction is restricted mainly to the Foreign Office (FCO) and the Lord Chancellor's Department. The Lord Chancellor's Department deals with individual cases of kidnapping to and from the United Kingdom as part of its role as the Central Authority for the purposes of the Hague and European Conventions. (In Scotland, the Central Authority is the Secretary of State working through the Scottish Courts Administration). The FCO, through its consular function, is intended to help parents recover their children either through diplomatic or logistical help. In practice, however, this help tends to be at best patchy.

**7.2.5** The experience of lawyers, referred to in *Home and away - child abduction in the nineties* is that the FCO offers little real help when a child is abducted to a country where neither the Hague nor the European Convention apply. It is totally unwilling to help when the children concerned are not UK subjects, even if they have been made wards of the English court. This is despite the fact that, under English law, such an order makes an infant the equivalent of a British citizen since he or she is placed in the custody of a High Court judge until the matter is resolved. The Foreign Office view is that attempts to recover abducted children represent private disputes in which it is inappropriate for a foreign government to intervene. In addition if the child holds the nationality of the country where it is being held and the abduction conventions do not apply, the Foreign Office considers the matter to be beyond its authority and is unwilling to become involved to any substantial extent. This attitude leaves children, whom the UK government has an obligation to protect, wholly defenceless.

**7.2.6** There is a need to persuade the FCO to play a more active role. The UK makes a great number of commercial treaties with countries. Few contain any provisions about human rights, and none about child abduction. While sometimes conditions of this nature would be inappropriate (the foreign state may well take its business elsewhere), there are plenty of situations for a country wishing to improve relations with the UK in which progress on child abduction could be made a quid pro quo. Where there is a known problem, such as in North Africa, the Government needs to have an active anti-child-kidnapping policy. States need to be told that the ratification of bi-lateral or multi-lateral treaties on the subject is a precondition to good relations. The FCO's current concentration on multi-lateral treaties at the expense of bi-lateral agreement may not be the right approach in all cases.

**7.2.7** The FCO should also take direct responsibility for the abduction of British children currently subject to UK court orders. It presently declines to do this on the basis that matrimonial disputes are a private matter. The ratification of the UN Convention on the Rights of the Child means that this is no longer the case. The FCO must take on a campaigning role to ensure that governments appreciate the need to make arrangements for the return of abducted children. They must also ensure that those facilities are put at the disposal of British citizens and those subject to UK court orders.

**7.2.8** Parents who approach the All Party Group and Reunite frequently complain that consular officials were unhelpful when their children were kidnapped in foreign countries. They said that assistance was not available to summon local police or obtain immediate local help. Consular staff, particularly in countries where child abduction is a major problem, need to know what to do when a panic-stricken parent tells them that his or her child has been stolen. Both emotional and financial support needs to be available for litigants abroad seeking to recover their children. Reports suggest that this has not been forthcoming and that diplomats have told parents not to bother trying to pursue such cases. This is not good enough. A programme of consular support needs to be prepared by embassies and consulates worldwide for which adequate funding must be made available. The fact that a child has dual nationality should not prevent the Foreign Office and its diplomatic representatives from taking the necessary action to protect British citizens.

**7.2.9** The Foreign Office should appoint, in each embassy in the non-convention countries, at least one person with specific responsibilities for child abduction matters. It should also produce guidelines on this topic and related problems. It is understood that the Foreign Office has agreed in principle to the latter course.

### ACTION REQUIRED FOR COMPLIANCE

**Compliance with Articles 11 and 35, the duty to combat illicit removal of children, requires that:**

- **the UK Government should expend more effort in encouraging other countries to ratify the international conventions on abduction;**

- **the UK Government should promote the conclusion of bi-lateral agreements with other countries;**

- **there should be greater support for parents through the Foreign Office and through the provision of financial assistance;**

- **the UK Government should seek to promote the establishment of a Commissioner for Abducted Children, with a representative in each state. Until that is achieved, the Foreign Office should appoint a senior diplomat to act as a Children's Ombudsman, to mediate and negotiate in individual cases;**

- **there should be a change of Foreign Office policy towards a more pro-active approach with regard to British children who also hold the nationality of the country to which they have been abducted;**

- **the Foreign Office should contact governments with bad records in child abduction matters, with a view to arranging meetings between parents and abducted children, and encouraging the creation of mediation and conciliation services which can result in an improvement in a situation;**

- **international bodies such as the European Union and the Commonwealth should be encouraged to address matters of child abduction.**

# 8 Prevention of abduction

## 8.1 The legal system

**8.1.1** Article 11 of the UN Convention obliges States Parties to take measures to combat the illicit **transfer** of children abroad. This means that domestic law must recognise the need to prevent child abduction and take measures to achieve that end. This involves matters of law, policy and practice. The Child Abduction Act 1984 made it a criminal offence to send one's own child abroad without the consent of the other parent or other people with custody. In England and Wales, an offence is committed whether or not there is a court order awarding custody (or residence) to anyone. In Scotland, the provisions of the Act apply only when there is a UK court order awarding custody of the child, or making him or her a ward of court, or prohibiting the removal of the child from the UK or any part of it.

**8.1.2** The situation in England and Wales has been affected by the introduction of the Children Act 1989 which aimed to reduce the number of court orders relating to children. Although the existence of a court order is not necessary to trigger the criminal provisions of the 1984 Act and the recovery provisions of the Hague Convention, the lack of an authoritative statement about custody rights makes it more difficult to enlist the assistance of the police under the 1984 Act and to persuade foreign courts that the removal was wrongful. The position is further complicated by section 1(13) of the Children Act, which allows anyone with a residence order to take the child abroad for any period up to one month without the permission of the other parent. This seems to negate the protection of the 1984 Act. Despite the Children Act's intention of reducing the use of wardship proceedings, these might still be the most effective way of preventing the removal abroad of children from England and Wales.

**8.1.3** In Scotland, children are protected by the criminal provisions only if there is a relevant court order in existence. This restriction discriminates against Scottish children, in breach of Article 2 of the UN Convention. A common situation, known to the Scottish Child Law Centre, is for a mother to fear an abduction - and even to have been threatened by the father that he will take the child abroad. The mother who merely fears abduction is afraid to seek a court order in case this makes the situation worse and causes hostility. The mother often has no evidence of the threat. Threats are made in private. She therefore lacks anything concrete to persuade the court that the making of an order is necessary.

**8.1.4** The importance of the criminal aspect of child abduction lies not so much in the capacity of courts to punish the abductor - as this may often disadvantage the child - but in its condemnation of the act as criminal, and the consequent bringing into play of the resources of the police force. If the police are notified of a potential wrongful removal of the child, they can act quickly to institute the port-stop procedure and apprehend the abductor with the child.

Compliance with Article 11, the duty to combat illicit removal of children, requires that:

- the loop-hole in the Children Act 1989 should be closed so that it should be possible to prosecute parents in Britain who take a child abroad for thirty days and during that time decide not to return the child;

- duty judges should always be available to ensure that court orders can be obtained when needed. In England and Wales there has been found to be a problem with the availability of judges between 4pm and 7pm, particularly on Fridays and the day before bank holidays. In addition, duty judges need to be equipped with portable telefax machines;

- lawyers, judges and police need to be better trained in the area of child abduction. Efforts should be made to help foreign courts understand the Children Act by printing guidelines on court orders.

## 8.2 The need for research

8.2.1 Investigation into ways of avoiding child abduction and then dealing with it when it occurs are hampered by the limited amount of empirical research done into the whole subject. Very little concrete information exists about why people abduct children and what can bring about the resolution of conflict arising from such behaviour. Most of the published studies are based on small, often unrepresentative samples, and none appears to have examined the problem in Britain.

Compliance with Article 11 requires that:

- better records are kept concerning prosecutions for child abduction and also records in Scotland of interdicts granted to stop children from being removed from the country. A central register of custody and access orders made or recognised in the UK should be maintained;

- further research is funded into the causes of child abduction.

## 8.3 Passport and exit restrictions

8.3.1 There are concerns about the current rules relating to passports and exit restrictions. The basic rule is that where an abduction is feared, the potentially threatened parent can apply under various legal provisions in relation to passports, such as Section 8 of the Children Act 1989, section 3 of the Law Reform (Parent and Child ) (Scotland) Act 1986, or section 37 of the Family Law Act 1986, for all the necessary orders relating to a child's passport and his or her right to leave the country.

8.3.2 It is not difficult, where a kidnapping is thought likely, to have a child's passport placed in the hands of a solicitor or specially endorsed. There is added security in retention of the parent's passport. However, most parents would legitimately complain if they had to hand over their documents in the same way. An alternative is to require the surrender of the parent's passport until the safe return is reported of the child from a contact visit. A requirement for the police to put out an all-ports alert during each access visit can also be inserted in a court order.

8.3.3 The main difficulty in this area is that the current way in which the passport system operates in the UK can prevent court orders being effective. Family passports need to be discontinued. Every child should have a passport in his or her own right. The lack of individual documents makes international child abduction much easier. If the current system is retained, photographs should appear in the passport of any child covered by it. Currently, only the name of a child travelling on a parent's passport needs to appear in that document. There also need to be restrictions on the number of passports on which a child can travel. At present, a child can have his or her own passport and be named on a parent's passport.

8.3.4 There is now provision for a parent to search the passport records to see if a travel document has been issued to a child. However, a period of three months may elapse before the issue of such papers shows up in a search. This period needs to be shortened to seven days.

8.3.5 At present, British visitors passports cannot be issued to children under the age of eight. An extension to end this restriction to all children would offer greater protection in line with Article 11.

8.3.6 Custody or similar orders should be marked on a child's passport. It should be possible for a court to require such a document to identify those whose consent is required for the removal of a child from the jurisdiction. Where a passport is marked in this way, evidence of the necessary consents would be required where an affected child leaves the country.

8.3.7 Publicity and formal status need to be given to the new if unofficial practice of the Marriages and General Department at St Catherine's House in London of annotating a child's birth certificate on request. This means that solicitors acting for the parent caring for the child will be notified if any attempt is made to obtain a duplicate copy of the certificate. A copy can be used to obtain a visitor's passport, even though a stop has been placed on the issue of an ordinary one. When a duplicate copy certificate has been requested, local registrars of births, death and marriages will be informed by St Catherine's House. The marking of birth certificates should be available in all court proceedings, not just as at present in extreme circumstances after a child has been made a ward of court.

8.3.8 The port-stop procedure can be an important tool in the prevention of a child's removal abroad but there are difficulties with its application. In *Home and away - child abduction in the nineties*, one suggestion was that where anything other than an individual passport and the necessary evidence of consent for the child to leave the country is presented, immigration officers should be instructed to check the central index to see whether a port-stop procedure has been set up with regard to the child. The procedure itself needs to be strengthened and publicised. It currently operates by telex. The introduction of telefax would allow photographs of the children concerned to be distributed which would increase the effectiveness of the service.

**8.3.9** It would be impractical in all probability to extend the stop notice system to visitor's passports. Stop notices need, however, to be available for children even in the absence of a court order. Often the slightest delay can make it impossible to prevent a child from being removed from the country. Passport stops which expire now after six months should remain unless removed by the agreement of all those with parental responsibility, or by the court.

**8.3.10** The quality of police work varies considerably in the whole area of child abduction. The most widely reported problem with port-alerts concerns the extent of the police's co-operation. In England and Wales, there is an automatic alert issued by the High Court Tipstaff following proceedings. However, the police often wrongly require a court order before they are prepared to act. In any event, police guidelines do need to be published, both for the assistance of the officers concerned and for the guidance of those who need to invoke their help.

**8.3.11** Before a port alert will be put out, the police officer has to be satisfied that an abduction is imminent, that is, likely to take place within 48 hours. The '48 hour' requirement for port-alerts is often difficult to meet. Bearing in mind the speed that is needed to stop a parent removing a child in a matter of hours, the police should be given wider discretion, or a system of the alert having to be justified within 48 hours of going out.

**8.3.12** In any event, the port-alert system does not apply to the removal of a child to the Isle of Man, the Channel Isles or Eire. There is a danger that a child will be removed through those islands and from there will be taken to another country. More generally, the government needs to study the overall effectiveness of the port-alert. The Working Party report indicates that it has failed even in high profile cases.

**8.3.13** Where a child has dual nationality, issue of a passport by an embassy or consulate within the UK can by-pass other restrictions. Some embassies and consulates are prepared to respect UK restrictions and refuse issue of passports to the children concerned. It would be helpful if the Foreign Office would collate information about embassy and consulate practice in this respect.

**8.3.14** There is also a need for an increase in the number of access centres where supervised visits can take place. There should be increased judicial control over the timetabling and conduct of family litigation to avoid unnecessary delay and uncertainty, and thereby further the best interests of the child.

## 8.4 The use of mediation in child abduction cases

**8.4.1** Mediation may have a role to play at several different stages in child abduction disputes. Mediation represents an attempt to settle disputes otherwise than by resorting to the legal process, by involving both parties to the dispute in their own negotiations to reach agreement. Such an approach is consistent with the requirement to promote the best interests of the child in line with Article 3. Specific practical issues may be sorted out even against a background of continuing conflict. Ideally, the parties should meet together with the impartial mediator on neutral ground if the full benefits of mediation are to be reaped. The benefits are the settlement

of the immediate dispute plus an improved capacity to negotiate (without the intervention of a third party) in the future. Shuttle mediation, where the mediator moves between the two separate parties or mediation over the telephone are often deployed successfully where it is not possible or desirable for the parties to engage in face-to-face negotiations.

**8.4.2** The advantages of mediation are:

- the decisions in mediation are made by those who have to live with them, rather than by a third party;

- voluntariness is a fundamental principle of mediation. A mediated agreement, because it is voluntarily consented to, is more likely to be satisfactory to the parties and therefore to be adhered to by them;

- even where no agreement is reached, mediation as a process may be of value in providing opportunities for improved communication;

- mediation allows discussion of all aspects of the dispute - legal, economic, practical and emotional. The parameters of exchanges are not limited by legal terms of reference. The parties' own perspectives and the issues, ethical, psychological, cultural, religious - that are relevant to them are given prominence in mediation;

- joint decision-making is the goal of mediation: mediation can provide a calm neutral forum for discussions, however fraught and painful, and the opportunity for each party to have his or her say in a safe environment;

- mediation is, in its nature, a forward-looking process involving the consideration of future options and their consequences. This is what makes mediation singularly appropriate to the negotiating of family disputes over children where future child care arrangements have to be determined and where co-operation between the parents is necessary to achieve this;

- mediation is a confidential process. The promise of confidentiality can nurture a potential for co-operation that might not be realised otherwise.

**8.4.3** Mediation can be beneficial where there are existing disputes over children, for example, in relation to residence and contact, where abduction is being contemplated and also following abduction. It is also important that respect for children's views is built into the mediation process.

### ACTION REQUIRED FOR COMPLIANCE

**Compliance with Articles 11 and 3, the duty to promote the best interests of the child, requires that:**

- **the Foreign Office should collate information about embassies and consulates within the UK which are prepared to respect UK restrictions by refusing issue of passports to children with dual nationality;**

- **secure Government funding is provided to ensure the continuation of out-of-court mediation services throughout the United Kingdom, many of which currently struggle to survive financially despite the increasing number of referrals. Existing mediation, advice and counselling services must receive greater publicity, emphasising their respective roles in preventing disputes concerning children. Posters and leaflets in different languages, the media and advertisements need to be used for this purpose;**

- mediators receive training in the relevant law and the causes and consequences of child abduction;

- mediators are recruited from a wider range of ethnic and cultural communities. Interpreters also have a significant role to play in some circumstances;

- a police pyramid of expertise in abduction problems needs to be set up with clear guidelines issued to the police and immigration officers indicating among other things that a court order is not necessary for them to act (although the situation is different in Scotland);

- family passports are abolished and British visitors passports should not be issued to minors. Court orders should be noted on both birth certificates and passports;

- more access or contact centres need to be created, with facilities for supervision.

# 9 Abduction to other jurisdictions within the UK

## 9.1 Background

**9.1.1** Abduction of children can be a problem, not just at international level, but between different legal jurisdictions within the UK. Article 11 which requires that children are protected from illicit transfer and non-return from abroad does also have application within the UK because of the difficulties of enforcing custody or residence orders between the different jurisdictions. Procedures for registration and enforcement of custody/residence orders from one UK jurisdiction in another are set out in the Family Law Act 1986. The Act sets out a scheme whereby a person obtaining a custody or residence order in one part of the UK can have it registered and recognised in other parts of the UK. However, in order to have it enforced, proceedings for enforcement need to be taken, involving new applications for legal aid (where relevant) in the new jurisdiction. Section 30 of the 1986 Act allows for the staying or sisting (suspending) of the enforcement proceedings by any person interested, on the grounds that he or she has taken, or intends to take, other proceedings in the UK or elsewhere which might affect the original order. However, problems have arisen in implementing the 1986 Act procedure.

## 9.2 Tracing the child

**9.2.1** Experienced solicitors can now obtain orders in 48-72 hours. The problem lies in tracing the child. Although section 33 of the Act gives the court power to order disclosure of a child's whereabouts, there are still cases where the child cannot be found. It has been suggested that the involvement of the police would be beneficial as they could assist tracing through, for example, car registration numbers. Access to social security files might also be considered. This is permitted to facilitate the tracing of absent fathers for the recovery of maintenance. It might also be available for the tracing of abducted children to secure their welfare.

**9.2.2** The police do not regard their intervention as appropriate in civil cases. However, they are often the most effective agents in tracing the child and ensuring a speedy return.

## 9.3 Enforcement and legal aid

**9.3.1** Time is of the essence in cases of child abduction. It seems cumbersome to require separate enforcement proceedings and separate applications for legal aid in the various jurisdictions. The aim should be the speedy return of the child to the jurisdiction from which he or she was taken. It is recommended that delivery orders from one part of the UK be made enforceable throughout the rest of the UK without the necessity for further court proceedings or legal aid applications. Legal aid should be awarded automatically in child abduction cases in all jurisdictions within the UK.

## 9.4 Overlapping jurisdiction

**9.4.1** In spite of the efforts of the 1986 Act to avoid duplication of jurisdiction, cases have arisen in which parties have found themselves embroiled in parallel cases in Scotland

and England. Parties can be involved in a race to establish jurisdiction in a place they see as favourable to them.

## 9.5 Conclusion

**9.5.1** The 1986 Act procedure is beset with practical difficulties. Abducting parents manipulate these deficiencies to their advantage and often to the child's detriment. The 1986 Act tries to reconcile the existence of different legal systems within one geographical and political entity. It does not work. Either (a) the unity of the UK should be recognised by making delivery orders directly applicable throughout the UK, and legal aid certificates transferable, as described above, or (b) the separateness of the jurisdictions should be recognised and consideration given to applying to abductions to other jurisdictions within the UK the principles which underlie the Hague Convention. The principles are :

(i) the notion of breach of custody rights rather than custody orders as a trigger for legal intervention when a child is taken from one part of the UK to another;

(ii) the primary objective being the prompt return of the child unless there is a grave risk of physical of psychological harm or the child will be placed in an intolerable situation. The wishes of the child should be considered in line with Article 13 of the Hague Convention and Article 12 of the UN Convention.

### ACTION REQUIRED FOR COMPLIANCE

**Compliance with Article 11 in the context of abduction within the UK requires that the Family Law Act 1986 is amended to achieve the aim of making court orders to hand over children directly enforceable throughout the UK without the need for further enforcement proceedings and applications for legal aid. If this cannot be done, the principles of the Hague Convention should be applied to abductions across the frontiers of the different legal jurisdictions that make up the United Kingdom.**

## Summary of action required for compliance

**1** Compliance with Article 4, the duty to implement the Convention to the maximum extent possible, requires that:

- legal aid should be made available to parents seeking to recover children from countries where such assistance is not available or adequate;

- child benefit should be continued after an abduction, or at least the costs of contact with the child and his or her return must be paid by the state;

- an International Children's Commissioner should be appointed with a representative in each state, to represent the interests of abducted children.

**2** Compliance with Article 2, the rights of all children to all the rights in the Convention without discrimination, requires that:

- interpreters, where necessary, are made available to help the independent person interact with the abducted child;

- Article 10(1)(a) of the European Convention is reconsidered on the basis that it may allow discrimination against children from certain countries;

- the application of the Child Abduction Act 1984 should be widened to Scottish children to cover cases where no court order is in existence.

**3** Compliance with Article 12, the right of children to express their views and have them taken seriously, requires that:

- there are informal arrangements for seeking and representing the abducted child's views. This could be achieved through the local offices of the International Children's Commissioner proposed above;

- legal aid should be provided automatically to allow independent representation of the abducted child in any country to which he or she has been taken;

- insofar as children abducted to the UK are concerned, an independent person should always be appointed to investigate and report on the child's circumstances, to advise the child of his or her rights, to present the child's views, and to help the child get independent legal representation if appropriate.

**4** Compliance with Article 9.3, the right to maintain contact with both parents, requires that a protocol is added to the Hague and European Conventions to facilitate return of a child removed by the custodial parent, in order that the child may continue to have access to the non-custodial parent.

**5** Compliance with Article 10.2, the right to family reunification, requires that procedures exist to enable children to apply for the right to leave the country. The Commissioner proposed above should be proactive in finding and advising children and supporting them if they want to leave the country to which they have been abducted.

**6** Compliance with Articles 11 and 35, the duty to combat illicit removal of children together with the duty to promote the best interests of the child (Article 3), requires that:

- the UK Government should expend more effort in encouraging other countries to ratify the international conventions on abduction;

- the UK Government should promote the conclusion of bi-lateral agreements with other countries;

- there should be greater support for parents through the Foreign Office and through the provision of financial assistance;

- the UK Government should seek to promote the establishment of a Commissioner for Abducted Children, with a representative in each state. Until that is achieved, the Foreign Office should appoint a senior diplomat to act as a Children's Ombudsman, to mediate and negotiate in individual cases;

- there should be a change of Foreign Office policy towards a more pro-active approach with regard to British children who also hold the nationality of the country to which they have been abducted;

- the Foreign Office should contact governments with bad records in child abduction matters, with a view to arranging meetings between parents and abducted children, and encouraging the creation of mediation and conciliation services which can result in an improvement in a situation;

- international bodies such as the European Community and the Commonwealth should be encouraged to address matters of child abduction;

- the loop-hole in the Children Act 1989 should be closed so that it should be possible to prosecute parents in Britain who take a child abroad for thirty days and during that time decide not to return the child;

- duty judges should always be available to ensure that court orders can be obtained when needed. In England and Wales there has been found to be a problem with the availability of judges between 4pm and 7pm, particularly on Fridays and the day before bank holidays. In addition, duty judges need to be equipped with portable telefax machines;

- lawyers, judges and police need to be better trained in the area of child abduction. Efforts should be made to help foreign courts understand the Children Act by printing guidelines on court orders;

- better records are kept concerning prosecutions for child abduction and also records in Scotland of interdicts granted to stop children from being removed from the country. A central register of custody and access orders made or recognised in the UK should be maintained;

- further research is funded into the causes of child abduction;

- the Foreign Office should collate information about embassies and consulates within the UK which are prepared to respect UK restrictions by refusing issue of passports to children with dual nationality;

- secure Government funding is provided to ensure the continuation of out-of-court mediation services throughout the United Kingdom, many of which currently struggle to survive financially despite the increasing number of referrals. Existing mediation, advice and counselling services must receive greater publicity, emphasising their respective roles in preventing disputes concerning children. Posters and leaflets in different languages, the media and advertisements need to be used for this purpose;

- mediators receive training in the relevant law and the causes and consequences of child abduction;

- mediators are recruited from a wider range of ethnic and cultural communities. Interpreters also have a significant role to play in some circumstances;

- a police pyramid of expertise in abduction problems needs to be set up with clear guidelines issued to the police and immigration officers indicating among other things that a court order is not necessary for them to act (although the situation is different in Scotland);

- family passports are abolished and British visitors passports should not be issued to minors. Court orders should be noted on both birth certificates and passports;

- more access or contact centres need to be created, with facilities for supervision;

- in the context of abduction within the UK, the Family Law Act 1986 is amended to achieve the aim of making court orders to hand over children directly enforceable throughout the UK without the need for further enforcement proceedings and applications for legal aid. If this cannot be done, the principles of the Hague Convention should be applied to abductions across the frontiers of the different legal jurisdictions that make up the United Kingdom.

# UK Agenda for Children

**14** International obligations

# Contents

**Acknowledgement**
This report is based on a paper produced by the UK Committee of UNICEF.

# 1 Introduction

**1.1** The Convention addresses in some detail the responsibilities of governments to fulfil obligations towards children not just in their own country but also abroad. These obligations comprise both the necessity of developing bi-lateral and multi-lateral international agreements necessary for the protection of children but also the importance of international co-operation in raising standards of care and protection for children. The preamble to the Convention provides the context for this obligation: *'Recognising the importance of international co-operation for improving the living conditions of children in every country, particularly in the developing world'*.

**1.2** The Convention emphasises that countries do not exist in isolation, nor do responsibilities for children rest exclusively with individual governments. Instead, every country must take a share in creating an environment throughout the world in which children's rights are respected. This report examines the international obligations contained in the Convention and assesses the extent to which they are currently being complied with by the UK government.

# 2 Implementation of economic, social and cultural rights

## Article 4

**2.1** Article 4 places an explicit obligation on the Government to pursue actively the implementation of the Convention both within its own jurisdiction and in an international context. The UK government funds an aid programme to the extent of £1.9 billion. However, this sum does not reach the target for aid of 0.7% of Gross National Product (GNP) from the industrialised countries agreed by the UN in the 1960s. Despite assurances made at the UN Conference on Environment and Development (the 'Earth Summit') 1992 that there would be a commitment to meeting that target, the amount spent on aid by the UK government represents only 0.31% of GNP. This places the UK 13th in the league table of donor nations[1].

**2.2** The UK government is currently proposing a freeze on the aid budget at its current level until 1996. Forecasts indicate that, at the rate of economic growth anticipated over the next three years, the aid budget will have dropped to 0.26% by 1996. This would represent the lowest level since the introduction of the target 0.7% and just over half the level of 0.51% which applied in 1979 when the Conservative government came into power. Furthermore the *Human Development Report 1992* shows that in 1990, out of a total allocation of 0.27% of GNP for overseas aid, only a fraction of this - 8.8% - was targeted at human priorities, the most basic needs of the poorest people - primary health care, primary education, clean water, safe sanitation and family planning[2]. UNICEF have estimated that for 25 billion dollars it would be possible to provide clean water, safe sanitation and primary education for all children, achieve control of the major childhood diseases, halve the rate of child malnutrition, and make family planning universally available[3]. They go on to argue that there should be a basic restructuring of aid programmes in order that at least 20% of the total goes directly to these basic provisions.

**2.3** However, the significance of the international aid programme does need to be seen in context. At present it only accounts for 5% of the total income of the Third World as compared with 80% represented by trade. Much of the aid programme is tied to goods and services used in projects that must be bought from the country giving aid. Nearly all UK bi-lateral aid is tied to buying British goods and, in addition, the UK imposes a local costs ceiling on many countries that limits the proportion of aid that can be spent on locally grown materials[4]. Similarly, policies such as protectionism, operated by the industrialised world, fail to offer developing countries a level playing-field in which to compete in the world market. During the 1980s the trading system played a central part in contributing to the falling living standards experienced by most developing countries - commodity prices fell, subsidised and protected agriculture in industrialised countries forced down world prices and those countries increased their levels of protectionism. The *1991 World Bank development report* commented that 'Unrestricted access to industrialised country markets would add 55 billion dollars to their export earnings - as much as they receive in aid'. In these and other ways, poor countries are inhibited in their ability to develop their economies and overcome the structural problems and historical weaknesses they face, and meanwhile children continue to suffer from the poverty which ensues[5]. If the UK government is to pursue its international obligations under the Convention, it needs to play an active part in beginning to challenge some of the trading practices which operate to perpetuate the poverty of many Third World economies.

**2.4** A commitment from the Government to argue for multi-lateral agencies like the World Bank to adopt a more responsible approach to international trade and production, the reduction of European Union (EU) tariffs on Third World goods and the removal of export subsidies on agriculture by rich countries would represent considerable progress in this respect. These measures would contribute to the creation of greater opportunities for developing countries to participate on more equal terms in the world markets and thus give children in those countries a better chance of seeing their rights to education, health care and an adequate standard of living realised.

**2.5** The UK government has an influential position on multi-lateral bodies such as the EU, the International Monetary Fund (IMF) and the Board of Executive Directors of the World Bank. Many of the policies prescribed by these bodies, such as the World Bank's structural adjustment policies, impact disproportionately on women and, in consequence, on children. There is evidence to show that structural adjustment has reduced employment and wages more for women than for men, deregulation of food prices together with lower family incomes has imposed greater pressures on many women's time, particularly in rural areas, as they struggle to provide for their families, and the worsening of health and educational services has had implications both for the health of women themselves and has also imposed increased burdens of care as they have sought to compensate for the loss of public facilities[6].

**2.6** All these changes have direct consequences for children as the most vulnerable members of society and in particular for their health, education and day-to-day care. A serious commitment to promoting children's rights in developing countries can only be ensured by addressing the rights of the child when undertaking any assessment of policies, such as those advocating structural adjustment, which have an impact on children's welfare. Without an explicit commitment to place children on the agenda of these bodies, their rights and their needs will inevitably fail to be acknowledged. It is imperative that decisions made by such powerful bodies are taken in the context of the best interests of children (Article 3) and with a full recognition of the necessity of respecting children's rights to life (Article 6), to the best possible health care (Article 24), to education (Article 28) and to an adequate standard of living (Article 27).

**2.7** The UK government should use its influence in bodies such as the World Bank and the IMF to ensure that the rights of children are placed at the centre of the agenda when they are advocating and prescribing policies for developing countries. Compliance with Article 4 and the obligation to implement the rights in the Convention to the '*maximum extent of their available resources and, where needed within the framework of international co-operation*' will necessitate a pro-active commitment to addressing the impact of policies such

as those of structural adjustment on the rights of children and ensuring that they are consistent with the principles and standards embodied in the Convention.

**2.8** In the same way that multilateral bodies must begin to accept and address the implications of the Convention, so too must countries seeking aid. One way forward would be to require that in all grant application bodies should address the rights of the child, setting out how the funds would be used to promote and enhance those rights. Children are powerless in the international arena and unless explicit measures are introduced to ensure that they are rendered visible and their rights are properly respected, they will continue to be marginalised to the interests of other groups. Such an approach could be seen as an extension of the recent statement by the Minister for Overseas Development that all non-governmental organisations' applications to the Overseas Development Agency (ODA) should include an analysis of the impact of the proposed project on women.

## ACTION REQUIRED FOR COMPLIANCE

**Compliance with Article 4, the obligation to implement the economic, social and cultural rights '*to the maximum extent of ... available resources and, where needed, within the framework of international co-operation*' requires:**

● **a firm commitment to the achievement of the 0.7% of GNP aid target as a matter of urgency with an equal commitment to ensuring that 20% of the total is allocated towards human priorities;**

● **a pro-active commitment to addressing the impact of policies such as those of structural adjustment on the rights of children and ensuring that they are consistent with the principles and standards embodied in the Convention. The UK government should use its influence in bodies such as the World Bank and the IMF to ensure that the rights of children are placed at the centre of the agenda when they are advocating and prescribing policies for developing countries;**

● **a commitment from the Government to argue for multi-lateral agencies like the World Bank to adopt a more responsible approach to international trade and production, the reduction of EU tariffs on Third World goods and the removal of export subsidies on agriculture by rich countries;**

● **that the ODA extend its ruling with regard to women to ensure that all appropriate grant applications address the rights of the child setting out how the funds would be used to promote and enhance those rights.**

# 3 International co-operation over information
## Article 17

**3.1** Article 17 states that governments must *'encourage international co-operation in the production, exchange and dissemination of ... information from a diversity of cultural, national and international sources'* with the aim of promoting the *'social, spiritual and moral well-being [of children] and [their] physical and mental health'*. Access to information is fundamental to the promotion of children's rights. Without information children lack the knowledge and, therefore, the power with which to challenge breaches of rights. Similarly, without information on children, governments are not able to evaluate the extent to which they are respecting children's rights and implementing the Convention. There are a number of universally accepted indicators for monitoring progress in respect of children's health and education - infant mortality rates, immunisation rates, attendance in primary education - and there is a growing international recognition of the need to collect this statistical data. *The Progress of nations*, a new publication by UNICEF, which draws together a global analysis of all the available data on these indicators, represents an important step forward in profiling the progress of countries in relation to these agreed standards and identifying where the gaps in information lie[7].

**3.2** Because there are, to date, accepted international indicators only in the fields of health and education, there are many rights in the Convention for which we have no consistently collected information against which to evaluate progress. For example, there are neither indicators nor much data on child labour, access to advocacy in the juvenile justice system, treatment of refugees or measures to counter discrimination in relation to gender, minority groups or disabled children. Without this data we cannot assess whether or not these rights are being respected. The UK government can play an important role in contributing to the international recognition of the significance of these developments and needs itself to demonstrate a commitment to them through the initiation of the relevant data collection within this country.

**3.3** Renewed membership and contributions to UNESCO would play an important part in furthering these debates. The UK government left UNESCO in 1985 and, although recent Parliamentary Questions indicate that the Government is reviewing the situation, there is no clear indication of a desire to rejoin as yet.

### ACTION REQUIRED FOR COMPLIANCE

**Compliance with Article 17 requires a commitment to identifying gaps in data collection of information pertaining to children's rights. Renewed UK membership of UNESCO would contribute to the UK being able to participate more fully in the process of developing certain international indicators of children's rights and pressing for the recognition of the value of collecting and analysing the necessary data with which to measure those indicators.**

# 4 International co-operation over inter-country adoption
## Article 21

**4.1** Article 21(b) states that *'inter-country adoption may be considered as an alternative means of child care if the child cannot be placed in a foster or an adoptive family or cannot in any suitable manner be cared for in the child's country of origin'*. Article 21(c) goes on to state that governments must ensure that *'the child concerned by inter-country adoption enjoys the safeguards and standards equivalent to those existing in the case of national adoption'*. Article 21(d) and (e) also require that no-one involved in inter-country adoption makes improper financial gain as a result and that bi-lateral or multi-lateral arrangements are established to ensure that placement of children in another country is carried out by competent authorities.

**4.2** There is concern amongst child welfare agencies in the UK that inter-country adoption is increasingly being used as a means for infertile couples from industrialised countries to obtain babies from developing countries. In other words, it is not a service for children needing families, but for couples wanting a child. This view is endorsed by the Department of Health and Welsh Office in their *Review of adoption law*[8]. A similar review is taking place in Scotland. The legislation on adoption in N Ireland is also comparable with that in England and Wales and the reviews will in due course lead to legislation which will apply throughout the UK.

**4.3** Inter-country adoptions are almost invariably trans-cultural and usually also trans-racial. It has been the policy of the Department of Health in its guidance to adoption agencies to encourage placements which take account of the child's race, culture, language and religion and where possible to place children in same-race families. Such an approach is consistent with the obligations in Article 8 to respect the right of children to preserve their identity, and in Article 30 to respect their right to enjoy their own culture and language and practice their own religion. Clearly, it is not possible in the context of inter-country adoption to require same-race placements. However, it is possible to require assessment of people seeking to adopt with a view to ensuring that they understand the importance of the child's right to identity and to have knowledge of and contact with her or his country and culture of origin. Compliance with Article 21(c) requires that children being adopted from abroad are protected by the same commitment to these rights as are children adopted in this country. The British Agencies for Adoption and Fostering (BAAF) have expressed concern that these standards are currently not universally applied and children are being brought into the country whose adoptive parents have not satisfactorily addressed the issues of identity and cultural implications for these children growing up in the UK. The White Paper *Adoption: the future*, published in 1993, does propose the introduction of a general requirement in adoption law that, in making decisions concerning adoption, local authorities and agencies should take account of issues of ethnicity and culture[9]. However, no reference is made to the specific needs of children adopted from abroad in this respect nor to the particular implications for adoptive parents.

**4.4** The Hague Convention on Inter-country Adoption (1993) requires that all placements in respect of inter-country adoption take place through an approved agency. The principles of this Convention are consistent with those contained in the UN Convention on the Rights of the Child. Private adoption placements in the UK were abolished by the Children Act 1975 and since that time all adoptions in this country have had to be arranged through authorised adoption agencies. This requirement was introduced to provide greater protection of children. However, the same principle does not currently apply to children adopted from abroad. It remains possible for a couple to adopt a child in another country through a private arrangement and to obtain entry clearance to bring the child into this country. These children are clearly not being offered the '*safeguards and standards equivalent to those existing in the case of national adoption*' (Article 21(c)).

**4.5** The *Review of adoption law* in England and Wales (and similarly in Scotland), acknowledges this inconsistency and emphasises that, ideally, all adoptions should be arranged on an agency to agency basis[10]. However, the Review concludes that it is not appropriate to prohibit all adoptions arranged on a private basis without the approval of an authorised adoption agency. Instead, they recommend that authorisation to proceed may be given where there is satisfactory evidence that the usual requirements have been met. The subsequent White Paper stresses that the UK government intends to ratify the Hague Convention (and indeed participated fully in the drawing up of the Convention), which would require legislation on this issue to achieve compliance but makes no explicit reference to its intention to introduce it. The position of the Government is therefore not fully clear. Certainly, a failure to prohibit private adoption placements would set up a clear distinction between the standards being applied in domestic and inter-country adoptions in contravention of Article 21(c). In Sweden, no child can be brought into the country unless he or she has been adopted through an authorised agency. The effect of this legislation has been to ensure that all children in inter-country adoptions are protected by the direct involvement of an approved agency both in their own country and in the country of adoptive parents.

### ACTION REQUIRED FOR COMPLIANCE

**Compliance with Article 21, the duty to ensure that children who are the subject of inter-country adoption are entitled to the same safeguards and standards as those that apply in national adoption requires that:**

● **all inter-country adoptions are undertaken through an approved agency in the country concerned. This would also be in accordance with the provisions of the Hague Convention to which the UK is a signatory;**

● **there are regulations setting out the obligations of adoption agencies undertaking assessments of people wishing to adopt from abroad to ascertain that they have understood the implications of a trans-racial and trans-cultural adoption and made a commitment to ensuring that the child has knowledge of his or her country of origin and, where possible and appropriate, contact with members of the birth family.**

# 5 International co-operation over disability
## Article 23

**5.1** Article 23.4 requires governments '*to promote, in the spirit of international co-operation, the exchange of appropriate information in the field of preventive health care and medical, psychological and functional treatment of disabled children ... taking particular account of the needs of developing countries*'. This right needs to be taken in conjunction with Article 24.4 and the responsibility to work internationally to achieve the realisation of the right of all children to the best possible health. Children in very poor countries are both at greater risk of disability and more vulnerable as a consequence of disability. Huge numbers of children suffer disabilities which could be eliminated through the provision of low-cost medications or improved diet. For example, vitamin A deficiency causes blindness which affects huge numbers of children in developing countries; a billion people, mostly children, suffer from a lack of iodine which causes reduced physical and mental capacity which could be avoided at the cost of only a few pence per child. Disabled children are a particularly vulnerable group whose needs are disproportionately affected by low ODA budgets and limited commitment to human priorities (see para 2.1). The performance of the UK government in relation to this Article should be measured against the level of ODA funding and the proportion of it targeted at human priorities, as well as their role within the EU, World Bank and other multi-lateral bodies.

**5.2** It is also imperative in providing aid in this field that care is taken to ensure that western models and assumptions about service provision are not imposed, but adapted by the users to suit their needs and culture. Medical aids need to be relevant both to the physical environment in which the child lives and also the cultural context. For example, wheel-chairs are of minimal value in mountainous regions without made up roads. Similarly, there must be recognition, of the extent to which the concept of learning disability is culturally determined according to the norms of the society and aid programmes must be developed in an appropriate social and cultural context. There is a need for a dialogue between countries about the form and nature of resources and services that are required to ensure that developments that are introduced reflect the situation in which disabled children are living.

### ACTION REQUIRED FOR COMPLIANCE

**Compliance with Article 23.4, the duty to exchange information and expertise in respect of children with disabilities must be undertaken with sensitivity and respect for the culture and environment in which the children are living. The Government should seek to share and disseminate knowledge and expertise as part of a dialogue with other countries which does not merely export practices operational within the UK.**

# 6 International co-operation over health

## Article 24

**6.1** Article 24.4 outlines governments' responsibilities '*to promote and encourage international co-operation with a view to achieving progressively the full realization of the right to [the best possible health and health care]*'. The continuation of a low ODA budget will affect UK obligations in relation to health. Of the current ODA budget, only a fraction of the 8.8% spent on human priorities actually goes to primary health care. Article 24 contains a range of goals also agreed by the UK government when they signed the World Summit Declaration and Plan of Action (30 September 1990). For example, reduction in infant mortality, provision of clean water, adequate nutrition and promotion of breastfeeding are all pledges of the World Summit and an increased aid budget should be targeted at working towards the attainment of those goals.

**6.2** Article 24.2(e) stresses that parents and children are supported in the knowledge of the advantages of breastfeeding. Breastfeeding has been dramatically reduced in many countries by the provision of free and low-cost supplies of infant formula to maternity units by manufacturers who ensure in this way that the baby is dependent on their product on leaving the hospital. The consequences of these marketing techniques have been widely documented: failure to breastfeed infants denies them the protections that breast milk provides, it imposes a high-cost food on mothers who have the capacity to feed their babies themselves, which would be healthier and cheaper and lack of access to clean water in many areas means that the baby is placed at considerable risk of infection and possible death. The detrimental effect on health and development pushed the World Health Assembly into adopting the Code of Marketing of Breast-milk Substitutes (1981). This has been adapted by the EU into two directives, one of which, on the marketing of formula outside the Community, has not yet been finalised.

**6.3** Article 24.3 states that governments must '*take all effective and appropriate measures with a view to abolishing traditional practices prejudicial to the health of children*' (see **UK Agenda Report 3 on physical integrity,** page 63 for a more detailed analysis of this issue). In the UK the practice of female genital mutilation amongst certain groups is a clear example of such a practice. The Prohibition of Female Circumcision Act 1985 makes it an offence to carry out any of the procedures which are known as female circumcision but which are more accurately described as female genital mutilation (FGM). The Act also makes it illegal to aid, abet, counsel or procure the carrying out of these procedures. The offence carries a maximum fine of £2,000. However, it appears no one has been prosecuted under this Act, possibly due to difficulties in acquiring evidence.

**6.4** In October 1991, the Government issued guidance on child protection in England and Wales entitled *Working together under the Children Act 1989.* This contains advice on the 1985 Act. The Children Act 1989 in England and Wales provides legal protection under section 47(1): local authorities have a duty to investigate if they have 'reasonable cause to suspect that a child who lives, or is found, in their area is suffering, or is likely to suffer, significant harm'. For female genital mutilation, care proceedings should only be used as a last resort. Section 8 of the Act can be used to prevent parents carrying out particular acts without the consent of the court, such as removing the child from the UK so that mutilation can be carried out abroad. Seeking a care or supervision order (section 31(1)) could also be considered.

**6.5** The effect of the guidance has been that social services are more active in combating this practice. But where the offence is carried out overseas, there is nothing the British legal system can do. There is a case in Cardiff where the father was warned not to remove the child from the UK, but did so. Investigations are currently stalled as the father refuses to have the child examined. If the court eventually finds against the father, then it will be a step in the direction of ensuring that British children are protected. However, Forward, a Department of Health funded NGO which has led campaigning against female genital mutilation, is concerned that there will still be inadequate protection for children who are not British, eg refugees who are here under 'exceptional leave to remain'.

## ACTION REQUIRED FOR COMPLIANCE

**Compliance with Article 24 requires that the UK government takes steps to ensure that:**

- **as a member of the EU, World Bank and other multi-lateral agencies involved in the support of macro-economic and structural adjustment programmes, it ensures that policies with which it is associated do not undermine the ability of a government to deliver health services to its citizens;**

- **it uses membership of the EU to see that the Code of Marketing of breast-milk substitutes is fully incorporated into any directive and subsequently into UK law. It should also support the UNICEF/ WHO Baby-Friendly Hospital Initiative both within the UK and overseas, in order to promote training of health personnel in the advantages of breastfeeding and correct techniques for assisting new mothers who wish to breastfeed. The UK government, together with other governments, has influence over the infant formula manufacturers, and should use it to encourage them to market their product responsibly;**

- **further resources are provided for training of social workers, teachers and others who are in contact with children at risk of female genital mutilation.**

# 7 International co-operation over the recovery of maintenance

## Article 27

**7.1** Article 27 requires governments '*to take all appropriate measures to secure the recovery of maintenance for the child from parents ... having financial responsibility for the child, both within the State Party and from abroad ... and shall promote the accession to international agreements ...*'. The UK does have reciprocal agreements with many countries and formal procedures exist for the recovery of maintenance. However, in practice, it is often extremely difficult to use these procedures to real effect and the numbers of women who actually benefit from maintenance when their former husband is abroad is low. These difficulties take on a greater significance in the context of the European Union Single Market and the likelihood of increased labour mobility and inter-country marriage.

### ACTION REQUIRED FOR COMPLIANCE

**Compliance with Article 27 and the responsibility on the Government to facilitate the recovery of maintenance requires that it encourages the European Union to consider the development of improved measures for the recovery of maintenance within member states if children are not to be financially disadvantaged as a consequence of the single market and greater labour mobility.**

# 8 International co-operation over education

## Article 28

**8.1** Article 28.3 requires that governments must '*promote and encourage international co-operation in matters relating to education, in particular with a view to contributing to the elimination of ignorance and illiteracy throughout the world ... particular account shall be taken of the needs of developing countries*'. UNICEF estimates that whilst 90% of children in developing countries start school, there is a massive dropout rate within the first few years. As a result there are an estimated 100 million children aged 6-11 not in school, over two thirds of them girls. The World Summit for Children in 1990, to which the UK was a party, established the goal of universal access to basic education including completion of primary education by at least 80% of the relevant school-age children by the year 2000. The UK government was also represented at the World Conference on Education for All held on 5-9 March 1990 at Jomtien, Thailand. The Conference adopted a World Declaration on Education for all which states: 'Substantial and long-term increases in resources for basic education will be needed'. At present, the aid from the UK as a percentage of all direct aid to education is only 4%, as compared with 54% from Sweden and 43% from the US.

### ACTION REQUIRED FOR COMPLIANCE

**A commitment to meeting the obligations under Article 28 is linked integrally to the level of commitment to the aid budget. Unless the UK government increases its contribution in line with the UN target of 0.7%, it will not be possible to meet our international obligations to contribute towards the elimination of ignorance and illiteracy.**

# 9 International co-operation to prevent sexual exploitation

## Article 34

**9.1** Article 34 states that governments must '*undertake to protect the child from all forms of sexual exploitation and sexual abuse ... and in particular must take all appropriate bilateral and multilateral measures [to protect children from unlawful sexual activity, prostitution, or exploitative use in pornographic performances]*'. This commitment has been affirmed by the European Parliament Committee on Legal and Citizens' Rights which, in a report on the European Charter of the Rights of the Child, states that: 'Every child must be protected against all forms of slavery, violence or exploitation. Appropriate measures shall be taken to prevent any child from being taken, abducted or exploited for the purposes of prostitution or pornography in the territory of the Community ... '.

**9.2** The sexual exploitation of children is a widespread phenomenon with a growing industry in child pornography. There is no reliable information on the extent of sex networks and rings in European countries but there is evidence of their existence. A study in Leeds in the UK revealed that there were 31 sex rings identified by the police over a two year period, involving 47 male perpetrators and 334 children[11]. In Germany it is estimated that there are about 100 private dealers in child pornography linked to paedophile networks. With border controls changing and inter-country mobility now much easier within Europe, the importing and exporting of pornographic materials will become easier unless there is effective harmonisation of legal measures and co-ordinated strategies to combat this trade.

**9.3** The use of modern technology in the distribution of pornographic material to children is also an increasing concern. The growth in numbers of home computers available to children and access to pornographic images via bulletin boards is now commonplace with little or no regulation of access to this material. This type of material is freely available from bulletin boards and is easily distributed and exchanged on floppy disc at low cost. The growth and development of cross satellite television has also increased the opportunities for children to be exposed to exploitative pornographic material. The UK government banned the use of decoders for the transmission 'Red Hot Television' (formerly 'Red Hot Dutch'). The company concerned is to take the case to the European Court of Justice and threatens to move the channel to a location outside the EU. The UK Government's case is that the channel risked causing serious harm to children's morals.

**9.4** Sex tourism is an industry which has grown rapidly in recent years. The Ecumenical Coalition on Third World Tourism have estimated that in 1991 several hundreds of thousands of children aged between 6-15 were being forced or sold into prostitution. It is estimated that 60% of all tourism in Thailand and 50% in Kenya, the Philippines and South Korea is sex tourism. Men who travel abroad to abuse children in this way evade any legal sanctions as it is not usually possible for a man to be prosecuted in his own country for an offence committed abroad.

---

## ACTION REQUIRED FOR COMPLIANCE

Compliance with Article 34 and the prevention of sexual exploitation and abuse of children requires:

- the UK government to press for effective legal protection for children against sexual exploitation in those countries where the trade in child prostitution is developing and for more effective prosecution of tourists abusing children in this way;

- a review of the issue of extra-territorial jurisdiction in order to consider the making of sexual abuse of children by UK citizens in other countries an offence liable to be prosecuted within the UK;

- within Europe, the harmonisation of legal measures throughout member states to ensure that possession of child pornography is an offence in all countries.

# 10 Protection of children affected by armed conflict

## Article 38

**10.1** Article 38.1 requires governments '*to respect and ensure respect for rules of international law applicable to them in armed conflicts*' and '*to protect civilian populations in armed conflicts*'. This places a clear obligation on governments to comply with international humanitarian law to which they are a party. It is worth noting that before the UN Convention was adopted in 1989, the International Committee of the Red Cross (ICRC) expressed concern that this Article is not as strong as provisions in other conventions, in particular the Geneva Conventions and two Additional Protocols which were added in 1977 (the first refers to international conflict and includes safeguards on recruitment and the second deals with non-international conflict and contains a section specifically on children; the UK has signed but not ratified the Protocols). However, Article 41 states that nothing in the UN Convention affects national or international laws '*that are more conducive to the realisation of the rights of the child*', so the weakness of this Article cannot diminish the effect of the additional Protocols once the UK has ratified them.

**10.2** UNICEF estimates that armed conflict throughout the world between 1980 and 1990 caused the deaths of 1.5 million children; a further 4 million were disabled and 10 million psychologically traumatized. Whereas civilian deaths during World War 2 represented 50% of the total, this has jumped to 75% in current conflicts because of the changing nature of war. The 1991 Gulf War saw a number of violations of humanitarian law which caused death and injury to child civilians. A recent report argues that the allied forces failed adequately to protect Iraqi civilians from the effects of the conflict. The worst attack causing civilian deaths was the bombing of the American air-raid shelter in Baghdad in which 310 people were killed including 130 children[12]. Clearly, the existing body of international law regarding humanitarian concerns in armed conflict has had only limited impact on the effective protection of children. Whilst the provisions of Article 38 are no stronger and are, in some respects, weaker than those of other relevant Conventions and Protocols, it can be used as a tool for raising awareness of the rights of children in circumstances of war.

**10.3** Article 38.4 states that governments must take '*all feasible measures to ensure the protection and care of children who are affected by an armed conflict*'. Humane provisions in respect of children displaced by war are clearly an important aspect of this care and protection. Better co-ordination between UK government departments, principally the Home Office, Foreign and Commonwealth Office and Department of Health is needed as current lack of communication between departments can lead to children not receiving appropriate humanitarian care in their country of origin and ending up being taken to third countries. UNHCR/UNICEF and the Refugee Council have stressed that it is preferable for children wherever possible to remain in their own country of birth. At present, no government department is responsible for keeping records as to who a refugee child is and where from, so that he or she can be reunited with his or her family

at the appropriate time. In the UK, the Red Cross offers a confidential tracing and registration service.

**10.4** The obligations under Article 38.4 also extend to children in the aftermath of war - children who have lost their family or their home, children who have been injured or disabled, children who have been emotionally and psychologically traumatised by the experience of war, as well as children who are vulnerable in the social, economic and political chaos which might prevail after a war. Children are particularly vulnerable in such circumstances, lacking both the physical and political power with which to ensure that their needs are met. For example, there has been considerable concern expressed over the impact of sanctions on children in Iraq, where shortages of essential medical facilities and drugs are likely to be having a seriously detrimental impact on children.

**10.5** Landmines litter many current and former war zones. According to the International Committee for the Red Cross, over 4 million may have been laid in Cambodia, 10 million in Afghanistan, a million in Kuwait; very few if any of these mines have self-destruct mechanisms so they remain active year after year[13]. Children are often the victims of landmines in rural areas where they are looking after sheep and cattle. Limiting their use is one of the aims of the 1981 Convention on Prohibitions and Restrictions on the Use of Certain Conventional Weapons which may be deemed excessively injurious or to have indiscriminate effects, also known as the Inhuman Weapons Convention. The UK has not yet ratified, although the Government took an active part in writing the Convention. The Convention came into force in December 1983. It is an 'umbrella treaty', acting through protocols of which I and II are relevant.

## ACTION REQUIRED FOR COMPLIANCE

**Compliance with the obligation to take all feasible measures to ensure the protection and care of children who are affected by armed conflict requires that:**

- **the Government ratifies the 1977 Geneva Protocols as a matter of urgency;**

- **the Government: (a) ratifies the UN Convention on prohibitions and restrictions on the use of certain conventional weapons; (b) calls for a review conference which can be done when the Convention is 10 years old (December 1993); (c) instates a moratorium on the production and export of landmine parts for a year or more, as the US did in October 1992;**

- **conditions of reconstruction and economic embargoes include consideration of the needs of children in the aftermath of war.**

# 11 Recovery and rehabilitation
## Article 39

**11.1** Article 39 states that governments '*shall take all appropriate measures to promote physical and psychological recovery and social reintegration of a child victim of: any form of neglect, exploitation, or abuse; torture or any other form of cruel, unhuman or degrading treatment or punishment; or armed conflicts*'. It further requires that such recovery and reintegration must take place in an environment which promotes '*the health, self-respect and dignity of the child*'. Recovery and rehabilitation for children involved in armed conflict needs to address the physical, developmental, social and psychological effects of their experiences[14]. The physical effects can include malnutrition, lack of health care, disability and sexually transmitted diseases. The developmental effects can include lack of affection and lack of schooling. The social effects can include the loss of family and the fear of returning home, whilst the psychological effects include the difficulties in coping with normal life, lack of trust, aggression, depression and anxiety. For rehabilitation to take place children need help in reintegrating with a family, and the recovery of a 'civilian' identity, adequate health care and the prospect of an economic future through education, training and income-generating schemes.

**11.2** Implementation of this Article requires that recognition is given to the experiences of armed conflict that have been undergone by many child refugees coming into the UK. All refugee children are suffering from the cumulative effects of some form of violence; be it torture, imprisonment, harassment, civil war, or the loss or death of parents and other family members. In addition they suffer from the loss of home, friends and culture when they come to the UK, where they may encounter for the first time racist violence and discrimination. At school they may receive no support for integration and have inadequate or non-existent provision of teaching of English as a second language. If parents are themselves suffering from the effects of violence and the shock of adapting to a new environment, then they are likely to be emotionally unavailable to their children. In extreme cases the parents' behaviour changes radically and children are disoriented and neglected. Often the apparent resilience of refugee children masks their inner suffering and their real needs may not become apparent. For unaccompanied children, the loss of their parents poses additional difficulties and suffering. Eventually some children may act out their feelings in anti-social ways which only worsens their situation, leaving them marginalised and stigmatised. If their needs and suffering continue to be unrecognised, then the effects become compounded and appropriate responses become more difficult to assess and provide (see **UK Agenda Report 11 on refugee children**, page 252 for a more detailed analysis of the experiences of refugee children).

**11.3** With few exceptions most local authorities are not providing the specialist treatment required for children with a refugee background. The Medical Foundation for the Care of Victims of Torture, an NGO, provides therapeutic treatment for child and adolescent refugees. They can only see a small number of children who may be in need of such services. In the first six months of 1993 they provided

counselling to 11 unaccompanied children. According to the Foundation, children's refugee background may seriously affect their school life if they are not provided with the opportunity to deal with the issues, and the cause of their problems is likely to go unrecognised by teachers and others involved in their case.

### ACTION REQUIRED FOR COMPLIANCE

**Compliance with Article 39, the duty to take measures to promote the social re-integration of child victims, requires that:**

- **community health services are properly resourced to cater for the mental health needs of refugee children;**
- **professionals such as teachers, health workers and social workers who work with refugee children are provided with appropriate training in order to be sensitive to the children's special requirements.**

# Summary of action required for compliance

1 Compliance with Article 4, the obligation to implement the economic, social and cultural rights *'to the maximum extent of … available resources and where needed, within the framework of international co-operation'* requires:

- a firm commitment to the achievement of the 0.7% of GNP aid target as a matter of urgency with an equal commitment to ensuring that 20% of the total is allocated towards human priorities;
- a pro-active commitment to addressing the impact of policies such as those of structural adjustment on the rights of children and ensuring that they are consistent with the principles and standards embodied in the Convention. The UK government should use its influence in bodies such as the World Bank and the IMF to ensure that the rights of children are placed at the centre of the agenda when they are advocating and prescribing policies for developing countries;
- a commitment from the Government to argue for multi-lateral agencies like the World Bank to adopt a more responsible approach to international trade and production, the reduction of EU tariffs on Third World goods and the removal of export subsidies on agriculture by rich countries;
- that the ODA extend its ruling with regard to women to ensure that all appropriate grant applications address the rights of the child setting out how the funds would be used to promote and enhance those rights.

2 Compliance with Article 17, the duty to encourage international co-operation in the exchange of information of benefit to children, requires a commitment to identifying gaps in data collection of information pertaining to children's rights. Renewed UK membership of UNESCO would contribute to the UK being able to participate more fully in the process of developing certain international indicators of children's rights and pressing for the recognition of the value of collecting and analysing the necessary data with which to measure those indicators.

3 Compliance with Article 21, the duty to ensure that children who are the subject of inter-country adoption are entitled to the same safeguards and standards as those that apply in national adoption requires that:

- all inter-country adoptions are undertaken through an approved agency in the country concerned. This would also be in accordance with the provisions of the Hague Convention to which the UK is a signatory;
- there are regulations setting out the obligations of adoption agencies undertaking assessments of people wishing to adopt from abroad to ascertain that they have understood the implications of a trans-racial and trans-cultural adoption and made a commitment to ensuring that the child has knowledge of his or her country of origin and, where possible and appropriate, contact with members of the birth family.

4 Compliance with Article 23.4 and the duty to exchange information and expertise in respect of children with disabilities must be undertaken with sensitivity and respect for the culture and environment in which the children are living. The Government should seek to share and disseminate knowledge and expertise as part of a dialogue with other countries which does not merely export practices operational within the UK.

5 Compliance with Article 24, the duty to promote international co-operation to achieve the right to the best possible health for children in developing countries, requires that the UK government takes steps to ensure that:

- as a member of the European Community, World Bank and other multi-lateral agencies involved in the support of macro-economic and structural adjustment programmes, it ensures that policies with which it is associated do not undermine the ability of a government to deliver health services to its citizens;
- it uses membership of the EU to see that the Code of Marketing of breast-milk substitutes is fully incorporated into any directive and subsequently into UK law. It should also support the UNICEF/WHO Baby-Friendly Hospital Initiative both within the UK and overseas, in order to promote training of health personnel in the advantages of breastfeeding and correct techniques for assisting new mothers who wish to breastfeed. The UK Government, together with other governments, has influence over the infant formula manufacturers, and should use it to encourage them to market their product responsibly;
- further resources are provided for training of social workers, teachers and others who are in contact with children at risk of female genital mutilation.

6 Compliance with Article 27, the responsibility on the Government to facilitate the recovery of maintenance, requires that it encourages the European Union to consider the development of improved measures for the recovery of maintenance within member states if children are not to be financially disadvantaged as a consequence of the single market and greater labour mobility.

7 A commitment to meeting the obligations under Article 28 is linked integrally to the level of commitment to the aid budget. Unless the UK government increases its contribution in line with the UN target of 0.7%, it will not be possible to meet our international obligations to contribute towards the elimination of ignorance and illiteracy.

8 Compliance with Article 34, the prevention of sexual exploitation and abuse of children requires:

- the UK government to press for effective legal protection for children against sexual exploitation in those countries where the trade in child prostitution is developing and for more effective prosecution of tourists abusing children in this way;
- a review of the issue of extra-territorial jurisdiction in order to consider the making of sexual abuse of children by UK citizens in other countries an offence liable to be prosecuted within the UK;
- within Europe, the harmonisation of legal measures throughout member states to ensure that possession of child pornography is an offence in all countries.

9 Compliance with Article 38, the obligation to take all feasible measures to ensure the protection and care of

children who are affected by armed conflict requires that:

- the Government ratifies the 1977 Geneva Protocols as a matter of urgency;

- the Government: (a) ratifies the UN Convention on prohibitions and restrictions on the use of certain conventional weapons; (b) calls for a review conference which can be done when the Convention is 10 years old (December 1993); (c) instates a moratorium on the production and export of landmine parts for a year or more, as the US did in October 1992;

- conditions of reconstruction and economic embargoes include consideration of the needs of children in the aftermath of war.

**10** Compliance with Article 39, the duty to take measures to promote the social reintegration of child victims, requires that:

- community health services are properly resourced to cater for the mental health needs of refugee children;

- professionals such as teachers, health workers and social workers who work with refugee children are provided with appropriate training in order to be sensitive to the children's special requirements.

# References

1. *The progress of nations*, UNICEF (1993)
2. *Human development report*, United Nations Development Programme, OUP (1992)
3. *The state of the world's children*, UNICEF (1993)
4. *Poverty or planet: a question of survival*, Jackson B, Penguin (1990)
5. *A raw deal: trade and the world's poor*, Madden P, Christian Aid (1992)
6. 'Can adjustment programmes incorporate the interests of women?' Stewart F, from *Women and adjustment policies in the Third World*, ed Afshar H and Dennis C, Women Studies at York/Macmillan Series (1992)
7. see reference 1
8. *Review of adoption law: report to the ministers of an inter-departmental working group*, Department of Health and Welsh Office (1992)
9. *Adoption: the future*, Department of Health, Welsh Office, Home Office and the Lord Chancellor's Department, HMSO (1993)
10. see reference 8
11. 'Prevalence of sex rings', Wild N J, *Paediatrics*, vol 83, no 4 (1989)
12. *Middle East watch: needless deaths in the Gulf War*, New York (1991)
13. *Landmines: a perverse use of technology*, ICRC (1992)
14. *Recovery and reintegration of children in armed conflict*, Statement for the meeting of the UN Committee on the Rights of the Child, Richman N, International Save the Children Alliance (1992)

# THE
# UNITED NATIONS
# CONVENTION
# ON THE RIGHTS
# OF THE CHILD

# THE CONVENTION ON THE RIGHTS OF THE CHILD

**Adopted by the United Nations General Assembly on 20 November 1989 and entered into force on 2 September 1990**

## Text

## PREAMBLE

*The States Parties to the present Convention,*

*Considering* that, in accordance with the principles proclaimed in the Charter of the United Nations, recognition of the inherent dignity and of the equal and inalienable rights of all members of the human family is the foundation of freedom, justice and peace in the world,

*Bearing in mind* that the peoples of the United Nations have, in the Charter, reaffirmed their faith in fundamental human rights and in the dignity and worth of the human person, and have determined to promote social progress and better standards of life in larger freedom,

*Recognizing* that the United Nations has, in the Universal Declaration of Human Rights and in the International Covenants on Human Rights, proclaimed and agreed that everyone is entitled to all the rights and freedoms set forth therein, without distinction of any kind, such as race, colour, sex, language, religion, political or other opinion, national or social origin, property, birth or other status,

*Recalling* that, in the Universal Declaration of Human Rights, the United Nations has proclaimed that childhood is entitled to special care and assistance,

*Convinced* that the family, as the fundamental group of society and the natural environment for the growth and well-being of all its members and particularly children, should be afforded the necessary protection and assistance so that it can fully assume its responsibilities within the community,

*Recognizing* that the child, for the full and harmonious development of his or her personality, should grow up in a family environment, in an atmosphere of happiness, love and understanding,

*Considering* that the child should be fully prepared to live an individual life in society, and brought up in the spirit of the ideals proclaimed in the Charter of the United Nations, and in particular in the spirit of peace, dignity, tolerance, freedom, equality and solidarity,

*Bearing in mind* that the need to extend particular care to the child has been stated in the Geneva Declaration on the Rights of the Child of 1924 and in the Declaration of the Rights of the Child adopted by the General Assembly on 20 November 1959 and recognized in the Universal Declaration of Human Rights, in the International Covenant on Civil and Political Rights (in particular in articles 23 and 24), in the International Covenant on Economic, Social and Cultural Rights (in particular in article 10) and in the statutes and relevant instruments of specialized agencies and international organizations concerned with the welfare of children,

*Bearing in mind* that, as indicated in the Declaration of the Rights of the Child, "the child, by reason of his physical and mental immaturity, needs special safeguards and care, including appropriate legal protection, before as well as after birth",

*Recalling* the provisions of the Declaration on Social and Legal Principles relating to the Protection and Welfare of Children, with Special Reference to Foster Placement and Adoption Nationally and Internationally; the United Nations Standard Minimum Rules for the Administration of Juvenile Justice (The Beijing Rules); and the Declaration on the Protection of Women and Children in Emergency and Armed Conflict,

## Unofficial summary of main provisions

## PREAMBLE

*The preamble: recalls the basic principles of the United Nations and specific provisions of certain relevant human rights treaties and proclamations; reaffirms the fact that children, because of their vulnerability, need special care and protection; and places special emphasis on the primary caring and protective responsibility of the family, the need for legal and other protection of the child before and after birth, the importance of respect for the cultural values of the child's community, and the vital role of international cooperation in achieving the realization of children's rights.*

# THE CONVENTION ON THE RIGHTS OF THE CHILD

| Text | Unofficial summary of main provisions |
|---|---|

*Recognizing* that, in all countries in the world, there are children living in exception-ally difficult conditions, and that such children need special consideration,

*Taking due account* of the importance of the traditions and cultural values of each people for the protection and harmonious development of the child,

*Recognizing* the importance of international co-operation for improving the living conditions of children in every country, in particular in the developing countries,

*Have agreed* as follows:

## PART I

### Article 1

For the purposes of the present Convention, a child means every human being below the age of eighteen years unless, under the law applicable to the child, majority is attained earlier.

**Definition of a child**

*All persons under 18, unless by law majority is attained at an earlier age.*

### Article 2

1.    States Parties shall respect and ensure the rights set forth in the present Convention to each child within their jurisdiction without discrimination of any kind, irrespective of the child's or his or her parent's or legal guardian's race, colour, sex, language, religion, political or other opinion, national, ethnic or social origin, property, disability, birth or other status.

2.    States Parties shall take all appropriate measures to ensure that the child is protected against all forms of discrimination or punishment on the basis of the status, activities, expressed opinions, or beliefs of the child's parents, legal guardians, or family members.

**Non-discrimination**

*The principle that all rights apply to all children without exception, and the State's obligation to protect chil-dren from any form of discrimination. The State must not violate any right, and must take positive action to pro-mote them all.*

### Article 3

1.    In all actions concerning children, whether undertaken by public or private social welfare institutions, courts of law, administrative authorities or legislative bodies, the best interests of the child shall be a primary consideration.

2.    States Parties undertake to ensure the child such protection and care as is necessary for his or her well-being, taking into account the rights and duties of his or her parents, legal guardians, or other individuals legally responsible for him or her, and, to this end, shall take all appropriate legislative and administrative measures.

3.    States Parties shall ensure that the institutions, services and facilities respon-sible for the care or protection of children shall conform with the standards estab-lished by competent authorities, particularly in the areas of safety, health, in the number and suitability of their staff as well as competent supervision.

**Best interests of the child**

*All actions concerning the child should take full account of his or her best interests. The State is to pro-vide adequate care when parents or others responsible fail to do so.*

### Article 4

States Parties shall undertake all appropriate legislative, administrative, and other measures, for the implementation of the rights recognized in the present Convention. With regard to economic, social and cultural rights, States Parties shall undertake such measures to the maximum extent of their available resources and, where needed, within the framework of international co-operation.

**Implementation of rights**

*The State's obligation to translate the rights in the Convention into re-ality.*

# THE CONVENTION ON THE RIGHTS OF THE CHILD

## Text

## Unofficial summary of main provisions

### Article 5

States Parties shall respect the responsibilities, rights and duties of parents or, where applicable, the members of the extended family or community as provided for by local custom, legal guardians or other persons legally responsible for the child, to provide, in a manner consistent with the evolving capacities of the child, appropriate direction and guidance in the exercise by the child of the rights recognized in the present Convention.

**Parental guidance and the child's evolving capacities**

*The State's duty to respect the rights and responsibilities of parents and the wider family to provide guidance appropriate to the child's evolving capacities.*

### Article 6

1.	States Parties recognize that every child has the inherent right to life.

2.	States Parties shall ensure to the maximum extent possible the survival and development of the child.

**Survival and development**

*The inherent right to life, and the State's obligation to ensure the child's survival and development.*

### Article 7

1.	The child shall be registered immediately after birth and shall have the right from birth to a name, the right to acquire a nationality and, as far as possible, the right to know and be cared for by his or her parents.

2.	States Parties shall ensure the implementation of these rights in accordance with their national law and their obligations under the relevant international instruments in this field, in particular where the child would otherwise be stateless.

**Name and nationality**

*The right to have a name from birth and to be granted a nationality.*

### Article 8

1.	States Parties undertake to respect the right of the child to preserve his or her identity, including nationality, name and family relations as recognized by law without unlawful interference.

2.	Where a child is illegally deprived of some or all of the elements of his or her identity, States Parties shall provide appropriate assistance and protection, with a view to speedily re-establishing his or her identity.

**Preservation of identity**

*The State's obligation to protect and, if necessary, re-establish the basic aspects of a child's identity (name, nationality and family ties).*

### Article 9

1.	States Parties shall ensure that a child shall not be separated from his or her parents against their will, except when competent authorities subject to judicial review determine, in accordance with applicable law and procedures, that such separation is necessary for the best interests of the child. Such determination may be necessary in a particular case such as one involving abuse or neglect of the child by the parents, or one where the parents are living separately and a decision must be made as to the child's place of residence.

2.	In any proceedings pursuant to paragraph 1 of the present article, all interested parties shall be given an opportunity to participate in the proceedings and make their views known.

3.	States Parties shall respect the right of the child who is separated from one or both parents to maintain personal relations and direct contact with both parents on a regular basis, except if it is contrary to the child's best interests.

4.	Where such separation results from any action initiated by a State Party, such as the detention, imprisonment, exile, deportation or death (including death arising from any cause while the person is in the custody of the State) of one or both parents or of the child, that State Party shall, upon request, provide the parents, the child or, if appropriate, another member of the family with the essential information concerning the whereabouts of the absent member(s) of the family unless the provision of the information would be detrimental to the well-being of the child. States Parties shall further ensure that the submission of such a request shall of itself entail no adverse consequences for the person(s) concerned.

**Separation from parents**

*The child's right to live with his/her parents unless this is deemed incompatible with his/her best interests; the right to maintain contact with both parents if separated from one or both; the duties of States in cases where such separation results from State action.*

# THE CONVENTION ON THE RIGHTS OF THE CHILD

## Text

## Unofficial summary of main provisions

### Article 10

1.    In accordance with the obligation of States Parties under article 9, paragraph 1, applications by a child or his or her parents to enter or leave a State Party for the purpose of family reunification shall be dealt with by States Parties in a positive, humane and expeditious manner. States Parties shall further ensure that the submission of such a request shall entail no adverse consequences for the applicants and for the members of their family.

2.    A child whose parents reside in different States shall have the right to maintain on a regular basis, save in exceptional circumstances, personal relations and direct contacts with both parents. Towards that end and in accordance with the obligation of States Parties under article 9, paragraph 2, States Parties shall respect the right of the child and his or her parents to leave any country, including their own, and to enter their own country. The right to leave any country shall be subject only to such restrictions as are prescribed by law and which are necessary to protect the national security, public order *(ordre public)*, public health or morals or the rights and freedoms of others and are consistent with the other rights recognized in the present Convention.

**Family reunification**

*The right of children and their parents to leave any country and to enter their own in order to be reunited or to maintain the child-parent relationship.*

### Article 11

1.    States Parties shall take measures to combat the illicit transfer and non-return of children abroad.

2.    To this end, States Parties shall promote the conclusion of bilateral or multilateral agreements or accession to existing agreements.

**Illicit transfer and non-return**

*The State's obligation to try to prevent and remedy the kidnapping or retention of children abroad by a parent or third party.*

### Article 12

1.    States Parties shall assure to the child who is capable of forming his or her own views the right to express those views freely in all matters affecting the child, the views of the child being given due weight in accordance with the age and maturity of the child.

2.    For this purpose, the child shall in particular be provided the opportunity to be heard in any judicial and administrative proceedings affecting the child, either directly, or through a representative or an appropriate body, in a manner consistent with the procedural rules of national law.

**The child's opinion**

*The child's right to express an opinion, and to have that opinion taken into account, in any matter or procedure affecting the child.*

### Article 13

1.    The child shall have the right to freedom of expression; this right shall include freedom to seek, receive and impart information and ideas of all kinds, regardless of frontiers, either orally, in writing or in print, in the form of art, or through any other media of the child's choice.

2.    The exercise of this right may be subject to certain restrictions, but these shall only be such as are provided by law and are necessary:

*(a)*    For respect of the rights or reputations of others; or

*(b)*    For the protection of national security or of public order *(ordre public),* or of public health or morals.

**Freedom of expression**

*The child's right to obtain and make known information, and to express his or her views, unless this would violate the rights of others.*

### Article 14

1.    States Parties shall respect the right of the child to freedom of thought, conscience and religion.

2.    States Parties shall respect the rights and duties of the parents and, when applicable, legal guardians, to provide direction to the child in the exercise of his or her right in a manner consistent with the evolving capacities of the child.

**Freedom of thought, conscience and religion**

*The child's right to freedom of thought, conscience and religion, subject to appropriate parental guidance and national law.*

# THE CONVENTION ON THE RIGHTS OF THE CHILD

## Text

## Unofficial summary of main provisions

3.    Freedom to manifest one's religion or beliefs may be subject only to such limitations as are prescribed by law and are necessary to protect public safety, order, health or morals, or the fundamental rights and freedoms of others.

### Article 15

1.    States Parties recognize the rights of the child to freedom of association and to freedom of peaceful assembly.

2.    No restrictions may be placed on the exercise of these rights other than those imposed in conformity with the law and which are necessary in a democratic society in the interests of national security or public safety, public order *(ordre public)*, the protection of public health or morals or the protection of the rights and freedoms of others.

### Article16

1.    No child shall be subjected to arbitrary or unlawful interference with his or her privacy, family, home or correspondence, nor to unlawful attacks on his or her honour and reputation.

2.    The child has the right to the protection of the law against such interference or attacks.

### Article 17

States Parties recognize the important function performed by the mass media and shall ensure that the child has access to information and material from a diversity of national and international sources, especially those aimed at the promotion of his or her social, spiritual and moral well-being and physical and mental health. To this end, States Parties shall:

*(a)*    Encourage the mass media to disseminate information and material of social and cultural benefit to the child and in accordance with the spirit of article 29;

*(b)*    Encourage international co-operation in the production, exchange and dissemination of such information and material from a diversity of cultural, national and international sources;

*(c)*    Encourage the production and dissemination of children's books;

*(d)*    Encourage the mass media to have particular regard to the linguistic needs of the child who belongs to a minority group or who is indigenous;

*(e)*    Encourage the development of appropriate guidelines for the protection of the child from information and material injurious to his or her well-being, bearing in mind the provisions of articles 13 and 18.

### Article 18

1.    States Parties shall use their best efforts to ensure recognition of the principle that both parents have common responsibilities for the upbringing and development of the child. Parents or, as the case may be, legal guardians, have the primary responsibility for the upbringing and development of the child. The best interests of the child will be their basic concern.

2.    For the purpose of guaranteeing and promoting the rights set forth in the present Convention, States Parties shall render appropriate assistance to parents and legal guardians in the performance of their child-rearing responsibilities and shall ensure the development of institutions, facilities and services for the care of children.

3.    States Parties shall take all appropriate measures to ensure that children of working parents have the right to benefit from child-care services and facilities for which they are eligible.

### Freedom of association

*The right of children to meet with others and to join or set up associations, unless the fact of doing so violates the rights of others.*

### Protection of privacy

*The right to protection from interference with privacy, family, home and correspondence, and from libel/slander.*

### Access to appropriate information

*The role of the media in disseminating information to children that is consistent with moral well-being and knowledge and understanding among peoples, and respects the child's cultural background. The State is to take measures to encourage this and to protect children from harmful materials.*

### Parental responsibilities

*The principle that both parents have joint primary responsibility for bringing up their children, and that the State should support them in this task.*

# THE CONVENTION ON THE RIGHTS OF THE CHILD

## Text

## Unofficial summary of main provisions

### Article 19

1. States Parties shall take all appropriate legislative, administrative, social and educational measures to protect the child from all forms of physical or mental violence, injury or abuse, neglect or negligent treatment, maltreatment or exploitation, including sexual abuse, while in the care of parent(s), legal guardian(s) or any other person who has the care of the child.

2. Such protective measures should, as appropriate, include effective procedures for the establishment of social programmes to provide necessary support for the child and for those who have the care of the child, as well as for other forms of prevention and for identification, reporting, referral, investigation, treatment and follow-up of instances of child maltreatment described heretofore, and, as appropriate, for judicial involvement.

**Protection from abuse and neglect**

*The State's obligation to protect children from all forms of maltreatment perpetrated by parents or others responsible for their care, and to undertake preventive and treatment programmes in this regard.*

### Article 20

1. A child temporarily or permanently deprived of his or her family environment, or in whose own best interests cannot be allowed to remain in that environment, shall be entitled to special protection and assistance provided by the State.

2. States Parties shall in accordance with their national laws ensure alternative care for such a child.

3. Such care could include, *inter alia,* foster placement, *kafalah* of Islamic law, adoption or if necessary placement in suitable institutions for the care of children. When considering solutions, due regard shall be paid to the desirability of continuity in a child's upbringing and to the child's ethnic, religious, cultural and linguistic background.

**Protection of children without families**

*The State's obligation to provide special protection for children deprived of their family environment and to ensure that appropriate alternative family care or institutional placement is made available to them, taking into account the child's cultural background.*

### Article 21

States Parties which recognize and/or permit the system of adoption shall ensure that the best interests of the child shall be the paramount consideration and they shall:

*(a)* Ensure that the adoption of a child is authorized only by competent authorities who determine, in accordance with applicable law and procedures and on the basis of all pertinent and reliable information, that the adoption is permissible in view of the child's status concerning parents, relatives and legal guardians and that, if required, the persons concerned have given their informed consent to the adoption on the basis of such counselling as may be necessary;

*(b)* Recognize that inter-country adoption may be considered as an alternative means of child's care, if the child cannot be placed in a foster or an adoptive family or cannot in any suitable manner be cared for in the child's country of origin;

*(c)* Ensure that the child concerned by inter-country adoption enjoys safeguards and standards equivalent to those existing in the case of national adoption;

*(d)* Take all appropriate measures to ensure that, in inter-country adoption, the placement does not result in improper financial gain for those involved in it;

*(e)* Promote, where appropriate, the objectives of the present article by concluding bilateral or multilateral arrangements or agreements, and endeavour, within this framework, to ensure that the placement of the child in another country is carried out by competent authorities or organs.

**Adoption**

*In countries where adoption is recognized and/or allowed, it shall only be carried out in the best interests of the child, with all necessary safeguards for a given child and authorization by the competent authorities.*

# THE CONVENTION ON THE RIGHTS OF THE CHILD

## Text

## Unofficial summary of main provisions

### Article 22

1. States Parties shall take appropriate measures to ensure that a child who is seeking refugee status or who is considered a refugee in accordance with applicable international or domestic law and procedures shall, whether unaccompanied or accompanied by his or her parents or by any other person, receive appropriate protection and humanitarian assistance in the enjoyment of applicable rights set forth in the present Convention and in other international human rights or humanitarian instruments to which the said States are Parties.

2. For this purpose, States Parties shall provide, as they consider appropriate, co-operation in any efforts by the United Nations and other competent intergovernmental organizations or non-governmental organizations co-operating with the United Nations to protect and assist such a child and to trace the parents or other members of the family of any refugee child in order to obtain information necessary for reunification with his or her family. In cases where no parents or other members of the family can be found, the child shall be accorded the same protection as any other child permanently or temporarily deprived of his or her family environment for any reason, as set forth in the present Convention.

### Refugee children

*Special protection to be granted to children who are refugees or seeking refugee status, and the State's obligation to cooperate with competent organizations providing such protection and assistance.*

### Article 23

1. States Parties recognize that a mentally or physically disabled child should enjoy a full and decent life, in conditions which ensure dignity, promote self-reliance, and facilitate the child's active participation in the community.

2. States Parties recognize the right of the disabled child to special care and shall encourage and ensure the extension, subject to available resources, to the eligible child and those responsible for his or her care, of assistance for which application is made and which is appropriate to the child's condition and to the circumstances of the parents or others caring for the child.

3. Recognizing the special needs of a disabled child, assistance extended in accordance with paragraph 2 of the present article shall be provided free of charge, whenever possible, taking into account the financial resources of the parents or others caring for the child, and shall be designed to ensure that the disabled child has effective access to and receives education, training, health care services, rehabilitation services, preparation for employment and recreation opportunities in a manner conducive to the child's achieving the fullest possible social integration and individual development, including his or her cultural and spiritual development.

4. States Parties shall promote, in the spirit of international co-operation, the exchange of appropriate information in the field of preventive health care and of medical, psychological and functional treatment of disabled children, including dissemination of and access to information concerning methods of rehabilitation, education and vocational services, with the aim of enabling States Parties to improve their capabilities and skills and to widen their experience in these areas. In this regard, particular account shall be taken of the needs of developing countries.

### Handicapped children

*The right of handicapped children to special care, education and training designed to help them to achieve greatest possible self-reliance and to lead a full and active life in society.*

### Article 24

1. States Parties recognize the right of the child to the enjoyment of the highest attainable standard of health and to facilities for the treatment of illness and rehabilitation of health. States Parties shall strive to ensure that no child is deprived of his or her right of access to such health care services.

2. States Parties shall pursue full implementation of this right and, in particular, shall take appropriate measures:

*(a)* To diminish infant and child mortality;

### Health and health services

*The right to the highest level of health possible and to access to health and medical services, with special emphasis on primary and preventive health care, public health education and the diminution of infant mortality. The State's obligation to work towards the abolition of harmful traditional practices.*

# THE CONVENTION ON THE RIGHTS OF THE CHILD

## Text

**Unofficial summary of main provisions**

*(b)* To ensure the provision of necessary medical assistance and health care to all children with emphasis on the development of primary health care;

*(c)* To combat disease and malnutrition, including within the framework of primary health care, through, *inter alia*, the application of readily available technology and through the provision of adequate nutritious foods and clean drinking-water, taking into consideration the dangers and risks of environmental pollution;

*(d)* To ensure appropriate pre-natal and post-natal health care for mothers;

*(e)* To ensure that all segments of society, in particular parents and children, are informed, have access to education and are supported in the use of basic knowledge of child health and nutrition, the advantages of breast-feeding, hygiene and environmental sanitation and the prevention of accidents;

*(f)* To develop preventive health care, guidance for parents, and family planning education and services.

3.　States Parties shall take all effective and appropriate measures with a view to abolishing traditional practices prejudicial to the health of children.

4.　States Parties undertake to promote and encourage international co-operation with a view to achieving progressively the full realization of the right recognized in the present article. In this regard, particular account shall be taken of the needs of developing countries.

## Article 25

States Parties recognize the right of a child who has been placed by the competent authorities for the purposes of care, protection, or treatment of his or her physical or mental health, to a periodic review of the treatment provided to the child and all other circumstances relevant to his or her placement.

## Article 26

1.　States Parties shall recognize for every child the right to benefit from social security, including social insurance, and shall take the necessary measures to achieve the full realization of this right in accordance with their national law.

2.　The benefits should, where appropriate, be granted, taking into account the resources and the circumstances of the child and persons having responsibility for the maintenance of the child, as well as any other consideration relevant to an application for benefits made by or on behalf of the child.

## Article 27

1.　States Parties recognize the right of every child to a standard of living adequate for the child's physical, mental, spiritual, moral and social development.

2.　The parent(s) or others responsible for the child have the primary responsibility to secure, within their abilities and financial capacities, the conditions of living necessary for the child's development.

3.　States Parties, in accordance with national conditions and within their means, shall take appropriate measures to assist parents and others responsible for the child to implement this right and shall in case of need provide material assistance and support programmes, particularly with regard to nutrition, clothing and housing.

4.　States Parties shall take all appropriate measures to secure the recovery of maintenance for the child from the parents or other persons having financial responsibility for the child, both within the State Party and from abroad. In particular, where the person having financial responsibility for the child lives in a State different from that of the child, States Parties shall promote the accession to international agreements or the conclusion of such agreements, as well as the making of other appropriate arrangements.

---

*Health and health services (continued)*

*Emphasis is laid on the need for international cooperation to ensure this right.*

**Periodic review of placement**

*The right of children placed by the State for reasons of care, protection or treatment to have all aspects of that placement evaluated regularly.*

**Social security**

*The right of children to benefit from social security.*

**Standard of living**

*The right of children to benefit from an adequate standard of living, the primary responsibility of parents to provide this, and the State's duty to ensure that this responsibility is first fulfillable and then fulfilled, where necessary through the recovery of maintenance.*

# THE CONVENTION ON THE RIGHTS OF THE CHILD

## Text

## Unofficial summary of main provisions

### Article 28

1. States Parties recognize the right of the child to education, and with a view to achieving this right progressively and on the basis of equal opportunity, they shall, in particular:

*(a)* Make primary education compulsory and available free to all;

*(b)* Encourage the development of different forms of secondary education, including general and vocational education, make them available and accessible to every child, and take appropriate measures such as the introduction of free education and offering financial assistance in case of need;

*(c)* Make higher education accessible to all on the basis of capacity by every appropriate means;

*(d)* Make educational and vocational information and guidance available and accessible to all children;

*(e)* Take measures to encourage regular attendance at schools and the reduction of drop-out rates.

2. States Parties shall take all appropriate measures to ensure that school discipline is administered in a manner consistent with the child's human dignity and in conformity with the present Convention.

3. States Parties shall promote and encourage international co-operation in matters relating to education, in particular with a view to contributing to the elimination of ignorance and illiteracy throughout the world and facilitating access to scientific and technical knowledge and modern teaching methods. In this regard, particular account shall be taken of the needs of developing countries.

**Education**

*The child's right to education, and the State's duty to ensure that primary education at least is made free and compulsory. Administration of school discipline is to reflect the child's human dignity. Emphasis is laid on the need for international cooperation to ensure this right.*

### Article 29

1. States Parties agree that the education of the child shall be directed to:

*(a)* The development of the child's personality, talents and mental and physical abilities to their fullest potential;

*(b)* The development of respect for human rights and fundamental freedoms, and for the principles enshrined in the Charter of the United Nations;

*(c)* The development of respect for the child's parents, his or her own cultural identity, language and values, for the national values of the country in which the child is living, the country from which he or she may originate, and for civilizations different from his or her own;

*(d)* The preparation of the child for responsible life in a free society, in the spirit of understanding, peace, tolerance, equality of sexes, and friendship among all peoples, ethnic, national and religious groups and persons of indigenous origin;

*(e)* The development of respect for the natural environment.

2. No part of the present article or article 28 shall be construed so as to interfere with the liberty of individuals and bodies to establish and direct educational institutions, subject always to the observance of the principles set forth in paragraph 1 of the present article and to the requirements that the education given in such institutions shall conform to such minimum standards as may be laid down by the State.

**Aims of education**

*The State's recognition that education should be directed at developing the child's personality and talents, preparing the child for active life as an adult, fostering respect for basic human rights and developing respect for the child's own cultural and national values and those of others.*

### Article 30

In those States in which ethnic, religious or linguistic minorities or persons of indigenous origin exist, a child belonging to such a minority or who is indigenous shall not be denied the right, in community with other members of his or her group, to enjoy his or her own culture, to profess and practise his or her own religion, or to use his or her own language.

**Children of minorities or of indigenous peoples**

*The right of children of minority communities and indigenous peoples to enjoy their own culture and to practice their own religion and language.*

# THE CONVENTION ON THE RIGHTS OF THE CHILD

## Text

### Article 31

1.  States Parties recognize the right of the child to rest and leisure, to engage in play and recreational activities appropriate to the age of the child and to participate freely in cultural life and the arts.

2.  States Parties shall respect and promote the right of the child to participate fully in cultural and artistic life and shall encourage the provision of appropriate and equal opportunities for cultural, artistic, recreational and leisure activity.

### Article 32

1.  States Parties recognize the right of the child to be protected from economic exploitation and from performing any work that is likely to be hazardous or to interfere with the child's education, or to be harmful to the child's health or physical, mental, spiritual, moral or social development.

2.  States Parties shall take legislative, administrative, social and educational measures to ensure the implementation of the present article. To this end, and having regard to the relevant provisions of other international instruments, States Parties shall in particular:

*(a)*  Provide for a minimum age or minimum ages for admissions to employment;

*(b)*  Provide for appropriate regulation of the hours and conditions of employment;

*(c)*  Provide for appropriate penalties or other sanctions to ensure the effective enforcement of the present article.

### Article 33

States Parties shall take all appropriate measures, including legislative, administrative, social and educational measures, to protect children from the illicit use of narcotic drugs and psychotropic substances as defined in the relevant international treaties, and to prevent the use of children in the illicit production and trafficking of such substances.

### Article 34

States Parties undertake to protect the child from all forms of sexual exploitation and sexual abuse. For these purposes, States Parties shall in particular take all appropriate national, bilateral and multilateral measures to prevent:

*(a)*  The inducement or coercion of a child to engage in any unlawful sexual activity;

*(b)*  The exploitative use of children in prostitution or other unlawful sexual practices;

*(c)*  The exploitative use of children in pornographic performances and materials.

### Article 35

States Parties shall take all appropriate national, bilateral and multilateral measures to prevent the abduction of, the sale of or traffic in children for any purpose or in any form.

### Article 36

States Parties shall protect the child against all other forms of exploitation prejudicial to any aspects of the child's welfare.

## Unofficial summary of main provisions

### Leisure, recreation and cultural activities

*The right of children to leisure, play and participation in cultural and artistic activities.*

### Child labour

*The State's obligation to protect children from engaging in work that constitutes a threat to their health, education or development, to set minimum ages for employment, and to regulate conditions of employment.*

### Drug abuse

*The child's right to protection from the use of narcotic and psychotropic drugs and from being involved in their production or distribution.*

### Sexual exploitation

*The child's right to protection from sexual exploitation and abuse, including prostitution and involvement in pornography.*

### Sale, trafficking and abduction

*The State's obligation to make every effort to prevent the sale, trafficking and abduction of children.*

### Other forms of exploitation

*The child's right to protection from all other forms of exploitation not covered in articles 32, 33, 34 and 35.*

# THE CONVENTION ON THE RIGHTS OF THE CHILD

| Text | Unofficial summary of main provisions |
|---|---|

## Article 37

States Parties shall ensure that:

*(a)* No child shall be subjected to torture or other cruel, inhuman or degrading treatment or punishment. Neither capital punishment nor life imprisonment without possibility of release shall be imposed for offences committed by persons below eighteen years of age;

*(b)* No child shall be deprived of his or her liberty unlawfully or arbitrarily. The arrest, detention or imprisonment of a child shall be in conformity with the law and shall be used only as a measure of last resort and for the shortest appropriate period of time;

*(c)* Every child deprived of liberty shall be treated with humanity and respect for the inherent dignity of the human person, and in a manner which takes into account the needs of persons of his or her age. In particular, every child deprived of liberty shall be separated from adults unless it is considered in the child's best interest not to do so and shall have the right to maintain contact with his or her family through correspondence and visits, save in exceptional circumstances;

*(d)* Every child deprived of his or her liberty shall have the right to prompt access to legal and other appropriate assistance, as well as the right to challenge the legality of the deprivation of his or her liberty before a court or other competent, independent and impartial authority, and to a prompt decision on any such action.

### Torture and deprivation of liberty

*The prohibition of torture, cruel treatment or punishment, capital punishment, life imprisonment, and unlawful arrest or deprivation of liberty. The principles of appropriate treatment, separation from detained adults, contact with family and access to legal and other assistance.*

## Article 38

1. States Parties undertake to respect and to ensure respect for rules of international humanitarian law applicable to them in armed conflicts which are relevant to the child.

2. States Parties shall take all feasible measures to ensure that persons who have not attained the age of fifteen years do not take a direct part in hostilities.

3. States Parties shall refrain from recruiting any person who has not attained the age of fifteen years into their armed forces. In recruiting among those persons who have attained the age of fifteen years but who have not attained the age of eighteen years, States Parties shall endeavour to give priority to those who are oldest.

4. In accordance with their obligations under international humanitarian law to protect the civilian population in armed conflicts, States Parties shall take all feasible measures to ensure protection and care of children who are affected by an armed conflict.

### Armed conflicts

*The obligation of States to respect and ensure respect for humanitarian law as it applies to children. The principle that no child under 15 take a direct part in hostilities or be recruited into the armed forces, and that all children affected by armed conflict benefit from protection and care.*

## Article 39

States Parties shall take all appropriate measures to promote physical and psychological recovery and social reintegration of a child victim of: any form of neglect, exploitation, or abuse; torture or any other form of cruel, inhuman or degrading treatment or punishment; or armed conflicts. Such recovery and reintegration shall take place in an environment which fosters the health, self-respect and dignity of the child.

### Rehabilitative care

*The State's obligation to ensure that child victims of armed conflicts, torture, neglect, maltreatment or exploitation receive appropriate treatment for their recovery and social re-integration.*

## Article 40

1. States Parties recognize the right of every child alleged as, accused of, or recognized as having infringed the penal law to be treated in a manner consistent with the promotion of the child's sense of dignity and worth, which reinforces the child's respect for the human rights and fundamental freedoms of others and which takes into account the child's age and the desirability of promoting the child's reintegration and the child's assuming a constructive role in society.

2. To this end, and having regard to the relevant provisions of international

### Administration of juvenile justice

*The right of children alleged or recognized as having committed an offence to respect for their human rights and, in particular, to benefit from all aspects of the due process of law, including legal or other assistance in preparing and pre-*

# THE CONVENTION ON THE RIGHTS OF THE CHILD

## Text

## Unofficial summary of main provisions

instruments, States Parties shall, in particular, ensure that:

*(a)* No child shall be alleged as, be accused of, or recognized as having infringed the penal law by reason of acts or omissions that were not prohibited by national or international law at the time they were committed;

*(b)* Every child alleged as or accused of having infringed the penal law has at least the following guarantees:

*(i)* To be presumed innocent until proven guilty according to law;

*(ii)* To be informed promptly and directly of the charges against him or her, and, if appropriate through his or her parents or legal guardian, and to have legal or other appropriate assistance in the preparation and presentation of his or her defence;

*(iii)* To have the matter determined without delay by a competent, independent and impartial authority or judicial body in a fair hearing according to law, in the presence of legal or other appropriate assistance and, unless it is considered not to be in the best interest of the child, in particular, taking into account his or her age or situation, his or her parents or legal guardians;

*(iv)* Not to be compelled to give testimony or to confess guilt; to examine or have examined adverse witnesses and to obtain the participation and examination of witnesses on his or her behalf under conditions of equality;

*(v)* If considered to have infringed the penal law, to have this decision and any measures imposed in consequence thereof reviewed by a higher competent, independent and impartial authority or judicial body according to law;

*(vi)* To have the free assistance of an interpreter if the child cannot understand or speak the language used;

*(vii)* To have his or her privacy fully respected at all stages of the proceedings.

3. States Parties shall seek to promote the establishment of laws, procedures, authorities and institutions specifically applicable to children alleged as, accused of, or recognized as having infringed the penal law, and in particular:

*(a)* The establishment of a minimum age below which children shall be presumed not to have the capacity to infringe the penal law;

*(b)* Whenever appropriate and desirable, measures for dealing with such children without resorting to judicial proceedings, providing that human rights and legal safeguards are fully respected.

4. A variety of dispositions, such as care, guidance and supervision orders; counselling; probation; foster care; education and vocational training programmes and other alternatives to institutional care shall be available to ensure that children are dealt with in a manner appropriate to their well-being and proportionate both to their circumstances and the offence.

## Article 41

Nothing in the present Convention shall affect any provisions which are more conducive to the realization of the rights of the child and which may be contained in:

*(a)* The law of a State Party; or

*(b)* International law in force for that State.

### *Administration of juvenile justice (continued)*

*senting their defence. The principle that recourse to judicial proceedings and institutional placements should be avoided wherever possible and appropriate.*

### Respect for existing standards

*The principle that, if any standards set in national law or other applicable international instruments are higher than those of this Convention, it is the higher standard that applies.*

# THE CONVENTION ON THE RIGHTS OF THE CHILD

| Text | Unofficial summary of main provisions |
|---|---|

## PART II

### Article 42

States Parties undertake to make the principles and provisions of the Convention widely known, by appropriate and active means, to adults and children alike.

### Article 43

1.    For the purpose of examining the progress made by States Parties in achieving the realization of the obligations undertaken in the present Convention, there shall be established a Committee on the Rights of the Child, which shall carry out the functions hereinafter provided.

2.    The Committee shall consist of ten experts of high moral standing and recognized competence in the field covered by this Convention. The members of the Committee shall be elected by States Parties from among their nationals and shall serve in their personal capacity, consideration being given to equitable geographical distribution, as well as to the principal legal systems.

3.    The members of the Committee shall be elected by secret ballot from a list of persons nominated by States Parties. Each State Party may nominate one person from among its own nationals.

4.    The initial election to the Committee shall be held no later than six months after the date of the entry into force of the present Convention and thereafter every second year. At least four months before the date of each election, the Secretary-General of the United Nations shall address a letter to States Parties inviting them to submit their nominations within two months. The Secretary-General shall subsequently prepare a list in alphabetical order of all persons thus nominated, indicating States Parties which have nominated them, and shall submit it to the States Parties to the present Convention.

5.    The elections shall be held at meetings of States Parties convened by the Secretary-General at United Nations Headquarters. At those meetings, for which two-thirds of States Parties shall constitute a quorum, the persons elected to the Committee shall be those who obtain the largest number of votes and an absolute majority of the votes of the representatives of States Parties present and voting.

6.    The members of the Committee shall be elected for a term of four years. They shall be eligible for re-election if renominated. The term of five of the members elected at the first election shall expire at the end of two years; immediately after the first election, the names of these five members shall be chosen by lot by the Chairman of the meeting.

7.    If a member of the Committee dies or resigns or declares that for any other cause he or she can no longer perform the duties of the Committee, the State Party which nominated the member shall appoint another expert from among its nationals to serve for the remainder of the term, subject to the approval of the Committee.

8.    The Committee shall establish its own rules of procedure.

9.    The Committee shall elect its officers for a period of two years.

10.    The meetings of the Committee shall normally be held at the United Nations Headquarters or at any other convenient place as determined by the Committee. The Committee shall normally meet annually. The duration of the meetings of the Committee shall be determined, and reviewed, if necessary, by a meeting of the States Parties to the present Convention, subject to the approval of the General Assembly.

## Unofficial summary of main provisions

### Implementation and entry into force

*The provisions of articles 42 - 54 notably foresee:*

*(i)    the State's obligation to make the rights contained in this Convention widely known to both adults and children.*

*(ii)    the setting up of a Committee on the Rights of the child composed of ten experts, which will consider reports that States Parties to the Convention are to submit two years after ratification and every five years thereafter. The Convention enters into force—and the Committee would therefore be set up—once 20 countries have ratified it.*

*(iii)    States Parties are to make their reports widely available to the general public.*

*(iv)    The Committee may propose that special studies be undertaken on specific issues relating to the rights of the child, and may make its evaluations known to each State Party concerned as well as to the UN General Assembly.*

*(v)    In order to "foster the effective implementation of the Convention and to encourage international cooperation", the specialized agencies of the UN (such as the ILO, WHO and UNESCO) and UNICEF would be able to attend the meetings of the Committee. Together with any other body recognized as "competent", including NGOs in consultative status with the UN and UN organs such as the UNHCR, they can submit pertinent information to the Committee and be asked to advise on the optimal implementation of the Convention.*

11.     The Secretary-General of the United Nations shall provide the necessary staff and facilities for the effective performance of the functions of the Committee under the present Convention.

12.     With the approval of the General Assembly, the members of the Committee established under the present Convention shall receive emoluments from United Nations resources on such terms and conditions as the Assembly may decide.

## Article 44

1.     States Parties undertake to submit to the Committee, through the Secretary-General of the United Nations, reports on the measures they have adopted which give effect to the rights recognized herein and on the progress made on the enjoyment of those rights:

(a)     Within two years of the entry into force of the Convention for the State Party concerned;

(b)     Thereafter every five years.

2.     Reports made under the present article shall indicate factors and difficulties, if any, affecting the degree of fulfilment of the obligations under the present Convention. Reports shall also contain sufficient information to provide the Committee with a comprehensive understanding of the implementation of the Convention in the country concerned.

3.     A State Party which has submitted a comprehensive initial report to the Committee need not in its subsequent reports submitted in accordance with paragraph 1 (b) of the present article, repeat basic information previously provided.

4.     The Committee may request from States Parties further information relevant to the implementation of the Convention.

5.     The Committee shall submit to the General Assembly, through the Economic and Social Council, every two years, reports on its activities.

6.     States Parties shall make their reports widely available to the public in their own countries.

## Article 45

In order to foster the effective implementation of the Convention and to encourage international co-operation in the field covered by the Convention:

(a)     The specialized agencies, the United Nations Children's Fund and other United Nations organs shall be entitled to be represented at the consideration of the implementation of such provisions of the present Convention as fall within the scope of their mandate. The Committee may invite the specialized agencies, the United Nations Children's Fund and other competent bodies as it may consider appropriate to provide expert advice on the implementation of the Convention in areas falling within the scope of their respective mandates. The Committee may invite the specialized agencies, the United Nations Children's Fund and other United Nations organs to submit reports on the implementation of the Convention in areas falling within the scope of their activities;

(b)     The Committee shall transmit, as it may consider appropriate, to the specialized agencies,the United Nations Children's Fund and other competent bodies, any reports from States Parties that contain a request, or indicate a need, for technical advice or assistance along with the Committee's observations and suggestions, if any, on these requests or indications;

(c)     the Committee may recommend to the General Assembly to request the Secretary-General to undertake on its behalf studies on specific issues relating to the rights of the child;

## Text

*(d)* the Committee may make suggestions and general recommendations based on information received pursuant to articles 44 and 45 of the present Convention. Such suggestions and general recommendations shall be transmitted to any State Party concerned and reported to the General Assembly, together with comments, if any, from States Parties.

## PART III

### Article 46

The present Convention shall be open for signature by all States.

### Article 47

The present Convention is subject to ratification. Instruments of ratification shall be deposited with the Secretary-General of the United Nations.

### Article 48

The present Convention shall remain open for accession by any State. The instruments of accession shall be deposited with the Secretary-General of the United Nations.

### Article 49

1.    The present Convention shall enter into force on the thirtieth day following the date of deposit with the Secretary-General of the United Nations of the twentieth instrument of ratification or accession.

2.    For each State ratifying or acceding to the Convention after the deposit of the twentieth instrument of ratification or accession, the Convention shall enter into force on the thirtieth day after the deposit by such State of its instrument of ratification or accession.

### Article 50

1.    Any State Party may propose an amendment and file it with the Secretary-General of the United Nations. The Secretary-General shall thereupon communicate the proposed amendment to States Parties, with a request that they indicate whether they favour a conference of States Parties for the purpose of considering and voting upon the proposals. In the event that, within four months from the date of such communication, at least one third of the States Parties favour such a conference, the Secretary-General shall convene the conference under the auspices of the United Nations. Any amendment adopted by a majority of States Parties present and voting at the conference shall be submitted to the General Assembly for approval.

2.    An amendment adopted in accordance with paragraph (1) of the present article shall enter into force when it has been approved by the General Assembly of the United Nations and accepted by a two-thirds majority of States Parties.

3.    When an amendment enters into force, it shall be binding on those States Parties which have accepted it, other States Parties still being bound by the provisions of the present Convention and any earlier amendments which they have accepted.

# THE CONVENTION ON THE RIGHTS OF THE CHILD

## Text

### Article 51

1.    The Secretary-General of the United Nations shall receive and circulate to all States the text of reservations made by States at the time of ratification or accession.

2.    A reservation incompatible with the object and purpose of the present Convention shall not be permitted.

3.    Reservations may be withdrawn at any time by notification to that effect addressed to the Secretary-General of the United Nations, who shall then inform all States. Such notification shall take effect on the date on which it is received by the Secretary-General.

### Article 52

A State Party may denounce the present Convention by written notification to the Secretary-General of the United Nations. Denunciation becomes effective one year after the date of receipt of the notification by the Secretary-General.

### Article 53

The Secretary-General of the United Nations is designated as the depositary of the present Convention.

### Article 54

The original of the present Convention, of which the Arabic, Chinese, English, French, Russian and Spanish texts are equally authentic, shall be deposited with the Secretary-General of the United Nations.

In witness thereof the undersigned plenipotentiaries, being duly authorized thereto by their respective Governments, have signed the present Convention.

# UK Declaration & Reservations
## UN Convention on the Rights of the Child
## UK Ratification

The Instrument of ratification contained the following reservations and declarations:

(a)     The United Kingdom interprets the Convention as applicable only following a live birth.

(b)     The United Kingdom interprets the reference in the Convention to "parents" to mean only those persons who, as a matter of national law, are treated as parents. This includes cases where the law regards a child as having only one parent, for example where a child has been adopted by one person only and in certain cases where a child is conceived other then as a result of sexual intercourse by the woman who gives birth to it and she is treated as the only parent.

(c)     The United Kingdom reserves the right to apply such legislation, in so far as it relates to the entry into, stay in and departure from the United Kingdom of those who do not have the right under the law of the United Kingdom to enter and remain in the United Kingdom, and to the acquisition and possession of citizenship, as it may deem necessary from time to time.

(d)     Employment legislation in the United Kingdom does not treat persons under 18, but under the school-leaving age as children, but as "young people". Accordingly the United Kingdom reserves the right to continue to apply Article 32 subject to such employment legislation.

(e)     Where at any time there is a lack of suitable accommodation or adequate facilities for a particular individual in any institution in which young offenders are detained, or where the mixing of adults and children is deemed to be mutually beneficial, the United Kingdom reserves the right not to apply Article 37(c) in so far as those provisions require children who are detained to be accommodated separately from adults.

(f)     In Scotland there are tribunals (known as "children's hearings") which consider the welfare of the child and deal with the majority of offences which a child is alleged to have committed. In some cases, mainly of a welfare nature, the child is temporarily deprived of its liberty for up to seven days prior to attending the hearing. The child and its family are, however, allowed access to a lawyer during this period. Although the decisions of the hearings are subject to appeal to the courts, legal representation is not permitted at the proceedings of the children's hearings themselves. Children's hearings have proved over the years to be a very effective way of dealing with the problems of children in a less formal, non-adversarial manner. Accordingly, the United Kingdom, in respect of Article 37(d), reserves its right to continue the present operation of children's hearings.

# COMMITTEE ON THE RIGHTS OF THE CHILD

## Eighth session

## CONSIDERATION OF REPORTS SUBMITTED BY STATES PARTIES UNDER ARTICLE 44 OF THE CONVENTION

Concluding observations of the Committee on the Rights of the Child: United Kingdom of Great Britain and Northern Ireland

1. The Committee considered the initial report of the United Kingdom of Great Britain and Northern Ireland (CRC/C/11/Add.1) at its 204th, 205th and 206th meetings (CRC/C/SR.204-206), held on 24 and 25 January 1995, and adopted* the following concluding observations.

### A. Introduction

2. The Committee appreciates the opportunity to engage in a constructive dialogue with the State party and welcomes the timely submission by the Government of the written responses to the Committee's list of issues (see CRC/C.7/WP.1). The Committee welcomes the additional oral information provided by the delegation of the State party which greatly assisted in clarifying many of the issues raised by the Committee. The additional oral information was particularly useful, in view of the Committee's observation that the initial report of the State party lacked sufficient information on the factors and difficulties impeding the implementation of various rights provided for in the Convention.

### B. Positive aspects

3. The Committee takes note of the adoption by the State party of a Children's Act applicable to England and Wales. The Committee also observes that the State party has extended the application of the Convention to many of its dependent territories. The Committee welcomes the intention of the State party to consider withdrawing the reservation it made to article 37 of the Convention as it relates to the procedures governing children's hearings in Scotland.

4. Moreover, the Committee welcomes the initiatives being taken by the State party to reduce the incidence of Sudden Infant Death Syndrome and to combat the problem of bullying in school. In addition, the Committee is encouraged by the steps taken to address the issue of the sexual abuse of children, including through the development of the 'Working Together' initiative which advocates and promotes an interdisciplinary approach to addressing this serious problem.

5. The Committee welcomes the information it received concerning the commitment of the Government to review its legislation in the area of the employment of children and to present new legislation in matters relating to the family, domestic violence and disability. Likewise, the Committee welcomes the measures being taken to pass further legislation in the area of adoption, including the intention of the Government to ratify the 1993 Hague Convention on Protection of Children and Cooperation in Respect of Intercountry Adoption. The Committee takes note of the Code of Practice for Children with Special Educational Needs which has statutory force and has been developed within the framework of the 1993 Education Act.

6. The Committee takes note of the Government's commitment to extend the provision of pre-school education. The Committee is equally appreciative of the recent initiative taken by the State party to require local authorities, in conjunction with health authorities and non-governmental organizations, to draw up Children's Service Plans.

### C. Principal subjects of concern

7. The Committee is concerned about the broad nature of the reservations made to the Convention by the State party which raise concern as to their compatibility with the object and purpose of the Convention. In particular, the reservation relating to the application of the Nationality and Immigration Act does not appear to be compatible with the principles and provisions of the Convention, including those of its articles 2, 3, 9 and 10.

8. The Committee remains unclear about the extent to which an effective coordinating mechanism exists for the implementation of the Convention on the Rights of the Child. It is concerned whether sufficient consideration has been given to the establishment of mechanisms, including of an independent nature, to coordinate and monitor the implementation of the rights of the child.

9. With respect to article 4 of the Convention, the Committee is concerned about the adequacy of measures taken to ensure the implementation of economic, social and cultural rights to the maximum extent of available resources. It appears to the Committee that insufficient expenditure is allocated to the social sector both within the State party and within the context of international development aid; the Committee wonders whether sufficient consideration has been given to the enjoyment of fundamental rights by children belonging to the most vulnerable groups in society.

---

* At the 208th meeting, held on 26 January 1995.

10. The Committee notes that the initial report of the State party contains little information on the difficulties experienced by children living in Northern Ireland and the effect on children of the operation of emergency legislation there. The Committee is concerned about the absence of effective safeguards to prevent the ill-treatment of children under the emergency legislation. In this connection, the Committee observes that under the same legislation it is possible to hold children as young as 10 for 7 days without charge. It is also noted that the emergency legislation which gives the police and the army the power to stop, question and search people on the street has led to complaints of children being badly treated. The Committee is concerned about this situation which may lead to a lack of confidence in the system of investigation and action on such complaints.

11. The Committee is concerned about the apparent insufficiency of measures taken to ensure the implementation of the general principles of the Convention, namely the provisions of its articles 2, 3, 6 and 12. In this connection, the Committee observes in particular that the principle of the best interests of the child appears not to be reflected in legislation in such areas as health, education and social security which have a bearing on the respect for the rights of the child.

12. With regard to article 2 of the Convention relating to non-discrimination, the Committee expresses its concern at the insufficient measures undertaken to ensure its implementation. In particular, it is concerned about the possible adverse effects on children of the restrictions applied to unmarried fathers in transmitting citizenship to their children, in contradiction of the provisions of articles 7 and 8 of the Convention. In addition, the Committee is concerned that children of certain ethnic minorities appear to be more likely to be placed in care.

13. Furthermore, in the light of article 6 of the Convention, the Committee expresses its concern at the health status of children of different socio-economic groups and those belonging to ethnic minorities.

14. In relation to the implementation of article 12, the Committee is concerned that insufficient attention has been given to the right of the child to express his/her opinion, including in cases where parents in England and Wales have the possibility of withdrawing their children from parts of the sex education programmes in schools. In this as in other decisions, including exclusion from school, the child is not systematically invited to express his/her opinion and those opinions may not be given due weight, as required under article 12 of the Convention.

15. The Committee notes with concern the increasing number of children living in poverty. The Committee is aware that the phenomenon of children begging and sleeping on the streets has become more visible. The Committee is concerned that the changed regulations regarding benefit entitlements to young people may have contributed to the increase in the number of young homeless people. The rate of divorce and the number of single-parent families and teenage pregnancies in the State party are noted with concern. These phenomena raise a number of issues, including as regards the adequacy of benefit allowances and the availability and effectiveness of family education

16. The Committee is disturbed about the reports it has received on the physical and sexual abuse of children. In this connection, the Committee is worried about the national legal provisions dealing with reasonable chastisement within the family. The imprecise nature of the expression of reasonable chastisement as contained in these legal provisions may pave the way for it to be interpreted in a subjective and arbitrary manner. Thus, the Committee is concerned that legislative and other measures relating to the physical integrity of children do not appear to be compatible with the provisions and principles of the Convention, including those of its articles 3, 19 and 37. The Committee is equally concerned that privately funded and managed schools are still permitted to administer corporal punishment to children in attendance there which does not appear to be compatible with the provisions of the Convention, including those of its article 28, paragraph 2.

17. The administration of the juvenile justice system in the State party is a matter of general concern to the Committee. The low age of criminal responsibility and the national legislation relating to the administration of juvenile justice seem not to be compatible with the provisions of the Convention, namely articles 37 and 40.

18. The Committee remains concerned about certain of the provisions of the Criminal Justice and Public Order Act 1994. The Committee notes that its provisions provide, *inter alia,* for the possibility of applying 'secure training orders' on children aged 12 to 14 in England and Wales. The Committee is concerned about the compatibility of the application of such secure training orders on young children with the principles and provisions of the Convention in relation to the administration of juvenile justice, particularly its articles 3, 37, 39 and 40. In particular, the Committee is concerned that the ethos of the guidelines for the administration and establishment of Secure Training Centres in England and Wales and the Training Schools in Northern Ireland appears to lay emphasis on imprisonment and punishment.

19. The Committee is equally concerned that children placed in care under the social welfare system may be held in Training Schools in Northern Ireland and may be placed in the future in Secure Training Centres in England and Wales.

20. The Committee is also concerned that The Criminal Evidence (N.I.) Order 1988 appears to be incompatible with article 40 of the Convention, in particular with the right to presumption of innocence and the right not to be compelled to give testimony or confess guilt. It is noted that silence in response to police questioning can be used to support a finding of guilt against a child over 10 years of age in Northern Ireland. Silence at trial can be similarly used against children over 14 years of age.

21. The situation of Gypsy and Traveller children is a matter of concern to the Committee, especially with regard to their access to basic services and the provision of caravan sites.

### D. Suggestions and recommendations

22. The Committee wishes to encourage the State party to consider reviewing its reservations to the Convention with a view to withdrawing them, particularly in light of the

agreements made in this regard at the World Conference on Human Rights and incorporated in the Vienna Declaration and Programme of Action.

23. The Committee would like to suggest that the State party consider establishing a national mechanism for the purpose of coordinating the implementation of the Convention, including between governmental departments and between central and local governmental authorities. Furthermore, the Committee suggests that the State party establish a permanent mechanism for the monitoring of the Children's Act and the Convention on the Rights of the Child throughout the United Kingdom. It is further suggested that ways and means be established to facilitate regular and closer cooperation between the Government and the non-governmental community, particularly with those non-governmental organizations closely involved in monitoring the respect for the rights of the child in the State party.

24. With regard to the implementation of article 4 of the Convention, the Committee would like to suggest that the general principles of the Convention, particularly the provisions of its article 3, relating to the best interests of the child, should guide the determination of policy-making at both the central and local levels of government. This approach is of relevance to decisions taken about the allocation of resources to the social sector at the central and local governmental levels, including with regard to the allocation of benefits to children who have completed compulsory schooling and have no full-time employment. The Committee notes the importance of additional efforts to overcome the problems of growing social and economic inequality and increased poverty.

25. With regard to matters relating to the health, welfare and standard of living of children in the United Kingdom, the Committee recommends additional measures to address, as a matter of priority, problems affecting the health status of children of different socio-economic groups and of children belonging to ethnic minorities and to the problems of homelessness affecting children and their families.

26. The Committee recommends that in line with the provisions of article 42 of the Convention, the State party should undertake measures to make the provisions and principles of the Convention widely known to adults and children alike. It is also suggested that teaching about children's rights should be incorporated into the training curricula of professionals working with or for children, such as teachers, the police, judges, social workers, health workers and personnel in care and detention institutions

27. The Committee would like to suggest that greater priority be given to incorporating the general principles of the Convention, especially the provisions of its article 3, relating to the best interests of the child, and article 12, concerning the child's right to make their views known and to have these views given due weight, in the legislative and administrative measures and in policies undertaken to implement the rights of the child. It is suggested that the State party consider the possibility of establishing further mechanisms to facilitate the participation of children in decisions affecting them, including within the family and the community.

28. The Committee recommends that race relations

legislation be introduced in Northern Ireland as a matter of urgency and is encouraged by the information presented by the delegation of the State party regarding the Government's intention to follow up on this matter.

29. The Committee would also like to suggest that a review be undertaken of the nationality and immigration laws and procedures to ensure their conformity with the principles and provisions of the Convention.

30. The Committee recommends that further measures be undertaken to educate parents about their responsibilities towards their children, including through the provision of family education which should emphasize the equal responsibilities of both parents. While recognizing that the Government views the problem of teenage pregnancies as a serious one, the Committee suggests that additional efforts, in the form of prevention-oriented programmes which could be part of an educational campaign, are required to reduce the number of teenage pregnancies.

31. The Committee is also of the opinion that additional efforts are required to overcome the problem of violence in society. The Committee recommends that physical punishment of children in families be prohibited in the light of the provisions set out in articles 3 and 19 of the Convention. In connection with the child's right to physical integrity, as recognized by the Convention, namely in its articles 19, 28, 29 and 37, and in the light of the best interests of the child, the Committee suggests that the State party consider the possibility of undertaking additional education campaigns. Such measures would help to change societal attitudes towards the use of physical punishment in the family and foster the acceptance of the legal prohibition of the physical punishment of children.

32. With regard to matters relating to education, the Committee suggests that children's right to appeal against expulsion from school be effectively ensured. It is also suggested that procedures be introduced to ensure that children are provided with the opportunity to express their views on the running of the schools in matters of concern to them. Further, the Committee recommends that the training curricula of teachers should incorporate education about the Convention on the Rights of the Child. It is recommended that teaching methods should be inspired by and reflect the spirit and philosophy of the Convention, in the light of the general principles of the Convention and the provisions of its article 29. The Committee would also like to suggest that the State party consider the possibility of introducing education about the Convention on the Rights of the Child into school curricula. Legislative measures are recommended to prohibit the use of corporal punishment in privately funded and managed schools.

33. The Committee also suggests that the State party provide further support to the teaching of the Irish language in schools in Northern Ireland and to integrated education schooling.

34. The Committee recommends that the emergency and other legislation, including in relation to the system of administration of juvenile justice, at present in operation in Northern Ireland should be reviewed to ensure its consistency with the principles and provisions of the Convention.

35. The Committee recommends that law reform be pursued in order to ensure that the system of the administration of juvenile justice is child-oriented. The Committee also wishes to recommend that the State party take the necessary measures to prevent juvenile delinquency as set down in the Convention and complemented by the Riyadh Guidelines.

36. More specifically, the Committee recommends that serious consideration be given to raising the age of criminal responsibility throughout the areas of the United Kingdom. The Committee also recommends the introduction of careful monitoring of the new Criminal Justice and Public Order Act 1994 with a view to ensuring full respect for the Convention on the Rights of the Child. In particular, the provisions of the Act which allow for, *inter alia*, placement of secure training orders on children aged between 12 and 14, indeterminate detention, and the doubling of sentences which may be imposed 17-year-old children should be reviewed with respect to their compatibility with the principles and provisions of the Convention.

37. Within the context of the law reform being considered with regard to matters relating to the employment of children, the Committee expresses the hope that the State party will consider reviewing its reservation with a view to its withdrawal. Similarly, the Committee expresses the hope that the Government may consider the possibility of becoming a party to ILO Convention No. 138.

38. The issues of sexual exploitation and drug abuse as they affect children should also be addressed on an urgent basis, including with regard to the undertaking of further measures to prevent them.

39. The Committee is of the view that the implementation of the provisions of article 39 of the Convention deserves greater attention. Programmes and strategies should be developed to ensure that measures are in place to promote the physical and psychological recovery and social reintegration of a child victim of, *inter alia*, neglect, sexual exploitation, abuse, family conflict, violence, drug abuse, as well as of children in the system of administration of justice. Such measures should be applied within the national context but also within the framework of international cooperation.

40. In addition, the Committee recommends pro-active measures for the rights of children belonging to Gypsy and Traveller communities, including their right to education, and that a sufficient number of adequately appointed caravan sites for these communities be secured.

41. The Committee also recommends that information on the implementation of the Convention in the dependent territory of Hong Kong be submitted to the Committee by 1996.

42. The Committee encourages the State party to disseminate widely the State party report, summary records of the discussion of the report within the Committee and the concluding observations adopted by the Committee following its consideration of the report. The Committee would like to suggest that these documents be brought to the attention of Parliament and that the suggestions and recommendations for action contained therein be followed up. In this regard, the Committee suggests that closer cooperation with non-governmental organizations be pursued.

# Children's Rights Office
Working towards a Children's Rights Commissioner

# Publications

From 1992 to 1995 the Children's Rights Development Unit
worked to produce an independent, in-depth report on UK
compliance with the Convention on the Rights of the Child.
The Children's Rights Office is now working to implement
the core recommendation of that analysis: that a statutory
Children's Rights Commissioner be appointed to monitor
and coordinate the implementation of children's rights
throughout the UK.

## UK Agenda for Children
A systematic analysis of the extent to which UK law, policy
and practice complies with the Convention on the Rights of
the Child
*1994, £20 plus £4 postage and packing*

## Building Small Democracies
Respecting children's civil rights within families.
*1995, £5 plus 50p postage and packing*

## Checklist for Children
Implementing the UN Convention on the Rights of the Child
through local authority policy and practice.
*1995, £11 plus £1 postage and packing*

## Child Health Rights
Implementing the UN Convention on the Rights of the Child
in the NHS: a practitioner's guide.
*1995, £5 plus 50p postage and packing*

## Making the Convention Work for Children
Explaining the history and structure of the UN Convention
on the Rights of the Child and its application in the UK.
*1995, £5 plus 50p postage and packing*

## My Rights in our World
A leaflet written by children in Northern Ireland on the UN
Convention on the Rights of the Child.
*1995, 5 copies £5 + £1 p and p, 20 copies £15 + £3.50 p and p*

## The Convention on the Rights of the Child
Background, full text, children's version plus concluding
observations of the UN Committee on the Rights of the Child
*1995, £3 recommended donation/A4 s.a.e. 45p (under 18, etc)*

*available from December 1996*

## Participation and Empowerment of Children and Young People: a practical handbook

*for further information please contact*

Children's Rights Office
235 Shaftesbury Avenue
London WC2H 8EL
Telephone 0171 240 4449
Fax 0171 240 4514